The Seven Weeks' War

The Seven Weeks' War

The Austro-Prussian Conflict of 1866

H. M. Hozier

LEONAUR

The Seven Weeks' War
The Austro-Prussian Conflict of 1866
by H. M. Hozier

First published under the title
The Seven Weeks' War

Leonaur is an imprint of Oakpast Ltd

ISBN: 978-1-78282-010-9 (hardcover)
ISBN: 978-1-78282-011-6 (softcover)

http://www.leonaur.com

Publisher's Notes

The views expressed in this book are not necessarily
those of the publisher.

Contents

To

Colonel Edward Bruce Hamley,

Royal Artillery,

Lately Professor of Military History, Strategy,

and Tactics at the Staff College,

Now Commandant of the Staff College,

This Faint Attempt to Chronicle the Events

of the German War of 1866

is

Dedicated

By

A Former Pupil

Preface to the First Edition

The only claim to consideration that the following pages can present is that for the most part they are the product of a personal eyewitness of some of the most interesting incidents of a war which, for rapidity and decisive results, may claim an almost unrivalled position in history. The author has attempted to ascertain and to advance facts. His object has been impartiality, his aim truth. Criticism from one so feebly competent to criticise would have been entitled to no respect, and has therefore been avoided. A few observations occasionally introduced are the results not of original thought so much as of communication with some whose positive abilities and experience entitle their opinions to be attentively weighed.

MAPS

The main features of the campaign of 1866 can be easily traced in any ordinary maps of Bohemia, Saxony or Moravia. Those who wish to study the details of the war, will find the maps published by the Prussian Staff at Berlin, in 1868, most lucid and serviceable. They are to be found in any large military library, and can be consulted at the Royal United Service Institution.

Prefatory Chapter

The results of the war of 1866 in Germany were the aggrandizement of Prussia, the formation of new Confederations and the disappearance of Austria as a Germanic power. To the eight provinces of which Prussia consisted in the spring of 1866 were added Hesse-Cassel, Nassau, Hanover, Schleswig-Holstein and Lauenburg. These were incorporated in the Prussian kingdom and raised its population to about 23,500,000.

At the same time arose under the leadership of Prussia the new North German Confederation, the harbinger of an united German Empire. It was sixty years almost to a day when the treaty of Prague was signed in 1866, since the Emperor Francis II. had announced to the *Diet* his resignation of the Imperial Crown: By that act, due to the victories of Napoleon I. over Germans, the oldest political institution in the world was extinguished, for this empire was that which the nephew of Julius won for himself from the powers of the East at the Battle of Actium, and which had preserved almost unaltered through eighteen centuries of time and through the greatest changes in extent, in power, and in character, a title and pretensions from which all meaning had long since departed.[1]

On the fall of Napoleon I. this empire was to a certain extent reconstituted by the treaty of Vienna as a Confederation of thirty-nine States. This Confederacy was extinguished in the war of 1866, and the treaty of Prague established the Confederation of the North German States, and led to the re-establishment of the Germanic Empire on a purer, more natural, and more homogeneous basis than it had ever possessed from the days of the Caesars. The treaty of Prague, however, was but the stepping-stone, not the key-stone of German Unity. North Germany numbering twenty-one States was indeed linked by

---

1. Bryce, Holy Roman Empire.

11

that treaty into a close connection with Prussia, who held the undivided leadership, the command of the German armies, and the power of peace and war north of the Maine.

South Germany did not hold itself together. Austria stood aloof, and appeared resolved henceforth to meddle no more in German affairs. Bavaria, Würtemburg, and Baden remained almost independent of each other, but each, on its own footing, concluded important treaties with Prussia. By that between Prussia and Bavaria, concluded on the 22nd August, 1866, these two powers mutually guaranteed the integrity of their respective territories with all the military forces at their disposal; and it was also established, that in case of war the King of Prussia should have the command-in-chief of the Bavarian army. The treaties between Prussia, Baden, and Würtemburg, were of the same tenure; they provided a strict military alliance and submission of the armies in time of war to the King of Prussia.

In Northern Germany, in the spring of 1867, a representative assembly elected by universal suffrage at the rate of one member for every 100,000 of the population, met at Berlin in February, and by the 16th April, had discussed and adopted a constitutional charter by which the whole of the States of North Germany were definitively united into a federal body. This charter, entitled the Constitution of the North German Confederation, consists of fifteen chapters, comprising seventy-nine articles, with a preamble declaring that the governments of the States enumerated, formed themselves into a perpetual Confederation for the protection of the territory and institutions of the union, and for the guardianship of the welfare of the German people.

The twenty-one States incorporated in this Confederation were, Prussia, Saxony, Mecklenburg-Schwerin, Mecklenburg-Strelitz, Oldenburg, Brunswick, Saxe-Weimar, Saxe-Meiningen, Anhalt, Saxe-Coburg-Gotha, Saxe-Altenburg, Waldeck, Lippe-Detmold, Reuss-Schleiz, Reuss-Greiz, Schwarzburg-Sondershausen, Schwarzburg-Rudolstadt, Schaumburg-Lippe, Hamburg, Lübeck, and Bremen. The executive power of the Confederation was vested in the Sovereign of Prussia: this ruler also, as the Lord President, managed the diplomatic intercourse of the Confederation with foreign powers; was the commander-in-chief of the army and navy, and had the prerogative of nominating ambassadors, of declaring war, and of concluding peace. It was his duty to enforce the observance of federal laws, and to compel negligent or disobedient members to fulfil their federal obligations, and to appoint all officers and civil functionaries. The contributions of the various States to the cost of the general administration of the Confederation, was regulated in proportion to the numbers of their population. The King of Prussia had also to appoint a Chancellor of the Confederation who should preside over the Federal Council. The chancellor selected was naturally the Count von Bismarck.

By the terms of the Constitution of the North German Confederation, the legislative power of the Union was vested in two representative bodies. One of these bodies is elected by the governments of the Confederate States, and is termed the Bundesrath, the other is elected by the population, and is termed the Reichstag. In the Bundesrath sit deputies from the governments of each State of the Confederation; the representative of Prussia has seventeen votes, that of Saxony four, and those from Mecklenburg-Schwerin and Brunswick two each. Besides smaller German estates and the three free-towns with one vote each. *All* together forty-two votes. The Reichstag is elected by universal suffrage for the term of three years and meets in annual session. To the Reichstag belongs the initiative of legislative acts; it is independent of the Bundesrath, but the members of the latter have the privilege of being present it its sittings to expose the views of their respective governments.

On account of the representations of the Emperor of the French, Saxony was not, on the conclusion of the war of 1866, so completely absorbed into the North German Confederation as her more northern neighbours. The King of Saxony, although a member of the Union, still retained the power of nominating officers, civil and military, in his kingdom, and the Saxon Army was not merged in that of the Confederation. It was, however, to be held under the supreme orders of the King of Prussia in case of war.

The conclusion of the war in 1866, and the treaty of Prague, were due in a great measure to the emperor of the French, whose offer to mediate between the contending powers, Austria hastily accepted, probably erroneously, as Count Bismarck had already made proposals for direct negotiations, in which no mention of the payment of a war indemnity was made. France was, however, only too eager to mediate; for French diplomatists for decades previous to 1870 held the creed, that the privilege of France was to arrange, and mould, to her own advantage, the domestic commotions of Germany. Prussia could not without folly at the close of a victorious campaign, risk all its glorious results by throwing down the gauntlet to France, and raising up on the

Rhine a new army of enemies, while unfriendly divisions were still frowning on the banks of the Danube and the Maine. She was perforce obliged to consent to French mediation, and French mediation was not disinterested.

It was the aim and object of France to oppose the unity of Germany, and to prevent the rise of a great and united nation on her own border. For this reason she stipulated for the semi-independence of Saxony, and caused a clause to be inserted in the treaty of Prague by which Prussia consented to cede to Denmark the northern portion of Schleswig. Austria, who at the time of the negotiation of the treaty of Prague was but the mouth-piece of France, stipulated when she retired from the German Confederacy, that the remaining Southern States should be formed into a Southern Confederacy. It was thus hoped to prevent the ultimate fusion of the Southern States with Northern Germany and Prussia, and to establish a power in Germany which jealousy of Prussia and the bitterness of defeat, might in an European conflict range upon the side of Prussia's enemies.

But the man who guided the foreign policy of Prussia was competent to foil the diplomatists of France. Confident of the difficulties which would defer the formation of the Southern Confederation, he assented to the Austro-French proposal, organised the Northern Confederation, which speedily acquired strength and consistency, and concluded between each of the Southern States individually, offensive and defensive alliances with Prussia. France, really by an attitude of desire to interfere in the internal arrangement of Germany, facilitated the conclusion of these treaties; and the fact that on the 6th August, 1866, she demanded the fortress of Mainz from Prussia under threat of war, though known but to a few men, had doubtless an important effect.

The cession of the fortress was refused, and when it was seen that Prussia was resolute the threat was not carried out, but an excuse made, which averred that the demand was wrung from the emperor when labouring under illness. The French army was then far from prepared for war, as it was not thoroughly completed with men, nor armed with a breech-loading weapon; and France failed to obtain after the war of 1866, territorial concessions from Germany, as signally as when before that war she proffered to declare against Austria, and attack her with 300,000 men, provided that Prussia would cede territory on the left bank of the Rhine.

While after the campaign of 1866 the North German Confederation almost daily increased in power and united sentiment, no progress was made in the formation of a Southern Bund. The States lying south of the Maine were too equal in size and resources. None was clearly preeminent, and to none would the others consent to accord pre-eminence.

An attempt was made at a conference held at Nördlingen in 1868, to form an agreement among the Southern States as to a very minor question,—the management of the federal fortresses of the South: yet even on this subject there was no concord, and the conference separated with the sole result of showing that it was almost impossible on any point to establish an harmonious understanding between the States of Southern Germany. At first, however, the relations between these States and Prussia were not quite satisfactory, for there were political parties who feared the preponderance of Prussia, and the probable absorption of the Southern States, but the attitude of France gradually forced the clear-sighted patriotism of the South to regard Prussia with friendly eyes, and the deep-seated desire of German unity swayed all except a few selfish and protectionist factions. Austria at first seemed inclined to harbour a desire of vengeance for the defeat of 1866, and to look upon France as a probable future ally.

But the publication of the fact that France had been willing to declare against her at the outbreak of the German war, did much to modify that feeling, and to turn her population, as well as her government, to the necessary task of internal, financial, and military reorganisation. The Prussian victories in 1866 were at the time looked upon in France with jealousy and disfavour. The crowning triumph of König-grätz was regarded by the excitable population of that empire as a direct step towards German unity, the aggrandizement of Prussia, and consequently as a menace to the ascendancy and control which for years the French had tacitly claimed in the internal affairs of Germany. In 1866 the claims of France to German territory were withdrawn; but in 1867 they were renewed in a form which, although less summary, still for a short time, threatened to disturb the peace of Europe. By the treaty of Vienna in 1815, the Grand Duchy of Luxemburg was given to the King of the Belgians, but at the same time was included in the Germanic Confederation.

On the separation of Belgium from the Netherlands, it was arranged by the treaty of London that Eastern Luxemburg and Limburg, to which the federal obligations of Western Luxemburg were transferred, should be handed over to the King of the Netherlands, while the King of the Belgians received full sovereignty over the western portion of Luxemburg. The King of the Netherlands refused to accede to this treaty, but after the French siege of Antwerp, Austria and Prussia, in behalf of the Germanic Confederation, enforced the provisions of the treaty, and the eastern portion of Luxemburg was formally included in the confederation. The town of Luxemburg was a most important fortress of Germany towards France, and from 1815 to 1867 was garrisoned by a Prussian garrison. In 1867, the King of Holland, Sovereign of Luxemburg, who had been excluded from the North German Confederation on its formation in 1866, made overtures for the sale of the fortress and territory, to France. To these the Emperor Napoleon lent a willing ear.

The arrangement soon became publicly known, and war between France and Prussia for the moment seemed imminent. The public feeling of Germany was allowed to become excited, although, had the leaders of Prussia desired, it is almost certain, that at the beginning of the complication, they could have yielded Luxemburg to France without being forced into war by the pressure of public opinion. Such was not, however, their desire; war with France was the readiest mode of completing German unity; and although Count von Bismark did not push forward such a war, he did not shrink from taking up the gauntlet if it were thrown down to him. He accordingly refused to abandon the defence of a fortress which had been confided to the guardianship of Prussia for half a century, and which was really situated on German ground, although not formally included in the North German Confederation. Some day the real history of the exclusion of Luxemburg from that confederation in 1866 may be known.

On the other hand, the emperor of the French having once expressed his readiness to purchase Luxemburg, could not withdraw, at the mere dictate of Prussia, without grievously wounding the sensitive pride of the French people, and raising into a storm the national jealousy of Prussia, which had been hardly concealed since the Battle of Königgrätz. Thus rulers seemed about to be forced into a war, which neither desired, by the populations over which they ruled; and this fact may well be considered by that hysterical school of politicians which maintains that wars are the work of rulers, and that in Republican institutions lies the best guarantee of enduring peace. To ward off the danger of war a conference was arranged. It was proposed by the King of Holland, sanctioned by the neutral powers, and met in London under the presidency of Lord Stanley, who was then the

Minister for Foreign Affairs. As the result of its deliberations the duchy was declared neutral, and its neutrality guaranteed by all the powers represented at the conference. Prussia withdrew her garrison from the fortress, and the fortifications were to be demolished. The concessions on the part of Prussia were not very material, as the fortifications had been erected prior to the introduction of rifled ordnance, and the great strength of the fortress lies in its natural position. Still war was for the moment averted, and many men believed that all difficulties were arranged between these two powers, that Austria was crippled, Russia unprepared, and that a lasting peace was really about to dawn upon Europe.

Those who looked below the surface could, however, perceive that France was but brooding over the insult which she chose to conceive had been offered to her, by the fact that Germany had shaken off her leading-strings, and that Germans chose to manage their own affairs without foreign interference. Those could also see that, in the apparent calm, not only was France pushing forward armaments and military organisation, but that Prussian administrators were quietly taking all necessary precautions in case of war, and studiously followed move with move. The war, which had been for long foreseen by these, broke out indeed suddenly, and surprised the world at large; but a few men in England had carefully watched how, in the spring of 1870, French agents were engaged in all our southern markets buying corn and forage. The excuses given for enormous purchases of this description were, that the season had been so dry in France that no harvest was expected; but this excuse was transparent, for had forage been so very scarce in France, French dealers would not have cared, simultaneously with an enormous rise in the price of forage, to have largely exported horses to France.

At the same time, too, a flotilla was secretly collected in the northern French ports capable of transporting 40,000 men and 12,000 horses. These things were, perhaps, known to and noticed by Prussian agents, but the British Government, against which the arrangements might have been equally directed, remained in a happy ignorance of any danger of war, and on the outbreak of hostilities, the Minister for Foreign Affairs, in his place in Parliament, stated that a few hours previously the British Foreign Office believed that there was not a cloud on the political horizon of Europe. Yet still, many Utopian Englishmen, in the face of these facts, contentedly argue that no preparations for the invasion of our country could be made without the government being fully aware of them.

During the years between the treaty of Prague and the outbreak of war with France, the Prussian military organisation had been extended to the troops of all the Northern States. The Prussian army, which fought in 1866, was increased by three *corps d'armée*. Of these the 9th was that of Schleswig-Holstein, the 10th that of Hanover, the 11th that of Hesse. The Grand Ducal Hessian, or 25th division, was placed in intimate connection with the last corps, while the semi-independent army of the kingdom of Saxony formed the 12th corps of the Confederation. The broad principles of the Prussian organisation, as far as regarded infantry, were proved so satisfactory in 1866, that they were extended after the Austrian war without alteration to the new *corps d'armée*. In the organisation of the cavalry, however, which was largely increased, the experience of 1866 dictated the necessity of a vital change. Hitherto the Prussian regiments of cavalry had always consisted of four squadrons in time of peace; on the outbreak of war the four squadrons took the field, and a *depôt* was formed to supply the necessary reinforcements of men and horses.

This system was found decidedly faulty during the Austrian war, and after the treaty of Prague the Prussian regiments were increased to five squadrons, of which four take the field, and one remains as a *depôt* to supply immediately the quick necessities of horses and men. To this change, and to the large increase of cavalry, is due, in no slight degree, the wonderful successes of the Prussian armies in 1870—71; for, as the emperor of the French himself stated, the Prussian cavalry formed an impenetrable screen, through which it was impossible for the enemy to discover the movements of the main armies, while every movement of the French armies was accurately and faithfully reported by the now famous Uhlans to the Prussian headquarters. In the important arm artillery, the Prussians, directly after the campaign of 1866, laid aside all muzzle-loading guns and adopted for their whole field-artillery breech-loading steel pieces made on Krupp's system.

Towards the end of 1869 some breech-loading bronze guns were turned out, took part in the subsequent war, and were so satisfactory that it is probable the whole field-artillery will be armed with bronze guns. The system of Prussian *Intendantur*, which had given such excellent earnest of efficiency in 1866, was naturally extended to the newly-formed *corps d'armée*. The *Intendantur* of Prussia must be clearly distinguished from the *Intendance* of France; the names are similar, but the systems are almost reverse: the Prussian system was proved excellent in two great wars, the French was paralysed under the first pressure of active service. It is fortunate that our country has adopted much more the Prussian than the French system of supply in the lately established department of Control

When the French Empire was threatened with war on account of the Luxemburg question in 1867, the nominal strength of the army was 600,000 men; but it was found that it would have been impossible, after providing for *depôts* and necessary detachments, to place much more than 150,000 men in line of battle. It was evident that the military system required reorganisation, and in 1868 the system of reorganisation elaborated by Marshal Niel became law. By this new system, which was, as its predecessor, based upon conscription, the forces of the empire were divided into three classes; the active army, the reserve, and the National Guard. The service under the colours was fixed at five years, after which the soldier was to enter the reserve for four years more. Young men who were not drawn for the active army were to serve four years in the reserve and five in the National Guard.

This system was inferior to the Prussian, because part of the reserve were not trained at all in the regular army, and the service in the ranks being five years instead of three, a smaller force of trained men could be annually passed into the reserve. Another distinction of great importance existed between the two military systems. In Prussia no man required for military service could purchase a substitute; in France any one liable to military service, by payment to the State of a sum of 2500 *francs*, was exempted, and the State undertook with the money so paid to replace him by another soldier. It is doubtful, however, whether the fund thus created was judiciously administered, and it is believed that the real strength of the French battalions was considerably inferior to the paper strength on the outbreak of the war. Nor was the system as laid down literally carried out, for it was objectionable to the people, and in such an exciteable and feverish population, it was not advisable to train the National Guard to a perfect knowledge of weapons and drill.

The result was, that although the reorganisation of 1868 theoretically placed more than 800,000 combatants at the disposal of the emperor, and raised the military forces of France to more than 1,200,000[2] men, the army fit to take the field at the commencement of the war mustered barely 400,000 soldiers. Of these 40,000 were at Cherbourg,

---

2. Active Army, 400,000 men; Reserve, 430,000 men; National Guard, 408,000 men.

preparing to embark on the flotilla which had been collected at the northern ports; 5,000 were at Rome, 10,000 in Algeria, 35,000 in Paris and at Châlons, 10,000 at Lyons, and about 30,000 at Marseilles, Toulouse, Rochefort, L'Orient, Bordeaux, Toulon, and in hospital. The force which could be sent towards the Rhine mustered thus barely 270,000 men. It was divided into eight corps and the Guards.

Against it there were ready to take the field on the German side, as soon as the rapid mobilization of the army was completed, the twelve corps of the North German Confederation, mustering at least 360,000 men, and the armies of Bavaria, Würtemburg, Darmstadt, and Baden, which were under the supreme command of the King of Prussia in virtue of the separate treaties concluded after the campaign of 1866, raised the field forces of that sovereign to over 500,000 combatants. These were well sustained by an effective and organised system of depôts and reserves, administered by an elastic and proved machinery, and handled by abstemious and well-trained officers. An iron discipline knit the Prussian soldiery together, previous victories gave entire confidence in the leaders, and a high sense of duty and self-denial pervaded the ranks.

In the French Army, on the other hand, there was much enthusiasm and great gallantry, but discipline had been allowed to lapse, the luxurious ideas which a rapid increase of wealth had fostered, pervaded some portion of the officers, while many of the others, raised from the ranks, were wanting in the high military education which alone gives to a leader the confidence of his followers, or fits him for the rapid decision and quick judgment that are every hour necessary in war. In armament the French troops were superior to the Prussians, for they were provided with the *chassepot* rifle, which, with the common advantage of being a breech-loading arm, was superior in range and accuracy to the needle-gun. The latter had been early adopted by the Prussian Government, which had been averse to incur the inconveniencies of a change of armament, except to secure a very clearly-defined advantage, and had apparently underrated the excellence of the *chassepot*.

Still the French advantage in this respect was more than compensated for by the hurried and excited manner in which the French troops, on more than one occasion, handled their weapons. On the other hand the Prussian soldier was more suitably equipped for European war than the French. Discarding the cumbrous equipment necessary for the formation of camps, or the refinements of cooking, the

Prussian troops were willing to trust during a campaign to the shelter which villages nearly always afforded in Western Europe, or, in case of necessity, to bivouac in the open air, while a small mess-tin carried by each soldier sufficed for his culinary wants.

The French soldier, on the contrary, was weighed down with *tentes d'abri*, heavy cooking apparatus, and an enormous kit. These were generally useless, frequently lost, always encumbrances; but an army accustomed to African or tropical war clings pertinaciously to the idea of canvas covering, fails to realize the different conditions under which campaigns must be conducted in Europe, and shudders at the idea of an exposure in war to which every true sportsman will willingly consent for pleasure. The French Army was heavily equipped on the experience of Africa, China, and Mexico, and it suffered heavily from this cause among others in France.

The actual declaration of war showed that, nevertheless, the men who administered the army and directed the policy of the empire, were of opinion that not only were the French forces able to cope with the Prussian in the field, but that they could be more rapidly placed upon the theatre of war.

In September, 1868, an insurrection broke out in the kingdom of Spain, which, joined by General Prim and Marshal Serrano, quickly developed into a revolution. At the end of that month Queen Isabella fled from the country to Biarritz. At the beginning of October Marshal Serrano entered Madrid at the head of the revolutionary army, and a provisional government was established, and General Prim named commander-in-chief of the army. The provisional government, in concert with the national representatives, decided that a constitutional monarchy should be the future form of Spanish government; but there was some difficulty in finding any man eligible to become King of Spain who would accept the position, and, till such a man could be found, Marshal Serrano was elected Regent of the Kingdom, with General Prim as his prime minister.

Several proposed monarchs had been named, but the throne remained vacant till, in the summer of 1870, General Prim, in the name of the Spanish Ministry, offered the Crown to the amiable and accomplished Prince Leopold of Hohenzollern-Sigmaringen, eldest son of the reigning Prince of Hohenzollern, who had in 1849 surrendered his sovereign rights to the King of Prussia. This prince, who had married in 1861 the sister of the King of Portugal, was in his thirty-sixth year, and a Roman Catholic by religion. He accepted the offer of the

Crown, subject to the approval of the Cortes, which was certain. The news of this acceptance was published in Paris on the 5th July, and the greatest excitement arose, as the nomination of Prince Leopold was there held to be the handiwork of Count von Bismarck, who contemplated to create in Spain a Prussian dependency which should threaten France from the south of the Pyrenees. French ministers declared in the Chambers that France could not tolerate such a result to negotiations which they said had been kept secret from the emperor of the French, and seemed by their expressions to have already made up their minds to war.

It may be correctly true that the negotiations with Prince Leopold were not officially notified by the Spanish Government to the Emperor Napoleon; but it is known that the French ambassador at Madrid had known of the probable election of this Prince for many months, and that the surprise which the French Government professed on the arrival of the official intimation was at the least disingenuous, or due to the neglect of their own agent The public mind in Paris, which had been secretly for a long time eager for war with Prussia, was only too glad to seize upon the Hohenzollern question and to urge the Imperial Government to hostilities; but the King of Prussia would not involve Europe in war for the sake of a family question; and by his influence, it is said, as head of the Hohenzollern family, and through the intervention of England, the candidature of Prince Leopold for the Spanish Crown was withdrawn, first by the prince's father, and afterwards by himself.

The danger of war seemed averted; but the desire for war ran high at Paris, and M. Benedetti, the French ambassador at Berlin, was directed to wait upon the King of Prussia, who was then at Ems, and obtain from him a pledge that His Majesty would never at any future time accede to the candidature of the prince. This the king refused to give, as he naturally reserved to himself freedom of action under future circumstances. The French ambassador being desirous of a further interview, the king sent an *aide-de-camp* to tell him that he could add nothing to what he had already said, and for further discussion referred him to Count von Bismarck. M. Benedetti naturally telegraphed the result of this interview to his own government. By the French Government the result of this interview was seized upon as an insult offered by the King of Prussia to the French ambassador, although the ambassador was ignorant himself of any insult. The news was published in Paris, and the war excitement rose to frenzy. The

King of Prussia, on the other hand, telegraphed to Count von Bismarck the account of the interview at Ems, who seemed quite ready to accept the French challenge, for he viewed the action of M. Benedetti as an insult to the King of Prussia; as such it was announced in Berlin. The mind of Germany was deeply incensed.[3]

The interview at Ems took place on the 13th July. On the morning of the 14th a cabinet council was held at St Cloud under the presidency of the emperor, and the two chambers expected a communication. None was however made; but on the 15th July a declaration was made in the *Corps Législatif* and Senate simultaneously of war against Prussia, which was rapturously applauded in both houses.

The same day the King of Prussia travelling from Ems was met by the crown prince at Brandenburg. They travelled together to Berlin, where they were met at the railway station by Herr von Thile, the Under Secretary of State for Foreign Affairs, with the telegraphed account of the speech made that day by M. Olivier, the French prime minister, in the chambers at Paris. The king, on reading the telegram, issued orders to General von Roon and General von Moltke, who had also come to receive His Majesty, that the whole army of the North German Confederation should be at once mobilized.

These officers drove direct from the station to their offices, and that night orders for mobilization were telegraphed to every part of the country. From the frontiers of Belgium to the Vistula, from the Baltic to the mountains of Silesia, that night the summons was sent out, and early next day the reserve and *Landwehr* men of Prussia were swarming to join their ranks. At the same time continuous trains of troops were hurrying towards Lorraine and Alsatia from all parts of France; troops were being conveyed from Algeria, and within a few days the French Army, available to take the field, was in the vicinity of Metz and Strasburg.

The French Government at the outbreak of the campaign had apparently hopes that some of the States of South Germany would separate from Prussia and join with France in the war. These hopes were speedily disappointed, for the whole of the German Powers rallied round Prussia, and so perfect was the machinery of mobilization and the railway transport of troops, that in twenty days more than 500,000 men were close down to the French frontier, and ready to advance to battle. The 7th and 8th corps were already on the frontier in a little

---

3. *The Franco-Prussian War*, edited by Captain H. M. Hozier, where full details of these various incidents will be found.

more than ten days, and the 3rd corps was fully equipped, completed, and ready to move in eight days.

During the twenty days which the German armies required to mobilize the French lost all advantage which the hasty declaration of war ought to have given. The army, instead of having been ready before the declaration of war, was unprepared to advance, and instead of dashing boldly into Germany, disturbing the mobilization of the various corps, and, perhaps, subduing the South before the North could come to its aid, lay inactive on the frontier, with detachments scattered from Thionville and Sierk to Belfort, with strong reserves at Metz. Had the war between France and Germany taken place before the events of 1866, their remissness might have not cost the French so dear; but the consolidation of the North German Confederation and the command-in-chief of the other German araiies, which was vested in the King of Prussia, allowed the mobilization of the whole German armies to be immediately undertaken without any of the diplomatic negotiations which would have been necessary before 1866.

In the first week of July the German armies concentrated On the right was General Steinmetz with the 1st Army in the direction of Birkenfeld: this army was composed of the 1st, 7th, and 8th Prussian corps. In the centre was Prince Frederick Charles with the 2nd Army, composed of the 2nd, 3rd, 4th, 9th, 10th corps, and the corps of the Prussian Guards, in the neighbourhood of Kaiserslautern. This prince had also under his command the 12th, or Saxon corps. On the left was the crown prince with the two Bavarian corps, the Würtemburg division, the Baden division, and the 5th and 11th Prussian corps in the neighbourhood of Speyer. The 6th corps was also moving up from Silesia to join the 3rd Army. It showed excellent taste and tact on the part of the advisers of the King of Prussia to counsel the commander-in-chief of the whole German forces to place the amiable, popular, and competent crown prince in command of the army in which the South German troops were enrolled.

The Prussian plan of the campaign was that the three armies should advance simultaneously in a south-easterly direction; the crown prince marching to the east of the Vosges mountains, the other two armies to the west of them. If the French army concentrated to hold the Vosges against the crown prince, the 1st and 2nd Armies would threaten its position in flank and rear; if, on the other hand, it concentrated against the 1st and 2nd Armies, the crown prince, bearing to his right, and pushing through the Vosges, would in his turn threaten his flank and rear. As the crown prince was to be engaged in a difficult and mountainous country, his army was accompanied only by one cavalry division in addition to the regiments of cavalry attached to infantry divisions. The other divisions of cavalry were attached to Prince Frederic Charles and General Steinmetz.

On the 3rd July, the general Prussian advance commenced. On the 4th, the French corps which occupied St. Avoid, a small town on the road from Metz to the frontier line of the Saar at Saarbrück, made a movement towards the latter place. The emperor and the Prince Imperial were present, and the French soldiery thought that the advance had at last really begun, and that they were upon the high road to Berlin. The movement was not, however, pushed; the supplies and provisions necessary for a campaign were not yet even collected in the rear of the army, and no proper system of issuing them to the troops, if the latter advanced, was yet in working order; the most necessary articles of field equipment were in some cases wanting, for the centralized system of military administration, which was the bane of the French army, prevented any rapid distribution of stores at the outbreak of a war. The French corps which advanced from St Avoid did not even cross the frontier in force, but confined itself to throwing some shells into the town of Saarbrück, and occupying the strong position of the heights of Spicheren, in front of Forbach.

Meanwhile, the German troops were swiftly, though silently, drawing down to the frontier, and in the early morning of the 6th the crown prince had massed his forces which he had marched from Landau by way of Schweighofen behind the dark woods that lie north of Weissenburg. Thence, soon after daybreak, he sprang upon the unsuspecting troops of General Douay, which formed the advanced guard of the corps of Marshal Macmahon, and drove them back with great loss on the main body at Worth. The same day the right division of the army of Prince Frederick Charles, who advanced by Homburg and Zweibrücken, together with the left division of General Steinmetz, stormed the heights of Spicheren, and drove the French occupants of that position in full retreat towards Metz.

On the 8th July, the crown prince, having marched by way of Sulz sous Forêts, came upon Marshal Macmahon at Worth, and after a severe battle there, in which the French leader showed great tactical resource, overthrew him completely, and the marshal retreated in great disorder on Nancy.

The Battle of Worth virtually decided the campaign. The heir to the crown of Prussia there tore from the brows of the French Army those laurels which a too credulous world had too uncritically accorded to it, and proved beyond doubt, that the army of France, however much animated with enthusiasm and gallantry, was unable to withstand the stem onset of the soldiery of Germany, directed with judgment and conducted with skill.

Three days after the Battle of Worth, the general advance of the German armies was continued. General Steinmetz moved by St Avoid, Prince Frederick Charles by way of Saar Union, and the crown prince by Merzweiler, Ingweiler, and Saarburg. At this place the right of the army of the crown prince united with the left of that of Prince Frederick Charles, and the strategical junction of the German armies on French soil was assured.

General Steinmetz then moved upon Metz, Prince Frederick Charles on Pont-à-Mousson, and the crown prince on Nancy, On the 14th, General Steinmetz came up with the French rearguard at Courcelles, and after a sharp action at that place forced it to seek shelter under the guns and within the outworks of the fortress of Metz. At the same time, Prince Frederick Charles threw bridges over the Moselle at Pont-à-Mousson, Novéant, and Corny.

On the 15th, he crossed the Moselle, and, with the heads of the 3rd (Alvensleben) and 10th (Voigt Rhetz) corps, occupied Gorze and Novéant.

On the 16th, the crown prince reached Nancy, and halted there, having detached a force to invest and besiege the fortress of Strasburg.[4] General Steinmetz was in front of Metz, on the eastern side. Marshal Bazaine, who commanded the whole French army which had been assembled, partly by design, partly by force of circumstance, within the forts of Metz, designed to move from that fortress with all his available strength towards Châlons. It was believed in the German camp that the French retreat had commenced on the previous day, and that some of the French Army had already got beyond the striking distance of Prince Frederick Charles. On the morning of the 16th, however, when the head of the 3rd Prussian corps debouched from the defile of Gorze on the elevated plateau, which to the west of Metz rises above the valley of the Moselle, with the intention of pursuing or attacking in flank the retreating French, it found the whole of Marshal Bazaine's army marching in retreat from Metz towards Vionville, and that the heads of its columns had not yet reached that place.

---

4. The Baden Division, and the division of *Landwehr* of the Guard.

General Stulpnagel, who commanded the leading Prussian division, immediately engaged the army of Marshal Bazaine; he was supported by the 6th division, which was following him, and these two divisions checked the whole French army, until Prince Frederick Charles brought up the 10th corps to their aid. The Prince threw the 10th corps across the road by which the French sought to retreat, and all through the long summer day a terrific battle was fought near Vionville. The French leader made one desperate attempt after another to break through; but the Prussian soldiers, though suffering frightful loss, sternly stood their ground, and at nightfall the Germans still held the road from Metz to Mars-la-Tour, and the French marshal was forced to fall back on Gravelotte. The remaining corps of Prince Frederick Charles were too far to the south to allow of their taking part in the battle of the 16th; but two German corps, with two divisions of cavalry, which were aided late in the evening by one division from General Steinmetz, held their ground against the 180,000 men that were marching under Marshal Bazaine.

On the 17th, the whole of the army of Prince Frederick Charles came up, and the bulk of the army of Steinmetz. The German troops took up a position extending from the head of the Gorze defile to St Marie aux Chênes, and the King of Prussia arrived upon the field. Marshal Bazaine, after falling back on Gravelotte on the 16th, took up a strong position there, which on the 17th he partly entrenched. Here on the 18th he was attacked by the German Army, and after a bloody battle was wholly cut off from the northern road to Verdun, and driven into Metz.

The army of Prince Frederick Charles, under whose orders General Steinmetz was now placed, immediately invested the fortress and the army within it; and in spite of bad weather, sickness, hardship, and numerous sorties, prevented the enemy from breaking out until the fortress and army capitulated on the 28th October.

After the Battle of Worth, the disorganised remains of the French troops which had been there defeated retreated in confusion to Châlons. Here they were reorganised as rapidly as possible by Marshal Macmahon, and were reinforced by all the levies which could be hurried up to their aid. The emperor in person, after leaving Metz, also retired to Châlons by way of Verdun. Counsel was then taken in the French camp, and it seems to have been decided that for military reasons the army should retreat upon Paris. But political circumstances would not permit the adoption of this course. On the departure of the Emperor Napoleon for the war, the empress had been nominated Regent, and after the first disasters of the campaign a cabinet had been formed, of which Count de Palikao was president. This cabinet did not venture to allow the emperor to return to Paris except as victorious; for popular feeling was running high, and a revolution might at any moment be provoked.

It was, therefore, under pressure of political circumstances, determined that the army at Châlons should make a movement by way of Rheims, Mézières, and Sedan, with the object of reaching Metz by way of Thionville, and of aiding the escape of Marshal Bazaine from the toils cast around him by Prince Frederick Charles. With many raw troops, and an improvised transport, this was a desperate cast; but the tardiness of French movements was not then appreciated, the rapidity of Prussian marching not yet thoroughly recognized, and the stake to be won by success possibly justified the hazard of the venture.

On the other side, as soon as the army of Marshal Bazaine was securely invested in Metz by the army of Prince Frederick Charles, the crown prince advanced in pursuit of Macmahon towards Châlons, from Nancy, by way of Vaucoureurs and Ligny. Avoiding the fortress of Toul, he left a force to besiege it. When the crown prince reached Ligny, the king arrived at Bar-le-Duc. Here it was ascertained by the advanced cavalry of the crown prince, chiefly through the medium of captured letters, that Marshal Macmahon was making a movement from Châlons and Rheims, to gain the northern line of railway by Mézières and Sedan in order to relieve Marshal Bazaine.

The direction of march which had been ordered for St. Dizier was immediately altered, and the crown prince began to move by St. Ménéhould and Grand Pré on Sedan, with the view of there falling upon the flank of the marching columns of the French marshal.

When Metz was invested, the 2nd, 4th, 5th, and 6th divisions of cavalry were detached from the army of Prince Frederick Charles, and attached to that of the crown prince. Now the Guards, the Saxon corps, and the 4th corps were also detached from the 2nd army, and formed into a fourth army, which was placed under the command of the crown prince on Saxony, and ordered to move from Metz by way of Verdun on Sedan, in order to head the French columns and check their advance into Lorraine.

These movements brought on the Battle of Sedan. On the 30th of August the Crown Prince of Saxony, moving down the right bank of the Meuse, surprised the French at Mouzon and drove them back; for the French army, instead of making forced marches of about twenty miles a day, on account of want of discipline among the new levies and the failure of transport arrangements, was only able to make about six. On the same day the crown prince also engaged the heads of Marshal Macmahon's columns at Beaumont and Donchery, and drove them in.

The French retired upon Sedan, and took up a position resting on that fortress, with their front upon the Meuse, and their flanks refused towards the Belgian frontier. It was anticipated in the German camp that they might possibly retreat into Belgian territory. Accordingly, Count von Bismarck sent a communication to the Belgian government to say, that if the French crossed the frontier and were not disarmed, the German troops would be forced to follow; but the Belgian Army had been already placed on a war footing, and with detachments was watching the frontier. These disarmed and made prisoner any isolated bodies which either purposely or accidentally entered armed upon Belgian soil.

On the 1st September the armies of the Crown Princes of Prussia and Saxony attacked, under the eyes of the King of Prussia, the position which the French had taken up at Sedan. The army of the Crown Prince of Saxony, crossing the Meuse by bridges which it threw during the previous night, extended its right towards the Belgian frontier, and drove in the French left The Bavarian corps of the army of the crown prince of Prussia assailed the French centre at Bazeilles, while the crown prince, pushing the 5th and 11th corps across the Meuse lower down the stream, not only drove in the French right, but extended his own flank so far as to touch the flank of the Guards who formed the right of the Saxon battle, surrounded the French completely, and entirely cut off their retreat from Belgium.

At the very commencement of the battle Marshal Macmahon was severely wounded, and the command devolved upon General Wimpfen, who had only just arrived on the theatre of war. All day the battle raged, the French fought gallantly—even desperately; but, pressed upon by the better-disciplined legions of Germany, they were pushed closer and closer to the ramparts of Sedan, while their adversaries gained a firm footing on all the heights which command and overlook the basin in which the fortress is situated. At last, hemmed in, surrounded, and exposed to the commanding fire of a numerous and superior artillery, no resource was left to the French army but capitulation.

A general of the emperor's staff was sent to the King of Prussia to propose terms for the army, and at the same time the emperor wrote a letter to the king, and proposed to surrender his sword. The terms announced were the unconditional surrender of the army and the fortress; but the officers were allowed to retain their swords, and to give their parole not to serve against Germany during the war. These terms were agreed to next day, and the whole French army was marched prisoner to Germany.

On the 2nd September the emperor had an interview with the King of Prussia and the crown prince, after which he went by way of Belgium to the *château* of Wilhelmshöhe, near Cassel, where he remained a prisoner on parole until the termination of the war.

After the halt of a few days, necessary for the completion of arrangements at Sedan, the armies of the crown princes, that of Prussia on the left and of Saxony on the right, marched for Paris by way of Attigny, Reims, Montmirail, and Coulommiers. There was no French army worthy of mention now in the field. Bazaine was invested with the bulk of the army of the Rhine in Metz; the emperor and Macmahon were prisoners on the road to Germany. The few troops who escaped from the general catastrophe at Sedan, or had been on the way to reinforce Marshal Macmahon, were hurried back to Paris to man the defences of the capital, which the cabinet had already taken vigorous measures to provision.

As soon as the news of the capture of the emperor and his army became known at Paris, revolution broke out. It might have been more prudent had the French nation deferred a change of government which must necessarily delay the progress of public business. It was not so. The change was made in the very face of the enemy. M. Gambetta and M. Jules Favre proclaimed the Republic in the *Corps Législatif*. The excited population, as if eager to drown the sense of national calamity in the storm of domestic politics, shouted rapturous applause. The imperial government was dissolved: the members of the cabinet fled the country, and the empress, hastily escaping from the palace of the Tuileries into which the mob broke, reached a seaport, and was conveyed to England in the yacht of an English private gentleman.

As there was no foe in the field to encounter, the German armies marched straight upon the capital At Coulommiers they separated, that of the crown prince of Saxony moving towards the north-east of Paris, that of the prince of Prussia towards the south-west The latter approached Versailles on the 19th September, encountered the garrison of the city that day at the strengthened posts of Villejuif, Chatillon, Plessis-Piquet, and Clamart, and after a tolerably sharp action drove it under the forts which surround the *enceinte*.

The 3rd and 4th armies then invested Paris, and encircled the city of luxury and light within a band of iron and of fire, which was not relaxed until the forts and guns of the defenders were surrendered to Prussian custody.

On the instalment of the Republic in Paris, M. Gambetta was appointed Minister of War, and General Trochu governor of the city. Every exertion was made to raise armies to resist the invader, and if possible to drive him from French soil, and the republican leaders were not lacking in energy. A large force was raised within the city, which at the termination of the siege mustered over 350,000 combatants. Conscripts were raised, arms and ammunition imported from abroad, clothing and stores purchased, and an army rapidly collected in the south-west, which obtained the name of the Army of the Loire. On the 19th of October the army in Paris was so far equipped and organised that General Trochu attempted to make a sortie and sally out of Paris; but the troops of the crown prince drove him back, and the siege continued. The Prussians at first did not attempt any active operations, but were content with strongly entrenching themselves, and trusting to hunger to enforce the capitulation of the place.

Early in November the French Army of the Loire had gained some consistency, and on the 9th of that month its vanguard drove the Bavarians, who had been sent to observe it, out of the city of Orleans. These fell back and took up a position in the vicinity of Toury; but had General d'Aurelles de Paladine, who commanded the French army, been in a position to immediately follow up his success, he might have raised the siege of Paris, as the crown prince would have had to call his troops together in order to oppose a French advance from the south. But the troops of the French general were too raw, and he was forced to wait in Orleans, where he threw up strong intrenchments, to organise them. He thus lost his opportunity.

Towards the end of October Metz capitulated, and the army of Marshal Bazaine was made prisoner. The army of Prince Frederick Charles was thus released for active service in the field. His army was divided: the 1st, 7th, and 8th corps were placed under the command of General Manteuffel, and sent to the north of France to repulse and break up French troops, which were being raised under cover of the various fortresses. Prince Frederick Charles himself, with the 3rd, 9th, and 10th corps, moved rapidly from Metz by way of Fontainebleau towards Toury, and, joining the Duke of Mecklenburg, who commanded at that place, formed a screen between the Prussian armies round Paris and the Army of the Loire.

At first Prince Frederick Charles was retained in observation; but the king decided towards the end of November that he should assume the offensive and advance upon Orleans. At the same time the French leaders came to a similar determination. M. Gambetta ordered General d'Aurelles de Paladine, who had now collected an army of 180,000 men, to advance upon Paris, and at the same time the garrison of Paris made a vigorous sortie towards the south. This sortie, which was at first partially successful, was subsequently repulsed with great loss, and all hopes of communicating with the Army of the Loire from Paris had to be abandoned. The failure of this sortie was not, however, known to General de Paladine; on the contrary, he believed that the Paris garrison had burst through the investing line, and he hastened to its assistance.

On the 28th November he moved a considerable force from his right flank on the village of Beaune-la-Rolande, where he fell upon the left flank of Prince Frederick Charles. The Hanoverians, who formed the garrison of Beaune, were for some time severely pressed, and at one period almost surrounded. They held firm, however, in the town, and repeated efforts on the part of the French storming-columns failed to carry the houses. In the afternoon Prince Frederick Charles himself came up with the 3rd corps to their aid; the French assailants of the town were taken in flank and reverse, and although they were commanded by General Bourbaki, were driven off with loss.

After his failure to penetrate the Prussian position at Beaune-la-Rolande, General de Paladine transferred the bulk of his army during the next few days to his left flank, and attempted, on the 1st December to advance by the main road from Orleans to Paris by way of Toury. A little to the north of Arthenay his advanced guard fell in with the corps of the Duke of Mecklenburg, and a severe action took place. Prince Frederick Charles also moved in this direction, and the whole forces of the two armies became engaged in front of Orleans. The French were everywhere pressed back, their entrenchments were stormed with the loss of many guns, and, after several days' fighting, Orleans was occupied by the Prussians on the 4th December.

The broken army of General de Paladine retired partly to the south and partly down the Loire. The columns which followed the latter route were under the command of General Chanzy, who stood to fight, and sustained for three days severe conflicts round Beaugency. He then retired towards Le Mans: the Army of the Loire was dispersed, and, the covering army of Prince Frederick Charles took up a position around Orleans.

While these events were taking place on the south-west of Paris, Prussian generals on the other hand occupied Amiens, and had repulsed the French troops in that direction. The sieges of fortresses in Alsace were being prosecuted, and many had surrendered. Prussian forces were also pushed towards Dijon to watch some hostile masses which were gathering in that direction.

The investment of Paris was steadily maintained, and preparations made for more active measures. Batteries were dug and armed, ammunition and ordnance brought up, and at the end of December a bombardment of the forts and city commenced.

Shortly afterwards the French armies of the provinces made another and a final attempt to relieve the metropolis. General Chanzy advanced from Le Mans, at the same time as General Bourbaki, moving rapidly towards the fortress of Belfort in Upper Alsatia, which was being besieged by a Prussian contingent, appeared to desire to raise the siege of that place, and then to strike against the great line of the Prussian communications with Germany.

At the same time as General Chanzy advanced from Le Mans, Prince Frederick Charles moved from Orleans with the intention of attacking him at Le Mans. The heads of the two armies, moving in opposite directions, came into collision accidentally at Vendôme. The French were defeated, and were pushed back, fighting hard, however, as they retreated. After five days, however, of constant battle, they were pushed through Le Mans, and that important strategical point captured with large supplies of food, arms, ammunition, rolling-stock, artillery, and many prisoners.

The Battle of Le Mans decided the fate of Paris. Provisions had already been getting very short, and the bombardment, although it did not appear to do much damage to the works, harassed the garrison. It was perceived that assistance from without could no longer be hoped for; for Bourbaki had been headed towards Belfort and defeated by General Werder, and General Manteuffel hurried across France to fall upon his flank. The greater part of the army of General Bourbaki was driven across the Swiss ironder and disarmed, after having suffered many privations and hardships. One more sortie was indeed made by the garrison of Paris, but more apparently with the idea of demonstrating the inutility of further resistance than with any serious ideas of success. On the 27th January an armistice was agreed to, which was prolonged in February, and ultimately led to the peace signed between Prussia and France at Frankfort in May, 1871.

A short time before the conclusion of hostilities a most important event in the history of the world took place at Versailles. The Battle of Sedan was the corner-stone of German unity. After that victory diplomatic negotiations were entered into between the Southern States and Prussia, which resulted in the entrance of the former into the North-German Confederation. But it was necessary for the solidity and stability of this augmented fabric, that some guide and superior should be raised who should stand before the world as the avowed and recognised head of the amalgamated German nation. Who could be so fit to sustain so august a post as the warrior-king—the commander-in-chief of the German forces, who had led those forces from victory to victory over the enemy of German unity? and where could his inauguration to the restored and emblazoned dignity of emperor of Germany be so well conducted as in the palace associated with the memory of the rape of Strasburg and the commencement of a settled French interference in Germany?

On the 21st January, 1871, King William of Prussia was proclaimed Emperor of Germany in the palace of Versailles, amid the cheers of the assembled German chieftains, and within the sound of the guns engaged in the bombardment of Paris.

This event was hailed throughout Germany as of equal importance with the result of the war, and well it might be, for it was the most certain guarantee of the future independence of Germany. It is possible that France may again rise to a high military position; the enthusiasm and gallantry of her soldiery may again carry her colours to her old frontier; she may become more powerful in arms than her late rival, and may even tear from Germany the left bank of the Rhine. This may be possible; but it is impossible that she ever again will be able to exert that ascendancy and interference in the internal affairs of the country which was more galling to the proud Germanic people than loss of provinces or disastrous defeats. From that the declaration of the empire of United Germany has saved Germany for ever, and that declaration could not have been made in 1871 but for the war which occurred in 1866.

Book 1

Chapter 1

Chapter Title

Who cares with foemen when we deal.
If craft or courage guide the steel?—Conington.

Although the animosity between Prussia and Austria which led to the outbreak of hostilities in 1866 had been the gradual growth of many years, the immediate causes of collision were the consequences of the war waged by Germany against Denmark in 1864. The results of this contest were embodied in the Treaty of Vienna of that year, by which King Christian of Denmark surrendered all his rights to the Elbe duchies of Schleswig and Holstein, and the duchy of Lauenburg, in favour of the Emperor of Austria and of the King of Prussia.[1]

The Danish war had been undertaken in the first instance by the Germanic Confederation, in consequence of a decree of Federal execution against the King of Denmark as Duke of Holstein, and, in virtue of that duchy, a prince and member of the confederation. The *diet* which passed this decree had intended that the execution should be carried out by amalgamated detachments of such troops of all the States included in the confederation as might be determined by the *diet*. Some of these troops actually marched into Holstein. But the occupation of the Elbe duchies by troops of the confederation, and the consequent establishment of these districts as an independent State, would not have suited the political purposes of Prussia.

The object of this power was not so much to free Holstein from the dominion of the Dane as to secure the harbour of Kiel for the new fleet which was to be formed in order to carry the black eagle of Brandenburg into a forward place among the naval ensigns of the world: but the *diet* was determined to carry out the execution;

1. For translation of Treaty of Vienna of 30th October, 1864, see Appendix 1.

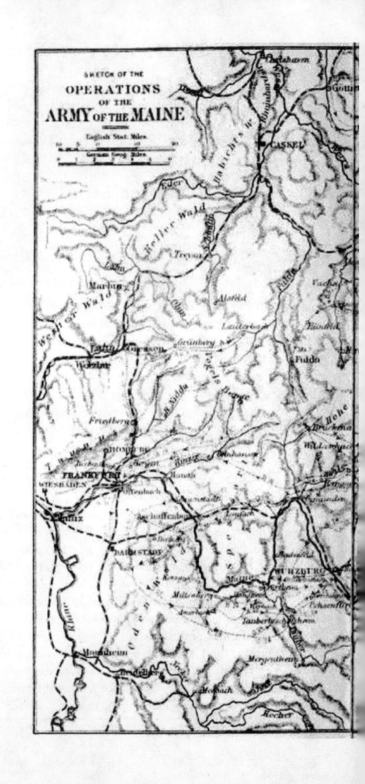

SKETCH OF THE
OPERATIONS
OF THE
ARMY OF THE MAINE

English Stat. Miles

German Geog. Miles

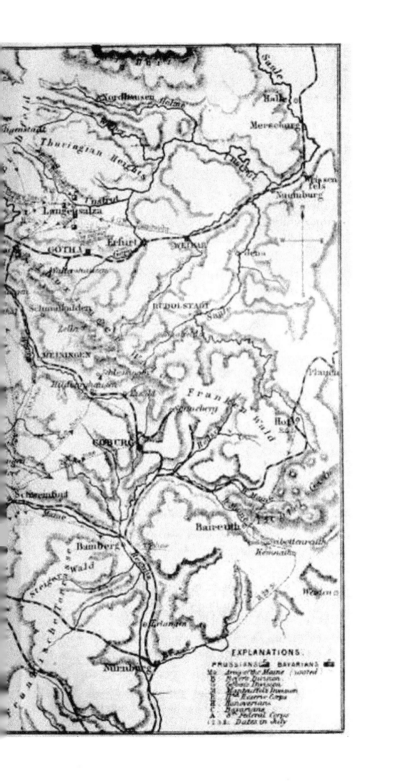

EXPLANATIONS.

PRUSSIANS ☐ BAVARIANS ☐ (routed)

	Army of the Maine
	Beyer's Division
	Goeben's Division
	Manteuffel's Division
	Reserve Corps
	Hanoverians
	Bavarians
	Federal Corps
12.14	Dates in July

and, if the troops of the Federal powers were once allowed to declare Schleswig-Holstein independent, the subjection of the duchies to the domination of Prussia would require a display of force and a violation of public opinion for which Count Bismark did not at that time consider himself strong enough. To annex an independent community, established under the auspices of the *diet*, with a popular and chosen prince, would have roused all Germany. The policy of the Cabinet of Berlin demanded that Schleswig-Holstein should not become independent yet.

Prussia was not, however, sufficiently confident in her strength to set aside at this time, with her own hand alone, the decrees of the *diet*. To have done so would have raised a storm against which she had no reason to suppose that she could successfully bear up. England was excited, and the warlike people of that country eager to rush to arms in the cause of the father of the young Princess of Wales. France was discontented with the insolence of the English Cabinet, but might have accepted a balm for her wounded pride in a free permission to push her frontier up to the Rhine. Austria would have opposed the aggrandizement of Prussia, and all Germany would have at that time supported the great Power of the South in the battle for the liberation of Holstein from the supremacy of the Hohenzollerns as eagerly as from that of the House of Denmark. The independence of Holstein, which could not be opposed by open force, had to be thwarted by stratagem.

Prussia sought the alliance of Austria with a proposal that those two great powers should constitute themselves the executors of the Federal decree, and put aside the troops of the minor States. Austria agreed, and rues at this hour the signature of that convention. Yet she had much cause of excuse. To allow Prussia to step forward alone as the champion of German national feeling would have been for Austria to resign forever the supremacy of Germany into the hands of her rival. Old traditions, chivalrous feeling, and inherited memories, caused Austrians to look upon their emperor as the head of Germany, the modern representative of the elected tenant of the Holy Roman Empire's crown and sceptre. Prussia was rapidly approaching to that supremacy with gigantic strides. Austria was already reduced to the position of being the advocate of German division and of small States, purely because amalgamation and union would have drawn the scattered particles not towards herself, but within the boundaries of her northern neighbour.

To permit Prussia to act alone in the matter of the Elbe duchies would have been to see her certainly obtain an important territorial aggrandizement, and also to lose the opportunity of creating another independent minor German State, which, if not a source of strength to Austria, might be a slight obstacle in the path of Prussia.

The war against Denmark was undertaken. The Danes, terribly inferior in numbers, organisation, equipment, armament, and wealth, after a most gallant resistance, lost their last strongholds; while a Western Power, which had certainly by insinuations, if not by facts or words, encouraged the Cabinet of Copenhagen into the delusion that other soldiers than Danes would be opposed to the German invaders of Schleswig, calmly looked on, and sacrificed in a few weeks the reputation which, fortuitously won on the plains of Belgium, had lived through half a century. The Danish war terminated in the treaty signed at Vienna on the 30th October, 1864, and the duchies of Schleswig, Holstein, and Lauenburg were handed over to the sovereigns of Austria and Prussia.

At this time the troops of Hanover and Saxony, which had been ordered by the *diet* to carry out the decree of Federal execution against the King of Denmark, were in Holstein. The next step in the policy of the great German Powers was to rid the duchies of their presence. On the 29th November, 1864, Austria and Prussia laid the treaty of peace with Denmark before the Germanic Diet, and proposed that, since the decree of Federal execution had been carried out, the presence of the Hanoverians and Saxons was no longer necessary in the duchies, and that both the troops and civil commissioners of these States should be required to vacate their position. This motion was opposed by the representative of Bavaria, and was negatived by a majority of one vote.

On the 30th November, however, the representative of Prussia announced in the *diet* that the claims of the prince of Augustenburg to the duchies would be settled by treaties between Austria and Prussia, and that these two powers would enter into negotiations with the pretender on the subject, but that, in the meantime, the Saxons and Hanoverians must retire from the disputed ground, and that notes had been sent by the Cabinet of Berlin to Dresden and Hanover, to demand the withdrawal of the contingents of those States. The representative of Hanover declared that his government was ready to withdraw its troops: the deputy of Saxony appealed to the decision of the *diet*. On the 5th December, 1864, the *diet* passed the motion proposed by Austria and Prussia, in opposition to a protest from the Bavarian representative. In consequence the troops and civil commissioners of Hanover and Saxony were recalled from the duchies by their respective courts, and Austria and Prussia took upon themselves the military and civil administration of Schleswig-Holstein.

Prussia stationed in the duchies six regiments of infantry, two of cavalry, and three batteries of artillery. Austria left there only the brigade Kalik, which was composed of two regiments of infantry, one battalion of rifles, two squadrons of cavalry, and one battery of artillery.[2]

The Austrian Government appointed Herr Von Lederer as civil commissioner, who was shortly afterwards recalled to Vienna, and replaced by Herr Von Hahlhuber. The Prussian civil commissioner was Herr Von Zedlitz. The Hanoverian and Saxon commissioners gave over the government of the duchies to the commissioners of the great powers on the 5th of December, who immediately entered upon their duties, and established the seat of government at Schleswig. The expulsion of the civil commissioners of the minor States, from the Elbe duchies was the last act of the Schleswig-Holstein drama in which Austria co-operated with Prussia. From this time she drew near again to the smaller States, which were now embittered against Prussia,

The administration of the duchies by the great powers was openly announced as only a temporary measure, and was regarded in this light by the whole world. Austria wished to give, up what she considered only a temporary trusteeship as soon as a possible, and proposed to place the Duke of Augustenburg provisionally at the head of the duchies, while the rival claims of the Houses of Augustenburg and Oldenburg to permanent occupation should be investigated. In Prussia, however, meanwhile the lust for increase of territory had been developed. It was discovered that the House of Brandenburg had itself claims to succession.

In a despatch of the 13th December, Count Bismark informed the Austrian Cabinet that Prussia could not accept the proposal to place the Prince of Augustenburg at the head of the duchies; and that such an act would forestall the claims of other pretenders, and would be viewed with disfavour by the courts of Oldenburg, Hanover, and Russia that an annexation of the duchies to Prussia could not indeed be carried out without the concurrence of Austria, but that such a step would be very advantageous to the interests of Germany in general,

---

2. The strength of the forces left would thus amount to about 12,000 Prussians and 5,200 Austrians, as troops left here were maintained on a peace establishment

and would not be antagonistic to those of Austria in particular; while Prussia's geographical position made it her special duty to insure the duchies against the recurrence of revolutionary disturbances. In this despatch the Cabinet of Berlin also proposed that in furtherance of this scheme the military organisation of the duchies should be assimilated to that of Prussia, and that their maritime population should be made available for recruiting the Prussian marines and navy.

By a despatch of the 21st December Count Mensdorf, the Austrian Minister for Foreign Affairs, answered the above despatch from Berlin, and said that Austria had undertaken the solution of the question in the interests of Germany; that the Austrian Cabinet was upon as friendly a footing with the Courts of Oldenburg, Hanover, and Russia, as was that of Prussia; that Hanover made no definite claims, but only expressed ideas of doing so; that the Austrian Cabinet would also investigate the claims of Oldenburg; but that Russia had lately declared that she would accept as authoritative only the decision of the Germanic Confederation on the question of succession; that if Prussia had wished to advance claims to the inheritance of the duchies, she ought to have done so before she made the declaration of the 28th May, in common with Austria, at the conference in London in favour of the Prince of Augustenburg.

As had already been remarked in Berlin through Count Karolyi,[3] Austria could agree to an incorporation of the duchies in Prussia only as an equivalent for an increase of her own German territory; that if Count Bismark spoke of the obligations of his own country, the Austrian Cabinet might say the same of itself; that Austrian blood had not been spilt to destroy the balance of power of the two great German States by a one-sided aggrandizement of Prussia. The despatch, in conclusion, let the Prussian Government understand that it ought to place no difficulties in the way of the rapid solution of this important question.

The Austrian Government was now in error. This despatch demonstrated that the avowed champion of the smaller States was about to betray their cause for the sake of individual advantage, and threw a trump card into the hand of Count Bismark. By some means this despatch was communicated to an Austrian newspaper, the *Presse*, and appeared openly in public print The Vienna police failed to discover from what sources the editor of the *Presse* had been supplied with a copy of the official document, but strong suspicions have ever since

---

3. Austrian Ambassador at Berlin.

prevailed that the publication was due to Prussian agency, which had acted with the object of shaking the confidence of the minor States in the leading power. In effect, several of the representatives of the smaller States sought from Count Mensdorf a declaration of what portion of territory the Austrian Government had in view in making the demand for an equivalent.[4]

During the winter several addresses were got up by Prussian partisans in the duchies, with the object of soliciting the Cabinets of Berlin and Vienna to agree to the incorporation of the duchies with the kingdom of Prussia. These were strongly negatived by protests directed to the Prussian House of Commons, and were generally considered to be due more to the electioneering tactics of Prussian agents than to any popular desire for annexation. Such of the late parliamentary representatives of the duchies as could meet together energetically protested against the addresses as exponents of the national will, but no means were taken for gauging the true desires of the population. No parliamentary estates were assembled to act as the mouth-piece of the influential and educated classes; no popular vote was allowed to declare the wishes of the people. Either step might have shown that the standard of Prussia was waving over a nation which aspired to hoisting the flag of independence.

Prussia, unable without a public violation of decency to monopolise the Elbe duchies, appeared in the early spring of 1865 desirous to lay aside the idea of annexation, and, instead, to pave the way for the accession of a prince to the government of the country, who might be a feudatory at least of the Court of Berlin. On the 21st of February, 1865, a despatch was sent by the Prussian Ministry to the Cabinet of Vienna, which professed to propose the measures which the Prussian Cabinet desired to see carried out in the duchies for the security of the interests of Prussia and of Germany, as well as what restraints should be placed upon the future sovereign of Schleswig-Holstein, both in his own and the general interest The substance of this despatch was,[5] that Prussia desired the following guarantees from the new State of Schleswig-Holstein, which was about to be established.

1. That this State should conclude a perpetual offensive and defensive alliance with Prussia, by which Prussia would guarantee the protection and defence of the duchies against every hostile

---

4. It is now supposed that the equivalent Austria wished to obtain was the county of Glatz, in Prussian Silesia.
5. For literal translation of this despatch see Appendix 2 B.

attack, while the whole naval and military power of the duchies should form an integral portion of the Prussian fleet and army.

2. The Prussian fleet—reinforced in the manner mentioned in Article 1—is to be entitled to the right of freely circulating and being stationed in all Schleswig-Holstein waters; and the Prussian Government is to have the control on the Schleswig-Holstein coasts of pilot dues, tonnage-dues, and lighthouse-dues.

3. Schleswig-Holstein is to pay Prussia a tribute, which is to be settled on an equitable basis, for the support of its army and navy, of which Prussia will undertake the whole administration. The Prussian Government will contract for the transport of war material, &c., with the Schleswig-Holstein railways, on the same terms as it does at present with the private[6] railway-companies of Prussia.

4. The fortresses of the duchies are to be regulated according to agreement between the Prussian and Ducal Governments, and, according to the requirements of the former, for general military purposes.

5. The duties of the new sovereign of Schleswig-Holstein with regard to the German Confederation remain the same as those of the former for Holstein. Prussia will find the Holstein Federal contingent out of parts of her army which do not form her own contingent

6. Rendsburg, in accordance with the wishes of all concerned, is to be declared a Federal fortress. Until that is done, it is to be occupied by Prussia.

7. Inasmuch as Prussia takes upon herself the duties of the military and maritime protection of the duchies, she requires that certain territories should be given up to her for the cost of fortifications, with full rights of sovereignty over them. The territories required would be at least—

   a. Sonderburg, with as much territory on both banks of the Sound of Alsen as may be necessary for a naval harbour at Hjörupshaff, and the security of the same.

   b. The territory necessary for the security of the harbour of Kiel, near the fort of Friedericsort

   c. Territories at both mouths of the proposed North Sea

---
6. Railways not in the hands of the government

and Baltic Canal, and, besides, the right of free navigation along this canal.

d. Schleswig-Holstein is to enter into the Zollverein,[7] and the administration of the railways and telegraphs of the duchies is to be amalgamated with that of Prussia.

These propositions showed that the government of Prussia was determined to attempt to establish Prussian supremacy in the Elbe duchies. The aims of the Cabinet of Berlin were clear to the Austrian Government; and Count Mensdorf, in the name of the latter, by a despatch of the 5th March, 1865, informed Count Bismark that a duke of Schleswig-Holstein, under such restrictions as would be entailed by an acceptance of the Prussian proposals, could not enter the Confederation of German princes on terms of equality, and with the power of a free vote in the *diet*; that the Prussian propositions were calculated to forward the special interests of Prussia alone, but; that Austria and the whole Germanic Confederation had a claim to the disposition of Schleswig-Holstein.

Austria in the same despatch, however, declared herself willing to concede to Prussia the right of occupation of Kiel harbour, and would agree to Rendsburg being declared a Federal fortress, to the commencement of a North Sea and Baltic Canal, and to the entrance of Schleswig-Holstein into the Zollverein. Further, Austria would not go; and she declared that treaties to settle the details of the above concessions could be entered into with profit only after the question of the sovereignty of the duchies was decided. Austria also expressed a wish to terminate negotiations from which there could be little hope that an agreement would result

---

7. The Zollverein, or General Customs Union, was entered into by most of the German States under the guidance of Prussia. The object of this union was to free the trade of Germany from the restrictions under which it lay from the conflicting interests and custom-house regulations of so many independent States. By the Zollverein Treaty, which was re-established on the 1st January, 1854, tolls or customs were collected once for all at the common frontier of the united States, and the produce divided among them in equitable proportions. The Zollverein included Prussia, and all the minor German States except Holstein, Lauenburg, and the principality of Lichtenstein. Austria was not included in the Zollverein, but became connected with it in 1853 by a commercial treaty with Prussia, by which both sides contracted to do nothing to prevent the free circulation of articles of trade in their respective territories, or the transit of any article of merchandise, except tobacco, salt, gunpowder, playing-cards, and almanacs; the principal of these exceptions, tobacco, being a government monopoly in Austria, and not in the other States.

Prussia and Austria had both spoken out their designs. That of Prussia was now manifestly the annexation of Schleswig-Holstein, that of Austria to thwart, hinder, and prevent the execution of Prussia's intention. Austria wished to carry out the project of establishing the duchies as a separate German State, under an independent prince, and thus to fulfil the object with which the German war against Denmark had been undertaken, and to satisfy the unanimous sympathy of Germany evoked for that war. This was doubly Austria's interest, in order to both impede the aggrandizement of her rival, and to I raise up another small State, a fresh unit of German nationality, a fresh obstacle to the German unity which she had found could not be effected under her own supremacy.

But the question of the Elbe duchies could not have been laid to rest in this condition, even if Austria and Prussia had both earnestly desired such a consummation. The whole Germanic people was nervously interested in its solution. In April, 1865, a motion brought forward in the *diet* at Frankfort by the representatives of Bavaria, Saxony, and Hesse Darmstadt, which proposed that Holstein should be given over to the prince of Augustenburg, was accepted by the majority.[8] This vote could, under the circumstances, have no practical result, but it showed that the current of feeling of the small States was setting strongly against the threatened preponderance of Prussia, and made Prussia feel that henceforth her policy must be antagonistic to, and subversive of the dynasties of the minor Germanic States.

Another element of discord had been in existence ever since Austria and Prussia had undertaken the joint government of the duchies, but it was not till the summer of 1865 that the quarrels between the commissioners of the two powers became so frequent and so stormy that they threatened to lead to a German war, through which the results of the conflict of 1866 might have been anticipated by a year. The Austrian Hahlhuber and the Prussian Zedlitz, engaged in a joint government, and primed by their own cabinets to support diametrically opposite lines of policy, could not fail often and seriously to disagree. The Austrian wished to encourage the expression of popular feeling in the duchies, and to support the manifestation of popular sympathy for the prince of Augustenburg: the Prussian desired to repress all expressions of political feeling, except such as emanated from the

---

8. This motion was brought forward on the 27th March, by Barons Von der Pfordten, Beust, and Dalwigk, the representatives of Bavaria, Saxony, and Hesse Darmstadt.

partisans of incorporation with Prussia.

These difficulties in the administration of the German provinces at the mouth of the Elbe were reflected in the society of Vienna and Berlin. Feelings rose high, and an appeal to arms seemed more than probable, when Prussia deemed it prudent to reopen negotiations with Austria. The celebrated personal meeting of the sovereigns of the two countries was arranged. The Emperor Francis Joseph and King William met at the little town of Gastein, on the banks of the Achen, about forty miles south of Salzburg, and from their interview originated the Convention of Gastein, which was concluded on the 14th, ratified on the 20th August, 1865. This convention consisted of the following heads:

1. Both Powers, Prussia and Austria, reserved to themselves the common sovereignty over the duchies Schleswig and Holstein, but Austria takes upon herself the provisional administration of Holstein, Prussia takes upon herself that of Schleswig.

2. Prussia and Austria will propose that a German fleet should be established, and Kiel declared a Federal harbour. Until the resolutions of the Germanic Confederation are carried out the navies of Prussia and Austria are to use the harbour of Kiel; but Prussia is to have the command in that harbour, to regulate the police there, and to acquire all territorial rights necessary for the security of this harbour.

3. Austria and Prussia will propose at Frankfort[9] that Rendsburg be declared a Federal fortress; until Rendsburg is recognised as a Federal fortress, it will be occupied by Austria and Prussia in common.

4. As long as the division of the administration of Schleswig and Holstein between Austria and Prussia endures, Prussia is to retain two high roads through Holstein, one from Lübeck to Kiel, the other from Hamburg to Rendsburg.

5. Prussia, on her side, takes upon herself the care of a telegraphic communication and postal line to Kiel and to Rendsburg, and also the construction of a direct railway from Lübeck by Kiel through Holstein, without raising claims to sovereign rights over the line.

6. Schleswig-Holstein is to enter the Zollverein.

---

9. The Parliament of the Germanic Confederation assembled at Frankfort.

7. The construction of the North Sea and Baltic Canal, with the results naturally accruing therefrom, is given over to Prussia.

8. With reference to the financial arrangements established by the Treaty of Vienna of the 30th October, 1864, all remains as of old. Only the duchy of Lauenburg is to pay no share in the expenses of the war, and the tributes of Schleswig and Holstein are to be divided in proportion to the amount of their populations.

9. The Emperor of Austria gives up the duchy of Lauenburg, with all rights as gained by the treaty of Vienna, to the King of Prussia, who will pay for this 2,500,000 Danish dollars in the Prussian silver currency, four weeks after the ratification of this Convention.

Thus by the Convention of Gastein the administration of the duchies was territorially divided between Prussia and Austria: Prussia obtained certain proprietary and administrative rights of great importance in Holstein; and, what is most notable, Austria sold her rights to the duchy of Lauenburg, which she had acquired by conquest in common with Prussia, and thus tacitly recognised the validity of the Austro-Prussian conquest of the Danish duchies, and of the right of either power to dispose of the conquest as it might desire, were the concurrence of the other obtained.

The Convention of Gastein was opposed on many sides. The princes of the small Thuringian states of Weimar, Meiningen, and Coburg protested against the clause by which Lauenburg was ceded to Prussia. The national party in Germany expressed loud disapprobation of the severance of Schleswig from Holstein. The French and English Ministers for Foreign Affairs in confidential notes expressed unfavourable opinions of the convention. The Prussian House of Commons was loud in its censure of the convention, and of the government which by concluding it menaced a heavy demand from the Prussian finances for the purchase of Lauenburg. The King of Prussia, however, paid for the ceded rights of Austria over the duchy out of his own private purse; the protestations of foreigners were disregarded; and, on the 15th September, Lauenburg was occupied by the Prussians.

In the few succeeding days the Prussian troops, except those whose retention in that duchy had been specially agreed to, withdrew from Holstein into Schleswig and Lauenburg. The Austrian force which had been in the two duchies concentrated itself in Holstein, under the

47

command of General Gablenz, who was made Governor of Holstein by the Emperor Francis Joseph. General Gablenz retained Herr Von Hahlhuber as Civil Commissioner, but after a short time the latter was replaced by Herr Von Hofman.

The King of Prussia nominated General Von Manteuffel as Governor of Schleswig, to whom Herr Von Zedlitz was attached as civil commissioner.

CHAPTER 2

Fruitlessness of the Gastein Convention

The Convention of Gastein silenced that portion of the German Press which had, during the summer of 1865, openly anticipated a rupture between Prussia and Austria, and had indulged in calculations as to which side Bavaria, Saxony, Hesse, and Hanover would be forced to espouse. It seemed that civil war between divisions of the Germanic people would be avoided; and for a time the two great Powers of Central Europe, by acting cordially in common, led many men to believe that community of interests and unity of policy was secured between them. Thus, when the *diet* assembled at Frankfort declared against the Convention of Gastein, the Governments of Austria and Prussia alike sent warning notes to the Frankfort Senate.

Again, when in November, 1865, the representatives of Bavaria, Saxony, and Hesse brought a motion before the *diet* which proposed that Austria and Prussia should now call an assembly of the estates of Schleswig and Holstein, which might participate in the solution of the question of the duchies, Austria and Prussia alike protested against this motion. Still, those who looked forward into the future foresaw that there were latent circumstances which foretold an approaching dissolution of the cordiality of the great Powers. One of these circumstances was the rising amity between Prussia and Italy; but more important was the jealousy for supremacy in Germany which the present position of affairs in the duchies was only too well calculated to rouse to action.

Prussia published, in the beginning of October, 1865, the opinion of the law officers of the crown with respect to the question of the duchies. This opinion was practically that all rights over the duchies originated in the Treaty of Vienna of the 30th October, 1864, and that all rightful claims of the House of Augustenburg to the crown of these provinces would have been annulled by this treaty, even if such claim had ever existed; but that, in fact, no rightful claim ever had existed

The Austrian administration in Holstein, notwithstanding this publication, allowed the rights of the Prince of Augustenburg to be continually treated of by the press, and at public assemblies, as a matter on which no doubt could be entertained, and suffered considerable agitation to take place in favour of his rights. The Prussian administration in Schleswig, on the other hand, allowed it to be understood that all such agitation would be regarded as treasonable, since it was calculated to thwart the aims of the temporary sovereign.

Nor was the Prussian Government disposed to look on calmly while the duchy of Holstein was permitted the right of free opinion and free discussion, the tide of which invariably seemed to set against the idea of incorporation with Prussia. On the 30th January, 1866, Count Bismark despatched a note to Vienna, in which he pointed out to the Austrian Cabinet how the conduct of its administration in Holstein must infallibly complicate the general relations between the two governments. This note was hardly despatched when a monster meeting of the Schleswig-Holstein Unions[1] at Altona gave the Prussian minister occasion to despatch a second, which is of peculiar interest.

In this note Count Bismark recalled to mind the happy days of Gastein and Salzburg, and expressed his belief, that Austria would be united with Prussia, not only in a conviction of the necessity of withstanding revolutionary ideas, but also in the plan of the campaign against such ideas; that affairs were now assuming a very serious aspect; that the bearing of the government of Holstein must be regarded as directly aggressive; and that the Austrian Government ought not to carry on against Prussia in the provinces the same agitation which it had united with the Prussian to quell at Frankfort The note went on to say that the Convention of Gastein had treated of the administration of the two duchies as only a provisional measure; but that Prussia had the right to advance that Austria, during the epoch of the provisional government, should maintain in Holstein the *status quo* in which she had received the province, in the same manner as Prussia felt herself bound to preserve this *status* in Schleswig.

The Prussian Government requested the Austrian to ponder upon the matter, and then to negotiate. Were a negative or evasive answer

1. Vereine.

returned, Prussia would be forced to adopt the conviction that Austria, prompted by a traditional antagonism, no longer wished to act harmoniously in union with her. This conviction would be painful, but Prussia must finally see her way clearly. If it were made impossible for her to act in concert with Austria, she must obtain full freedom for her own policy in order to contract closer alliances in other directions for the advancement of her own immediate interests.

The negative and evasive answer was returned in a note from Count Mensdorf, on the 9th of February, in which this minister, in the name of Austria, declined the responsibility for the national assemblies, because the duchies were only under a provisional government The count added, that Austria was well aware she did not occupy Holstein as an acquisition, but that so long as the provisional government might last, she considered herself perfectly free in the administration of the duchy, and could admit no control from any quarter.

This despatch from Vienna was the first step towards the development in a crisis of the political circumstances which now followed rapidly, one after the other. Austria saw in the Prussian declaration a hidden threat of war, and an open reference to an intended alliance with her mortal foe, Italy, and believed that she was threatened with an imminent and simultaneous attack on both her northern and southern frontiers. This belief was strengthened by the apparent fact, that a council was held at Berlin, on the 28th of February, under the presidency of the king, to which the chief of the staff of the army. General Von Moltke, and the military Governor of Schleswig, General Von Manteuffel, were summoned.

Austria accorded no faith to the most pacific assurances on the part of Prussia that these fears were groundless. Nor was her confidence m the peaceful intentions of her rival established by the denial of a rumour which had gained public credence, and which asserted that the question discussed at this council had been whether, under the aspect of political circumstances, Prussia ought to prepare herself for the war which might be the result of their development; nor by the assertion that no preparations for war of any kind had been made in Prussia. Austria, anxious at the same time for her position in Germany and Italy, full of mistrust and anger against Prussia, badly directed and counselled, perhaps also instigated by the embittered enemies of Prussia in Germany, began early in the month of March her preparations not only for a war, but also for a struggle of which the intended object was to support the Germanic Confederation against Prussia.

CHAPTER 3

Commencement of the Preparations For War

Open antagonism between Prussia and Austria was declared by the exchange of notes which was mentioned towards the end of the last chapter.

Prussia had acquired full freedom for her own policy by the Austrian answer to her declaration of the 26th of January, and men in Germany looked around anxiously to see what use Count Bismark would make of this liberty. For a time the wary minister gave no signal of what he was about to do. Many expected that, face to face with the strong military power of Austria, and with the sentiment of all Germany hostile to him, he would be obliged to treat with Vienna.

The solution of a conflict between different States depends ultimately always upon strength. Prussia, therefore, naturally desired to reinforce her strength, and to replace the alliance which had been broken by some new alliance.

But where to turn for the new alliance? In Germany there was no hope of finding friends among the governments, for these were all interested in the maintenance of small States, and naturally antagonistic to national community. Nor were the people of Germany at this time at all disposed to regard Count Bismark as their champion, or accept him as the leader of a national party. The late quarrels between the Prussian minister and the Prussian Commons, the press prosecutions in Prussian territory instigated by the Government over which he presided, the conservative tendencies of his views on taxation, marked him out more as the enemy than the harbinger of a free national unity. The people of Germany were at this time no allies of the counsellor of the head of the House of Hohenzollern.

As no alliance could be found in Germany, the Prussian minister looked abroad, and there saw, in the south-western frontier of the territories of the *Kaiser*, a natural ally to join hand-in-hand with Prussia against Austria. This was the newly formed, hardly consolidated kingdom of Italy. This ally could boast no long list of victories borne on the banners of its soldiery, its traditions did not reach seven years back, its army was composed of raw levies; but its people were feverish, eager, and covetous to gain Venetia, and to inflict a blow upon the detested Austrian.

Before the conclusion of the Convention of Gastein, in the middle of the year 1865, when at that time a rupture of the alliance between Austria and Prussia appeared possible, the latter power had drawn near to the young kingdom of Italy, and had entered into negotiations for the conclusion of a commercial treaty between the Zollverein and that kingdom. The larger number of the minor States which belong to the Zollverein[1] had not yet recognised the kingdom of Italy, and their rulers had no desire now to do so, for the recognition of a sole sovereign of the united peninsula would be tantamount to a recognition of the advantage of the concentration of the small States which had, previously to 1859, been independent portions of Italy, and of the superfluous character of their reigning dynasties. On the other side, Italy would not enter into negotiations with a confederation of which most of the component States still denied her title-deeds of kingdom. Prussia stepped in as mediator. Italy was happy to be recognised The small States of the Zollverein were forced into agreement with the proposals of Prussia. Count Bismark threatened to dissolve the Zollverein. The mere threat drove a probe into the mercantile classes of all Germany; the interests of the monied aristocracy was brought to bear on the governments; and on the 31st December, 1865, a commercial treaty between the newly recognised kingdom of Italy and the Zollverein was signed.

When the prospect of a war between Prussia and Austria arose in the spring of 1866, came Italy's opportunity to complete the work which had been commenced at Magenta, to secure and unite to herself the only province which, still under the rule of the foreigner, prevented her from being free from the Alps to the Adriatic. Italy naturally drew as close to Prussia as she possibly could. Austria requires a long time to mobilize her army, and had begun her preparations for war in the middle of February. Public attention was directed to

1. See chapter 1.

them by a council of war held at Vienna on the 10th March, to which Feldzeugmeister Benedek was summoned from Verona. At this council the party in favour of war was strongly predominant; and decided that Austria was strong enough to take the field against Prussia and Italy at the same time, provided that measures were taken to isolate Prussia in Germany, and to draw the States of the confederation to the Austrian side.

At this council too high an estimate appears to have been formed of the strength of Austria, and far too low a calculation made of the powers of Prussia; for the opinion of the council seems to have been that Austria could only emerge from such a war as a decisive victor. Italy was so detested, that all Austrians wished for an Italian war; and, with justice, among the Austrian soldiery a proud contempt was entertained for the Italian Army. It was considered that Prussia, weakened by an internal political conflict, could not unite her contending parties in a common 'foreign policy. Nor was a high opinion entertained of her military resources and organisation. The professional papers and periodicals of Austria ingeniously demonstrated that Prussia, however hardly pressed, could not place her normal army on a complete war-footing, because trained men would be wanting. The writers of these articles calculated that the battalions of infantry could only be brought into the field with a muster-roll of eight hundred men; no consideration was paid to the *Landwehr*,—in fact, doubts were in some cases thrown upon the existence of *Landwehr* soldiers at all, and those who believed in their existence entertained no doubts of their certain disloyalty.

It was also calculated that the Prussian Army would have to make such strong detachments for the garrisons of fortresses that a very small force would be left for operations in the field. These false calculations, the first step and perhaps the most certain to the bitter defeat which ensued, were due to defective information, and to the absence from the War Office of Vienna of those detailed accounts of foreign military statistics, deprived of which any country that undertakes a military measure of any kind necessarily gropes in the dark. To isolate Prussia from Germany, and to entangle her in a strife against overwhelming numbers, the plan of Austria was to draw the Germanic Confederation into a decisive action against Prussia, in order that the confederation might be implicated in the question in dispute between Austria and Prussia concerning Schleswig-Holstein. Austria was certain of gaining, by the vote of the minor States, a majority in the Germanic Diet against the aims and objects of Prussia, If Prussia bowed to the decision of this majority, her position of power in the Confederation would for a long time be shaken, but if she refused to accept this decision, then would arise a favourable opportunity to declare Federal execution against Prussia, and to crush her with the whole forces of the confederation.

After this council of war, the Austrian preparations were secretly pushed forward. The fortresses, especially Cracow, were strengthened and prepared for defence, and the troops in Bohemia were reinforced. These armaments and military movements excited the attention of Prussia. Questions were asked: Austria answered that the population of Bohemia had broken out in riots against the Jews, and that the Imperial Government was necessarily obliged to send troops into the disturbed districts for the protection of its Jewish subjects. The Prussians averred that, by a singular coincidence, the care and protection of the Jewish subjects drew the troops suspiciously dose to the frontier, while the Jews chiefly resided in Prague, the capital and almost the central point of the province of Bohemia.

The Austrian Army in a mobilization, before the war of 1866,[2] had to be increased from the 269,000 men, whom it mustered on a peace footing, to 620,000. It therefore required the recall of over 350,000 men on furlough, or soldiers of reserve, to complete its strength. This increase of force could only conveniently be made in the recruiting districts of each regiment, because the men who were called in for each regiment must be clothed and armed by the fourth battalion, which was always stationed in time of peace as a weak *depôt* in the recruiting district.

In March, 1866, the quarters of many regiments of the Austrian Army were changed, so as to bring the battalions into the vicinity of their recruiting *depôts*; and several regiments from Italy, Gallicia, and Hungary, which could conveniently receive their full complement of men only in Bohemia, Moravia, or Austrian Silesia, were moved into those provinces. By these means the Austrian forces in Bohemia were, by the end of March, reinforced by about twenty battalions of infantry and several regiments of cavalry, which were, however, to avoid suspicion, still retained upon a peace footing; while the purchase of horses, and the completion of fourth battalions to full strength, commenced in various parts of the Imperial dominions.

---

2. The Austrian Army, in consequence of the disastrous results of the campaign of 1866, has been reorganised. The text alludes to the former organisation of the army.

At the same time the Austrian Government took steps to strengthen the fortresses in Italy, and to protect, in case of war, the coasts of Istria and Dalmatia. In the same month an extraordinary but very secret military activity commenced in Wurtemberg and Saxony. All ideas of armament were officially denied by Austria, but the Prussian agents did not fail to observe their existence. The King of Prussia had already taken action, and issued a decree by which the authors of any attempts to subvert his own authority or that of the Emperor of Austria in the Elbe duchies, were threatened with imprisonment This decree was published by General Von Manteuffel in the duchy of Schleswig on the 13th March, and gave occasion for the Austrian ambassador at the Court of Berlin to ask Count Bismark, on the 16th March, whether Prussia seriously intended to break the Convention of Gastein. Count Bismark answered No, and added that he could make no further answer by word of mouth, as oral conversations were easily liable to be misunderstood, and that, if the Austrian ambassador desired any further information on the subject, it would be better that he should put his interrogations in writing. This was not, however, done.

Directly after the council of war at Vienna, on the 10th, March, Austria had taken steps to array the minor States against Prussia, and to secure their co-operation. In a circular despatch of the 16th March, the States of the Germanic Confederation which were inclined towards Austria were warned of the warlike attitude of Prussia, and were cautioned to take heed to the armament of their contingents and to their completion to war strength, since Austria had an intention to soon bring before the Germanic Diet a motion for the mobilization of the Federal army.

The movement of troops in Bohemia daily excited the apprehensions of Prussia. There still rankled in that country, the memory of 1850, when she, unprepared, suddenly found herself opposed to Austria fully armed, and was forced to submit to) the terms dictated to her at Olmütz. Count Bismark had, however, provided that no such fate should befall her in 1866.

Although he knew well the position in which he stood with regard to the minor States, he considered it advisable to force from them a declaration of their policy. In a despatch of the 24th March he declared that, on account of the armaments of Austria, Prussia was also at last obliged to take measures for the protection of Silesia; for, although Austria at present spoke in peaceful terms, it was to be feared that these would alter as soon as her preparations for war were completed.

Prussia, he added, could not, however, remain content with measures calculated for her momentary safety alone; she must look into the future, and seek there guarantees for that security which she had in vain anticipated from her alliance with Austria. Prussia, of course, under these circumstances, looked in the first place towards the other German States; but her perception ever became clearer that the Germanic Confederation in its present form did not fulfil its aim, not even did it do so when Austria and Prussia were united, much less would it when these two powers were disunited.

If Prussia now were attacked by Austria, she could not expect the support of the Germanic Confederation: she could only rely upon the goodwill of the single States which had promised her their help without reference to the bonds of the confederation. In this despatch, therefore, Prussia wished to ask with what feelings she was regarded by individual States; and, that she might prove their sincerity towards her, she would in any case desire a reform of the political and military constitution of the confederation.

This despatch of Count Bismark, which was really only a question to the minor States of how they would act in case of a war between Prussia and Austria, was answered by their respective governments in almost identical terms. With one accord they pointed to the Eleventh Article of the Charter of Constitution of the Germanic Confederation, by which all States members of the confederation bound themselves never to make war against each other, but to bring their differences before the Germanic Diet, which was to be the mediator and arbiter between the disputants. How worthless any such article can be to restrain physical by moral force was never more clearly demonstrated than in the late struggle, when the Germanic Confederation was shivered to pieces in the shock of battle of its contending members.

Prussia now saw it was time to make her preparations for war. Austria had earlier begun to arm, but the more elastic military organisation of Prussia, the constant attention—sprung from the knowledge of her statesmen that, sooner or later, a German war would take place— which had for many years been devoted to her army, more than compensated for the start of a few weeks which Austria had gained.

By decrees of the 27th and 29th of March the first armaments were ordered in the provinces most exposed to attack from Austria. The battalions of the five divisions which garrisoned the provinces contingent with the Austrian and Saxon frontiers were placed on the highest peace footing, but not yet increased to war strength. Five brigades of field artillery were, however, fully completed; and the armament of the fortresses of Glatz, Cosel, Neisze, Torgau, Wittemberg, Spandau, and Magdeburg commenced. Prussia, confident in the rapidity with which her whole army could be mobilized, was able to limit herself to these purely defensive augmentations, which entailed an increase of only about 20,000 men to the army always maintained in time of peace. She deferred till the last necessary moment the raising of the army to war strength, in order as long as possible to leave the men, who must be called into the ranks, to their trades, professions, and labours. Of this increase of the army no secret was made; the decree which ordered it was openly published and commented upon in the daily press.

On the 31st March, Count Mensdorf, the Austrian Minister for Foreign Affairs, announced to the Cabinet of Berlin that all movements of troops in Bohemia had really taken place only in consequence of the riots against the Jews, and that the Emperor Francis Joseph had never contemplated an attack on Prussia.

On the 6th April Prussia announced in answer that she had not been the first to arm, and that now she only had taken defensive measures. The Austrian Government replied on the following day that no overwhelming concentration of troops had taken place in Bohemia, in fact nothing to approach what the Austrian organisation could place in the field if a great war were in prospect; that no extraordinary purchase of horses had been made, and that the number of men who had been on furlough recalled to the ranks was not worthy of mention; that any discussion as to priority of armament was rendered superfluous by the declaration of the emperor, that he had never contemplated an attack on Prussia; that the Cabinet of Vienna desired only a similar declaration on the part of King William; and that, since no preparation for war had been made in Austria, it was only necessary that Prussia should repeal the armaments which had been decreed at the end of March.

On the 15th April, Count Bismark sent a note to Vienna, in which, without argument, he assumed that Austria had armed, and had commenced to arm before Prussia, and expressed his opinion that Austria should be the first to commence to disarm.

On the 18th Count Mensdorf replied, and promised that Austria would move the troops quartered in Bohemia from those positions in which Prussia had considered that they were intended for an attack upon Silesia.

Count Bismark, on the 21st April, remarked in reply that, on authentic news being received of the disarming of Austria, Prussia would follow step by step in the same course. Scarcely, however, had Austria named the 25th of April as the termination of all military proceedings which might be supposed to be intended against Prussia, than the promise of disarmament was stultified by the announcement that, although Austria would disarm in Bohemia, she was compelled to take decisive measures for the defence of Venetia against Italy.

Prussian partisans argue that the armament of Venetia was an equal threat against Prussia as the armament of Bohemia, but this was not necessarily the case. Six hundred thousand Austrian soldiers south of the Danube would require as long a time to be moved to Saxony as would suffice to mobilize the whole Prussian Army. But Prussia was allied with Italy, and although she chose to fancy that Austrian troops in the Tyrol might be intended to act upon the Elbe, in reality she saw in them the means given to Austria to crush an army allied to Prussia, after the defeat of which Austria might turn her undistracted forces against her German enemies.

There is no doubt that Italy had already armed, and was fully prepared to take advantage of the opportunity of a war between Prussia and Austria to attack Venetia. The open threat that Venetia would be assailed at the first favourable moment would alone have been ground sufficient for Austria to declare war against Italy, and to sweep away an army which was avowedly maintained only to strike her in the hour of trouble. On the 22nd April the soldiers of reserve and men on furlough were called up for the regiments in Venetia, and measures were taken to prepare for the field an army to act against the Italians.

These steps called forth a despatch from Count Bismark, in which Prussia took her new ally under her protectorate, and demanded that Austria should not only disarm in Bohemia and Moravia, but also in Venetia. To this Austria did not consent, and Prussia made an advance in her armaments. This was accelerated by the discovery that some of the minor States were secretly treating at Bamberg, which aroused the suspicion that a coalition was being formed against Prussia. On the 24th April, the infantry of five Prussian *corps d'armée*, as well as the whole of the cavalry and artillery, were increased to war strength, but as yet were not mobilized.[3]

---

3. The term mobilization is applied to the administrative acts which supply a collection of soldiers with the transport, commissariat, &c., which render them fit to be moved into and act in the field.

On the 26th April, Austria again reverted to the Schleswig-Holstein question, and proposed to submit the definitive decision of this question to the Germanic Confederation, and to hand over the duchies to the Prince of Augustenburg. Both these propositions were declined by Prussia on the 7th May, when Count Bismark remarked that the competency of the Confederation to decide in these international questions could not be recognised, and that the whole question could be most simply and easily settled by coming to an understanding with Austria, for the reform of the Constitution of the Confederation by the speedy assembly of a German Parliament, as had already been proposed by Prussia on the 9th April.[4]

Matters were daily approaching a crisis, and Prussia was determined to be ready for the conflict which would probably soon break out The King of Prussia, on the 4th May, had already ordered the five *corps d'armée*, which had been augmented to war strength, to be mobilized; and ordered the soldiers of reserve of the other [5] four *corps d'armée* to be called in, so as to place these also upon a war strength. On the 7th May, these four corps also received orders to be mobilized; so that now the whole of the war army, as provided for by the regulations of the Prussian service, were called under arms. The mobilization was effected with wonderful rapidity and precision. At the end of fourteen days, the 490,000 men who formed the strength of this army stood on parade, armed, clothed, equipped with all necessities for a campaign, and fully provided with the necessary transport trains, provision and ammunition columns, as well as field hospitals. The rapidity with which these trains were provided might almost be accepted as proof that, for several years, Prussia had foreseen that her policy would not, for any great length of time, conduct her along the paths of peace.

On the 19th May, the concentration of the Prussian army might have commenced, and actually by the end of May the troops had taken up their positions in the frontier provinces, a triumph for the Prussian machinery of mobilization. The rapidity with which this army was called together, equipped, and transported to its positions on the frontier cannot be too highly admired, especially when it is considered that more than 250,000 of the soldiers had been suddenly called in from the reserve and *Landwehr*. Prussian authors, with complacency, point to the army collected upon the frontier at the very

4. See beginning chapter 4.
5. See Military Organisation, Book 3, chapter 1.

beginning of June, and indignantly demand how Europe can suppose that Prussia incited the war, when, if she wished to make an attack upon Austria, she could have done so at this moment with such a great advantage. For, although the Austrian armaments had been commenced ten weeks earlier than the Prussians, they were still in a very backward state, and the Austrian army was still far from ready to open the campaign.

But was Prussia really so moderate as her advocates would have the world believe? Was it desire of peace or fear of failure which stayed her hand, and held her marshalled corps on the north of the mountain frontier of Bohemia? It may have been both, but the results of the war show that the latter entered into the calculations of those who planned the Prussian strategy. The army was ready, and might have attacked Austria, but it would in its advance have exposed its communications to the assault of the minor States, and, until forces were prepared to quell these, the main army could not assume the offensive. This appears to have been the probable cause why the troops were not at once concentrated, and pushed immediately into Bohemia.

As it was, at the very beginning the Prussian Army confined itself to taking up defensive positions to cover the provinces most exposed to attack, especially towards Bohemia. The Austrian Army of the North had commenced its concentration in Bohemia on the 13th May, and Feldzeugmeister[6] Benedek had there taken over the command-in-chief of it on the 18th. The 1st, 5th, and 6th Prussian *corps d'armée* [7] were posted in Silesia, the 2nd and 3rd corps in Lusatia, and the 4th corps round Erfurt. The Guards corps was still left at Berlin, and the 7th and 8th corps were retained in Westphalia and the Rhine provinces respectively.

Several of the minor States—such as Bavaria, Hesse Darmstadt, and Nassau—had also ordered their armies, and their contingents of Federal troops, to be mobilized during the month of May; others— as Saxony, Electoral Hesse, Würtemburg, and Hanover—had commenced the augmentation of the military peace establishments by the recall of men on furlough, or soldiers of the reserve.

Italy had early in the year commenced preparations for an attack against Venetia as soon as war might break out between Austria and Prussia. At the beginning of May the Italian armaments assumed a more definite form; and, in order to enlist more closely national feel-

6. General of Artillery.
7. See Book 3, chapter 1.

ing in the probable struggle, on the 8th of that month a decree was published at Florence for the formation of twenty volunteer battalions, to be placed under the immediate command of General Garibaldi All party contests, all political animosities, in Italy were silenced. The whole nation drew together for a common assault upon its traditional enemy when he should be encumbered by the heavy pressure of Prussia upon his northern frontier. The crowds of volunteers that flocked to Garibaldi's standard were so great that, at the end of May, the number of battalions had to be doubled. On this Austria raised a compulsory loan in Venetia of twelve million gulden, which so embittered and excited Italian feeling that it seemed doubtful whether King Victor Emanuel would be able to keep his people in hand, or prevent excitable individuals from precipitating a contest for which the moment had not yet arrived.

Thus the nations were making ready for war, each, with its hand on its sword, moving heavy masses of troops to convenient positions near the frontiers of its probable antagonist. Before detailing the positions these masses assumed, or attempting to show how they were guided into the shock of battle, it is necessary to cast a glance over the diplomatic sparring which preceded the military conflict

CHAPTER 4

Prussia's Motion For Reform of Germanic Confederation

As was referred to in a previous chapter, Prussia brought forward, on the 9th April, in the Germanic Diet a motion for the reform of the confederation. The essence of this motion consisted in a desire that a German Parliament should be assembled by means of universal and direct suffrage, in order to introduce that unity into the central power which naturally must be wanting to the *diet*,—an assembly of delegates of the various States, who acted in accordance with the instructions of their cabinets. Prussia desired that the day for the assembly of this parliament should be at once fixed; and declared that when this point was settled she would bring forward special motions. She wished also to employ the time which must intervene before the assembly of this parliament in taking measures to secure the accord of the other governments to the measures which she would bring forward.

The Prussian motion was not very agreeable to the other governments; but it would not have been prudent to reject it altogether. The constitution of the Administrative Assembly of the Germanic Confederation was notoriously and avowedly imperfect, and few men in Germany, either among sovereigns or subjects, would not have rejoiced in its reform and reorganisation. But very few Germans desired that the ideas of this reform, and the projects for its completion, should emanate from Prussia, and still less from Count Bismark.

The *diet*, on the 21st April, decided that the motion should be referred to a specially-chosen committee. And on the 26th this committee was elected

The object of many of the German Governments was now to put off indefinitely the calling together of the parliament Count Bismark, in a despatch of the 27th, recognised that this was the aim of many, and expressed his opinion that the step the *diet* had already taken in referring the motion to a committee could hardly have any other result than to postpone a solution of the question until the Greek *Kalends*. He said that at this time growing animosities required the completion of the work of reform; and that on this work depended the maintenance of peace, and the dissolution of the uneasiness which at present penetrated all minds.

On the 11th May the President of the Prussian Cabinet communicated confidentially to the committee of the *diet* the ground-plan of the changes which he considered ought to be made in the constitution of the confederation. These were: the completion of the central power by means of a German Parliament, extension of the legislative competency of the new central power, removal of all restrictions on trade and commerce of every sort which then separated the Germanic States from one another, the organisation of a common system for the guardianship of German trade abroad, the foundation of a German navy, an improved establishment of the German land-forces, so that their general efficiency might be improved, while the expenses of individual States might be diminished.

These proposals were, doubtless, good and worthy of regard; but there were too many interests which would be affected by their adoption to allow such measures to be immediately accepted by the *diet* Long time would have been required to pass a motion entailing such great alterations through the *diet*; and the demand of Count Bismark for a speedy reform of the constitution of the confederation, far from removing, aggravated the chances of war. While the steps for the reform of the Federal Constitution dragged slowly along, the preparations for war were rapidly developed, and, a few days after the despatch of Count Bismark's confidential communication to the committee of the *diet*, the decree was issued for the mobilization of the whole Prussian Army.[1]

1. Rüstow, Der Krieg von 1866 in Deutschland.

CHAPTER 5

Breach of Convention of Gastein

Oh what a tangled web we weave,
When first we venture to deceive.

It was after Prussia proposed a reform of the Federal Constitution that Austria reopened the Schleswig-Holstein question, after a long silence had been maintained on that subject between the two great powers.[1]

On the 26th April, Count Mensdorf sent a despatch to Count Karolyi, the Austrian ambassador at Berlin, the contents of which were to be communicated to Count Bismark, which earnestly pressed Prussia again to turn her attention to the matter of the Elbe duchies. This despatch was naturally not agreeable to the Prussian Government, for in it Austria assumed that Schleswig-Holstein should be given over to the Prince of Augustenburg, which solution of the question would have been the most unfavourable of all to the interests and intentions of Prussia. In a letter of the 1st May, Count Bismark expressed anew his views on the question to Baron Werther, the Prussian ambassador at Vienna, and endorsed the contents of this letter by a note of the 7th May, in which he expressed the strong desire of Prussia to hold fast to the Treaty of Vienna and the Convention of Gastein, by which the introduction of any third party, as for instance of the Germanic Confederation, into the government of Schleswig-Holstein was prohibited.

Count Bismark further declared that Prussia had no intention to renounce the rights she had acquired over Schleswig-Holstein to a third party without consideration for her own interests, or for those of Germany in general: but that she was always ready to treat with Austria as to the conditions on which she would renounce the question

---

1. See chapter 2.

of the rights to the duchies of the Elbe which she had acquired by the Treaty of Vienna. In conclusion, the Prussian minister added the wish that Austria might act in harmony with Prussia in the question of the reform of the Federal Constitution.

For the first time in the diplomatic proceedings Prussia had now openly repudiated the idea that her hold upon Schleswig was temporary or provisional She now insisted upon the right of conquest to that duchy, as sealed by the Peace of Vienna of October, 1864.

To this despatch Austria returned no answer. The din of armaments on all sides rose every day more loudly. All Germany, Austria, and Italy were hunting on their harness, and rapidly becoming great camps; and men foresaw that almost any attempt to secure peace would probably only precipitate a conflict

Austria had, on the 4th May, entirely broken off negotiations with Prussia on the subject of disarmament [2] Count Mensdorf had declared that it was superfluous to argue the question of priority of argument; that it was impossible for Austria to disarm in Venetia, on account of the agitation in Italy; and that Austria, by preparing to resist an attack on her south-eastern frontier, was protecting not only her own individual interests, but those of all Germany, and that no German State should look askance at preparations made in such a cause.

The government of Saxony was much disturbed by the Prussian interrogation as to why that country was arming, and the concomitant demand that these armaments should cease. Fearful of an attack. Saxony, on the 5th May, proposed a motion in the Frankfort Diet, the object of which was that the *diet* should promptly decree, with reference to the proceedings of the Prussian Government, that the internal peace of the confederation was to be preserved.

On the introduction of this motion, the Prussian representative declared that Prussia had no intention to attack Saxony, and that all the armament which had taken place in his country had only been prompted by purely defensive considerations.

Nevertheless, on the 9th May, the *diet* passed the Saxon motion by a majority of ten over five votes.

The middle States, at the head of which stood Bavaria, under this threatening aspect of affairs, earnestly desired to effect a compromise. They felt that, since Prussia had not been the only State to arm, it would be unfair if she only were required to declare the object of her armament They therefore proposed a motion in the *diet* to the effect

2. See chapter 4.

that all governments which had armed should be required to state their reasons for having done so. This motion was passed on the 24th May, and on the 1st June the statements were to have been received. The 1st June was an important landmark in the development of the diplomatic crisis; but, before reviewing its incidents, it is necessary to glance at external influences which were exerted in the vain, and perhaps only apparent, endeavour to preserve peace in Germany.

While in Italy the whole population were clamorous for war; while Prussia, the author and originator of the whole disturbance, by her disregard of the rights of the prince in whose nominal cause she had taken up arms in 1864, was pointing out her increased battalions as purely a defensive police for the security of her territory; and while the war party in Austria, eager to wipe out on the Mincio the memory of Solferino, and proudly confident of the power of the military empire to sweep away with one hand the feverish soldiery of Victor Emanuel, while with the other it shattered the legions of Prussia, urged the Cabinet of Vienna not to yield an item: Russia and England, led and accompanied by France, entered upon the diplomatic theatre. These three great powers made a common attempt to avert the war by despatching, on the 28th May, almost identical notes to Austria, Prussia, Italy, and the Germanic Confederation. In these notes it was proposed that the five great powers should join in a conference, at which the Germanic Confederation should also be represented, in order to settle by treaty the three main questions which menaced the peace of Europe. These questions were that of the Elbe duchies, of the tranquillity of Italy, and of the reform of the Federal Constitution of Germany.

The possibility of peace being maintained by these means was from the beginning extremely doubtful: even in the event of all the parties interested consenting to submit their causes to this European jury. Almost the utmost that could be expected from a conference would be that the points of dispute might be defined, and in this manner that the theatre of war might be limited.

On the 29th May, Prussia accepted the proposal for the conference. Italy followed this example; also the Germanic Confederation. Of what validity these acceptances were, may however be calculated from the fact that at the time of the acceptance the confederation informed its representative, Herr Von der Pfordten, that the project had already practically fallen to the ground.[3]

3. *Rüstow, Der Krieg von 1866 in Deutschland und Italien.*

Austria was only willing to join the conference on condition that no territorial alterations should be there discussed. This proviso was absolutely necessary for Austria. If territorial changes were to be discussed, few could doubt but that a proposal would be made for the cession of Venetia to Italy, and of the Elbe duchies to Prussia. If these cessions took place, Austria would lose as much without a blow, in her own diminution and the aggrandizement of her German rival, as could at that time have been anticipated from the most disastrous issue of the imminent war. It does not appear that it was any desire of war on the part of Austria which made her couple her expressions of readiness to join the conference with this condition, which appears on the contrary to have been advanced from a perhaps too honest desire to meet the wishes of the great powers.

To this communication of Austria the mediating powers replied that, in their opinion, the disputant governments should be allowed full freedom for the discussion, and if possible for the solution, of every relevant question at the conference.

Thus matters stood on the 1st June, the day appointed by the Federal Decree of the 24th May as that on which the German Powers were to make their declarations concerning their armaments.

The *diet* was assembled at Frankfort The Austrian representative rose, and declared that Austria could look back with a calm conscience on her steady endeavours to preserve an unity with Prussia in the question of the Elbe duchies. The Emperor Francis Joseph had conceded the uttermost title that the dignity of Austria and the rights of the Germanic Confederation would allow. Prussia had made unjust proposals, and had expressed the intention of prosecuting and carrying out these proposals by force. As Prussia had threatened, after the peace of Vienna, to compel the Federal troops to evacuate Holstein, so she had also threatened Austria concerning the question of the duchies with force, and had relied on the support of foreign opponents of the Imperial State.

At the time of the Convention of Gastein Prussia had renewed this attempt, because Austria would not consent to administer Schleswig-Holstein according to the policy of annexation. Threatened on two sides, Austria had been compelled to place herself in an attitude of defence. The preparations against Italy might rest unchallenged at Frankfort Austria would recall her troops that had been raised against Prussia, provided that the latter did not intend to make an attack on Austrian territory, or on any State allied to Austria, and would give security against the recurrence of the danger of war. This security would depend for Germany, as for Austria, on the fact that in Germany not force, but treaties and right ruled, and that Prussia also, although an European Power, should respect the peace and the decrees of the confederation, and further that the Schleswig-Holstein question should be settled, not for the interest of an individual claimant, but according to the rights of those provinces and Federal rule.

On the 24th August, 1865, Austria and Prussia had promised to communicate to the confederation the result of their negotiations in reference to Schleswig-Holstein. Austria now was fulfilling this promise. That she must now declare that all her endeavours to obtain a solution of the question of the duchies which would be agreeable to the confederation had been of no avail, and that now, in the first place, Austria yielded up everything further on this point to the decree of the confederation, and in the second place had already ordered her commissioner in Holstein to assemble the estates of that duchy in order to obtain an expression of the wishes of the people as to their future fate.

Austria thus attempted to undo what she had assisted in doing by the Treaty of Vienna and the convention of Gastein. But, in order to make restitution for her disregard of right in these two agreements, she was now obliged to break the Convention of Gastein, in handing over to the confederation, which she had declared incompetent in this international question, the decision of the future fate of the duchies. Her second step, by which she ordered her commissioner, Field Marshal Gablenz, to convene the Holstein Estates, was also, if not an actual breach of the convention, a virtual one, because by the convention, although the administration of the duchies was divided, the rights of the two sovereigns to the common supremacy were still as much extant as ever.[4]

After the Austrian declaration, the representative of Prussia at the *diet* rose, and said that the mobilization of the Prussian Army had only taken place in consequence of the Austrian armaments; only if these armaments were annulled, and if at the same time the other Germanic States which were allied with Austria restored amicable relations between themselves and Prussia, could Prussia herself disarm. On these conditions she would disarm immediately. Prussia had only taken defensive measures. If the Germanic Confederation was not in a position to give Prussia guarantees for the maintenance of peace, if

4. See chapter 1.

the members of the confederation resisted those reforms of the Federal Constitution which were universally recognised as necessary, the Prussian Government must accept the conclusion that the confederation did not attain its object, and could not fulfil the most important of its aims, and that with regard to further Federal revolutions, Prussia would act on this conviction.

The Prussian representative further defended his government against the Austrian conception of the circumstances connected with the Schleswig-Holstein question, and advanced in support of his assertion the many declarations which Prussia had made with reference to this question.

The speeches of the two representatives of the great German Powers were the main events of the assembly of the *diet* of the Germanic Confederation at Frankfort on the 1st June, 1866. The reports of these speeches were immediately telegraphed to every town in Germany, and caused great excitement. Men foresaw that a war would result by the shock of which the political circumstances and peculiar constitution of the Fatherland would be shaken to their very foundations; but no one almost supposed the outbreak of war to be so near. It was believed that Austria was much superior as a military power, certainly at the outbreak of a war, to Prussia, but she was not yet ready, and it could not be supposed that she would urge matters on till her preparations were complete. Nor did sage men, who, wondering by what fatuous madness Count Bismark was driving his government into a one-sided struggle, looked impartially upon the course of events, ever imagine that Prussian temerity would be wild enough to anticipate the necessity of defence through bearding a more than respected adversary by commencing the attack.

Count Bismark saw, however, in the steps that Austria had lately taken, in her summons to the Holstein Estates, and in the publication of her intentions with regard to the Elbe duchies, the final severance of the Cabinet of Vienna from his policy. No longer could Austria be persuaded to stand beside him in a common slight against, or oppression of, the body of the Germanic Confederation. Austria had resumed her position as the champion of the individuality of small States. The spoilers had ultimately quarrelled over the allotment of their prey. The Convention of Gastein was broken through and trampled upon.

Against the breach of this convention, Count Bismark sent a protest to Vienna; but, in anticipation of the answer he would receive to this protest, signed on the 4th June a despatch to the Prussian plenipotentiaries at foreign courts. This despatch accused Austria of giving provocation to war; and attributed to the Austrian Government the intention of recruiting its finances by forced contributions from Prussia, or by an honourable bankruptcy.

Count Bismark at the same time took a step more likely to be productive of important results than either protests or protocols The concentration of the Prussian army was resumed. The *corps d'armée* of the Guard was sent to Silesia, the eighth *corps d'armée* and one division of the seventh corps were forwarded by railway from the banks of the Rhine to the neighbourhood of Halle.[5] In Berlin a reserve *corps d'armée* was formed of the four regiments of the *Landwehr* of the Guard, and of four other *Landwehr* regiments, while all available artillery and cavalry was drawn together, organised, and mobilized as quickly as possible.

---

5. How it came that Prussia was able to leave the frontier of the Rhine totally undefended during the campaign, when it was evident from the subsequent demand made by France that the government of the Tuileries had a jealous eye upon Rheinland, has remained one of the mysteries of the war. The explanation as far as yet can be discovered appears to be as follows:—In 1865 Count Bismark paid a visit to the Emperor of the French at Biarritz, and there hinted broadly that in case France would stand aloof, and allow Prussia to work her way in Germany, compensation might be given. for France's tranquillity by the cession of the Rhine provinces. The emperor, who expected, like everyone else, that the contest would be, if not favourable to Austria, certainly long and doubtful, anticipated that at a certain stage he would be able to step upon the theatre of war, and demand, from whichever side he espoused, the possession of the Rhine provinces of Prussia. He gave no distinct assurance to Count Bismark of neutrality, but the count left Biarritz with a tolerable certainty that France would not interfere, at least at the commencement of a war, and without giving any distinct promise to the emperor of territorial compensation. When the campaign terminated as abruptly as it did, the Emperor of the French wished to claim the price of his neutrality, but Prussia was then in a condition to enter on a campaign with France, whose armies were not armed with breech-loaders, and refused to entertain any ideas of territorial cession.

BOOK 2

CHAPTER 1

First Bloodless Conflict in Holstein

The good old rule sufficeth me,
The stern and simple plan—
Let those take who have the power,
And let those keep who can.

Notwithstanding the protests of Count Bismark, the Austrian Civil Commissioner of Holstein, General Von Gablenz, issued a decree on the 5th June, 1866, by which the estates of Holstein were summoned to meet on the 11th of that month at Itzehoe. It was, however, known at Berlin (on the same day as that on which the despatch to the plenipotentiaries of Prussia at foreign courts was signed) that Austria was about to bring forward a motion in the *diet* for Federal execution against Prussia. Accordingly, on the 6th June, Prussia published a more special protest against the assembly of the Holstein Estates, as well as a declaration that Prussia would consider such an encroachment on the Convention of Gastein as a direct breach of that agreement, and that in consequence not only was the convention a dead letter, but that the common occupation and administration of the duchies must be resumed as before that convention.

Orders were accordingly despatched from Berlin to General Manteuffel, the Prussian commissioner in Schleswig, that as soon as General Gablenz summoned the Holstein Estates to meet, he should enter Holstein with his Prussian troops in order to again resume the common administration of the two duchies. Orders were given to General Manteuffel to avoid any conflict with the Austrian troops; and to assure General Gablenz that the inruption of Prussian troops into the duchy over which he was appointed to represent the Austrian Emperor, was undertaken quite in a friendly spirit. General Manteuffel accordingly informed General Gablenz beforehand of his intention of invading Holstein, and issued this proclamation to the people of the duchy of Schleswig:—

Gottorp, June 7.

Inhabitants of the Duchy of Schleswig,—
Since my assumption of office here I have always acted towards you with frankness. Never have I had any reason to repent of that course, and I now address myself to you again with the same frankness. The rights of sovereignty which His Majesty my king and master has over the duchy of Holstein have been endangered by proceedings with which you are all acquainted. The most sacred interests of your country are placed in jeopardy, for never have the estates of either of the duchies been called together except in view of an assembly of the general representation of an undivided Schleswig-Holstein. I am charged by His Majesty the King with the protection of those menaced rights, and for that reason I have today ordered the entry of troops into Holstein, as I have announced to the Imperial Governor of the duchy of Holstein that this military measure has only a purely defensive character.

Inhabitants of the Duchy of Schleswig,—I have learnt to know and to esteem the spirit of order and legality with which you are animated, and I now give you a proof of this esteem. At this moment Schleswig is being almost denuded of troops. You will prove that the attitude which you have hitherto maintained has not been induced by fear, but by the loyalty of your character. But you, too, in your turn have learnt to know me, and you know that I am faithfully and heartily devoted to the interests of this country. You will with confidence accept my word. No doubt of the power or of the will of Prussia could find root in your minds. Let us have faith in each other.

The Governor of the duchy of Schleswig,
E. Manteuffel,
Lieutenant-General
Aide-de-Camp to His Majesty the King of Prussia.

General Gablenz did not wait for the inruption at Kiel, where his headquarters had hitherto been, but suddenly left that town, and concentrated the whole of his forces, which consisted of the infantry brigade of Kalik and one regiment of dragoons, at Altona. The government of Holstein and the Prince of Augustenburg followed him quickly.

On the morning of the 8th June the Prussian troops crossed the Eider, without paying any attention to a protest launched against their proceedings by General Gablenz, and moved slowly southwards. General Manteuffel had under his command in Schleswig two brigades of infantry and one brigade of cavalry, and he crossed the frontier of Holstein with all his disposable force. Austria was naturally unwilling to resume the common administration of the two duchies as it had existed previous to the Convention of Gastein, and accordingly, by order of his government, General Gablenz concentrated his troops in the south-western corner of the duchy. General Manteuffel, who had marched into Holstein on the 8th June, on the 11th prevented the assembly of the Holstein Estates at Itzhoe by taking military possession of that town, closing the House of Assembly, and placing a guard over the door with fixed bayonets.

General Gablenz, assailed by far superior numbers, and unable to be of any more use in Holstein, on the night between the 11th and the 12th June withdrew his troops to Hamburg, and thence despatched them by railway through Hanover, Cassel, and Frankfort to the Austrian Army of the north in Bohemia. From this bloodless conflict in Holstein arose the first Prussian victory, gained by the knowledge of the great rule of war, which teaches that to reap success great numbers must be hurled upon the decisive point, and that in order that these superior numbers may be forthcoming, rapidity of concentration, organisation, and locomotion of troops are vitally required. This bloodless victory, and the consequent evacuation of Holstein by the Austrians, had an important effect on the subsequent incidents of the war.

The abandonment of Holstein added only five battalions of infantry, two squadrons of cavalry, and one battery of artillery to the Austrian army in the field; while the same event left the whole of the Prussian division of General Manteuffel—which consisted of twelve battalions of infantry, eight squadrons of cavalry, and six batteries of artillery—free and at the disposition of the Prussians for the further prosecution of operations.

The assembly of the Holstein Estates, and the delivery of the opinion of the southern Elbe duchy with regard to its future fate, was prevented by the inroad of the Prussians. The Prince of Augustenburg departed from the province. The Prussian Government appointed

Herr Von Scheel-Plessen as Supreme President of Schleswig-Holstein. Supreme President is the title of the highest civil administrator of a Prussian province. Scheel-Plessen entered upon the duties of his new office on the 11th June; while the non-consulted duchies looked on sulkily upon the Prussian assertions of right The duchies came under Prussian rule when Scheel-Plessen assumed his office. This was all very arbitrary, forcible, and dependent upon main strength, but the Prussian virtual annexation of Schleswig-Holstein had one good effect. It settled the question of the Elbe duchies; and, as far as the Seven Weeks' War is concerned, neither reader nor author will be again troubled with the intricate problem of the true rights of succession to "Schleswig-Holstein sea-surrounded."

CHAPTER 2

Final Rupture Between Prussia and Austria

On the 11th June, 1866, an Extraordinary Assembly of the *diet* was summoned.

The representative of Austria advanced the proposition at this sitting, that Prussia had broken the Convention of Gastein, and threatened the peace of the Germanic Confederation, by marching her troops into Holstein. He proposed in consequence for the restoration of peace, that the whole of the army of the confederation, with the exception of the three *corps d'armée* [1] which, by the Federal Constitution, Prussia was bound to put into the field, should be mobilized in such form of principal, contingents, and reserves within fourteen days, that the troops should be able then to march within fourteen hours.[2] That care was to be taken for *depôt* contingents, and that the appointment of a commander-in-chief was to take place as soon as the decree was passed; and that the supervision of all these matters was to be given , over to the *diet*, which was to act in concert with the military commissioner of the Germanic Confederation.

The representative of Prussia at the *diet* declared that he was not authorized to make any statement upon the motion which had been brought forward, the purport of which was entirely new to him.

The Austrian representative, who filled the post of President of the *diet*, urged an immediate decree in favour of the motion; and the Assembly, although the representative of Mecklenburg brought to no-

---

1. The 4th, 5th, and 6th *corps d'armée* of the Federal army.
2. Could a British Army be mobilized and be placed in such a state within fourteen days as to be able to march in twenty-four-hours? Yet this rapidity of mobilization was not sufficient to oppose the Prussian organisation.

tice, that even on the most unimportant questions, when for instance only the disbursement of one hundred *gulden*[3] was under consideration, three sittings were required, one for the introduction of the motion, one for the discussion, and one for the final vote, the majority of the Diet decreed that the final vote on the Austrian motion should be taken on the 14th June. Whoever recalls to mind the many years which the *diet* consumed ere it passed the vote of Federal execution against Denmark, can hardly doubt that the deeds of Prussia had been replete with some peculiar enormity in the eyes of the princes of the small states to arouse so enthusiastic a zeal in such an usually torpid body as the Germanic Diet

---

3. Equal to about 10*l.*

Breakup of the Germanic Confederation

Destruction hangs o'er yon devoted wall,
And nodding Ilion waits th' impending fall.

Pope.

The history of mankind informs us that a single power is very seldom broken by a confederacy.—Johnson.

Before the 14th June arrived, Count Bismark sent a definite and final project to the governments of the various States which were members of the Germanic Confederation. The first article of this project of reform expressed:

That the territory of the confederation was to consist of those States which had hitherto been included in the Confederation, with the exception of the dominions of the Emperor of Austria, and of the King of the Netherlands.

While, then, Austria wished to enlist the governments of the Germanic Confederation in war against Prussia, Prussia desired to exclude Austria from the confederation. As for the government of the Netherlands, it had wished for nothing more for a long time than to be allowed to withdraw from the confederation its two duchies which were included within that political league.[1]

The next article treated of the Parliament, the common concerns of Germany, and of the privileges of the new confederation. The German war navy, with a common German budget, with the Federal harbour of Kiel and of the Bay of the Jahde, were proposed to be placed

---

1. The duchies of Luxembourg and Limburg.

under the supreme command of Prussia, while the land forces of the new confederation were to be divided into two Federal armies, an army of the north, and an army of the south. The King of Prussia was to be commander-in-chief of the northern army, the King of Bavaria that of the southern, both in peace and war.

In peace the commander-in-chief of either army was to superintend the efficient organisation and administration of his own army; and, in urgent cases, he was to be able to call out his army within the boundaries of his own part of the Federal territory, conditionally with the subsequent approval of the confederation. For each of the two Federal armies there was to be a common budget. The administration of either army was to be conducted under the superintendence of the commander-in-chief, and to either army the States included in its portion of the Federal territory were each to contribute their proportionate quota of soldiers. Each government was to pay the expenses of its own contingent of the Federal army. All expenses of the military budget were to fall on the military chest of that army to which the budget was specially applied The relations of the new confederation with the empire of Austria were to be settled by special treaties.

These were the principal points of the project of reform proposed by Count Bismark on the 10th June. This project surprised the majority of the German States in a very unpleasant manner. The 14th June arrived, the day for the final vote in the *diet* upon the Austrian motion.

The representative of Prussia in the *diet* protested against the motion being entertained, and declared that both in form and substance the motion was subversive of the ideas of the Confederation.

The votes were, however, taken, and the Austrian representative carried his motion by a majority of nine over six votes. The details of the voting were as follows:—For the Austrian motion there voted,—

The first *curia*, Austria.

The third, Bavaria.

The fourth, Saxony.

The fifth, Hanover.

The sixth, Wurtembuig.

The eighth, Electoral Hesse (Hesse-Cassel).

The ninth, Hesse-Darmstadt.

The sixteenth (Lichtenstein, Waldech, the two Reuszc, Lippe,

Lippe-Schaunburg, Hesse-Homburg).

Of the thirteenth *curia* (Brunswick and Nassau), Nassau.

Of the twelfth *curia* (Saxe Weimar, Saxe Altenburg, Saxe Coburg, and Saxe Meiningen), Saxe Meiningen.

Of the seventeenth *curia* (the four free towns, Hamburg, Lübeck, Bremen, and Frankfort), Frankfort.

Against the Austrian motion there voted,—

The seventh *curia*, Baden.

The eleventh *curia*, Luxembourg and Limburg (belonging to the Netherlands).

The twelfth *curia*, with the exception of Saxe Meiningen.

Of the thirteenth *curia*, Brunswick.

The fourteenth *curia*, the two Mecklenburghs.

The fifteenth *curia*, Oldenburg, Anhalt, and the two Schwurzburgs.

The seventeenth *curia*, with the exception of Frankfort.

In this voting, Prussia did not give a voice, as her representative had protested against any entertainment of the motion, and did not vote: and the tenth *curia*, Holstein Lauenburg, had no representative. The vote of the thirteenth *curia* was cancelled, because Brunswick voted against Nassau, and thus there was no majority in this *curia*.

Thus the results were that the 7th, 11th, 12th, 14th, 15th, and 17th *curiae*, therefore six *curiae*, voted against Austria; the 3rd, 4th, 5th, 6th, 8th, and 9th, besides the representative of Austria himself, for the Austrian motion. The vote of the 16th *curia* was recorded in favour of the motion, but, as appeared afterwards, accidentally. Each of the seven small States which composed this *curia* had an equal voice within the *curia*, and the vote of the *curia* was that of the majority of the component members.

On the 14th June, the representative of this *curia* who voted in the *diet*, and who was the delegate of Schaunburg-Lippe, declared that Lippe-Detwold, Waldeck, and Reusz of the younger line, therefore three-sevenths of the total, wished to vote against the Austrian motion; that he had not received full instructions from his own government, and must, consequently, give the vote of the *curia* for the Austrian motion. As soon as this was known, however, the government of Schaunburg-Lippe notified to the Prussian Government that it had also intended to vote against the Austrian motion, and thus disowned the act of its own delegate. It was then too late, for the vote had been given, and the motion passed. But had the government of Schaunburg-Lippe been a little more careful in sending definite instructions to its representative, and had Prussia voted, the Austrian motion would have been thrown out by a majority of eight over seven votes, and the event which plunged Central Europe into immediate war might have been certainly postponed, possibly evaded. On such tiny circumstances do the destinies of nations hang.

As the votes were actually recorded, the Austrian motion was carried by a majority of nine over six voices.

After the Austrian representative, the president of the *diet*, had declared the result of the voting, nine votes for Austria against six, the Prussian representative stated that it was now his duty to publish to the *diet* the resolutions of Prussia. The Austrian motion was in itself a negation of the Federal Constitution, and must necessarily be regarded by Prussia as a breach of the community of the confederation. The Federal Constitution recognised Federal execution against members of the confederation only in particular cases, which were clearly defined. These cases were entirely neglected in the Austrian motion. The position which Austria had assumed with regard to Holstein came in no manner under the protection of Federal treaties. On this account Prussia had refused in any way to take action on the Austrian motion, and not taken any precautions to oppose the Austrian intention.

According to the ideas of Prussia, the *diet* would not have for a moment listened to the Austrian proposals, but would have cast out the motion without any second thought upon the matter. Since the *diet* had, however, acted in a manner so contrary to all expectation; since Austria had been actually arming for three months, and had called the other members of the confederation to her aid, and since hereby the Act of Confederation, the chief object of which was to secure the internal tranquillity of Germany, was entirely invalidated, Prussia must consider the rupture of the Germanic Confederation as completed, and must view that confederation as dissolved and abrogated. Prussia did not, however, despise the national necessities for which that confederation was instituted, nor did she wish to unsettle the unity of the Germanic nationality; therefore she wished to declare herself ready and desirous to form a new confederation with those States which might be willing to unite with her in a Federal union on the basis of the reform proposed for the confederation on the 10th June. In conclusion, the Prussian delegate asserted the claims of his government to a share of all rights which sprang from the former constitution, and, having protested against the disbursement of any Federal moneys without the consent of Prussia, quitted the assembly.

The Germanic Confederation, established in 1815, was broken up at this moment. The declaration of internal war had virtually been proclaimed among its members.

The first action of Prussia in consequence of the decree of the *diet* of the 14th June, was to send a summons to the three States the territories of which lay within or close to the Prussian provinces, and which had voted against Prussia on the 14th June. These States were Hanover, Saxony, and the Electorate of Hesse. This summons required that the governments of these States should immediately reduce their troops to the peace establishment, which had existed on the 1st March, and should agree to join the new Prussian Federation on the basis of the reform proposed on the 10th June. If these governments declared, within twelve hours, their agreement to these demands, Prussia undertook to guarantee their sovereign rights within the boundaries of the proposed Federation; otherwise, Prussia announced her intention to declare war.

The three governments hesitated, and made no reply. On the evening of the 15th June, Prussia declared war against these three countries. No formal declaration of war was made against Austria, but at a later date the intention to commence hostilities was communicated to the Austrian outposts.

On the 17th June, the Austrian war manifesto was published; on the 18th, the Prussian; on the 20th, Italy, who had entered into an offensive and defensive alliance with Prussia, declared war against Austria and Bavaria. Diplomacy had now done its work, and the conflict was removed from the field of politics to the theatre of war.

Subjoined, for facility of reference, is a tabular list of the principal features of the political prologue.

October 20th, 1864. Treaty of Vienna.

August 14th, 1865. Convention of Gastein.

March 12th, 1866. First preparations of Austria for war in Bohemia and Moravia.

March 30th, 1866. First preparations of Prussia.

April, 1866. Negotiations concerning these armaments.

April 23rd, 1866. Great armament of Austria in Venetia.

April 26th, 1866. Proposal of Austria to submit the questions in dispute to the *diet*

May 7th, 1866. Declaration of Prussia of the *diet* to decide in international questions, and suggestion of the desirability of the reform of the Confederation.

Until *May 28th,* 1866. Armaments in all Germany and Italy.

May 28th, 1866. Proposal of a conference by the three great non-Germanic European Powers.

May 29th, 1866. Prussian acceptance of this proposal

June 1st, 1866. Austrian acceptance under conditions which render the conference impossible.

June 1st, 1866. Submission of Schleswig-Holstein question to the *diet*

June 5th, 1866. Summons by General Gablenz for assembly of Holstein Estates.

June 10th, 1866. Prussian proposal for the reform of the Federal Constitution.

June 11th, 1866. Austrian motion for the decree of Federal execution against Prussia.

June 14th, 1866. Acceptance of the Austrian motion by the *diet*

June 15th, 1866. Declaration of war by Prussia against Hanover, Electoral Hesse, and Saxony.

June 20th, 1866. Declaration of war by Italy against Austria and Bavaria.

CHAPTER 1[2]

The War Strength of Prussia

Before it is possible to enter upon a review of the military operations of the war, it is necessary to glance at the organisation, administration, and numbers of the forces which were at the disposal of the
belligerent powers. The question of the numerical strength of an army
in the field is always an extremely difficult one. Before a campaign,
sometimes the demands of strategy require that the strength of troops
should be exaggerated, sometimes the contrary. The casualties of every
skirmish, the sickness incident to every day's march and every night's
exposure, reduces the number of soldiers under arms. Hazy distinctions between combatants and non-combatants, different modes of
reckoning, the exclusion or inclusion of artillery and administrative
services in returns, the non-completion of battalions up to their normal strength, all throw great difficulties in the way of gaining an accurate appreciation of the number of men engaged on either side in
particular actions. It appears, therefore, advisable to sketch here the
organisation and regulated normal strength of the armies engaged in
the war, and to attempt, at necessary points in the narrative, to calculate and compute from the most trustworthy authorities the actual
numbers present on particular occasions.

The kingdom of Prussia before the war of 1866 had, with an area
of about 127,350 square miles, a population of over nineteen million
souls. The yearly revenues, according to the latest budgets, amounted

1. It may be a relief to the general and not professional reader to be made aware that
an omission to read this book, which is almost entirely technical, will not interrupt
the continuity of the narrative.

2. In the prefatory chapter to the second edition, will be found a sketch of the
changes made in the Prussian military system between the termination of the campaign of 1866 and the commencement of the late war with France.

to about 21,600,000*l*., and the expenditure of the government was always confined within its income. The National Debt in 1864 amounted to about 42,000,000*l*. The State chest in 1862 contained, from the surplus of estimated over actual annual expenditure, and from some other minor sources, a sum of about 2,500,000*l*. The financial economy of Prussia is superior to that of any nation in Europe. The army has lately cost in time of peace about, 6,300,000*l*. annually, the navy about 6,450,000 *l*.

The Prussian Army which took the field in the war of 1866 consisted of eight *corps d'armée* of troops of the line, and of the *corps d'armée* of the Guard. Each *corps d'armée* is organised with the intention of being a perfectly complete little army of itself, so that without inconvenience it can be detached from the main army at any time. Each *corps d'armée* of the line in time of war consists of two divisions of infantry, one division of cavalry, sixteen batteries of artillery, and a military train. Each division of infantry is composed of two brigades, each of which has two regiments, and, as each regiment contains three battalions, in a division of infantry there are twelve battalions; to every infantry division is also attached one regiment of cavalry, of four squadrons, and one division of artillery, of four batteries, making the total strength of the force under the command of every infantry divisional general twelve battalions, four squadrons, and four batteries.

A cavalry division consisted of two brigades, each containing two regiments, and, as every regiment had four squadrons, the division contained sixteen squadrons; it had also two batteries of horse artillery attached to it.

The reserve of artillery consisted of one division of field artillery, which formed four batteries, and of two batteries of horse artillery, besides an artillery train for. the supply of ammunition.

This gives the strength of a *corps d'armée* as twenty-four battalions of infantry, twenty-four squadrons of cavalry, and sixteen batteries of artillery. Besides this, however, each corps has one battalion of rifles and one battalion of engineers, besides an engineer train for the transport of materials for making bridges, and a large military train, which carries food, hospitals, medicines, fuel for cooking, bakeries, and all the other necessaries of not only life, but of the life of an army, the members of which require not only the same feeding, clothing, and warming as other members of the human race, but who will not be denied bullets, powder, shot and shells, saddlery for their horses, and who from the nature of their life are more liable to require medicines, bandages, splints, and all hospital accessories than other men.

If we do not consider the train when we are calculating the number of combatants who actually fall in, in the line of battle, every battalion may be considered to consist of 1,002 men. Thus the force of infantry and engineers in a *corps d'armée* numbers over 26,000, and on account of men absent through sickness may in round numbers be calculated at this figure. Each squadron of cavalry may be calculated at 140 mounted men, which makes the whole cavalry force about 3,300 men. Each division of four batteries of horse artillery brings into the field 590 actual combatants, and each of field artillery the same, so that the whole artillery force of a *corps d'armée* is about 2,350 men. The actual number of combatants with a *corps d'armée* is in this way seen to be 31,650 men, which may be stated in broad numbers at 31,000. The Guard *corps d'armée* differs chiefly from the Line corps in having one additional rifle battalion, one additional Fusilier regiment, and two additional cavalry regiments, which increase its strength by about 5,150 actual combatants; the total number of combatants in this corps may be safely assumed as 36,000 men, in round numbers.[3]

If we turn, however, to the list furnished by the military authorities, we find that the army was said to consist of 335,000 men, with 106,500 horses, of which only about 70,000 belonged to the cavalry and artillery, and that it was accompanied by a waggon train of 8,950 carriages, of which only 3,500 belonging to the artillery performed any service on the field of battle.

What has then become of these 55,000 men, 36,500 horses, and 5,450 carriages which form the difference between the returns we find of an army on paper and the actual number of men engaged on the field of battle? This difference represents the moving power of the combatant branches; it is this difference that feeds the warriors when they are well, that tends them when wounded, and nurses them when struck down with disease. Nor are these the only duties of the noncombatant branches. An army on a campaign is a little world of itself, and has all the requirements of ordinary men moving about the world, besides having an enemy in its neighbourhood, who attempts to oppose its progress in every way possible. When the line of march leads to a river, over which there is either no bridge or where the bridge has been destroyed, a bridge must be immediately laid down, and, accordingly, a bridge train is necessarily always present with the army.

---

3. This paragraph is still correct, except that the squadron now always musters 150 mounted men.

When a camp is pitched, field bakeries have to be immediately established to feed the troops; field telegraphs and field post-offices must be established for the rapid transmission of intelligence. A large staff must be provided for, which is the mainspring that sets all the works in motion. And these are only ordinary wants, such as any large picnic party on the same scale would require. When we consider that 200 rounds of ammunition can easily be fired away by each gun in a general action, that every infantry soldier can on the same occasion dispose of 120 rounds of ball cartridge, and that this must be all replaced immediately; that all this requires an enormous number of carriages, with horses and drivers; that outside of the line of battle there must be medical men, their assistants, and nurses; that within it and under fire there must be ambulance waggons, and men with stretchers to bear the wounded to them; and that forty *per cent* of the infantry alone in every year's campaign are carried to the rear, we may understand how the large difference between the number of actual fighting men and of men borne upon paper is accounted for.

We have seen that each *corps d'armé* may be safely estimated at 30,000 combatants, and that of the Guard at 36,000, without taking into consideration those large artillery and engineer trains which would be requisite were the army to undertake the siege of any considerable fortress. It only remains now to consider whether this strength may always be reckoned upon as constant; and it appears that this may be done in consequence of the admirable system of Prussian organisation. By this system, as soon as a *corps d'armée* is put on a war footing, there is a *depôt* battalion formed for each regiment, a *depôt* company for each battalion of rifles, a *depôt* squadron for each cavalry regiment,[4] a *depôt* division for the artillery of each *corps d'armée*, a *depôt* company for each engineer battalion, and a *depôt* for the military train. These *depôts* remain in their barracks, and supply all vacancies made in the ranks of the corps to which they belong. Nor is it at all difficult for them to do so, because in consequence of the system of recruiting pursued in this country these *depôts* do not consist entirely of raw recruits, but partly of men who have served for some time in the army, and who have, after leaving the regular ranks, been annually put through a course of training.

In Prussia, with the exception of clergymen and a few others, every man in the year in which he becomes twenty years old is liable to

---

4. The *depôt* squadron for each regiment of cavalry is now maintained in time of peace, (as at time of first publication).

military service for five years, three of which he spends in the regular army and two in the reserve. On completion of this service he is placed in the first levy of the *Landwehr* for seven years, and afterwards in the second levy of the *Landwehr* for seven years more. When it is necessary to raise the regular army to a war footing, the reserve is first draughted into the ranks, then the first levy of the *Landwehr*, and afterwards, if necessary, the second levy.[5] If the *Landwehr* is exhausted the *landsturm* is called out, and in this case every man between sixteen and fifty is liable for service.

Each *corps d'armée* of the line in time of peace is quartered in one of the eight provinces of the kingdom; its recruits are obtained from that province, and its *Landwehr* are the men in the province who have served five years and who have been dismissed from actual service, but are subjected to an annual course of training. The provinces to which the different *corps d'armée* in 1866 belonged were:—1, Prussia Proper; 2, Pomerania; 3, Brandenburg; 4, Prussian Saxony; 5, Posen; 6, Silesia; 7, Westphalia; 8, Rhine Provinces. The Guards are recruited from men of a certain stature from all the provinces, and the *Landwehr* of the Guard consists of the men who have formerly served in it.

Prussia, after the successes of Frederick the Great, was content to suppose that the military organisation which had served her so well in the Seven Years' War was perfect, and required little or no modification to enable it to continue superior to that of other European Powers; but while she reposed complacently on the laurels of Rossbach and Leuthen, military science had rushed forwards, and she was rudely roused from her repose by the crushing defeat of Jena. Under enormous difficulties, and with the greatest secrecy, a new organisation was then introduced into the Prussian Army. The terms of peace dictated by Napoleon after the Jena campaign allowed the Prussian Army to consist of only 42,000 men, but no stipulation was made as to how long these men should serve.

In order to secure the means of striking for independence on the first favourable opportunity, General Scharnhorst introduced the *Krümper* system, by which a certain number of soldiers were always allowed to go home on furlough after a few months' service, and recruits were brought into the ranks in their place. Those drilled were in their turn sent away on furlough and other recruits brought in for training. By means of this system at the beginning of 1813 not only could the existing regiments be filled up to proper war strength, but

5. After 1866 the distinction between the two levies of *Landwehr* ceased.

fifty-one new battalions were raised from prepared soldiers. This force, however, was totally insufficient for the great struggle against Napoleon; so in February, 1813, volunteer *Jäger* detachments were formed which mustered together about 10,000 men, and in March the raising of a *Landwehr* was decreed, which in five months after the signature of the decree was able to take part in the war with a strength of 120,000 men.

Thus in August, 1813, Prussia possessed an army of 250,000 men, of whom 170,000 men were ready to take the field, while the remaining 80,000 formed reserve and *depôt* troops and supplied garrisons. This army fought in the war of independence, and formed the first nucleus of the existing military organisation of the kingdom,—an organisation which, dating from a terrible misfortune, the bitter experience of which has never been forgotten, has since been constantly tended, improved, and reformed, and with careful progress been brought to such a high pitch of excellence that in 1866 it enabled the Prussian troops to march and conquer with an almost miraculous rapidity, to eclipse in a few days the glories of the Seven Years' War, to efface the memory of Jena by thundering on the attention of the startled world the suddenly decisive victory of Sadowa, and to spring over the ashes of Chlum into very possibly the foremost place among the armies of the world.[6]

After Prussia had regained her position as a great power it was necessary that she should have an army of a strength similar to that of the armies of other great powers, and therefore with a muster-roll of about half a million of men. At this time the other great powers kept the greater part of their soldiery in peace, as in war, in the ranks, and only allowed a few trained veterans, who together amounted to about one-fourth of the total strength of the army, to be absent on furlough. But Prussia was then the smallest of the great powers, and had neither such a large population nor revenue as the others. Thus, she had, in the first place, not sufficient men; in the second place, not enough money to maintain an army on a similar system, and could in peace keep together only a much smaller portion of her soldiery than her possible enemies could. This portion of her army was organised on the following system:—

The country was required every year to grant 40,000 recruits, each of whom served for three years under the standards and for two years in the reserve; so the standing army amounted to 120,000 men, and

6. The events of 1870—71, have not belied this paragraph, written in 1867.

by calling in the reserves could be raised immediately to 200,000 men. Bat, to complete the requisite number of 500,000 soldiers, 300,000 more were necessary, and in time of peace the kingdom could afford to maintain only very small *depôts* for these additional troops. The war of independence had shown that the *Landwehr* system, by which men were allowed to retire from service, but still remained liable to be called up for duty, was capable of effecting good service, and in case of need of supplying the men who could not be kept in time of peace in the regular army. Therefore this system was retained, and by the decree of the 3rd of September, 1814, the Prussian army was organised definitively on the *Landwehr* system.

By this system every Prussian capable of bearing arms was without exception liable to military duty, and to serve from his 20th to his 23rd year in the standing army, from his 23rd to 25th in the reserve, from his 25th to 32nd in the first levy of the *Landwehr*, and from his 32nd to 39th in the second levy. The *landsturm* was to consist of all men capable of bearing arms between seventeen and forty-nine years of age who did not belong either to the standing army or to the *Landwehr*. From the *Landwehr* battalions and squadrons were raised which formed *Landwehr* regiments, and these were united for annual exercise or service in brigades and divisions with regiments of the line. *Landwehr* men who had belonged to *Jäger* battalions, to the artillery, or to the engineer service, were not formed into separate corps; but in case of being called up were to return into the ranks of the regiments in which they had formerly served.

By this system, with an annual supply of 40,000 recruits, Prussia was enabled to hold in readiness for war an army which consisted of three distinct parts.

1. The standing army of 120,000 men, raised in war by the recall of the reserves to 200,000 men, and with *Landwehr-Jägers*, artillerymen, and pioneers, to 220,000 men.

2. The first levy of the *Landwehr*, including only infantry and cavalry, of which, in peace, only small depôts, numbering together about 3,000 men, were maintained, but which, on the mobilization of the army for war, supplied considerably over 150,000 men, even allowing liberally for deaths, sickness, emigration, and other causes of reduction.

The standing army and the first levy, after detaching 30,000 men to strengthen the garrisons of fortresses, formed together the field army of 340,000 men, and besides, from their surplus men and recruits, could leave at home a force of depôt troops amounting to about 50,000 men.

3. The second levy of the *Landwehr*, from which no exercise or training was required in time of peace, but which in war was called upon to furnish 110,000 soldiers, who, with the 30,000 above mentioned from the standing army and first levy, garrisoned the fortresses of the country, and could, in case of urgent necessity, be supported by the *landsturm*.

From these three sources—1, the field army; 2, *depôt* troops, formed by the standing army and first levy of the *Landwehr*; 3, garrison troops, formed by the surplus of the first levy, the second levy of *Landwehr*, and in case of need from the *landsturm*—Prussia could for war raise 530,000 men, of whom in time of peace hardly one-fourth were present with the standards. The standing army during the time that this organisation remained intact consisted of forty-five infantry regiments, ten light infantry battalions, thirty-eight cavalry regiments, nine artillery regiments, and nine divisions of engineers.

The great advantage of this system was that in peace it necessitated but a small expense, and required but few men to keep up an army which on the outbreak of war could be raised quickly to a large force. As it was arranged after the War of Independence it endured without alteration during the reigns of Frederick William III. and Frederick William IV.

But in the campaigns which the Prussian army undertook in 1848 and 1849, and again when the army was mobilized in 1850 and 1859, the disadvantages of an organisation so entirely based upon the *Landwehr* system became apparent in a high degree.

The energetic spirit with which the Prussian people rushed to arms against Napoleon I. can only, under very peculiar circumstances, agitate a whole nation, and make every individual willing and anxious to sacrifice his personal comfort and convenience in order to respond to the call of his government, and serve with alacrity in the ranks of the army. Such circumstances seldom occur, and are due either to the insupportable weight of a foreign domination—as was the case in Prussia from 1807-12—or to some strong patriotic stimulus such as has knitted the people of the same country together during the late campaign; but this spirit is seldom found at the outbreak of an ordinary war, engaged in for ordinary political reasons.

It was found on the mobilization in 1848 that a great portion of the *Landwehr* soldiers obeyed only unwillingly the call to arms, because it interfered with their private occupations; that they sometimes, weaned by long ease from military ideas, showed a want of discipline, and that, thinking more for their wives and families than for their duty to the State, they did not always acquit themselves properly in action.

Besides, there was this disadvantage that the *Landwehr*—therefore, about half of the field army, newly embodied—prevented the divisions from being immediately prepared to take the field, a delay which is terribly prejudicial to an army in these times, when troops are forwarded to the theatre of war by the rapid means of railway transport The officers and non-commissioned officers of the *Landwehr* were also little used to their duties, and at the very moment of mobilization a great number of them were necessarily transferred to the line, and others brought from the regular army to supply their places. These numerous alterations of their leaders at such an important time were alone sufficient to impair materially the efficiency of the troops.

Besides these disadvantages, the existing system had brought about a great injustice in the distribution of military service, as in 1815 only 40,000 recruits were yearly called for to support the standing army of 140,000 men, while in the meantime the population had increased from 10,000,000 to 18,000,000; so that about one-third of the lads who should proportionately have entered the service were entirely free of duty, and those who did enter were liable to be recalled to the ranks for a longer period of their life than was really necessary; for if, instead of 40,000 recruits, 63,000 were, as easily could be, called up every year, men, instead of being liable to be put into the standing army on the outbreak of war for twelve years (from twenty to thirty-two), need only be liable for seven years (from twenty to twenty-seven). In direct ratio with the increase of population the national revenues had also increased from 50,000,000 to 93,000,000 *thalers*, and so admitted of an increase of the standing army and of the military expenses.

There were thus three grounds for a reform in the *Landwehr* system, and therefore King William I., while still Regent, introduced in 1859 and 1860 a reorganisation of the army, which up to 1865 formed a bone of contention between the Prussian Ministry and the Radical party in the Lower House, but the success of which in the war of 1866 completely silenced, if not thoroughly convinced, even its tax-paying opponents of its wonderful excellence and elasticity. By this reorganisation of 1859, as it is usually called, the first levy of the *Landwehr* was no longer, as a rule, to be sent into the field; and to attain this object the standing army, including the reserves, was to be increased by as many men as the first levy of the *Landwehr* formerly provided—in fact, to be nearly doubled.

The time of service in the *Landwehr* was diminished by two years, and that in the reserve in return to be lengthened by two years. The *Landwehr* still remaining in two levies, but composed only of men from twenty-seven to thirty-eight years old, was, as a rule, with its first levy alone to perform the duty which had hitherto been performed by the second levy,—namely, to garrison the fortresses. In case of necessity the government still, however, retained the power of calling up the second levy to aid in this duty.

By this organisation a recruit who joined the Prussian service served for three years (from nineteen to twenty-two)[7] in the regular army; for five years (from twenty-two to twenty-seven) in the reserve; and for eleven years (from twenty-seven to thirty-eight) was liable to be called up for duty as a *Landwehr* man.

By this reorganisation the total war strength of the field army was slightly increased, and its efficiency most materially improved; the war strength of the *depôt* troops was, on account of the necessity of great rapidity in modern warfare, more than doubled; that of the garrison troops was improved, and could now, by calling up the second levy, be made twice as great as it was formerly. These reforms also allowed the standing army to be increased by thirty-six regiments of infantry, nine battalions for the fusilier regiments, ten cavalry regiments, and five divisions of garrison artillery. Sufficient time had not yet elapsed on the outbreak of the Austrian war for this reorganisation to be thoroughly carried out, and still eight of the ten cavalry regiments had not been formed, and their place was supplied during that campaign by twelve *Landwehr* cavalry regiments, and as yet only one of the divisions of garrison artillery had been formed.

During the campaign of 1866 the elasticity of this organisation was clearly manifested. In a wonderfully short time the large armies which fought at Königgrätz were placed on a war footing, and brought about 260,000 combatants into the very field of battle, besides the necessary detachments which must be made by a large army to cover communications, mask fortresses, and so on; but the detachments made from the Prussian Army were very small compared to those which would have to be separated from an army organised on a different system; for as the field army advanced the *depôt* troops moved up in rear, and formed both *depôts* and reserves for the first line, while some of the garrison

7. From the 1st January of the year in which he became twenty years old.

troops of *Landwehr* came up from Prussia, and formed the garrisons of Saxony, Prague, Pardubitz, and all the other points on the lines of communication. At the same time General Mülbe's corps, formed for the most part of reserve and *depôt* soldiers, pushed up to Brünn, and was hastening to take its place in the first line, when its march was stopped by the conclusion of the long armistice.

While the armies of Prince Frederick Charles, the crown prince, and General Herwarth were being supported in Bohemia, Moravia, and Saxony, General Falkenstein, with a number of Line regiments and a force of *Landwehr*, was driving the war forwards to the Main; and the Prince of Mecklenburg, with the second reserve corps, was pushing on against Bavaria. Nor was Prussian territory left without its garrisons: *Landwehr* battalions were in Kosel, Neisse, Berlin, Torgau, Magdeburg, Königsberg, and all the other garrison towns of the country, while under their shelter recruits were being drilled, and more *Landwehr* embodied to march forward into the conquered countries. The armies which were on the Marchfeld in front of Lundenburg and in Bavaria did not form a thin front line, which, once broken or turned, would have been driven back even to the Elbe; their rear was guarded and supported by large forces of strong and firm battalions, lately embodied, but from their nature quickly trained, and composed of well-grown old soldiers who were thirsting to be sent against the enemy, and on whose well-knit frames disease or the hardships of war could make little impression.

Though the part of the Prussian organisation which refers to the recruiting of the army and to the filling up of the ranks in case of war has had a great deal to do with the success of the Austrian campaign, on account of the facility and rapidity with which by its means the army could be mobilized and brought upon a war footing, the portion of the Prussian organisation which relates to the combination of the recruits so obtained in pliable bodies, which can be easily handled, easily moved, yet formed in such due proportions of the different arms as to be capable of independent action, did not fail to be appreciated most fully by those who, with its assistance, gained such tremendous results. This portion of the military organisation of the Prussian army is so simple that almost every man in the ranks can understand it.

Jealous of expense in time of peace, it allows for a wide expansion, without hurry and without confusion, on the outbreak of war. It provides for, at the same time, the broadest questions and the most minute details, and is so clearly laid down and so precisely defined, yet at the same time admits of so much elasticity, that the Prussian officers can find no words strong enough to express their praise of it

England, in fact, in 1866, hardly wakened up to realize that the Prussian army then was very different from that which at the beginning of this century was destroyed on the fatal day of Jena, or that then it only resembled the army which marched so well to our aid at Waterloo, in patriotic feeling and in the rudiments of its organisation. Prussia seems now about to spring into the position she held one hundred years' ago, when Frederick had made her the first military power in the world, and England was introducing her military system into the germs of the army which marched through the Peninsula, and at Waterloo shattered the legions which Blücher annihilated. Would that England now would take some hints for the organisation of her army from the victors of Königgrätz, and would adopt the experience which has been won on the plains of Bohemia, before military progress is forced upon her by a disaster more fatal, perhaps, than that of Klostersevern![8]

In peace everything is always kept ready for the mobilization of the army, every officer and every official knows during peace what will be his post and what will be his duty the moment the decree for the mobilization is issued, and the moment that decree is flashed by telegraph to the most distant stations every one sets about his necessary duty without requiring any further orders or any explanations.

When a war is imminent the government decrees the mobilization of the whole army, or of such a portion as may be deemed necessary. In preparing for the Austrian campaign, the whole field army and the first levy of *Landwehr* were mobilized before the invasion of Saxony. A part of the second *Landwehr* levy was also mobilized immediately the troops of Prince Frederick Charles stepped across the Saxon frontier; and on the day of the great battle near Königgrätz, without any exertion, Prussia had over 600,000 men under arms. Every commanding general mobilizes his own *corps d'armée*; the "*Intendantur*" the whole of the branches of the administrative services; the commandants of those fortresses which are ordered to be placed in a state of defence take their own measures for strengthening the fortifications and for obtaining from the artillery *depôts* the guns necessary for the armament of their parapets. All orders are sent by telegraph, or, where telegraphic communication does not exist, by mounted orderlies. The mobiliza-

---

8. It is hardly necessary to notice that since this was written in 1867, England has made a great advance in military improvement.

tion of the whole army is soon complete in every branch; the infantry is ready in a fortnight from the time the decree is signed

The process of the mobilization may be classed under the following fire beads:—1, The filling in of the field troops to their war strength; 2, the formation of *depôt* troops; 3, the formation of garrison troops and the arming of the fortresses; 4, the mobilization of the field administration; 5, the formation of the headquarter staffs, &c., who are to remain in the different districts to supply the places of those who march to the seat of war.

The completion of the rank and file of the field troops to war strength was effected by drawing in some of the reserve soldiers, who supply half the total war strength of the infantry, one-third of that of the artillery, and one twenty-fifth of that of the cavalry. The cavalry has, of course, on account of being maintained in such force during peace, a superabundance of reserve soldiers available on a mobilization; these, after the men required for the cavalry itself have been drawn from them, are handed over to the artillery and military train, so that these services thus obtain many valuable soldiers, well accustomed to mounted duties. The reserve soldiers who are to be enrolled have orders sent to them through the commanding officer of the *Landwehr* of the district in which they live, who can avail himself of the services of the provincial and parochial civil authorities to facilitate the delivery of these orders.

The men are, immediately on the receipt of their orders, required to proceed to the headquarters of the *Landwehr* of the district, where they are received, medically inspected, and forwarded to their regiment, by an officer and some non-commissioned officers of the regiment which draws its recruits from the district officers who are required to fill up vacancies in the regular army in a mobilization are obtained by promoting some of the senior non-commissioned officers. *Landwehr* officers obtain their commissions much in the same way as do military officers in England, but no *Landwehr* officer can be promoted to the rank of captain unless he has been attached to a regular raiment for two months' duty; and no *Landwehr* officer can be a field officer unless he has before served for some considerable time in the regular army. Many of the officers of the *Landwehr* are officers still on the strength of the regular army, who are detached to the *Landwehr* on its mobilization.

On a mobilization, the whole army required in 1866 about 88,000 horses more than it had in time of peace; in order to obtain these quickly the government has the power, if it cannot buy them readily from regular dealers, to take a certain number from every district, paying for them a price which is fixed by a mixed commission of military officers and of persons appointed by the civil authorities of the district

Each regiment of field artillery forms nine ammunition columns, in each of which are waggons to carry reserve ammunition for infantry, cavalry, and artillery, in the proportions in which experience has shown that ammunition is usually required In the field these ammunition waggons follow directly in rear of the field army, but are kept entirely separate from the field batteries, the officers of which are justly supposed to have enough to do in action in superintending their own guns, without being hampered with the supply of cartridges to the cavalry and infantry.

Every battalion of engineers forms a column of waggons which carries tools for intrenching purposes, and also a heavy pontoon train and a light field bridge train for which all is kept ready during peace. If a portion of the army is mobilized merely for practice, or goes into camp for great manoeuvres, as is done nearly every summer during peace, one, or perhaps two or three, engineer battalions make their trains mobile, in order to practise the men and to accustom them to the use of the *matériel*. Arms and ammunition which are required to complete the war strength of regiments are supplied from the artillery *depôts*.

Officers are allowed soldier servants on a more liberal scale than in the English army, but no officers' servants are mustered in the company; they form, with all the non-combatant men of each battalion of infantry, the train which is attached to every battalion: this consists of the officers' servants and the drivers of the regimental waggons; everyone else borne on the muster-roll draws a trigger in action, so that the muster-rolls actually show the number of rank and file who are present, and do not include any of the followers, who often never come up into the line of battle at all. On service the captain of every company is mounted, and is required to have two horses, to aid in the purchase of which he is allowed a certain sum of money by the State.

The strength of an ordinary battalion on active service is one field-officer, four captains, four first lieutenants, nine second lieutenants, one surgeon, one assistant-surgeon, one paymaster, one quarter-master, 1002 non-commissioned officers and privates. The train attached to this battalion is, besides officers' servants, the drivers of the ammunition waggon, which has six horses; of the *Montirung Wagon*, which carries the paymaster's books, money chest, and a certain amount of material for the repair of arms and clothing, and is drawn by four horses; a hospital cart with two horses, an officers' baggage waggon with four horses, and men to lead four pack-horses, each of which carries on a pack-saddle the books of one company.

The baggage of a cavalry regiment on service consists of one medicine cart with two horses, one field forge with two horses, four squadron waggons, each with two horses, one officers' baggage waggon, with four horses; the total strength of a cavalry regiment being 23 officers 659 men, of whom 600 fall in in the ranks, 713 horses, and seven carriages.

The nine ammunition columns which are formed by each artillery regiment for the supply of ammunition to the artillery and infantry of the *corps d'armée* to which the regiment belongs are divided into two divisions, one of which consists of five columns, and has a strength of two officers, 175 men, 174 horses, and 25 waggons; the second, consisting of four columns, has two officers, 173 men, 170 horses, and 24 waggons. This division is made to facilitate the despatch of the two divisions separately to the ammunition *depôt* to have the waggons refilled after their first supply of cartridges has been exhausted, or to allow one division to be detached with each infantry division, in case of the *corps d'armée* being divided, as was the case in this war with the third and fourth corps, in which case four columns can conveniently be attached to each infantry division, and one column to the cavalry division of the corps.

The reserve ammunition park from which these ammunition columns are replenished, is also divided into two divisions, each of which has a strength of nine officers, 195 men, 264 carriages, and is further subdivided into eight columns of 33 waggons each. It is brought into the theatre of war either by railway or water carriage, or by means of horses hired in the country where the war is being conducted. It generally is one or two days' march in rear of the army. In the campaign of 1866 on the day of the great battle, the ammunition reserve park of the army of Prince Frederick Charles was at Turnau, to which place it had been brought by railway.

A siege train for attacking fortresses is not generally organised at the beginning of a war, unless the general plan of the campaign should be likely to lead the army into a country where fortresses exist, which could not be either neglected or masked, and which must be reduced.

If a siege train is organised, it is formed with especial reference to the fortresses against which it is to act, and follows the army in the same manner as the reserve ammunition park. At the beginning of the 1866 campaign the Prussians had no siege train with the army, but directly the Battle of Sadowa had been won a siege train was organised, perhaps to be employed against the fortresses on the Elbe, though such small places scarcely merited such an attention from so large an army, perhaps for an attack on Olmütz. When the fortifications of Floridsdorf were found looming in front of the advance on Vienna, the siege train was ordered up to be ready for the attack of the Austrian works covering the Danube, but it was halted as soon as the four weeks' armistice was agreed upon. The want of siege trains was, however, felt.

The garrison of Theresienstadt, a fortress which had been totally neglected, sallied out and broke the railway bridge on the line of communication between Prague and Turnau. Had their communication been thus broken during the active campaign, and not during the armistice, it must have seriously inconvenienced the Prussians. Had Theresienstadt been masked, the sally of the garrison would have been probably prevented; but had it been properly besieged, the garrison would have been kept within their works, and the direct line of railway between Prague and Dresden would have been at the service of the Prussian Army for almost its entire length.

It is thus that the Prussian Army is formed in peace, that its field forces can be made ready to march in a few days in case of war, and that the troops in the field are supplied with the powder and shot which give them the means of fighting. But, *l'art de vaincre est perdu sans l'art de subsister*. An organisation of even more importance lies still behind—the organisation of the means of supplying the warriors with food when in health, with medicine and hospitals when diseased or wounded, and for filling up the gaps which are opened in the ranks by battle or pestilence; an organisation which has always been found to be more difficult and to require more delicate handling than even strategical combinations, or the arraying of troops for battle.

The Prussian Army could in 1866 enter the field with 342,000 men in its ranks; but, as is well known, no army, nor any collection of men, can maintain its normal strength for a single day; in such a host, even of young healthy men, ordinary illness would immediately cause a few absentees from duty, much more so do the marches, the hardships, and the fatigues to which a soldier is exposed on active service before the first shot is fired. Then as soon as an action takes place, a single day adds a long list to the hospital roll, and the everything sees in the ranks many gaps which in the morning were filled by strong soldiers, who are now lying torn and mangled or dead on the field of battle. The dead are gone forever; they are so much power lost out of the hand of the general; nor can an army wait till the wounded are cured and are again able to draw a trigger or to wield a sabre.

Means must be taken to supply the deficiencies as quickly as possible, and to restore to the commander of the army the missing force which has been expended in moving his own army through the first steps of the campaign, or in resisting the motion of his adversary. What is the amount of such deficiencies may be estimated from Prussian statistics, which have been compiled with great care, and from the experience of many campaigns; these state officially that at the end of a year's war forty *per cent* of the infantry of the field army, twenty *per cent* of the cavalry, artillery, and engineers, and twelve *per cent* of the military train would have been lost to the service, and have had to be supplied anew.

It is for the formation of these supplies of men, and for forwarding them to the active army, that *depôts* are intended. The *depôts* of the Prussian army are formed as soon as the mobilization takes place, and it is ordered that one half of the men of each *depôt* should be soldiers of the reserve, who, already acquainted with their drill, can be sent up to the front on the first call; the other half of each *depôt* consists of recruits who are raised in the ordinary way, and of all the men of the regiments belonging to the field army which have not been perfectly drilled by the time their regiment marches to the seat of war. The officers of the *depôts* are either officers who are detached from the regular army for this duty, or are officers who have been previously wounded, and who cannot bear active service, but can perform the easier duties of the *depôt*, besides young officers, who are being trained to their duty before joining their regiments.

Between the reorganisation of 1859 and the war of 1866, the number of *depôt* troops kept up during a war was quite doubled; formerly every two infantry regiments had one *depôt* battalion, and every two cavalry regiments one *depôt* squadron. When the army was reorganised, it was foreseen that this amount of *depôt* troops would never be sufficient in case of a war of any duration or severity, so by the new regulations each infantry regiment had one *depôt* battalion of 18 officers and 1,002 men; each rifle battalion, a *depôt* company of 4 officers and 201 men; each cavalry regiment, a *depôt* squadron of 5 officers,

200 men, and 212 horses; each field artillery regiment (96 guns), a *depôt* division of one horse artillery battery, and three field batteries, each of four guns, with 14 officers, 556 men, and 189 horses; every engineer battalion, one *depôt* company of 4 officers and 202 men; every train battalion, a *depôt* division of two companies, which muster together 12 officers, 502 men, and 213 horses.

All this was required to feed the army in the field with supplies of men to take the places of those who pass from the regimental muster roll into the lists of killed, died in hospital, or disabled; for those who are only slightly wounded return to their duty either in the *depôt* or at once to their battalions, as is most convenient from the situation of the hospital in which they have been.

As a rule, four weeks after the field army has marched, the first supply of men is forwarded from the *depôts* to the battalions in the field. This first supply consists of one-eighth of the calculated yearly loss which has been given above. On the first day of every succeeding month a fresh supply is forwarded. Each of these later supplies is one-twelfth of the total calculated yearly loss. If a very bloody battle is fought, special supplies are sent at once to make up the losses of the troops that have been engaged.

The troops in *depôt* are provided with all articles of equipment with which they should take the field. When a detachment is to be sent to the front, all who belong to one *corps d'armée* are assembled together; the infantry soldiers are formed into companies of 200 men each for the march, the cavalry into squadrons of about 100 horsemen, and are taken under the charge of officers to the field army, thus bringing to the front with them the necessary reserves of horses. The places in the *depôts* of those who have marched away are filled up by recruiting.

An army, though of great strength and well provided with supplies of men, cannot always be sure of taking the initiative, and by an offensive campaign driving the war into an enemy's country. There is no doubt that an offensive campaign is much better for a country and much more likely to achieve success than a defensive one: it was much better for the Prussians in 1866 to cover Berlin in Bohemia than in Brandenburg, in 1870 in Alsatia than in Rhineland; General Benedek would have preferred to cover Vienna indirectly by an attack on Prussian Silesia rather than in a defensive position at Königgrätz; Napoleon justly saw that the proper point to defend Paris in 1815 was not on the Marne, but in Belgium.

But political reasons or want of preparation often force an army to be unable to assume the offensive, and with the loss of the initiative make a present to the enemy of the first great advantage in the war. In this case the theatre of war is carried into its own territory, when an army requires fortresses to protect its arsenals, dockyards, and its capital, to cover important strategical points, or to afford a place where, in case of defeat or disaster, it may be reorganised under the shelter of fortifications and heavy artillery. It was well seen in the war of 1866 that small fortresses do not delay the progress in the field of a large invading army, which can afford to spare detachments to prevent their garrisons from making sallies. Josephstadt and Königgrätz did not delay the Prussian armies for a day, though they are both strong places, and would possibly have stood a long siege; but they were both masked by detachments, the loss of which from the line of battle was hardly felt by the main body, and, though no trenches were opened and no guns mounted against them, the great line of the Prussian communications passed in safety within a few miles of their paralysed garrisons.[9]

It was also demonstrated by that war that fortifications which inclose a town of any size are comparatively useless, unless the defensive works are so far in front of the houses as to preclude the possibility of the bombardment of the city. Towns are now so rich, both in population and wealth, that few governments would dare to expose their subjects to the loss of property and risk to life which a bombardment must entail Prague, though surrounded by ramparts, struck the Austrian colours without firing a shot, because the Prussian guns would at the same time have played upon the defenders of the parapets, the unprotected citizens, and the rich storehouses of its merchants.

The Spielberg at Brünn, if it stood alone, might make a strong resistance to the passage of an invader, but the white flag of truce waving from its flagstaff, instead of the war standard of Austria, greeted the Prussian vanguard, because the emperor could not have borne to hear that its spires, its palaces, and large manufactories had crumbled to the ground under Mecklenburg's artillery. But it would be rash to jump to the conclusion that fortresses, and even fortified towns, are no longer of use in war. Fortresses are useful as supports to the flanks of an army: if Benedek had lain along the river from Josephstadt to Königgrätz, the junction of the two Prussian princes would have been long delayed, perhaps prevented. The guns of Königgrätz materially checked

9. In the same manner, in 1870, even Strasburg, Phalsburg, Bitche, Toul, and Belfort did not, although besieged, delay the progress of the invaders.

the pursuit of the Austrian legions defeated at Sadowa. What Olmütz did to save the army of the north from a total disorganisation, and to allow General Benedek, under its cover, to make his preparations for the masterly move by which he carried it to Vienna, is well known.

Whenever a capital is distinctly the objective point of an invader, as would be the case if an enemy's army were ever to be allowed to land on the shores of our own England, strong works round the city, but so far in advance of the houses as would prevent their being reached by the besieger's shells, become a necessity, between and behind which the defenders army, if worsted in a battle, might be restored, and wait until the attacking troops had shattered themselves against the in-trenchments. And though the earthworks at Floridsdorf had little to do with the sudden cessation of hostilities, there can be no doubt that if Vienna had been properly fortified on every side Austria might, with a very fair chance, have struck another blow before she suffered herself to be excluded from the confederation of the German people.[10]

As long as fortresses exist they require garrisons, but the troops which are formed in Prussia on the breaking out of a war are not intended, in case of an offensive campaign, only to hang listlessly over the parapets of fortified places. When an army pushes forward into a foreign country, it leaves behind it long lines of road or railway over which pass the supplies of food, clothing, medicines, and stores, which are vitally import- ant to the existence of an army. With an unfriendly population, and an enemy's cavalry ready always to seize an opportu-nity of breaking in upon these lines of communication, of charging down upon convoys, and destroying or burning their contents, and of thus deranging seriously what might be called the household econo-my of the army, it is necessary, especially on lines of railway, that strong garrisons should be maintained at particular points, and that patrols should be furnished for nearly the whole line.

Towns have to be occupied in rear of the front line, *depôts* of stores have to be guarded and protected, convoys have to be escorted, tel-egraph lines watched, the fortifications which may fall garrisoned. To detach troops for the performance of all these duties dribbles away the strength of an army: if the Prussian armies which crossed the frontier into Bohemia and Moravia had been obliged to make all these detachments, how many fighting men would have mustered on the Marchfeld? Very few. If these armies had waited till troops were

10. The fortifications of Paris allowed time In 1870-71 for three separate attempts to raise the siege of the capital.

formed at home after the course of the campaign had been seen, how long would it have required to march to the Rossbach? Probably the advanced guard would have still been upon the Elbe when it was actually on the Danube. To provide for these duties, and to allow the main armies to push forward in almost unimpaired strength, Prussia forms on the mobilization of the field army her so-called garrison troops.[11]

In the formation of these garrison troops, there is a drawback from the general excellence of the Prussian military organisation, which arises from the *Landwehr* system. The men of the first levy of the *Landwehr* form, when alone called out, as many battalions as do the united levies when nearly the whole of the second levy is also called out In both cases there are 116 battalions, which consist each of 402 men of the first levy, and are only filled up to their full strength of 1,000 men by men of the second levy. On account of this arrangement, if only the men of the first levy are required, a large number of weak battalions are formed, which are more expensive and more difficult to handle than would be a smaller number of full battalions.

It would appear much simpler to have a certain number of battalions composed entirely of men of the first levy, and the rest entirely of men of the second levy; but in Prussia this simplicity cannot be obtained because it is considered advisable to have a *Landwehr* battalion for every recruiting district, and only to enrol the men of the district in their own battalion. If, however, treble the population which inhabits one of the present recruiting districts were included in one district, it would be quite easy to have three battalions of *Landwehr* for each district, one completely composed of men of the first levy, the second of the first men. of the second, and the third of the later men of the second levy, who now complete the battalions up to their full strength.[12]

In some respects, which are easily seen, the Prussian *Landwehr* resembles the British Militia, but there are two vital differences between our organisation and that of Prussia. The first is, that in England when a militia regiment is formed it is made up of men who are not old soldiers, and consequently, if the regiment is for some years disembodied, all its late recruits know nothing of their work except what they can pick up in the short period of annual training; so that in course of

---

11. These were even more necessary in France, where the bitterly hostile feeling of the inhabitants and the Franc-Tireur organisation required constant watching.
12. This has to a certain extent been improved since 1866.

time, if a regiment remains for many years without being embodied, the mass of the ranks contain men who from want of training are un-qualified to step on the very outbreak of a war into the line of battle. In the second place, the *Landwehr* of the first levy is as much an at-tendant and concomitant of an army in the field as the park of reserve artillery, and it is this which makes the *Landwehr* so valuable, because it thus takes up the duties which otherwise would have to be performed by detachments from the active army.

If the Prussian armies in the Austrian campaign had been obliged to leave detachments in Leipsic, Dresden, Prague, Pardubitz, and along the railway from Görlitz to Brünn, besides troops in Hanover, Hesse, and on the lines of communications of the armies which were fight-ing against the Bavarians, how many troops would have formed the first lines of battle either on the Danube, or in the theatre of war near the Main? It is probable that the number of *Landwehr* men employed on foreign soil, in Saxony, and in guarding and garrisoning the rear of the armies which were concentrated between the Thaya and the Danube, would be underestimated at 103,000, exclusive of the corps of the regular army which was watching Olmütz. If this estimate be at all correct, the armies which were collecting, together 225,000 regular troops, for the attack upon Vienna, would, unless they had had these *Landwehr* behind them, have been reduced to under 125,000 men. In fact, an English army under the same circumstances would have been shorn of almost half its strength.

When a Prussian army with its unimpaired strength is preparing to fight a battle in an enemy's country, when supplies of men are already coming up in anticipation of the losses which the action will cause, and when its lines of communication are guarded and secured by the garrison troops in its rear, it musters an enormous number of soldiers, who must every day be provided with food, without which a man can neither fight, march, nor live; and not only must it provide for itself alone, but also for the prisoners of the enemy who may fall into its hands,—not only food, but hospitals, medicines, and attendants for the sick, surgeries, assistants, and appliances for the wounded, and the means of conveying both sick and wounded from the places where they fell helpless to convenient spots where they may be tended and healed at a safe distance from the danger of battle, or of being taken in case of a sudden advance of the enemy.

It is extremely difficult from mere figures to realize what a gigantic undertaking it was to supply even food alone to the armies which fought in the Austrian campaign—more difficult still to appreciate the difficulties in the late campaign in France. The difficulties of such a task may be conceived if we remember that the front line of the Prussian armies in front of Vienna mustered nine times the number of British troops with which Lord Raglan invaded the Crimea; that close behind this line lay General Mülbe's reserve corps, and a corps of the Army of Silesia, which was watching Olmütz, and that these two corps alone were stronger by 4,000 men than all the British, German, and Spanish troops that fought at Talavera; that behind them again was a large mass of *Landwehr*; that during the siege of Sebastopol the British army was stationary, and had the great advantage of sea transport to within a few miles of its camps, while in the late campaigns the Prussian Army had been moving forward at an enormously rapid rate, and that the men to be fed in the front line alone numbered about 250,000 in Austria[13]—a population as large as that of the twelfth part of London.

It would be a bold man who would undertake to supply the twelfth part of the whole population of London with tomorrow's food—a bolder still who would undertake the task if this portion of the population were about to move bodily tomorrow morning down to Richmond, and would require to have the meat for their dinner delivered to them the moment they arrived there, and who, without railway transport, agreed to keep the same crowd daily provided with food until moving at the same rate they arrived at Plymouth; and yet a general has to do much more than this in giving food to his men,— he has, besides the ordinary difficulties of such a task, to calculate upon bad roads, weary horses, breaking waggons, the attacks of an enemy's cavalry; he has not only to get the food to the troops, but in many cases he has to provide it in the first place; he has to keep his magazines constantly stocked, to increase the amount of transport in exact proportion as his troops advance; to feed not only the fighting men, but all the men who are employed in carrying provisions to the combatants, to find hay and corn for all the horses of the cavalry and for the horses of the transport waggons, and to arrange beforehand so that every man and horse shall halt for the night in close proximity to a large supply of good water.

This is not the lightest nor the least of a general's duties. It was the proud boast of England's great soldier that "many could lead troops, he could feed them." When the enemy is in front, and any moment

---

13. In France, towards the end of the siege of Paris, over 500,000.

may bring on an action, a general has little time to turn his mind to the organisation of a system of supply. Then he must sift intelligence, weigh information, divine his adversary's intentions almost before they are formed, prepare a parry for every blow, and speed a thrust into any opening joint of his antagonist's harness. The means of supplying troops ought to be given ready into the hands of a general; they should be all arranged and organised beforehand, so that he has but to see that they are properly administered and made use of.

The transport which follows a Prussian army in the field, exclusive of the waggons of each battalion, the artillery and engineer trains, and the field telegraph divisions, is divided under two heads, both of which are under the control of the *Intendantur*. The first but smaller portion is kept for the use of the commissariat branch, and is usually retained solely for the supply of food to men. The second portion carries the medicines and hospital necessaries for the sick and wounded, together with the means of carrying disabled men, food for horses, stores to supply magazines, and all *matériel* except munitions of war and regimental equipment

The first portion for use of the commissariat branch consists in the first place of a certain amount of waggons, which are in time of peace always kept ready in case of war, and immediately on the mobilization of the army are provided with horses and drivers from the military train, who are entirely under the control of the *intendant-general*. Each army has an army *intendant*; each corps has with its headquarters an army *intendant*, and an *intendantur* officer is attached to each division. These officers, with their subalterns and assistants, form the first links of the chain by which a general draws food to his troops. The provision columns of each *corps d'armée* which are always retained in peace ready to be mobilized, consist of five provision columns, each of which has 2 officers, 98 men, 161 horses, and 32 waggons. If the *corps d'armée* is broken up into divisions, a certain portion of these columns accompanies each infantry division, the cavalry division, and the reserve artillery.

The 160 waggons which form these columns carry three days' provisions for every man in the *corps d'armée*; as soon as the waggons which carry the first day's supply are emptied, they are sent off to the magazines in rear, replenished, and must be up again with the troops to supply the fourth day's food, for in the two days' interval the other waggons will have been emptied. As it is easier to carry flour than bread in these waggons, each *corps d'armée* is accompanied by a field bakery, which consists of 1 officer and 118 men, 27 horses, and 5 waggons, which are distributed among the troops as may be most convenient; and as the horses of both the provision columns and field bakeries have very hard work, a *depôt* of 86 horses, with 48 spare drivers, accompanies each *corps d'armée*.

These provision columns thus carry three days' provisions, but in a country where supplies are not very abundant they can do nothing in the way of collecting food; their duty is simply to bring provisions from the magazines where they are gathered together, and to carry them to the troops. It is evident, therefore, that as the army advances these magazines must advance also, and that means must be provided for keeping the magazines full. The collection of food in such magazines entails an enormous amount of transport; this transport is obtained by hiring waggons and carts at home in the country where the war is being carried on, or in the countries near it. Waggons hired in the country are also used for carrying forage for the horses of the cavalry and artillery from the magazines to the front, for the provision columns only carry food for the men.

When the army of Prince Frederick Charles advanced from Saxony, it made its first marches as if in a totally desert country as far as the supply of provisions was concerned, because the Prussian generals knew it was quite possible that the Austrians might, in order to retard their progress, lay waste the country. Immense magazines were accordingly collected at Görlitz and in Saxony, which, as the army advanced, were brought forward by railway and by long trains of country waggons to places where they could be conveniently reached by the provision waggons and forage carts. These magazines were constantly replenished both by food and forage brought by railway from the interior of Prussia, or by requisitions levied on Saxony and Bohemia of food and forage, for which the commissariat paid by cheques which the fortune of war afterwards allowed to be defrayed from the war contributions paid by the Austrian and Saxon Governments.

Had the fate of arms been different, of course Saxony and Austria would have provided that these cheques should be honoured by the Berlin Exchequer. When it was found that the country was not laid waste, the provision waggons in some cases were filled in the neighbourhood of the troops by requisitions, but this was found not to be so good a plan as to send them back to magazines where the provisions were collected ready for them, because the time taken up in gathering together driblets of food and forage from each village, and the great distances over which waggons had to move, imposed an enormous amount of work on both the men and horses.

Although the requisition system was very useful, it was only regarded as an auxiliary means of supply, for the armies moved prepared every day to find that the country in front of them might be devastated, and Prussia and Saxony were always looked upon as the real sources of supplies; and this was absolutely necessary, because it would have been impossible to feed such a large force as the Prussian armies presented by requisitions alone, for requisitions cannot conveniently be made at great distances from the direct line of communications, and in a very short time the quarter of a million of men who were in the front line alone would have eaten up everything in the country around them if they had been dependent on that tract of country only for supplies. Then, even if the troops could have got food from more distant places, the villagers and country people would have starved; but it is the interest of a general to make his requisitions so that they do not drive the inhabitants to destitution, for terrible sickness always follows in the train of want, and, if pestilence breaks out among the people of the country, it is certain immediately to appear in the ranks of the invading army.[14]

The trains which accompany the medical department of a *corps d'armée* into the field consist of three heavy hospital trains, each of which has 14 surgeons, 114 men, 69 horses, and 11 waggons, and twelve light divisional hospital trains, each with 13 surgeons, 74 men, 56 horses, and 11 waggons. Each light train carries medicines, materials, instruments, and ambulances for 200 sick. Each *corps d'armée* has, besides, three detachments of sick-bearers, who, on the day of battle, are divided among the troops; each battalion has also sixteen men appointed as assistant sick-bearers, who, with the regular sick- bearers, carry the wounded to the rear; no other man is ever allowed to quit the ranks under fire.

When a man is struck, he is taken immediately a short distance out of fire to where the battalion surgeons are waiting; they hastily bind up his wound, he is then placed in an ambulance waggon and carried to the light divisional field hospital, which is kept out of fire about a couple of miles in the rear, The surgeons here perform any necessary operation that is absolutely required, but men are only kept here until

14. In the campaign in France, the system of requisitions was ultimately abandoned. Stores which were wanted were purchased, and the cost recovered by money contributions levied on the occupied towns and districts.

a sufficient number arrive to fill a large ambulance waggon, which, as soon as filled, is sent off to the heavy hospital trains which are established in the villages in the rear. At the beginning of the Battle of Sadowa the regimental surgeons were occupied in every sheltered nook of ground on the hill of Dub, the divisional hospitals were behind that hill and in Milowitz, the heavy hospitals were in and about Höritz. When the Austrians retreated and the Prussian troops advanced, the divisional hospitals followed; and, before the Austrian guns had ceased firing, were established in Sadowa, Chlum, and Lipa, and all the other villages in the field whither the indefatigable sick-bearers were rapidly bringing in both Austrian and Prussian wounded.

When the field army, the *depôt* and garrison troops, and the provisional and medical department trains have been mobilized, the Prussian Army is fit to take the field. The necessary commandants and staffs of the districts where the *depôt* troops are stationed are composed either of officers detached from the regular army or of invalid officers. When the army takes the field, its movements must be directed not only so as to pursue the original plan of the campaign, but also so as to keep pace with the enemy's combinations, and the movements of its different parts must be guided by orders from the directing general.

The above is a sketch of the general system on which the Prussian Army is normally organised. How such an army is worked in the field, how its resources are made available, and how it achieves the objects for which it has been mobilized, must depend in a great measure upon the skill of the general to whose direction it is entrusted. What an army so organised can effect when its motions are guided by a skilful hand, the rapid victories of the late campaign have shown. When the field army enters on the theatre of war, the organiser and administrator has done with it; his province is then to take care that its recruits are forthcoming and its supplies are ready when required.

But when an army is handed over to the general who is to use it, he has a right to expect that when he receives his divisions he shall also receive the means of manoeuvring them; and when he assumes the command of his corps he shall be provided with every appliance which can help him to move them in the combination and unison without which different bodies of troops are not an army, but a series of scattered detachments, which must be easily defeated in detail, or in isolation taken prisoners by an active and energetic enemy. After the plan of a campaign has been once decided upon, the means by which a general moves his troops into positions where they may act most advantageously, and from which they may strike the heavy blows that will gain a speedy and profitable peace—for a peace is the ultimate object of all wars—may be classed under the heads of Information, Intelligence, and the Transmission of Orders. Information of the enemy's preparations, of the number of troops be can put into the field,—how those troops will be armed, organised, and administered,—should be obtained by the government of the country to which the army belongs, and communicated to the general when he takes the command of the army.

To acquire this information concerning foreign armies during peace every country in Europe devotes a special department of its War Office, which is ever busy collecting and compiling statistics of every foreign army, because, however friendly the relations of any two countries may be, it can never be known how long they may remain so. As soon as hostilities are imminent, a War Office has little chance of obtaining much information from inside the lines of the probable enemy; then the duty of collecting information devolves upon the general himself who must, by every means he can avail himself of, discover, as far as possible, every position and intention of his adversary's troops. For this purpose, during war, spies are generally employed. Spies have a dangerous task, and not an honourable one; consequently, except in very rare and extreme cases, officers will not accept the invidious duty, and it is often extremely difficult to find persons who will consent to act as spies sufficiently conversant with military matters to make their information worth having.

Money is the great means of obtaining good spies; needy adventurers and unscrupulous men will, if well paid, do the work, and, for the sake of a sufficient sum, run the risk of the certain death which awaits them if discovered in disguise within the hostile outposts. Even if it were accurately known how the Prussian information was derived from within the Austrian lines during the 1866 campaign, it would be too delicate a subject to enter upon; but it may be stated here, though such a statement is hardly necessary, that all the absurd rumours circulated at the beginning of the campaign, which implied that Austrian officers were guilty of the hideous crime of betraying the movements of their army to the enemy, were utterly without foundation, and were cruel libels against brave men who, however unfortunate in the result of the war, won the admiration of every rank in the Prussian Army by their gallantry, chivalrous bearing, and courage, not only on the field of battle, but in all the trying incidents to which a disastrous campaign gives rise. It is not proper even to express a guess as to how information was collected, but the Austrians dealt out death with no sparing hand among suspected persons found within their lines, so probably they had cause to imagine that there were spies in the midst of their troops.

The information collected from spies is not, in most cases, completely trustworthy. In the first place, the men who undertake this duty are nearly always mercenary wretches, who will sell friend and foe alike as best suits their own interests; in the second place, spies are seldom sufficiently acquainted with military matters not to exaggerate movements of slight importance, and miss observing vital combinations. To test the accuracy of their reports intelligence is collected by means of reconnoitring officers, who, either alone or attended by a few troopers, get as close as they can to the enemy's posts; observe as far as possible, without the use of disguise and in full uniform, the positions of his troops; and, when discovered and pursued by his patrols, fight or ride to bring their intelligence safe home to their own outposts. Intelligence is also culled by every *vedette* and every advanced sentinel, but the reconnoitring officer is the main source.

To reconnoitre well requires not only a brave but a very able officer, with a quick eye, a ready memory, and a great knowledge of the indications which tell the presence of hostile troops, and allow an estimate to be formed of the force in which they are. Two Prussian officers of the staff of Prince Frederick Charles, the afternoon before the Battle of Königgrätz, boldly approached the Austrian lines, observed the positions of the Austrian troops, and, though both pursued and assaulted by cavalry, got safe home, and brought to their general certain intelligence which allowed him to frame the combinations that resulted in the morrow's victory. When the reconnoitring officer regains the shelter of his own outposts, he must either personally bring or by some means send his intelligence as quickly as possible to headquarters. The plan usually pursued in European armies has been for the officer himself to ride quickly to his general, and to be the first bearer of his intelligence.

When a general receives intelligence, he has to weigh it, consider it, and often strike the balance between conflicting information. He has then to move his own divisions in accordance with his deductions, and must send word to any cooperating force of what he has heard, and what he is about to do. Undoubtedly, the quickest way for a reconnoitring officer to despatch his reports to his general, and for the general to communicate with his own divisions and with his colleagues, would be by electric telegraph; but it would be almost impossible for a reconnoitring officer to communicate with headquarters by electricity. Reconnoitring expeditions are made so suddenly and so uncertainly that, quick as the Prussian field telegraph is laid down, this means of communication is hardly available with the outposts. Nor is the electric telegraph easily used to communicate with every division; it might be so used, but its application would require a number of extra waggons to be attached to every division, and would bring a confusing number of lines into the office of the chief of the staff.

During the late campaign, orders were sent to the divisional commanders by mounted officers, who were attached to headquarters for this special purpose. Besides these officers a certain number of picked troopers are selected from every cavalry regiment, and formed into a special corps at the beginning of a campaign, and a certain number attached to every general. These troopers form the general's escort, and act as orderlies to carry unimportant messages. When an officer is sent with an important order, one or two of these soldiers are sent with him, in case of his being attacked to act as a defence as far as possible, to yield up a horse to him in case of his own breaking down, or, in case of his being killed, to carry the order themselves to its destination, or, at any rate, to prevent its falling into the hands of the enemy if the officer is wounded and likely to be taken. During the campaign the communications between headquarters and divisions were kept up by means of mounted officers; but communications between the headquarters of each army and the king were maintained by means of the field-telegraph.

For this purpose a field-telegraph division is attached to the headquarters of each army. It consists of three officers, one hundred and thirty-seven men, seventy-three horses, and ten waggons. Two of the waggons contain batteries and instruments, and are fitted up as operating rooms; the other eight waggons each contain the wires and means of putting them up over five miles of country; thus each division can, with its own materials, form telegraphic communication over forty miles. These forty miles are, however, seldom all required, for the lines of the communications of armies usually run along railways, and as far as possible the permanent wires are repaired by the men of the division, and made use of for the telegraphic communication of the army.

Each division carries with it five miles of insulated wire for the purpose of laying through rivers or lakes if these should come in the way of the line. The wires are coiled inside each waggon on rollers, from which they can be uncoiled as the waggon moves along, or in bad ground the roller can be transferred to a stretcher, which is carried between two men. The poles are exceedingly light, and about ten feet high, so that where the wire crosses roads it may pass clear over the heads of mounted men. As it is equally culpable in war to prevent communication by unfair means within the lines of an army as it is to seek to obtain the same in disguise between the enemy's sentries, any enemy not in uniform, or any one in the enemy's pay who is detected cutting the telegraph wire, is regarded as a spy, and treated accordingly.

During the war of 1866 this organisation had not been entirely introduced into the Prussian Army, and the arrangements for the prosecution of the war consequently slightly differed from those which would have been made if time had allowed the regulated organisation to have been thoroughly introduced into the service.

It may be convenient to subjoin here a summary statement, compiled carefully from the best authorities, of the organisation and strength of the Prussian Army, which was employed for the various purposes of the war.

Every Prussian who was twenty years old entered the army as a soldier without distinction of rank or wealth. Time of service was with the colours three years, in the reserve five years, and in the *Landwehr* eleven years.

I.—INFANTRY.

a. GUARD.—4 Regiments of Foot Guards of three battalions each	=	12 batts.	=	12,024 men
4 Regiments of Grenadiers of the Guard	=	12 ,,	=	12,024 ,,
1 Regiment of Fusiliers	=	3 ,,	=	3,006 ,,
9 Regiments of the Guard	=	27 batts.	=	27,054 men
b. LINE.—52 Regiments of Infantry (13—32 and 41—72) of three battalions, each	=	156 batts.	=	156,312 men
12 Regiments of Grenadiers (1—12).	=	36 ,,	=	36,072 ,,
8 Regiments of Fusiliers (33—40)	=	24 ,,	=	24,048 ,,
72 Regiments of the Line . .	=	216 batts.	=	216,432 men

114

1 Batt. of Jägers of the Guard	=	1 batt.	=	1,002 men
1 Batt. Schützen . . .	=	1 ,,	=	1,002 ,,
8 ,, Jägers of the Line	=	8 ,,	=	8,016 ,,
10 ,, of Riflemen . .	=	10 ,,	=	10,020 men
The total Infantry · . .	=	253 batts.	=	253,506 men

The armament of the Infantry regiments was the needle-gun with the ordinary bayonet; that of the Fusilier regiments the fusilier musket, which only differed from the ordinary needle-gun in being rather shorter and lighter; that of the *Jägers* the needle-rifle with sword-bayonet

2.—CAVALRY.

a. GUARD—1 Regiment of *Garde du Corps* of four squadrons	=	4 squad.	=	600 horsemen
1 Regiment of Cuirassiers	=	4 ,,	=	600 ,,
3 Regiments of Uhlans	=	12 ,,	=	1,800 ,,
2 Regiments of Dragoons	=	8 ,,	=	1,200 ,,
1 Regiment of Hussars .	=	4 ,,	=	600 ,,
8 Regiments of Cavalry of the Guard . .	=	32 squad.	=	4,800 horsemen
b. LINE. —8 Regiments of Cuirassiers	=	32 squad.	=	4,800 horsemen
12 Regiments of Uhlans .	=	48 ,,	=	7,200 ,,
12 Regiments of Hussars (of which eight had 4 squadrons, and four had 5 . . .	=	52 ,,	=	7,800 ,,
8 Regiments of Dragoons (of which four had 4, and four had 5 squadrons) . . .	=	36 ,,	=	5,400 ,,
40 Regiments of Cavalry of the Line . . .	=	168 squad.	=	25,200 horsemen
Total of Cavalry . .	=	200 squad.	=	30,000 horsemen

The armament of the *Cuirassier* regiments was *cuirass*, helmet, sabre, and pistol; that of Uhlans, lance, sword, and pistol; of Dragoons and Hussars, sword and needle-carbine. *Cuirassiers* and Uhlans were heavy, Dragoons and Hussars light cavalry. The horses were all of Prussian breed, mostly from good English sires and grandsires.

3.—ARTILLERY.

1.—1 Brigade of Artillery of the Guard, three divisions of field batteries, of which each consists of four batteries of 6 guns *	=	72 guns
1 Division of Horse Artillery of the Guard, consisting of six batteries of 4 guns each	=	24 ,,

Total Field Artillery of the Guard . . . $=$ 96 guns

---

* Of these 4 batteries were armed with the rifled 6-pounder gun.
4   ,,   ,,   ,,   4   ,,
4   ,,   ,,   smooth 12   ,,

2.—8 Brigades of Artillery of the Line = 144 batteries . $=$ 768 guns

Total of Field Artillery 162 batteries . . $=$ 864 guns
2 Divisions of Garrison Artillery called out = 18
batteries . . . . $=$ 96 ,,

4.—SPECIAL TROOPS.

1 Battalion of Pioneers of the Guard . . . . $=$ 1,002 men
8   ,,   ,,   Line . . . $=$ 8,016 ,,

9 Battalions of Pioneers = 36 companies . . . $=$ 9,018 men

5.—MILITARY TRAIN.

1 Battalion of Military Train of the Guard of two
companies . . . . $=$ 1,226 men
8 Battalions of Military Train of the Line . . $=$ 9,808 ,,

Total Military Train . . . . . . $=$ 11,034 men

DEPÔT TROOPS.

Each regiment of Infantry on being mobilized formed a *depôt* battalion, each regiment of Cavalry a *depôt* squadron, each *Jäger* battalion a *depôt* company, each brigade of artillery a *depôt* division, each battalion of Pioneers a *depôt* company:—

81 *depôt* battalions of Infantry   = 81,162 men.
10 ,,   companies of *Jagris*   = 2,500 ,,
48 ,,   squadrons   = 7,200 ,,
 9 ,,   divisions of Artillery (228 guns) = 7,400 ,,
 9 ,,   companies of pioneers   = 2,250 ,,
                                   ——————— men
Total of *Depôt* troops   =100,512 men

Thus the strength of the Prussian regular army at the commencement of the campaign was—

Infantry   253,504 men
Cavalry   30,000 ,,
Artillery   35,100 ,, with 864 guns
Pioneers   9,108 ,,

116

Train	11,034 ,,	
Non-combatants with		
regiments, &c.	18,000 ,,	
Depôt troops	100,512 ,, with 228 guns	
Officers	13,000 ,,	

Total about 473,600 men, with 100,000 horses and 1,092 guns.

The *Landwehr*, the first levy of which formed the troops of reserve supports, and for garrison duties in support of the regular army, and consisted of men between twenty-eight and thirty-two years of age, was organised as follows:—

Infantry.—
4 Regiments of *Landwehr* of the Guard, each of three battalions.
32 Regiments of *Landwehr* battalions, each of three and eight independent battalions.
  Totalling 116 battalions = 118,900 men

At first the majority of the battalions were formed 500 strong, and at a later period raised only to the strength of 800 men by calling up some of the second levy of the *Landwehr*, so that the actual strength of the *Landwehr* did not reach 118,900 men. Of these one hundred and sixteen battalions, twenty-four were amalgamated together in the first reserve *corps d'armée*; the remainder were used as garrisons for fortresses and for the maintenance of occupied territories.

The cavalry of the first levy of the *Landwehr* consisted of twelve regiments:—

1 Heavy Cavalry Regiment of				
4 squadrons	= 4 squad. =	600 horsemen	
5 Regiments of Uhlans	= 20	,,	= 3,000	,,
1 Regiment of Dragoons	= 4	,,	= 600	,,
5 Regiments of Hussars	= 20	,,	= 3,000	,,

                                              7,200
During the course of the war 7 more regiments
  of four squadrons each were formed = 4,200   ,,

      Total *Landwehr* Cavalry   =11,400   ,,

The remainder of the *Landwehr* of the second levy, after the battalions above mentioned had been filled up to war strength, was only called out in special cases, and by particular orders. The men were then either sent to increase the strength of the battalions under arms, or could be formed in independent regiments, which could consist of one hundred and sixteen battalions of infantry, and one hundred and forty-four squadrons of cavalry.

The regiment of infantry consisted of three battalions, each of four companies. Each company consisted of two divisions. The formation for parade was in three ranks; in action the third rank men of the whole battalion acted as skirmishers, or three of each company formed a third two-rank deep division of the company.

Each squadron of Cavalry was formed of four divisions; the formation was always in double rank.

The Prussian fleet, which till within the last few years has never aspired to any very distinguished place amongst those of the great maritime powers, consisted at the beginning of the war of eight screw *corvettes*, namely—

The *Arcona*	28 guns,	400	horse-power
Gazelle	28 „	400	„
Vincta	28 „	400	„
Nymph	17 „	200	„
Augusta	14 „	400	„
Victoria	14 „	400	„
Hertha	28 „	400	„
Medusa	17 „	200	„

of also eight gunboats of the first-class, each of which had three guns, and was of 80 horse-power; of fifteen gunboats of the second class, each of which mounted two guns, and was of 60 horse-power; of also four steam despatch-boats, namely—

The *Eagle*	4 guns,	300	horse-power
Loreley	2 „	120	„
Grief	2 „	120	„
Grille	2 „	160	„

of also two paddle-wheel steamers—

Arminius	4 guns,	300	horse-power
Cheops	3 „	300	„

Thus the whole steam-fleet mustered altogether only 245 guns.

Of sailing-vessels Prussia possessed the frigates *Gepin*, 48 guns;

Thetis, 36; and the *Niobe*, 26: the brigs *Rover*, 16 guns; *Mosquito*, 16; *Hela*, 6: the schooners *Ilitis* and *Leopard*, and the guard-ship *Barbarossa*, of 9 guns, as well as thirty-four sloops of 2 guns each, and four yawls of 1 gun each.

The *personnel* of the fleet was formed of a ship's complement division of 1,882 men, among whom are included officers, officials, and boys; of a dockyard division of 589 men; and of the marines (infantry and artillery), who numbered 952 men.

CHAPTER 2

The War Strength of Austria

Since its last war the government of Austria has decided upon a total reorganisation of its army. It is therefore only necessary here to show as briefly as possible the organisation of the Austrian Army as it existed at the beginning of the campaign, more with a view to deduce therefrom the actual number engaged, than to take any special notice of a system which the most bitter experience has proved to be grievously faulty.[1]

The empire of Austria had at the beginning of the war an area of about 294,000 square miles, and a population of about 35,000,000 inhabitants, of many nationalities, such as German, Slave, Magyar, and Czech. Its annual receipts amounted to 48,850,000*l*., its annual expenditure to almost 52,100,000*l*., so that every year there was a considerable deficit. To the army and navy 11,700,000*l*. were annually devoted. The national debt amounted in April 1864 to 309,600,000*l*., and must since that time have increased by at least 20,000,000*l*.

The Austrian Army consisted of—

INFANTRY

80 Infantry regiments of the Line (1—80)
1 Imperial regiment
32 Battalions of Feldjägers (1—32)
14 Border Infantry regiments (1—14)
    (*Grenz Infanterie-regimenter*)
1 Border Infantry battalion (Titler).

---

1. The new organisation of the Austrian Army since 1866, has been shown in some able letters which have appeared at intervals in the *Times* during the last three years, (as at time of first publication).

CAVALRY

12 Cuirass regiments (1—12)
2 Regiments of Dragoons (1—2)
14 Regiments of Hussars (1—14)
13 Regiments of Uhlans (1—13)

ARTILLERY

12 Regiments of Artillery (1—12)
1 Regiment of Coast Artillery

SPECIAL TROOPS

2 Regiments of Engineers
6 Battalions of Pioneers

TROOPS OF ADMINISTRATION

10 Sanitary companies
48 Transport squadrons
Besides other Administration troops and departments.

TROOPS FOR PROVINCIAL DEFENCE.

10 Regiments of *Gens-d'armes* A military police corps
The Tyrolean Provincial corps
Againsal Provincial Rifle battalions
Volunteer Companies of Sharpshooters and *Landsturm*

Each regiment of infantry of the line consisted in peace of four battalions and a *depot*. The fourth battalion to which the *depôt* was attached remained in peace in the district to which the regiment belonged, and served as a *depôt* battalion, while the three first battalions were, as a rule, quartered in a totally different province than that from which their recruits were drawn. In time of war the *depôt* was formed into a *depôt* division, and the fourth battalion was sent into some fortress as a garrison battalion, while the three first battalions were sent into the field to join the army of manoeuvre.

Each battalion mustered, or ought to have mustered, in war, 1,018 combatants, divided among six companies. Every two companies formed the so-called division: each company consisted of two subdivisions.

The Imperial regiment of *Jägers* had in war six battalions and one *depôt* battalion. Each battalion mustered in six companies 1,011 combatants, as did also each battalion of Feldjägers.

The whole of the duty of the Military Borderers was divided into three portions. The first levy formed the regular border infantry regiments and the Titler battalion: the second, the armed population, was only formed for service in its own particular province, and consisted of, in all, 22,000 men. The third levy was only specially called upon in cases of urgent necessity, and formed a force of about 28,000 men.

In war, each regiment of the Military Borderers of the first levy consisted of three battalions, each of six companies. The first eight regiments formed, at the outbreak of a war, one battalion of four companies as a *depôt*; three others formed an independent division for the same purpose. Of these eleven regiments three battalions could be put into the field in war; of the remaining three of the fourteen border regiments two battalions could only be put in the field; the Titler battalion sent one battalion into the field, so that forty battalions of Military Borderers were with the field army.

For the defence of fortresses there were left, after the army of operation took the field, eighty-four battalions of infantry regiments, and eleven Border battalions, in all about 100,000 men.

The Tyrolean Provincial corps, as well as the Border troops which did not join the army, were retained in their own particular provinces.

The principal weapon of the Infantry of the Line and of the Border regiments was a rifled musket on Lorenz's system, with a bayonet The *Jägers* had a rather shorter musket, the rifling of which had a slightly sharper twist than that of the line.

Cavalry,—The *cuirass* regiments, which were originally *cuirassiers*, but had previously to the war of 1866 laid aside the *cuirass*, formed the whole of the heavy cavalry. Each *cuirass* regiment, with the exception of the eighth, the old Dampier *Cuirassiers* (which, on account of privilege derived as early as 1619, had never been reduced, and still contained six squadrons), consisted of five squadrons. Every light cavalry regiment consisted of six squadrons. At the outbreak of the war each regiment of cavalry left one of its squadrons as a *depôt* squadron at home. The squadron contained one hundred and forty-nine mounted men. The whole cavalry mustered 29,000 sabres.

Artillery.—The field artillery consisted of twelve regiments, of which nine were formed to accompany the *corps d'armée* of infantry; the remaining three were intended to form the army artillery of reserve, and to be attached to the cavalry of reserve.

The regiment of coast-artillery was divided into four battalions, of which the first and second battalion had in war each five active companies, two mountain batteries of eight guns, and one *depôt* company. The third and fourth battalions each had six active companies and one *depôt* company.

The heavy batteries of the field artillery were armed with muzzle-loading rifled 8-pounder guns; the light with muzzle-loading rifled 4-pounder guns; the mountain batteries with rifled 3-pounders. Garrison artillery of the latest pattern consisted of rifled breach-loading guns, 6-, 12-, 24-, and 48-pounders; but there are still many smooth-bored guns and howitzers in the armaments of the fortresses.

An Austrian *corps d'armée*, as a rule, consisted of four brigades of infantry, four squadrons of cavalry (one attached to each infantry brigade), four 4-pounder field batteries (one attached to each infantry brigade), a reserve artillery, two companies of engineers, and two companies of pioneers, with four bridge-trains, besides administrative services. To an army which would be formed by the amalgamation of several of these *corps d'armée*, would be attached several brigades of light cavalry, each of which consisted of two regiments; therefore ten squadrons, and one 4-pounder battery of horse-artillery, some divisions of reserve cavalry, an army reserve of artillery, a reserve of engineers, and all necessary administrative services.

Recruiting,—In each year in Austria from 80,000 to 85,000 recruits were called into the army. The time of service was ten years, of which the last two were spent in the reserve.

In the Infantry the recruit was kept from one to three years with the colours, in the cavalry seven or eight years, in the engineers and artillery three years: he was, after his period of actual presence with his corps expired, dismissed to his home on furlough, and called out annually for military exercise till he had accomplished eight years' service, when he was transferred to the reserve.

In case of war the men on furlough were called in to fill up the ranks of the army of operation, the men of the reserve to join the *depôt* and garrison corps.

The tactical unit in the infantry was the division of two companies, in the cavalry the squadron, in the artillery the battery of eight guns. It was laid down as a rule by the Austrian regulations, that in action every division of troops was to retain a dependent reserve.

The Austrian Army was divided according to nationalities, thus—

123

	German.	Poles.	Hungarian.	Italian.	Siebenbürger.	Borderers.	Mixed.
Infantry .	23 regts.	13	23	7	7	7	
Jägers .	27 batts.	4	3	2	2	—	
Cavalry .	12 regts.	13	11	—	1	3	1
Artillery	— regts.	1	—	—	—	—	12

Subjoined is a summary, calculated from the best available authorities, of the Austrian troops available for the army of operation at the commencement of the war:—

1.—INFANTRY.

a. LINE.—80 Regiments of three battalions of three companies.

	Peace Strength.		War Strength.
1 Battalion	= 470	=	1,018
80 Regiments	= 240 batts.	=	244,480 combatants

b. JÄGERS.—One Imperial Jäger regiment of six battalions of six companies, and thirty-two Feldjäger battalions of six companies.

1 Battalion	= 627	=	1,011 combatants
38 Battalions		=	38,420 ,,

c. BORDERERS.—Eleven Regiments of three battalions, three of two battalions, and one independent battalion.

1 Battalion	=	956 combatants
40 Battalions	=	38,240 ,,

2.—CAVALRY.

12	Cuirass regiments of four squadrons . .	=	7,142
	1 extra squadron . . .	=	149
2	Regiments of Dragoons of five squadrons .	=	1,490
14	,, Hussars of five squadrons . .	=	10,430
13	,, Uhlans of five squadrons of 114 horsemen	=	7,410
			26,621

Austrian Navy,—Austria had done more for her navy within the few years which immediately preceded the war, than would have been anticipated from the small extent of her sea-coast, and her little interest in European commerce. The Austrian Navy mustered twenty-eight screw-vessels, namely—

1 line-of-battle ship,
5 frigates,
7 armour-plated frigates,
2 *corvettes,*
7 second-class gunboats,
3 third-class gunboats
3 schooners,
12 paddle-wheel steamers,

besides sixteen sailing-vessels, of which two were frigates, three *corvettes*, three brigs. The above formed the Austrian fleet of seagoing vessels; but for the navigation of interior waters, and for the defence of the coast, there were ten screw-steamers, sixteen paddle-wheel steamers, and thirty-five guard-ships.

The steam fleet of seagoing ships numbered forty vessels, which carried 651 guns, amounted to 11,475 horse-power, and were manned by 7,772 men.

The sailing fleet of seagoing vessels, which was only practically valuable for purposes of transport, consisted of eighteen vessels, with 225 guns, and 1,804 men.

The twenty-six vessels on the inner waters had together 72 guns, 1,511 horse-power, and 961 sailors; while the thirty-five guard-ships mounted 115 guns, and bore 1,060 sailors.

War Strength of the Remaining States of Germany

Bavaria.—Population, 4,700,000; area, 34,750 square miles; revenue, 4,700,000*l*.; national debt, 34,300,000*l*. In Bavaria the time of military service was six years. It was allowed to find substitutes for military service. The time of actual presence with the colours is twelve months in the first year, eight in the second, three in the third, and fourteen days in the fourth. Except for this time, the soldier was sent home on furlough.[1] The army consisted of—

INFANTRY.

16 Regiments of three battalions of six companies,
    1 battalion   = 1,950 men
8 Battalions of *Jägers*   =   668 ,,
           Total   50,768 men

armed with Podewil's muskets and sword-bayonet. [2]

CAVALRY.

3 Regiments of *Cuirassiers*
6 Regiments of Light horse
3 Regiments of Uhlans
            1 regt. of 4 squadrons = 591 horsemen
    12 Regiments = 7,620 horsemen

Cuirassiers armed with iron *cuirass* and helmet, straight sword, and pis-

---

1. This organisation was modified after the war of 1866, and will probably be even more modified in consequence of that of 1870—71.
2. In 1870, partly armed with the Werder rifle.

tol; the other regiments with bent sabre and pistol; Uhlans with lances.

ARTILLERY.

Four Regiments, of which—

No. I and II each 2 6-pounder batteries of 4 guns = 16 guns
                   3 12 pounder batteries of 4 guns = 24 „
   III Horse Artillery, with 4 12-pounder
              batteries of 6 guns   = 24 „
   IV 2 6-pounder batteries of eight guns   = 16 „
     2 12-pounder batteries of eight guns   = 16 „

              Total   96 „

The 6-pounders were rifled on the Prussian system; the 12-pounders were smooth-bore.

Engineers.—One regiment of eight companies, 1,380 men.

The army had divisions, brigades, regiments, and battalions. Tactical units were the company in two ranks, the squadron, and the battery. The formation for battle of the Bavarian infantry battalion was four Fusilier companies in line, and the two light companies in column in rear of the wings.

Saxony,—Area, 6,775 square miles; population, 2,225,000; revenue, 2,100,000*l.*; debt, 9,600,000*l.* The time of service in Saxony was six years in the line and two years in the reserve.

INFANTRY.

16 Battalions of four companies, 1 battalion = 983 men
4 Battalions of Jägers of 4 Companies, 1 bat. = 999   „
         Total   19,752 men

armed with Podewil's muskets and sword-bayonet

CAVALRY.

1 Guard regiment and 3 Line regiments of five squadrons,
1 regiment   = 803 men
         Total   3,217 men.

ARTILLERY.

1 Regiment of field-batteries, with 22 6-pounder
           rifled guns   = 22 guns
6 rifled 1 2-pounder batteries   = 36 „

1 Horse Artillery regiment of 2
      batteries of 6 guns   = 12 „
                                —

        Total   70 „

SPECIAL TROOPS.

One company of Engineers and two of Pioneers.

The army was divided into two divisions, each of which had two brigades. One brigade consisted of two regiments and one battalion of *Jägers*. Besides these divisions, there was a cavalry division of two brigades, each of two regiments, and a corps of artillery; the infantry fought in three ranks, with a reserve formation out of the third rank in rear of the wings.

Hesse-Cassel.—Area, 4,350 square miles; population, 740,000; revenue, 500,000*l.*; debt, 1,400,000*l.*

Military service was universal, and for a period of ten years, of which five years were spent in the line and first levy of reserve, five in the second levy. The time of actual presence with the standards varied from twenty-one to thirty-four months.

INFANTRY.

2 Brigades of 2 regiments of 2 batts. of 4 companies = 879 men
1 Jäger battalion   = 619 „
1 Schützen   = 387 „
        Total   8,614 men

armed with the Prussian needle-gun.

CAVALRY.

Garde du corps (sword and pistol)   = 264 horsemen
2 Regiments of Hussars (sword and carbine) = 521   „
        Total   1,306 horsemen

ARTILLERY.

1 rifled 6-pounder battery   6 guns
I smooth 6-pounder battery   6 „
½ smooth 12-pounder battery   4 „
1 Horse Artillery 6-pounder   6 „
                         —

        Total   22 „

ENGINEERS.

1 company of Pioneers.

Hanover.—Area, 17,450 square miles; population, 1,890,000; income, 3,750,000*l.*; debt, 7,200,000*l.*

Recruiting conducted by conscription: time of service seven years, in the cavalry ten years.

INFANTRY.

Two divisions, each of two brigades, each of two regiments and one light battalion = 8 regiments, and four light battalions = 18,000 men.

CAVALRY.

2 Cuirassier regiments	= 1,000 horsemen
4 Dragoon ,,	= 1,000 ,,
2 Hussar ,,	= 1,000 ,,
Total	3,000 ,,

ARTILLERY—50 guns.

Würtemburg,—Area, 8,875 sq. miles; population, 1,720,000; revenue, 1,500,000*l.*; debt, 7,500,000*l.*

The contingent of Würtemburg formed the first division of the eighth corps of the Germanic Confederation.

Recruiting conducted by conscription, but substitutes allowed. Time of service twelve years, six of which were passed in the line, six in the *Landwehr.* Time of actual presence with the standards about eighteen months.

INFANTRY.

1 Division of 2 brigades of 4 regiments, each
of 2 battalions (4 companies)
16 Battalions (1 battalion   = 851 men) = 13,616 men
2 Battalions of *Jägers* (1 battalion = 849 men) = 1,698   ,,

Total   15,314   ,,

armed with Podewil's musket

CAVALRY.

1 Brigade of 4 regiments, each in 4 squadrons
1 Regiment = 714 to 880 horsemen
            Total   3,271
of which one regiment acts as a *depôt*

ARTILLERY.

1 Regiment:—

2 Horse Artillery 4-pounder batteries of 8 guns	= 16 guns
2 light field 6-pounder batteries of 8 guns	= 16 „
2 heavy field 12-pounder batteries of 6 guns	= 12 „
3 siege batteries	— „
Total	44 „

ENGINEERS.

210 men on a war footing.

Baden,—Area, 6,950 square miles; population, 1,400,000; revenue, 1,700,000*l.*; debt, 10,800,000*l.*

The contingent formed the second division of the eighth corps of the army of the Germanic Confederation.

INFANTRY.

5 Regiments of two battalions
2 Fusilier Battalions.
1 Battalion of *Jägers*
            = 10,745 men

armed with Podewil's musket

CAVALRY.

3 Regiments of Dragoons, each of 4 squadrons
            = 2, 100 horsemen.

ARTILLERY—38 guns.

Hesse-Darmstadt,—Area, 3,800 square miles; population, 860,000; revenue, 950,000*l.*; debt, 2,000,000*l.*

The army of Hesse-Darmstadt formed the third division of the eighth corps of the Germanic Confederation.

INFANTRY.

Two brigades, each of two regiments, each of two battalions, each in five companies.

8 Battalions (1 battalion = 831 men) = 6,648 men
1 Battalion of *Jägers*   =   594 ,,

    Total   7,242 ,,

armed with Podewil's musket

CAVALRY.

1 Brigade of 2 regiments.
1 Regiment = 648 horsemen.
Total 1,296 horsemen.

ARTILLERY.

1 Horse Artillery battery, with four smooth
 and 2 rifled 6-pounder guns   = 6 guns
3 Field-batteries of 6 guns   = 18 ,,
(One 12-pounder battery, one rifled
 6-pair one smooth 6-pounder battery) —
    Total   24 ,,

ENGINEERS—1 company.

Nassau.—Area, 2,137 square miles; population, 460,000 inhabitants.

INFANTRY.

1 Brigade of 2 regiments, each of 2 battalions.
  1 Battalion = 1033 men.
4 Battalions   = 4,132 men
1 Battalion of Jägers   =   809 ,,

    Total   4,941 ,,

ARTILLERY.

1 rifled 6-pounder battery of 8 guns = 8 guns
1 smooth-bore battery   = 8 ,,

    Total   16 ,,

The contingents of the other minor states are so small that it would be tedious to enter into their composition in detail. The military of those which voted for the Austrian motion on the 14th June in the

Diet were:—

Saxe-Meiningen	2,000 men
Reusz Grez	400 „
Frankfort-on-Maine	1,000 „
Total	3,400 „

Of those which voted against the Austrian motion:—

The Saxon Duchies	7,500 men
Mecklenburg	7,500 „
Oldenburg	3,500 „
Lübeck, Bremen, Hamburg	3,600 „
Anhalt	2,000 „
The two Lippes	1,200 „
Waldech	800 „
Reusz-Schleiz	700 „
The two Schwarzburgs	1,800 „
Total	28,600 „

Brunswick, Lemburg, and Luxembourg also voted against Austria, but the two former put no contingents in the field; the contingent of the last took so much time in its mobilization that it was not ready for employment until very nearly the conclusion of peace.

CHAPTER 41

War Strength of the Kingdom of Italy

The kingdom of Italy, had with an area of 116,750 square miles a population of about 21,775,000 inhabitants. Since the formation of this monarchy, in 1860, its finances had never been in anything but the most unsatisfactory condition.

Large armies and fleets had been maintained at a ruinous expense, and have both proved their incapacity to accomplish the purposes for which they were intended; large numbers of useless officials, who did no public work worthy of the name, and served as impediments more than as facilities to the transaction of business, were suffered to live idly on the resources of the State. In the year 1864 the revenue of the country amounted to 27,000,000*l*., the expenditure of the government to nearly 37,000,000*l*., and since that year this annual deficit had remained about constant

In the year 1864 9,280,000*l*. were spent upon the army, and 2,500,000*l*. upon the navy.

The Italian Army, according to the latest organisation previous to 1866, consisted of:—

INFANTRY.

8 Regiments of Grenadiers (Nos. 1—8).
72 Regiments of Infantry of the Line (Nos. 1—72)
5 Regiments of Bersaglieri (Nos. 1—5).

The regiments of grenadiers and of the line differed only in some

---

1. The kingdom of Italy is at present, (as at time of first publication), engaged in the reorganisation of its military forces, so that this chapter must be regarded solely as a record of the past.

slight details of clothing from each other. A regiment of either consisted of the regimental staff, four battalions, and a *depôt*.[2]

Each battalion consisted of four companies, and each on a war footing mustered four officers and 149 men. Thus the effective strength of each regiment amounted to, with the staff, 81 officers and 2,453 men, or altogether 2,534 men; and the eighty regiments of Grenadiers and of the Line amounted in all to 202,720 combatants.

The *depôts* remained at home to find and drill recruits, and then forward them to the troops in the field. Each *depôt* consisted of 14 officers and 61 men.

Every regiment of Bersaglieri consisted of a staff, eight field battalions, each of four companies and a *depôt* division. The companies of the Bersaglieri were of the same strength as those of the Line. Thus the effective strength for war of each regiment of Bersaglieri amounted to 152 officers and 4,872 men, or altogether to 5,024 men. The five regiments therefore would afford 25,120 combatants.

The Bersaglieri were armed with short rifles and sword bayonets: the rest of the infantry with Minié rifles and ordinary bayonets,

CAVALRY.

4 Regiments of Cavalry of the Line (heavy).
7 Regiments of Lancers.
7 Regiments of Light horse.
1 Regiment of Guides.

With the exception of the regiment of Guides, all the regiments of cavalry had six field squadrons and a *depôt* squadron.

Each squadron on a war footing mustered 5 officers, 145 men, 112 horses. The regimental staff consisted of 11 officers, 7 men, and 18 horses. The regiment therefore numbered 41 officers, 877 men, and 738 horses. A regiment might accordingly be considered to bring about 700 sabres into the field.

This would give for the effective force on a war footing of the eighteen regiments (exclusive of the Guides) 12,600 sabres. The *depôt* of a regiment consisted of 14 officers and 59 men. The regiment of Guides, which was chiefly intended to furnish orderlies for general officers, consisted of seven squadrons, and had altogether 60 officers, 1,074 men, and 858 horses. The Heavy Cavalry as well as the lancers carried the lance,

---

2. According to the organisation of 1865.

ARTILLERY.

1 Regiment of Pontoniers, who, in the Italian service as in the
French, are included among the Artillery.
3 Regiments of Garrison Artillery, Nos. 2, 3, 4.
1 Regiments of Field Artillery, Nos. 5, 6, 7, 8, 9.
6 Companies of Artificers.

The regiment of Pontoniers had nine companies on a war footing;
each regiment of Field Artillery had sixteen field-batteries and two
depôt batteries; each regiment of Garrison Artillery had sixteen companies and two *depôt* companies. Two batteries of the fifth regiment
were Horse Artillery batteries. Except these, the Italian army possessed
no horse artillery. From the five field regiments there could be placed
in the field eighty field-batteries, each of six guns, forming a total artillery force of four hundred and eighty guns.

These guns were all rifled, and were divided into batteries of
8-pounders or 16-pounders.

ENGINEERS,

Two regiments of Sappers. Each regiment on a war footing had
eighteen field companies and two *depôt* companies.

MILITARY TRAIN.

Three regiments. Each regiment had on a war footing eight
companies and one *depôt* company. Each of the field companies
mustered 8 officers, 330 men, and 420 horses.

ADMINISTRATIVE TROOPS

were divided into seven companies, which contained all the
hospital attendants and commissariat soldiers.

The total strength of the Italian Army in the field was thus:—

Infantry	202,720
Bersaglieri	25,120, with 480 guns
Cavalry	13,000

Organisation,—In time of war the army was divided into divisions.
Each division consisted as a general rule, of:—

2 Brigades of Infantry, each of two regiments;
2 Battalions of Bersaglieri;
1 Regiment of Light Cavalry;

3 Batteries of Artillery (two 8-pounder batteries
and one 16-pounder battery);
1 Company of Sappers.

Such a division would quite bring into the field a force of 10,000 Infantry and 700 cavalry, with 18 guns.

Several such divisions, generally three or four, were amalgamated into a *corps d'armée*, for which a special reserve was then formed. This reserve consisted of one battalion of Bersaglieri, four squadrons of cavalry, and a 16-pounder battery for each division, which were deducted from the strength of the division. A company of sappers, and a company of pioneers with a bridge train to throw a bridge over three hundred yards, was added to a *corps d'armée*.

An army was formed by the conjunction of several *corps d'armée*, and had an additional force of reserve artillery and engineers, with a pontoon train capable of constructing a bridge six hundred yards long. A division of reserve cavalry was formed out of the four Heavy Cavalry regiments, which were divided into two brigades, and of the two Horse Artillery batteries of the service.

Recruiting,—The recruiting of the Italian Army was conducted by conscription; substitutes were, however, allowed About 50,000 recruits were levied annually before the war. These were divided into two portions proportionately to the vacancies in the ranks. The recruits of the first portion served for eleven years, of which the first five were spent under the standards; those of the second portion were called out and then dismissed, but were liable to military service for a period of five years.

Besides the regular army, a National Guard existed in Italy. This was of the character of a *burgher* guard, and existed for the most part only upon paper. It was intended, however, after 1866, to form, in case of war, a mobilized National Guard of 220 battalions, mustering about 110,000 men, to act as garrison troops.

There existed also a corps of *Carabineers* who did the duty of a *gendarmerie*, and numbered over 20,000 men, but these would rarely be ever available against an external enemy, as to them were entrusted all the police duties of the Peninsula.

At the beginning of the war the Italian forces were strengthened by the formation of volunteer corps to serve under General Garibaldi; of these there were forty-two battalions. As with all irregular troops, it was extremely difficult to discover what number these corps mustered, but they may apparently be safely calculated as 35,000 men.

Italian Fleet.—The Italian fleet consisted of:—

1 screw line-of-battle ship;
13 screw frigates;
7 steam frigates of the second class, of which six were ironclad;
2 sailing frigates of the second class;
8 steam *corvettes* of the first rank, of which two were ironclad;
2 sailing corvettes of the first rank;
17 corvettes of the second and third rank;
14 smaller vessels;
8 screw gunboats;
25 transport vessels.

The number of guns mounted on these vessels amounted to 1,524; the number of men employed in them was 14,000 officers, seamen, and engineers.

The infantry of the Marine consisted of two regiments organized on the same principles as those of the Infantry of the Line, and clothed and armed in the same manner as the Bersaglieri.

BOOK 4

CHAPTER 1

Prelude of the War

The Germanic Confederation possessed five Federal fortresses, originally raised to protect Germany against an invasion from France. These were Mainz, Luxembourg, Landau, Rastadt, and Ulm. At the end of May the garrisons of Mainz and Rastadt, in accordance with the constitution of the Confederation, were composed of a mixed force of Austrian and Prussian and some other Federal troops. When it became evident that war was likely to break out between the great German Powers, Bavaria proposed in the *diet* on the 1st June, that the Prussian and Austrian garrisons should be withdrawn from these fortresses, as well as from the free town of Frankfort, which was occupied in a similar manner, and that the guardianship of these places should be handed over partly to the troops of the States in which these places were situated, partly to the reserve division of the Federal army.

To prevent the bloodshed which would have in case of war ensued between the soldiers of these mixed garrisons, the motion was unanimously accepted. It was determined that Mainz should be held for the Confederation by troops of Bavaria, Saxe Weimar, Saxe Meiningen, Anhalt, Schwarzburg, and the two *Lippes*; Rastadt by those of Baden, Saxe Altenburg, Coburg Gotha, Waldech, and Reusz; and that a Bavarian division should remain in Frankfort

The Prussian and Austrian troops were, in accordance with this resolution, withdrawn from the fortresses of the Confederation. The Prussians were assembled under the command of General Von Beyer at Wetzlar. The Austrians were attached to the 8th Federal corps, which was placed under the command of Prince Alexander of Hesse, an Austrian general who had gained distinction at the Battle of Montebello in 1859.

On the 14th June, when Prussia declared the Germanic Confederation dissolved, war became inevitable. Prussia had at this time concentrated her main armies on the frontiers of Saxony and in Silesia. In rear of these lay the hostile States of Hanover and Hesse-Cassel, the troops of which might either act against the communications of the Prussian armies, or by withdrawing south of the Maine unite with the Bavarians and Austrians, and swell the armies of these two powers with their contingents. In front of the right wing of the Prussian main line lay the hostile kingdom of Saxony, which if left unoccupied would have formed a convenient ground for the *débouché* from the Bohemian mountains of the Austrian columns, covered by the Saxon army. In order to prevent the forces of the two former States from causing annoyance to the rear of her armies, and to seize the initiative in Saxony, Prussia took most rapid measures.

The decree against Prussia had been passed at Frankfort on the 14th June.

A telegraphic summons was despatched to the three States of Saxony, Hesse-Cassel, and Hanover, which demanded that they should immediately reduce their armies to the peace establishment which had existed on the 1st March, and should agree to the Prussian project of the 10th June for the reform of the Germanic Confederation. If the three States agreed to this demand, Prussia would undertake to guarantee to them their sovereign rights; if they did not within twelve hours consent to do so, war would be declared.

The governments of these States did not reply. Prussia declared war against them on the evening of the 15th June, and on the 16th Prussian troops invaded their territories.

Position of Prussian Troops at the End of the First Fortnight of June.— Prussia had commenced her preparations for war on the 27th March, when five divisions had been placed on a war footing, five brigades of artillery been strengthened, and the fortresses in Silesia and the province of Saxony armed. The mobilization of the whole army had been decreed on the 7th May, and on the 19th of that month the concentration of troops in Silesia, Lusatia, and Thuringia had begun. On the 1 st June the *corps d'armée* of the Guard had been sent to Silesia, and the 8th corps and 14th division despatched to Halle: a reserve corps was at the same time formed at Berlin. The main Prussian armies were composed of three principal sections:—

1st. The First Army, under the command of Frederick Charles,

139

which consisted of the and *corps d'armée* (Pomeranian), 3rd (Branden-burg), 4th (Saxony), and of a cavalry corps formed of fifteen regi-ments. It lay round Heyerswerda and Görlitz.

2nd. The Second Army, under the command of the Crown Prince of Prussia, which consisted of the Guard corps, the 1st corps (Prus-sia), the 2nd (Poland), the 6th (Silesia), and of a cavalry corps of seven regiments. It lay in Silesia,

3rd. The Army of the Elbe, under the command of General Her-warth von Bittenfeld, which consisted of the 8th corps (Rheinland), and the 14th division of the 7th corps (Westphalia), as well as a cavalry corps of three regiments.

In rear of these was the reserve corps in Berlin, under the com-mand of General Mülbe, which consisted of two divisions of *Landwehr* and six regiments of Landwehr cavalry. A third division of *Landwehr* was also in course of formation at Berlin.

By the 15th June Prussia had prepared troops for the invasion of Saxony, Hanover, and Cassel. The First Army and the Army of the Elbe, which was stationed round Halle and Torgau, were designed to act against Saxony. Hesse-Cassel and Hanover were to be invaded by the then separated divisions, which after the occupation of these States were united under the command of General Vogel von Falckenstein, and on the 1st July named the Army of the Maine.

On the morning of the 15th June, the troops destined to act against Hanover consisted of the division which General von Manteuffel had mobilized in Schleswig, and with which he had invaded Holstein. Af-ter the Austrians quitted the latter duchy this division had been con-centrated at Harburg, where it was supported by a flotilla of Prussian gunboats on the Lower Elbe and on the coast of the North Sea. A sec-ond division was also collected for the same purpose under General von Falckenstein, near the fortress of Minden, in that portion of the Prussian province of Westphalia which projected into the southern boundary of the kingdom of Hanover.

The greatest part of this division was formed by the 13th division, one division of the Westphalian *corps d'armée*. The Prussian garrisons which had been withdrawn from the Federal fortresses were united with some other detachments, and formed into a division under Gen-eral Beyer, which numbered 17,000 men. It was posted at Wetzlar, in the Prussian enclave, that was surrounded by the territories of Hesse-Cassel and Nassau.

Positions of the Austrian Army at the End of the First Fortnight of June.—
Feldzeugmeister Von Benedek, the hero of San Martino, assumed the
Supreme command of the Austrian Army of the North on the 18th
May, and spread the seven *corps d'armée* and five divisions of cavalry, of
which it was composed, between Cracow and the Elbe, along the lines
of railway which run through most parts of the Austrian provinces.
These seven corps were:—

The 1st, under the command of Count Clam Gallas, which was
posted at Prague,

The 2nd, under Count Thun Höhenstadt, at Olmütz.

The 3rd, under the Archduke Ernst, at Brünn,

The 4th, under Count Festetics, at Teschen.

The 6th, under Baron Ramming, at Olmütz.

The 8th, under the Archduke Leopold, at Brünn.

The 10th, under Count Huyn, afterwards under Count Gablenz,
with only nine battalions, at Bömisch Trübau.

The cavalry divisions attached to this army were:—

The 1st light cavalry division (Baron Edelsheim), consisting of six
regiments and three batteries of horse artillery.

The 2nd light cavalry division (Prince Thurn and Taxis), four regiments and two batteries.

1st reserve division of cavalry (Prince Schleswig-Holstein), six regiments and two batteries.

2nd reserve division of cavalry (Von Zajtsek), six regiments and
two batteries.

3rd reserve division of cavalry (Count Coudenhove), six regiments
and two batteries.

Positions of the Austrian Army of the South.—The Austrian army of
the South consisted of three *corps d'armée*, and was under the command of the Archduke Albrecht One of these held Eastern Venetia and
Istria, while the other two were posted in the renowned quadrilateral
formed by the fortresses of Peschiera and Mantua on the Mincio, and
Verona and Legnano on the Adige.

The third *corps d'armée*, under the Archduke Ernst, served as a general reserve, which might be either directed against Italy, or sent into
Bohemia, as circumstances required.

Positions of the Italian Army.—The Italian Army was divided into
four *corps d'armée*. The first of these, under Giovanni Durando, was
stationed in the middle of June at Lodi. It consisted of four divisions,

and was intended to act upon the Lake of Garda and the Upper Mincio. The second of these divisions, under Cuchiari, was at Cremona. It consisted of three divisions, and was designed to act upon the Lower Mincio, and against Mantua. The third, under Delia Rocca, was posted in rear of the two former on both sides of the Po, with its headquarters at Placenza. It contained four divisions. The fourth, under Cialdini, consisted of five divisions, and had its headquarters at Bologna, where it was intended to operate on the Lower Po and Lower Adige.

The campaign on the Mincio did not commence quite so soon as hostilities in Germany. It is necessary, in order to preserve the clearness of the narrative, to disregard the Italian campaign until the course of events in Germany has been tolerably developed. It is sufficient here to mention that Italy declared war against Austria on the 20th June.

Army of Saxony.—The army of Saxony had been mobilized, and was by the end of the first fortnight of June ready to take the field. It was distributed through the kingdom of Saxony, with its main body in Dresden and Pima,

Army of Hanover.—The army of Hanover was totally unprepared for war, and was for the most part peaceably garrisoned in the neighbourhood of the town of Hanover.

Army of Bavaria—The Bavarian army was concentrated, in the middle of June, between Bamberg and *Würzberg*, under Prince Charles of Bavaria, in three divisions of infantry, one reserve brigade of infantry, one corps of reserve cavalry, containing eight regiments and two batteries, one corps of reserve artillery of ten batteries.

Eighth Federal Corps.—The eighth corps of the Federal army was formed at Frankfort, but not with great alacrity. The Government of Baden was by no means eager to put its troops into the field against Prussia, but was obliged to do so for fear of the duchy being over-run by its powerful neighbours in case of refusal to do so. When this corps was formed, it occupied Frankfort, and was placed under the command of Prince Alexander of Hesse. The troops which composed it were:—

Those of Würtemburg, 14,000 men and 42 guns.

Those of Baden, 12,000 men and 38 guns.

The troops of Hesse-Darmstadt, 10,090 men and 24 guns.

The Nassau brigade, 5,000 men.

An Austrian division, formed from the garrisons which had withdrawn from the Federal fortresses, and mustered 12,000 men.

The total strength of this corps was in round numbers fifty-three thousand infantry, thirty-three squadrons, and one hundred and fourteen guns.

CHAPTER 2

Prussian Occupation of Hanover

On the evening of the 15th June, Prussia declared war against Hanover, Hesse-Cassel, and Saxony. The two former States, unless their armies were quickly disabled, could hinder effectually the Prussian communications between Berlin and the Rhenish provinces. An Austrian occupation of Saxony would have much facilitated operations against the open province of Brandenburgh and against Berlin, while it would have seriously impeded a Prussian advance into Bohemia, Against these States, then, it was necessary, that Prussia should act with immediate energy, in order, if possible, to disarm, certainly to occupy, them before she could turn her attention against her principal enemy Austria, and the States allied thereto. By excellent combinations punctually carried out this result was obtained. In the course of a few days three of the most important middle States of Germany were completely overrun by Prussian troops: and their sovereigns driven from their capitals and countries as if by a thunderbolt.

The Prussian invasion of Hanover and Hesse-Cassel was effected by combined movements from different points far apart: the enterprise was accordingly attended with considerable difficulty. It was very undesirable to weaken the main Prussian armies on the frontiers of Saxony and Silesia by the smallest detachments. Orders were accordingly sent to General Falckenstein, who was in Westphalia, to invade these States with both his divisions, and to occupy them. Göben's division was to be directed from Minden on Hanover, to which town that of General Manteuffel from Harburg was also to march. Beyer s division was ordered at the same time to invade Hesse-Cassel from Wetzlar. The Hanoverian army was not yet mobilized, that of Cassel was but a weak contingent, so that it was calculated that it would be quite possible, with these three Prussian divisions, to bring superior numbers to bear upon any decisive point

It was however necessary, in order to carry out these combinations, to withdraw all the troops from Holstein, where demonstrations in favour of the Prince of Augustenburg might cause trouble. In order to insure tranquillity in that duchy, several *Landwehr* battalions were despatched to Altona and Lauenburg, as soon as the invasion of Hanover was resolved upon. Wetzlar was evacuated, but the 8th Federal corps at Frankfort was not yet sufficiently organised to cause any apprehension, as for several days it would be unable to make a movement forward.

The rapid progress of affairs and the Prussian declaration of war on the 15th had caused great excitement in Hanover. When the Austrian troops, round which the army of Hanover might have rallied, had been withdrawn from Holstein, all idea of defending the capital of that kingdom had been given up; and on war being declared, it was determined to save the army by a movement towards the south, where it might unite with the Bavarians. This movement was made on the night of the 15th, chiefly by railway to Göttingen, but with such hurry that many important articles of equipment were forgotten: such were the reserve ammunition and the field dispensaries. On the morning of the 16th. King George of Hanover followed his troops and collected them round Göttingen.

General Falckenstein broke up from Minden at daybreak on the 16th, and on the 17th, at five o'clock in the afternoon, the first Prussian troops, after two forced marches, entered the town of Hanover. The railways from Hanover northwards towards Lüneburg, eastwards to Brunswick, and westwards to Minden, as well as the line behind the retreating army of King George, had been broken up by the Hanoverians. The main body of the division of General Manteuffel had a long portion of railway to restore, and was obliged to wait the resumption of transport along the line, so that it did not reach Lüneburg until the evening of the 18th.

Here two battalions of the 25th regiment were placed on the railway, and pushed up to the capital: the remainder of the division reached the town on the next evening.

18th.—The government of the country was immediately taken under Prussian superintendence, and no opposition could be made by a population which was surprised, and totally unfit to defend itself, as its members were untrained to the use of arms.

At the same time the Prussian navy had commenced operations. A battalion of the 25th regiment was, at ten o'clock on the evening of the 17th June, placed on board of the two transport vessels, *Loreley* and *Cyclops*, which belonged to the Prussian squadron on the Lower Elbe, and on a private steamer which belonged to a merchant of Harburg. The vessel steamed down the Elbe, and, at one o'clock on the morning of the 18th, arrived at Twietenfelt Here the battalion was disembarked, and immediately moved against the small fortress of Stade.

At its head marched a detachment of seamen from the transport fleet, who were destined to act as pioneers. About three o'clock in the morning, the small column reached the neighbourhood of Stade. It was observed by a Hanoverian cavalry outpost, which immediately galloped back to alarm the unsuspecting garrison. The Prussians pursued as quickly as they could; but when they reached the place, the gates were already closed.

The sailor-pioneers rushed forward to the gate, and smote upon it heavily with their axes. After a few vigorous blows it gave way a little. The axes were more vigorously plied, and in a few minutes the door fell with a crash across the roadway. Over the obstacle the Prussian infantry dashed into the town, and were received by shots directed from a few of the garrison who had located themselves in some of the houses. These shots did little execution, and the Prussians pushed on towards the market-place. Here some forming detachments of Hanoverians opened fire upon them, and a slight skirmish ensued. This was terminated by the commandant of the place, who, finding his men outnumbered, and in immediate danger of being surrounded and captured, ordered them to cease firing, and demanded a parley. This was granted by the Prussian commander; in a few minutes terms of capitulation were agreed upon, and Stade by the fortune of war ceased to be a fortress of the King of Hanover.

On the 19th June, Fort William and the batteries on the Weser, which were evacuated on the appearance of the Prussian flotilla, were occupied; and two days later, in a similar manner, Emden and the coast batteries on the Ems fell into the hands of the invaders. Thus on the 22nd June, the Prussians were in possession of the whole of Hanover with the single exception of the southern enclave of Göttingen.

In consequence of these vigorous and energetic measures, all the Hanoverian provisions of weapons and ammunition for the war fell into the hands of the Prussians, as well as the whole field equipment for the army in the way of waggons and *matériel*. These gains amounted to sixty cannon, ten thousand new rifled small arms, eight hundred waggons, and a large quantity of gunpowder. These losses were of great detriment to the Hanoverian cause, and gave into the hands of Prussia instruments of offence which her generals knew full well how to turn to account

The Hanoverian army halted at Göttingen,—paralysed, it was unable to move, and had to be organised. Had it been in a fit state of preparation for war, it might on the 16th or 17th have reached Cassel, and by the Cassel and Bebra railway effected a retreat in safety to the south. As it was, however, on account of the tardy measures and want of foresight of the Hanoverian Ministry, the brave soldiery of which it was composed were forced, after a display of great gallantry, valour, and devotion, to succumb to a catastrophe which will be treated of in another portion of this history.

CHAPTER 3

Prussian Occupation of Hesse-Cassel

The Electoral Prince of Hesse-Cassel was fortunate enough to save his army from falling into the hands of the enemy, but could not prevent the invasion of his country. The troops of Cassel, on the receipt of the Prussian declaration of war, immediately prepared to retire from Cassel towards the Maine. On the 16th the retreat was commenced; and that day, chiefly by means of the railway, they reached the neighbourhood of Fulda, This movement could not be prevented by the Prussians, for the nearest Prussian troops were those at Wetzlar, and the railway between Cassel and Marburg had been broken up. On the 19th June the army of Hesse-Cassel reached Hanau, and secured its communication with the eighth corps of the Federal army at Frankfort.

The territory of Hesse-Cassel did not, however, escape an invasion. On the night of the 15th June, General Beyer concentrated his troops, which numbered 17,000 combatants, on the frontier of Hesse-Cassel at Gieszen, and began his march into Hessian territory on the morning of the 16th at two o'clock. At Gieszen he published a proclamation, in which he announced to the people that Prussia had been obliged to declare war against the elector, but that the war was only to be carried on against the government, not against the country, which, on the contrary, was about to behold the dawn of better days and more fortunate circumstances.

On the 16th Beyer's advanced guard reached Marburg. The Prussian pushed through this town, and during the next two days urged his troops by forced marches towards Cassel. He sent a detachment to his right against the railway which leads from Cassel by Bebra to Hersfeld and Eisenach, and broke up the line at Melsungen. His object in this was to prevent the retreat to the south of any Hessian troops which might still be in the north of the electorate. He was, however, too late to attain this object, as Cassel had been cleared of its garrison on the night of the 16th, and it was already at Hanau.

On the evening and during the night of the 19th the Prussian troops passed into Cassel, the capital of the electorate, which is about eighty miles, or five long ordinary marches, from Wetzlar. The elector had not gone away with his troops, but had remained at his castle of Wilhelmshöhe, which was long renowned for the orgies held there by Jerome, King of Westphalia. On the night of the 22nd the Prussian envoy. General von Röder, made fresh propositions to him. Of these the principal was that the Elector should agree to the Prussian project for the reform of the Germanic Confederation. The latter did not, however, feel able to comply with the Prussian demands, and on the 22nd was taken as a State prisoner to the Prussian fortress of Stettin on the Oder, where a portion of the old castle of the dukes of Pomerania was given up to him as a residence.

Shortly afterwards cholera broke out at Stettin, and permission was given him to go to Königsberg, in East Prussia; of this permission, however, he made no use. Hesse-Cassel was now in the power of the Prussians. A more important result of the invasion was that the Prussian General Beyer was established in the rear of the Hanoverian army at Göttingen, which, without preparation, commissariat, military train, or reserve ammunition, was thus exposed to attack by a force nearly as large as its own, in its flank if it attempted to move southwards, in its rear if it turned to bay and faced its pursuers from the north. The Hanoverian army was already practically disarmed, paralysed, and prisoners.

CHAPTER 4

Prussian Occupation of Saxony

The troops designed for the invasion of Saxony were the army of the Elbe and the First Army. The former was to advance from the north, the latter from the east On the evening of the 15th June, when the Saxon Government had rejected the Prussian ultimatum, and received the declaration of war, the retreat of the Saxon army commenced, in order to gain Bohemia by way of Bodenbach, and there to unite with the Austrians. The funds from the treasury and the royal plate had already been packed up, and the waggons in which they had been placed accompanied the army.

Means were also adopted to impede as much as possible the advance of the Prussian troops. Saxon pioneers were set to work upon the railways which lead from the frontier upon Dresden. Of such railways there are two, that which follows the valley of the Elbe and joins the Leipsic line at Rieza and that which from Görlitz leads by Bautzen upon the capital of Saxony. At nightfall the Saxon pioneers commenced their work, but in the dark, and under constant apprehension of being broken in upon by the Prussian advanced guards, they made but little progress. The rails were taken up, but were neither carried away, nor twisted, nor broken so as not to be again immediately available. At eleven o'clock at night the wooden bridge which carries the railway branches to Leipsic and Chemnitz across the Elbe, near Rieza, was set on fire by means of petroleum. Its destruction was not accomplished, for only two piers were burnt, and the whole bridge was again made passable within a few days.

While the work of destruction went slowly on in Saxony that night, heavy masses of Prussian troops were drawing together, and dosing down to the very frontier line of that kingdom. Between Görlitz and the border on the west, Prince Frederick Charles marshalled three strong *corps d'armée*. On the north General Herwarth von Bittenfeld divided his force into three columns, which were to advance by Strehla, Dahlen, and Wurzen, on the left bank of the Elbe. During the few dark hours of the short summer night, the last preparations for the invasion were made. The main bodies were collected together about midnight, and the soldiers piled arms to rest and wait for dawn.

Few slept; a dull and heavy murmur continually rose from the crowded columns, and told the subdued but deep excitement which pervaded the hearts of the men; and this excitement was not without a cause, for the soldiers thought that the Austrian was in Dresden, and that there would be a battle on the morrow. At last the first faint streaks of dawn appeared; the troops eagerly fell into their ranks, and before the sun had risen the advanced guards were pushing briskly over Saxon ground.

The pioneers engaged upon the railway fled before the invaders' columns, fortunate to avoid being taken. Bittenfeld, from the north, reached Rieza about nine o'clock, and occupied that town in force. Two pontoon bridges were thrown across the Elbe below the town, a portion of the troops crossed, and marched on to Grossenhain, while the rest were directed up the left bank of the river, towards Meissen. Hardly had Bittenfeld's troops established themselves in Rieza, when a detachment of the field railway corps came up, who immediately commenced the restoration of the lines which had been removed, while pioneers were set to repair the burnt portions of the bridge.

In the meantime, the columns of the First Army were advancing in Lusatia. A detachment entered the town of Löbau, which was found without any garrison. The railway bridge here was not blown up, though it had been mined. The lines were, however, torn up, and laid in confusion on the way; but the Prussians employed the country people immediately to restore the railway. Bautzen was also occupied. Here the line had again been torn up, but was quickly repaired. But Prince Frederick diaries moved cautiously, for the passes of Reichenberg and Gabel were on his left To cover his communication with Görlitz, and to shield his left flank, he pushed a strong detachment along the Zittau road to a point a little beyond Ostritz.

On the 17th a detachment was thrown out on the right to feel Bittenfeld's left, and the prince pushed troops to Bisschofswerda, on the Dresden road, while Bittenfeld's advanced guard occupied Meissen. On the 18th a simultaneous advance was made on the capital. The advancing columns met with no opposition, and that afternoon the

Prussian colours were hoisted over Dresden.

The Prussian outposts were then pushed forward without encountering any opposition up to the frontier of Bohemia. Leipzic and Chemnitz were occupied, and the line of railway between Leipzic and Plauen, as well as that between Dresden and Chemnitz, secured by Prussian troops. On the 20th June the whole of Saxony was in the undisturbed possession of the troops of Prince Frederick Charles and of Herwarth, except where the Saxon standard floated above the virgin fortress of Königstein.

At the time of the inruption into Saxony, Prince Frederick Charles of Prussia issued this address to the inhabitants:—

> His Majesty the King of Prussia, my most gracious master, having been compelled to declare war against the King of Saxony, a portion of the troops under my command have today crossed the frontier between Prussian and Saxon Lusatia.
>
> We are not at war with the people and country of Saxony, but only with the government, which by its inveterate hostility has forced us to take up arms.
>
> Private property will be everywhere respected by my troops, who are also directed to protect every peaceful citizen from injury.
>
> I intreat you to repose confidence in our intentions, and to be assured that my soldiers, by strict discipline and good fellowship, will alleviate the hardships of war as much as possible. Provisions will never be exacted without a due receipt for them.
>
> Frederick Charles, General of Cavalry.
>
> Headquarters, Görlitz, June 16, 1866.

The administration of the country was undertaken by Royal Commissioners; but the Saxon officials and organs of administration were retained. A kindly feeling soon sprang up between the soldiery and the inhabitants, although there were occasional disturbances with the officials, chiefly with regard to the war contributions of fuel and forage which the country was required to furnish. The excellent discipline of the Prussian soldiery showed itself conspicuously in Saxony. The fears and prejudices of the inhabitants subsided more and more every hour, and the Prussians within a few days regarded themselves and were regarded as if in a friendly country.

At this time, as a security against the chances of an Austrian attack, and as a support for further operations, the reserve corps of General

Mülbe was ordered up from Berlin to Dresden. The positions of the armies about to be engaged in hostilities were, on 30th June, after the occupation of Saxony, as shown in the sketch over the page.

The Prussian dash into Saxony was a great military success. It gave Prince Frederick Charles the advantage of being able to attack the Austrians on a narrow front, if they should issue from the passes of the mountains, instead of being obliged to fight them on their own terms in an open country, as would have been the case had they been allowed to occupy this kingdom. At that moment the Prussian patrols and pickets were pushed close up to the Austrian frontier, the issue of the narrow defile which the Elbe cleaves in the Iron Mountains was secured, the Saxon troops had retired into Bohemia, and without pulling a trigger the Prussian army had, by the rapid action of its chief, gained as great advantages as could have been looked for from a victorious battle in this part of the theatre of war. There was only one point in Saxony where Saxon troops were still found, and where the Saxon standard was still hoisted.

The little fortress of Königstein, situated on an isolated sandstone cliff on the left bank of the Elbe, about nine miles from the Austrian frontier, was still occupied by a Saxon garrison. Inaccessible, from the steepness of the rock on which it stands, and at a considerable distance from the surrounding heights, this fortress has never been reduced. From the hill of Lilienstein, which stands on the opposite side of the river, and has a command over the fortress of more than 150 feet, Napoleon attempted to bombard Königstein, but his artillery was not heavy enough to send shot over the 3,000 yards which separate the summit of the two hills. With their rifled cannon the Prussian artillery could now easily, from the hill of Lilienstein or from that of Paffenstein on the opposite side, have engaged the guns of the fort on equal terms; but the Prussian commander did not deem it worthwhile to drag artillery to the top of these steep hills in order to force the capitulation of the small garrison of 1,200 men, who, in the event of Saxony remaining in his possession, must fall into his hands, and, in case of his being obliged to retire, could add so little to the force of his enemies. Königstein, guarded by its escarpments and impossibility of approach, was still allowed to retain its reputation for impregnability.

In most of the villages and hamlets of Saxony, certainly in all those which lay on roads leading to the frontier, Prussian soldiers were billeted; cavalry and artillery horses filled the farmsteadings of the border farmers, and field guns and artillery carriages were parked on many a

153

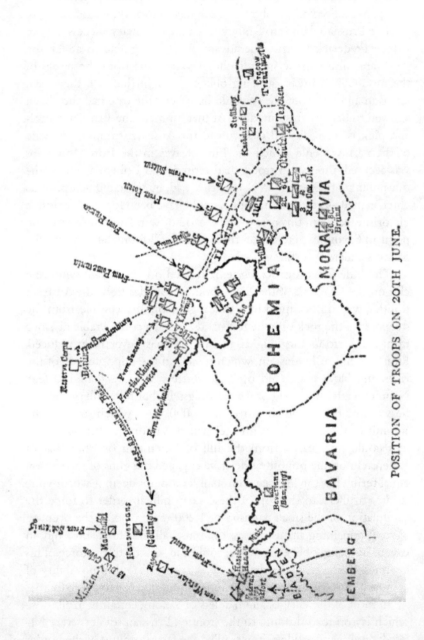

POSITION OF TROOPS ON 20TH JUNE.

village green. But the Saxons had no complaints to make, and, as far as could be judged from appearances, seemed highly to approve the occupation of their county by the Prussian army. The Saxon peasantry and the soldiers were on the most friendly terms, and a stranger who did not know the Prussian uniform, in passing through the villages, would have supposed that the troops were quartered among the people of their own country. As soon as the Prussian vanguards crossed the frontier, Prince Frederick Charles issued a most stringent order, in which he insisted upon the troops showing every respect for private property and for the comfort of the inhabitants. This order was strictly observed both by officers and men. The kind-hearted soldiers brought with them none of those horrors which too often follow in the train of an army which occupies a strange country.

On the contrary, had it not been for the swords and bayonets of patrols which glittered in the sun along every road, the scene was one of perfect peace. In some places the men were helping the peasantry to carry the hay harvest, in others they might be seen working in the cottage gardens, and nearly always were spending money in the village shops; the bare-legged country urchins got taken up for rides on the cavalry or artillery horses as they went to be watered, or were invited, half afraid, to peep into the muzzle of a rifled gun; only when, with the contempt bred by the familiarity, some too adventurous youngster tried to introduce a handful of cornflowers into the mouth of a piece of ordnance, was he warned off the precincts of the battery by the reluctant sentry.[1]

The Prussian military authorities took care to make the inconveniences of the existing state of affairs sit as lightly as possible on the inhabitants of the country in which the troops where quartered. Passenger traffic on the railways of Saxony was soon resumed, except where the broken bridge of Rieza caused a gap. Telegraphic messages were received at the bureaux, and were certainly and regularly delivered.

The successful occupation of the kingdom of Saxony gave the Prussian leader also great moral, material, and strategical advantages. His adversaries had seen the energy and vigour with which the Prussian blows were delivered. Two armies were established on hostile territory, which facilitated the supply of provisions to these large masses of troops. The theatre of war for the armies was also transferred to foreign soil. But the main advantages were gained in reference to the whole theatre of the war throughout Germany. The wide semicircle

---

1. It must be remembered that this was a war of Germans against Germans.

in which the Prussian Army had been spread along the Saxon and Bohemian frontiers, was much contracted by the advances of Prince Frederick Charles and Herwarth. The communication between the individual armies was much facilitated by the possession of the Saxon railways, and an invasion of Bohemia was rendered possible, because the frontier passes of the mountains were secured; while in the case of its being necessary to act on the defensive, the Erz-Gebirge and the Lusatian hills afforded much superior military positions to any along the quite open frontier between Saxony and Prussia.

The invasion of Saxony brought immediately conditions of open war between Prussia and Austria. Saxony appealed to the *diet* at Frankfort, from which Prussia and several other States had since 14th June withdrawn their representatives. The remaining members of the *diet* decreed, on the 16th June, that Austria and Bavaria should give aid against Prussia; not only to Saxony, but also to Hanover and Hesse-Cassel. Austria declared herself ready to devote all her military forces to the support of the States which had been invaded by Prussian troops. This declaration was regarded by Prussia as an open and official announcement of a declaration of war. That Austria also intended it to be such was shown by the publication, on the 17th June, of this war manifesto of the emperor:—

To My Peoples.

While engaged in a work of peace, which was undertaken for the purpose of laying the foundation for a Constitution which should augment the unity and power of the empire, and at the same time secure to my several countries and peoples free internal development, my duties as a sovereign have obliged me to place my whole army under arms.

On the frontiers of my empire, in the south and in the north, stand the armies of two enemies who have allied with the intention of breaking the power of Austria as a great European State.

To neither of those enemies have I given cause for war. I call on an Omniscient God to bear witness that I have always considered it my first, my most sacred duty, to do all in my power to secure for my peoples the blessings of peace.

One of the hostile powers requires no excuse. Having a longing to deprive me of parts of my empire, a favourable opportunity is for him a sufficient cause for going to war.

Allied with the Prussian troops, which are now up in arms against us, a part of my faithful and valorous army two years ago went to the shores of the North Sea. I entered into an alliance with Prussia for the purpose of upholding rights secured by treaties, to protect an imperilled German race, to confine within the narrowest possible limits an unavoidable war, and by means of an intimate connexion of the two central European Powers—whose principal duty it is to maintain the peace of Europe—to obtain a lasting guarantee for the peace of my empire, of Germany, and of Europe.

Conquests I have never sought for. Unselfish in my alliance with Prussia, I did not, in the Vienna Treaty of Peace, seek to obtain any advantage for myself. Austria is not to blame for the series of unfortunate complications which could not have arisen had Prussia been equally disinterested and equally mindful of her Federal duties. Those complications were brought about for the furtherance of selfish purposes, and, consequently, could not be done away with by my government in a peaceful way. The state of affairs became more and more serious.

Even when it was notorious that the two hostile States were making preparations for war, and that there was an understanding which could only be based on an intention to make in common an attack on my empire, I, being mindful of my duties as a sovereign, remained in a state of profound peace, as I was willing to make all those concessions which were compatible with the welfare and honour of my peoples. But when I saw that further delay would not only render it difficult to ward off the intended blow, but also imperil the safety of the monarchy, I was obliged to resolve on making those heavy sacrifices which are inseparable from preparations for war.

The assurances given by my government of my love of peace, and the repeated declarations which were made of my readiness to disarm at the same time with Prussia, were replied to by propositions which could not be accepted without sacrificing the honour and safety of the monarchy. Prussia not only insisted on complete disarmament in the northern provinces of the empire, but also in those parts of it which touch on Italy, where a hostile army was standing, for whose love of peace no guarantee could either be given or offered.

The negotiations with Prussia in respect to the Elbe duchies clearly proved that a settlement of the question in a way compatible with the disunity of Austria, and with the rights and interests of Germany and the duchies, could not be brought about, as Prussia was violent and intent on conquest. The negotiations were therefore broken off, the whole affair was referred to the Bund, and at the same time the legal representatives of Holstein were convoked.

The danger of war induced the three powers—France, England, and Russia—to invite my government to participate in General Conferences, the object of which was to be (*sein sollte*) the maintenance of peace. My government, in accordance with my views, and, if possible, to secure the blessing of peace for my peoples, did not refuse to share in the conferences, but made their acceptance dependent on the confirmation of the supposition that the public law of Europe and the existing treaties were to form the basis of the attempt at mediation, and that the powers represented would not seek to uphold special interests which could only be prejudicial to the balance of power in Europe and to the rights of Austria. The fact that the attempt to mediate failed because these natural suppositions were made is a proof that the conferences could not have led to the maintenance of peace.

The recent events clearly prove that Prussia substitutes open violence for right and justice.

The rights and the honour of Austria, the rights and the honour of the whole German nation, are no longer a barrier against the inordinate ambition of Prussia. Prussian troops have entered Holstein; the estates convoked by the Imperial *Stadtholder* have been violently dissolved; the government of Holstein, which the Treaty of Vienna gives to Austria and Prussia in common, has been claimed for Prussia alone; and the Austrian garrison has been obliged to give way to a force ten times as strong as itself.

When the German *Bund*, which saw in the measure no infraction of the Federal laws, accepted the Austrian proposition to 'mobilize' the Federal troops, Prussia, who prides herself on being the defender of the interests of Germany, resolved to complete the work she had begun. Violently severing the tie which unites the German races, Prussia announced her secession from the *Bund*, required from the German Governments the acceptance of a so-called project of Reform, which in reality is a division of Germany, and now she employs military force against those sovereigns who have faithfully discharged their Federal duties.

The most pernicious of wars, a war of Germans against Germans, has become inevitable, and I now summon before the tribunal of history, before the tribunal of an eternal and all-powerful God, those persons who have brought it about, and make them responsible for the misfortunes which may fall on individuals, families, districts, and countries.

I begin the war with confidence, arising from the knowledge that my cause is a just one, and with the consciousness of the power which is possessed by a great empire when the prince and the people have one and the same thought—that the rights of their country must be steadfastly upheld. My heart beats high at the sight of my gallant and well-appointed army—the bulwark against which the force of the enemies of Austria will be broken—and of my faithful peoples, who are full of loyal confidence and self devotion.

The pure fire of patriotic enthusiasm burns with equal strength and steadiness in all parts of my vast empire. Joyfully do the furlough men and reserves take their places in the ranks of the army; numerous volunteers present themselves; the whole of the able-bodied population of the countries which are most exposed are preparing to take the field, and everything that can possibly be done to assist the army and provide for its necessities is willingly done. All the inhabitants of my kingdoms and countries have one and the same feeling—the feeling that they belong to one and the same nation, that unity gives strength, and that a gross violation of justice has been committed.

It is doubly painful to me that the settlement of the questions relative to the internal constitution of the empire has not yet made so much progress that I, at this important moment, can assemble around my throne the representatives of all my peoples. Although I am now deprived of this support, my duty as a sovereign has become clearer, and my resolution stronger, that for all future time my empire shall have the benefit of it.

We shall not be alone in the struggle which is about to take place. The princes and peoples of Germany know that their liberty and independence are menaced by a power which listens but to the dictates of egotism, and is under the influence of an ungovernable craving after aggrandizement, and they also know that in Austria they have an upholder of the freedom, power, and integrity of the whole of the German Fatherland. We and our German brethren have taken up arms in defence of the most precious rights of nations. We have been forced so to do, and we neither can nor will disarm until the internal development of my empire and of the German States which are allied with it has been secured, and also their power and influence in Europe.

My hopes are not based on unity of purpose, on power alone, I confide in an almighty and just God, whom my house from its very foundations has faithfully served, a God who never forsakes those who righteously put their trust in Him. To Him I pray for assistance and success, and I call on my peoples to join me in that prayer.

Given in my residence and metropolis of Vienna, on this 17th of Tune, 1866.

Francis Joseph (M.P.).

On the same day the following general order was also issued to the Austrian Army of the North by Feldzeugmeister Benedek:—

Headquarters, Olmütz

Soldiers,—We are on the eve of grave and sanguinary events. As in 1859, you are collected in great numbers around our flag. Soldiers, we have now to repair in the eyes of the world the faults of that period; we have to punish an arrogant and faithless enemy. I have the full and entire conviction that you are aware of and are worthy of this mission. Have also confidence in me, and be assured that on my part I will exert my best efforts to bring this campaign to a speedy and glorious termination. We are now faced by inimical forces, composed partly of troops of the line and partly of *Landwehr*. The first comprises young men not accustomed to privations and fatigues, and who have never yet made an important campaign; the latter is composed of doubtful and dissatisfied elements, which, rather than fight against us, would prefer the downfall of their government.

In consequence of a long course of years of peace, the enemy does not possess a single general who has had an opportunity of learning his duties on the field of battle. Veterans of the Mincio and of Palestro, I hope that with tried leaders you will not allow the slightest advantage to such an adversary. On the day of battle the infantry will adopt its lightest campaign accoutrement, and will leave behind their knapsacks and camping material, in order that they may be able to throw themselves with rapidity and promptitude upon the heavily-laden enemy. Each soldier will receive his flask filled with wine and water, and a ration of bread and meat easily to be carried. The officers will discontinue the use of their wide scarves, and all the useless insignia of their ranks, which but renders them too distinguishable in action.

Every man, without distinction of name or position, shall be promoted whenever he shall distinguish himself on the field of battle. The bands will place themselves in rear of the front of the respective positions, and will play heroic pieces for the warlike dance. The enemy has for some time vaunted the excellence of their firearms, but, soldiers, I do not think that will be of much avail to them. We will give them no time, but we will attack them with the bayonet and with crossed muskets. When, with God's help, we shall have beaten and compelled to retreat our enemies, we will pursue them without intermission, and you shall then find repose upon the enemy's soil, and those compensations which a glorious and victorious army has a right to demand.

BOOK 5

CHAPTER 1

Theatre of German War

Whoever casts a glance upon the map of Central Europe must at once observe the range of mountains which, starting from the Black Forest, passes through Germany from west to east, separates the basin of the Danube from the plain through which the Weser, the Elbe, and the Oder glide to the German and Baltic seas, and terminates in the chain of the Carpathian Hills. This range about midway divides into two branches near the source of the Saale, which again join together near the east of the county of Glatz, and enclose in the so-formed quadrilateral the kingdom of Bohemia. On the north of these mountains lie the kingdoms of Saxony and Prussia; on the south the territories ruled by the Emperor of Austria. Bohemia, although a dependency of the Austrian empire, is geographically separated from the valley of the Danube, in which lie the majority of the provinces of the *Kaiser*, by the hills of the Bohemian Forest and the mountains of Moravia.

The advanced post of Austria towards the north, it stands as a strong bastion against an invasion of the empire from that direction, and is also a most valuable base of operations from which to hurl troops against the valleys of the Elbe or the Oder. It was this position of Bohemia which caused the destruction of Napoleon in 1813, when Prussia and Russia held the Elbe, and Austria from Bohemia menaced his right flank. If he quitted his central position at Dresden to march on the Elbe, the Austrians issued from Bohemia, and cut off his communication with the Rhine; if he advanced against Bohemia, as soon as he passed the northern mountains of that province the allies debouched from the line of the Elbe, and separated him from France. It was a consequence of the natural configuration of Bohemia that, after having prevented the junction of his enemies by the victory of

Dresden, the great Napoleon was surrounded at Leipsic.

In the midsummer of 1866, Bohemia was again about to play an important part in a European war. Austrian troops were collected there. Beyond the Erz-Gebirge, or Iron Mountains, and the Riesen-Gebirge, or Giant Hills, which form the Bohemian frontier on the north, lies in the first place the kingdom of Saxony, but beyond this again are the southern provinces of Prussia, from which two Prussian armies available for service in the field had now advanced. In the event of war, Saxony appeared likely to be the first battlefield, if the Austrian general should assume the offensive. But in a life-and-death struggle between the great German Powers it was impossible that the theatre of war could be restricted to one tiny kingdom; the area of operations on the contrary extended nearly throughout the district which spreads from the sea on the north to the Danube on the south, from the Rhine on the west to the Vistula on the east.

This is a district not unacquainted with war. After the last attempt to overthrow an established monarchy in England it was the scene of that Seven Years' strife through whose baptism of blood Prussia advanced into the hierarchy of the great powers of Europe. It was repeatedly trodden under foot by the conquering legions of the First Emperor of the French, and it was in its very centre that the battle was fought which led to the first overthrow of his power. Its wide extent is inhabited by two distinct races, and is the seat of two antagonistic creeds. The Teutonic race prevails in the north, and the generally established religion is Protestant; the Slavonic blood predominates in the south, owns the Catholic faith, and politically was under the sway of the *Kaiser*.

The basin of the Elbe is the central geographical division of Germany. This basin is divided into two; that of the Upper Elbe forms a plateau surrounded by mountains, and is the kingdom of Bohemia; that of the Lower contains Saxony and the central provinces of Prussia. The upper basin is in general ill cultivated, and little has been done to develop its resources. It possesses, however, forests, considerable iron mines, and breeds horses which are valuable in war. Its roads, except one or two main *chaussées*, are few, mountainous, and bad; but it is a country easily defensible, for its forests, mountains, and rivers present at every point obstacles to an invading army. The lower basin of this river is, on the other hand, a country of plains, marshes, and small lakes: not very fertile, but well cultivated, thickly populated, and opened up by a multitude of roads. The Elbe, entering it from a close defile between the mountains of Northern Bohemia, runs through its whole length, passing by the fortress of Königstein, Dresden, the capital of Saxony, and the fortified town of Wittenberg. This river, within Prussian territory, supported by the fortresses of Torgau and Magdeburg, forms a strong line of defence against an army advancing on Berlin from the west, but one which can easily be turned from Bohemia.

The basin of the Oder, bounded on the south by the mountains which overhang Braunau, Glatz, and Troppau, contains on the upper course of the river the province of Prussian Silesia. The river itself forms an angle near Breslau, which allows of its being used as a line of defence for the eastern districts of the kingdom of Prussia against an attack from either the south or west This line is supported by the fortresses of Glogau, Küstrin, and Stettin. The country through which the Oder flows is in general flat, marshy, and woody; the land is fertile only in pasture, but is well cultivated, and inhabited by an active and industrious population.

The basin of the Weser, in which lies the western portion of the kingdom of Hanover, is bounded on the south by the mountains of the Thuringian Forest and the Hartz, and is in general sandy and covered with thickets; its principal riches are flocks and herds. The Danube, the southernmost of the four rivers which were introduced into the theatre of war in Central Germany, runs through a plain which lies on the south side of the Bohemian and Moravian mountains.

Starting from the confluence of the Main with the Rhine at Mayence, following upwards the valley of the former river, skirting the southern slopes of the Thuringian Forest, passing along the summits of the Erz-Gebirge, the Riesen-Gebirge, and the mountains of Moravia, and terminating at the southernmost point of Upper Silesia, runs the line which geographically divides Northern from Southern Germany. This line now divided from one another the territories occupied by the troops of the two great parties into which the Germanic Confederation was rapidly splitting. By the sudden *razzia* made by her troops into Hanover, Hesse-Cassel, and Saxony, and by surrounding the Hanoverian troops, Prussia secured free communication between her Rhenish provinces and Berlin, disarmed the hostile forces in her rear, and divided the whole of Germany into two distinct areas for military operations.

These northern and southern areas, separated by the central geographical line of Germany, were now in the possession of the troops of the northern and southern antagonists respectively.

The Prussian occupation of Saxony had also the effect of separating the troops of the southern league quartered on the east of the line of the Saale from those assembled on the west, and divided Germany into an eastern and western theatre of war.

On the western theatre the Prussian troops which had invaded Hanover and Hesse-Cassel were ranged against the Hanoverians, the Bavarians, the troops of Cassel, and those of the eighth Federal corps.

On the eastern theatre the main armies of Prussia were drawn up against that of Austria with its Saxon allies, where they occupied, positions in Saxony and Silesia on the one side, on Bohemia and Moravia on the other. Between Bohemia and Saxony lie the chains of the Iron and Giant Mountains; between Moravia and Silesia, a part of the Giant chain, the mountains of Schweidnitz, and the Sudetic hills. These mountains as a rule are steep towards Prussia, and slope more gently towards Bohemia. They consist of several parallel ridges, and are of very unequal heights, sometimes falling as low as a thousand feet, sometimes, raising their peaks high into the air, they tower over spurs themselves fifteen hundred feet high.

On the west of Bohemia the Fichtel Mountains divide the passes which lead from North Germany into Bohemia from those which by the sources of the Saale lead in the neighbourhood of Hof and Eger into Bavaria. This feet added to the importance and to the value of the Prussian occupation of Saxony, for the presence of the troops of Prince Frederick Charles in that kingdom, if it did not entirely prevent, certainly threw great difficulties in the way of a junction between the Austrians and Bavarians, and placed the Prussians in about the advantageous position of having broken the line of the armies of the South German States.

The south-western frontier of Bohemia is formed by the hills of the Bohemian Forest; the south-eastern by the mountains of Moravia, The eastern theatre of operations lay between the mountains which separate Bohemia and Moravia from Saxony and Prussia and the Danube.

In this theatre two main lines of railway exist, and show the lines along which the troops on either side would draw together, in order to repel an offensive movement of the enemy. The northern line is that which runs from Oderberg, by Oppeln, Brieg, Breslau, and Görlitz to Dresden and Leipzic; the southern is that which leads from Prerau by Olmütz and Pardubitz to Prague. These lines at three points are joined to each other by lines from Dresden to Prague, from Löbau to Türnau, and from Oderberg to Prerau.

Within Bohemia lies the important quadrilateral of railways be-

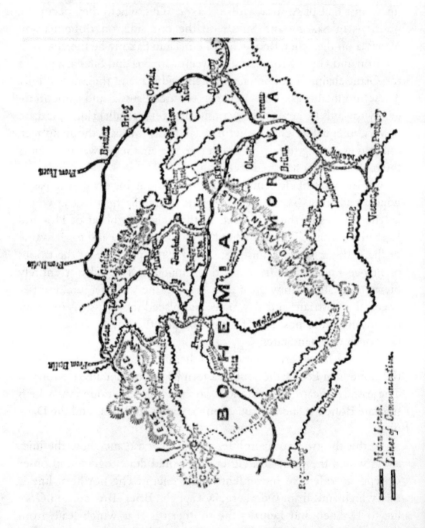

tween Prague, Türnau, Josephstadt, and Pardubitz, from which lines lead to Leipzic, Dresden, Berlin, Görlitz, Breslau, Cracow, Vienna, Pilsen, Nüremberg, and Regensburg, and which, in consequence, forms a highly advantageous position for the concentration of troops.

The fortresses enclosed in this theatre are, on the Austrian side, Cracow on the Vistula, Olmütz on the March, Josephstadt and König-grätz on the Upper Elbe, Prague on the Moldau, and Theresienstadt on the Eger. On the Prussian side are Kosel on the Oder, Neisse on the Neisse, Glatz, Schweidnitz,. and Torgau, on the Elbe. From Sch-weidnitz, which is of little importance as a fortress, to Torgau, the distance is about one hundred and fifty miles.

After the Prussian occupation of Saxony, the main armies of the two great Powers were separated by the mountains along which run the northern frontier lines of Bohemia and Moravia. The Prussian army consisted of three principal parts, which all received orders from the king as commander-in-chief of all the forces, and numbered, inclusive of the reserve corps of General Mülbe in Dresden, about 280,000 combatants, with 900 guns.

The Austrian Army, on the south of the mountains, mustered about 245,000 combatants, with 600 guns, to which was added the Saxon army, that had retired into Bohemia, with a force of 25,000 combat-ants, and 60 guns.

Plan of Operations.—The Austrian Army was not in such a forward state of preparation for taking the field as the Prussian. Feldzeugmeister Von Benedek had not apparently anticipated such extreme rapidity and energy of movement as was exhibited by the Prussians, and had before the outbreak of hostilities announced his intention of assuming the offensive, and of invading Prussian territory, when he had given most humane and praiseworthy directions to his own troops for their behaviour in the enemy's country. An Austrian invasion of Prussia may be effected by either of two routes: the first leads over the Lusatian mountains to Bautzen and Görlitz to Berlin; the second by the val-ley of the Oder into Silesia. An offensive movement by the first route would have given the Austrians the advantage of seizing Saxony, and of covering the passage of the Bavarians by the passes of the Saale to Wittenberg, where the whole of the invading army might have been united. The other route did not offer these advantages, and in it lay as obstacles the Prussian fortresses of Glatz, Neisse, and Kosel.

The rapid invasion of Saxony by Prussia, and the consequent retreat of the Saxons, appears to have determined the Austrian commander to relinquish any attempt of crossing the mountains into that kingdom. His army was concentrated round Brünn and Olmütz; he could not draw it together in time to seize the passes into Saxony; and he appears to have then determined to act upon the defensive, and to hold one portion of the Prussian troops in check, while he threw himself with strong force on the others issuing from the mountain passes, in order to crush them in detail.

To secure a favourable position for this operation, he concentrated his army towards Josephstadt. He sent one *corps d'armée* with the Saxon troops to cover the issues of the passes from Saxony, there to check the armies of Prince Frederick Charles. With his forces from Josephstadt he intended to hold the crown prince in issuing from the mountains, and to reinforce Clam Gallas to crush Prince Frederick Charles at Gitschin. On the 19th June the Austrian movements with this aim commenced: that day the headquarters of Feldzeugmeister Von Benedek were moved from Olmütz to Böhmisch Trüban, and on the 23rd June his army occupied the following positions:—

The 1st corps, the Saxons, the brigade Kalik, and the 1st light cavalry division, were posted under the supreme command of Count Clam Gallas, amounting altogether to nine brigades, with 60,000 men, on the left bank of the Iser, between Weisswasser, Münchengrätz, and Türnau, in order here to check the enemy advancing from the northwest. The 4th and 8th corps, and 1st division of reserve cavalry, were at Josephstadt; the 10th and 6th corps were pushed forward to the Silesian frontier on the north-east of Josephstadt; the 3rd corps and the 2nd and 3rd divisions of reserve cavalry were held in reserve north of Pardubitz; the 2nd corps and the 2nd light cavalry division formed the extreme right of the Austrian line at Böhmisch Trüban. By this

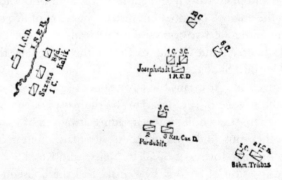

disposition of his troops, Feldzeugmeister Benedek held a force much superior to that of the crown prince, immediately opposite to the defiles leading to Silesia, and covered the ground on which all the roads from Saxony and lower Silesia unite together in Bohemia, so that he actually stood in front of the point where the armies of Prince Frederick Charles and of the crown prince must unite.

Prussian Plan of Operations.—How and why Prussia assumed the offensive in Saxony has been already seen. To increase the advantages gained by the possession of this kingdom, it was extremely desirable to push forward into Bohemia, and thus diminish, by a concentration forwards, the extent of the arc covered by the different armies. Political and financial reasons also required a speedy termination of the war. It was determined in the Prussian councils to assume the offensive.

An invasion of the Austrian dominions from the positions of the Prussian armies could be effected in two ways: by the first the armies could cross the north-eastern and north-western frontiers of Bohemia, and be directed to unite in the north of Bohemia. By the second plan the Elbe Army and the First Army could have been ordered to cross the frontier, and to move on Prague, while the Second made an offensive movement against Olmütz. The latter plan was considered too dangerous; by its prosecution the communications between the two armies would have been entirely broken; and if Benedek had ignored the Second Army he could have fallen with much superior forces on Prince Frederick Charles, and overthrown him, when the distance from Olmütz to Vienna would not have been less than that from Josephstadt to Berlin.

The first plan was accordingly adopted; and in order to carry it out, it was determined that the Army of the Elbe, acting as the extreme right wing of the Prussian advance, should move from Dresden by Neustadt, and over the mountains by the passes of Schluckenau or Gabel. The First Army, which formed the centre of the invading forces, was to move with the cavalry corps from Zittau, Görlitz, and Löbau, by the passes of Krottau Friedland and Neustadtl or Reichenberg. The Second Army, as the left wing, was to move from Landshut and the county of Glatz through the passes near Schatzlar or Trautenau, and through the pass of Nachod or Skalitz.

The First Army and the Army of the Elbe were to unite near the Iser, and to gain together the left bank of that river towards Gitschin. The Second was to gain the right bank of the Elbe. When these points were gained, the two armies would be in close communication, and could act in conjunction along the line of railway leading by Pardubitz and Brünn to Vienna.

The distance from Schluckenau to the county of Glatz, along which the Prussian front extended, is about one hundred miles. The Army of the Elbe and the First Army, which were to move through passes only about thirty or thirty-five miles distant from each other, could unite on the Iser in four marches, and immediately assail the enemy with four and a half *corps d'armée*, if the Austrians attempted to make an offensive movement towards Silesia, The circumstances of the country, and the strategical situation, threw more difficulties in the way of the Second Army during its defiling through the mountains, and there was considerable danger that it might be attacked while still isolated. On this account the Army of Silesia was made stronger by one *corps d'armée* than the First Army, and was to commence its movements four days later, so as to allow the Austrian attention to have been distracted by the presence of Prince Frederick Charles in Bohemia, and to permit of the complete junction of the First Army and of the Army of the Elbe on the Iser.

To hold the Austrian commander as long as possible in uncertainty as to the points at which the army of the crown prince was about to break into Bohemia, and, if possible, to make him remove his guards from the passes by which the descent was really to be effected, a false demonstration was made by the Second Army. This army had been concentrated round Landshut and Waldenburg, but on the 15th June, the crown prince, leaving only one *corps d'armée* in its original position, moved two of his remaining three corps thirty miles to the south-east, and there placed them in position near Neisse, sent at the same time the Guards to Brieg, and shifted his own headquarters to the fortress of Neisse, in order to make the Austrians believe that the Army of Silesia intended to await attack in a defensive position near the fortress, or to break out southwards from that point upon Olmütz.

The possession of Saxony and of the passes over the Iron Mountains, enabled the defence of that kingdom to be entrusted to the single reserve corps of General Mülbe. In case, however, that Austrian raids might be made into Saxony, or to oppose the Bavarians in case they might attempt by way of Hof into that country, fortifications were thrown up round Dresden.

On the left wing of the Prussian base of operations. Lower and Middle Silesia were covered from an Austrian attack by the nature of the Prussian offensive movement as well as by the fortresses of Glatz and Neisse. That portion of Silesia, however, above Oppeln, which penetrates into Austrian territory, was exposed to hostile attacks from Oderberg and from Galicia. In order not to weaken the armies of operations by detaching troops to protect this portion of the province, new and peculiar means were adopted. Two scouting parties were formed which were to support each other; and in case of formidable attack, to withdraw into the fortress of Kosel. One of these was under General Knoblesdorf, and consisted of three battalions of infantry, some battalions of *Landwehr*, a regiment of cavalry of the line, and one battery. Its headquarters were at Ratibor. The other consisted of *Landwehr* only, and mustered six battalions, two regiments of cavalry, two companies of *Jägers*, and one battery. It was commanded by Count Stölberg, and stationed at Nicolai. These parties were not only intended to watch the frontier and oppose an irruption by the Austrians, but were also to annoy the enemy beyond the frontier, and to break up his railway communications.

As a consequence of these arrangements, a lively war of detachments was soon developed along the Upper Silesian frontier, the details of which afford many interesting records of personal adventure, and the results of which demonstrated that the Prussian possesses in rapidity, subtlety, and endurance, all the qualities necessary for the accidents of petty warfare. Each detachment protected well its own position of the frontier, and only at a few points did the enemy succeed in effecting momentary sallies: they kept the Austrian troops in Western Galicia in check, and did considerable damage to their enemy. In one instance they destroyed the railway from Oswiecin to Oderberg so thoroughly, that the communication from Cracow to Bohemia as well as to Vienna was completely broken.

CHAPTER 2.

Passage of the First Army Through the Mountains

On the 23rd June the Army of the Elbe and the First Army were to cross the Bohemian frontier. When it is considered that not only the concentration and advance of the troops had to be arranged after the occupation of Saxony, but also the supply of provisions and ammunition, the establishment of hospitals, and the bringing up of reserves, it seems wonderful that these two armies could have been ready in so few days to take the field.

The southern boundary of Saxon Lusatia runs forward for a distance of about fifteen English miles within the general line of the Bohemian frontier of Austria. In the salient angle of Saxony formed by this peculiar tracing of the border line stands within Saxon territory the frontier town of Zittau. This town covers the issue of the passes which lead from Reichenberg and Friedland in Bohemia, through the mountains into Lusatia, and commands the railway which by the pass of Reichenberg runs from Türnau to Bautzen. About six miles to the northeast of Zittau and about seventeen south-west of Görlitz the village of Hirschfeld is situated on the Neisse, at a point where this river receives a small affluent called the Kipper. To this village the headquarters of the First Army were moved on the 22nd June.

Directly to the south were clearly seen the bold swelling masses of the Bohemian mountains, which here rise higher than in any part of the chain except where the Schneekoppe looms over the passes which lead into Silesia. The break in the mountain line which shows the defile through which passes the road to Reichenberg could be distinctly seen from here. Many eyes were often turned towards the gap in the clear relief of the hills against the sky, and many sought to know whether Prince Frederick Charles had come south to force that pass, or expected the Austrians to issue from it But those who had that day marched along the seventeen miles of dusty road from Görlitz could have little doubt with what object the First Army had advanced; the amount of transport which stretched in almost a continuous line for twelve miles of the way, told clearly that it was attached to an army destined for more than the mere defence of a frontier.

Prince Frederick Charles on the 22nd broke up his quarters at Görlitz, drew the First Army together, and launched it by the two roads which lead through Zittau and Seidenberg respectively, towards the Austrian frontier. The headquarter staff left Görlitz about three in the afternoon, and pushed along a road crowded with marching troops and military carriages to Hirschfeld. The road from Görlitz to that place was covered with an almost unbroken stream of infantry regiments, batteries of artillery, cavalry detachments, military carriages, and a long line of country waggons as supplementary transport, while the thick cloud of dust, which rose about a mile and a half to the left, showed that an equally strong column was pushing forward by the Seidenberg road. The heat was great, and the dust, rising in dense clouds from beneath the feet of the men and horses, or wheels of the carriages, hung heavily upon the marching columns; but the men stepped out cheerily, for they were anxious to advance, and they did not seem to suffer from fatigue. The regiments marched in with drums and fifes playing, ranks closed up, no stragglers, and the men keeping step so well that, but for the dust on their clothes and appointments, they might have been imagined to be going for instead of returning from a march.

The *chaussée* leading from Görlitz to Zittau is broad enough to allow four carriages to pass. The march was excellently arranged; there was no confusion, and no halts had to be made except those which were necessary to allow the men to rest The carriages of the military train were scrupulously kept to one side of the road, so as to leave the rest clear for die troops. Its own baggage marched in the rear of each battalion, but it was not much; only one waggon with the reserve ammunition, a cart for the officers' baggage, three or four packhorses to carry the paymaster's books, and the doctors' medicine carts. The soldiers marched strongly; their faces were lit up with excitement, for they knew that every pace brought them nearer to the enemy, and they longed for battle. The country people on the road or working by the wayside exchanged kind words with the men, and expressed many good wishes for their success, and did so with sincerity, for the Prussian soldiers who had been billeted in the Saxon hamlets had made themselves great favourites with the villagers.

Never was a march better conducted. The standing crops which fringed the road for almost its entire length were in no single place either trampled down or passed through. The road was crowded and dusty, but the men never left it, and, if there was a halt where corn grew by the wayside, no soldier went further from the line of march than to sit on the narrow fringe of grass which separates the *chaussée* from the cultivated ground, and in no case were the field, intruded upon. The staff officers, too, with a wise provision for the comfort of the troops, and with a careful regard for the farmers, had arranged that halts of long duration should be made by alternate regiments at places where the hay had been cut and carried home, and the short grass could, without itself suffering any harm, afford relief to the heated feet of the soldiers.

The road about a mile south of Görlitz descends a steep hill, formed by the spur of the Landeskrone, which runs down to the edge of the Neisse, and on which the town of Görlitz is built It then runs along the valley as far as Ostritz; on the right are wide unenclosed fields covered with rich crops, which terminate on the low line of hills that fringes the valley towards the west; on the left runs the slow stream of the Neisse, shrouded in willows; beyond the river a chain of gentle elevations separates its valley from that formed by the Rolte rivulet, up which runs the road from Görlitz by Seidenberg to Friedland. A mile south of Ostritz a chain of hills, standing directly across the road, forms a defile through which the river winds with a narrowed stream, the road bends to the right, and goes over a hill thickly covered with fir-trees, but soon descends again, and at Hirschfeld rejoins the course of the river. Two good military positions for an army retreating on Görlitz are afforded on this road—that behind Hirschfeld, where in front of the hill a rivulet crosses the way; and a second where, in front of Görlitz, the road dips down into the valley.

The Prussian troops were on the night of the 22nd in force in Zittau and Seidenberg, and the troops were placed along the road which connects those two towns. Headquarters were established in a very picturesque, but not over-clean, Saxon village. Prince Frederick Charles and his staff occupied the village inn; the square in front, half market-place, half green, was crowded with the carriages of the military train. Soldiers were billeted in every cottage, and chargers stood

174

in every stable. The little hamlet was a continual scene of busy turmoil; horses were being attended to, arms were being cleaned, and the men were making ready for tomorrow's march; while now and then a distant trumpet on the left told that the evening watches were being set by the troops that lay towards the frontier.

The resources of this little village were sorely taxed by the sudden inroad of hungry men; the common room of the inn was filled with a multitude of soldiers hungry with a long day's march. Each man bought a large piece of bread and a junk of meat, and retiring to a side table, or bench, cut it up with his pocket-knife, and made a hearty meal. The regimental officers fared no better than their men. The campaign had already begun, and a great deal of the outward distinctions of ranks had been, as is always the case, shaken off, but the real discipline was unimpaired.

The health of the army was excellent; the sick only averaged 2½ *per cent*, which would be a remarkably small number even in a period of profound peace. The sanitary arrangements were so good that there seemed to be every chance of this small proportion of illness being maintained.

The surgeons, hospital attendants, and sick-bearers wore on their left arm a white band with a red cross, as a mark of their profession and their neutrality.

No declaration of war against Austria was made by Prussia; but on the morning of the 23rd, at daybreak, Prince Frederick Charles sent one of his *aides-de-camp*, Major von Rauch, to announce to the commander of the nearest Austrian post that he in the course of the day intended to pass the Bohemian frontier. Von Rauch, as is usual in such cases, accompanied by a trumpeter, whom he caused constantly to sound, and himself waving a white handkerchief, fell in with one of the Austrian patrols, which was furnished by Radetzky's hussars. The patrol fired on the staff officer, fortunately without effect; he boldly rode up to it, and on explaining the object of his visit, was conducted blindfold to the commandant of the advanced post, which was Reichenberg; this officer, of course, apologized for the mistake which his patrol had made, and the *aide-de-camp*, after a long and early ride, was escorted back to within a short distance of the Saxon frontier, where he soon met the advancing columns of his own army.

Prince Frederick Charles, late on the night of the 22nd, issued the following General Order to the First Army:—

Headquarters, Görlitz, June 22.

Soldiers!—Austria, faithless and regardless of treaties, has for some time, without declaring war, not respected the Prussian frontier in Upper Silesia. I therefore, likewise, without a declaration of war, might have passed the frontier of Bohemia. I have not done so. I have caused a public declaration to be sent, and now we enter the territory of the enemy in order to defend our own country.

Let our undertaking rest with God. Let us leave our affairs in the hands of Him who rules the hearts of men, who decides the fate of nations, and the issue of battles. As it stands written in Holy Writ—'Let your hearts beat to God, and your hands on the enemy.'

In this war are concerned—you know it—the maintenance of Prussia's most sacred rights, and the very existence of our dear native land. Her enemies have declared their intention to dismember and to destroy her. Shall the streams of blood which your fathers and mine poured out under Frederick the Great, in the War of Independence, and which we ourselves latterly shed at Düppel and Alsen, have been spilt in vain? Never! We will maintain Prussia as she is, and by victories make her stronger and mightier. We would be worthy of our fathers.

We rely on the God of our fathers, who will be mighty in us, and will bless the arms of Prussia.

So, forward with our old battle cry, 'With God for King and Fatherland! Long live the King!'

Frederick Charles, General of Cavalry.'

On the morning of the 23rd the Prussian armies crossed the frontier of the Austrian territories. General Herwarth von Bittenfeld, with the Army of the Elbe, marched by the high road from Schluckenau to Rumburg. Prince Frederick Charles, with the 4th *corps d'armée*, followed by the 2nd corps, and the cavalry corps, advanced along the road and railway leading from Zittau to Reichenberg, while the 3rd corps moved from Seidenberg and Marklissa over the passes of Schönwald and Neustadtl on Friedland.

The troops were early under arms, and fell into their ranks a little after daybreak, under a steady downfall of drizzling rain. They had to march many miles from their billets to the places where they were to form columns for the advance, but they stepped out well over the slippery grass and sloppy roads, and were all ranged in proper order close to the Austrian frontier, but still on Saxon ground, a little after 7. At 6 the commander-in-chief left his last night's quarters at Hirschfeld, and by the Zittau road reached the frontier a little before 8. The frontier is marked on the road by a tollhouse, in front of which a long bar supplies the place of a gate. This bar balances near its end furthest from the tollhouse on a pivot, and, by means of a weight at the end of its shorter arm, can be raised almost perpendicularly upwards when the road is to be left open for a free passage.

On this bar are painted the alternate black and gold stripes which are the distinctive colours of Austria. The bar was raised that day, but not quite in a vertical position; high enough to allow a man on horseback to ride under it, it still sloped over the road. It was here that Prince Frederick Charles took up his position to watch his troops march over the border. He had hardly arrived there before he gave the necessary orders, and in a few moments the Uhlans, who formed the advanced guard of the regiments that marched by this line, were over the frontier. Then followed the infantry.

As the leading ranks of each battalion arrived at the first point on the road from which they caught sight of the Austrian colours that showed the frontier, they raised a cheer, which was quickly caught up by those in the rear, and was repeated again and again till, when the men came up to the tollhouse and saw their soldier prince standing on the border line, it swelled into a roar of rapturous delight, which only ceased to be replaced by a martial song that was caught up by each battalion as it poured into Bohemia. Their chief himself stood by the roadside calm and collected; but he gazed proudly on the passing sections, and well he might, for never did an army cross an enemy's frontier better equipped, better cared for, or with a higher courage than that which marched out of Saxony that day. Ever and *anon* he would call from a passing battalion some officer or soldier who had before served under him, and with a kindly inquiry or cheerful word, won a heart, for soldiers love officers who take an interest in diem.

Everywhere the prince was greeted by the troops with loud cries of joy; as he rode along the way by which the regiments were marching they cheered him continuously. At one point his reception was peculiarly remarkable. A Pomeranian regiment (the 2nd), which had served under him when he was a divisional general, had piled its arms for a halt, and the men were lying down by the side of the road to rest Suddenly the word was passed among them that the prince was coming; with one accord they sprang as if by magic to their feet, made two long lines along the road through which he might pass, and gave him such a cheer as only old soldiers can.

The concentration of the troops and the advance into Bohemia were most excellently managed. This same army had exactly a week before entered Saxony, prepared to fight in that country; within that time Saxony had been entirely occupied, and within six days the majority of the troops were again concentrated, and began their march into Austria. The advance was conducted in this way:—The troops the previous night were concentrated on the frontier; on the morning of the 23rd, on the right, Herwarth von Bittenfeld pushed forward two columns from Dresden by Schluckenau and Rumburg; Prince Frederick Charles advanced from Saxony; his troops marched in five columns; the column on the right followed the high road from Zittau; the right centre column marched along the railway lying to the left of that road; the centre column followed a road to the left of the railway. The left centre column marched by the Seidenberg road, and the left column by the Marklissa road east of this highway.

Thus on a broad front, and by several roads all within a distance which would allow the different corps to concentrate in a very few hours, the army moved to the front well in hand and without inconvenience to the troops. The march within Austrian territory was distinguished by the same regard for private property that was so scrupulously observed in Saxony. The Austrian villagers at first looked on the irruption of the army of the northern Germans half in fear, half in curiosity, but soon they came to be on speaking terms with the soldiers, and then were quickly seen supplying them with drinking water and doing them other good services.

The castle of Grafenstein, in which the headquarters were fixed on the night of the 23rd, is the property of Count Clam Gallas, who commanded the first Austrian corps in Bohemia; it is beautifully situated on the top of a hill, covered with thick foliage, which rises abruptly from the low ground of the valley of the Neisse. The count had not left much furniture for the use of his unexpected guests, as nearly all the moveables were sent away some time before to Vienna, but a stock of mattresses were found in the house which the servants good-naturedly lent to the temporary occupants, and a prince of Prussia and his staff were accommodated in the rooms of an officer who was waiting to fight a battle with their army beyond the mountains.

Two of Radetzky's hussars were taken prisoners; they were out with a patrol and came into collision with a patrol of the Prussian regiment of Magdeburg hussars; in the skirmish the horses of these two Austrians were shot, and the men were taken. They were the first prisoners of the war. The rapid concentration of the Prussian army produced some feats in marching, which were quite extraordinary for troops who had only just taken the field. The 5th Pomeranian Hussars marched three days successively for long distances, and on the 22nd made fifty English miles; they were again on the line of march on the 24th, with horses in excellent condition, and the men looking as if they had only just turned out of barracks.

The Prussians were now on the northern slopes of the mountains, and one day's march would, without opposition, take them through the passes. The highest hills were now so close that with a glass the stems of the fir-trees which clothed them could be easily distinguished. The road to Reichenberg lay straight and open before them. The march of the 23rd was different from that of the preceding day; it was a march which showed that the enemy might be found in front The heavy baggage and reserve commissariat transport was all a day's march in rear; the only carriages which were present in the column of route were the guns and waggons of the artillery, the hospital carnages, and the few waggons which are necessary to regiments when actually about to fight.

The advanced posts, on the evening of the 23rd, were pushed forwards about seven miles; there were vigilant patrols and pickets out, and all was provided for against a surprise. These precautions are of course always necessary with an army in the field; in the present case their utility was not put to the test, for the Austrians were not in force in the neighbourhood.

Count Clam Gallas, to whom the Austrian commander had entrusted the guidance of the Austrian and Saxon troops on the Iser, had only pushed patrols of light cavalry up to and beyond Reichenberg. Several skirmishes took place between them and the Prussian hussars, dragoons, and lancers, who formed the advanced scouts in front of each column, in which the Austrian cavalry was generally outnumbered and obliged to retire.

It rained steadily all the night of the 23rd, and the morning brought no improvement in the weather, but the troops were in high spirits, and appeared to care nothing for the wet. On the 24th the army of Prince Frederick Charles marched by three roads: the left column by way of Eisniedel on Reichenberg; the centre by Kratzkau on the same town; while General von Bittenfeld came from the mountains, and moved upon Gabel. Some of the regiments halted at Reichenberg, and were billeted in the town for the night; others were pushed through and took up positions in front Many battalions had to bivouac that evening; but, although the ground was moist and damp from incessant rain, the weather was warm, and the troops did not take much harm from their first night in the open. The army was now drawn together and concentrated round Reichenberg; for General von Bittenfeld at Gabel was only twelve miles to the right

On the night of the 24th, the Prussian advanced posts near Kratz-kau could see the light of the Austrian bivouac fires, and the next morning the Magdeburg hussars who cleared the way for the army had a skirmish with some of Radetzky's Austrian hussars. Shots were exchanged, two of the Prussians were wounded and five of the Austrians were wounded, with two killed. A combat was expected at Reichenberg. Three Austrian cavalry regiments, Lichtenstein's hussars, Radetzky's hussars, and the hussars of the regiment of Hesse-Cassel, were known to be in front of the Prussian advance, and it was anticipated that in the fine strategical position of Reichenberg the Austrians might stand to fight; for this town covers the junction of roads which leads over the mountains by Gabel, Grottau, Friedland, and from Hirschberg. But the Austrian cavalry retired through the town, and it was occupied about ten o'clock by the Prussian advanced guard; and Prince Frederick Charles, without a blow, gained the south side of the mountains, and commanded the issues of the passes.

The march of the 24th, although over a hill country, was not over a severe road, for the summit of the mountain chain dips so deeply into the gorge which forms the defile of Reichenberg, that the road through the pass both ascends and descends with a moderate gradient; on either side of the way the mountains rise high, but not steep, for the whole character of this range is more rounded and swelling than bold and sharp. As the army passed between the hills in the early morning, the tops were shrouded in a dense mist, which occasionally lifted high enough to show the lower parts of the dense fir woods which clothe the upper mountain sides, but never to afford a glimpse of their summits.

The rain fell heavily and without ceasing; it battered down the grain which grew in the fields by the wayside, and filled the mountain watercourses with rushing mud-coloured streams; there was no wind to give it a slanting direction, and it came straight down on the men's helmets, only to roll off in large drops upon their backs and shoulders, but it did not seem to depress the spirits of the troops; they stepped along cheerily, marching as well as they did the first day they left their garrisons, and many of the soldiers said that they preferred the wet weather to heat. All along the line of march the commander of the army was loudly cheered.

When Prince Frederick Charles reached the market-place of Reichenberg, he halted to await the arrival of the troops who had marched by the Friedland road. The town looked dull, for as it was Sunday the shops were all shut, and at first the Bohemians seemed inclined to remain in their houses; but the bands of the marching regiments roused their curiosity, and they soon collected and lined the street in dense crowds to see the troops go by. The soldiers who had arrived early and had been dismissed from their ranks joined in the crowd, and a common language soon made them great friends with the townspeople. Many tales are told of the dreadful devastation to which a country is subjected by the plunderers of an invading army.

So far as the Prussian Army had yet advanced into Bohemia the soldiers had treated the Austrians with the greatest kindness; as in the British service, everything that a soldier wished to buy must be scrupulously paid for, and there seemed to be no desire among the men that it should be otherwise; in fact, the troops were much more plundered than plunderers, for the cigar merchants and public-house keepers were driving a most prosperous trade, and took very good care that they themselves did not suffer, for the soldiers were unaccustomed to Austrian currency, and had to pay an equivalent of Prussian coin.

Reichenberg was, on the morning of the 24th, occupied by the Prussians about ten o'clock. Before evening nearly the whole army, attended by artillery and waggons, marched through the narrow winding streets of a town which to these artificial disadvantages for free locomotion adds the natural one of being built upon a steep hill; still there was no confusion in the marching columns, and, although the troops had to move by different streets and were sometimes obliged to march in and out of the town by country lanes and narrow paths, no column took a false direction or made an unnecessary halt; yet the Quartermaster-General von Stülpnagel had only a few minutes allowed him in which he could arrange his plans.

The column which had marched by the Friedland route was brought through the market-place and past the commander-in-chief. This corps was composed of men of the province of Brandenburg;

they were taller than the average of the Prussian infantry, but were not so thick and stout, and did not look so strong as the sturdy Pomeranians; but they had intelligent faces, and could readily be seen to be, as they were, men of an education superior to that which is usually found in the ranks. The regiment of the late king led; the men bore his cipher on their shoulder cords, instead of a number. The whole corps marched magnificently.

After a wet day and a long journey they came up the hill of Reichenberg with ranks closed up, with as perfect a step as on a holiday parade, and went swinging along as if they could not know fatigue; yet they were heavily encumbered, for every man carried his knapsack, the weight of which tells severely against a soldier's marching, and might, in a country where transport is plentiful, be carried for him. After the late king's regiment came the 64th, Prince Frederick Charles's own: the faces of the soldiers showed that they recognised their colonel, and they went past him without cheering, for in the town the men marched as on parade, but with that appearance which is more pleasing to a soldier than any acclamations.

The headquarters were established in the *schloss* or castle of Reichenberg, another of the properties of Count Clam Gallas, who thus twice became the involuntary host of Prince Frederick Charles. Here a curious scene was afforded: the castle stands on a hill, overlooks the picturesque town, and commands a beautiful view of the plains and mountains beyond it The side of this hill below the castle was covered with carefully-tended turf, and luxuriant shrubberies. The place seemed only fit to be the quiet home of a country gentleman, but up and down its gravelled avenue chargers were being led ready saddled for the *aides-de-camp*, who were waiting to carry out the evening orders; military train horses were being led to water, soldiers, in stable dress, were hurrying about, mounted dragoons were in attendance as orderlies, and near the door of the castle stood the horse of the officer of Uhlans, who had brought in the last report from the outposts.

On the afternoon of the 24th, the Thuringian regiment of Uhlans, who are much the same as lancers, took up outpost duty, and one squadron of them had a skirmish with some of Radetzky's hussars. The hussars were led by a staff officer, who came too near the Prussian infantry picket, and the deadly needle-gun shot the first officer who fell a victim to this war. The hussars and Uhlans mutually charged each other, and in the *mêlée* which ensued, two Prussian officers and seventeen men were wounded. The Austrian loss was not ascertained.

The possession of Reichenberg allowed Prince Frederick Charles to open railway communication with the Silesian and Saxon lines, which was of great importance in the supply of the army's necessities. The railway from Reichenberg to Zittau was almost immediately restored, for to each Prussian army was attached a corps of pioneers, architects, and railway officials, who followed the advancing army, laid down the lines torn up by the enemy, and rapidly reorganised the working of the line for the purposes of military transport

Two other excellent institutions of the Prussian Army were quickly established, and put in working order at every halting-place; they were the Field Telegraph and the Field Post-office. As soon as it was determined where headquarters were to be fixed for the night, the field telegraph division started off to the nearest permanent telegraph station where the line could be fixed in working order; from this starting point they carried a single line along the side of the shortest road to the head quarter house, and generally by the time the chief of the staff arrived at his quarters he found his telegraph ready, by which he could get information or send his orders. The field post-office was established also at headquarters, but had branch offices at the headquarters of each *corps d'armée*; it carried the private letters of soldiers and officers, as well as official despatches, and sent out a mail nearly daily.

This was a greater convenience than the field telegraph, but the latter was one of the neatest appliances of modern science to the art of war which it is possible to conceive. The whole of its apparatus was carried in some light waggons; one contained the batteries and needles, and was used as a small room in which the telegraphist worked; the other waggons carried the poles and wires, with the implements for putting them up. The wires were coiled round revolving discs, which were fitted in the waggon, so that the wire could be passed as the waggon went along, or the disc could be transferred to a stretcher earned between two men, so that it might be laid off the road in places where it was desirable to cut off corners. The detachment who laid the lines were all instructed in repairing damage done to the permanent wires. When it is remembered that on the morning of the 23rd the Austrians were close up to the frontier, and that at midday the castle of Grafenstein, five miles from the nearest permanent station, was in direct telegraphic communication with Berlin, some idea can be formed of the advantages which this apparatus gives to an army in the field

The headquarters of the First Army halted at Reichenberg on the

25th, to allow the cavalry that came by the Friedland road which had covered the march of the column to come in. During the day the outposts were pushed forward, but the Austrians were not felt

Count Clam Gallas had drawn his army together on the south of the line of Iser, round Münchengrätz. The Poschacher brigade, supported by the light cavalry, was posted as his advanced guard on the northern side of the river, and was pushed forward along the road to Reichenberg. This was the same Austrian brigade which had in Schleswig, in 1864, on account of the sturdy manner in which it stormed and occupied the Königsberg, gained the name of the "iron brigade." It was now destined to commence the contest against its former allies in the

Combat of Liebenau

The Austrian brigade occupied the hills south of the village of Liebenau, about half way between Reichenberg and Türnau, and had pushed detachments into the village itself.

The road from Reichenberg to Türnau crosses a range of hills which separates the valley of the Upper Neisse from the country beyond, and drops down from this range by some sharp zigzags to the valley in which lies the village of Liebenau.

This village is built on the banks of a stream which forms a defile through a second range of hills lying between Liebenau and Türnau. This rivulet, in the part of its course above the village of Liebenau, runs at right angles to the defile, and forms a valley between the two hills which lie north of Liebenau towards Reichenberg, and those which lie to the south towards Türnau. The railway from Liebenau to Türnau passes through the defile formed by the stream which runs through the village; but the road turns to the left and ascends the southern range, passing near the top between a steep cutting through rocks. This cutting is about 100 yards in length, and here the road is only about 30 feet wide.

The hills are on their side covered with thick plantations of fir trees; but when the traveller leaving Liebenau has by the road gained the summit of the range which lies south of the village, he finds before him a wild plateau extending for about two miles in the direction of Türnau. This plateau was this morning covered with high-standing crops of wheat and barley, already whitening for the harvest The road runs through the cornfields, and at the end of the plateau drops down by a gentle slope into the valley of the Iser. From the brow of this

184

slope Türnau can be seen lying on the river towards the left front The *Schloss* of Sichrow, standing on the very edge of the Liebenau defile, is directly on the right, and the view to the front is bounded by the fir-clad and fantastically rocky hills which form the southern boundary of the valley of the Iser, while on the left the church of Gentschowitz stands raised on a knoll above the general plain, and looking down upon the orchards and cottages of the little hamlet which clusters round its foot

Between the bottom of the slope which falls from this flat plain into the valley and the Iser, and about half way between the foot of the hill and the river itself, there runs a low range of hills, having an elevation considerably inferior to that of the plateau. On this lower range, immediately surrounded by orchards, but in the midst of a wide-stretching corn land, lies the village of Kositz.

On the evening of the 25th the Prussian advanced posts were pushed forward to the tops of the range of hills which bound the valley of Liebenau on the north. The next morning General von Horne, who with the 8th division held the outposts, had advanced early to occupy Liebenau. As his advanced guard entered the village, the Austrian rear-guard were discovered tearing up the pavement, in order to form a barricade across the narrow street through which the high road runs. On the approach of the advanced guard they retired to the hill over which the road to Türnau passes south of the village. Here the Austrians took up position; their artillery, placed on the brow of the hill, looked down upon the village of Liebenau, which Horne had just occupied, and their cavalry covered the guns.

But they were not in force. They had little infantry, and their main strength appeared to be only four regiments of cavalry, with two batteries of horse artillery. Horne's division passed through the village, and began to ascend the hill, while General von Hann came down to Liebenau with the Prussian cavalry, and the field artillery took up a position on the hills which bound the Liebenau valley on the north. Thus the guns of the Austrians were on the southern, those of the Prussians on the northern range, which form the valley of Liebenau; the valley between them is about 600 yards wide, and there seemed to be an opportunity for a smart combat. Down in Liebanau, between the opposed batteries, were the wings of Horne's divisions, and columns were already issuing from the village, making their way along both the railway and the *chaussée*, while the skirmishers were getting among the short spruce firs that clothe the hill beside the road.

A little before nine o'clock Prince Frederick Charles and his staff came upon the hill where the artillery was placed. It was almost exactly the same hour when a flash of fire, with a heavy puff of white smoke on the Austrian hill, showed that their artillery had opened, and a rifle shell came whistling over the heads of Horne's division. The Prussian artillery answered, and for a few minutes the hills echoed with the noise of their rapid discharges; while the smoke, drifting but slowly on the lazy breeze, hid from sight the opposite guns, though the quick reports and the whistling of the shells told that they were not idle. But the Prussian guns were too numerous. Horne's division was pushing up the hill, and the Austrian artillery had to retire. Then the Prussian cavalry pushed forward by the road, and in a short time, eight fine cavalry regiments were formed on the northern edge of the plateau. The Thuringian Uhlans, the Uhlans of the Prince of Hohenlohe, and the dragoons of the Prince of Mecklenburg were extended to the left, while the Brandenburg hussars of Ziethen, conspicuous by their red uniform, were nearer the road. On the right of the cavalry was the horse artillery, and Prince Frederick Charles, himself a cavalry officer, was in the front

The retreat of the Austrians could be traced by the broad paths trampled down in the corn, and every now and then they halted, their artillery came into action, and two or three rounds were fired at the forming lines. When Prince Frederick Charles had completed his dispositions he ordered the advance, and the troops pressed forward. The cavalry and artillery moved on the plateau, while Horne's infantry, on the right, made for the *Schloss* of Sichrow and the woods around it The cavalry pushed on quickly, and the guns moved well with it, but every now and then halted and came into action. The Austrians, inferior in numbers and already retiring, could not hope to stand against the force thus displayed, and they drew quickly over the plateau, making for the hills of Kositz. Three regiments of cavalry were launched after them, and went dashing through the corn, but did not reach the retiring troops before the latter had quitted the plateau, and then the woods and broken ground on the side of the slopes impeded their progress.

As soon as the Austrians gained the Kositz hills their artillery opened, and poured shells briskly into the advancing lines, but the gliding motion of the advancing troops and the undulating ground deceived their aim, for only about twenty casualties occurred When the Prussian guns gained the southern brow of the plateau, they opened on the Austrian batteries; a smart cannonade ensued, but the Austrians were ultimately silenced Yet they did well, for they made good their retreat; but had not the Prussian horse been detained by having to pass through the narrow street of Liebenau, the field artillery which that day fired into the Prussian ranks would probably have gone as a trophy to Berlin.

It is evident that the Austrian commander had not calculated on the rapid advance of General von Horne. His dispositions for the defence of the Liebenau position were incomplete; the street of Liebenau was not rendered impracticable, for the workmen were disturbed by the Prussian advance guard, and in the cutting which the road leading from the village passes through at the top of the hill leading on to the plateau, although the trees which stood by the wayside had been cut down, they were not formed into *abattis*, nor was the cutting blocked by waggons or any barricade. The Austrians retreated across the Iser, and broke the bridge of Türnau, but the Prussians after the combat occupied that town with Horne's division, while the main body of the army bivouacked on the plateau, and one division occupied Gablenz, which lies five miles to the north-east

On the same day the 14th division, which belonged to the Army of the Elbe, occupied Böhmisch Aicha, and assured free communication between Prince Frederick Charies and General Herwarth von Bittenfeld.

The plateau that looks down on Liebenau was sadly changed in the course of the day. The corn was trampled down by the feet of horses and the wheels of artillery; dead horses lay dotted here and there over the plain, while large holes in the ground showed where shells had struck and burst But these marks were not frequent, for the Austrian shells often penetrated into the earth without bursting, and several were dag out by the soldiers in the afternoon. Nor was the practice of their artillery good. The Ziethen hussars, whose red uniforms drew their fire, were at one time exposed to a heavy cannonade; but though above fifty shells struck the ground around them, not one fell among their ranks, not at that time had they a man touched.

The result of the combat of Liebenau was not over-valued in the Prussian Army; the officers on that side did not despise their enemy, and they fully recognised the fact that it was to superior numbers that the Austrians yielded. They had great confidence in their chief and in the needle-gun and their rifled cannon, but they had no vain assurance. They knew that the Austrian Army was a good one, and they determined to omit nothing that their skill or science could suggest to let their troops meet it on the best of terms.

The Austrians retired to Podoll in order to hold that important point, where not only the road to Münchengrätz but also the railway between Türnau, Kralup, and Prague crosses the Iser.

General Horne, after the action of Liebenau, pushed forward to the Iser and occupied Türnau, the junction of the railway from Reichenberg with that to Prague. After a bridge of pontoons had been thrown across the river here in order to replace the one broken by the Austrians, he determined to occupy the bridges of Podoll five miles below Türnau. The movement by which he effected this brought on the

ACTION OF PODOLL

The railway and high road which lead down the valley of the Iser from Türnau to Münchengrätz run for a distance of about five miles from the former town on the north side of the river, but on reaching the village of Podoll cross to the south bank by two bridges, which are about 200 yards distant from each other, that of the railway being on the right, and that by which the road crosses on the left of a person, looking towards Münchengrätz. The railway bridge is constructed of iron; that which carries the road across the stream is made of wood, and lies on a level with the causeway, which is raised on an embankment about ten feet above the fiat meadows lying alongside it The Iser is at Podoll near upon 100 yards wide, and runs with a deep but fast stream between steep banks, which only rise about four feet above the level of the water.

By the side of the road and on the banks of the stream grow large willow-trees, planted at equal distances from each other, and at about ten yards apart. Three roads lead from the plateau of Sichrow to the high road that runs down the valley of the Iser. That on the east, a country road, which leaves the plateau near the *Schloss* of Sichrow and joins the highway near the village of Swierzin, almost at an equal distance between Türnau and Podoll; in the centre the *chaussée* from Liebenau strikes into the high road halfway between Swierzin and Türnau, and the road from Gentschowitz on the west joins it close to this town.

On the afternoon of the 26th, Prince Frederick Charles threw a light pontoon bridge over the river a little below the broken bridge of Türnau, and occupied the town with a small force without opposition. Part of Horne's division marched at the same time by the country road on the east, occupied the village of Swierzin, and pushed its advanced guard towards Podoll. The troops directed on this point consisted of two companies of the 4th *Jäger* battalion, the 2nd and fusilier battalions of the 31st regiment, and the 1st battalion of the 71st. The *Jägers*, who were leading, got to within three-quarters of a mile of Podoll-bridge before they came into collision with Austrian outposts, but here they found the enemy, and a sharp action ensued, for the Austrians had six battalions in the village, and meant to hold the place and cover the passage of the river.

It was about 8 o'clock, and the dusk of the evening was rapidly closing in, when the *Jägers* first felt their enemy. On the right-hand side of the road, about half a mile before the bridge, stands the first house of the village. It is a large square farmhouse, with windows without glass, but with heavy gratings. The Austrians had occupied it in force, and their outlying pickets, as they retired before the advancing Prussians, formed line across the road beside it. As soon as the *Jägers* came within sight the garrison of the farmhouse and the formed-up pickets opened a bitter fire upon them. From the grated windows and from the line of soldiers in the road there came one rapid volley, which told severely on the Prussian riflemen, but these went quickly to work, and had fired about three times before the Austrians, armed only with muzzle-loading rifles, were able to reply.

Then the noise of musketry rose high, occasionally swelling into a heavy roar, but sometimes falling off so that the ear could distinguish the separate reports. But this did not last Major von Hagen, commanding the 2nd battalion of the 31st, which was following the *Jägers* on the first sound of the firing, had put his troops into double quick time, and was soon up to reinforce the riflemen. It was now nearly dark, and the flashes of the rifles, the reports of the shots, and the shouts of the combatants were almost the only indications of the positions of the troops; yet it could be seen that the rapid fire of the needle-gun was telling on the Austrian line in the road, and the advancing cheers of the Prussians showing that they were gaining ground.

Then while the exchange of shots was still proceeding rapidly between the window-gratings of the farmhouse and the Prussian firing parties, who had extended into a cornfield on the right of the highway, there was a sudden pause in the firing on the road, for the *Jägers*, supported by the 31st, had made a dash, and were bearing the Austrians back beyond the farmhouse to where the cottages of the village closed on each side of the road, and where the defenders had hastily thrown some hewn down willow-trees as a barricade across the way.

Then the tumult of the fight increased. Darkness had completely closed in, and the moon had not yet risen; the Prussians pressed up to the barricade, the Austrians stoutly stood their ground behind it, and, three paces distant, assailants and defenders poured their fire into each other's breasts. Little could be seen, though the flashes of the discharges cast a fitful light over the surging masses; but in the pauses of the firing the voices of the officers were heard encouraging their men, and half-stifled shrieks or gurgling cries told that the bullets were truly aimed. This was too severe to endure. The Prussians, firing much more quickly, and in the narrow street, where neither side could show their whole strength, not feeling the inferiority of numbers, succeeded in tearing away the barricade, and slowly pressed their adversaries back along the village street.

Yet the Austrians fought bravely, and their plans for the defence of the houses had been skilfully though hastily made; from every window muskets flashed out fire, and sent bullets into the thick ranks of the advancing Prussians, while on each balcony behind a wooden barricade *Jägers* crouched to take their deadly aim; but in the street the soldiers, huddled together and encumbered with clumsy ramrods, were unable to load with ease, and could return no adequate fire to that of the Prussians, while these, from the advantage of a better arm, poured their quick volleys into an almost defenceless crowd.

As the battle in the street was pushed inch by inch towards the Iser, the Austrians, in every house which the foremost ranks of the Prussians passed, were cut off from their retreat, and were sooner or later made prisoners, for the houses of the village do not join on to each other, but are detached by spaces of a few yards, and there is no communication from one house to the other except by the open street The whole of the Prussian force was now up, and extending between the houses which the first combatants had passed by, cut off the escape of their garrisons, and exchanged shots with the defenders.

With shrieks and shouts, amid the crashing of broken windows, the heavy sounds of falling beams, and the perpetual rattle of the firearms, the battle was heavily pressed down the narrow street, and about half-past eleven the moon came up clear and full to show the Austrian rearmost ranks turning viciously to bar the Prussians from the bridge. The moonlight, reflected in the stream, told the assailants that they were near the object of their labour, and showed the Austrians that now or never the enemy must be hurled back. Both sides threw out skirmishers along the river bank, and the moon gave them light to direct their aim across the stream; while on the first plank of the bridge the Austrians turned to bay, and the Prussians pausing some short paces from them, the combatants gazed at each other for a few moments. Then they began a fiercer fight than ever. The discharges were more frequent, and in the narrower way the bullets told with more severe effect.

Herr von Drygalski, leading the fusilier battalion of the 31st, a lieutenant-colonel of only two days' standing, went down with two bullets in his forehead, and a captain at his side was shot in both legs; many men fell, and the grey horse of a Prussian field-officer, with a ball in his heart, fell heavily against the wall, kicking amid the ranks; but he was soon quieted forever, and at that moment men regarded but little such wounds as could be inflicted by an iron-shod hoof, even in the agonies of death. The Austrians stood gallantly, and made an attempt to set fire to the bridge; but the difference of their armament again told upon them here; and it is said that, galled by their hard fortune, they charged with the bayonet, but that the Prussians also took kindly to the steel, and this charge caused no change in the fortune of the fight: certain it is that the defenders were ultimately obliged to retire across the bridge.

While this combat was proceeding slowly along the street, another fight was carried on upon the railway almost with an equal progress, and with an almost similar result. A party of the Austrians fell back from the point where shots were first exchanged, and where the railway crosses the road, along the line. They were pushed by some Prussian detachments, but neither side was here in strong force, and the principal fighting was done upon the road; but here, too, the needle-gun showed its advantage over the old-fashioned weapons of the Austrians, for the latter fell in the proportion of six to one Prussian. The railway bridge was not broken, but the lines were torn up by the retiring troops, and the line was not passable by trains.

The Prussians pushed over both bridges after the retreating Austrians; the latter threw a strong detachment into a large unfinished house, which stood by the *chausée* about a quarter of a mile beyond the bridge, and again made a stand, but not of long duration; they had lost many killed, wounded, and prisoners; many of their officers were dead or taken; but they stood till they could gather in all the stragglers who had escaped from the houses of the village, and, harassed by the pursuing Prussians, drew off sullenly by the main road to München-grätz. Thus terminated a contest which, fought upon both sides with the greatest vigour and determination, yet resulted in a clear victory for the Prussians; for, when the last dropping shots ceased, about four o'clock in the morning, there were no Austrian solders within three miles of Podoll-bridge except the wounded and the taken.

There was no artillery engaged on either side; it was purely an infantry action, and the Prussians derived in it great advantage from the superiority of their arms over that of their opponents, not only in the rapidity, but in the direction of their fire, for a man with an arm on the nipple of which he has to place a cap, naturally raises the muzzle in the air, and in the hurry and excitement of action often forgets to lower it, and only sends his bullet over the heads of the opposite ranks, while the tidier armed with a breech-loading musket keeps his muzzle down, and if in haste he fires it off without raising the butt to his shoulder, his shot still takes effect, though often low, and a proof of this is that very many of the Austrian prisoners were wounded in the legs.

The road to Podoll was next morning crowded with hospital wag-gons and ambulance cars bringing in the wounded; every cottage in the way was converted into a temporary hospital, and the little village of Swierzin was entirely filled with stricken men. The sick-bearers, one of the most useful corps which any army possesses, were at work from the very beginning Of the action. As the combatants passed on these noble-minded men, regardless of the bullets and careless of per-sonal danger, removed with equal hand both friend and enemy who were left writhing on the road, and carried them carefully to the rear, where the medical officers made no distinction in their care for both Austrian and Prussian.

Not only was it those whose special duty is the care of the wound-ed who alone were doing their best to ease the sufferings of those who had suffered in the combat; soldiers not on duty might be seen carrying water for prisoners of both sides alike, and gladly affording any comfort which it was in their power to give to those who over-night had been firing against their own hearts! Nor is this wonderful; for after the flush of the battle was over, and the din of the musketry had died away, the men of the Prussian Army could not forget that one common language linked them to their adversaries, and that, after all, it was probably German blood which, flowing from an Austrian breast, trickled over the white livery of the House of Hapsburg.

In the village the utmost disorder gave evidence of the severity of the contest Austrian knapsacks, *shakos*, clothes, and arms were scattered about in wild confusion. Dead horses lay in the ditches by the roadside. White coats and cloaks, which had been thrown off in the hurry of the fight, lay scattered along the road; the trees which had formed the Austrian barricade were still on the side of the street, and many held a bullet. The cottages had been ransacked of their furniture, and their beams and roof-trees had been torn down to form defences for the doors and windows; while along the street and upon the banks of the river lay objects which in the distance look like bundles of untidy uniform, but which on nearer approach were seen to be the bodies of slain soldiers. Sometimes they lay in groups of twos or threes, twisted together as if they had gripped one another in their mortal agony, and sometimes single figures lay on their backs, staring with livid countenance and half-closed hazy eyes, straight up against the hot morning sun. The dark-blue uniform with red facings of Prussia, and the white with light-blue of Austria, laid side by side, but the numbers of the latter much preponderated, and on one part of the railway three Prussian corpses opposite nineteen Austrian formed a grisly trophy of the superiority of the needle-gun.

Close on 500 unwounded Austrian prisoners were next morning marched up to headquarters, and the Austrian loss in killed and wounded was very considerable. The Prussians lost two officers dead, and seven or eight wounded. The medical officers officially reported that the proportion of wounded Austrians to wounded Prussians was as five to one. Thus the needle-gun told both on the battlefield and in the hospital.

On the 27th the headquarters of the First Army halted at the castle of Sichrow. There had been no skirmishing; but white smoke curling up from beyond some fir woods beside the Iser told that the bridge of Mohelnitz, about five miles below Podoll, which the Austrians had set on fire to obstruct pursuit, was burning steadily.

The results of the actions of Liebenau and Podoll were, that two of the important passages of the Iser, those of Türnau and Podoll, fell into the hands of the First Prussian Army. That of Münchengrätz still was in the hands of the Austrians, but was soon also to be seized from their grasp. The Army of the Elbe had advanced on the 23rd by Schluckenau, and on the 26th the fourteenth division, under the command of General Mündter, had been pushed to Bömisch Aicha in order to feel Prince Frederick Charles's right

Count Clam Gallas had only opposed a few hussar regiments to the advance of General Herwarth von Bittenfeld, so that this general met with no serious opposition in issuing from the mountains. On the 27th, the day after the night action of Podoll, his eighth corps, which was advancing from Gabel by Niemes, in the direction of München-grätz, first fell in with any serious hostile force. The Prussian advanced guard, consisting of two squadrons and two battalions of Schöler's brigade, which, followed by the whole 8th corps, was on the march from Hayda, pushed forward on a reconnaissance as far as Hühnerwasser.

The Austrians, bound only to furnish intelligence, and ordered not to engage seriously, retreated, after a slight skirmish to Münchengrätz, and evacuated the right bank of the Iser, thus permitting a full communication to be opened between the Army of the Elbe and that of Prince Frederick Charles. The two armies were able on the following day to advance in concert, so as to take possession of the whole line of the Iser.

Count Clam Gallas, after the skirmish at Hühnerwasser, withdrew the greater part of his force to the left bank of the Iser, occupied Münchengrätz in force, and made preparations for the destruction of the bridge over the river on the west of the town. The Prussian plan to seize that place brought on the

ACTION OF MÜNCHENGRÄTZ

On the 27th Prince Frederick Charles halted in the position of Sichrow, and made his dispositions for his further advance. The seventh division had occupied Türnau, where the engineers had quickly thrown a pontoon bridge over the Iser, to replace the permanent one, which had been burnt by the retiring Austrian cavalry. The eighth division, under General Horne, occupied the village and bridge of Podoll; the sixth division, under General Manstein, moved forward to the support of Horne. The main body of the army was on the plateau of Sichrow, and General Herwarth von Bittenfeld, after a sharp skirmish, in which he took many prisoners, seized Hühnerwasser.

The road and railway which lead from Türnau to Jung Bunzlau cross the Iser near together at the village of Podoll, and run beside each other on the southern side of the river to a point about three miles below Münchengrätz; about a quarter of a mile below Podoll the hills which form the plateau of Sichrow, turning southwards, come close to the northern bank of the Iser, and form a chain of heights which descend with a steep slope to the water's edge. The hills which form the southern boundary of the valley of the Iser rise to a height of about 500 feet in the Muskey Berg, which, running parallel to the road for a mile of its length from its extremity nearest Podoll, then trends southwards and strikes the road from Münchengrätz to Unter Bautzen at the village of Bossin. The Muskey Berg presents towards the river on its upper part a rocky, precipitous front; below this the *débris* fallen from the rocks has accumulated and formed a slope, which, although steep, would, were it not for the precipice above, be still practicable for light infantry.

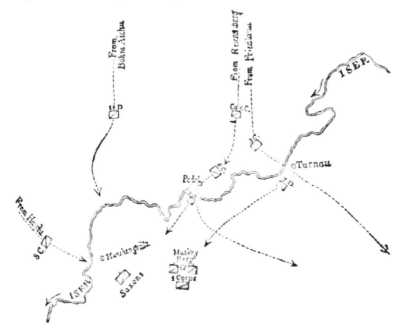

Gitschin

This lower slope is covered with a dense forest of fir trees; the summit of the hill is in general a flat plateau, clothed with greensward, but near the edge of the precipice fir trees are thickly planted, and form a belt along the summit, with an average breadth of loo paces, while, conspicuous near the place where the hill line turns towards Bossin, stands a high solitary cone rising 100 feet above the plateau, bare of trees, but covered with green grass. Opposite this high cone of the Muskey Berg, and close to the river, but still on the southern bank, lies the isolated hill of the Kaczowberg. It is considerably lower than the Muskey Berg range, and is not wooded. Its length is about 500 yards, and its longitudinal direction is at right angles to that of the stream. The distance between the summits of the Muskey Berg and the Kaczowberg is about two miles, and through the valley between these two hills run the road and railway from Podoll to Münchengrätz. Between these hills the valley is a dead flat plain.

It was at the time of the action richly cultivated, intersected by rows of fruit trees, and covered with wheat, barley, clover, and potato patches. No hedges divided the different farms, but brooks and ditches made the ground very difficult for the action of cavalry. Looking from the bridge of Podoll along the valley towards Münchengrätz, the Muskey Berg lies to the left front, the Kaczowberg to the right front; between them are seen in the distance the *schloss* and spires of the town, but further view is stopped by a low range of elevations, topped by dwarf plantations, which lie between the roads from Münchengrätz to Fürstenbrück, and from Münchengrätz to Jung Bunzlau, and runs from the village of Bossin to that of Wessely.

The Austrians had thrown up a redoubt and a battery for eight guns on the Kaczowberg; the latter would have enfiladed the Podoll road, but no guns were in it, for the Prussian advance had been rapid, and there was not time to arm the work. Still, it was expected that the enemy would stand here, and the Prussian commander advanced prepared to fight He intended to strike for no meagre victory. He formed a plan by which to capture the whole opposing force; but, though skilfully designed and punctually executed, his adversary did not stand quite long enough to allow of its complete development, for the Austrian commander sacrificed his position and the town of Münchengrätz, after a sharp combat, but without a regular battle.

The Prussian leader calculated that if he made a demonstration of a careless march towards Münchengrätz by the high road and railway, the Austrians who might be on the Muskey Berg would lie there quiet till the heads of his columns had passed their position, in order that their artillery might take the marching troops in reverse, and that he might himself in the meantime turn their position. By the same bait he also hoped to hold his adversaries on the Kaczowberg until their retreat was cut off. To effect this double object the 7th division was to move from Türnau by a road on the south side of the Iser, which at the village of Wschen crosses the road from Podoll to Sobotka, at Zdiar. It was then to take the Austrians on the Muskey Berg in rear, for this hill slopes gently on its reverse side towards a rivulet which forms the little lake of Zdiar. The division was afterwards to push on over the hill and strike the road from Münchengrätz to Fürstenbrück, between the village of Bossin and the former place.

On the right bank of the river General Herwarth was to advance from Hühnerwasser on Münchengrätz, cross the Iser, and occupy the town, throwing out at the same time the fourteenth division to his left, which by Mohelnitz and Laukewitz should take in reverse the defenders of the Kaczowberg. The divisions of Horne and Manstein were to push down the main road from Podoll, while strong reserves closed down to Podoll. A division of infantry was to cross at Hubelow and attack the Kaczowberg in front, while a division of cavalry kept the communications open between the divisions on the right bank of the river. A strong division of cavalry was also sent from Türnau to scour the country towards Jicin, in the direction of Josephstadt

About eight o'clock on the morning of the 28th, Prince Frederick Charles, with General von Voigt-Rhetz, his chief of the staff, and General Stülpnagel, his quartermaster-general, came down to the bridge of Podoll, and almost immediately the *Jägers*, who formed the advance guard of Horne's division, crossed the bridge, but not before an opening cannonade in the direction of Münchengrätz told that Bittenfeld was already engaged. On a hill upon the northern bank there was a convenient spot from which to see the whole theatre of the combat, and here the Prussian staff went to watch the course of the action.

There was not a cloud upon the sky, and the sun poured down a tremendous heat; thick clouds of dust rose from the columns on the road, but this line was only followed by the artillery, the train, and the main body of the regiment. As the *Jägers* passed the bridge they threw out skirmishers to the right and left, who went in a long wavy line pushing through the standing corn. The cavalry scouts clustered thickly on the flanks of the skirmishers, and horsemen in more solid formation followed in their rear. It was a fine sight; the long line of rifles extending almost across the valley, felt carefully through the crops. The Uhlans, with their tall lances and fantastic pennants, hovered about the flank, and the heavy masses on the road pushed on steadily behind the centre of the light troops.

But attention was called towards Münchengrätz, where the progress of Bittenfeld's attack could be traced by the puffs of white smoke which rose from the discharges of the artillery. The Prussian cannonade was seen to be slowly advancing, and that of the Austrian to be retiring, while a heavy cloud of black smoke rising close beside the town showed that the Austrians had retired from the right bank of the river and had burnt the bridge. For a short time the fight was stationary, but in about a quarter of an hour a bright flash of flame and a much heavier smoke rising from the Austrian line told that an ammunition waggon had exploded. Their battery then ceased firing, and rapidly retired, while a quick advance of the Prussian cannonade showed that Bittenfeld's pioneers had quickly thrown . their bridge, and that his corps was across the Iser. But the Austrians did not go far, for in a short time they were again in action in the direction of the Jung Bunzlau road, and one battery was drawing off towards Fürstenbrück.

It then seemed that Bittenfeld had halted; the cannonade ceased in this direction. The view of the Muskey Berg from the position occupied by the staff is extremely beautiful, but it was not the sandstone cliff's of the opposite mountain, nor even the advancing Prussians in the plain, that General Voigt-Rhetz, the chief of Prince Frederick Charles's staff, was so carefully scanning with his glass,—he saw a group on the highest point of the cone of the Muskey Berg which looked like a general's staff, and he smiled quietly as he saw his adversaries getting entangled in the toils which had been so carefully woven for them. The heads of the Prussian columns were some way past the hill, and were pushing steadily towards Münchengrätz, when the well-known puff of smoke rising from the dark firs on the Muskey Berg plateau showed that the Austrians had opened fire upon them. The battery on the hill did not appear to be of more than four guns, and at first they fired slowly, nor did they do much execution.

Their shells, projected from so great a height, went straight into the ground, and did not ricochet among the troops; but they were well aimed, and in most cases burst at the proper moment, and every now and then a man went down. As soon as the Austrian guns opened fire the troops in the road were turned into the fields, and moved on in open order; the train waggons were also hurried on to the softer ground, and halted separately where best concealed. Four Prussian batteries quickly opened fire, but the Austrian guns stood high, and the height of the hill deceived their aim; at first their shells fell short, but soon they got the range; still the fir-trees and rocks protected the Austrian gunners, and the batteries in the plain seemed to do little execution.

Orders were soon sent to them to cease firing, for the enemy's guns did not much harass the marching troops, and other means were taken for clearing the hill A squadron of Uhlans was directed to pass close along the foot of the Muskey Berg, so that the guns on the plateau could not be depressed sufficiently to hurt them, and were to gain a steep path which leads to the summit between the highest point and Bossin, while an infantry brigade was to support the movement; but before this plan could be carried into execution the seventh division was heard engaged on the reverse side, and the Austrian battery quickly limbered up and retired. The guns were not intercepted by the seventh division, but here General Franzecky made 600 prisoners from the infantry which was on the hill to support the battery.

While the seventh division was still engaged behind the Muskey Berg, four Austrian guns appeared on the summit of the hill, between Bossin and Wessely, and opened fire against the Prussian columns, who were now again advancing over the plain. But Franzecky was pushing towards them, and his artillery threatened to enfilade them, so that they soon had to retire. The seventh division then struck the road between Münchengrätz and Bossin, and attacked the latter village. Bittenfeld had already pushed towards it from Münchengrätz, and supported this attack. The first round of Franzecky's artillery set fire to a house, which began to burn fiercely, and the flames were soon communicated to the next, for most of the cottages in this country are built of wood, which, dried in the hot summer sun, readily takes fire.

After a sharp skirmish the Austrians were driven from the village and retired in the direction of Fürstenbrück, and they left here 200 prisoners, and General Herwarth von Bittenfeld had already captured 200. The Austrian soldiers who had been taken chiefly belonged to Italian regiments, and showed no disposition to fight; twenty-five of them in one mass laid down their arms to Lieutenant von Bülow, who, being one of Prince Frederick Charles's *aides-de-camp*, was returning from delivering an order, and saw these men separated from their regiment. He collected about half-a-dozen train soldiers and rode up to them, when they surrendered without offering any resistance.

The Austrians made no attempt to hold the Kaczowberg. The only points they attempted to defend were the Muskey Berg, Münchengrätz, and the village of Bossin. They lost at least a thousand prisoners, and about three hundred killed and wounded.

With the occupation of the village of Bossin ended the combat of Münchengrätz, in which by a series of strategical movements, with little fighting, and slight loss—for the Prussian killed, wounded, and missing did not number 100—Prince Frederick Charles gained about twelve miles of country, and took 1,000 prisoners, turned the strong position of the Kaczowberg, and effected his secure junction with the corps of General Bittenfeld.

The headquarters of the Army of the Elbe and of the First Army were established at Münchengrätz. The majority of the inhabitants had fled from the town; the army had outmarched its provision trains, and there was nothing to be bought in the place. On account of actual necessity the soldiers were allowed to take what eatables they could find in the place, but little had been left, for the Austrian Army was there the night before, and their commissariat appears to have been as miserably corrupt as it was in the Italian campaign. The prisoners reported that they had had nothing to eat for two days, and begged for a morsel of bread; but the Prussian Army was hard set itself for provisions, and there was but little to give away. Nor were the Austrian hospital arrangements such as they ought to have been. Twenty-six wounded men were found here when the Prussians marched in, lying in a cottage on a floor covered with blood, untended, with their wounds undressed, and saying that they had had no nourishment for forty-eight hours; no surgeon had remained with them, nor was their condition reported to the Prussian commander; fortunately they were discovered accidentally by a Prussian staff officer.

Hospital necessaries were scarce, but Prussian medical men were sent to attend them, and application was made to the magistracy of Münchengrätz to supply linen with which to dress their wounds. These are reported to have refused to assist in alleviating the sufferings of their fellow-countrymen, who were shot down in defending the very passage to their own town, till Count Stöhlberg, a Prussian officer of *cuirassiers*, roused by their barbarity, drew his sword on the *burgomaster*, and threatened him with death unless the wants of the wounded men were attended to, when the necessary materials came forth. The Prussian troops were very weary. They had marched and fought that day (the 28th) over a long distance and in a heavy country. There was little water away from the river, and the soldiers had suffered much from thirst; but they marched nobly.

Few stragglers were ever seen, except those who had fallen fainting out of the ranks, and were lying half stupefied by the roadside; but none lay long without succour, for the *krankenträger*, or sick-bearers, hovered with their water-bottles round the flanks and in the rear of the marching as well as of the fighting battalions, and gave a willing aid to all that needed it

The army of Prince Frederick Charles was now concentrated

round Münchengrätz; two divisions were near or in Bossin: a large force covered the left at Zehrow and south of Türnau, and threw its outposts towards Sobotka. The force in front of Prince Frederick Charles was the Austrian first *corps d'armée*, the brigade Kalik, which had lately returned from Holstein, and the cavalry division of General Edelsheim. To these the Saxon Army was joined, and the whole allied force was under the command of Prince Albert, Crown Prince of Saxony.

By the actions of Liebenau, Hühnerwasser, Podoll, and Münchengrätz, the whole line of the Iser was won by the Prussians, and a great strategical advantage gained, the distance from the Second Army which had on the 27th commenced its advance from Silesia, was still, however, great; for from thirty to thirty-five miles lay between the left wing of Prince Frederick Charles and the extreme right wing of the crown prince: difficulties still existed which had to be overcome before the junction of the two armies could be effected. Count Clam Gallas, on being driven from the line of the Iser, retired to Gitschin, and there took up a defensive position. Before tracing the means which Prince Frederick Charles adopted to dislodge him from this point, it is desirable to cast a glance over the preceding actions.

The actions of Liebenau and Hühnerwasser were fought by the Austrians merely as reconnaissances, and may be passed over in silence. But why did Count Clam Gallas neglect to defend Türnau at all, and hold Podoll with only a single brigade? It was undoubtedly his object to hold the line of the Iser and to there check his enemy for as long a time as possible. Münchengrätz is, at the most, but twelve miles distant from Türnau; he had 60,000 men at his disposal, and could therefore have well held the whole line had he thrown up the necessary intrenchments. It seems, however, that the Austrian general committed the great error of despising his enemy. Had he ranged part of his army on the plateau south of Türnau and Podoll, broken the bridges at these places, and thrown up earthworks to impede the passage of the river, and at the same time collected the other part or his force at Münchengrätz, and there made similar defensive preparations, the line of the Iser might, indeed, still have been forced by the Prussians, but only by the employment of their whole strength; and, probably, only after the lapse of a considerable amount of time.

Had it been forced, the Austrian retreat from both points to Sobotka would have been secure. Had it not, the Prussians would have been compelled to seek for a passage further to the north at Eisenbrod or Semil, and to have made a flank march in a country which in that direction is broken into ravines and hollows by the spurs of the Giant Mountains. It might be urged against such dispositions that by breaking the bridges Count Clam Gallas would have deprived himself of all chance of assuming the offensive in case of a favourable opportunity. His duty and object, however, was not to crush but to detain Prince Frederick Charles: the defeat of the Prussian First Army was to have been effected by the arrival of Feldzeugmeister Benedek himself with overwhelming forces, before or after having disposed of the crown prince.

The Austrian position on the Muskey Berg was tactically strong, but strategically weak. By the surrender of Türnau, Count Clam Gallas exposed the right flank of that position, and allowed his retreat to Gitschin to be threatened.

CHAPTER 3

Action of Gitschin

The fourth Prussian corps, consisting of the seventh and eighth divisions, had been sharply engaged at Podoll and Münchengrätz, and was allowed to halt at the latter place on the 29th June. That evening it marched as the reserve of the First Army, which moved from the Iser towards Gitschin by three roads—the left from Türnau by Rowensko, the centre from Podoll by Sobotka, the right from Münchengrätz by Ober Bautzen on Sobotka, while the Army of the Elbe moved on the right wing of the First Army by Unter Bautzen and Libau.

On the evening of the 28th, the fifth division was pushed forward from Türnau as far as Rowensko, on the road to Gitschin, where it halted for the night, with the sixth division a short distance in rear of it The same evening the third division, with the fourth in rear, was pushed to Zehrow, on the road from Podoll to Sobotka; and its advanced guard, consisting of the 14th regiment and two companies of the second *Jäger* battalion, in the course of the night occupied the defile of Podkost, after a sharp skirmish.

On the afternoon of the 29th, the fifth division broke up from Rowensko at two o'clock, and advanced towards Gitschin. The third division, which had a longer march before it, left Zehrow for the same place at mid-day.

The distance from Türnau to Gitschin is about fifteen miles; from Münchengrätz to the same town about twenty miles; and Podoll to Podkost about six miles.

Four roads lead from the town of Gitschin, almost towards the four points of the compass; that of the north to Türnau, of the west to Sobotka, of the south to Kosteltz, and of the east, but bending south-wards, to Höritz. From the Kosteltz road to the Türnau road runs, about three miles' distance from Gitschin, a semicircular range of steep broken hills; on their slopes and summits spruce and silver firs grow in thick woods which occasionally reach down into the cultivated ground. Here and there upon these hills are patches of corn or clover land, while at various intervals there are little villages, which generally consist of ten or twelve large wooden cottages separated from each other, and standing in orchards. Near the foot of the range of hills the ground is much broken up by shallow ravines and gullies.

The Austrian first corps and the Saxons held an excellent position along this range of hills, the right flank of which rested on Eisenstadt, and the left on the Anna Berg, a prominent elevation on the south side of the Sobotka road. In the centre were the heights of Brada, which had been strengthened. The reserve was drawn up between these hills and the town of Gitschin.

Where the road from Sobotka passes through the hills they dip down so as to form a narrow pass, and the fir forests on each side run down close to the road. On the Sobotka side of the woods there is a ravine about 100 feet deep, but with banks not so steep but that the road can descend and ascend them in a direct line. A quarter of a mile from this ravine, and nearer Gitschin, the road drops again into a similar hollow, but here the forest has retired from the side of the *chaussée*, and the ground is covered with standing crops, among which fruit trees are thickly studded. At about the same distance further on towards the town, a third break in the ground causes another sharp undulation of the roadway.

On the Gitschin side of this hollow ground, partly on the bank, but more on the brow of the slope, and on the more level country beyond, stands the little village of Lochow, forming a clump of houses with low walls, but having high thatched roofs, which just rise above the tops of the orchard trees that cluster closely among and around the cottages. A quarter of a mile beyond the village lies the last break in the ground, for beyond this a flat plain stretches to the little river which, passing the town of Gitschin on its Lochow side, falls into the Iser near Türnau. This last ravine is rather deeper and wider than the others; at the bottom there is a rivulet, which the road, after descending the Lochow bank, crosses by a low stone bridge, and then runs straight up the opposite side of the *nullah*, as it might be termed in Indian phrase, to gain the level plain.

The 2nd corps of General von Schmitt, which marched from the neighbourhood of Podoll, struck at Sobotka the road from München-grätz to Gitschin. General von Schmitt there changed the direction of his march to the left, and advanced towards Gitschin. He moved with his two divisions at some distance apart; that of General von Werder, or the 3rd division, led the way. Von Werder's advanced guard consisted of the 2nd battalion of *Jägers* and the 3rd battalion of the 42nd regiment. In the rear of these followed the three battalions of the regiment of the late King of Prussia (the 2nd), the two remaining battalions of the 42nd, and one battalion of the 14th regiment, with one six-pounder and two four-pounder field batteries.

A strong Austrian force held the wood behind the first ravine, with its sharpshooters behind the trunks of the fir-trees, with the view of compensating for the inferiority of their rifle to the Prussian needle-gun. Behind each marksman two soldiers were placed, whose only duty was to load their rifles and hand them to the picked men to whom the firing was entrusted. The Austrian artillery was placed behind the wood, so that it could bring a cross-fire on the opening in front through which the *chaussée* passes, and strike heavily on the Sobotka bank of the ravine and the open country beyond. As the Prussian advanced guard approached the ravine, the Austrian batteries opened fire upon them, and the marksmen from behind the trees also soon commenced a biting fire. The *Jägers* and the men of the 42nd quickly spread out as skirmishers, and, regardless of the withering fire to which they themselves were exposed, showered bullets from their quickly-loaded arms against the defenders of the wood, while some of their artillery, quickly brought into action, tried to silence the Austrian guns.

But the fight was unequal, the sharpshooters behind the trees could rarely be seen, and the fire of the Prussians did not tell much upon their concealed enemies; nor were their guns in sufficient force to en-gage successfully the more numerous Austrian pieces. The *Jägers* from among the trees were aiming well; the men of the 42nd were falling fast, and it seemed that the defenders would be able to hold the wood. But the rest of the Prussian division was coming up; more artillery was already in action; and the Austrian gunners began to fire with less effect The regiment of the King of Prussia soon arrived. The Prus-sian soldiers, unable to make much impression with their fire on the riflemen in the trees, were already anxious to come to close quarters, and then General von Werder sent his men forward to take the woods with the bayonet They were carried, but not without loss, for the Austrians retired from tree to tree, and only when pressed beyond the last skirt of the wood retired under cover of their guns and reserves to take up a position on the further brow of the next ravine.

The musketry fire recommenced. The opponents stood on either bank of the hollow, and poured volley after volley into each other's ranks, while the artillery, from positions on the flanks of both lines, sent their shells truly among their adversary's infantry. But here the needle-gun had more success, for the Austrians stood up clear against the sky, and soon the white uniforms began to go down quickly. No troops so ill-armed could have stood before the murderous fire which the Prussians directed against the opposite line. The Austrians did all that men could do; but, after losing fearfully, were obliged to fall back, and take up their third position in the village of Lochow, and on the Anna Berg. The 42nd regiment and the second *Jäger* battalion were sent against the Anna Berg, while the 2nd and the 14th attacked the village.

It was now about seven o'clock in the evening; the combat had already lasted almost two hours, but here it was renewed more fiercely than ever. The Prussians, encouraged by their success—brave soldiers and bravely led—eagerly came to the attack. With hearts as big, and with officers as devoted, the Austrians stood with a desperate calmness to receive them. On both sides the fighting was hard; but at any distance the Austrian rifle had no chance against the needle-gun, and at close quarters the boyish soldiers of the *Kaiser* could not cope with the broad-shouldered men of Pomerania, who form the *corps d'armée*, one division of which was here engaged. Yet for three-quarters of an hour the little village of Lochow was held, and the continuous rattle of the rifles and the heavy cannonade of the guns remaining almost stationary told the determination of the assault and the stoutness of the defence. But the Austrians were slowly forced from house to house and from orchard to orchard, and had to retreat to their last vantage ground on the top of the Gitschin bank of the fourth ravine.

And here both sides re-engaged in the fight with the utmost fury. The defenders felt that this was their last standing point, and on its maintenance depended the possession of Gitschin; the assailants knew that success here would almost certainly bring them to the object of all their exertions. The Prussian line soon formed on the top of the opposite bank to that held by the Austrians, and then began to fire rapidly against the brow where the Austrians stood. The latter returned the fire, but from necessity more slowly; still their guns smote the Prussian troops heavily, and the shells bursting in front of the assailants' line, caused many casualties. But the Pomeranians were highly excited, and it is said that a heavy mass of the Prussians dashed down the road and rushed up the opposite slope with their rifles at the charge. A fierce struggle ensued. The strong men of Pomerania pressed hard against their lighter opponents, and pushed them beyond the brow of the slope on to the level plain; yet the lithe and active Austrians fought hard, and strove to drive their bayonets into the faces of their taller antagonists; but strength and weight told, for their more powerful adversaries urged them back foot by foot till a gap was clearly opened in the defenders' line.

The musketry bullets had also told sharply on the Saxons and Austrians, and they were obliged to retire. They drew off across the plain towards Gitschin, but not in rout; slowly and sullenly the Saxon rearguard drew back, suffering awful loss in the open plain, where the needle-gun had a fair range; but they fought for every yard of ground, ever turning to send among the advancing Prussians shots which were often truly aimed, but which formed no sufficient return for the showers of bullets which were rained upon themselves. For long the plain was the scene of the advancing combat, and it was not until near midnight that General von Werder occupied Gitschin. In the town the Austrians did not stand; they held some houses at the entrance for a short time, but these were carried, and then they retired rapidly towards the south. In their haste they left their hospitals, and here, as in Lochow, Von Werder's division took a large number of prisoners.

But this was not the only combat that evening. On the northern side of Gitschin the Austrian position extended beyond the Türnau road, to cover the town against the Prussians advancing from the direction of Türnau. The range of hills which runs round the northwestern side of Gitschin drops with a steep slope down to the Türnau road, near the village of Brada, and sends out a much lower prolongation of the range which runs at right angles to the direction of the road, and beyond it, as far as the river that passes by Gitschin and joins the Iser near Türnau. Over this lower spur the road runs, and on its summit lies on the Prussian right of the road, and close to it, the village of Podultz; while further to the right and on the top of the high hills is the village of Brada, standing about 300 yards further southwards than Podultz.

The 5th division, under General Tümpling, on the afternoon of the 29th, advanced from Rowensko, and about half-past four o'clock came within 2,000 yards of the village of Podultz. His division consisted of the 8th, 12th, 18th, and 48th regiments, with four batteries of artillery. As the Prussians advanced they saw the village of Podultz close to the road, and on their right, standing on the top of the gentle ascent by which the road rises to the top of the lower spur, on the other side of the road, and about three hundred yards from it nearer to the advancing division by two hundred yards than Podultz, the village of Diletz lying in the plain; while high on their right they could see the chimneys of Brada above the thick fir wood which, lying on the hill side, in front of that village, runs down nearly to Podultz, and trace by the different colour of the foliage the ground occupied by its orchards.

The three villages and the fir wood were held by Austrian and Saxon troops, supported by seven batteries of artillery, which were placed both on the spur and on Brada hill, while behind the spur were hidden three of Austria's finest cavalry regiments—the hussars of Radetzky, of Lichtenstein, and of the Austrian regiment of the King of Prussia. In front of the village of Brada and of the fir wood an abattis was constructed which ran down the steep slope nearly as far as Podultz. As soon as the Prussians came within range the Austrian batteries opened upon them; the Prussian guns replied, and under the cover of their artillery the columns advanced to the attack of the position. The 8th and 48th regiments advanced against the village of Diletz, which was garrisoned by the 1st, 2nd, 3rd, and 4th Saxon battalions, and where, as the prisoners reported, the Crown Prince of Saxony himself took part in the fight The Fusilier battalion of the 48th engaged the garrison of the village, while the rest of the regiment with the 8th turned towards Eisenstadt, but were sharply attacked by an Austrian column, and driven back to Zames. Both columns were exposed to a very hot fire.

After a severe struggle both villages were carried, though that of Podultz, set on fire by a shell, was burning when the Prussians occupied it Then General Edelsheim, who commanded the Austrian cavalry, with a desperate valour attacked the burning village, but the horses would not face the flames,, and the Prussian infantry from behind the blazing houses fired on the disordered squadrons and killed many troopers. After taking Podultz the 12th and 18th regiments pushed past Brada, leaving it to their right, and made for the Lochow road, in order to cut off the retreat of the Austrians, who were retiring from Lochow on Gitschin. The Austrian cavalry charged the advancing Prussians, but the latter received them without forming square, and the horsemen recoiled broken by their steady fire. The Austrian troops in Brada and the Saxons and Austrians in Diletz were quite separated by the capture of the village of Podultz, and the former were almost entirely taken; the latter were cut off from retreat in large numbers, for Von Werder was pressing towards Gitschin, the roads were crowded, and the little river formed on the right of the broken allies a wide extent of marshy ground, which it was almost impossible to cross. The loss of the Saxons between Diletz and Gitschin was tremendous; they fell thickly, and the ground was covered with corpses.

The Prussians suffered much, but they fought most bravely, and, with only four regiments and half as many guns as their opponents, carried a very strong position held by a much superior force; for the Prussians had in the field but 16,000 men, and the allied strength in the first line was estimated at 30,000. Under a crushing fire they advanced to the attack of Podultz and Diletz, and the vacancies in the muster-roll show how fearfully they suffered; but every man who fell on the Prussian side was trebly avenged, and a long broad track of fallen enemies marked the line of march of the four regiments who fought near Diletz. But though the Austrian position was strong, it was badly occupied. The troops on the hill of Brada seem to have been so enclosed in their defensive works that they could make no counter attack on the Prussian columns engaged at Podultz, nor could they attack in flank the 12th and 18th regiments as they passed. Many officers fell on both sides. General Tümpling, who commanded the Prussian division, was wounded, fortunately not severely.

The field of Diletz was thickly strewn with killed and wounded. Here the Prussians lay more thickly than at Lochow, for the more numerous artillery of the defenders ploughed with terrible effect through the dense columns of the assailants as they advanced to the attack. But between Diletz and Gitschin the ground was covered with broken arms, knapsacks, *shakos*, and fallen men, who were mostly either Saxons or Austrians, for here the needle-gun was more used than artillery.

The Prussians took about 7,000 prisoners in the two combats, many officers, and the Austrian loss in killed and wounded was about 3,000, so that the actions of that evening withdrew 10,000 soldiers from under the Austrian colours.

The Prussian headquarters were moved to Gitschin. The town had been almost entirely deserted by the inhabitants, the streets were filled with military carriages and marching troops, while a Prussian garrison bivouacked under the colonnade which runs all round the market-place.

On the afternoon of the 30th, the strategic object of the movements of the two Prussian armies was achieved, for communications were opened in Bohemia between Prince Frederick Charles and the crown prince. A regiment of dragoons sent from Gitschin that day to feel for the Second Army found the advanced troops of the crown prince at Arnau, and sent back intelligence that he had secured the passages of the Upper Elbe at Arnau and Königinhof. The Ziethen regiment of hussars in the front defeated an Austrian regiment, and captured a convoy of about fifty waggons on the same day.

Count Clam Gallas sent to Benedek to announce the defeat of his force at Gitschin, his incapability of any longer holding the First Prussian Army in check, and that he was retreating hastily on Königgrätz. This report reached the Austrian commander-in-chief early on the morning of the 30th, and had an important effect on the dispositions which he was making against the army of the crown prince. It is now necessary to trace the course by which the Second Army gained the position in which its outposts were found by the cavalry of Prince Frederick Charles on the 30th June.

BOOK 6

CHAPTER 1

Passage of the Army of Silesia Through the Mountains

The First Army and the Army of the Elbe, united under the command of Prince Frederick Charles, on the 30th June, opened communication in Bohemia with the Second Army, which had marched through the mountains from Prussian Silesia, under the command of the Crown Prince of Prussia. It is necessary now to follow the steps by which the Crown Prince brought his army successfully through the passes of the Sudetic Hills.

The crown prince had been appointed commander-in-chief of the Second Army on the 19th May, and on the 2nd June was also named Military Governor of Prussian Silesia. On the 4th June he moved his headquarters from Berlin to that province. The Second Army consisted of the corps of the Guards, and the first, fifth, and sixth *corps d'armée* of the line.

When the crown prince assumed the command in Silesia, he fixed his headquarters at the castle of Fürstenstein. At this time the fifth corps lay round Landshut, the sixth round Waldenburg, the cavalry division round Striegau, and the first corps, which was on the line of march from Görlitz, was moving to Hirschberg and Schönau. The independent corps, under General Knobelsdorf and Count Stölberg,[1] had pushed detachments close up to the Austrian frontier. The fortresses of Glatz, Neisse, Cosel, and Glogau were armed, and new fortifications were thrown up round Schweidnitz.

As has been already noticed, the Army of Silesia in the course of the second week of June, in order to deceive the Austrian commander,

---

1. See Book 5 end of chapter 1.

and to secure the safety of Prussian Silesia against a hostile invasion, took up a defensive position, on the 10th of that month, near the fortress of Neisse, behind the line of the river of that name. At the same time the corps of the Guards joined the Second Army from Berlin, and was posted at Brieg, but left one division to watch the passes of the mountains on the west of the county of Glatz, and to keep open the communications with the First Army, which was near Görlitz.[2]

At this time six of the Austrian corps which Feldzeugmeister Benedek held at his disposal were posted in Austrian Silesia and in Moravia. Political events developed themselves rapidly. The decree of the *diet*, the declaration of war by Prussia against Saxony, and the irruption of General Herwarth von Bittenfeld and of Prince Frederick Charles into that country, followed each other in quick succession. The Saxon army retired into Bohemia, and the Austrian troops began moving towards Josephstadt.

On the evening of the 19th of June, the crown prince received orders from the king, through General von Moltke, the chief of the staff of the army, to leave only one corps on the Neisse, to move the first corps to Landshut, and to station the two other corps in such positions that they might be ready, either in conjunction with the first corps, to move into Bohemia, in order to effect a junction with the First Army, or, if it were necessary, to be equally ready to strengthen the corps on the Neisse.

As the Austrian troops kept moving into Bohemia, it became hourly more probable that the Prussian Second Army would be required to cross the mountains into that province. In order to lead the Austrian staff to believe that this movement was not contemplated, the sixth corps was drawn entirely to the left bank of the Neisse, and received orders that it should, immediately on the outbreak of hostilities, make a strong demonstration against the Austrian frontier in that direction. Officers were at the same time sent to prepare quarters for all the corps on the right bank of the Oder, as if a general movement in that direction was intended

On the evening of the 20th June, a further order came from the king, which directed the crown prince to send intimation in writing to the commanders of the several Austrian outposts, that Prussia considered Austria's bearing at Frankfort as a virtual declaration of war.

As soon as the existence of war between the two great powers was actually recognised, the crown prince issued the following general

2. See Book 4, chapter 4.

order to his troops:—

Soldiers of the Second Army!—You have heard the wods of our king and commander-in-chief! The attempts of His Majesty to preserve peace to our country have proved fruitless. With a heavy heart, but with strong confidence in the spirit and valour of his army, the king has determined to do battle for the honour and independence of Prussia, and for a new organisation of Germany on a powerful basis. I, placed by the grace and confidence of my royal father at your head, am proud, as the first servant of our king, to risk with you my blood and property for the most sacred rights of our native country. Soldiers! for the first time for fifty years a worthy foeman is opposed to our army. Confident in your prowess, and in our excellent and proved arms, it behoves us to conquer the same enemy as our greatest king defeated with a small army. And now, forward with the old Prussian battle-cry—'With God, for King and Fatherland.'

(Signed)   Friederich Wilhelm.

On the 22nd of June the crown prince received from the king the order to prepare to assume the offensive in Bohemia, in order to join the First Army in the direction of Gitschin.

This order had been anticipated by the crown prince. On the previous day he had sent a letter by post, to request permission from the king to move towards his right At the same time he expressed a wish to be allowed to send the sixth corps, which had been ordered to remain near Neisse, into the county of Glatz. By this disposition the sixth corps would both be available for the defence of its native province, Silesia, and, if necessary, could more easily be joined to the main army than from its previous position.

On the 23rd June the crown prince received by telegraph permission to move the sixth corps as he desired. He had, however, on the 22nd, already acted before receiving this permission. That day he sent the sixth corps from Neisse in the direction of Olmütz. This corps crossed the Austrian frontier, and moved through the highland border districts of Friedberg, Freywalde, and Zuchmantel, while the soldiers everywhere spread the news that they formed the advanced guard of the entire army of the crown prince. Some slight skirmishes between the advanced guards and some Austrian hussars ensued without much damage to either side.

In consequence of this demonstration, however, Feldzeugmeister Benedek held the second and third Austrian corps between Hohenmauth and Bömisch Trübau in such a position that they could not be opposed to the Prussian columns at the point where the latter really crossed the frontier. On this day, the 22nd June, the headquarters of the crown prince remained at Neisse; the fifth corps was in the neighbourhood of Ottmachau; the corps of the Guards was drawn together round Münsterberg; the first corps was at Landshut, the sixth corps, as already stated, over the Austrian frontier, and engaged in its demonstration against Austrian Silesia.

The Second Army was now moved into positions which would facilitate its irruption into Bohemia; and on the 25th June, its one hundred and twenty-five thousand warriors were posted, so that the first corps was at Schömberg, the Guards at Schlegel, the fifth corps between Glatz and Reinerz, the first brigade of the sixth corps at Glatz, and the remainder of the sixth corps at Patschkau, the cavalry division at Waldenburg. On the same day the crown prince changed his headquarters from Neisse by way of Camenz to Eckersdorf,

The staff of the crown prince knew that the Austrian first corps and the army of Saxony were engaged against Prince Frederick Charles, and that the second Austrian corps had pushed forward towards the county of Glatz. It was, therefore, correctly argued, that only four Austrian corps could be opposed to the Prussians in issuing from the mountains; but even under these circumstances the march of the Army of Silesia through the passes was exposed to great difficulties, and to considerable danger.

The county of Glatz forms a salient bastion of hills in the highland frontier between Prussian Silesia and Bohemia. From Glatz four great roads lead into the Imperial dominions: the first on the north-west by Wünschelburg to Braunau, the second on the west by Reinerz to Nachod and Josephstadt, the third on the south by Mittelwalde to Gabel and Wildenschwert, the fourth on the south-east by Wilhelmsthal to Altstadt On .the east of the county of Glatz, a road runs from Neisse by Ziegenhals and Würbenthal in the direction of Olmütz, and on the west of the county a road runs from Landshut by Liebau to Trautenau and Josephstadt The passage of the frontier by the Second Army had necessarily to be effected by one of the six frontier passes. The strategical intention of effecting a junction as soon as possible in Bohemia with the First Army, determined the selection of the three roads to Trautenau, Braunau, and Nachod, the directions of which also afforded to the Army of Silesia the advantage of being able to make its advance in three columns, which could afford to each other mutual assistance in case of any one being attacked by the enemy.

The roads on either flank were good. That by Reinerz and Nachod led through a defile five miles in length, and it was only beyond Nachod that troops who marched through it could deploy. The pass to Braunau in the centre had the advantage that the Bohemian frontier at this point advanced for a space of twenty miles. In consequence of this geographical configuration it was the least liable to be blocked or broken up by the enemy, and the troops that marched by it were the least likely to be impeded in their formation after debouching. They would consequently be available to support either of the flank columns in case of opposition being made to their issue from the mountains. After passing the mountains, the junction of the Army of Silesia with that of Prince Frederick Charles could only be effected by a flank move to the right. In order to facilitate this subsequent movement, the plan of the passage of the army of the crown prince was determined as follows:—

The right wing, which consisted of the first corps, was to move, followed by the cavalry division, from Landshut by Liebau on Trautenau. The fifth corps on the left was to occupy the pass of Nachod.

The corps of the Guards in the centre was to move by the intermediate road from Wünschelburg on Braunau, in order to act as a reserve to either of the flank corps, or if necessary to occupy the pass of Eypel. The sixth corps was to remain for a short time on the south of the fortress of Neisse, but as soon as possible was to be withdrawn from this position and to be advanced to Reinerz to support the fifth corps. The protection of Upper Silesia was handed over to the detachments under Count Stölberg and General Knobelsdorf. After passing the mountains the whole army was to make a wheel to its left, pivoted on Nachod and Skalitz, to seize the railway from Josephstadt to Türnau, and along that line gain its junction with the First Army.

To carry out the preliminaries of this plan, on the evening of the 26th June the first Prussian corps was stationed at Landshut with its advanced guard at Liebau. The guards occupied Münsterberg with advanced posts at Frankenstein and Silberberg. The fifth corps was at Ottmachau with its advanced guard at Lewin. The main body of the sixth corps was near Zuchmantel.

The Austrian commander thought that he had secured the left

wing of his whole army by the first Austrian corps and the Saxons under Count Clam Gallas, and on the 26th June held his remaining forces in the following positions:—The tenth Austrian corps was at Pilnikau, the fourth at Königinhof, the sixth moved that day from Opocna to Skalitz, the eighth was in the rear of Josephstadt, the second further south in reserve, and the third round Bömisch Trübau.

It is naturally difficult to say what was the intention of Feldzeugmeister Benedek: if, however, he had the idea of at any time assuming the offensive, he ought to have with might and main attacked the heads of the Prussian columns with overwhelming masses as they issued from the mountains. He was bound at any cost to prevent the passage of the fifth corps, which was the pivot of the Prussian Army, and on the same terms to defeat the first corps and the Guards before they could reach the line of the Aupa, It must have been on the defeat of the army of the crown prince that he depended to be able to assume the offensive with superior numbers against the First Prussian Army and the Army of the Elbe.

Early in the afternoon of the 26th of June, the first Prussian corps was concentrated near Liebau, the corps of the Guards round Wünschelburg, and the fifth corps at Lewin.

That evening the heads of the columns of the Guards pushed across the frontier at Tunschendorf and Johannisberg, under the direction of the crown prince in person. The troops cheered loudly as they stepped upon Austrian ground. Some detachments of the third regiment of Uhlans of the Guard had a little beyond the frontier a skirmish with some of the Austrian Windischgrätz dragoons and Mexican Uhlans, in which the Prussians had the advantage. Certainly Austrian prisoners and captured horses were brought into the Prussian headquarters, and the cavalry of the Second Army acquired the idea that it was fully equal if not superior to the horsemen opposed to it. The Guards bivouacked that night between Politz and Braunau.

On the left wing, the fifth corps the same evening was pushed forward towards the frontier in the direction of Nachod. The bridge over the little river Metau, which forms here the boundary line, had been broken; and as the Prussian scouts approached the river, two Austrian vedettes with two infantry sentries could be made out hidden behind some willow-trees at the Bohemian end of the bridge. These were dislodged by a few Prussian *Jägers*, who forded the river and pushed on in pursuit At a toll-house about four hundred yards further on they were checked by the fire of two Austrian field-guns, and were driven back to the river, where the Prussian pioneers were already engaged in the repair of the broken bridge. Two Prussian guns were quickly brought up, and after a few shots being exchanged the Austrian pieces withdrew, with their escort of two squadrons of cavalry and about ninety foot soldiers. General Löwenfeld, who commanded the leading division of the fifth Prussian corps, sent his *Jägers* in pursuit, and secured without opposition the town of Nachod, and the strong castle which about three-quarters of a mile from the Metau covers the issue of the pass, and could have been easily held, by a handful of determined men, for at least two days against the whole Prussian Army.

After these preliminary movements on the 26th, on the 27th commenced the series of brilliant operations by which the army of the crown prince wrestled its way through the mountains.

Chapter 2

Passage of the Right and Central Columns of the Army of Silesia Through the Mountains

The first corps, which formed the right column of the army of the crown prince, was under the command of General von Bonin. This officer ordered his advanced guard to advance from Liebau at four o'clock on the morning of the 27th, and to follow the road by Golden-Oels to Trautenau. At the latter town it was to halt until the main body arrived at Parschnitz in the road between Schömberg and Albendorf, then it was to move forward upon Arnau. The reserves of infantry and of artillery were to follow the advanced guard, the reserve of cavalry the main body.

The march commenced Hostile dragoons were descried in front of the heads of the columns, but did not yet attack. The main body first came up to the advanced guard, which had halted at Parschnitz at eight o'clock, about ten, when the latter was ordered to move forward, and soon commenced

The First Action of Trautenau

The town of Trautenau lies on the River Aupa, in a basin almost surrounded by mountains: by the river the ground is wet and marshy, on the hillsides it is rough and broken, so that it is nowhere particularly favourable for the action of cavalry or artillery.

The great heat made the Prussian troops suffer much from fatigue and thirst on their march, and they were weary when they reached the town of Trautenau. But the Austrians were in the town, and General von Bonin was forced to attack them, as his road to join the crown prince, who was with the left column, led through Trautenau. The head of the advanced guard broke down the barricade on the bridge over the Aupa. The infantry fight soon began in the streets, and the Austrians were pushed back gradually from house to house. But the Austrians reinforced their troops, and then maintained their position, till the Prussians, calling up more battalions, again got a little the better of the combat. Both sides suffered heavily, and the Prussians gained ground but slowly, for from every house and from every corner hidden marksmen poured bullets into the ranks of the battalions that tried to push along the streets.

When all the Prussian reinforcements had arrived, a general attack was made, and the Austrians were pushed out of the houses into the open country beyond. The Prussians pursued and followed step by step their slowly-retreating enemies. Beyond the town one of Austria's most celebrated cavalry regiments, the Windischgrätz dragoons, stood waiting to sweep the Prussian battalions from the open ground if they issued from the shelter of the houses. These dragoons have long held a high reputation, and, for a record of brave deeds done by the regiment, alone in the Austrian army wear no moustache. The Prussian infantry could not advance, and it seemed that the houses of Trautenau had been won in vain. But assistance was at hand.

The 1st regiment of the Prussian Dragoons came trotting along the main street, deployed into line almost as they debouched from the town, and with their horses well in hand, and their sword-points low, bore in a steady canter straight down upon the Austrian cavalry; these did not wait inactive to receive the attack, but rushed forward to meet their foes; no shots were exchanged, not a saddle was emptied till the close. When within a few yards of each other, both sides raised a cheer, and, welcoming the hug of battle, the two lines rushed upon each other. Horse pressed against horse, knee against knee, swords went up quick and came down heavily on head-piece or on shoulder, points were given and received, blows quickly parried were returned with lightning speed; here an Austrian was borne to the ground, there a Prussian was sent reeling from his seat, and for a few minutes the mass of combatants swayed slowly backwards and forwards. But then, as if some mighty shell had burst among them, the Austrian soldiers flew scattered from the *mêlée*, and the Prussians riding hard after them drove them from the field, but themselves being under the fire of small arms suffered a heavy loss.

The Austrian infantry, which consisted of Mondel's brigade of the tenth Austrian corps, formed on a hill called the Capellenberg, which afforded a strong position beyond the town. This hill could only be scaled by the assailant infantry with great difficulty. Notwithstanding the unfavourable nature of the ground, and the strong resistance of the defenders, the right wing of the Prussian advanced guard under Colonel Koblinski, which consisted of two battalions of the 41st regiment and a company of *Jägers*, gained the Capellenberg between twelve and one o'clock.

The Austrians retired a short distance. The Prussian commander ordered eight battalions to advance from Parschnitz, cross the Aupa, and attack the right flank of the Austrian position. These battalions had great difficulties to encounter: the wooded hills close to the Aupa could only be traversed in extended order, and as soon as the open ground was gained they suffered much from some hostile skirmishers concealed in the standing corn.

Notwithstanding these disadvantageous circumstances, they gained ground. About three o'clock the advanced guard seized the village of Hohenbruck, south of Trautenau, and the brigade on the left wing occupied the heights on the west of the road from Trautenau to Rognitz. It was now three o'clock, the Austrians had retired, and General von Bonin considered that the action was over.

The retreat of the Austrians had, however, been but a tactical manoeuvre, and for once in the history of war a tactical retreat resulted in an advantage to the general who had made it, though even in this case the gain was only of a temporary nature. About half-past three o'clock the action began again. General Gablenz, who commanded the tenth Austrian corps, had advanced from Pilnikau with his whole force, and at that hour made a heavy attack on the Prussian troops, who were already weary with a hot march and a lengthened combat General Gablenz directed some of his battalions against the Prussian front, and with others made a movement against General Bonin's left flank. At half-past four o'clock the Austrians recovered Hohenbruck, and at five the Prussian troops commenced their retreat

In order to cover this movement General Barnekow, with the 43rd Prussian regiment, occupied the commanding hills and plantations which lie on the north of the Capellenberg, supported by the 3rd regiment of Grenadiers, which was posted on the hills lying further back. The 43rd stopped the Austrian pursuit, though with great loss to its own strength, for an hour and a half, but they had to be withdrawn a little after six o'clock. The grenadiers again brought the Austrians up, and stayed their advance until all the Prussian troops had gained an unpursued retreat

General von Bonin had intended to hold the line of the Aupa on the north of Trautenau, but General Gablenz pressed upon him, and he was forced to continue his retreat to the same position as he had occupied on the morning of the day of the action, keeping his rear-guard at Golden-Oels, about three miles from Trautenau.

The cavalry division of the army, which was to have followed the first corps through the mountains as soon as the defile was cleared, remained at Schömberg.

The first Prussian corps lost in this action, in killed and wounded, sixty-three officers and twelve hundred and fourteen men; the Austrian tenth corps, according to Austrian returns, lost one hundred and ninety-six officers and five thousand five hundred and thirty-six men; a terrible disparity in numbers! The Austrian infantry, with a muzzle-loading arm, had indeed gained a victory over an enemy equipped with a breech-loading weapon, but at such a sacrifice as made success almost as costly as defeat.

General Gablenz did not pursue beyond Trautenau. He kept his advanced guard there for the night, and bivouacked at Neu-Rognitz. His corps was considerably shaken by its victory, of which it was soon to be deprived by the fortune of war.

The corps of the Guards had crossed the Bohemian frontier at Steinethal on the evening of the 26th, and had pushed forward the second division by Braunau, as far as Weckelsdorf. On the 27th June this corps was to move in a south-westerly direction, in order to open the communication between the first corps, which was advancing against Trautenau on the right, and the fifth corps at Nachod on the left. At mid-day the first division of the Guards was to march on Eypel. At Qualitch, the general commanding this division hearing the heavy firing at Trautenau halted, and sent an offer of assistance to General von Bonin.

Then the Prussian infantry of the first corps, advancing on the road beyond Trautenau, were everywhere pressing the Austrians back, when a staff-officer came up to the commander of the first corps, and told him that the Prussian Guard was ready to come to his assistance. General von Bonin thought his victory already secure, and declined the proffered aid. For another four hours he did not want it, for the Prussians kept advancing slowly, steadily, pressing the Austrians back, but at four o'clock large reinforcements of artillery came up upon the

Austrian side, and General von Bonin ordered his retreat

The first division of the Guard corps, ignorant of the failure of the first corps at Trautenau, continued its march, and in the evening reached the neighbourhood of Eypel, on the Aupa, while the second division moved to Kosteletz, about five miles to the south-east of that place. The reserve artillery and heavy cavalry were still one day's march in rear. The Prince of Würtemburg, who commanded the Guards, received in the night intelligence from the crown prince, and instructions to move to its relief—of the result of the action at Trautenau, and he immediately gave orders that at daybreak the next morning his corps should cross the Aupa, attack the corps of General Gablenz, and thus disengage the first Prussian corps, and restore the broken communication with General von Bonin. According to the disposition of the Prince of Würtemburg, the first division of the Prussian Guard was to advance by Eypel, in a westerly direction, and the second division to move from Kosteletz to Eypel, to serve as a support to the first division.

The first division, under General Hiller, defiled over the Aupa at Eypel on the 28th June, at five in the morning, and threw out cavalry patrols in the direction of both Trautenau and Königinhof. These patrols discovered that General Gablenz was bivouacked with the main body of his corps at Neu-Rognitz, about two miles south of Trautenau, and that he held the latter town with a strong advanced guard. His position was therefore pointed northward against the first Prussian corps, and his right flank was now threatened by the advance of the Guards from Eypel. The Prussian patrols also discovered that the baggage of the corps of General Gablenz was drawing off towards Königinhof, but was still five miles distant from that town. Under these favourable strategical conditions, the first division of the Guards received orders immediately to advance by Standenz, to attack the enemy in the direction of Königinhof, while the second division, as a reserve, was advanced beyond the defile of Eypel. At the same time two battalions of the Franz Grenadiers were sent forward towards the north-west against Trautenau, in order to cover the right wing of the advance. These dispositions led to the

ACTION OF SOOR

General Gablenz desired to change his front to the right, in consequence of finding his right wing thus threatened. To cover this evolution he ranged his whole artillery, covered by Knobel's brigade, on the hills between Neu-Rognitz and Burgersdorf. In this he succeeded, and extended his right wing to Prausnitz, where he gave his hand to Fleischhacker's brigade of the fourth Austrian corps, which had been sent to his assistance. The advance of the two Prussian grenadier battalions against Alt-Rognitz threatened, however, to cut off from him the brigade which he had posted in Trautenau.

The Prussian advanced guard, under Colonel Kessel, which consisted of four battalions of the fusiliers, one company of the *Jägers* of the Guard, two companies of the pioneers of the Guard, the fourth squadron of the hussars of the Guard, and one 4-pounder battery, came upon the Austrian position before the whole of General Gablenz's guns were formed. It was, however, received by a hot fire from twenty-four pieces, which had already taken up their position. The single Prussian battery engaged these guns with considerable rashness, while the infantry attacked the plantations west of Standenz, and drove the Austrian position slightly in.

Soon the guns of General Gablenz were all in position, and sixty-four pieces opened a withering fire on the six Prussian guns, which, however, held their ground, though with great loss. While the Fusiliers and the *Jägers* of the advanced guard sought to gain some ground, some of the battalions of the Prussian main body, under General Alvensleben, came up, and hurried into the action wherever they were most required. Next arrived the first and second battalions of the Fusiliers, and the second company of the *Jägers* of the Guard, who moved in the direction of Burgersdorf and Alt-Rognitz. After these followed the Second regiment of Grenadiers, and with them came a very welcome field-battery, which immediately opened fire to support the only Prussian battery as yet in action.

Burgersdorf and the plantations near it were now captured by the Prussians, and at that moment the rest of the Prussian infantry and the remainder of the artillery came into play. The action then became general. The Prussian infantry advanced, and stormed the rising ground on which the Austrian battalions stood, but at an awful sacrifice; men fell every moment, and officers went down so quickly that hardly a company reached the summit commanded by its captain. But the Guards pressed on, and the Austrians had to retire from position to position, while the Prussians advanced steadily, urging them backwards. The Austrian corps of Gablenz was then defeated, for the troops could not rally under the fire of the needle-gun, and every battalion which retreated was routed.

The two Prussian battalions which had been detached towards Trautenau to cover the right wing had been during this time heavily engaged. As they moved towards Trautenau, some columns were seen advancing towards them. It was uncertain at first whether these were some of the troops of the first Prussian corps, or some of the Austrians from Trautenau. The doubt was soon dispelled. As they approached, it became clear that, while three of the Austrian brigades of the corps of General Gablenz were resisting the front of the Prussian attack, the remaining brigade, that of Grivicics, had been ordered to sally from Trautenau against the Prussian right wing, and to it the advancing columns belonged—a movement which, but for the precautions of the Prince of Würtemburg, would have had an important influence on the action.

The two Prussian battalions withstood the attack of this brigade with the greatest courage. The greater part of the officers and one-third of the soldiers of these battalions were laid on the field, either dead or dying, but they held their ground until the second division of the Guards, which had been held in reserve, could hurry up to their assistance. This division coming up, drove the brigade of Grivicics back into Trautenau, cut it off from the main body of Gablenz's corps, stormed the town, and captured there a stand of colours and over three thousand prisoners.

General Gablenz withdrew the rest of his corps along the road to Königinhof. The Prussians were too much fatigued to pursue in force: and the Austrian brigade of Fleischhacker, which belonged to the fourth corps, was allowed to pass the night at Soor unmolested as a rearguard, while the first division of the Prussian Guards bivouacked opposite to it at Burgersdorf. The next morning this brigade also re-tired at daybreak, towards Königinhof. The Guards had but eleven hundred men in killed and wounded in this action. The Austrians left behind them five thousand prisoners, three standards, and ten guns.

By the successful issue of this action the communication with the first corps which had been broken on the 27th by its failure at Trautenau, was completely re-established.

On the morning of the 29th, the crown prince caused the first corps, which had been defeated at Trautenau on the 27th, to march past before him through that town, where the victory of the Guards on the 28th had opened a free passage for it

The Guards on the 29th moved from Burgersdorf and Trautenau, on Königinhof and Rettendorf. Early in the morning of that day, one of the regiments in issuing from Burgersdorf had a skirmish with some detachments of scattered Austrians who had been cut off from their corps, and passed the night in the woods.

As the advanced guard of the first division of the Guards approached Königinhof, it again fell in with the army, and a combat ensued which terminated in the

Capture of Königinhof

The advanced guard of the first division of the Guards, consisting of four battalions of Fusiliers, two companies of *Jägers*, and two field batteries, broke up from Burgersdorf at mid-day on the 29th, and were ordered to advance and occupy the town of Königinhof. The brigade of Fleischhacker, which belonged to the fourth Austrian corps, was posted as garrison of the place, and had drawn up several infantry columns, covered by skirmishers, in the cornfields on the north of the town. The Prussian riflemen quickly engaged them: the slow shots of the muzzle-loading arms did little execution against the rapid discharges of the needle-gun, and these advanced columns were soon driven to seek shelter in flight.

The defence of the houses was entrusted to the Austrian regiment of Coranini, and here took place a hot contest, for this gallant corps defended each yard of every street, and each window of every house. The Fusiliers of the Prussian Guards pressed on, overthrew their opponents in the streets, and, dashing past the loopholed houses, occupied the bridge over the Elbe. The majority of the defenders were still in the town, and were completely surrounded. Nothing was left to them but to lay down their arms. The Prussians here captured four hundred prisoners and two standards.

The weak remnant of the Coranini regiment retreated to Miletin. The Prussian Guards were concentrated in the neighbourhood of Königinhof, and the first Prussian corps advanced to Pilnikau.

Feldzeugmeister Benedek had in the meantime drawn the second Austrian corps to the vicinity of Josephstadt It arrived, however, too late to aid in a defence of the line of the Elbe at Königinhof. That important point for the passage of the river was already in the possession of the Prussian Guards, when, on the 30th June, Count Thurn appeared with his corps on the heights south of the Elbe, at Königinhof. This Austrian general could do nothing more than open an ineffectual cannonade against the Prussian corps of the Guards, on the 30th June. That day one division of the latter corps bivouacked near Gradlitz, on the left bank of the Elbe, about two miles out of Königinhof, and the same day the first Prussian corps advanced to Arnau, on the river, about seven miles to the north of the same place.

It is now necessary to trace the passage of the left column of the crown prince's army through the mountains, and to show how, on the 30th June, it was able to effect a junction with the right and central columns on the banks of the Elbe.

CHAPTER 3

Advance of the Left Column of the Army of Silesia

To the fifth Prussian corps, which formed the head of the left column of the army of the Crown Prince, and which he himself most closely directed, was the most difficult task given. Only one narrow road leads from the county of Glatz to Nachod, which beyond the Bohemian frontier runs in a winding course near the town of Nachod, through a difficult defile. A *corps d'armée*, with all its trains and baggage advancing by one road, forms a column of march twenty miles long. If only the combatants themselves and the most necessary train, such as ammunition columns and field hospitals, form the columns, it still will stretch over ten miles; so that if the head of the column is attacked as it issues from a defile where the troops cannot move off the road, the rearmost battalion will not be able to support the most advanced until four hours have passed

In order to ensure the safe issue from the mountain passes, the advanced guard of the fifth corps, under General von Löwenfeld, was pushed forward as far as Nachod on the evening of the 26th June. The Austrians held the defile with a very weak force, and did not stand obstinately in the Castle of Nachod, so that the Prussian advanced guard occupied that strong post with very slight opposition. General Ramming, who had been posted with the sixth Austrian corps and a portion of the first division of reserve cavalry at Opocna, about ten miles to the south of Nachod, marched on the 26th towards Skalitz, by order of Feldzeugmeister Benedek. He was intended next day to fall upon the head of the Prussian fifth corps as it issued from the pass, and drive it back into the defile. At the same time the eighth Austrian corps under the command of the Archduke Leopold was posted on

227

the railway to Josephstadt, in order to act as a reserve to General Ramming. The next day the advanced guard of the Prussian fifth corps brought on the

ACTION OF NACHOD

On the 27th, the same day that the first corps was defeated at Trautenau, as the advanced guard of the fifth Prussian *corps d'armée* was, about ten o'clock in the morning, moving out of Nachod towards Skalitz, in order to take up a position covering the strategical point where the roads to Josephstadt and Neustadt branch, its patrols observed heavy Austrian columns advancing by the road from Neustadt, and two Austrian *cuirass* regiments drew up across the road to bar the way against the Prussian infantry. These were supported by two Austrian infantry brigades, while a third stood in the rear as a reserve. The Prussians were then in a dangerous position, for the road through the defile of Nachod behind them was choked with the carriages of the artillery, and only a few battalions and two squadrons had gained the open ground.

General von Löwenfeld, who commanded the advanced guard, threw his infantry into a wood which was beside the road, where, protected by the trees to a certain extent from the shells of the Austrian guns, they maintained their position until their artillery had cleared the defile. At the same time the small body of Prussian cavalry who were with the infantry charged straight down the road against the centre of the line of the *cuirass* regiments. The Austrians numbered eight times as many sabres as the Prussians, and their cavalry bore the highest reputation in Europe. All expected to see the Prussians hurled back, broken and destroyed, by their collision with the Austrian line, but the result was far different; the Prussian squadrons thundered down the road, and seemed merely by the speed at which they were galloping to cut clean through the centre of the line of *Cuirassiers*; but, though they were thus successful in their first onslaught, they were quickly assailed in flank and rear by overwhelming numbers, and with difficulty escaped without being cut to pieces.

Many, however, managed to shake themselves free from the *mêlée*, and, galloping back, rallied under the protection of the fire of their infantry in the wood; but the Austrians pressed forward, and they had to retire; and it seemed that the issue of the defile would be lost, for Austrian infantry were quickly coming up, and were preparing to attack the wood held by the Prussians. At the first intelligence of the advance of the enemy the crown prince in person hurried up to the front. Then upon Löwenfeld's battalions depended not only the safe passage of the fifth corps through the defile, but also the preservation of the whole of the artillery, for so crowded with carriages was the road that, had the Austrians pressed on, every gun and waggon must have fallen into their hands. But the infantry proved worthy of the trust placed in them, and nothing availed to dislodge them from the trees, though the shells went whistling in quick succession through the trunks, and the splinters carried away the branches above the heads of the soldiers, and tore up the turf beneath their feet

The crown prince was in Nachod when the firing commenced, but he pushed his way with difficulty through the crowded defile, and came to his advanced guard in order himself to be with his soldiers in their time of trial. Behind him followed as quickly as possible the battalions of the main body of the corps, and the guns of the artillery were also pushed forward; but the road was long and crowded, and both regiments and guns made their way with difficulty. In the meantime the Austrians pressed hard upon the little band in the wood, and seemed as though they would pass it by, and close the defile with their columns. But before they could do so the battalions of the main body gained the end of the defile, and the Prussian guns began to come quickly forward, for waggons and all encumbrances had been pushed off the road into the ditches to facilitate the free passage of the troops going into action.

The newly-arrived troops reinforced those in the wood, and the artillery replied to the Austrian batteries; but at noon the battle was still stationary, and the Prussians had not advanced their position since the beginning of the fight, for the Austrian cavalry stood prepared to charge the Prussian infantry if it attempted to move forward on the open ground. The crown prince knew that on breaking that cavalry line depended the passage of the fifth corps into Bohemia, and he sent against it the Eighth Prussian regiment of Dragoons, and the first Uhlan regiment. It was as exciting moment The Prussians, nerved by the importance of the issue of their charge, and with the eyes of their infantry upon them, sprang forward readily: the Austrian horsemen, proud of their high renown, and eager to wipe out the memory of the former skirmish, also bounded forward as soon as they saw the Prussians approaching. The two lines met about half way, for one moment formed a tangled struggling crowd, and then the Prussian Uhlans, with their lance-points low and heads bent down, were seen pursuing.

The most famous cavalry in Europe had been overthrown.

Before and during this charge both divisions of the fifth Prussian corps had cleared the defile, and scarcely had the effect of the cavalry charge been seen than General Steinmetz, who commanded the whole corps, determined to assume the offensive. Then, in rear of their cavalry, the Prussian infantry and artillery dashed forward. Some of the battalions turning aside, marched against the village of Wisokow, already in flames from a Prussian shell, with their bayonets at the charge. Among the burning houses the Austrians waited for them: a sharp struggle ensued, but the village was carried, and the Austrians were driven out of it.

In the meantime the Austrian heavy horsemen had rallied, and again returned to the charge. This time they advanced with skill as well as courage, and bore down on the flank of the Uhlans; but their approach was seen, and before they reached the Prussian line it had quickly changed its front, and met the advancing squadrons face to face. Again the Austrians recoiled, but now without a chance of rallying; they were broken and scattered, and the Uhlans, spreading out in pursuit, went dashing in small knots over the plain after them, and captured two guns from their horse artillery. This cavalry charge decided the fortune of the day, and the Austrians retired, pressed by the Prussian infantry.

General Steinmetz, who commanded the fifth corps, which was here engaged, led forward all his troops, leaving only three battalions of the royal regiment in reserve, and pushed the enemy back. But his men, after a long march and a severe action, were too fatigued to pursue in mass, so they were halted, and the cavalry and one or two battalions alone followed up the pursuit; but they did well, for they brought back 2,000 prisoners and three guns, besides the two taken by the Uhlans; and these were not the only trophies, for three sets of infantry colours were taken by the Prussians, and the standards of the Austrian *cuirassiers* fell into the hands of the Uhlans. The crown prince thanked General Steinmetz on the field in the name of the king for the victory, and well the general and his troops merited the compliment, for all the first part of the action was fought with twenty-two battalions against twenty-nine, and with an inferior force of cavalry and artillery.

This victory cost the Prussians a loss of nine hundred men killed and wounded; among the latter were the two generals, Von Ollech and Von Wunck. The fifth Prussian corps, notwithstanding that on the

27th it had marched over fifteen miles through a narrow defile, and been engaged in action for eight hours, was still so strong and so confident that General Steinmetz resolved to resume the attack the ensuing day without loss of time.

General Ramming, who had deservedly the reputation of being one of the most able and talented generals of the Imperial army, after having engaged the Prussians at Nachod, with his whole force retreated to Skalitz on the evening of the 27th. On arriving at that place he sent a despatch to the headquarters of the army, in which he requested that the eighth Austrian corps, which was posted at Josephstadt, might be allowed to assist him with two brigades. Feldzeugmeister Benedek thereupon ordered that the eighth corps should advance to Skalitz, and be prepared to engage in the first line, while that of General Ramming should form its reserve. Both corps were placed under the command of the Archduke Leopold. One brigade of the Prussian sixth corps, which was to follow the fifth corps through the defile of Nachod, had reached Nachod on the evening of the 27th, and was ready that day to advance with General Steinmetz. General Steinmetz determined to advance. At the same time the Austrian general replaced the sixth corps by the eighth corps at Skalitz, in order to oppose the Prussians and drive them back. Hence arose the

Action of Skalitz

The Austrians were soon forced to quit all hopes of the offensive, and to assume the defensive energetically in front of Skalitz, on the road and railway, which are flanked on the north and south by two woods. The country was entirely unfavourable for the action of cavalry. Either side brought up as much force as possible. The battle swayed hither and thither, but ultimately the superior strength and armament of the Prussian soldier told against his weaker antagonist

On the north of the railway the 37th and 58th Prussian regiments and 4th Dragoons with three batteries advanced; while on the south the King's own regiment, though exposed to a terrible fire of artillery, gained the wood on the south of the town, and here succeeded in sustaining the assaults of far superior numbers, until the 6th, 46th, and 52nd and 47th regiments could come up to its aid, and join with it in an attack on Skalitz.

This attack was made about 3 p.m. On the north side of the town the 6th and 52nd regiments advanced, and along the high road the 7th, 37th, 58th, and 47th regiments.

The Austrian position was forced, and the Archduke Leopold compelled to fall back to a strong position behind the Aupa, where he intended to hold his ground, supported by his numerous artillery. This position was however also carried by the Prussians, who there took many prisoners, and by it they gained the command of the defile of the Aupa.

General Steinmetz, by this victory, captured four thousand prisoners, eight guns, and several stands of colours. On this day, the 28th, depended whether the Army of Silesia would effect its issue from the mountains, or fail in the attempt. The corps of the Guards was engaged at Trautenau, the fifth corps at Skalitz. The crown prince, in person, could not be present at either action. He was obliged to choose a position between the two, whence he could proceed to any point where his presence might be necessary. He accordingly posted himself on a hill near Kosteletz, where the heavy cavalry of the Guard took up its position on coming through the hills, and where it was joined at a later period of the day by the reserve artillery of the Guard. The time passed heavily on that hill of Kosteletz.

The thunder of cannon rose ever louder from Skalitz on the south, and from the direction of Trautenau on the north. With anxious ears the commander-in-chief and his staff listened to the progress of the cannonade, and with eager eyes scanned the positions of the eddying clouds of white smoke which rose from the engaged artillery. It was the intention of the crown prince, if an unfavourable report of the progress of the action on either side was brought to him, to repair to that point, and in person to encourage his pressed troops. But every orderly officer, every *aide-de-camp*, brought the intelligence that the battles in both places were going well for the Prussians.

At last, between three and four o'clock, the commander-in-chief received the positive report from General Steinmetz that he had stormed Skalitz, and driven back two of the enemy's corps. No longer had the crown prince to give a thought to this side. He immediately started for Eypel, in order to be present at the action in which the Guards were engaged. At this place the news reached him that the Guard had also victoriously achieved its task, and not only had forced the defile from Eypel, but had also opened the pass from Trautenau. Here, then, were the three issues from the mountains, the defiles of Trautenau, Eypel, and Nachod, popularly called the gates of Bohemia, in the secure possession of the Second Prussian Army, and the junction of the hitherto separated corps almost certain to be effected on the following day. To accomplish the junction of his united army with that of Prince Frederick Charles, the crown prince ordered the advance the next morning to be made as far as the Elbe.

The quarters of the crown prince on the night of the 28th were fixed at Eypel, where he heard for the first time that the first corps had only returned on the 27th from Trautenau to their former bivouac, and were fit to advance again on the 29th, having halted there on the 28th. The report of General von Bonin had not before reached headquarters, and all that was heard of the first corps was that it had not assisted the Guards in the action of the 28th.

The crown prince immediately ordered General von Bonin to advance at daybreak on the 29th, from Trautenau to Pilnikau.

On the 29th June, General Steinmetz, with the fifth and sixth corps, was to advance from Skalitz in a westerly direction, towards Königinhof, as far as Gradlitz, in order to approach the other corps of the crown prince, so that the whole Army of Silesia might be united on the Elbe before commencing general operations in concert with the First Army. Fresh forces of the enemy opposed this march, and took post in a situation which caused the

ACTION OF SCHWEINSCHÄDEL

The Austrian troops, which here opposed the advance of the Prussian fifth corps, were those of the fourth corps, under the command of General Festetics, whom Feldzeugmeister Benedek had sent forward from Jaromirz, after he had withdrawn the 6th and the 8th corps. Of this corps there were present only three brigades, for one brigade had been detached to Königinhof, where on the same day it was engaged in an action against the leading battalions of the Prussian Guard, as has been already noticed. General Steinmetz attacked, and after an action of three hours, which consisted of little more than a cannonade, the Austrians were driven back, and retreated under the guns of the fortress of Josephstadt, which opened hotly upon the advancing Prussians. General Festetics made his retreat in good time, in order not to suffer a loss similar to that which had befallen the other Austrian corps which had been engaged at Trautenau and Skalitz. Early as he retired, however, he lost eight hundred prisoners.

General Steinmetz, after pushing the retreating Austrians close up to Josephstadt, did not venture to press further in this direction, as by pursuing such a course he would have been exposed to be cut off and isolated from the other corps of the crown prince. He detached, accordingly, one brigade, to observe the garrison of Josephstadt, and moved the remainder of his corps to Gradlitz, about two miles east of Königinhof, in order to concentrate with the rest of the Army of Silesia, He arrived there on the night of the 29th June, and took up a position near the division of the Guards, which was already stationed there.

The sixth Prussian corps, which followed the fifth corps by the defile of Nachod, from the county of Glatz, had only sent forward one brigade to aid the corps of General Steinmetz in the actions of the 28th and 29th June. It reached Gradlitz, however, late on the 30th June, so that now three corps of the Army of Silesia were concentrated in the vicinity of Königinhof. The first corps had reached Arnau, where there is also a bridge over the Elbe, about seven miles to the north of Königinhof. Thus the army of the crown prince, four days after its inroad into Bohemia, had successfully united its divided columns of advance, and had made itself master of the line of the Elbe from Arnau to near Josephstadt Four Austrian corps had been repulsed, three of which were decidedly defeated, and had lost ten thousand prisoners, twenty guns, five colours, and two standards to the crown prince.

On the 30th of June a cavalry regiment, sent out from Gitschin by Prince Frederick Charles, fell in with the outposts of the corps of the crown prince at Arnau. Communications between the two main armies were now established in Bohemia, and their secure junction almost certain. For the sake of simplicity, it may be here advisable to give briefly a general sketch of the steps taken each day by the two armies from the time of their crossing the Austrian frontier to bring about their common concentration.

SUMMARY OF THE ADVANCE OF THE THREE PRUSSIAN ARMIES INTO BOHEMIA FOR CONCENTRATION

On the 23rd June, the army of Prince Frederick Charles advanced in three columns from Zittau, Görlitz, and Laubau, towards Reichenberg.

The same day the Army of the Elbe advanced from Saxony.

On the 24th, Prince Frederick Charles occupied Reichenberg, and concentrated his three columns, which had passed through the mountains.

On the 26th, the advanced guard of the fifth corps (Army of Silesia) seized Nachod in the evening, and the Guards crossed the frontier of Bohemia by the Wünschelburg road.

The same evening Prince Frederick Charles secured the passage of the Iser at Türnau and Podoll, and the Army of the Elbe occupied Hayda and Bömisch Aicha.

On the 27th, the first corps of the crown prince's army seized Trautenau, but was defeated and driven back by General Gablenz.

The fifth corps of the crown prince's army defeated General Ramming in the action of Nachod.

The Army of the Elbe, after a skirmish, occupied Hühnerwasser.

On the 28th, the Army of the Elbe and Prince Frederick Charles defeated the corps of Count Clam Gallas at Münchengrätz, and secured the line of the Iser.

The Guards, under the crown prince, defeated General Gablenz at Soor, and cleared the issue from the Trautenau defile for the first corps.

The fifth corps defeated the Archduke Leopold at Skalitz.

On the 29th, the Guard corps stormed Königinhof; and the fifth Prussian corps drove General Festetics from Schweinschädel. The crown prince concentrated his army on the left bank of the Elbe.

The army of Prince Frederick Charles that night stormed Gitschin.

On the 30th, communications were opened between the army of Prince Frederick Charles round Gitschin and the first corps of the army of the crown prince at Arnau.

OBSERVATIONS

For some reason, political or military, Benedek did not assume the offensive. He threw this advantage into the hands of his adversaries. It is supposed that political causes and the request of the Germanic Confederation prevented the Austrian general from taking this line of action, and carrying the war into Saxony.

After having determined to fight on the defensive, he intended to check one portion of his enemy's armies with a detachment, while with superior forces he threw himself upon the other. The lines of operation of the Prussian armies, convergent from separate bases, gave him a favourable opportunity to reap successful results from such a course. He could either send a detachment to hold Prince Frederick

Charles while he assailed the crown prince, or could hold the latter while with the mass of his army he threw himself upon the former. To hold the crown prince, however, while he attacked Frederick Charles was much more hazardous than to adopt the alternate line.

The crown prince, if he beat the detachment left to bar his way, could sweep down upon the Austrian communications with Vienna ere Benedek had laid his grasp upon the First Prussian Army. If this had been his intention, he should have held the Castle of Nachod and the passes at Trautenau and Eypel. If, on the other hand, he intended to delay Frederick Charles, the line of the Iser should have been tenaciously held between Türnau and Münchengrätz. None of these things were done. Inferior forces of the Austrians were exposed at almost all points to superior forces of the Prussians; while the masses, which cast at the proper moment to either side would have turned the scale, oscillated vaguely backwards and forwards under vacillatory or contradictory orders.

On the evening of the 26th June Benedek knew that the crown prince was on the frontier, and that Prince Frederick Charles was close to the Iser. His corps at this time were stationed, the tenth at Pilnikau, the fourth at Königinhof, the sixth near Skalitz, while of the three others, two were south of Josephstadt and one as far off as Böhmisch Trübau. On the 27th, after Türnau on the Iser had been evacuated without a blow by Clam Gallas, and the passage of that stream at Podoll stormed by Frederick Charles, Benedek appears to have made no movement to support with his reserves his corps at Nachod or Trautenau against the crown prince, or to send reinforcements to Clam Gallas.

On the 28th, the crown prince determined to retrieve the misfortune of his right on the previous day, by energetically attacking the position of the Austrian corps; while at the same time the fifth corps, supported by the sixth, should move against Skalitz. Benedek had had only two corps engaged on the previous day. One of these had been defeated at Nachod and driven back to Skalitz, but had by no means been routed.

The other had well held its own and had repulsed its assailants. As yet the Austrian commander had lost nothing so important that he might not hope, by vigorous action on the 28th, to gain a decided success, and with one blow to turn the fortune of the campaign, and the destiny of Austria.

The first Prussian corps was not on the morning of the 28th sufficiently recovered from its repulse on the previous day to engage at all. The fifth corps was able to engage, but was supported only by one brigade of the sixth, because the three remaining brigades of that corps were still in the defile through the mountains.

Thus, the crown prince had only the two divisions of the Guard corps, the fifth corps, and one brigade of the sixth corps ready to go into action on the morning of the 28th, in all about 67,000 men.

General Benedek ought to have known on the 27th by daybreak, that he had nothing to fear in the direction of Olmütz, for the demonstration of the sixth Prussian corps made in that direction on the previous day had been withdrawn. He could therefore on the 27th have moved the third corps from Böhmisch Trübau to Josephstadt that day, and would then have had six corps, about 150,000 men, ready to push into action energetically on the morning of the 28th, and with them to drive the crown prince back into the defiles. This great opportunity, however, was missed. The sixth Austrian corps at Skalitz was indeed reinforced by the eighth; but the tenth corps was left without reinforcements at Trautenau, so that, although he had a force at hand double that of his adversary, on the morning of the 28th only three corps, about 70,000 men, were placed in position to come under fire.

It is natural to inquire why Benedek did not employ on the 28th the three corps which did not come into action that day. The reason, as far as can be gathered, appears to be, that Benedek made the vital error of attempting to check the crown prince when he was already past the defiles, and in a position to threaten the Austrian communications, with a detachment, while he directed his principal blow against Prince Frederick Charles. At this time the distance between the two Prussian armies was about forty miles. They were too far separated to afford each other mutual assistance. The distance from Benedek's headquarters[1] to the Iser was nearly fifty miles; that from the same place to Skalitz, about eight miles; to Trautenau about twenty.

At the two latter places the crown prince was thrusting against the Austrian detachments. The Prussian Second Army was thus at less than half the distance from the mass of Benedek's troops than was the First Army. It was also in a more favourable position to sweep down on a vital point of Benedek's line of communication with Vienna than was the First. Clearly every exertion should have been made to crush the crown prince on the 28th. The *feldzeugmeister*, however, designed to hold the crown prince by three corps while he made his great at-

1. Josephstadt.

tempt against Prince Frederick Charles. Orders were sent to the commanders of the corps at Trautenau and Skalitz, not to compromise themselves in a serious action, but to retreat slowly, if pressed by superior numbers. These orders were neglected. If they had been observed, it is doubtful whether the crown prince would not have pushed them back, and concentrated his army on the Austrian communications, before Benedek had time to strike down Prince Frederick Charles, and return with his main force to support his troops in front of the Second Army.

The result of the neglect of the orders of the commander-in-chief was, however, that the three Austrian corps engaged on the 28th near Josephstadt were severely mutilated for further operations. Intending to support Clam Gallas and the Saxons before he knew of the unfortunate issue of the combats of Nachod and Skalitz, Benedek instructed them to stand firm at Gitschin; and promised to support them with his third corps on the 29th, and ultimately with other corps. This despatch was received at the Saxon head-quarters about mid-day on the 29th. The Saxons and Clam Gallas took up a strong position to fight at Gitschin. When they were already engaged, and had compromised themselves in a serious action with the leading divisions of Prince Frederick Charles, a second despatch arrived from Benedek.

This had been written after the results of Trautenau and Skalitz on the 28th were known to him. In it he ordered the crown prince of Saxony to fall back slowly before Prince Frederick Charles, while he himself collected his forces on the heights above Königinhof to oppose the Second Army. By the crushing defeat at Gitschin, the left flank of this position was laid open to the Prussian First Army, and the Austrian commander was reduced to make fresh dispositions, unable any longer to prevent the junction of the two Prussian armies on the ground upon which at the outbreak of hostilities he himself stood. Thus, by a neglect to strike boldly on his nearest adversary, Benedek sacrificed all the advantages which he had possessed from a central situation, and the separate lines of operation of his antagonists. To the superior armament of the Prussians a degree of importance has rather hastily been awarded, which seems not to be wholly merited. The needle-gun came into action under certainly favourable circumstances.

At Podoll the Prussians armed with breech-loaders fired upon the troops of Clam Gallas while the latter were crowded together in the narrow street of a village. At Nachod the soldiers of Steinmetz fired from the cover of a wood upon their Austrian assailants in the open. In both cases the rapid discharges told fearfully upon the men who were armed with the more slowly loaded weapons. The consequence was that the Prussians gained a great moral victory at the very beginning. They found confidence, their opponents lost heart. Yet in the subsequent operations the difference of armament had little physical effect, Superior strategical capabilities, superior organisation, and greater activity seemed to have been more powerful in gaining the junction of the Prussian armies than superior armament. Yet the Prussian leaders hazarded much by their two convergent lines of operation. The result is but another proof of the old maxim that "*in war he is the victor who makes the fewest errors.*"

BOOK 7

CHAPTER 1

Operations Preceding the Battle of Königgrätz

After his unsuccessful attempts at Soor and Skalitz on the 28th, to prevent the issue of the columns of the crown prince from the mountains, Feldzeugmeister Benedek determined to take up a strong position on the right bank of the Upper Elbe, in order to prevent the passage of that river by the Army of Silesia.

The Elbe, which runs in a course nearly directly from north to south between Josephstadt and Königgrätz, forms almost a right angle at the former fortress. Its upper course above that place lies from north-west to east. Parallel to the stream, and about one mile from it, a chain of hills thickly wooded with fir-trees rises with a steep ascent, and forms the southern bank of the valley. About halfway up the hillside runs the railway which leads from Josephstadt to Türnau. It was along these heights that the Austrian commander designed to draw up his troops, in such a manner as to bar the passage of the Upper Elbe against the crown prince, and to command the bridges of Arnau, Königinhof, and Schurz.

The right wing of the troops under the immediate command of Benedek rested on the fortress of Josephstadt, and his position extended along the heights towards Daubrowitz, while his extreme left was formed and covered by the first corps and the Saxons under Count Clam Gallas at Gitschin. In Königinhof he left one brigade, and at Schweinschädel three brigades of his fourth corps, in order to check the advance of the crown prince while he was making his dispositions. These troops were, as has been already said, driven in by the Prussians on the 29th, when they retired and formed a portion of the new Austrian line near Josephstadt.

On the night of the 29th Prince Frederick Charles stormed Gitschin, and defeated Count Clam Gallas, who retired in disorder towards Königgrätz. The loss of Gitschin exposed the left flank of Benedek's intended position. As soon as he heard the news of Count Clam Gallas's failure on the morning of the 30th, he was obliged to make new arrangements to oppose the advance of the enemy towards Vienna.

Of his eight corps, five—namely, the first corps, the Saxons, the sixth, eighth, and tenth—had been decidedly beaten, and had suffered great loss both in men and *morale*. The fourth corps had also been under fire and suffered, though to a much less serious extent. Two corps only remained to the Austrian commander which were thoroughly intact. He had no hope of any supports, reserves, or reinforcements. His left flank was exposed, and no course remained open to him except to retire before he was cut off from his line of communication with Vienna, and to accept battle from his adversary in a chosen and prepared position. The Austrian army had suffered a loss of about forty thousand men since the opening of the campaign in its attempts to prevent the junction of the Prussian armies. Notwithstanding this, its bravery and power of endurance were still great. High hopes were entertained that Benedek's generalship would retrieve all previous failures by a decisive victory.

The Austrian commander felt himself unequal to assume the offensive. He was forced to seek a defensive position, and could choose one in either of two entirely distinct manners. If he desired a purely defensive position he might withdraw behind the Elbe, and take up the line of that river between the fortresses of Josephstadt and Königgrätz; or, what would perhaps have been better, he might have concentrated his army behind the Adler, between Königgrätz and Hohenbruck. Here his left flank would have been secured by the fortress, his right by the Adler, and he would have covered a safe retreat and source of supply in the railway between Pardubitz and Böhmisch Trübau.

On the other side he might choose a defensive position, where he would still retain the power of assuming the offensive. This appears to have been his object. He hoped in a great battle to repair the misfortunes of the last few days, and then on his side to advance as an assailant. Whether he would have done better to have taken up an entirely defensive position until the confidence of his army was restored is a question which few could decide. He has been blamed for not doing so, but in war success is generally regarded as the sole criterion of merit Fortune declared against Benedek. He did not reap success.

On the afternoon of the 30th June, he issued orders for the whole army to retire towards Königgrätz, and to concentrate in front of that fortress. This retreat along crowded country roads was attended with considerable difficulty, and it was not till the night of the 2nd July that his whole force was assembled in front of Königgrätz, where it took up a position between that town and the little river Bistritz.

On the Prussian side four divisions of the First Army, and part of that of General Herwarth von Bittenfeld, had not yet been under fire. Of the Second Army three brigades had not as yet pulled a trigger. The first corps had had time to recruit itself after its defeat at Trautenau, and the remainder of the troops were flushed with victory, high of courage, and eager for battle. In order to complete effectually the junction between the army of the crown prince, which on the 30th June had concentrated on the left of the Upper Elbe, with that of Prince Frederick Charles, which, with the Army of the Elbe as its right wing, was halted that day round Gitschin, the Second Army would require to make a wheel to its left, pivoted on Gradlitz.

To carry out this movement, on the 1st July the first corps, which formed the right wing of the Army of Silesia, advanced from Arnau to Ober Prausnitz, and threw its advanced guard forward to Zelejow on the road to Miletin. The cavalry division took post at Neustadtl. The first division of the Guards occupied Königinhof, while its advanced guard seized the plateau of Daubrowitz, on the bank of the Elbe. The second division of the Guards, the reserve artillery, and the heavy cavalry of the Guard halted at Rettendorf, while the fifth and sixth corps concentrated round Gradlitz. The headquarters of the crown prince were in Königinhof. The Prussian generals thought that Feldzeugmeister Benedek would accept battle on the left bank of the Elbe, with his flanks resting on the fortresses of Josephstadt and Königgrätz, which lie ten miles apart along the river, and with his front covered by the stream; or that, if he did not do so, he would cross the Elbe at Pardubitz, and take up a position there behind the river.

Under this idea two and a half Prussian corps were held on the left bank of the Elbe both to observe the fortress of Josephstadt and to be prepared vigorously to oppose any attack made from behind the cover of that fortress against the line of communication of the crown prince with Silesia.

Prince Frederick Charles, on the 1st July, pushed forward from

Gitschin. The Army of the Elbe formed his right wing, and occupied Smidar and Hoch Wessely. The sixth division, with the fifth in its rear, occupied Miletin; the seventh and eighth, Höritz; the third and fourth, with the cavalry corps and the reserve artillery corps, were bivouacked along the road from Gitschin to Höritz. The headquarters of the prince were at Kammenitz.

The small *château* and village of Kammenitz lie on the northern slope of an isolated hill, which stands on the left-hand side of the road from Gitschin to Höritz, about half-way between the two towns. The headquarters of Prince Frederick Charles were moved here on the evening of the 1st July from Gitschin.

From the hill south of the village of Kammenitz a wide view could be obtained of the undulating plain which, richly cultivated and studded with villages and fir-woods, stretches southwards for nearly thirty miles. Near to Kammenitz, the smoke of the bivouac fires and the glitter of the sunlight on the piled arms marked the position of the Prussian troops, but no Austrian outposts could be made out. During the march of that day a sudden thunderstorm came on, and the rain fell heavily for an hour; the road, crowded with thousands of waggons and military carriages, ran into ruts under the excessive transport, and the convoys of Austrian wounded, who had been perforce deserted by their retreating friends, jolted painfully along towards the hospitals which had been established at Gitschin.

The maimed soldiers suffered much, for every time the waggons rocked some wound was opened afresh, or some bandage came undone, but they bore it patiently, and their guardians did all they could to alleviate their sufferings. The different coloured facings of the wounded told that many Austrian regiments had been engaged in the late combats, for the uniforms of the different infantry regiments could be distinguished, besides those of hussars and riflemen.

On the night of the 1st the main body of the First Army lay between Kammenitz and Höritz. General von Bittenfeld had occupied Smidar on the fight flank, and Jung Bunzlau[1] was also occupied in the same direction. The head of the columns of the Second Army had crossed the Upper Elbe, and the whole Prussian force was free for operations in Bohemia, for the Hanoverians had laid down their arms near Erfurth, and there were now no hostile troops in Northern Germany.[2]

---

1. On the railway between Münchengrätz and Prague.
2. See *post.*

The inhabitants of the towns had mostly fled on the approach of the Prussian Army, but the country villagers, unable to afford to pay for transport, had been obliged to remain in their houses. Nor did they suffer by doing so, for the Prussian soldiers behaved well, and there was no plundering where the inhabitants remained. In the towns where there was no one to sell, the commissariat was obliged to take the necessaries of life, for the marches had been long, the roads had been crowded with troops, and the provision trains had not always been able to keep up with the army. But the soldiers never used force to supply their wants. Forage for the horses was taken from the barns of the large landed proprietors, who had deserted their castles and *châteaux*; but the men paid for what they had from the peasantry: unable to speak the Bohemian language, they by signs made their wants understood, and the peasantry, as far as lay in their power, supplied them readily, for none were found so ignorant as not to appreciate Prussian coin.

The villagers were invariably kindly treated; no cottages had been ransacked, their poultry yards had been respected, their cattle had not been taken away from them, and, though the women of this province are beautiful, no Bohemian girl had cause to rue the invasion of her country. Yet the inhabitants of a land where a war is carried on must always suffer; troops must move through the standing corn, cavalry and artillery must trample down the crops; hamlets must be occupied, defended, and assaulted, and a shell, intended to fall among fighting men, must often unintentionally set fire to a cottage, which, blazing fiercely, communicates the flames to others, and thus a whole hamlet is often destroyed. Then the ejected cottagers have little hope of anything but starvation, for a vast army with its many hundred thousand mouths eats up everything in the country, and can spare little after its own necessities are supplied to give away in charity.

The proprietors of the burnt houses sometimes wandered about the fields dejected and desponding, sometimes stood staring vacantly at the cinders and charred timbers which marked the place where a few days ago stood their homes; the little money that was given to them by kind-hearted officers might keep off the pangs of hunger for a short time, but was no compensation for the heavy losses they had sustained, for often their cottage and their cowhouse and a little field was all their wealth, and since these were gone and their crop destroyed, they had nothing. The young men even in the country districts had nearly all fled south, frightened by a report that the Prussians would make them join the ranks; for this report there was never a foundation, for no recruits had been demanded or received in the countries occupied by the armies.

Brilliant success had attended the skilful plans laid for the prosecution of this campaign by the Prussian leaders. The army of Prince Frederick Charles had fought five severe combats without a reverse, and had secured a favourable position in which to fight a great battle. The crown prince fought severe actions on the 27th, 28th, and 29th, and had now secured his junction with Prince Frederick Charles, bringing with him as trophies of his victories 15,000 prisoners, 24 captured guns, six stands of colours, and two standards.

The places where there had been fighting did not long retain the more ghastly signs of the combat; the wounded were always removed as quickly as the *krankenträger* could work, and though broken boughs, burnt houses, and down-trodden corn marked for a few days the places where the hostile troops had been engaged, the broken arms and castaway knapsacks were soon removed, and the graves dotted among the fields, each with a wooden cross at the head, alone told the spots where soldiers had fallen. And these, too, soon disappeared, for the sun and the rain rapidly diminished the mounds of newly-turned earth, and it will soon be impossible to distinguish the positions of the graves from the other parts of the fields. But this will matter little to those who sleep below. The wounded merited greater commiseration. The hospital resources of the Prussian Army had been tasked to the utmost for more wounded prisoners had been taken than could have been anticipated.

Every available house and the churches in Gitschin had been converted into hospitals, but still there was more room required; nor would the few remaining inhabitants help to assist the wounded Austrian soldiers; in vain did the Prussian staff entreat, imprecate, and threaten; the towns-people who were still at Gitschin would not even carry some of the coffee which they had in abundance to give to the wounded, and these from the scarcity of provisions in the army fared badly. As the news spread abroad in the country that the Prussians did not pillage and murder, the people began to return to their houses, but they all appeared to be totally callous to the sufferings of their fellow-countrymen.

The Austrian medical men and hospital attendants who were captured at Gitschin worked hard, and were aided powerfully by the Prussian officers, but they had few materials with which to supply the wants of so many; and though none went totally unprovided for, and none were entirely neglected, a little trouble on the part of the inhabitants would have tended materially to the comfort and cure of many.

The inhabitants pleaded as an excuse that the Austrian soldiery had treated them badly, and had pillaged; but this did not seem true, for the houses bore no signs of having been plundered, and if plundering had been allowed in the Austrian Army the prisoners would, not have had to complain of want of food. Railway traffic was already opened to Münchengrätz, but the army had now left the line of railway, many miles of road separating it from the nearest station; and in those miles of road lay the difficulty of supplying the troops with provisions. The railway trains easily brought enough to any station, but at this time the roads were required for the marching columns, and everything had to give way for the passage of the troops.

The army carried no tents; sometimes at night the soldiers were billeted in villages, but more often slept in the open air. As soon as a regiment arrived at the place where it was to pass the night, the rifles were piled four together resting against each other, and the knapsacks were taken off and laid on the ground beside them. The men quickly lighted their fires and began cooking their rations; a couple of stones or a few bricks formed their field stoves, and their whole cooking apparatus consisted of the one tin can which they carry with them. This serves for both boiling the water for coffee and for making their meat into a thick soup, which they seem to prefer to roasted food.

As soon as it got dark each man lay down to sleep wrapped in his cloak with his knapsack for a pillow, and the muffled figures lay as regularly in the bivouac as they stood in the ranks on parade. The officers lay separate in groups of two or three, and in rear of the battalion the horses were picketed and champed at their bits uneasily all night long, and seldom seemed to lie down. When a village was occupied a rush was made to secure mattresses, but these were only used by the luxurious. The men, as a rule, appeared to prefer straw, and if they could get plenty of it were quite content to sleep in the open air. General and staff officers usually contrived to get into houses, and then there was a heavy drain on the sleeping accommodation of the establishment.

One had a pillow, another a mattress, a third a couple of blankets, and beds were made on the floor on the most advanced shake-down principles, but all slept soundly, for the day's work was long and tiring, and the march generally begun at early morning. The proprietors of

246

most of the large houses had not only left them, but had taken most of their furniture with them, so that the temporary occupants were entirely dependent on what little had been left behind, and had to make it up by borrowing from the nearest cottages.

On the 30th June the king left Berlin, and on the afternoon of the 1st July arrived at Gitschin, where in person he assumed the supreme command of the three Prussian armies in Bohemia, It was decided by him that the troops should halt on the 2nd July, to recover from the great fatigues they had lately undergone.

A council of war was ordered to assemble at Gitschin, to which Prince Frederick Charles and the crown prince were summoned. It was decided that on the 3rd the First Army should send a reconnaissance towards Königgrätz, that the Second should send a strong detachment towards Josephstadt, and if possible cut that fortress off from communication with the army of Feldzeugmeister Benedek; while the remainder of the troops halted in their actual positions.

These plans were, however, entirely altered within a few hours.

CHAPTER 2

Battle of Königgrätz

When Prince Frederick Charles left Kammenitz on the morning of Monday, the 2nd July, to attend the council of war summoned by the king to meet at Gitschin, he sent out two officers to reconnoitre beyond Höritz; both fell in with Austrian troops, and had to fight and ride hard to bring their information home safely. Major Von Ungar, who went in the direction of Königgrätz, escorted by a few dragoons, came upon a large force of Austrian cavalry and *Jägers* before he got to the little river Bistritz, over which the road from Höritz to Königgrätz crosses, about halfway between those two towns.

A squadron of cavalry made an immediate dash to catch him, and he and his dragoons had to ride for their lives; the Austrians pursued, and those best mounted came up to the Prussians, but not in sufficient numbers to stop them, and after a running skirmish, in which Von Ungar received a lance thrust in the side which carried away most of his coat, but hardly grazed the skin, this reconnoitring party safely gained the outposts of their own army. More on the Prussian right the other reconnoitring officer also found the Austrians in force, and was obliged to retire rapidly. From the reports of these officers, and from other information which Prince Frederick Charles received at Kammenitz on his return from the council of war held at Gitschin, he inferred that the Austrian commander had the intention of advancing the next day from the Bistritz, with the object of attacking the First Prussian Army with superior force, before its junction with that of the crown prince was practically effected.

Prince Frederick Charles, in order to secure a favourable position in which to accept this probable attack, resolved immediately to move his army forward beyond Höritz, and sent orders to General Von Bittenfeld to advance with the army of the Elbe to Neu Bidsow, and be prepared thence to fall upon the left wing of the Austrian column of advance, while he himself assailed its leading divisions; At the same time he sent Lieutenant Von Normand with a letter to the crown prince, asking him to push forward in the morning from Miletin with one corps, and attack the right flank of the Austrians while he himself engaged them in front.

There was some fear that the Austrian cavalry patrols and detachments which were prowling about would intercept the *aide-de-camp* and stop the letter, but Von Normand succeeded in avoiding them, and got safely to the crown prince's headquarters at one o'clock on the morning of the 3rd, and rejoined Prince Frederick Charles at four to report the success of his mission, and to bring to the leader of the First Army an assurance of the co-operation of the Second. Had this *aide-de-ca*mp been taken prisoner or killed on his way to Miletin, his loss would have probably influenced the whole campaign, for on that letter depended in a great measure the issue of the battle.

The commander of the First Army sent at the same time his chief of the staff. General Von Voigt Rhetz, to acquaint the king at Gitschin with the steps he was prepared to take, and to solicit his approval of them. The king expressed his entire approbation of the plan of Prince Frederick Charles, and sent an officer of his own staff to order the crown prince to advance in the morning against the Austrian right, not with one corps alone, but with all his available forces. An officer of the king's staff was also sent to General Herwarth von Bittenfeld, with an endorsement of the order already signed by Prince Frederick Charles.

Long before midnight the troops were all in motion, and at half-past one in the morning the general staff left Kammenitz. The moon occasionally shone out brightly, but was generally hidden behind clouds, and then could be distinctly seen the decaying bivouac fires in the places which had been occupied by the troops along the road. These fires looked like large will-o'-the-wisps as their flames flickered about in the wind, and stretched for many a mile, for there were 100,000 soldiers with the First Army alone, and the bivouacs of so great a force spread over a wide extent of country. Day gradually began to break, but with the first symptoms of dawn a drizzling rain came on, which lasted until late in the afternoon. The wind increased and blew coldly upon the soldiers, for they were short of both sleep and food, while frequent gusts bore down to the ground the water-laden corn in the wide fields alongside the way.

The main road from Höritz to Königgrätz sinks into a deep hollow near the village of Milowitz. On the side of this hollow furthest from Höritz, is placed near the road the village of that name, and on the left of the road, on the same bank, stands a thick fir wood. A little after midnight the army of Prince Frederick Charles was entirely concealed in this hollow, ready to issue from its ambush and attack the Austrians if they should advance.[3] Soon after dawn, a person standing between the village of Milowitz and the further hill of Dub could see no armed men, except a few Prussian *vedettes* posted along the Dub ridge, whose lances stood in relief above the summit, against the murky sky. A few dismounted officers were standing below a fruit-tree in front of Milowitz, with their horses held by some orderlies behind them. These were Prince Frederick Charles and his staff. All was still, except when the neigh of a horse, or a loud word of command as the last divisions formed, rose mysteriously from the hollow of Milowitz.

Until nearly four o'clock the army remained concealed. No Austrian scouts came pricking over the hill of Dub, no enemy's skirmishers were detected in the corn by the side of the high road. Prince Frederick Charles began to fear that the Austrian commander meant to slip away from the encounter, and to steal behind the Elbe, where his right flank would be covered by Josephstadt, from the assault of the Army of Silesia.

To hold the Austrian Army in front of the Elbe was absolutely necessary for the success of the Prussian plans, and Prince Frederick Charles resolved, with his own army alone, to engage the whole of Benedek's forces, and clinging to the Austrian commander, to hold him on the Bistritz until the Prussian flank attacks could be developed. A few short words passed from the commander of the First Army to the chief of his staff; a few *aides-de-camp*, mounting silently, rode quietly away; and, as it were by the utterance of a magician's spell, one hundred thousand Prussian warriors springing into sight as if from the bowels of the armed earth, swept over the southern edge of the Milowitz ravine, towards the hill of Dub.

The head of the eighth division was on the main road to Königgrätz, while the third and fourth divisions spread through the corn lands on its right The fifth and sixth divisions followed the eighth in reserve. A brigade of cavalry served on the left of the eighth division

3. The eighth division and cavalry, with the fifth and sixth divisions in rear, were on the left of the road, while the third and fourth divisions were behind the villages of Bristau and Stracow respectively, in the same hollow.

to connect the main army with the seventh division under Franzecky, which had been sent straight from Miletin to Cerekwitz, in order to cover the left flank of the First Army.

About four o'clock in the morning of the 3rd July, the army began to advance, and marched slowly up the gentle hill which leads from Milowitz to the village of Dub, two miles nearer Königgrätz. The corn lay heavy and tangled from the rain, upon the ground; the skirmishers pushed through it nimbly, but the battalions which followed behind in crowded columns toiled heavily through the down-beaten crops, and the artillery horses had to strain hard on their traces to get the wheels of the gun-carriages through the sticky soil. At six the whole army was close up to Dub, but it was not allowed to go upon the summit of the slope, for the ridge on which Dub stands had hidden all its motions, and the Austrians could see nothing of the troops collected behind the crest. Perhaps they thought that no Prussians were near them, except ordinary advanced posts; for the cavalry *vedettes* which had been pushed forward thus far over night remained on the top of the ridge, as if nothing were going on behind them.

From the top of the slight elevation on which the village of Dub stands, the ground slopes gently down to the River Bistritz, which the road crosses at the village of Sadowa, a mile and a quarter from Dub. From Sadowa the ground again rises beyond the Bistritz, and to the little village of Chlum, conspicuous by its church tower standing at the top of the gentle hill, a mile and a half beyond Sadowa. A person standing that morning on the top of the ridge saw Sadowa below him, built of wooden cottages, surrounded by orchards, and could distinguish among its houses several water-mills, but these were not at work, for all the inhabitants of the village had been sent away, and a white coat here and there among the cottages was not a peasant's blouse, but was the uniform of an Austrian soldier; three quarters of a mile down the Bistritz a big red-brick house, with a high brick chimney near it, looked like a manufactory, and some large wooden buildings alongside it were unmistakeably warehouses; close to these a few wooden cottages, probably meant for the workmen employed at the manufactory, completed the village of Dohalitz.

A little more than three quarters of a mile still further down the Bistritz stood the village of Mokrovous,—like most Bohemian country villages, built of pine-wood cottages enclustered in orchard trees. The *château* of Dohalicka stands midway between Dohalitz and Mokrovous, on a knoll overhanging the river. Behind Dohalitz, and

251

between that village and the high-road which runs through Sadowa, there lies a large thick wood; many of the trees had been cut down about ten feet above the ground, and the cut down branches had been twisted together between the standing trunks of the trees which were nearest to the river, to make an entrance into the wood from the front extremely difficult.

On the open slope between Dohalitz and Dohalicka along the ground there seemed to run a dark dotted line of stumpy bushes, but the telescope showed that these were guns, and that this battery alone contained about sixty pieces. Four miles down the Bistritz, from Sadowa could be seen the house-tops of Nechanitz, above which rose the dark fir-woods that clustered round the castle of Hradek. Looking to the left, up the course of the Bistritz, the ground was open between the orchards of Sadowa and the trees which grow round Benatek, a little village about two miles above Sadowa, except where, midway between these villages, a broad belt of fir-wood runs for three-quarters of a mile. Above and beyond these villages and woods on the course of the river, the spire of Chlum was seen; below it a few houses, gardens, and patches of fir-wood; and a little to the left, rather down the hill, the cottages of the hamlet of Cistowes, and on the side of the main road the orchards, and the house-tops of Lipa.

On the extreme left, at the foot of the hills, lay the larger village of Horenowes, above which stood on the bare plateau what appeared to be a large single tree.[4]

The air was thick and hazy, the rain came down steadily, and the wind blew bitterly cold, while the infantry and artillery were waiting behind the brow of the hill near Dub. At seven o'clock Prince Frederick Charles pushed forward some of his cavalry and horse artillery. They moved down the slope towards the Bistritz at a gentle trot, slipping about on the greasy ground, but keeping most beautiful lines; the lance flags of the Uhlans, wet with the rain, flapping heavily against the staves. At the bottom of the hill the trumpets sounded, and in making their movements to gain the bridge the squadrons began wheeling and hovering about the side of the river, as if they courted the fire of the enemy. Then the Austrian guns opened upon them from a battery placed in a field near the village at which the main road crosses the Bistritz, and the Battle of Königgrätz began.

Feldzeugmeister Benedek had drawn up the Austrian Army to ac-

---

4. The supposed solitary tree was in reality two trees, but was taken to be one by both Prussian armies, and from the fortress of Königgrätz.

cept battle in this position seen from the Dub hill. His centre lay in front of Chlum, where the hills attain their greatest height; in his front was the marshy stream of the Bistritz. Batteries had been thrown up in some positions favourable for bringing a heavy artillery fire to bear against his assailants, and the ranges of different distances from these batteries marked by poles and barked trees.

Little was spared to bring the artillery, the best arm of the Austrian service, into action with every advantage.[5] The villages were also barricaded and prepared with abattis for infantry defence, but not sufficiently. The right flank of the Austrian position was covered to a certain extent by the Trotina brook, which flows through a deep marshy ravine into the Elbe, but little had been done by the engineer to aid in opposing the passage of this naturally strong feature. The left wing was supported by the wood and castle of Hradek, while the left centre was strengthened by possession of the villages of Problus and Prim. Feldzeugmeister Benedek had formed his army in the following order of battle:—

The Saxons on the left wing held Problus, with an advanced guard in Nechanitz; in rear of them stood the eighth corps, the first light cavalry division, and the second division of reserve cavalry at Prim.

In the centre, the tenth corps was posted round Langenhof, the third corps round Cistowes, and the fourth corps at Maslowed, with a detachment in Benatek.

On the right wing, the second corps and the second division of light cavalry were at Sendrasctz, while on the extreme right flank the *Schwarz-gelb* brigade held the Trotina.

As reserves, the first corps was posted on the left of the main road near Rosnitz, the sixth corps on the right of the road on the south of Rosberitz; in rear of these were the first and third divisions of reserve cavalry.

The first shot was fired about half-past seven. The Prussian horse artillery, close down to the river, replied to the Austrian guns, but neither side fired heavily, and for half an hour the cannonade consisted of but little more than single shots. At a quarter before eight the King of Prussia arrived on the field, and very soon after the horse artillery were reinforced by other field batteries, and the Prussian gunners be-

---

5. The great loss of Austrian guns was due to the horses and limbers being sent under cover of the hill out of fire. When the Prussians advanced only the lightest guns could be saved, and nearly one third of the Austrian pieces engaged fell into the hands of the victors.

gan firing their shells quickly into the Austrian position. As soon as the Prussian fire actively commenced Austrian guns seemed to appear, as if by magic, in every point of the position; from every road, from every village, from the orchard of Mokrovous, on the Prussian right, to the orchard of Benatek, on their left, came flashes of fire and whizzing rifle shells, which, bursting with a sharp crack, sent their splinters rattling among the guns, gunners, carriages, and horses, often killing a man or horse, sometimes dismounting a gun, but always ploughing up the earth, and scattering the mud in the men's faces.

But the Austrians did not confine themselves to firing on the artillery alone, for they threw their shells up the slope opposite to them towards Dub, and one shell came slap into a squadron of Uhlans, who were close beside the king; burying itself with a heavy thud in the ground, it blew up columns of mud some twenty feet in the air, and, bursting a moment after, reduced the squadron by four files.

As soon as the cannonade in front became serious, the guns of the seventh division began to bombard the village of Benatek, on the Austrian right. The Austrians returned shot for shot, and neither side either gained or lost ground. In the centre, too, the battle was very even; the Prussians pushed battery after battery into the action, and kept up a tremendous fire on the Austrian guns, but these returned it, and sometimes with interest, for the Austrian artillery officers knew their ground, and every shell fell true; many officers and men fell, and many horses were killed or wounded. More *krankenträgers* were sent down to the batteries, and always returned carrying on stretchers men whose wounds had been hastily bound up under fire, but who seemed to be too much stunned to suffer much from pain.

Gradually the Prussian cannonade appeared to get stronger, and the Austrian batteries between Dohalitz and Dohalicka retired higher up the hill, but the guns at Mokrovous still stood fast, and the Prussians had not yet crossed the Bistritz; many guns were now turned on Mokrovous, and at ten o'clock the battery there was also obliged to retire a little.

While this cannonade had been going on, some of the infantry had been moved down towards the river, where they took shelter from the fire under a convenient undulation of ground.

The eighth division came down on the left-hand side of the causeway, and, under the cover of the rising in the ground, formed its columns for the attack of the village of Sadowa; while the third and fourth divisions, on the right-hand side of the road prepared to storm

Dohalitz and Mokrovous. A little before their preparations were complete the village of Benatek, on the Austrians' right, caught fire, and the seventh division made a dash to secure it, but the Austrians were not driven out by the flames, and here for the first time in the battle was there hand-to-hand fighting. The 27th regiment led the attack, and rushed into the orchards of the village; the burning houses separated the combatants; they poured volley after volley at each other through the flames; but the Prussians found means to get round the burning houses, and, taking the defenders in reverse, forced them to retire with the loss of many prisoners.

It was ten o'clock when Prince Frederick Charles sent General Stülpnagel to order the attack on Sadowa, Dohalitz, and Mokrovous. The columns advanced covered by skirmishers, and reached the river bank without much loss, but from there they had to fight every inch of their way. The Austrian infantry held the bridges and villages in force, and fired fast upon them as they approached. The Prussians could advance but slowly along the narrow ways and against the defences of the houses, and the volleys sweeping through the ranks seemed to tear the soldiers down. The Prussians fired much more quickly than their opponents, but they could not see to take their aim; the houses, trees, and smoke from the Austrian discharges shrouded the villages.

Sheltered by these, the Austrian *Jägers* fired blindly where they could tell by hearing that the attacking columns were, and the shots told tremendously on the Prussians in their close formations; but the latter improved their positions, although slowly, and by dint of sheer courage and perseverance, for they lost men at every yard of their advance, and in some places almost paved the way with wounded. Then, to help the infantry, the Prussian artillery turned its fire, regardless of the enemy's batteries, on the villages, and made tremendous havoc among the houses. Mokrovous and Dohalitz both caught fire, and the shells fell quickly and with fearful effect among the defenders of the flaming hamlets; the Austrian guns also played upon the attacking infantry, but at this time these were sheltered from their fire by the houses and trees between.

In and around the villages the fighting continued for nearly an hour; then the Austrian infantry, who had been there, driven out by a rush of the Prussians, retired, but only a little way up the slope into a line with their batteries. The wood above Sadowa was strongly held, and that between Sadowa and Benatek, teeming with riflemen, stood to bar the way of the seventh division. But General Franzecky, who commanded this division, was not to be easily stopped, and he sent his infantry at the wood, and turned his artillery on the Austrian batteries. The seventh division began firing into the trees, but found they could not make any impression, for the defenders were concealed, and musketry fire was useless against them. Franzecky let them go, and they dashed in with the bayonet.

The Austrians would not retire, but waited for the struggle, and in the wood above Benatek was fought out one of the fiercest combats which the war has seen. But the wood was carried. The Austrian line of advanced posts was now driven in on the Bistritz, but its commander had formed his main line of battle a little higher up the hill, round Lipa, still holding the wood which lies above Sadowa.

Then the Prussian artillery was sent across the Bistritz, and began to fire upon the new Austrian position. At the same time the smoke of General Herwarth's advance was gradually seen moving towards the Austrian left. He had at Nechanitz found the brigade of Saxon troops which formed the advanced front of the corps at Problus, with some Austrian cavalry, and was driving them towards Problus and Prim, himself following in such a direction that it appeared he would turn the Austrian left flank. But the Austrian commander seemed determined to hold his position, and heavy masses of infantry and cavalry could be seen on the upper part of the slope.

By eleven o'clock the eighth division of the Prussian infantry had taken the village of Sadowa, the fourth that of Dohalitz, and the third that of Dohalicka. The eighth division was now sent against the wood, which, above these places, runs along the side of the Sadowa and Lipa road, while the third and fourth divisions attempted to bear the battle up the hill towards Lipa, and to attack the left flank of the wood. The Prussians advanced against the nearest trees, but did not at first make much impression, for the Austrians being here again concealed, the fire of the needle-gun did not tell, and a whole battery placed at the far end of the wood fired through the trees, and told on their ranks with awful effect.

But the assailants fought on, at last broke down the obstacles at the entrance, and then dashed in. The fighting continued from tree to tree, and the Austrians made many a rush to recover the lost position of the wood, but in this close fighting their boyish troops went down easily before the strong men of the eighth division; but when the defenders drew back a little, and their artillery played into the trees, the Prussians suffered fearfully, and about halfway up in the wood the fight became stationary.

For two hours more it continued so; in vain Horne, who commanded the eighth division, strove to push along the road or through the trees to storm the battery beyond. The fire was too terrible, and his men became gradually exhausted.

A few minutes after the Prussians had occupied the villages along the Bistritz, Feldzeugmeister Benedek was informed that the sixth Prussian corps belonging to the army of the crown prince was threatening his right flank. He sent orders that this attack should be checked or detained, and appears to have calculated that the crown prince could be held in check until he had time to inflict a severe blow upon the army of Prince Frederick Charles. With this aim he made his preparations for a counter-attack between Problus and Lipa, which was to be made as soon as his artillery had shaken the Prussian line sufficiently. Sixty-four guns were stationed between Lipa and Streselitz to fire on the third and fourth Prussian division, and some of the reserves of cavalry and infantry were moved up to positions favourable for making the counter-attack.

At this time the Austrian artillery were making splendid practice, and about one o'clock, the whole battle line of the Prussians could gain no more ground, and was obliged to fight hard to retain the position it had won. At one time it seemed as if it would be lost, for guns had been dismounted by the Austrian fire, and in the wooded ground the needle-gun had no fair field, and the infantry fight was very equal.

Then Prince Frederick Charles sent the fifth and sixth divisions forward. They laid down their helmets and knapsacks on the ground, and advanced to the river. The king was now near to the Bistritz, and the troops cheered him loudly as they marched into the battle. They went over the Sadowa bridge, disappeared into the wood, and soon the increased noise of the musketry told they had begun to fight; but the Austrian gunners sent salvo after salvo among them, and they did not push the battle forwards more than a few hundred yards, for they fell back themselves, and they could not reach the enemy. Not only did the fragments of the shells fly about among them, scattering death and awful gashes among their ranks, but the portions of the trees, torn by the artillery fire, flew thickly about, huge ragged splinters that caused even more frightful wounds.

Herwarth, too, was checked upon the right The smoke of his musketry and artillery, which had hitherto been pushing forward steadily, stood still.

He had marched with his three divisions from Smidar to Nechanitz, and had made himself master of this village at the same time as the divisions of Prince Frederick Charles had occupied the hamlets further up the Bistritz. The Saxon artillery withdrew to the heights by Problus and Prim, and to an intrenchment beside the Hradek wood. Then here also the battle came to a standstill. It required a long time to bring the artillery over the Bistritz, for the Saxons had broken the bridge at Nechanitz, no ford could be found, and the banks of the river were too marshy to allow of the guns being dragged through the stream.

About one o'clock Herwarth's pioneers had repaired the bridge, and his artillery had been brought across the river. He then directed the fourteenth division, commanded by General Münster, against Problus through Lubno as his left wing. In his centre he sent the fifteenth division, under General Canstein, against Prim, while the sixteenth division, under General Etzel, made a wide sweep to the right, in order to turn the left of the Austrian position at the Castle of Hradek. Problus and Prim were strengthened with barricades and abattis. The Saxons and the eighth Austrian corps fought nobly. A hot battle ensued here, which lasted till past three o'clock.

Affairs did not apparently go more favourably for the Prussians in the centre. The whole of the First Army was severely engaged, with the exception of eight batteries of artillery and the cavalry which was still held in reserve. The reserve artillery of Prince Frederick Charles was sent a little distance up the Bistritz, in order to bring a fire against the flank of the Sadowa wood, to search out the defenders, and if possible to dismount the guns in the batteries in front of Lipa. But, notwithstanding, the Austrians clung obstinately to the trees.

Franzecky's men, cut to pieces, could not be sent forward to attack the Sadowa wood, for they would have exposed themselves to be taken in rear by the artillery on the right of the Austrian line formed in front of Lipa. The First Army was certainly checked in its advance. The Prussian commanders began to look anxiously to the left for the coming of the crown prince. Some Austrian guns near Lipa were seen to be firing towards the Prussian left, and it was hoped they might be directed against the advanced guard of the Second Army, but at three o'clock there were no signs of Prussian columns advancing against Lipa. The generals became manifestly uneasy, and they drew Horne's division out of the Sadowa wood. Cavalry was also formed up, so that it would be available either for the pursuit of the Austrians, or for retarding their pursuit

When Prince Frederick Charles sent the night before the battle to request the co-operation of the crown prince, the latter sent back an answer that he would be on the field at two o'clock. More than faithful to hi» promise, he was there with two corps at half-past twelve, and his artillery was engaged with the batteries on the Austrian right at that hour. But the fire from the Austrian batteries was so terrible that he could not attack with his infantry till something had been done towards silencing the enemy's guns. The generals directing the first attack could see nothing of the crown prince's infantry, as they were hidden in the undulations of the ground. The *aide-de-camp* despatched from the Second Army to tell the king that the crown prince was engaged had to make a long detour, and did not reach the generals directing the front attack till late in the afternoon.

Hence arose great uneasiness in the front, for from the direction of the Austrian guns they might have been firing against the seventh division, which formed the left of the front attack, and as nothing could be seen of the crown prince's troops it began to be feared that he had been stopped by some accident As time went on anxiety increased, for it was felt that the Austrian position was too strong to be taken by a front attack alone. Glasses were anxiously directed to the left, but the day being wet there was no dust to show where columns marched, and nothing could be seen to indicate the advance of the Second Army against the Austrian right. The king himself gazed steadfastly through his glass, looking in vain through the misty air. No glimpse could be caught of Prussian riflemen on the slope to the left of Lipa, and no battalions could be seen; the guns also were out of sight, for they were on the reverse side of the Lipa ridge, or were hidden from the position of the staff by the wood that runs from Benatek up the slope towards Lipa.

The anxiety of the Prussian generals at Sadowa was, however, groundless. While they were still unaware that the crown prince was upon the field of battle, some of his soldiers were already in the very heart of the Austrians' position, and holding their ground against repeated attempts by superior numbers to dislodge them.

Advance of the Crown Prince.—On receiving the request from Prince Frederick Charles to move against the Austrians' right, and the subsequent order from the king to the same effect, the crown prince issued orders to the troops to march early on the 3rd July. His orders were not sent out till nearly five in the morning, but before seven the heads of his columns had begun to move. On his left wing the sixth corps crossed the Elbe above Jaromir, and marched in two columns towards the Trotinka.

The twelfth division, under General Proudzinsky, which moved down the Elbe close to the river, was fired upon by the fortress of Josephstadt, and had to leave one brigade to observe the garrison of that place. On the right wing the first corps, followed by the cavalry division, was ordered to march in two columns by Zabres and Grosz-Trotin to Grosz-Bürglitz. In the centre, the corps of the Guards was to move from Königinhof on Jericek and Lhota. The fifth corps was to follow the sixth corps as a reserve, and to march two hours later from the Elbe to Choteborek. All baggage and train were to be left behind.

The crown prince knew nothing of the Austrian position. Where he should find the Austrian flank, in what force, and how defended, were questions which he and his chief of the staff could only answer on the actual field of battle, and on the spur of the moment. The rain had already fallen heavily for some time when the Second Army commenced its march. The crown prince witnessed the passage of the Elbe at Königinhof by a portion of the Guards, and then hastened forward with his staff to place himself at the head of the column. The steep roads leading up the high bank of the valley of the Elbe to the plateau of Daubrowitz, slippery and heavy with the rain, tried severely the strength of both men and horses.

Directly after passing Daubrowitz the commander-in-chief of the Second Army saw from smoke arising from a cannonade, and from burning houses in the direction of Sadowa, that the First Army was already engaged. The wind was blowing towards the battle, so that he could not hear the cannonade, and could not tell in which direction it was moving. He directed the head of his column upon Choteborek. The view extended with every step forward, and it soon became apparent that a great battle was being waged. At a quarter-past eleven the crown prince had reached the chain of hills to the west of Choteborek with the first division of the corps of the Guards close behind him.

In front of Choteborek the ground formed a low trough about two miles wide, in which there were many soft and marshy places. Beyond this trough lay the hill of Horenowes, conspicuous with its single tree, and at its foot the village of that name. Beyond this hill the view was shut out, but on its western side the eye could range clearly down the valley of the Bistritz, where it was easy to distinguish the situations of the antagonistic lines of battle by the smoke of a great number of batteries in action, and by the flames of several burning villages. It could be seen that the seventh division, which formed the left wing of the First Army, was fighting an unequal battle in front of Benatek, and was already in need of support.

Towards Grosz-Bürglitz and Welchow, where the two wings of the Second Army were to debouch, heavy woods shut out the view. It was certain, however, that if these two corps, in execution of the orders which had been given them, had reached those places, the further march of the Second Army would conduct it against the right flank and partly into the rear of the enemy's position. Already the army of the crown prince occupied a similar position with regard to the First Army, as that of Blücher to the British line on the day of Waterloo.

The crown prince despatched officers to ascertain the real positions of the first and sixth corps. Hardly had they left his side when a report came in from General Von Mutius with the intelligence that the sixth corps had already reached Welchow, and in consequence of the heavy cannonade he had ordered it to push on in the direction of the firing. It was this advance which, reported to Benedek, was his first intimation of the advent of the crown prince, and which he ordered to be held in check by his second corps. Fortune had ordained that the sixth corps should have been casually prepared to advance, because, in consequence of the order which it had received to make a reconnaissance against Josephstadt, it had already crossed the Elbe when the second order for an advance beyond Josephstadt reached it.

In a short time the fifth corps was also reported by General Steinmetz to be approaching Choteborek. No news had come in from the first corps, but it was known that on account of its longer march its arrival could hardly yet be expected.

The crown prince determined, with the first division of the Guards, which he held available, to seize the hill of Horenowes. In order to do so, he was obliged to advance across the marshy hollow, where his troops would be exposed, without any cover, to the fire of the Austrian guns, which would have plenty of time to collect on the hill in large quantities while the Prussians were traversing the low ground. To save his men as much as possible, the regiments were ordered to spread out and to march singly on the Horenowes hill, where their chief pointed out the conspicuous trees as their goal.

It was a remarkable circumstance that the columns of the Guards could descry no Austrian patrols or outposts to oppose their path. One battery of artillery alone could be seen upon the Horenowes hill. It was clear that the advance of the Guards would turn the line of Austrian guns, which, posted between Horenowes and Maslowed, were playing on Franzecky, and would take some pressure off his struggling division. As the Guards advanced, these guns were seen to change their position, and at half-past eleven forty Austrian pieces were ranged beside the single tree, to fire against the advancing columns of the Second Army. At ten minutes to twelve the first shell was discharged from these batteries against the Prussian Guards.

The advanced guard of the first division of the Prussian Guards, under General Alvensleben, had bivouacked the previous night at Daubrowitz. It had pushed on in the morning by Burglitz and Zizelowes, and had debouched from the latter place in the direction of Horenowes, at a quarter-past eleven. A quarter of an hour later, five 4-pounder batteries of the Guard opened fire against an Austrian battery, and compelled it to quit its position between Horenowes and Benatek. A 6-pounder Prussian battery at the same time opened upon the Austrian artillery, which was beginning to form on the east of Horenowes, while the infantry advanced by Wrchwitz, for the attack of that village. The other troops of the division followed up this attack by way of Jericek.

The second division of the Guard had lain the previous night at Rettendorf, considerably in rear of the first division. Its march had been consequently delayed, and the reserve artillery of the Guard corps, as well as the heavy cavalry of the Guard, arrived at the scene of action before this division. Its direction was by Choteborek to Lhota.

At eleven o'clock the reserve artillery of the Guard was marching on the left rear of the first division. The ground heavy with rain, and the high corn which wound itself round the wheels of the guns, tired the horses excessively. In front of Jericek, six batteries opened fire, to signal by their noise to the First Army that the crown prince was near at hand. But this salvo was not distinguished by the staff of Prince Frederick Charles amidst the general din of battle, and, as the range was very great, little harm was done to the Austrians by i.t

By the time that General Alvensleben advanced against Horenowes, the sixth corps had, on the left, commenced an assault against Racicz. Of this corps, one brigade of the twelfth division, consisting of six battalions, four squadrons, and two batteries, under General Proudzynski, led the way by Roznow and Nesnasow. When the eleventh division, consisting of twelve battalions, eight squadrons, and four batteries, under General Zastrow, reached Welchow, the former had only encountered a few detachments of Austrian cavalry. General Mutius then ordered it to keep the enemy in sight, and in its further advance to communicate with the eleventh division, which he directed against the heights of Horenowes.

A report was now brought to that general that it was urgently desirable that he should send some artillery as quickly as possible to support Franzecky's division. Four batteries immediately pushed forward at a trot, covered by the 4th regiment of Hussars, crossed the Trotinka at Luzan, and at half-past eleven opened upon the Austrian artillery stationed on the east of Horenowes. The two brigades of the eleventh division in the meantime advanced in *échelon*, left in front, and supported by the 8th Dragoons crossed the Trotinka with great difficulty to the south-east of Luzan, and advanced under a heavy artillery fire to the attack of Racicz.

The twelfth division directed its march against Smiritz by Roznow, while a squadron of its cavalry regiment, which had been pushed forward in the direction of Smiritz, reported that there were Austrian regiments of cavalry in its front.

On the approach of the first division of the Guard to Horenowes, and of the eleventh division to Racicz, and when both wings of the position of their artillery began to be threatened, the Austrians commenced evacuating their position, and had entirely withdrawn from it by one o'clock. By the same hour the villages of Horenowes and Racicz fell into the hands of their assailants, after short contests. The greater portion of the troops which had garrisoned these places retired in the direction of Sendrasitz, while the first division of the Guard pressed forward to the trees on the east of Horenowes, and the eleventh division pressed upon the retreating Austrians on the south of Racicz.

The small resistance which the army of the crown prince here met with appears to be due to the fact that when General Franzecky carried the village of Benatek, the Austrian fourth corps moved forward to oppose him, drove the battle back, and remained engaged with his division in the Maslowed wood. The Austrian second corps was thus alone exposed to the onset of the whole of the crown prince's army, and was pushed back by its attack to Sendrasitz. These two Austrian movements caused a gap in Benedek's line of battle, through which the Prussian Guards penetrating, seized Chlum, the key of his position, and turned the fortune of the day.

On the advance of the Prussian Guards to Horenowes some Austrian battalions took up a position on the hill east of Maslowed. The Guards immediately marched against this hill, and carried it without meeting with any serious resistance. The village of Maslowed, which lay to their right, was evacuated, and half a company of Prussian riflemen occupied it without drawing a trigger. The sixth corps in the meantime engaged the main body of the second Austrian corps, which had furnished the garrisons for Horenowes and Racicz, at Trotina, Sendrasitz, and Nedelitz, and finally forced it to withdraw across the Elbe at Lochenitz. By this contest, which was of quite an independent nature, the left wing of the Prussian Guard was covered while it took the direction of the village of Chlum, guided by the church tower, which forms the highest landmark in the field.

In this way the Prussian Guard marched a distance of about two thousand paces along the rear of the position of the fourth Austrian corps, which was now being pushed back by Franzecky in the Maslowed wood. An Austrian brigade showed itself between Maslowed and Lipa, the Prussian advanced guard formed up to its own right and attacked it; while the main body, under Colonel Von Obernitz, pushed on to Chlum, and the fusilier regiment, under Colonel Von Kessel, threw itself into Rosberitz.

The first Prussians who arrived in Chlum saw on the reverse side of the hill, between themselves and the fortress of Königgratz, the whole of the Austrian reserves, mustering about 40,000 men. Between them and their comrades of the First Army were the Austrian corps engaged near Lipa, and in the Sadowa wood. Twelve battalions of the Prussian Guards was the whole force at hand to hold the key of the battle against the whole reserve of the enemy.

A fierce battle soon began round Rosberitz and Chlum, which were seized by the Prussian Guard at a quarter before three o'clock. At five minutes before three an *aide-de-camp* reported to Feldzeugmeister Benedek, who was between Chlum and Lipa, that the Prussians had occupied the former village. The Austrian commander could not credit this unexpected intelligence, and hastened himself in person to ascertain its truth. On approaching Chlum he was received by a withering volley, which told with severe effect upon his staff, and convinced him of the veracity of the report He immediately hastened to send up some reserves to retake the place.

About three o'clock the Army of the Elbe carried Problus, and Feldzeugmeister Benedek was obliged to send two brigades of the nearest Austrian corps, the first, to reinforce his front while he directed one brigade against Chlum, and one against Problus. At the same time the Saxon artillery of the reserve, which was on the further side of the highway from Rosberitz, opened with terrible effect on the Prussians in that village, and prepared the way for an attack by the sixth Austrian corps.

The position of the Prussian Guard became every moment more critical. The few battalions in Rosberitz could not hold their ground, and were driven out of the village, having lost among other officers Prince Anton of Hohenzollern. The reserve artillery of the Prussian Guard under the Prince of Hohenlohe laboured up to the aid of the battalions in Chlum, and, coming into action, smote heavily upon the thick masses of the Austrian reserves which were preparing to attack the houses. Three times they attacked, twice they almost reached the orchard and churchyard, but were received at a few paces distance by such a volley from the needle-guns that nearly the whole of the attacking force was either killed or wounded.

By the time of the third attack the advanced guard of the reserve division of the Prussian Guard had come up to the support of the battalions who were already in occupation. The third attack was repulsed, and at the same moment the battle was won. The first Prussian corps and the fifth corps, with the cavalry of the Second Army, was pressing up towards Chlum and Rosberitz, bringing a reserve of 50,000 fresh soldiers into the heart of Benedek's position; while the main body of the second division of the Guards dashed against the wood of Lipa, and the batteries of Chlum.

As yet the Prussian generals at Sadowa were in ignorance of the progress of the crown prince, for his other divisions were on the reverse side of the hill of Chlum, and the attack of the second division of the Guard could alone be seen from the front. First a swarm of black dots stealing across the fields showed the advance of the skirmishers, and the Austrian sharpshooters, who had been lying among the corn, could be seen running before them to gain the shelter of their own lines; close behind the skirmishers followed the heavy columns of infantry, looking like small black squares gliding along the sides of the hill. The Austrian guns played sharply on them, but they pushed forward without wavering till within a short distance of the batteries; then a few rapid volleys of musketry sent up a cloud of smoke, which, hanging heavily in the misty air, shut out the view; but the sudden silence of the Austrian guns told that the Prussians had closed, and that the batteries had been stormed.

The ground leading up to them was steep, and the gunners sent round after round into the storming columns, till the leading ranks were close to the muzzles of the guns; the riflemen who were ensconced in intrenchments beside the batteries, to defend them, sent biting volleys into their assailants; but, caring nought for the fire of the infantry or the steepness of the ground, the Prussians dashed straight at the guns, and both gunners and sharpshooters had to turn and fly. Then the deadly needle-gun opened its fire on the fugitives, and with such precision that the ground was covered with dead or wounded Austrians lying thick together. In one place forty corpses lay on less than an acre of ground, and the wounded appeared to be to the dead as three to one.

The Austrian defeat was now inevitable. As soon as the crown prince sent his infantry against the Lipa wood, the First Army sprang forward, and, with loud cheers and drums beating, went dashing up the hill. The Sadowa road was cleared as if by magic, and the battalions went straight against the Austrian batteries. No heed was given to take the guns in flank; the soldiers felt certain of victory, and sought it by the shortest road. Though disordered by the broken ground, and out of breath with the rapid ascent, so quickly did they advance that the Austrian gunners had no time to limber up, but were forced to desert their pieces and seek safety for themselves and their horses in flight. Most of the guns which had been placed in batteries were taken, but those which acted as field artillery, admirably handled, were quickly withdrawn, and were already fast forming on a further ridge by Rosnitz to cover the retreat of the infantry.

The Prussians paused but a few moments among the taken guns and then rushed on in pursuit The summit of the ridge was quickly gained, and there before them they saw the whole hollow ground between them and Rosnitz filled with running white uniforms. The victorious battalions commenced a rapid fire upon them, and men dropped quickly from the flying ranks, rolling over and over as they fell on the sloping ground. The sixth corps, which the crown prince had directed more against the Austrian rear, caught the fugitives in flank, and raked the running ranks with their fire. The Prussian artillery was also quickly up, unlimbered, and came into action on the summit of the ridge, and sent its shells bursting with a horrible precision among the heads of the flying soldiers. And yet the Austrians kept their formation, and never let their retreat become a rout. Such a retreat under such circumstances is as creditable to the valour of the Austrian soldiers as a battle won.

The Prussian cavalry, unable to leave the road till it got to nearly the top of the hill, on account of the woods by the side of the way, was not up till the Austrian infantry had got half way across the hollow which separates Chlum from the further ridge of Rosnitz, and there the Austrian batteries had taken up their position and began to play upon the pursuing troops. Then, for a few minutes. Prince Frederick Charles, who was leading the hussars and dragoons, had to leave them to make his general dispositions for attacking the new position taken up by the Austrian artillery, and the cavalry immediately got out of hand. By single squadrons, by single troops, and even only in knots of a few horsemen, they rushed with wild impetuosity at different points of the retreating infantry; but the Austrian guns sent shells rapidly among them, and the infantry, though running, still kept its formation, and turned, when they came too close, to stand and deliver volleys which emptied many a saddle.

Nor were the Austrian cavalry off the field, though they could not face the tremendous fire of the Prussians to charge and cover the retreat of their infantry; but when attacked by the enemy's cavalry, and when thus the guns could not fire upon them, they fought hard, and sacrificed themselves to cover the retreat. Then, as the squadrons of the 3rd regiment of Prussian Dragoons were rushing forward to chaise some battalions firing near the village of Wsester, an Austrian *cuirass* brigade, led by an Englishman in the Austrian service of the name of Beales, charged them in flank. They drove the Prussians back, and, smiting them heavily with their ponderous swords, nearly destroyed the dragoons; but Hohenlohe's Prussian Uhlans, seeing their comrades worsted, charged with their lances couched against the Austrians' flank, and compelled them to retire. Pressed hard by the lancers they fell back, fighting hard, but then Ziethen's hussars charged them in the rear.

A fierce combat ensued; the Austrian horsemen struck strongly about them, fighting for their lives; but the lancers drove their lances into their horses, while the hussars, light and active, closed in upon them, and only ten Austrians are reported to have escaped unwounded from the *mêlée*. Beales himself was borne wounded to the ground. But the Austrian artillery was not long able to hold its new position;

the fire of the Prussian guns and the dispositions which were being made to attack it compelled it to retire. It then drew off slowly, but on every successive ridge came into action, and fired against the pursuers to check them, and gain for its own infantry time for retreat. Some Prussian horse artillery and cavalry followed it, and till after nightfall the pursuit went thundering towards the Elbe, and drew the fire of the heavy guns of the fortress. The Austrian cavalry retired to Pardubitz, and the remainder of the army by seven or eight bridges, thrown across the river between that place and Königgrätz, got beyond the stream by night without severe loss.

The Prussian cavalry slowly followed in pursuit along both roads. The wounded who were lying on the ground shrieked with fear when they saw the cavalry galloping down towards them, but Prince Frederick Charles took care that they should be avoided, and at one time checked the pursuit in order to move his squadrons around, and not go through, a patch of standing corn, where many wounded Austrians had taken refuge. These, when they saw the lancers coming, thought they were going to be massacred, and cried piteously, waving white handkerchiefs as a sign of truce; but they had no cause to fear. Large numbers of prisoners were taken, for the pursuit was continued to the Elbe, and it was not till nine o'clock that all firing had ceased, though the main body of the army halted about seven.

As the princes returned, the battalions cheered them for their victory; but they left the pursuit of their enemies and the cheers of their own victorious troops to look after the hospital accommodation provided for the wounded. These lay in immense numbers in the field; the dead too laid thick, but all they required was done on the morrow. Every cottage in the neighbourhood that had not been burnt was full of wounded. Austrians and Prussians lay side by side, but the *krankenträger* were still out, and all were not collected till late the next morning. Conspicuous in the hospitals, working diligently in their voluntary labour, were the Knights of St John of Jerusalem. This Order of Knighthood, renewed lately for the succour of the weak and suffering, had sent here a large hospital establishment, under the direction of Count Theodore Stölberg.

From the voluntary contributions of the knights, hospitals were maintained in the nearest towns and in the field, all necessary hospital stores were carried, by the Order, and means of transport accompanied the army, hospital nurses were provided, and by their aid many wounded were carefully attended to who could not have been looked after by the ordinary arrangements.

The Battle of Königgrätz was a great victory for the Prussians, though its full advantages were not known by them until the following day. One hundred and seventy-four guns, twenty thousand prisoners, and eleven standards, fell into the hands of the conquerors; the total loss of the Austrian army by the disaster of the 3rd July amounted to almost forty thousand men, while that of the Prussians was not ten thousand. The morale of the Austrian army was destroyed, and their infantry found that in open column they could not stand against the better-armed Prussians. The Austrians had hoped to be able to close with the bayonet, and so amend the effects of the fire of the needle-gun; but the idea of the superiority in the use of the bayonet in which the Austrian army prided itself, is one of those vanities which are common to every nation, and this war proved that at close quarters the stronger men of Prussia invariably overcame the lighter and smaller Austrians.

The Austrian and Saxon troops engaged amounted to about two hundred thousand men, with six hundred guns.[6] The Prussian army in the field mustered in round numbers two hundred and sixty thousand combatants, with eight hundred and sixteen guns, but of them the fifth corps, one brigade of the sixth corps, and all but the advanced guard of the first corps, in all about sixty thousand men, never fired a shot. Thus the number of casualties were about one thirteenth of the number of men actually engaged.[7]

The highest proportionate loss of the Prussian Army fell upon Franzecky's division, which lost two thousand out of a little over fourteen thousand men. The greatest loss on the Austrian side was incurred by the troops who attempted to retake Chlum, and by those who had to retire out of the Lipa and Sadowa woods after the crown prince had developed his attack. The artillery on both sides appeared to fail in causing such numerous casualties as might have been anticipated from so large a number of rifled guns. Nor did the infantry fire tell except at close quarters. Whether this was due to the inferior

6. This estimate of the Austrian force is based on an able letter written from Olmütz after the battle by the special correspondent of the *Times*, in which that writer states that Benedek had then collected one hundred and sixty thousand of the defeated army at Olmütz. This with the Austrian loss would give the above figure.
7. The following list of the proportion of casualties to combatants, in some of the most famous battles of the last two centuries, is extracted from a careful essay written for the professional papers of the Royal Engineers by Lieutenant-Colonel Cooke, R. E.

Name of Battle.	Year.	Numbers.		Killed and Wounded.	
		On each side.	Total.	Number.	Proportion to total Forces.
Malplaquet.	1709	. . . . . .	180,000	18,250 Allies.	. .
Hohen Friedberg.	1745	70,000 P. 70,000 A.	140,000	5,000 9,000	1/10
Prague . .	1757	64,000 P. 74,000 A.	138,000	16,000 8,000	1/6
Rosbach .	1757	22,000 P. 55,000 A.	77,000	500 2,800	1/23
Breslau . .	1757	25,000 P. 60,000 A.	85,000	5,000 6,286	1/8
Lissa. . .	1757	36,000 P. 80,000 A.	116,000*	5,000 6,574	1/10
Zornsdorf .	1758	32,000 P. 50,000 R.	82,000	11,385 21,531	1/4 to 1/3
Hoch Kirch	1758	50,000 A. 30,000 P.	80,000	5,000 7,000	1/7
Marengo .	1800	28,127 F. 30,850 A.	58,977†	7,000 6,800	1/4
Austerlitz .	1805	90,000 F. 80,000 R. & A.	170,000‡	12,000 11,000	1/7
Jena . . .	1806	100,000 F. 100,000 P.	200,000§	14,000 20,000	1/6
Preussic Eylau . .	1807	85,000 F. 75,000 R.	160,000	30,050 25,000	1/3
Friedland .	1807	80,000 F. 50,000 R.	130,000	10,000 17,000	1/5
Talavera .	1809	52,000 E. & S. 50,000 F.	102,000	5,928 7,200	1/8
Wagram .	1809	150,000 F. 130,000 A.	280,000	24,000	1/12
Salamanca .	1812	. . . . . .	90,000	8,000 E. 22,800 F. ‖	1/3
Borodino .	1812	125,000 F. 125,000 R.	250,000	80,000	1/3
Leipsic . .	1813	150,000 F. 280,000 Allies	430,000	50,000 ¶ not known.	. .
Vittoria . .	1813	70,000 E. &c. 27,000 F.	97,000	10,000	1/10
Waterloo .	1815	67,600 E. &c. 68,900 F.	136,500	14,000 not known.	. .
Magenta .	1859	48,090 F. & S. 61,640 A.	109,730	4,000 5,700	1/11
Solferino .	1859	135,234 F. & S. 163,124 A.	298,358**	14,415 13,020	1/11

* 21,000 Austrian prisoners missing.
† 1,000 French and 3,000 Austrian prisoners.
‡ 19,000 Austrian prisoners.
§ 20,000 Prussian prisoners.
‖ Includes missing.
¶ Includes some prisoners.
** 2,770 Allies and 9,290 Austrians missing.

shooting power of the needle-gun or to the practical disadvantage of aiming under fire seems to be uncertain.

The number of cartridges fired by the Prussian Army in the battle barely exceeded one per man on the ground. Hardly any soldier fired so many as ninety, and few more than sixty.[8] The average number of rounds fired by the artillery of Prince Frederick Charles's army, was forty-two per gun, and no gun of that army fired more than eighty rounds. In the artillery of the Guard, the thirteen batteries engaged fired one thousand seven hundred and eighty-seven rounds, being an average of twenty-three per gun; one battery fired eighty-one rounds per gun.

On the evening of the battle, an officer of the Ziethen hussars, who were forward in the pursuit, rode as far as the gates of Königgrätz, and, finding there were no sentries outside, rode in; the guard, immediately on seeing him in his Prussian uniform, turned out and seized him, when, with a ready presence, he declared he had come to demand the capitulation of the fortress. He was conducted to the commandant, and made the same demand to him, adding that the town would be bombarded if not surrendered within an hour; the commandant, unconscious that he was not dealing with a legitimate messenger, courteously refused to capitulate; but the hussar was conducted out of the town, passed through the guard at the entrance, and got off safely without being made a prisoner.

That night the Prussian Army bivouacked on the field, where the main body remained the next day in order to allow the troops time to rest after their great fatigues.

The appearance of the field of battle the next morning showed the severity of the fight. The wounded had all been removed, but few of the dead had been buried, for the number of wounded was so great that every man who could be spared from duty was required to look after them. All night long the *krankenträger* had been at work, and had been assisted by a large number of soldiers. Every village near the field of battle had all its standing houses converted into hospitals, and all the surgeons in the army had been busy all night long. In the woods and in the broken ground the bodies of Austrians and Prussians were tolerably equal in number, generally lying in groups of four or five of either nation together, marking the spot where a shell had burst; but

---

8. At the Battle of Borodino, one of the most sanguinary contests on record (see preceding page), the French are said to have fired 1,400,000 cartridges, which would be at the rate of about 10 per man.

in the open ground and down the reverse side of the Chlum hill the Austrians lay terribly thick, and hardly a Prussian uniform was to be seen.

Wherever the Austrians fought unprotected by cover, and wherever the Prussian riflemen, armed with needle-guns, could see their enemies, the disproportion of the dead became immediately apparent The corn was trodden down all over the field as flat as if it was straw laid on a stable floor, and the ground was ploughed up and dug into holes with shells.

On the top of the hill of Chlum, and near the village, stood a large number of the captured guns, with all their waggons and carriages beside them, and on the slope away from Sadowa the rest were placed under the charge of the corps of the Guard. Everywhere about the field, fatigue parties were digging large trenches in which the Austrian and Prussian killed were laid side by side, clothed in their uniforms. No other tombstone was put to mark each grave than a plain wooden cross, on which was written the number of each regiment that lay below. The officers were placed in single graves near the men. But here and there a few were seen silently carrying some comrade to a more retired spot.

On one part of the field a Prussian general with his staff was burying his son, who had fallen in the attack on the Austrian right. Close by, the wife of a private soldier who had found her husband's body on the field had had it buried by some soldiers, had hung some oak branches on the little wooden cross at the head, and was sitting on the freshly-turned earth, sobbing her heart out, with his shattered helmet in her lap. She had followed his regiment, in order to be near him, from the beginning of the campaign, through all the long marches the army had made.

The less severely wounded were moved to Höritz, from which, on the approach of the Prussians, the inhabitants had nearly all fled. The vacated houses were converted into hospitals, and at nearly every window and every door men were hanging about listlessly, with heads or arms bound up, with a half stupefied look, as if they had not yet recovered from the stunning effects of the blow which had disabled them. Many were Austrians, and prisoners of war; but the greatest liberty seemed to be accorded to them, for they were allowed to wander about the streets, and to mix freely with the Prussian soldiers.

Long columns of unwounded prisoners were being marched continually through the town on their way to the rear. The Austrians looked dejected and unhappy, yet marched stolidly and silently along; but the prisoners from the Italian regiments laughed and talked cheerily, and on them their imprisonment sat lightly.

Here and there an Austrian officer, prisoner on parole, strolled moodily about, stopping every now and then to return the courteous salutations of the Prussian officers who passed by. To ease the anxiety of their friends at home, they wrote letters to announce that they were not killed, but taken, and these were sent with a flag of truce to the Austrian lines. The greatest courtesy and kindness were shown by the Prussian officers to their unfortunate prisoners, and every attempt was made to make them feel their position as little as possible. Several Austrian officers wounded mortally on the field requested Prussian officers to send their last message to their families, requests which it is needless to say were readily complied with.

Field-Marshal Gablenz came to Höritz the day after the battle from the Austrian headquarters, to ask for an armistice as a preliminary to peace. It was impossible that Prussia could grant an armistice at this moment, when the Austrian Army was still in the field, and any pause in the operations of the campaign would be used to collect troops from the Italian frontier and from the distant provinces of the empire in order to oppose the Prussian armies. Nor could peace be concluded by Prussia without the concurrence of Italy, for a treaty existed between the Cabinets of Berlin and Florence, by which neither could make peace without the sanction of the other.

The field-marshal accordingly returned to his own lines without obtaining any result from his mission.

The actual junction of the two armies of the crown prince and of Prince Frederick Charles was effected on the battlefield of Königgrätz, and the Austrians had now lost the chance they had of falling upon each army separately.

As the consequence of the defeat of Königgrätz, Austria on the 4th July ceded Venetia to the Emperor of the French, who was nominally to hold the province, although it was virtually then, and practically in the following October, given to the kingdom of Italy.

Observations on the Battle of Königgrätz

The details of a great battle are, as a general rule, less perfectly known the more closely the time at which they are criticised approaches to the date of the action. While the men are still living on whom disclosures would draw an inconvenient censure, the govern-

273

ment of a country which has suffered a great reverse in war is naturally unwilling to gratify the curiosity of the world by the publication of information which can only be certainly found in its own official archives. Without such information it is impossible to make any observations on the causes or conduct of incidents in war with an assured certainty. It is necessary to attempt to lift the veil which shrouds such events during the lifetimes of the principal actors with only a hesitating and a faltering touch, and to acknowledge that any conclusions based upon a crude knowledge of facts are enunciated with diffidence. If correct they are fortuitous, if incorrect their fallacies will be exposed by future information.

The position taken up by Feldzeugmeister Benedek in front of Königgrätz has been severely criticised It does not, however, appear that the river in his rear was any disadvantage to him, although his army was defeated, and had its flank turned by a strong force. The Austrian commander took the precaution to throw bridges over the river. With plenty of bridges a river in rear of a position became an advantage. After the retreating army had withdrawn across the stream, the bridges were broken, and the river became an obstacle to the pursuit. Special as well as general conditions also came into play. The pursuing Prussians could not approach with impunity the heads of the Austrian bridges.

The heavy guns of the fortress scoured the banks of the river both up and down stream, and, with superior weight of metal and length of range, were able to cover the passage of the Austrians. The position was otherwise acknowledged on all sides to be a good one, carefully chosen; and though the villages were not completely barricaded and loopholed, this omission was probably due to the extreme rapidity of the movements of Prince Frederick Charles. A great disadvantage was the fact that the presence of two opponent armies acting from divergent bases against the Austrian position caused, as all such conditions always must cause, Feldzeugmeister Benedek to fight with his army drawn along two sides of an angle. One side was from Prim to Maslowed, the other from Maslowed to Lochenitz. By such a formation a defeat or even a repulse of either wing must necessarily allow the successful enemy to penetrate into the rear of the other. Or a success and advance of one or both wings must leave a gap at the salient angle.

Two questions have attracted more notice with reference to the battle than others. These are, first—Why did Benedek allow the crown prince to come down so heavily upon his right flank? and secondly, How did the first division of the Prussian Guard manage to get into Chlum unobserved? The answer to the first question appears to be that the Austrian general was deceived as to the position of the crown prince.[9] On the 30th June he knew that the crown prince was on the Elbe, because from the heights above Königinhof the Prussians were that day cannonaded by an Austrian battery. Between the 30th and the 2nd, the crown prince pushed troops across the river at Arnau and Königinhof, and directed the heads of their columns towards Miletin. On the afternoon of the 2nd, two of Prince Frederick Charles's divisions occupied Miletin. Late on the night of the 2nd, one of these divisions of Prince Frederick Charles's army was ordered to move to Milowitz, while the other moved to Cerekwitz. It seems probable that these movements were reported to Benedek by his spies, but erroneously.

It would appear that he was told that the main body of the crown prince's army had joined Frederick Charles at Miletin, and that the mass of the united armies on the night of the 2nd was moving towards its own right to make a concentrated attack against Benedek's left near Nechanitz, with the object of driving in his left, and of cutting him off from Pardubitz and the railway to Vienna. The spies would not fail to notice that some of the crown prince's troops were still at Königinhof, and near Gradlitz. Their presence there would be accounted for by the supposition that they were left to watch Josephstadt, to hold the line of the Elbe, and prevent a raid against the crown prince's line of communication with Silesia until he had changed that line for the one by which Frederick Charles communicated with Saxony.

This ideal cause of the Austrian conduct on the 3rd July appears to be borne out by the following general order which, as it is said, Benedek issued late on the night of the 2nd: so late that it only reached his second corps on the Trottina at four o'clock on the morning of the day of the battle. This order would seem to have been dictated when the Feldzeugmeister heard that the Prussians were moving to their own right from Miletin. It was as follows:—

The Saxon corps will occupy the heights of Popowitz and Tresowitz, the left wing slightly refused and covered by its own cavalry. To the left of this corps and somewhat to the rear, the

---

9. This theory is entirely based on hypothesis, and must be accepted only for what it is worth.

first light cavalry division will take post, on the extreme left flank of Problus and Prim. On the right of the Saxons the tenth corps will take its position; on the right of the tenth the third will occupy the heights of Chlum and Lipa. The eighth corps will serve as immediate support to the Saxons. The troops not named above are only to hold themselves in readiness while the attack is confined to the left wing. Should the hostile attack assume greater dimensions, the whole army will be formed in order of battle.

The fourth corps will then move up on the right of the third to the heights between Chlum and Nedelitz; and on the extreme right flank next to the fourth the second will take post.

The second light cavalry division will take post in rear of Nedelitz, and there remain in readiness. The sixth corps will take post on the heights near Wsetar; the first near Rosnitz. Both these corps will be in concentrated formation. The first and third cavalry divisions will take post at Sweti. In the event of a general attack the first and sixth corps, the five cavalry divisions, and the reserve artillery of the army, which will be posted in rear of the first and sixth corps, are to serve as the reserve of the army.

The retreat, if necessary, will be made by the high road to Hohenmauth, without disturbing the fortress of Königgrätz.

The second and fourth corps must at once cause pontoon bridges to be thrown across the Elbe. The second corps will throw two between Lochenitz and Predmeritz. The first corps will also throw a bridge.

As a digression it may be noticed in passing that these bridges mentioned in this order were ready by mid-day. The organisation of the Austrian Army cannot have been so very bad as some are now fain to suppose.

By the general tenor of this order, it appears that the *feldzeugmeister* fully expected to be attacked on his left, for much the same reason as Wellington at Waterloo fully expected to be assailed on his right. The part of the order which relates to the fourth and second corps shows that he contemplated the possibility of an attack on his right; but not from a very large force. Probably the reports of the spies induced him to believe that the first corps and the Guards at least of the army of the crown prince had joined Prince Frederick Charles, and that only two corps, or sixty thousand men, were at the most on the Elbe. He knew that the two main bodies of these latter two corps must defile over the river, and march fifteen miles over very bad roads and an extremely difficult country, before they could feel his right In the meantime he might have disposed of the adversaries in his front The conduct of the Austrian general during the action seems also to confirm this. Had he known that at ten o'clock Prince Frederick Charles sent only four divisions across the Bistritz, he would hardly have failed to bear down upon them with greatly superior numbers, and crush them at once, before the arrival of their assistants.

From the time of the attack on Benatek until the arrival of the crown prince, Franzecky was exposed across the Bistritz, separated by a wide interval from Horne's division in the Sadowa wood The country favourable for the action of cavalry. Franzecky had with him only one regiment of hussars. The Prussian reserve cavalry could not have crossed the stream, on account of its marshy banks, to his assistance. Twenty thousand Austrian horsemen were at Benedek's command. He held them inactive. Yet the hero of San Martino was not the man to miss to strike a blow if he thought he could do so with safety. He must have imagined Franzecky much stronger than he really was. Probably the Austrian staff imagined that the crown prince's corps, which here joined Frederick Charles, were the assailants of Benatek.

If there is any ground for the above supposition, how much must the conclusion reflect upon the Austrian system of reconnaissances and patrols. From the high bank above Königinhof, a staff officer lying hidden in the fir-wood could, almost with the naked eye, have counted every Prussian gun, every Prussian soldier that the crown prince moved towards Miletin. The eyes of the Austrian Army on more than one occasion during the campaign failed. Their patrol system was very much inferior to that of the Prussians. Its inferiority seems to have been due to the want of military education among the officers to whom patrols were entrusted.

In the Prussian Army special officers of high intelligence were always chosen to reconnoitre. Properly so, for the task is no easy one. An eye unskilled, or a mind untutored, can see little, where a tried observer detects important movements. A line of country, or a few led horses, will tell the officer who is accustomed to such duty more than heavy columns or trains of artillery will disclose to the unthinking novice. The Prussian system never failed, never allowed a surprise. The Austrians were repeatedly surprised, and taken unprepared. Yet the outpost system of the latter during the Italian war of 1859 merited the praise of the Emperor of the French, and was by him pointed out to his own army as a model of superiority.[10] The military development of Prussia had not yet been fully appreciated.

Another fact which may aid to corroborate the theory advanced above, is the telegram in which Feldzeugmeister Benedek first announced to Vienna the loss of the battle In this he said that some of the enemy's troops, under cover of the mist, established themselves on his flank, and so caused the defeat Probably at that time he thought that the troops that got into Chlum were a detachment from those engaged at Benatek. If the Austrian general had suspected any attack from the direction of Königinhof, he would surely have watched the country in that direction with his cavalry, but the troops of the crown prince did not fall in with a single patrol till they actually came into collision with the Austrian line of battle.

How the Prussian Guards were allowed to get into Chlum appears inexplicable. From the top of Chlum Church tower the whole country can be clearly seen as far as the top of the high bank of the Elbe. A staff-officer posted there, even through the mist, which was not so heavy as is generally supposed, could have easily seen any movements of troops as far as Choteborek. A person near Sadowa could see quite distinctly Herwarth's attack at Hradek, and, except during occasional squalls, there was no limit to the view over the surrounding country except where the configuration of the ground or the heavy smoke overcame the sight. From the top of Chlum Church there was a clear view over all the neighbouring hills, and the top of the spire generally stood out clear over the heavy curtain of hanging smoke which, above the heads of the combatants, fringed the side of the Lipa hill from Benatek to Nechanitz.

So little apprehensive, however, was Benedek of an attack on his right, that he stationed no officer in the tower; and himself took up a position above Lipa, where any view towards the north was entirely shut out by the hill and houses of Chlum. No report appears to have reached him of the advance of the Guards, yet they were engaged at Horenowes, and passed through Maslowed. From that village, without opposition, they marched along the rear of the Austrian line, apparently unobserved, until they flung themselves into Chlum and Rosberitz. It seems that the fourth corps to whom the defence of the ground between Maslowed and Nedelitz was entrusted, seeing their comrades

10. General Order of the emperor after the Battle of Solferino.

heavily engaged with Franzecky in the Maslowed wood, turned to their aid, and pressing forwards towards Benatek quitted their proper ground.

A short time afterwards the second Austrian corps was defeated by the Prussian eleventh division, and retreated towards its bridge at Lochenitz. The advance of the fourth corps, and the retreat of the second, left a clear gap in the Austrian line, through which the Prussian Guards marched unmolested, and without a shot seized the key of the position. Once installed they could not be ejected, and the battle was practically lost to the Austrians.

The Prussian pursuit was tardy, and not pushed. The men were fatigued, and night was coming on. The Austrian cavalry was moving sullenly towards Pardubitz. The Prussian cavalry of the First Army had suffered severely. The Elbe lay between the retreating Austrians and the victorious Prussians. The victory, although fortuitously decisive, was not improved to such advantage as it might have been.

CHAPTER 3
Defence of Silesia

Before proceeding to review the events which have in the mean-time been taking place in the western theatre of war, it is requisite to cast a glance upon the operations of the two Prussian corps which had been left to guard the province of Silesia. On the concentration of the Austrian Army in Bohemia, a corps of 6,000 men, under General Trentinaglia, had been left at Cracow. Two Prussian independent corps had, as was already noticed, been stationed at Ratibor and Nicolai, to shield south-eastern Silesia, against a probable attack from this corps. The former was commanded by General Knobelsdorf, and consisted of the 62nd regiment of Infantry, the 2nd regiment of Uhlans, a few battalions of *Landwehr*, and one battery. The latter, under General Count Stölberg, was formed of *Landwehr* alone, and mustered six battalions, two regiments of cavalry, two companies of *Jägers*, and one battery.

The corps of Knobelsdorf was to defend the Moravian frontier, that of Stölberg the Gallician; and both, in case of attack by over-whelming numbers, were to fall back under the protection of the fortress of Kosel.

On the 21st June, Stölberg's corps obtained its first important al-though bloodless success. That day it marched rapidly, many of the men being conveyed in waggons to Pruchna, blew up the railway viaduct there, and so destroyed the communication between General Trentinaglia and the main Austrian Army.

On the 24th and 26th June, as well as on the intermediate days, several Austrian parties made demonstrations of crossing the frontier near Oswiecin. Large bodies of troops appeared to be in the act of concentration at that place, and General Stölberg determined to assure himself of the actual strength of the Austrians there by a reconnaissance in force.

To aid this, General Knobelsdorf sent a part of his troops to Myslowitz, to cover the rear of Stölberg's corps while it marched on Oswiecin,

At the latter place. General Stölberg found a considerably superior force of the enemy. He seized the buildings of the railway station, placed them hastily in a state of defence, and determined by making a long halt here to force the Austrians to develop their full force.

After he had achieved this object, General Stölberg retired to his position near Nicolai. The detachment at Myslowitz had at the same time to sustain an action there, and fulfilled completely its purpose of holding the enemy back from Oswiecin.

On the 30th June, Stölberg's detachment was so weakened by the withdrawal of his *Landwehr* battalions, which were called up in order to aid in the formation of a fourth battalion to every regiment, that it could no longer hold its own against the superior Austrian force near Myslowitz. It retired accordingly nearer to Ratibor, in the direction of Plesz, and undertook from here, in connexion with General Knobelsdorf, expeditions into Moravia against Teschen, Biala, and Skotchau, annoyed the Austrians considerably, and made the inhabitants of Moravia regard the war with aversion.

BOOK 8

CHAPTER 1

Operations In the Western Theatre of the German War

As has been already shown in a preceding chapter,[1] the Prussian troops which had invaded Hanover and Hesse-Cassel occupied on the 19th June the following positions:—

The divisions of General Goeben and General Manteuffel were in the town of Hanover, and that of General Beyer in Cassel. Of the allies of Austria the Hanoverian army was at Göttingen, the Bavarian in the neighbourhood of Würzburg and Bamberg, the eighth Federal corps in the vicinity of Frankfort. The latter consisted of the troops of Würtemberg, Baden, Hesse-Darmstadt, Nassau, and Hesse-Cassel, to which an Austrian division was added. We have seen under what disadvantages the Hanoverian Army left Hanover, and commenced its southward march. Its formation and preparations began only at Göttingen, and they were necessarily conducted under every untoward circumstance. The soldiers of the reserve, and those who had been absent on furlough, nobly responded to the call of their king, and made their way through the country which was in Prussian possession, and sometimes even through the lines of the enemy, to join the ranks at Göttingen. By their firm determination to reach their regiments they afforded an earnest of the gallantry and courage which they afterwards displayed upon the field of battle. By the arrival of these men, the army at Göttingen mustered about twenty thousand combatants, with fifty guns.

Southern Germany expected great deeds of the Bavarian Army. It might have thrown serious difficulties in the way of the Prussian

---

1. See Book 4, chapter 2.

successes, had not an uncertainty and vacillation pervaded all its operations. Prince Charles of Bavaria, the commander-in-chief, under whose orders the eighth Federal Corps was also afterwards placed, seems to have conducted his campaign without a definite strategical object, and without energy in its prosecution. Against him in command of the Prussian Army of the Maine[2] was a general gifted with prudence and clear foresight, who pursued his aim with an iron vigour. The Bavarian is a smart soldier in time of peace, and conducts himself well in battle: but the ranks of Bavaria do not contain such intelligence as do those of Prussia, for men drawn for military service are allowed to provide substitutes, so that only the poorer and less educated classes of society furnish recruits for the army.

The eighth Federal corps did not assemble either with zeal or rapidity. The troops of the Grand Duke of Baden not only came very late to the place of concentration, but when actually in the field were handled in a manner which gave rise to grave suspicions of the affection of their government for the South-German cause. The kernel of this miscellaneous corps was formed by an Austrian division composed of the troops which had been withdrawn from the fortresses of Rastadt, Mayence, and Frankfort. Even if the princes of the small states which furnished their contingents to the eighth corps had made clear to themselves the end or object of the war which they had undertaken, their reasons for the quarrel had not penetrated the lower ranks of their armies. The troops had no idea, no knowledge, of the causes for which they were to shed their blood, and markedly in this respect contrasted with the Prussian soldiery, which held that the honour, integrity, and even existence of its fatherland was in jeopardy.

The Federal troops did not fail in bravery, but no enthusiasm thrilled through their ranks. Individual bodies were doubtless animated by a high courage, and in many cases displayed a heroic devotion to their leaders and their princes. But the mass did not work evenly; a want of harmony existed amongst its heterogeneous units, which, in combination with the clouded plans of its chiefs, facilitated the task of General von Falckenstein. There was also dissension in the councils of the leaders. Prince Alexander not only habitually disagreed with his superior, Prince Charles, and so originated causes of disaster; but himself was often engaged in paltry squabbles with the lieutenants who commanded the different contingents.

---

2. This name was only given on the 1st of July to the Prussian divisions amalgamated together under the command of General Vogel von Falckenstein.

The Hanoverian Army had marched from its capital almost totally unprepared to undertake a campaign. It stood in dire need of several days' rest in order to be organised, and to allow time for the formation of a transport train, as well as for the clothing and armament of the soldiers of reserve who had been recalled to the ranks, and for the horsing of part of the artillery. On this account it was forced to halt until the 20th June at Göttingen, and the favourable moment for its unmolested march to unite with the troops of Bavaria was allowed to slip away.

On the 19th June, by the successful occupation of Cassel by Prussian troops, the ultimate retreat of the Hanoverians was first endangered. On the same day the Prussian General von Falckenstein set out from Hanover with Goeben's division in pursuit of them. The Hanoverian army had gained a start of almost seventy miles on General von Falckenstein, which was of the more importance, inasmuch as the latter could not make use of the railroads, which had been torn up and broken.

The King of Hanover determined to move in a south-easterly direction, and to attempt to reach Bavaria by passing through Prussian territory on the road which leads by Heiligenstadt and Langensalza, and then by Gotha or Eisenach, or to unite with the Bavarians in the neighbourhood of Fulda, The roads in this direction through the mountains of the Thuringian Forest are very convenient, and by no means difficult. Had the march been pushed on with certainty and rapidity, there seems to have been no reason why it should not have been successful in its issue. The portion of the Prussian province of Saxony through which the line of march lay from Heiligenstadt to Langensalza was entirely denuded of Prussian troops.

The only force to oppose the progress of the retreating army on this road was the contingent of Saxe-Coburg Gotha, at Gotha. This consisted, however, of only two battalions. It seems, therefore, that the direction proposed for their route offered considerable chances of success, if on the one side the Hanoverians had forced their marches, and on the other the Bavarians had pushed forward by Coburg in strength, in order to effect a junction with their threatened allies. But neither the Hanoverian nor Bavarian leaders acted energetically.

The Prussian staff, on the contrary, took most prompt measures to cut off the Hanoverian retreat, and to occupy the principal points on their line of march with troops. The Duke of Coburg had declared openly and decidedly on the side of Prussia, and his troops were in consequence at the service of the Prussian Government On the 20th June, Colonel von Fabeck, the commandant of the Coburg contingent, received a telegraphic order from Berlin to post himself with his two battalions at Eisenach, because it was expected that the Hanoverians would there first attempt to break through. Three battalions of *Landwehr*, one squadron of *Landwehr* cavalry, and a battery of four guns, were sent from the garrison of Erfurt to reinforce him. A battalion of the fourth regiment of the Prussian Guard, which had reached Leipsic on the 19th, was also despatched to his aid, a detachment of which, on the 20th, rendered the railway tunnel near Eisenach, impassable.

At the same time General Beyer, pushing forwards from Cassel towards Eisenach, occupied the passages of the River Werra, between Allendorf and that place.

The idea of uniting with the Bavarians, by moving from Heiligenstadt by Eschewege and Fulda, was under these circumstances, given up by the King of Hanover. On the 20th of June such is said to have been his intention, and on that day he moved his advanced guard from Göttingen to Heiligenstadt. On the 21st he ordered his whole army to move upon Gotha, and crossed the Prussian frontier with his troops, after taking leave of his people by means of a proclamation, in which he mournfully expressed his hope soon to return victorious at the head of his army, to the land which he was then temporarily forced to quit

General Arentschild, on entering Prussian territory near Heiligenstadt, issued a proclamation in which he disavowed any intention of treating the country in a hostile manner, and declared that he only desired to be allowed to march through without interruption. The Hanoverian army, dependent for its subsistence upon requisitions, moved but slowly. On the 22nd it occupied Mühlhausen, and on the 23rd Grosz-Gottern. From this place advanced guards were pushed forward on the one side towards Erfurt, on the other to the railway between Eisenach and Gotha. The latter found that this line was already occupied by the Prussians. On the 24th the Hanoverian army reached Langensalza.

In the meantime Colonel Fabeck, the commander of the Coburg contingent, quitting his position at Eisenach, approached Gotha, and occupied the road by which the Hanoverians might have broken through in this direction. A second squadron of *Landwehr* cavalry and a *depôt* battalion were sent from Erfurt to reinforce him; and a second battalion of the fourth regiment of the infantry of the Prussian Guard was hurried up from Berlin. One battalion of this regiment occupied Weimar, and the other Eisenach.

On the 24th June, the force opposed to the Hanoverians at Gotha consisted only of six weak battalions, two squadrons, and four guns. There can hardly be any question but that, if the King of Hanover had marched rapidly on Gotha that day, Colonel von Fabeck would have been quite unable to hold his position. But the Hanoverian leaders failed to take advantage of this last opportunity. The king rejected a proposal made by Colonel von Fabeck, that his army should capitulate; but applied to the Duke of Coburg, and asked him to act as a mediator with the Prussian Government. The Hanoverians desired a free passage to Bavaria, and were in return willing to pledge themselves to take no share in the war in Germany during six months. The Duke of Coburg insisted that this time should be extended to a year, to which the Hanoverians assented, and the duke telegraphed a report of the negotiations to Berlin.

Had the Hanoverians obtained these terms, their intention was to move into Italy, and there to act on the Austrian side against the Italians,—a, course of action which would have recalled to memory the past times in which the Electors of Hanover sent so many of their subjects to combat in the cause of the republic of Venice.

The King of Prussia, immediately on the receipt of the telegram of the Duke of Coburg, despatched his adjutant-general, General von Alvensleben, to Gotha, to treat with the King of Hanover. In the meantime an armistice was agreed upon, which was to expire on the morning of the 25th. This armistice was violated, doubtlessly by some misunderstanding, on the night of the 24th, by the Hanoverians, who advanced to the Gotha and Eisenach railway, and broke up the line near Frötestadt. General von Alvensleben sent a proposal from Gotha to the King of Hanover that he should capitulate. To this no answer was returned; but the king expressed a wish that General von Alvensleben should repair to his camp, in order to treat with him.

This wish was complied with early on the 25th, when an extension of the armistice was agreed upon, and General von Alvensleben hurried back to Berlin for further instructions. It was not at this time the interest of the Prussians to push matters to extremities. Their troops were widely scattered, and the small force at Gotha was unequal to engage the Hanoverian army with any chance of success. The Hanoverians seem to have been ignorant of how small a body alone barred the way to Bavaria, and to have hoped that time might be afforded for aid to reach them. On the night of the 24th a messenger was sent to the Bavarian headquarters at Bamberg to report the situation of the Hanoverian army, and to solicit speedy assistance. To this request Prince Charles only replied that an army of nineteen thousand men ought to be able to cut its way through. In consequence of this opinion only one Bavarian brigade of light cavalry was advanced on the 25th of June to Meiningen, in the valley of the Werra, while a few Bavarian detachments were pushed forward along the high road as far as Vacha.

This procedure of Prince Charles of Bavaria was alone sufficient to condemn him as a general He held his army inactive, when, by a bold advance, not only could he have insured the safety of the Hanoverians, but could in all probability have captured the whole of his enemy's troops at Gotha. Thus he would have saved nineteen thousand allies, have captured six thousand of his adversary's men, have turned the scale of war by twenty-five thousand combatants, have preserved to his own cause a skilled and highly trained army, proud of high and ancient military reputation, which the faults of politicians had placed in a most precarious and unfortunate position.

On the 25th Prussian troops were closing in upon the devoted Hanoverians; but telegraphic orders were forwarded from Berlin to all their commanders not to engage in hostilities until ten o'clock on the morning of the 26th. Colonel von Döring was despatched to Langensalza by the Prussian Government, with full powers to treat with the King of Hanover; he proposed an alliance with Prussia, on the basis of the recognition of the Prussian project for reform of the Germanic Confederation, and of the disbandment by Hanover of its army. To these terms King George would not agree; deserted by his allies, to them he was still faithful, and still expected that the Bavarians must come to his aid. He refused to entertain any proposition for the capitulation of his array, and demanded a free and unimpeded passage into Bavaria.

In the meantime, while the king treated, the Bavarians remained inactive, and while the Hanoverian army was fatigued by marching and countermarching within its lines, the troops of Prussia closed round it. On the 25th June the Prussian divisions of Goeben and Beyer reached Eisenach. The same day General Flies, who had been despatched by General Manteuffel with five battalions and two batteries, reached Gotha by means of the railway which runs through Magdeburg and

Halle. On the same evening the Prussian troops at Gotha were rein-forced by two battalions of the 20th regiment of *Landwehr*, and a *depôt* battalion from the garrison of Magdeburg. General Flies immediately assumed the command of the Prussian and Coburg troops at Gotha, and pushed his advanced guard that evening to Warza, halfway be-tween Gotha and Langensalza.

Round this place the Hanoverian army lay. The opportunity of forcing its way into Bavaria, while the two battalions of Coburg were alone at Gotha, had been lost By the morning of the 26th, forty-two thousand Prussians were placed on the south, west, and north, within a day's march of its position, and all hopes of escape into Bavaria, or of aid from its southern allies, appeared to be vain.

On the 26th the armistice expired at ten o'clock in the morn-ing, but the Prussian commander-in-chief did not immediately com-mence hostilities. His dispositions were not yet perfected. That day the Hanoverian army drew more closely together, either with the object of accepting battle, or, as some say, with the intention of moving by Tennstedt, and endeavouring to join the Bavarians by a circuitous route.

That evening the Hanoverians took up a position between the vil-lages of Thämsbrück, Merxleben, and the town of Langensalza. None of these places were well suited for defence, and no artificial fortifi-cations were thrown up on the southern side of the position, where General Flies lay. On the northern side a few insignificant earthworks and one battery were erected, to guard the rear and right flank of the army against the Prussian corps under General Manteuffel, which lay in the direction of Mühlhausen. The soldiers were weary with march-ing and privations, but eager to join battle with the Prussians, who of late years had spoken in a disparaging and patronising tone of the Hanoverian army, which, since the battle of Langensalza, has been exchanged for one of high respect and admiration.

There had been a false alarm in the Hanoverian lines of an advance by the enemy in the night between the 26th and 27th June; but an attack was not expected on the 27th. This day had been appointed by royal command to be observed as a solemn day of fast and humilia-tion throughout Prussia, and the Hanoverian leaders appear to have imagined that on this account the Prussian generals would not attack. In this they were deceived, for before evening there had been fought the bloody

The Prussian troops on the morning of the 27th occupied the following positions:—

The division of General Manteuffel was at Mühlhausen; that of General Beyer at Eisenach; that of General Goeben had one of its brigades, that of General Wrangel, pushed forwards towards the northwest of Langensalza, and the other brigade, that of General Kummer, at Gotha; while the corps of General Flies was concentrated on the south of Langensalza, at Warza. General Flies, who commanded five battalions of infantry of the Prussian line, one *depôt* battalion, two battalions of the Duke of Saxe-Coburg-Gotha, and five battalions of *Landwehr*, with three squadrons, in all about twelve thousand men,[3] with twenty-two guns, advanced from Warza, and attacked the Hanoverian position on that forenoon.

General Flies has been censured by military critics for making this attack so early, while, as will be seen in the sequel, his colleagues were still too far distant to render him assistance during the action which he thus precipitated. He has not, however, failed to find defenders of the course he pursued. It has been urged that the object of his attack was to hold the Hanoverian Army on the Unstrut, and if this were his only object he was successful Hanoverian sources of information, however, hardly allude to the supposition that King George was about to move to Tennstedt; and, unless General Flies had strong reasons for believing that his adversary meditated the immediate execution of such a movement, he was hardly justified in exposing himself to an unnecessary chance of disaster.

It has also been said that General Manteuffel on the north was to fire two cannon as a signal to General Flies that he was ready to attack, and that the Hanoverians, having discovered this arrangement, gave the signal at an early hour from their own batteries. The Hanoverians, however, assert that their artillery only fired its first shot after General

---

3.

3 Battalions, 11th Regiment ⎫ (1,000 per Battalion) . .	5,000
2 ,, 25th ,, ⎬	
2 ,, Saxe Coburg-Gotha (900 per Battalion) .	1,800
Depôt Battalion 71st Regiment (400 per Battalion) . .	400
2 Battalions, 20th Landwehr Regiment ⎫	
2 ,, 32nd ,, ,, ⎬ (800 per Battalion)	4,000
1 Battalion, 27th ,, ,, ⎭	
3 Squadrons (150 horsemen each)	450
	11,650
Gunners	600
	12,250

Flies' infantry attack had been well developed.

The position occupied by the Hanoverian army on the morning of the 27th lay along the sloping side of the line of hills which rises from the left bank of the River Unstrut The right wing and centre rested on the villages of Thämsbrück and Merxleben; the left wing between the villages of Nägelstadt and Merxleben. The third brigade (Von Bülow) formed the right wing; the fourth brigade (Von Bothmer) the left; while in the centre was posted the first brigade (Von de Knesebeck), which at the beginning of the action was held in rear of the general line. The village of Merxleben, and the ground in front of it, was occupied by the second brigade (De Vaux), which had its outposts pushed as far as Henningsleben, along the road to Warza. The artillery and cavalry of the reserve were posted behind Merxleben, near the road to Sundhausen, where the scanty *depôts* of ammunition and stores were established. The front of the position was covered by the river, which with its steep banks impeded at first the Prussian attack, but afterwards was an obstacle to the offensive advance and counter-attack of the Hanoverians.

At about nine o'clock on the morning of the 27th, the two Coburg battalions which formed the advanced guard of General Flies' column reached Henningsleben, and attacked the Hanoverian outposts there. These withdrew to Langensalza, occasionally checking their pursuers by the fire of their skirmishers. One Hanoverian battalion remained for a short time in Langensalza, but then the whole Hanoverian troops, which had been pushed along the Gotha road, withdrew across the Unstrut to Merxleben, and the Prussians occupied Langensalza before ten o'clock.

General Flies then made his arrangements for an attack on the main Hanoverian position. His artillery was very inferior numerically to that of the enemy, so he relied chiefly on his infantry fire. He sent a small column to make a feint against Thämsbrück, while he advanced two regiments of infantry against Merxleben, and detached a column of *Landwehr* to his right, in order to outflank, if possible, and turn the Hanoverian left.

On the Hanoverian side the first gun was fired between ten and eleven, from a battery of rifled 6-pounders attached to the second brigade, and posted on the left of Merxleben. The first brigade was immediately pushed forward to the support of the second brigade, and took up its position on the right of that village.

By a singular error, the Hanoverians failed to hold a wood and bathing-establishment close to the river, on the right bank, opposite Merxleben. Into these the Prussian regiments advancing against the village threw themselves. Sheltered by the cover, they opened a biting musketry fire against the Hanoverian gunners and troops near the village, which lasted till the end of the battle, caused great loss in the Hanoverian ranks, and made an issue from the village and a passage of the bridge most difficult and dangerous. The first gunshot of the Hanoverians was quickly followed by others, and in a few minutes the whole of the Prussian and the greater part of the Hanoverian pieces were engaged, when the roar of the guns, the explosions of bursting shells, and the rapid crackling of small arms, rose loud in the rough harmony of war.

The Prussian column on the right pressed forward against the Hanoverians' left, seemed to be bearing against their line of retreat, and threatened to turn their flank. The Hanoverian leader seized the opportunity, and resolved to attack with vigour the widespread Prussian line.

The first brigade in the centre, with the third brigade on its right wing, advanced at mid-day from Merxleben. The fourth brigade on the left wing moved forward at the same time against the Prussian right, but here the banks of the river were steeper, and the time occupied in descending and ascending the banks, as well as in wading through the stream, prevented more of this brigade than one battalion of rifles from at first taking a share in the onset The rest of the Hanoverian troops, however, supported by their artillery, pressed steadily forward, and bore down upon the Prussians, who retreated. Many prisoners were taken, but not without severe loss to the assailants, who soon occupied the wood and bathing-establishment beside the river.

The Prussians then drew off from every point, and a favourable opportunity occurred for a vigorous pursuit But the disadvantage of a river in front of a position now became apparent. The cavalry could not ford the stream, nor approach it closely, on account of the boggy nature of its banks, and had to depend upon the bridges at Thämsbrück, Merxleben, and Nägelstadt. The Duke of Cambridge's regiment of dragoons issued from the latter village, and dashed forward quickly, but unsupported, against the Prussian line of retreat, and took several prisoners. As soon as the heavy cavalry of the reserve had threaded its way across the bridge of Merxleben, it also rushed upon the retreating Prussians. Two squares were broken by it, and many prisoners made, while Captain von Einein, with his squadron of *cuirassiers*, captured a

Prussian battery. But the horsemen of Hanover suffered fearfully from the deadly rapidity of the needle-gun, and Von Einein fell in the midst of his captured cannon.

The cavalry pursued the Prussians as far as Henningsleben, but a further pursuit, or an advance of the infantry even so far, was impossible, on account of the fatigue of both men and horses, and the scarcity of provisions and ammunition.

About five o'clock the pursuit terminated, and the Hanoverians, masters of the field of battle, posted their outlying pickets on the south of Langensalza,

The total loss of the Hanoverians in killed and wounded was one thousand three hundred and ninety two. The Prussians lost nine hundred and twelve prisoners, and probably about the same number as their enemies in killed and wounded. It is said that the Hanoverian infantry engaged did not number more than ten thousand men, because the recruits were sent to the rear, and during the day one thousand men were employed in throwing up earthworks. The Hanoverian cavalry consisted of twenty-four squadrons, of which eighteen certainly took part in the pursuit, and must have mustered at least nineteen hundred sabres. The artillery in action on that side consisted of forty-two guns. The Prussian force, as has been shown before, numbered about twelve thousand combatants, with twenty-two guns. It is extremely questionable how far General Flies was justified under these circumstances in precipitating an action.

The Battle of Langensalza was of little avail to the gallant army which had won it The troops of Hanover were now too intricately involved in the meshes of Falckenstein's strategy.

This general, on the 28th, closed in his divisions, and drew them tightly round the beleaguered Hanoverians, who, by the action of Langensalza, had repulsed but not cut through their assailants. The division of General Manteuffel and the brigade of General Wrangel were pushed into the Hanoverian rear, and took up positions at Alt-Gottern, Rothen-Heiligen, and Bollstedt. The division of General Beyer was advanced from Eisenach to Hayna. General Flies was at Warza, and the brigade of General Kummer at Gotha was held ready to move by railway to Weimar, in order to head King George, in case he should march to the eastward on the left bank of the Unstrut. Forty thousand hostile combatants were knitted round the unfortunate monarch and his starving but devoted troops.

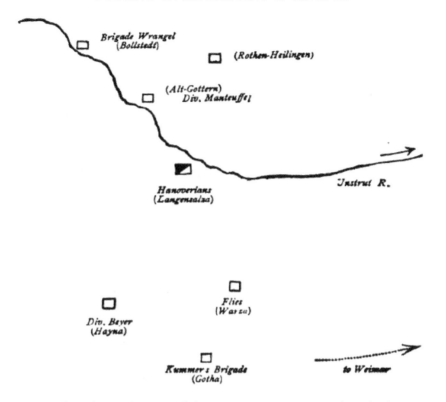

When these positions of the Prussians were reported to the king, he determined to avoid a holocaust of his soldiery. An action could hardly have been successful; it must have been desperate. The terms of capitulation which had been formerly proposed by Prussia, were agreed to on the evening of the 29th. Arms, carnages, and military stores were handed over to the Prussians: the Hanoverian soldiers were dismissed to their homes: the officers were allowed to retain their horses and their swords, on condition of not again serving against Prussia during the war. The king himself and the crown prince were allowed to depart whither they pleased, except within the boundaries of Hanover.

Political errors, and the supineness of Prince Charles of Bavaria, had at one stroke of the pen made a whole army captive, and blotted out from the roll of independent states one of the most renowned of continental principalities.

This disaster of the Hanoverian Army was due in a less degree to the uncertain action of its leaders than to the improvidence of its administrators, and the blindness of the political guardians of its country. Still there is no doubt that, on the days preceding the 25th June, the army of King George could easily have forced its way through the small knot of its enemies at Gotha, and have secured a safe retreat, provided only that it had been directed to march boldly forward. Its subsequent conduct at Langensalza compels us to believe that its organisation at this time must have been sufficiently advanced to allow it to take this course. For the reasons that it did not do so its military directors must be responsible.

Yet, whoever is to blame for the calamitous results of its expiring campaign, none can regard, without a feeling of sympathy and emotion, the last struggles of a proud and high-minded soldiery, who bore up ineffectually for days against privation, hardship, and superior numbers; who even hoped against hope; who rallied round their king in the hour of his misfortune, and strove to carry him, by the pressure of their bayonets, through the clustering bands of hostile combatants. Hanoverians may well look with a mournful satisfaction on Langensalza. British soldiers may justly feel a generous pride in the last campaign of an army which mingled its blood with that of their ancestors on the battlefields of Spain and Belgium, and not unworthily rank the name of the battle which closes the last page of Hanoverian history with Salamanca, Talavera, Quatre Bras, and Waterloo.

CHAPTER 2

Campaign on the Maine

When Prussia determined upon war, she resolved to throw herself
with her main force upon Austria, since that power was the leader and
backbone of the coalition against her. With the intention of crushing the Austrian army in Bohemia and Moravia, the whole of the
regular *corps d'armée* of the Prussian service were directed upon those
countries. Westphalia and the Rhenish provinces were denuded of
their regular troops, which were marched to the Austrian frontier. To
protect the western provinces of Prussia from the allies of Austria, to
overrun Hanover and Hesse-Cassel, and then to act against the allies
of Austria in the south-west of Germany, was the task entrusted to
General Vogel von Falckenstein. He was provided with an army hastily
collected together from the Elbe duchies, and from the garrisons of
the neighbouring fortresses.

With this army, General von Falckenstein had to be prepared to
take the field against the Bavarians and the seventh corps of the late
Germanic Confederation. Previous to engaging with these adversaries, he was forced to occupy Hanover and Hesse-Cassel, and to pursue
and disarm the Hanoverian troops. These preliminaries cost the Prussian general the loss of fourteen days of valuable time, and allowed the
eighth Federal corps to assemble its heterogeneous constituents, and
organise them round Frankfort. There can be no doubt but that if, on
the 18th or 19th June, General Falckenstein had been able to concentrate his divisions near Wetzlar, and to have marched immediately
upon Frankfort, he would have entirely prevented the collection of
the troops of Baden, Würtemberg, and Hesse, and have annihilated in
detail their separated divisions.

On the other hand, fortune favoured Falckenstein, inasmuch as
that during this fortnight the main armies of his opponents remained

inactive, and, with the exception of some petty demonstrations, began to develop no energy until quite the end of June, when he himself, after the capitulation of the Hanoverians, was free to turn his unrestricted attention to them, and had concentrated his whole army at Gotha and Eisenach.

The army thus assembled under General von Falckenstein consisted of three divisions. These were the division of Lieutenant-General von Goeben, which consisted of the 13th, 53rd, 15th and 55th regiments of Infantry, with the 8th regiment of Hussars, and 4th regiment of cuirassiers. It mustered in all, at this time, about thirteen thousand men, with twenty-four guns, and was divided into two brigades, one commanded by General Kummer, the other by General Wrangel. One division was the division of General von Beyer, which had been formed from the garrisons of the Federal fortresses of Mayence, Rastadt, Luxemburg, and Frankfort-on-Maine, and consisted of the 19th, 20th, 30th, 32nd, 34th, 39th and 70th regiments of Infantry, with the 9th regiment of Hussars,—altogether twenty-one thousand five hundred men, with forty-two guns.

Another the division of General von Manteuffel, which had formerly garrisoned the duchy of Schleswig; it consisted of the 25th, 36th, 11th, and 59th regiments of Infantry, and the 5th and 9th Dragoons,—in all thirteen thousand men, with thirty guns. The command of this division was shortly afterwards given to General von Flies. To the Army of the Maine were also attached two battalions of the duchy of Saxe-Coburg, one of Oldenburg, and one of Lippe-Detmold, which numbered together about two thousand five hundred combatants. General von Falckenstein had thus under his orders as nearly as possible fifty thousand men, with ninety-six guns.[1] The battalions of *Landwehr* and the *depôt* troops which had fought at Langensalza were not retained with the army, but were dismissed to rejoin the garrisons of those fortresses from which they had been taken.

Opposed to the Prussian Army of the Maine stood, after the capitulation of the Hanoverians, the seventh and eighth corps of the Germanic Confederation. The seventh Federal corps consisted of the army of Bavaria, which was under the command of Prince Charles of Bavaria, who was also commander-in-chief of the two corps. The Bavarian Army was divided into three divisions, each of which consisted

---

1. Later five fourth battalions, a newly-raised rifle battalion, and three newly-raised *Landwehr* cavalry regiments, as well as the Oldenburg-Hanseatic brigade, consisting of seven battalions, six squadrons, and two batteries, reinforced this army.

of two brigades. A brigade was formed of two regiments of infantry of the Line, each of three battalions; a battalion of light infantry, a regiment of cavalry, and a battery of artillery. There was also a reserve brigade of infantry, which consisted of five line regiments and two battalions of rifles. The reserve cavalry consisted of six regiments, the reserve artillery of two batteries. The first division was under the command of General Stephan, the second under General Feder, the third under General Zoller. The infantry of the reserve was commanded by General Hartmann, the cavalry by a prince of the House of Thurn and Taxis. The whole army numbered over fifty thousand sabres and bayonets, with one hundred and thirty-six guns.[2] The chief of the staff of Prince Charles was General von der Tann, who was a tried commander of a division.

The Bavarian Army in the middle of June was posted along the northern frontier of its own kingdom in positions intended to cover that country from an invasion from the north or east Its headquarters were at Bamberg, its extreme right wing at Hof, and its extreme left wing near the confluence of the Franconian Saale with the Maine, between Schweinfurt and Gemünden.

The eighth Federal corps, under the command of Prince Alexander of Hesse, consisted of the Federal contingents of Würtemberg, Baden, Hesse, and a combined division; which included the Austrian auxiliary brigade and the troops of Nassau. The whole corps mustered forty-nine thousand eight hundred sabres and bayonets, with one hundred and thirty-four guns. (See table following). Prince Alexander assumed the command of this corps on the 18th June, and established his headquarters at Darmstadt.

The elector of Hesse-Cassel had sent his troops to the south as soon as the Prussians invaded his territory. By a decree of the *diet* of the 22nd June, they were placed under the orders of the commander of the eighth Federal corps. On account of their rapid retreat from

---

2. Each battalion of the line mustered on paper 950 men; each rifle battalion 668; and each regiment of cavalry 591 horsemen. This would give a total of 58,036 combatants; but from this number several deductions have to be made for sickness and incomplete battalions. The number stated in the text has been carefully compiled from the comparison of many authorities. Theoretically, Bavaria possessed a large force of *Landwehr*; but as the *cadres* of the *Lanawehr* battalions were not maintained in peace, and no arrangements made for their clothing or armament in case of the outbreak of a war, these auxiliary troops never paraded during the earlier operations of the war, except upon paper; and only once during the whole of the campaign, near Bayreuth, did a detachment of these troops take a part in any action.

* The Order of Battle of this eighth Federal corps was :—

1st (Würtemberg) Division.—Lieutenant-General von Hardegg.

 1st Infantry Brigade (1st and 5th Regiments and 3rd Jäger Battalion). —Major-General von Baumbach.

 2nd Infantry Brigade (2nd and 7th Regiments and 3rd Jäger Battalion). —Major-General von Fischer.

 3rd Infantry Brigade (3rd and 8th Regiments and 1st Jäger Battalion). —Major-General Hegelmeier.

 Cavalry Brigade (1st, 3rd, and 4th Regiments).—Major-General Count von Scheler.

 Artillery, Six Batteries of Eight Guns.

2nd (Baden) Division.—Prince William of Baden.

  Infantry.—Commander, Lieutenant-General Waag.

 1st Brigade (Grenadier and 5th Regiments and a Jäger Battalion).— Major-General von la Roche.

 2nd Brigade (2nd and 3rd Regiments and Fusilier Battalion).— Colonel von Neubronn.

 Cavalry, 1st, 2nd, and 3rd Dragoons.

 Artillery, Five Batteries of Six Guns.

3rd (Hesse-Darmstadt) Divison.—Lieutenant-General von Perglas.

 1st Brigade (1st and 2nd Regiments and one Jäger Company).—Major-General Frey.

 2nd Brigade (3rd and 4th Regiments and one Jäger Company).—Major-General von Stockhausen.

 A Battalion of Sharpshooters was attached to the Division.

 Cavalry Brigade (two Regiments of Light Horse).—Prince Louis of Hesse.

 Artillery, Four Batteries of Six Guns.

4th (Combined) Division.—Lieutenant-Field-Marshal Count Neipperg.

 Austrian Brigade.— Major-General Hohn.

  Three Battalions of the 16th Infantry Regiment (Italians).

  One Battalion of the 49th ,, ,,

  One ,, ,, 21st ,, ,,

  One ,, ,, 74th ,, ,,

  The 35th Jäger Battalion.

  Two Batteries of Eight Guns.

 Nassau Brigade (1st and 2nd Regiments and a Jäger Battalion).— Major-General Roth.

 Artillery, two Batteries of Eight Guns.

To this division were attached two squadrons of the Hussars of Hesse-Cassel.

Cassel, their preparations for war were interrupted, and little could as yet be expected from them in the open field. On the 29th June, when Prince Alexander received orders for an advance of his corps, he directed the Hesse-Cassel contingent, on this account, to retire to Mainz, there to cover the Rhine, and the country in the immediate vicinity of that fortress. Two squadrons of hussars alone he retained as the divisional cavalry of his fourth division. These, as well as the troops of Hesse-Darmstadt, were ready for action. The troops of Würtemberg and Baden still wanted time; those of Baden particularly: for their duchy entered only unwillingly into the war against Prussia. Würtemberg had sent an infantry brigade, a regiment of cavalry, and two batteries on the 17th June, to Frankfort These were intended to unite with the troops of Hesse-Darmstadt already assembling there, and to form a guard for the Rump Diet which still held its sittings at that town.

The next Würtemberg brigade joined the corps only on the 28th June, the last brigade on the 5th July. On the 17th June the government called up its furlough and reserve soldiers, and organised its division. The first Baden brigade reached Frankfort on the 25th June, where the Austrian brigade had arrived only a few days before. The rest of the troops and the transport trains did not come in till the 8th July. The 9th July can be considered to have been the first day on which the eighth Federal corps was first ready to take the field. While these minor governments were still assembling their small contingents, the troops of Prussia had long been in possession of Saxony and Hesse, had caused the surrender of the Hanoverian Army, and already inflicted a crushing defeat on the main forces of Austria,

The Bavarian Army lay along the Maine, with its first division towards Hof, its fourth towards Gemünden. The Bavarian Government was anxious to make an advance upon Berlin, by way of Hof; but the general strategical movements of all the allies of Austria were, in virtue of a convention concluded between Austria and Bavaria on the 14th June, directed from Vienna, The directing genius decided against any offensive movement in a north-easterly direction: and insisted strongly on a junction of the Bavarian and eighth Federal corps between Würzburg and Frankfort, in order to then move against the Prussian provinces, on the north-west. The aim of Austria was to compel Prussia to detach strong bodies from her troops engaged with Benedek, and so to weaken her main army. The Bavarian and eighth corps when united were to have the name of the West German Federal Army.

On the 21st June, Prince Charles of Bavaria heard that the Hanoverians had moved from Göttingen. On the 23rd he knew certainly that they had marched to Mühlhausen and Langensalza. On the 25th for the first time he made any movement of importance. On that day the Bavarian army was set in motion towards the north. That evening the advanced guard of the first cavalry brigade entered Meiningen: the main body reached that town in the night between the 26th and 27th. Communications with the Hanoverians had been cut off and Prince Charles, uncertain of their exact position, on the 28th had ordered his columns to move towards Fulda. News reached him, however, of the commencement of the battle of Langensalza, and, changing the direction of his march, he moved towards Gotha.

The same evening a despatch arrived from Vienna which urged a rapid advance of the Bavarians. Forced marches were ordered, and the troops, to raise their enthusiasm, received double pay for the first two days. On the 29th, the first division, followed by the second, reached Hilburghausen; the fourth, followed by the third, pushed past Meiningen. It was only when the advanced guards had reached Zella, in the Thuringian Forest, that they received counter-orders: for Count Ingelheim, the Austrian ambassador at the court of King George, had arrived with the intelligence that the Hanoverians had laid down their arms. Thus the forced marching of two days had been lost, and the Bavarian army had commenced its campaign without result or glory, on account of too tardy an assumption of the initiative.

On the 29th the riflemen and light horsemen who formed the advanced guard of the first division reached Schleusingen; on the 30th the main column entered that place. The forced marches of the 29th and 30th had fatigued the troops. The constant succession of orders and counter-orders had wearied them, for they saw that all their exertions were neutralized by altered commands, or by changes in the direction of the line of march. Before the commencement of actual war their confidence in their leaders had waned, for the men saw no grounds for the fatigues laid upon them. The capitulation of the Hanoverians dispirited them, the more so as it was popularly attributed to the vacillation, the cowardice, sometimes indeed to the treachery, of the Bavarian Army. Still the prince hoped to unite with the eighth Federal corps by a flank march to his left, along the roads which lead by Giessen to Hünfeld, and by Hildern to Fulda. The success of this movement was however prevented, as will be afterwards seen, by the sudden appearance of the Prussians.

The eighth Federal corps had, by the 27th June, assembled about 39,000 men, with eighty guns.[3] Since another Würtemberg brigade, another cavalry regiment, and two more batteries were expected to come in on the following day, it considered itself strong enough to assume the offensive, and the following orders were issued for the 28th June:—

The troops of Hesse-Darmstadt were to form the advanced guard, with two brigades of infantry, two rifled 6-pounder batteries, a regiment of cavalry, and a bridge train. The first and fourth divisions formed the main body: each consisted of two brigades of infantry; the first division had three batteries of artillery and a regiment of cavalry attached to it; the second had two batteries of artillery, a regiment of cavalry, and two squadrons of Hesse-Cassel hussars attached. The reserve consisted of five battalions of the Bavarian brigade of La Roche, six regiments of cavalry, and thirty-four guns, of which sixteen were rifled. The advanced guard on the 29th June took up a position around Friedberg, about eighteen miles north of Frankfort, with its right on the River Nidda,

On the 30th the commander-in-chief broke up his headquarters at Frankfort, and ordered a general advance. He intended to move upon Alsfeld, a town which, on the Schwalen, still in the territory of Hesse-Darmstadt, lies close to the frontier of Hesse-Cassel. Prince Alexander considered himself secure from any attack on his left flank by Prussian detachments from the Rhine provinces because of the troops of Hesse-Cassel in Mainz. The division of Baden on the 1st July occupied Giessen, and paid a short visit to the Prussian town of Wetzlar, and on the 2nd July Prince Alexander held a position from Giessen eastwards to Grünberg, on the road to Alsfeld.

Here he received a despatch from Prince Charles of Bavaria, which had been sent from Meiningen on the evening of the 30th June. This altered the direction of the march of the eighth Federal corps.

It does not appear clear whether Prince Alexander, in his design of an advance to Alsfeld, was acting in compliance with an order from Prince Charles of Bavaria, or whether on his own responsibility he moved forward to cover the territory of Hesse-Cassel from invasion. The direction of the movement shows, however, that he who ordered

3. 1st Division, 5,200 Infantry, with 1,100 Cavalry and 16 Guns.

2nd	,,	4,500	,,	240	,,	6 ,,
3rd	,,	10,000	,,	2,600	,,	24 ,,
4th	,,	12,000	,,	1,000	,,	32 ,,

it, be he who he may, was singularly ill-furnished with intelligence of his enemy's movements. By making for Alsfeld Prince Alexander not only would have exposed his right flank and his line of communication to the head of Falckenstein's columns, but would have increased the difficulties of his junction with Prince Charles.

As it was, at the time that Prince Charles sent to change the line of march of the eighth corps, these difficulties were already formidable enough. An interval of between eighty and ninety miles separated the two bodies: and not only did the valley of the Fulda as well as that of the Werra intervene, but rugged hills rose between them, such as the Vogels-Berg and the Hohe Rhön. It did not need such a keen general as Falckenstein to perceive the advantages he would derive if he drove the Prussian Army as a mighty wedge between these separated corps, and hurled himself with full force on the nearest ere the other could arrive to its assistance.

In his own immediate command Prince Charles showed vacillation and uncertainty. He did not strive with all energy to liberate the Hanoverians, and unite them with his own force. Nor when he found himself too late to achieve this object did he take rapid measures for a concentration with the eighth corps. On the contrary, instead of making towards his left, he drew away to his right, apparently with the object of crossing another difficult mountain country, the Thuringian forest, and placing that obstacle also between himself and his allies, while he left the valley of the Werra open to his antagonist as a groove down which to drive the wedge that should separate the Bavarians entirely from Prince Alexander.

On the evening of the 30th June he for the first time appears to have decided upon a concentrative movement. He then issued orders that both corps should seek to unite at Fulda. To accomplish this, the Bavarians were to move in a westerly, the Federals in an easterly, direction. The latter began to move with this object on the 3rd July. Prince Alexander moved with his first and third division that day to Ulrichstein, a small town on the northern issues of the Vogels-Berg. With his second division he occupied Giessen and Wetzlar to secure his line of communication with Frankfort, and sent his fourth division to Friedberg. His cavalry was sent out to scour the country towards Alsfeld and Marburg. He evidently expected his enemy by the railway from Marburg, and took these precautions to cover his flank march. On the 4th July headquarters remained inactive at Ulrichstein, and some patrols alone pushed forward. Here again was a lack of energy and clear-sightedness. Portions of any army which are separated, and desire to concentrate in the presence of an enemy, should exert all their powers to do so, and not waste a single hour, far less halt on the second day of the march.

How false these news were became soon apparent. On the 4th July news came to the headquarters of Prince Alexander, that strong Prussian columns were moving on Fulda from Hünfeld and Gerza, towns which lie between the Werra and the Fulda. An advance of the eighth corps prepared for battle, and with all precautions, was ordered for the next day. During this, however, the Prussian and Bavarian troops had come into contact

General Falckenstein had, after the capitulation of the Hanoverians on the 29th of June, concentrated on the 1st July his three divisions at Eisenach. To this united corps was given the name of the Army of the Maine. On the 2nd July, Falckenstein took the main road which leads from Eisenach by Fulda to Frankfort, and reached Marksahl that day. His intention was to press the Bavarians eastwards. These occupied a position at that time with their main body near Meiningen, on the west of the Werra. Two divisions were posted on that river, near Schmalkalden, to cover the passage of that stream against a Prussian corps which was expected from Erfurt. The cavalry was intended to open communications with the eighth corps in the direction of Fulda.

On the night of the 2nd July, the same night that the troops of Prince Frederick Charles in Bohemia were moving towards the field of Königgrätz, a Bavarian reconnoitring party fell in with one of Falckenstein's patrols. On the 3rd July the Prussian reconnoitring officers brought in reports that the Bavarians were in force round Wiesenthal, on the River Felde. It was clear to Falckenstein that this position was held by the heads of the Bavarian columns which were moving to unite with the eighth corps. The Prussian general could not afford to permit the enemy to lie in a position so close and threatening to the left flank of his advance. He ordered General Goeben to push them back on the following morning, by forming to his left, and attacking the villages on the Felde in front, while General Manteuffel's division should move up the stream, and assail them on the right flank. The third division, that of General Beyer, was in the meantime to push its march towards Fulda.

ACTION OF WIESENTHAL

The Bavarian general, on the 3rd of July, having obtained information of the vicinity of the Prussians, concentrated his army. That evening he occupied the villages of Wiesenthal, Neidhartshausen, Zella, and Diedorf, with considerable strength. His main body bivouacked round Rossdorf, and in rear of that village.

At five o'clock in the morning of the 4th July, General Goeben sent Wrangel's brigade against Wiesenthal, and Kummer's against Neidhartshausen. The latter village, as well as the neighbouring heights, were found strongly occupied by the enemy. They were carried only after a long and hard battle, the scene of which was marked by numbers of Prussians killed and wounded. Towards noon the Bavarian detachments which had been driven from Neidhartshausen and Zella received reinforcements. Prince Charles determined to hold Diedorf. He ordered a brigade to advance beyond this village, and take up a position on the hills on the further side. The Prussians opened a heavy fire of artillery and small arms from Zella upon the advancing Bavarians. Under this fire the latter could not gain ground, and no change in the positions of the combatants took place at this point, until the termination of the action.

In the meantime a severe combat had been fought at Wiesenthal. At the same time that General Kummer left Dermbach, he detached two battalions to his left, which were to occupy the defile of Lindenau, while Wrangel's brigade advanced against Wiesenthal. Wrangel's advanced guard consisted of a squadron of cavalry and a battalion of infantry, which moved along the road in column of companies. Hardly had it reached the high ground in front of the village, when it was sharply assailed by a well-directed fire of bullets and shot. The heavy rain prevented the men from seeing clearly what was in their front, but they pressed on, and the enemy was pushed back into the barricaded village, and up the hills on its southern side. Before the Prussian advanced guard reached Wiesenthal the rain cleared up. The Bavarians could be seen hurrying to evacuate the place, and taking up a position with four battalions, a battery, and several squadrons at the foot of the Nebelsberg.

The Prussian battalion from Lindenau had arrived on the south flank of Wiesenthal Another battalion came up with that of the advanced guard, and the Prussians occupied the village. The Prussian artillery also arrived, and came into action with great effect against a Bavarian battery posted on the south-west of Wiesenthal. At the same time the needle-gun told severely on the Bavarian battalions at the foot of the Nebelsberg. Three of these retired into the woods which cover the summit of that hill, while the fourth took post behind the rising ground. Swarms of Prussian skirmishers swept swiftly across the plain in front, and made themselves masters of the edge of the wood. But the Bavarians held fast to the trees inside, and would not be ousted. Two fresh batteries of Bavarian artillery, and several new battalions, were seen hurrying up from Rossdorf. At this moment it was supposed that Manteuffel's cannonade was heard opening in the direction of Nornshausen. This was in truth but the echo of the engaged artillery. But the Prussian columns hurried forward, and dashed with the bayonet against the wood-crested hill. The Bavarians awaited the charge, and their riflemen made serious impressions upon the advancing masses. But the men of Westphalia rushed on.

After a short, sharp struggle, the hill was carried; and the Bavarians fled down the reverse slope, leaving hundreds of corpses, grisly sacrifices to the needle-gun, to mark the line of their flight. General Goeben had achieved his object. He halted his troops, and prepared to rejoin Falckenstein. Leaving a rearguard of one battalion, three squadrons, and a battery to cover his movement, and the removal of the killed and wounded, he withdrew his two brigades to Dermbach. The Bavarian march to unite with the eighth corps had been checked; and Falckenstein had lodged his leading column securely between the separated portions of his adversary's army. The Bavarians in the night, finding their road barred, retired, to seek a junction with Prince Alexander by some other route.

They did not, however, move over the western spurs of the Hohe Rhön, in the direction of Brückenau, whence they might have stretched a hand to Prince Alexander, who on the night between the 5th and 6th July was only seven miles from Fulda. They preferred to move by the woods on the eastern side of the mountains towards the Franconian Saale and Kissingen. Thus they made a movement which separated them from their allies, instead of bringing the two corps close together. Prince Alexander had sent an officer to the Bavarian camp. He was present on the 4th July at the action of Wiesenthal, and returned to the headquarters of the eighth Federal corps with a report of the failure of the Bavarians. On the receipt of this intelligence, Prince Alexander appears to have abandoned all hope of effecting a junction with Prince Charles north of the Maine. He faced about, and moved back to Frankfort, a town which, until its subsequent occupation by the Prussians, appears always to have had a singular attraction for the eighth Federal corps.

On the 4th July, the same day that General Goeben pressed the Bavarians back at Wiesenthal, the leading division of Falckenstein's army had a singular skirmish in the direction of Hünfeld. As General Beyer, who commanded the Prussian advanced guard, approached that town, he found two squadrons of Bavarian cavalry in front of him. Two guns accompanied these squadrons, which opened fire on the advancing Prussians. The weather was wet, and a clammy mist held the smoke of the cannon, so that it hung like a weighty cloud over the mouths of the pieces. A Prussian battery opened in reply. The first shot so surprised the Bavarians, who had not anticipated that there was artillery with the advanced guard, that the cuirassiers turned about, and sought safety in a wild flight They left one of their guns, which in their haste had not time to be limbered up. Beyer pressed forward, and found Hünfeld evacuated by the enemy. Indeed it is said that these *cuirassiers*, who had been pushed forward by Prince Alexander to open communications with Prince Charles, were so dismayed by one well-aimed cannon-shot, that many of them did not draw rein till they reached Wurzburg.

Prince Alexander withdrew towards Frankfort Falckenstein pushed forward on the 6th; he occupied Fulda with Beyer's division, while Goeben and Manteuffel encamped on the north towards Hünfeld. The object of the Prussian advance was obtained. On the 5th July the Bavarians and the eighth Federal corps were separated from each other by only thirty miles; on the 7th seventy miles lay between them.

Prince Alexander left the Würtemberg division to hold the passes of the Vogels-Berg towards Giessen. The Bavarians, after the action of Wiesenthal, drew back and took up a position in the neighbourhood of Kissingen, on the Franconian Saale.

General Falckenstein, on the 7th, united his whole army at Fulda. He had the choice of attacking either of his separated enemies. To pursue the eighth Federal corps by Giessen, would probably allow it to unite with the Bavarians by moving up the Maine. To advance directly upon Frankfort with the Bavarians on the Saale in his flank and rear, and with the defiles of Gelnhausen, occupied by the eighth corps, in his front, would be extremely hazardous.

Prince Charles was also considered the more formidable antagonist, and the one upon whom it was the more necessary to inflict a heavy blow.

On the 8th July General Falckenstein commenced his march from Fulda. He did not turn towards Gelnhausen, as was expected in the

Bavarian camp, but moved against the position of Prince Charles. On the 9th the Prussian Army reached Brückenau, and orders were given for a flank march to the left, over the Hohe Rhön, against the Bavarians on the Saale. Beyer's division moved as the right wing along the road to Hammelburg; Goeben advanced in the centre towards Kissingen; and Manteuffel on the left upon Waldaschach. On the morning of the 10th July, at nine o'clock, Beyer's division, which had received very doubtful intelligence of the presence of the Bavarians in Hammelburg, began its march towards that town.

About eleven the head of the advanced guard fell in with the first patrols of the enemy's cavalry in front of Unter Erthal, a small village on the road from Brückenau, about two miles south of Hammelburg. These retired on the Prussian advance, but unmasked a rifled battery, posted beyond the houses. A Prussian field-battery quickly unlimbered and came into action. Under cover of its fire an infantry regiment made a dash at the bridge by which the road from Brückenau crosses the Thulba stream. The bridge was not seriously defended, and after a short cannonade the Bavarians drew back to Hammelburg. At mid-day three Prussian batteries topped the Hobels Berg, and after a few rounds from the guns the infantry rushed down with loud cheers to carry the houses. This was, however, not an easy task. The Bavarian General Zoller held the town with something over three thousand men; he determined to bar the passage of the Saale. The odds were too unequal. The Prussians numbered about fifteen thousand men. Yet the Bavarians clung with a high courage to the houses, and opened a biting fire of small arms on the assailants. Their artillery, too, supported well the infantry defence.

Two Prussian infantry regiments threw out skirmishers, and attempted to put down the fire of the Bavarian riflemen. But these were protected by the cover of the houses; and the defenders' artillery from the hill of Saalch splintered its shells among the ranks of the Prussian sharpshooters. The fight did not gain ground for about an hour. After that interval two more Prussian regiments and two additional batteries came into play. Heavily the Prussian pieces threw their metal upon the Bavarian guns at Saalch. The fire of the latter grew weaker and weaker. They were rapidly being silenced by superior force. Some houses, kindled by the Prussian shells, at the same time caught fire, and the town began to burn fiercely in three places. Still the Bavarians clung to the bridge, and stood their ground, careless equally of the flames and of the heavy cannonade. Beyer sent forward his *Jägers* to storm the place.

No longer could the defenders endure the assault. The quick bullets of the needle-gun rained in showers among the burning buildings, scattering fire and death among the garrison. The defence had to be abandoned; and the Bavarians, pursued by salvos of artillery, drew off to the south-east, and the Prussians gained the passage of the Saale at Hammelburg.

On the same day as General Beyer fought the action of Hammelburg on the right, Falckenstein's central column was heavily engaged with the main body of the Bavarians at the celebrated bathing-place of Kissingen. On the 5th July eighty Bavarian troopers, flying from Hünfeld, passed in hot haste through the town. The visitors and the inhabitants were much alarmed, but the *burgomaster* quieted them by a promise that he would give twenty-four hours' warning if the place was in danger of being attacked by the Prussians. This assurance had more weight, because even on the 8th July Bavarian staff-officers sauntered about the Kurgarten as quietly as if in a time of the most profound peace. Some of the troops which had been quartered in Kissingen and its neighbourhood were on the 9th sent to Hammelburg. All appeared still, and yet the inhabitants of the neighbouring villages were already flying from their homes to avoid the Prussians. The Bavarian intelligence department does not appear to have been well managed.

By mid-day on the 9th it was too late for the *burgomaster* to give his warning that the Prussians were already near. The Bavarians concentrated about twenty thousand men, and took up their position. The visitors and inhabitants could not now retire, and had to remain to be the involuntary witnesses of an action. Those who lived in the Hotel Sauner, which lies on the right bank of the Saale, were allowed to move into the less exposed part of the town. None were permitted to quit the place for fear of their conveying intelligence of the Bavarian dispositions to the enemy. The wooden bridge over the Saale, as well as the two iron ones, were destroyed, but of one iron one in front of the Alten Berg the supports were left. It was through the assistance of these that the Prussians gained the first passage of the river; for they knew the localities well, as many of their staff-officers had frequently visited the fashionable watering-place of Kissingen. The stone bridge was barricaded hastily as well as possible, and its approach protected by two 12-pounder guns. Five battalions, with twelve guns, held the town itself. The Bavarians had chosen a very strong position; they held the houses next to the bridge as well as the bank of the Saale beyond the bridge. Their artillery was posted on the Stadt Berg, but not on the important Finster Berg. A battery on the latter hill would have prevented the Prussians from gaining the passage of the river from the Alten Berg. Behind the village of Haussen guns were also in. position. All the bridges outside of Kissingen were destroyed, and all points favourable for defence occupied by infantry. General Zoller commanded the Bavarians.

On the 10th July, at early morning, Prussian hussars appeared. Columns were soon afterwards descried on the roads towards Klaushof and Garitz on the west of Kissingen; and a battery came into position on a hill between Garitz and the river. At half-past seven in the morning, the Bavarian guns near Winkels and the two 12-pounders at the bridge opened on the leading Prussian columns, which consisted of General Kummer's brigade. Kummer's artillery replied, and in a short time the rattle of musketry, mingling with the heavier booming of the guns, told that he was sharply engaged.

The main body of Goeben's division had in the meantime reached Schlimhoff. Here it received orders to detach three battalions by Poppenroth and Klaushof, who were to attack Friedericshall under the command of Colonel Goltz. When General Wrangel's brigade approached Kissingen, it received orders to advance on the right wing of Kummer's brigade, to seize the Alten Berg, and if possible, by extending to its right, to outflank the Bavarian position. A squadron was sent at the same time to reconnoitre the ground beyond Garitz. A battalion was despatched as an advanced guard against the Alten Berg; and a battery of artillery came into action on the northern spur of that hill. The Alten Berg was quickly cleared of Bavarian riflemen by the Prussian *Jägers*.

A company under Captain von Busche was then sent against the bridge on the south of Kissingen, which the Bavarians had partially destroyed, but where the piers had been left standing. Tables, forms, and timber were seized from some neighbouring houses, and with secrecy and rapidity the broken bridge was so far restored that before mid-day. men could cross it in single file. Von Busche led his company over the stream, and then directed his men against a road on the further side, from the cover of which the enemy's marksmen annoyed them considerably. This company was followed by a second, and as quickly as possible a whole battalion was thrown across the stream. The battalion gained the wood on the south-east of Kissingen; here a column was formed, and under cover of many skirmishers advanced against the town. More men were pushed across the repaired bridge, and soon two and a half Prussian battalions were engaged in a street fight among the houses. The remaining portion of Wrangel's brigade was at this time directed in support of Kummer against the principal bridge. Infantry and artillery fire caused the Prussians severe losses, but they pushed on towards the barricade. Their artillery outnumbered that of the defending force, and, protected by it, the battalions carried the bridge.

The army of Bavaria boasted to have had at that time a hundred and twenty-six cannon. Of these only twelve came into action at Kissingen, five at Hammelburg. The rest were uselessly scattered along the bank of the Saale, between these two places.

The passage of the stream by the Prussians decided the action. They secured the Finster Berg and the Bodenlaube, with the old castle of that name, and pushed forward with loud cheers into the heart of the town. Here the Bavarian light infantry fought hard, and, suffering heavy sacrifices themselves, inflicted grievous loss on the Prussians. The Kurgarten, held by three hundred riflemen, were stormed three times by Wrangel's men without success. It was carried on the fourth assault. A young lieutenant, who commanded the Bavarians, with the whole of his men, refused quarter, and died in the place they had held so well At a little after three the whole town was carried.

The Bavarians did not yet renounce the combat. The corps which retreated from Kissingen took up a position on the hill east of the town, and renewed the battle. Wrangel's brigade received orders to clear the hills south of the road which leads to Nudlingen, of the enemy. This was to be effected by the fusilier battalion and the second battalion of the 55th regiment. The first battalion of the same regiment cleared the way, and, extended as skirmishers, advanced along the road. The other troops followed in reserve. The Bavarians had taken up a position on both sides of the road, and greeted the Prussians with an artillery fire from the Sinn Berg. They fought well, and not till seven o'clock did Wrangel occupy Winkels. The Bavarians were supposed to be retiring, and Wrangel's troops were about to bivouac, when a report came in from the 19th, which had occupied the outposts, that the Bavarians were advancing in force.

Two battalions of the 55th, a 12-pounder battery, and a squadron of hussars, were immediately sent to reinforce the outlying troops, while two companies of the 55th were sent into the hills on the right to menace the left flank of the enemy's advance. The battery and squadron advanced at a trot General Wrangel in person went to the out-posts, and was receiving the reports from the commanding officer of the 19th, when some rifle bullets came from the southern hill into the closed columns of the regiment. The Bavarians, under Prince Charles himself, had come down with nine fresh battalions of their first division. They had seized the hills which lie on the north of the road, and were pressing rapidly forward under the cover of their artillery. The Prussian cavalry and battery, as well as the 19th regiment, were pushed back. The 55th, coming up, threw themselves into a hollow road, and, under the protection of their fire, the retreat was for a time checked Prince Charles urged on, however, superior forces, and those, too, had to retire.

The Prussians now took up a position on the heights south-east of Winkels, where two batteries came into play. The retreating battalions halted here, and the fight stood still. One battalion of the 19th regiment and two companies of the soldiers of Lippe were sent by Wrangel into the hills on the north of the road, while the second battalion of the 55th was pushed up there on its southern side. As soon as these flanking troops had gained their positions, the whole brigade advanced in double-quick time, with drums beating. The charge succeeded, though the loss was great. The Bavarians were driven back. The Prussians regained their former position, and Prince Charles relinquished his attack.

The Prussian left column, which was formed by Manteuffel's division, on the 10th July also secured the passage at Waldaschach, about five miles above Kissingen, and at Haussen. At neither place did the Bavarians make any obstinate stand.

The Bavarians appear to have been surprised on the Saale. The Prussian march, previous to the battle of Kissingen, was so rapid that they did not expect an attack till the following day. In consequence, their whole force was not concentrated on the river. The troops which held Kissingen and Hammelburg were unsupported, while those which should have acted as their reserves were too far distant to be of any service. The latter, on the other hand, arrived so late that their comrades had already been defeated, and they themselves, instead of acting as reinforcements, met with only a similar fate to those first engaged. The Bavarian staff were unprepared. They had no maps of the country, except one which the chief of the staff, General von der Tann, borrowed from a native of one of the small towns near the field.

CHAPTER 3

The Actions on the Maine

When Prince Alexander of Hesse turned to retreat on the 5th July, he might still, by a rapid march along the road which leads from Lauterbach to Brückenau, have made an attempt to unite with the Bavarians before they were attacked at Kissingen by the Prussians. This course he appears, however, to have considered too hazardous. He retired to Frankfort, and on the 9th July concentrated his troops round that town. His first division was at Frankfort: the second in some villages north of the town, on the river Nidda; the third division at Bergen, and the fourth at Bockenheim. The reserved cavalry was towards Friedberg; the reserve artillery across the river, in Offenbach. The two banks of the Maine were connected by a bridge, which leads from Frankfort to Offenbach.

Frequent alarms made it evident how little steadfast confidence pervaded the Federal corps of Prince Alexander. The news of the victory won by the Prussians at Königgrätz was widely circulated through the ranks by the Frankfort journals. Every moment reports were rife that Prussian columns were advancing towards Frankfort from Wetzlar, or Giessen; and once an officer, by spreading the alarm, caused a whole division to lose its night's rest, and to take up a position in order of battle.

At this time the eighth Federal corps was not practically fit to take the field. Such confusion reigned in the fortress of Mainz, that whole regiments marched into the town and took up quarters on their own account, without any report being made to the commandant. Newly appointed officers, surgeons, and hospital assistants, had to seek for their regiments without being able to obtain accurate intelligence of their whereabouts from any one. No firm union existed between the different divisions of the eighth corps. The corps had not been concentrated for twenty-four years, and the divisions were totally different in uniform, administration, and organisation. The hussars of Hesse-Cassel were dressed and accoutred so similarly to Prussian cavalry, that the Austrians fired upon them at Aschaffenburg. The small arms were of different calibres. The four field batteries of the third division were equipped on four different systems.

The day after the victory of Kissingen, General Falckenstein could turn his attention against this heterogeneous mass without fear of any assault on his rear by the Bavarians. The latter retired in such haste, after the Battle of Kissingen, towards the Maine, that Manteuffel's division, which was sent in pursuit, could not feel them. On the 11th July, General Falckenstein ordered Beyer's division to march by way of Hammelburg and Gelnhausen on Hanau. This it accomplished, without, as was anticipated, falling in with the Würtemberg division at Gelnhausen. The latter only held this place till the 14th July, and then retired in great haste, without throwing any obstacle in the way of the advancing Prussians, either by breaking the bridges, or by any other means.

The division of General Goeben was directed at the same time through the defile of the Spessart upon Aschaffenburg. Here the passes were not held nor barricaded. Notwithstanding the presence in this district of large numbers of foresters, no abattis or entanglements were placed across the road. None of the almost unassailable heights were occupied, either to prevent the direct progress of the Prussians, or to threaten their line of march in flank. The railway which was still serviceable was not used to convey the small number of riflemen and guns, which at Gemünden, as at many other points, would have thrown great difficulty in Goeben's way. Manteuffel's division followed Goeben's, and scoured the country in the direction of Würzburg.

Between Gemünden and Aschaffenburg, the River Maine makes a deep bend to the south. Into the bow thus formed, the mountainous region of the Spessart protrudes, through which the road and railway lead directly westward from Gemünden to the latter town. On the 13th July, the leading brigade of Goeben's division, that of Wrangel, was approaching Hayn, when a report came in from the squadron of hussars, which was clearing the way, that some of the enemy's cavalry and infantry were advancing towards that place from Laufach, a station on the railroad nearer to Frankfort than Hayn.

It was soon discovered that these were troops of Hesse-Darmstadt The fusilier battalion of the 55th regiment was pushed forward to gain the top of the defile, up which the brigade was then moving. It advanced in columns of companies and, without difficulty, pushed back two hostile battalions which it encountered. The village of Laufach was taken, and the railway station occupied, while three battalions and a squadron were sent forward to seize a cutting beyond the station, and to relieve the fusiliers. The relief had not been fully carried out when the enemy, with eight or nine battalions and two batteries assumed the offensive. The assailants mustered about eight thousand men. The battalion of the 55th threw itself into a churchyard surrounded by walls, and placed itself on the defensive.

The village of Frohnhöfen in front was occupied by three companies, supported by six companies posted on the hills on the right, and seven on those on the left of the railway. The remaining troops of the brigade took up a position in front of the station, as a reserve. The enemy attacked all points; so that, by degrees, nine companies had to be sent up to Frohnhöfen. The most severe attack was made on the right wing. General Wrangel was obliged to send his two remaining battalions and a battery to this point. All his available troops were now engaged, and the fight for some time was very even. At last, however, all the assaults of the Hessians were repulsed, and a counter attack made by three battalions and a squadron supported by the fire of a 12-pounder battery had great success.

The Hessians drew off from all points towards Aschaffenburg, and left more than one hundred prisoners, as well as the greater portion of five hundred killed and wounded, in the hands of the victors. The latter also captured the majority of the knapsacks of their assailants, who had taken them off at the beginning of the action, and on retreating left them lying on the ground. The advantage of the needle-gun in a defensive position, was well demonstrated at Laufach. Whole ranks of corpses of its enemies lay in front of the position, and until early morning wounded men were found. On the Prussian side the loss was very small, in all hardly twenty men, and one officer.

The commander-in-chief of the eighth corps was this day uncertain whether he should defend Frankfort. His troops were in scattered positions, and instead of a large concentrated mass of troops, only small detachments were pushed out to meet the enemy. The division sent in haste to Frohnhöfen, only brought one of its four field batteries into action, and used only one or two squadrons of its whole cavalry to attack the Prussians. The two brigades of infantry came in haste without rations, and after one another under fire. There was no commander-in-chief, the leader of each brigade acted for himself, and led his troops by the most direct road against the enemy with great valour, but with little judgment. The blame for all these errors is apparently due to General von Perglas, the commander of the Darmstadt division, who allowed his troops to advance in closed masses unprotected by artillery against a wood in which the Prussians, well covered, had firmly planted themselves.

The advantages of ground, disposition, and leading were all on the side of the Prussians, who gained their success, although very weary from a long march, without any exertions worthy of mention. They had quickly, but so skilfully availed themselves of each local advantage and cover for the defence of their line by infantry and artillery fire, that all the reckless bravery of the Hessians had no other result than to inflict upon themselves very severe losses. Among these were a regimental commander, a major of the staff, and thirty killed or wounded company officers. After the action of the 13th July, Wrangel's brigade bivouacked at Laufach, with a strong advanced post of three battalions round Frohnhöfen.

On the 14th, at seven in the morning, the further march on Aschaffenburg was to commence. The care of the enemy's wounded on the previous day, the collection of scattered arms, and waiting for the return of the patrols which had been sent out at dawn, delayed the start for half an hour. The reports of the latter told that the enemy was retreating from Hösbach. A squadron of hussars was sent forward to occupy that village. The infantry of Wrangel's brigade followed along the main road with flankers pushed out far on the right and left. On the hill of Weiberhofen, Wrangel's brigade fell in with that of General Kummer, which had moved by a route on the south of the railway.

A report soon was brought in that the enemy was advancing strong detachments from Hösbach. Colonel von der Goltz, the commander of the vanguard, was immediately ordered to take up a position on the heights south of the main road, under cover of which the brigade formed for battle in the valley. General Kummer was ordered with his brigade to move along the railway towards Aschaffenburg. General Goeben was in command of the two united brigades. The advance guard had hardly formed when a further report announced that the enemy was drawing back. General Goeben then ordered a general advance. He moved Wrangel's brigade along the road, Kummer's on the railway embankment; at the same time he drew a hussar and *cuirassier* regiment from the reserve, and covered his right flank by moving them through the open fields on the south of the road. Hösbach was found unoccupied by the enemy, as was also Goldbach.

On the further side of the latter village the infantry fire opened. The 15th and 55th Prussian regiments pushed forward to the wooded bank of the Laufach stream. The Federal troops here consisted of the Austrian division under General Count Neipperg, formed of troops which had originally garrisoned Mainz, Rastadt, and Frankfort There were also some of the Hesse-Darmstadt troops here. The infantry fire of the Federal soldiers caused the Prussians little loss; but an Austrian battery, posted on a hill south of Aschaffenburg, and admirably served, annoyed them much. The Prussian artillery could find no favourable position from which to attack this battery with clear advantage, and the Austrian guns for some time had the best of the action. At last three battalions of the 15th Prussian regiment were pushed along the stream nearer to the village of Daurm, and made themselves masters of a hill on which stood a tower surrounded by a wall. Protected by this, the infantry succeeded by its musketry fire in forcing the enemy's artillery to retire. The advance of some Federal cavalry was also stopped by the same means before the squadrons could attack.

As soon as the Austrian battery drew back, a general advance was made against Aschaffenburg, which is surrounded with high wall that offered the Austrians cover, and a convenient opportunity for defence. The Prussian artillery coming into action on the top of a hill soon showed itself superior to that of the Austrians. After long firing in the environs of the town, and the gardens which lay in front of the walls, the Prussians advanced to storm, and although they were received with repeated salvos, forced their enemy out of his strong position without suffering very severe loss. At the railway station there was a sharp combat, but at no other point was the resistance very determined. The town of Aschaffenburg has only two gates. In consequence, as the retreating Austrians were hurrying towards the bridge over the Maine a block occurred. The Prussians pushing forward, entered the city with the rearmost ranks of the enemy, and made two thousand prisoners. These were for the most part Italians, who defended themselves without much energy. General Goeben occupied the bridge by which the railway to Darmstadt crosses the Maine, with three battalions, two squadrons, and a battery. These pushed reconnaissances towards Frankfort The rest of his troops he cantoned in the town of Aschaffenburg.

The losses of the Prussians in the capture of the town were not severe. Those of the Federal troops were considerable; as there were many killed and wounded, besides the large number of prisoners. A large quantity of material of war fell also into the hands of the conquerors. A regiment of hussars of Hesse-Cassel, which Prince Alexander had attached to his Austrian division, lost five officers and one hundred and eight non-commissioned officers and men, in its attempt to cover the retreat of the infantry through the streets.

While General Goeben advanced towards Aschaffenburg, and gained there the passage of the Maine, General Beyer's division pushed towards Frankfort, by way of Gelnhausen, The easily defensible passage of the Kinzig, near this town, was found unoccupied by the Federal troops, and on the 17th, Beyer reached the neighbourhood of Hanau without ever having seen an enemy.

During the action of Aschaffenburg, Prince Alexander, instead of supporting his Austrian division, which was engaged there, remained with the mass of his troops inactive at Seiligenstadt. Yet he could by vigorous action have been much superior in numbers to Goeben at the former town, have saved the passage of the river, and perhaps pushing Goeben and Manteuffel backwards, by bearing on their right, have urged them into the bend of the Maine, and severed them from Beyer and their line of communication with the north. This page of the history of the campaign of the leader of the Federal corps is but a repetition of the perpetual tale of opportunities lost and advantages neglected. The advantage of positions was always on the side of the Federal corps, yet these advantages were sacrificed, always with loss to the Federal side, to which the casualties in the Prussian ranks by no means corresponded. The lives of soldiers were to all appearance trifled away and wasted, by strategical ignorance and absence of energy on the part of their leader.

The immediate result of the victorious advance of the Prussian army of the Maine was the evacuation of Frankfort and the line of the Maine, by the eighth Federal corps, and its occupation by the Prussians. On the 16th July, General Falckenstein entered the town at the head of Goeben's division, and was able to report to the king that all the lands north of the Maine were in Prussian possession. General Falckenstein had within fourteen days defeated two armies, of which each was as strong as his own, in two great, and several minor actions; and, in a country by no means very advantageous for the offensive, had manoeuvred so as to separate his two adversaries, who on the 5th July were within thirty miles of each other, by a distance of sixty miles.

The following is a summary of the operations north of the Maine:—

Bavarians,—From the 15th to 25th June, halted near Schweinfurt In the meantime the Hanoverians were surrounded, and obliged to capitulate.

On the 25th June they made various movements, with the object of effecting a junction with the eighth Federal corps.

On the 12th July they again returned to Schweinfurt, after having been pushed away from their allies by Falckenstein, at Wiesenthal and Kissingen.

The Eighth Federal Corps.—From the 15th June to the 12th July occupied strategical positions round Frankfort

On the 5th July it made a partial march on Fulda. Some of its cavalry fell in with some Prussian patrols, and it retreated rapidly to the Maine.

On the 13th and 14th July the actions of Laufach and Aschaffenburg were fought, while Prince Alexander lay at Seiligenstadt

On the 14th July Prince Alexander concentrated rearwards, on the south of the Maine.

On the 13th July, when the Prussians reached Laufach, not more than thirty miles from Frankfort, the residuary members of the mutilated Germanic Diet retired from the ancient city on the Maine, where of old the rulers of the Holy Roman Empire were elected and crowned. Their business had, since the outbreak of hostilities, been chiefly confined to making protests against Prussia. The days when the Confederation could enforce its decrees were, however, past, and the *diet* had found a very different patient of Federal execution from the Dane. Its protests were now all spent shot. A few of the deputies, however, still held together, and styled themselves, in diplomatic language, the *diet* and Confederation of Germany.

These, on the 13th July, quitted Frankfort with the documents from the Archives of the Bund, and journeyed to Augsburg, where the black, red and gold flag of the Germanic Confederation was hoisted over the inn of the sign of the Three Moors.

The last Bavarian battalion left Frankfort on the 14th, and the headquarters of the eighth Federal corps were established that night at Dieburg, a station on the railway between Aschaffenburg and Darmstadt

On the 15th, Prince Alexander drew near to the south, and concentrated his corps on the Odenwald. This day his light cavalry opened communications with Prince Charles's corps at Würzburg, by the left bank of the Maine, and the road through Moltenberg and Werbek.

On the 15th, the Senate of Frankfort published a proclamation to the inhabitants, in which it was announced that the *diet* which usually held its sittings in the free city, had temporarily withdrawn; that the city would act as an open town, and that there appeared to be no danger of any injury to the lives or property of any of the inhabitants. The construction of earthworks, which had been commenced by the Federal troops, was abandoned, and all was prepared for the advent of the Prussian conquerors. At Darmstadt the Russian flag was hoisted on the palace of the Grand Duke of Hesse-Darmstadt, who in person started for Munich.

Wrangel's brigade, after the capture of Aschaffenburg, was pushed forward by forced marches to Hanau. About five o'clock on the evening of the 16th July, the first Prussians arrived near Frankfort, brought in a train from Aschaffenburg. They got out of the carriages a short distance from the city gates, and took up a position on the Hanau road. This advanced guard consisted of a regiment of *cuirassiers* and a regiment of hussars. At seven a patrol of the hussars, led by an officer, halted before the city gate. In another quarter of an hour the head of the vanguard, consisting of one squadron of cuirassiers and the remaining hussars, passed in. The populace were for the most part sullenly silent. A few insulting cries to the Prussians were occasionally heard from some of the windows, but the soldiers took no notice of them. In a few minutes the Generals Vogel von Falckenstein, Goeben, Wrangel, and Tresckow, surrounded by the officers of the staff, rode in at the head of the main body. The bands of the regiments played Prussian national airs. Before ten o'clock the whole line of march had entered. The telegraph and post-offices were occupied. The railway station was garrisoned, and guards established over all the principal buildings. The free town of Frankfort was virtually annexed to the Prussian monarchy.

On the 17th July, the remainder of Falckenstein's troops entered the town, and some troops were pushed forwards south of the city, who captured a Hessian bridge train.

General Vogel von Falckenstein established his headquarters in Frankfort, and published a proclamation in which he announced that he had assumed temporarily the government of the duchy of Nassau, the town and territory of Frankfort, and the portions of Bavaria and

Hesse-Darmstadt, which his troops had occupied The civil functionaries of these districts were retained in their posts, but were directed to receive no order except from the Prussian commander-in-chief. Several of the Frankfort papers which had always been distinguished for strong anti-Prussian feeling were suppressed. The eleven armed unions [1] which had existed in the city, were abolished; and the functions of the senate and college of *burghers* established by a general order. Six millions of *gulden* [2] were demanded from the town as a war contribution, and after much grumbling paid by the citizens. When, afterwards, on the 20th July, a second additional contribution of twenty millions of *gulden* [3] was demanded, an universal cry of indignation and horror was raised.

In the meantime, General von Roeder had been appointed governor of the town, to whom the *burgomaster* represented, on the 23rd July, that the town had already furnished six millions of *gulden*, and about two millions of rations, and requested to appeal against the subsequent contribution to the King of Prussia. So much did this misfortune of his city weigh on the *burgomaster* that the same night he committed suicide. The town sent a deputation to Berlin which treated so effectually, and was so powerfully supported by the opinions of the foreign press, that the contribution was not insisted upon by the king. Frankfort shortly afterwards was united definitely to Prussia, when the first contribution of six millions was not actually returned to the citizens, but was retained by the government to be expended in public works for the benefit of the city.

General Falckenstein, at Frankfort, issued the following general order to his troops:—

Soldiers of the Army of the Maine!—On the 14th of this month at Aschaffenburg, we have fulfilled the second portion of our task. On that day the right bank of the Maine, as far as our arms reached, was cleared of the enemy. Before we advance to new deeds, it behoves me to express to you all my recognition of the manner in which you have made the numerous exertions necessary for our success. Yet it is not that alone which I have to praise. It is your valour, and the energy with which, in six great and several smaller actions, you have hurled yourselves upon the enemy, knitted victory to your banners, and made

---

1. Vereine.
2. £600,000.
3. £2,000,000

thousands of your adversaries prisoners. You defeated the Bavarians in two brilliant engagements at Wiesenthal, and Zella on the 4th of this month, crossed the Rhön mountains in order again to spring upon the Bavarian Army at the four different points of Hammelburg, Kissingen, Hausen, and Waldaschach: everywhere you were victorious.

So soon as the third day after the bloody storming of Kissingen, the same division had crossed to the Spessart to engage the eighth Federal corps. The victory of the thirteenth division over the division of Darmstadt at Laufach, and the capture of Aschaffenburg from the united Federal and Austrian troops on the 14th, were the earnings of its bravery and its toils. On the 16th Frankfort was occupied by it I must express to this division my special thanks. Fortunate to be generally at the head of the corps, and so the first to come into collision with the enemy, it showed itself as worthy of this honourable post, as did the intelligence and energy of its leader to take advantage of his opportunities.

Headquarters,   Von Falckenstein,
Frankfort, 14th July, 1866. Commander-in-Chief of the Army

CHAPTER 4

The Campaign South of the Maine

The day that General von Falckenstein published his general order to the troops, the Army of the Maine lost its commander. The difficult state of affairs in Bohemia, caused by the animosities of political parties, which, till the Prussian invasion, had been kept down by the strong hand of the Austrian Government, had, on the removal of that pressure, sprung forth into full life. The importance of the communications of the main Prussian armies with the provinces of Saxony and Silesia, which were threatened by the three fortresses of Theresienstadt, Josephstadt, and Königgrätz, led the King of Prussia to appoint General Falckenstein as military governor-general of that province.

Lieutenant-General von Manteuffel assumed the command of the Army of the Maine in Falckenstein's place. The division which General Manteuffel had commanded was placed under General Flies. On the 18th July Wiesbaden was occupied by the Prussians; and on the 20th Kummer's brigade was pushed southwards as an advanced guard and entered Darmstadt, but the main body of the army halted at Frankfort until the 21st. While he waited at Frankfort General Manteuffel received reinforcements. These consisted of three battalions, three squadrons, and two batteries of Oldenburg, two battalions of Hamburg, one of Lübeck, one of Waldeck, which was detached to watch the fortress of Mainz, one of Bremen, one of Schwarzburg-Sonderhausen.

Besides these contingents of the allies of Prussia, he also received five fourth battalions of Prussian troops, which remained as the garrison of Frankfort, the ninth *Jäger* battalion, and three reserve regiments of *Landwehr* cavalry,—in all fifteen battalions, twelve squadrons, and twelve guns, which mustered over twelve thousand combatants. Of these, five thousand men were left to hold the line of the Maine at Frankfort, Hanau, and Aschaffenburg. The remainder raised the active army to a strength of sixty thousand combatants.

At the same time a second reserve corps was formed at Leipsic and placed under the command of the Grand Duke of Mecklenburg-Schwerin. It consisted of the division of Mecklenburg-Schwerin, which numbered four battalions of infantry, one battalion of *Jägers*, four squadrons, and two 6-pounder batteries, and of a combined Prussian division, which was placed under the command of General Horne, who had formerly commanded the eighth division of the army of Prince Frederick Charles. Horne's combined division consisted of the fourth regiment of the Prussian Guard, the fourth battalions of five regiments of the line, two battalions of Anhalt, two regiments of *Landwehr* cavalry, and eight batteries. This second reserve corps mustered in all about twenty-three thousand combatants. It was intended to enter Bavaria by way of Hof, and either to act against the rear of the united Bavarian and Federal corps, while engaged with General Manteuffel, or to force the Bavarian army to form front towards the east, and prevent Prince Charles of Bavaria from acting in concert with Prince Alexander against Manteuffel.

By the 21st July, the railway from Frankfort to Cassel had been repaired by the railway detachment of the Army of the Maine, and was available throughout its whole length, not only for military transport, but also for private traffic On that day, the main body of the Army of the Maine quitted Frankfort, and moved towards the south. Beyer's division at the same time advanced from Hanau by Aschaffenburg to the south. The Bavarians had not occupied the road from Würzburg to the passage of the Maine at Heidenfeld. The eighth Federal corps was reported to be in retreat through the Odenwald, by Höchst and Moltenberg. Further information told that the Bavarians were concentrated, and in position near Würzburg.

It then appeared probable that part of the eighth Federal corps intended to hold the defiles of the Odenwald, and the line of the Neckar, while the remainder of its troops joined the Bavarians near the Tauber. To take advantage of two roads, in order to move quickly, and if possible to press upon Prince Alexander before he was firmly linked with the Bavarians, and to shield his right flank against any detachments lurking in the Odenwald, General Manteuffel moved Goeben's division by Darmstadt on Könieg, while Flies and Beyer pushed up the valley of the Maine by Wurth. At the same time he sent a strong reconnaissance up the right bank of the river against Heidenfeld. Frankfort and Aschaffenburg were firmly occupied.

On the 23rd July, the Army of the Maine occupied a position near Moltenberg and Amorbach. Along its whole front it could firmly feel the eighth Federal corps. It was found that the enemy was in force on the Tauber, and that his advanced posts were pushed over the river as far as Hundheim. On the 24th two actions took place on the Tauber, an affluent of the Maine, which falls into the latter stream below Wertheim. General Manteuffel moved against the Tauber in three columns. On the left Flies' division advanced on Wertheim. The two columns on the right were under General Goeben. Of these, that on the left consisted of the Oldenberg brigade and the battalion of Bremen, which moved upon Werbach against the division of Baden. That on the right, consisting of the remaining troops of Goeben's division, with Wrangel's brigade in front, marched on Tauberbischofsheim. Beyer's division was moved on Dermbach as the reserve.

At Tauberbischofsheim the Würtemberg division, under General Hardegg was posted, to hold the place itself, and then issue from the valley on the road towards Würzburg, in case of an attack by the Prussians. The artillery fire of the advanced guard brigade of Goeben's divisions caused great loss among the defenders, and soon forced them to retire from the village. General Hardegg withdrew his troops, but endeavoured to hold the Prussians in the houses, and to prevent the advance of their batteries. By blowing up the bridge over the Tauber, he for a time prevented the progress of the Prussian artillery. After a hot combat, which lasted three hours, the Würtembergers were relieved by the fourth division of the eighth Federal corps. The action increased in fury, but ultimately the Prussians gained the passage of the Tauber at Bischofsheim, and pushed their outposts a short distance along the road to Würzburg.

The action at Werbach afforded the brigade composed of the Oldenburgers and the battalion of Bremen, its first opportunity to display its efficiency. As soon as the Prussian advanced guard, which attacked Bischofsheim, met with opposition, this brigade was pushed against Werbach. The enemy evacuated Hochhausen, which lies on the left bank of the river, without firing a shot, but set himself stolidly to oppose the passage of the stream at Werbach. The attacking troops had marched for twelve hours on the 23rd July, and on the 24th had been moving from five o'clock in the morning until two in the afternoon. They found their opponents in a good position, from which they themselves were exposed to a heavy cannonade. The Oldenburg artillery opened, and with such a good effect, that it soon got the fire of the opposite batteries under. These did not make good practice: the loss they inflicted was most trivial. The infantry, which had been hidden behind some rising ground, and in a wood, then advanced to the attack of the village of Werbach, threading their way through the intricate vineyards which clothed the slope down to the Tauber.

After a short time spent in skirmishing, the Oldenburgers rushed to the assault, part forcing their way over the barricades, part wading through the water of the stream, which rose breast high against them. Their losses were heavy, but their rush successful They carried the houses, and drove the defenders clean through the village, and themselves covered by the houses, commenced a murderous fire on the retreating columns. The combat at Werbach not only secured to General Manteuffel the passage of the stream at that point, but had a more important result. The division of Baden retreated so far after its failure here, that the position in which the Federal corps had determined to fight on the Tauber on the following day had to be evacuated.

At Wertheim, General Flies forced back the Hessians, whom he found posted there, and secured the passage of the Tauber at this point also.

The commander of the eighth Federal corps, when he perceived that he could no longer hold the line of the Tauber, fell back to Gerscheim, a village half way between Tauberbischofsheim and Würzburg, and about seven miles from either place. Here he determined, on some wooded heights, to await the Prussians. In the meantime the Bavarian army, following the road from Würzburg to Aschaffenburg, closed towards the eighth corps, and taking post on the north at Helmstadt, and Utingen, formed with it a long line of battle, in rear of which lay Würzburg and the Maine.

General Manteuffel was obliged to attack the allied corps in this position, although they were numerically much superior to him. He formed the intention of strengthening his right, and pivoting himself on Wertheim, to act with vigour against the allied left. He hoped thus to push his adversaries off the road to Würzburg, and to force them into the elbow which the Maine forms north of that place. There cut off from their communications, and with the river in their rear, they would have had almost no resource except that of capitulating.

On the 25th, the Prussian commander-in-chief drew forward Beyer's division, which had hitherto remained in reserve in rear of his left wing, and placed it between those of Goeben and Flies. The Army of the Maine now formed a line of battle about ten miles long, but only Goeben and Beyer were to attack on the 25th. Flies was to hold himself at Wertheim as the pivot of the army. Goeben was to attack the eighth Federal corps; Beyer the Bavarians. General Kummer's brigade, on the 25th, marched as the advanced guard of Goeben's division. When that officer had passed a wood lying a short distance in front of Gerscheim, he made out the enemy—Würtembergers, Nassauers, and Austrians drawn up on the north of the road in order of battle. Their superiority in artillery was very considerable; they had eight batteries, six regiments of cavalry, and about seventy thousand infantry, while Kummer had only six battalions, four squadrons, and two batteries. Wrangel's brigade had marched towards the right, in order to act against the enemy's left flank.

The Oldenburg brigade, with the reserve, were behind, but at so great a distance that their arrival on the ground could not be calculated upon for an hour. Nevertheless General Kummer determined at once to attack. His two batteries came into position, some infantry occupied the wood beside him, the rest of the foot soldiers and the cavalry formed in order of battle, and his artillery opened fire. The enemy replied from forty pieces, and after a cannonade which lasted three-quarters of an hour, compelled the Prussian guns to retire. Prince Alexander of Hesse immediately sent some infantry against the wood, but the Prussians held the trees firmly, and from the cover slaughtered their assailants with their quickly-loaded arm.

At this time the Oldenburg brigade and the reserves came up, and Wrangel was seen advancing against the enemy s left. The artillery fire of the allies told little on the Prussian troops, and caused but slight loss in proportion to the number of guns engaged. Wrangel's appearance on his left, and Kummer's steady hold of the wood, made the enemy begin slowly to retire. The Oldenburg artillery joined to Kummer's two batteries, fired heavily upon their slowly retreating columns. The allied batteries, halting at every favourable spot, came into action, and it was not till nightfall that the cannonade ceased. By that time the Prussians had occupied and passed beyond Gerscheim. On the same day, Beyer advanced against the Bavarians, who were in position near Helmstadt, by way of Bottingheim and Neubrunn.

In front of Bottingheim he fell in with some cavalry patrols. At Neubrunn some infantry made its appearance. This was the advanced guard of the Bavarian main body, which was about to advance against Werbach. This infantry Beyer attacked sharply, and drove back towards Helmstadt. In rear of Neubrunn the retiring Bavarians were reinforced, and halted in a swelling plateau, much dotted over with plantations. The battle now began in earnest The Prussian advanced guard moving towards Mädelhofen found an unoccupied plantation on the Bavarian left Pivoted on this it wheeled up to its left, and moved against Helmstadt. At the same time Beyer's main body moved straight upon that village. The Bavarians could not maintain themselves in that place, but their artillery, which drew off towards Utingen, took up a position beyond Helmstadt, from which their guns rained a hot fire of shells upon the heads of the Prussian columns. The Prussian artillery, covered by numerous skirmishers in the plantations, engaged the Bavarian guns. About three hours after the beginning of the fight the enemy's artillery drew off to Utingen, and so left the road to Mädelhofen, the most direct route to Würzburg open to Beyer's left wing.

The Prussian division then made a concentrated attack against a wood near Mädelhofen, under cover of which heavy masses of Bavarian infantry were preparing for an attack towards Neubrunn. At the same time, Beyer's two regiments of cavalry dashed against the Bavarian horse, which in front of the wood were covering the formation. A severe hand to hand combat took place. The Bavarian horsemen were finally, however, overcome, and forced to quit the field. While the cavalry were engaged, some of the Prussian infantry pushed the Bavarian battalions back to Waldbrunn. The whole of Beyer's division then moved against the plantations near Mädelhofen and Waldbrunn, but the enemy drew off so quickly that Beyer concluded the action had terminated, and ordered his troops to bivouac.

It was not so, however. Hardly had the Prussian regiments taken up their positions for the night, than an attack opened upon their left rear in the direction of Helmstadt. A part of the Bavarian Army had, unperceived, advanced in this direction from Utingen, and now opened a second action with a heavy cannonade. Beyer quickly changed his front left back, forming a reserve of the two regiments which had previously been upon his right. His artillery, as soon as it had taken up its new position, opened fire against the line of Bavarian guns, which was continually pushing more and more in the direction of Neubrunn, in order to outflank the Prussian position.

This fire, however, did little towards silencing the Bavarian batteries. The Prussian reserve, which had a long distance to travel, was far from the left wing. Every moment the attack of the enemy's infantry might be expected. Matters seemed very critical. But the Bavarians did not attack. After a time his reserve reached Beyer's left. He then ordered a general advance, which was successful. Prince Charles of

Bavaria was forced back to Roszbrünn, where he halted General Beyer calculated upon for an hour.

Nevertheless General Kummer determined at once to attack. His two batteries came into position, some infantry occupied the wood beside him, the rest of the foot soldiers and the cavalry formed in order of battle, and his artillery opened fire. The enemy replied from forty pieces, and after a cannonade which lasted three-quarters of an hour, compelled the Prussian guns to retire. Prince Alexander of Hesse immediately sent some infantry against the wood, but the Prussians held the trees firmly, and from the cover slaughtered their assailants with their quickly-loaded arm. At this time the Oldenburg brigade and the reserves came up, and Wrangel was seen advancing against the enemy's left. The artillery fire of the allies told little on the Prussian troops, and caused but slight loss in proportion to the number of guns engaged. Wrangel's appearance on his left, and Kummer's steady hold of the wood, made the enemy begin slowly to retire.

The Oldenburg artillery joined to Kummer's two batteries, fired heavily upon their slowly retreating columns. The allied batteries, halting at every favourable spot, came into action, and it was not till nightfall that the cannonade ceased. By that time the Prussians had occupied and passed beyond Gerscheim. On the same day, Beyer advanced against the Bavarians, who were in position near Helmstadt, by way of Bottingheim and Neubrunn. In front of Bottingheim he fell in with some cavalry patrols. At Neubrunn some infantry made its appearance. This was the advanced guard of the Bavarian main body, which was about to advance against Werbach. This infantry Beyer attacked sharply, and drove back towards Helmstadt. In rear of Neubrunn the retiring Bavarians were reinforced, and halted in a swelling plateau, much dotted over with plantations. The battle now began in earnest.

The Prussian advanced guard moving towards Mädelhofen found an unoccupied plantation on the Bavarian left. Pivoted on this it wheeled up to its left, and moved against Helmstadt At the same time Beyer's main body moved straight upon that village. The Bavarians could not maintain themselves in that place, but their artillery, which drew off towards Utingen, took up a position beyond Helmstadt, from which their guns rained a hot fire of shells upon the heads of the Prussian columns. The Prussian artillery, covered by numerous skirmishers in the plantations, engaged the Bavarian guns. About three hours after the beginning of the fight the enemy's artillery drew off to Utingen, and so left the road to Mädelhofen, the most direct route to Würzburg open to Beyer's left wing. The Prussian division then made a concentrated attack against a wood near Mädelhofen, under cover of which heavy masses of Bavarian infantry were preparing for an attack towards Neubrunn.

At the same time, Beyer's two regiments of cavalry dashed against the Bavarian horse, which in front of the wood were covering the formation. A severe hand to hand combat took place. The Bavarian horsemen were finally, however, overcome, and forced to quit the field. While the cavalry were engaged, some of the Prussian infantry pushed the Bavarian battalions back to Waldbrunn. The whole of Beyer's division then moved against the plantations near Mädelhofen and Waldbrunn, but the enemy drew off so quickly that Beyer concluded the action had terminated, and ordered his troops to bivouac.

It was not so, however. Hardly had the Prussian regiments taken up their positions for the night, than an attack opened upon their left rear in the direction of Helmstadt. A part of the Bavarian Army had, unperceived, advanced in this direction from Utingen, and now opened a second action with a heavy cannonade. Beyer quickly changed his front left back, forming a reserve of the two regiments which had previously been upon his right. His artillery, as soon as it had taken up its new position, opened fire against the line of Bavarian guns, which was continually pushing more and more in the direction of Neubrunn, in order to outflank the Prussian position. This fire, however, did little towards silencing the Bavarian batteries.

The Prussian reserve, which had a long distance to travel, was far from the left wing. Every moment the attack of the enemy's infantry might be expected. Matters seemed very critical. But the Bavarians did not attack. After a time his reserve reached Beyer's left. He then ordered a general advance, which was successful. Prince Charles of Bavaria was forced back to Roszbrünn, where he halted. General Beyer bivouacked near Helmstadt Goeben's division halted for the night on the road between Gerscheim and Würzburg, with its outposts at Kist. When Prince Charles's attack against Beyer, near Helmstadt, was developed, General Flies moved forward from Wertheim to support Beyer. He did not arrive on the field before the termination of the battle, but he took a position for the night at Utingen, and patrolled towards Roszbrünn.

This action cost the Prussians about three hundred and fifty officers and men, who were placed *hors de combat*. The Bavarians lost seventeen officers and two hundred and thirty-nine men killed and wounded, besides three hundred and sixty-three prisoners, who for the most part were wounded.

Prince Alexander, on the evening of the 25th, withdrew his corps to Würzburg, and took up a position under shelter of the fortress. Prince Charles appears to have received no information of this retreat, for on the morning of the 26th, he not only held his position at Rosz-brünn, where his rear and his communication with Würzburg were already threatened by Goeben, but he also advanced against Utingen to attack Flies. He must in so doing have believed that the eighth Federal corps still covered his left, and held the road from Tauber-bischofsheim to Würzburg. As soon as the Bavarian attack on Flies was announced by their cannonade, Beyer detached some of his regiments to act against Prince Charles's flank. This attack, supported vigorously by a simultaneous advance of Flies against his front, forced the Bavarian commander to retire; not, however, without inflicting very severe injury on the Prussians.

Goeben, on the 26th, pushed his advanced guard towards Würzburg, and soon discovered by his patrols that Prince Charles, after leaving only a few light troops in front of the town, and a strong garrison in the houses on the left bank of the river, had drawn the mass of his troops across the Maine, and posted them in the town on the right bank, and in the citadel.

On the 28th, the Bavarian and the eighth Federal corps concentrated, and took up a position at Rottendorf, a village which lies in the angle of the Maine, five miles east of Würzburg. General Manteuffel that day drew his whole army together in front of Würzburg, with Goeben's division in advance, so that Kummer's brigade was opposite Marienberg, Wrangel's on its right, and the Oldenburg contingent on its left. Kummer pushed his skirmishers close up to Marienberg, and with them forced the enemy to quit some earthworks which they had begun to throw up. The whole artillery of the Army of the Maine was then posted on the right and left of the road, and opened a cannonade on the houses, to which the enemy's guns actively replied. The arsenal and the castle of Marienberg were set on flames, after which the batteries ceased firing.

The day after that cannonade a flag of truce was sent from the Bavarians to General Manteuffel, who announced that an armistice had been concluded between the King of Prussia and the Bavarian Government. The cessation of hostilities rescued the allied army from a very precarious position in the elbow of the Maine, where it was all but cut off from the territories which it had been intended to defend.

General Manteuffel had gained a free scope for action over the whole of Bavaria, Würtemberg, and Baden, because the River Maine was placed between those countries and the troops of Prince Charles. This general, to defend those countries, would have required to cross a swift river in face of a strong and already victorious enemy, no easy task for an army which had already lost confidence in its leader.

<h2 style="text-align:center">OBSERVATIONS</h2>

The most interesting manoeuvre of the Prussian Army of the Maine, after it had occupied Frankfort, was the movement by which General Manteuffel advanced against the Tauber. The army marched southwards in the formation A. As soon as certain information was received that the enemy was on the Tauber, the division wheeled to the left, and stood opposed to the enemy in the formation B. The right wing (2), Flies' division, had then Goeben's division (1) as a reserve, and could with great strength urge the enemy back towards the Maine, while Beyer's division at Wertheim prevented him from pushing out in that direction. As long as General Manteuffel could prevent the allies from marching up the Tauber he held an advantage over them, for the second reserve corps was coming down to Nürnberg against their rear. If the enemy did move up the Tauber in spite of his dispositions, General Manteuffel, by wheeling division C to the right, restored the order of march, in which he had advanced from Frankfort, for further operations.

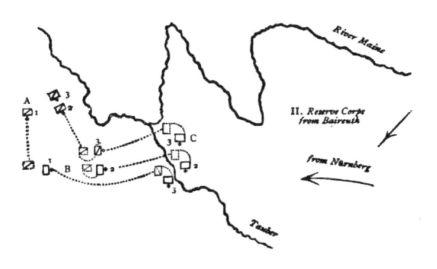

It is difficult to perceive with what object Prince Charles, after the action on the Tauber, withdrew in the direction of Wurzburg, and afterwards took up a position in the bend of the Maine. He could hardly have wished here to fight a pitched battle, while General Manteuffel on one side of him, and the second Prussian reserve corps on the other, were not separated by more than sixty miles, and when he left the initiative of attack in the hands of his adversaries. Nor could he have the intention of conveying his troops by railway by way of Bamberg, Nürnberg, and Regensburg to Vienna. His road in that direction was threatened, and before he could have moved half his army, the remainder would have been waylaid by the second reserve corps.

The strength of the Bavarian and eighth Federal corps, which mustered together at least one hundred thousand men, was frittered away in isolated conflicts, instead of being concentrated for a great battle. Such conflicts could have had no important result, even if they had been successful. On the Tauber, the eighth corps fought alone, unsupported by the Bavarians. On the 25th, the whole right wing of the Bavarians came under fire, only in the evening, for the first time; and there was no harmony of either conduct or action between the Bavarians and the troops of the eighth corps. On the 26th, Prince Charles made an offensive movement without any support from Prince Alexander, and apparently without any idea that the latter had withdrawn to Würzburg.

CHAPTER 5

Occupation of Franconia by the Second Reserve Corps

On the 18th July the Grand Duke Frederick Franz of Mecklen-burg-Schwerin assumed the command of the second Prussian reserve corps at Leipsic On the same day he ordered this corps to move upon Hof, in Bavaria, On the 23rd, the third battalion of the fourth regiment of the Guard crossed the Bavarian frontier, and captured a detachment of sixty-five Bavarian infantry. This battalion was pushed by forced marches from Leipsic to Werdau, thence by railway to Plauen. At the latter place waggons were raised by requisition from the country people, and the battalion conveyed in them by night to within, two miles of Hof. Two companies rushed into the town, while the others, making a circuitous march, sought to gain the exit on the further side, and thus to surround and capture the whole of the Bavarian garrison. The greater part of these, however, made their escape by a railway train which happened to be ready, and an outlying detachment of sixty-five non-commissioned officers and men were alone taken prisoners.

On the 24th July, the headquarters of the Grand Duke of Mecklenburg reached Hof. Here he published a proclamation to the inhabitants of Upper Franconia, in which he informed them that his invasion of their country was only directed against their government, and that private property and interests would be perfectly respected by his troops. In consequence, he was able to draw from the inhabitants the means of supplying his men with rations.

The head of the Prussian advanced guard reached on the 28th, the provincial capital Baireuth. The Bavarian garrison of this town had been withdrawn by telegraphic orders from Munich: and wisely so. Its numbers were far too small to have fought an action with any chance of success, and any resistance against the invaders could only have served to imperil the lives and property of the inhabitants. Nürnberg had also, from fear of the fate with which it was threatened, solicited the Bavarian Government to allow it to be declared an open town.

On the 29th July, the grand duke in person reached Baireuth, and there reviewed his troops. Bavaria, which had always aspired to a special consideration in the Germanic Confederation, because she claimed to be the leader of the Middle States, displayed no military force at all proportionate to her pretensions. No force worthy the name opposed this invasion of Franconia. One only of four brigades of reserve which were in course of formation, but, as yet, were hardly clothed in uniform, badly equipped and miserably organised, had been despatched from Munich towards the Saxon frontier. For any efficient protection of the country it was much too weak, and the *Landwehr*, which had so much been vaunted by the Bavarian press, as a strong defensive organisation, barely existed upon paper, and was practically of no account The second reserve corps advanced unmolested, as if in time of profound peace, and was received by the people always with friendship, sometimes with tokens of lively sympathy. The Bavarian brigade of reserve retired to Kemnath.

A false telegraphic despatch, which announced that an armistice had been concluded between Prussia and Bavaria, led the reserve battalion of the regiment of the Bavarian guard to again advance, on the 28th, towards Baireuth. This advance was made without any precaution. As soon as it approached near the town it was told by the Prussian officer who commanded the advanced guard of the second reserve corps that the intelligence of an armistice was unfounded. It did not, however, by a forced march, attempt to withdraw itself beyond the reach of danger, but retired to St Johann's, barely three miles from Baireuth, and there calmly took up its quarters for the night As could hardly otherwise happen, it was there fallen upon, and fled during the night to Seidenburg, and on the 29th to Seibottenreuth.

Here it was overtaken by the fusilier battalion of the 4th regiment of the Prussian Guard, which, in company with some Mecklenburg cavalry and *Jägers*, had been despatched from Baireuth in pursuit, and was totally routed. Of the nine hundred and fifty men, of whom the battalion had been composed, hardly five hundred succeeded in escaping from their pursuers, and, by the sacrifice of their knapsacks and many of their arms, gaining a railway station between Seibottenreuth and Nürnberg. This was the only opportunity which the second reserve corps had of being engaged.

On the 31st July, the Prussian advanced guard moving forwards occupied the ancient city of Nürnberg, from which the dynasty of the Hohenzollerns was originally transferred to Brandenburg. On the first August, the main body reached the same place. Here the Grand Duke of Mecklenburg was only separated from Würzburg by a distance of sixty miles, and could insure his junction with General Manteuffel without any danger from the eighth Federal corps or the Bavarian army. Other reinforcements were also on the way to General Manteuffel, for on the 27th July the first Prussian reserve corps had been despatched from Bohemia, by way of Pilsen, into Bavaria, and had already occupied Weiden and Waldsassen. The armistice, however, which commenced on the 2nd of August, and which had been granted by Manteuffel, on the 30th July, to Prince Alexander and Prince Charles, put an end to all further operations, and, in all probability, prevented both the army and the capital of Bavaria from falling into the hands of the Prussians.

The Prussian troops were everywhere victoriously pressing forward, and every day their enemies were more paralysed, and daily the total disruption of the Germanic Confederation became more complete.

On the 28th July, Baden received a new ministry, which declared that, after the 31st July, the grand duchy would no longer consider itself as belonging to the late confederation. The grand ducal representative at the spectral phantom of the *diet* was recalled, and the fortress of Rastadt was declared to belong to the Baden Government The troops of Weimar, which formed its garrison, were dismissed to their homes.

On the 1st August, Heidelberg and Mannheim, Ludwighofen, Mergentheim, and Erlangen, were occupied by Prussian detachments. The South-German Governments lost all hope, and sought by negotiations for an armistice. Lines of demarcation between the armies were agreed upon, and the war on the western theatre was finally put an end to by settled conventions.

Bavaria at first gained merely a purely military suspension of hostilities, but Herr von der Pfordten, who had been despatched to the King of Prussia at Nikolsburg,[1] by the Bavarian Government, obtained one for three weeks, which was to date from the 28th July. Within that time peace was concluded at Berlin.

---

1. See Book 9, chapter3.

Before the definite conclusion of the armistice, the Prussian troops had occupied the Bavarian territory at three points, they had also crossed the frontiers of Baden and of Würtemberg. Darmstadt had long held a Prussian garrison. Würzburg, as one of the conditions of the suspension of hostilities, received a Prussian corps of four thousand men on the 2nd August; the fortress on the Marienberg alone remained in the hands of the Bavarians. On the 1st August, General von Manteuffel, at Würzburg, concluded an armistice with General von Hardegg, for Würtemberg; on the same day he also concluded one for Hesse-Darmstadt, and on the 3rd a plenipotentiary from Baden came to Würzburg, and there obtained one from Manteuffel for the Grand Duchy. The headquarters of the Army of the Maine were established at Würzburg during the truce, where they remained until the 22nd August

The King of Prussia despatched, on the 1st August, the following telegram to the Army of the Maine, through General Manteuffel:

I charge you to express to the troops of the Army of the Maine my entire satisfaction with their valour and behaviour. I thank the generals, the officers, and all the soldiery. With me the armies in Bohemia, Moravia, and Austria send to their Prussian and German comrades greeting and goodwill.

At the same time the order of *"Pour le Mérite"* was sent by the king, with an autograph letter to the Grand Duke of Mecklenburg.

The end of the struggle was notified by General von Manteuffel to his army, in the following general order:—

Headquarters, Würzburg,
August 2nd, 1866.

Soldiers of the Army or the Maine!—By the victories of the arms of Prussia, the enemy has been compelled to seek for an armistice. His Majesty the King has granted it. I do not speak to you of the hardships which you have cheerfully suffered, nor of the bravery with which you have everywhere fought. But I recall to your memory the days of actions and the results of your victories. After that, under your skilful and esteemed leader, General von Falckenstein, you had seized Hanover, Hesse-Cassel, and all the broad territories as far as Frankfort-on-the-Maine; had compelled the Hanoverian army to capitulate; had defeated the Bavarians on the 14th July at Zella and Weisenthal, on the 10th July at Hammelburg, Kissingen, Friedericshall, Hansen, and Waldaschach; on the 11th July the troops of Hesse-Darmstadt at Oerlenbach; on the 13th these again at Laufach, and on the 14th the Austrians at Aschaffenburg, you made your victorious entry into Frankfort.

After a short rest, again you sought the foe; on the 23rd you defeated the troops of Baden at Hundheim; on the 24th, the Austrian, Würtemberg, Hesse-Darmstadt, and Nassau division at Tauberbischofsheim, and the troops of Baden at Werbach; on the 25th, the whole concentrated eighth Federal Corps at Gerscheim, and the Bavarians at Helmstadt, the latter on the 26th, also at Roszbrünn; and today, after twenty victorious greater or minor combats, have entered Würzburg as conquerors. The result of those victories is that not only the countries north of the Maine have been won, but that the power of your arms has smitten heavily on Hesse-Darmstadt, and deep into Baden and Würtemberg, and has freed a portion of our land, which could not be directly protected by our army from the presence of an enemy.

The Würtembergers had occupied Hohenzollern, and had driven away our officials. They must now quit that principality;[2] the black and white flag waves again over the town of Hohenzollern. I must express my thanks to the generals, commanders, officers, and to all the rank and file. I also thank the military surgeons for their unremitting and self-sacrificing care of the wounded, both under fire and in the hospital, as well as to the non-combatant departments for their successful administration of the army's supplies. Soldiers of the Army of the Maine! I know that you are thankful to God, and I expect that during the armistice your recognised manliness and careful behaviour towards the inhabitants of the country will be worthy of the Prussian name.

The relics of the *diet* quickly approached dissolution. On the 1st of August the small knot of diplomatists which at the hotel of the Three Moors, at Augsburg, still assumed the functions of that august body, were deserted by the ambassadors of England, France, Spain and Belgium; while the Russian representative remained at Augsburg only on account of illness. The sitting of the 4th August acknowledged the end of the last shadow of the Germanic Confederation. Prince Charles of

---

2. The principalities of Hohenzollern.

Bavaria reported the conclusion of an armistice with Prussia by the governments of Austria, Bavaria, Würtemberg, and the Grand Duchy of Hesse; and reported at the same time, that he resigned the command-in-chief of the western Federal army, which had been bestowed on him by the decree of the *diet* of the 27th June.

Brunswick had very tardily placed its troops on a war footing, but by the beginning of August they were attached to the second Prussian reserve corps. That State a short time previously declared its withdrawal from the confederation.

The remaining members of the *diet* annulled the protests which had been made against Prussia, and decreed that no obstacle should be offered to the North-German troops in the Federal fortresses in retiring to their homes.

On the 28th July, the troops of Saxe-Meiningen had already been permitted by the Governor of Mainz to leave that fortress, which, in virtue of the subsequent treaties of peace, was occupied by and given over entirely to Prussia on the 26th August

This decree was the last act of the *diet* of the Germanic Confederation, which was constructed after the fall of the first French Empire. By it, it practically published its own death warrant

BOOK 9

CHAPTER 1

Prussian Advance From Königgrätz to Brünn

Feldzeugmeister von Benedek had headed in person the troops with which he attempted to retake Chlum after the Prussian Guards had possessed themselves of that village, and so turned the scale of the Battle of Königgrätz. After his three attacks on the burning houses and the garrisoned churchyard had been repulsed, he saw that all was lost, and himself in vain attempted to find a soldier's grave on the field of battle, and with his blood to wash out the memory of his misfortune. The rapid advance of the whole Prussian army forced the Austrians speedily to retreat. During the night of the 3rd of July, in great disorder, having but half of its artillery, with its staff separated and scattered, the defeated army pushed across the crowded bridges over the Elbe, and wearily dragged itself in the direction of Hohenmanth. Benedek himself retreated to Holitz, on the road to this place, and there on the morning of the 4th, made the best arrangement he could for the safety of his troops.

Their losses in men, *matérial*, and guns rendered it impossible for him to think of any new dispositions until they were thoroughly reorganised. To carry out such a reorganisation he must seek a place of shelter, and the cover he desired was to be found under the guns, and behind the intrenchments of Olmütz. With the exception of the tenth corps, which had suffered most severely, and which he therefore despatched by railway directly to Vienna, he ordered the remainder of his army to move on the intrenched camp at Olmütz, while he left his first light cavalry division to watch the road from Pardubitz to Iglau, and his second to delay the enemy, if possible, on that from Pardubitz

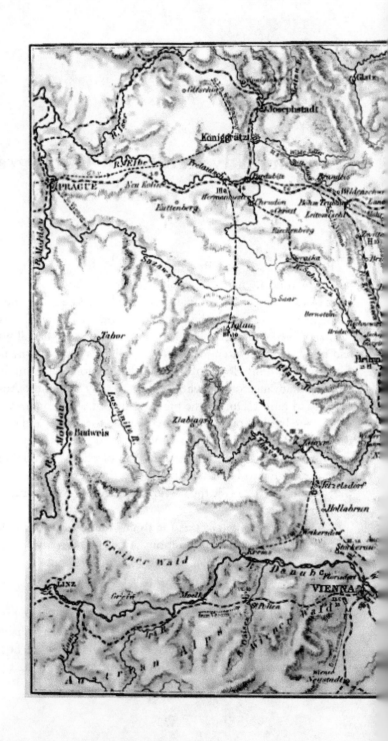

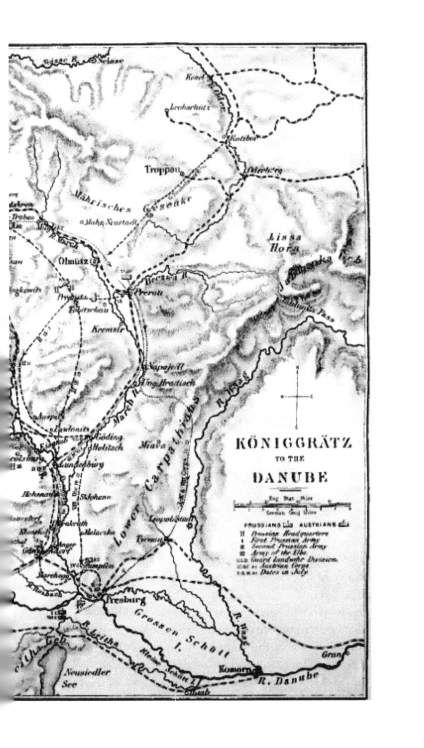

KÖNIGGRÄTZ
TO THE
DANUBE

PRUSSIANS   AUSTRIANS

    Prussian Headquarters
I.   *First Prussian Army*
II.   *Second Prussian Army*
III.   *Army of the Elbe*
   Guard Landwehr Division.
   Austrian Corps.
   Dates in July.

to Brünn.

On the 4th July he also sent Field Marshal Gablenz, one of the most able of the Austrian generals, to the Prussian headquarters, in order to treat for a suspension of hostilities, as a preliminary to the conclusion of peace. This was a new proof of the desperate condition of the Austrian army. Gablenz reported himself on the 4th July at mid-day, at the outposts of the crown prince's army, and received permission to go to the king's headquarters. He was blindfolded in passing through the army, as is the custom of war, and accompanied by a Prussian officer, was conducted to Höritz. When he reached that town the king was absent, as he had gone to visit his troops on the field of battle. General Gablenz was taken to meet him, and fell in with the king between Sadowa and Chlum, who at first took him for a wounded Austrian general, and was about to condole with him, but being informed of his mission, ordered the bandage to be removed, and requested the Austrian general to return with him to Höritz. Here Gablenz expressed Benedek's desire of an armistice, but no truce could be granted, for Prussia and Italy were mutually bound to agree to no suspension of hostilities without a common agreement General Gablenz returned unsuccessful to the Austrian headquarters.

Equally unsuccessfully did the Austrian Government endeavour to make a separate peace with Italy. It determined, however, to leave only garrisons in the fortresses of the Venetian quadrilateral, and to transfer all the remaining troops of the Army of the South from the Mincio to the Danube, to shield its capital against its northern enemy.

The Prussian Army the night of the Battle of Königgrätz, bivouacked on the field. The following afternoon it began to move forward, to seize the passages over the Elbe. The Second Army on the left was directed upon Pardubitz. It left behind it the sixth *corps d'armée* to watch the fortresses of Josephstadt and Königgrätz. No siege against these places was undertaken. Yet the town of Königgrätz was nearly destroyed On the 5th July, the day after the Prussian armies had marched from the vicinity of the fortress, the commander of the troops left to mask the place, opened a cannonade on the town from some of the Austrian guns, which had been captured in the battle. The shells burst among the dry houses, and the place would soon have been in flames had not a gun from one of the bastions opened with singular effect upon the Prussian gunners and compelled them to withdraw.

The army of Prince Frederick Charles, and that of Herwarth, were both directed upon Przelautsch. At the same time the division of

Landwehr of the Guard, which had followed in rear of the main armies, was despatched to Prague, the capital of Bohemia. The Austrian garrison did not attempt to defend this town, and the Imperial lieutenant transferred the seat of the government of the province to Pilsen. The Prussian soldiery here found a very welcome booty in twenty-seven millions of cigars, which, as tobacco in Austria is a government monopoly, were confiscated for the benefit of the Prussian troops. On the 8th July, this division reached the ancient town on the Moldau, and hoisted the Prussian flag upon the Hradschin, the palace of the kings of Bohemia. On the 11th, General Mülbe took the command of the place, having moved the first Prussian reserve corps from Saxony into Bohemia.

The first division of the *Landwehr* of the line remained in Saxony, to which later a newly-formed second division was added. The detachments made from the Prussian main armies for masking fortresses, and escorts of prisoners, as well as the losses in battle and from sickness, were replaced by a portion of eighty-one new battalions, which had been lately formed out of the troops left at the regimental *depôts*. The first line armies, when they moved from the Elbe, were of the same, or rather superior, strength to those which ten days before had crossed the Bohemian frontier.

In consequence of the Battle of Königgrätz, Feldzeugmeister Benedek resigned the command of the Austrian Army of the North, and the Archduke Albrecht, the victor of Custozza, was appointed to the supreme command of the whole army. Until its arrival on the Danube, however, Benedek commanded the Army of the North. Count Clam Gallas had been ordered to give up his command after Gitschin, and the chief of the staff, Field Marshal Baron Henikstein, had, before the 3rd July, been ordered to cede his post to Major-General Paumgarten, who had hitherto commanded in Gallicia. The latter reached the army the evening before the battle of Königgrätz, but did not interfere with the dispositions of his predecessor.

One feeling alone existed in the army of Benedek. He possessed the admiration of his officers, and the love of his men. This affection towards him only increased in the hour of his misfortune in the camp. But the populace of Vienna blindly raged against him, and failing to perceive the negligence and errors of the ministers and administrators who had sent the army into the field in its unprepared condition, inveighed in unmeasured terms against the unfortunate general who had commanded it.

343

On the evening of the 4th July, the armies broke up from the bivouac they had occupied near the field of Battle of Königgrätz, and advanced towards the Elbe.

On the 5th, they crossed the river; the First Army, under Prince Frederick Charles, at Przelautsch; the Second, under the crown prince, at Pardubitz. The march was begun the previous evening. After going a short way the troops halted for the night, and slept by the side of the road. Early on the morning of the 5th they again set forward, and reached the Elbe late in the afternoon. The villages along the road had been mostly deserted, for the inhabitants had fled south with the retreating Austrian army. The houses looked desolate, with their doors and windows wide open, and shutters flapping mournfully in the wind, while there still remained in the street in front vestiges of the hasty packing up of such articles as could be carried away.

A stray dog or two were seen here and there, which still stood on the threshold and barked at the soldiers as they marched by; but even these were rare, and often the poultry had invaded the dwelling rooms, and were roosting among the furniture. For twenty-five miles the army marched through a luxuriantly fertile country, but almost entirely deserted; sometimes one or two peasants stood by the side of the road staring vacantly at the passing troops, or a few women might be found in a village who, half frightened by the sight of the soldiers, supplied them with the drinking water which they everywhere requested. But the people had no cause to fear; they would have done better to remain, for some of the troops had to be billeted in the houses along the road, and when the inhabitants were not present, the soldiers took what they required, and there was no one to receive payment for what they consumed.

The children did not seem so timid; they were present along the roads in large numbers, for the cherries were just ripening, and they took advantage of the panic among their elders to make a raid on the trees which grew in long strips by the side of the way. With them the soldiers soon became great friends. The boys ran along the battalions with their caps full of the fruit, and got coppers in exchange for handfuls of it; the sellers, exulting in the pockets full of coin they soon collected, seemed to have no scruples as to whose property it rightfully was, but laughed with delight at this unexpected result of the war.

But for the most part the country in front of the army was still and silent No church clocks sounded, for their guardians had fled. There was no one to wind them up, and the hands stood motionless on the dials. No horses neighed, for they had all been taken to carry away the flying inhabitants, or perhaps to aid in dragging off the retreating Austrian guns. The flowers before the wayside shrines of the Madonna were dried up and withered, for the votaries who were wont to renew them had fled, fearful of the invading army. The cattle had been driven away, and the pastures were vacant. Broad belts of corn, trodden flat to the ground, showed the lines along which the Austrian battalions had hurried, and here and there lay a knapsack or ammunition pouch which some fatigued fugitive had cast away as an impediment to his flight.

But where the army marched all was bustle and noise; the infantry tramped monotonously along the roads, while the cavalry spread in bending lines through the fields, and behind the combatants toiled long trains of waggons, which carried the stores of this large army. Along every road and every lane foot soldiers marched, and cavalry occupied the intervals between the heads of the columns—all pointing southwards, towards the Elbe. For miles on either side could be seen the clouds of dust raised by the marching troops; in some places it rose from trees and woods, in others from among houses, or from the hard straight roads leading through the wide corn land, where the hot July sun poured its rays straight down upon the soldiers' heads and made them suffer much from heat and thirst.

As the foremost troops neared the Elbe all ears listened eagerly for the sound of cannon, for it was thought that if the Austrians could bring their troops under fire again they would oppose the passage of the river, and whether they did so or not would be accepted as a criterion of how much they had suffered by the defeat at Königgrätz. The heads of the columns steadily advanced nearer and nearer to the line of willows which marked the course of the stream. No cannon sounded, no rifle even was discharged, and it seemed that the advanced guard must have passed unopposed. At last the news came back that the passage was secured, and that there were no signs of the enemy on the opposite bank. Soon the troops closed down to the river and filed across the wooden bridge which, with four arches, spans the muddy stream; and the black and yellow stripes on its parapets were the only visible signs that the Prussian Army was in the dominions of the emperor of Austria.

Prince Frederick Charles occupied Przelautsch about six on the evening of the 5th, and almost at the same time the crown prince entered Pardubitz. The line of the Elbe was now secured as a basis for future operations, and the Austrian railway communication between Vienna and Prague was cut. At the latter town there were said to be only four Austrian battalions, and it was expected to be evacuated by them and occupied by the Prussians within a few days.

As was the case. Then, notwithstanding the fortresses of König-stein in Saxony, and Josephstadt, Königgrätz, and Theresienstadt in Bohemia, the Prussian armies, after making some necessary repairs, obtained railway communication from Pardubitz and Przelautsch by way of Prague and Reichenberg with their own country, which was of great importance to them in their further advance.

The towns of Przelautsch and Pardubitz were entirely filled with Prussian soldiers. On every door was written in chalk the name of the regiment and company to which the house was allotted, and the number of men which it was to accommodate. The numbers appeared enormous for the size of the house, fifty or sixty men were sometimes billeted in a small house with four rooms, but the soldiers managed well enough so long as they could get straw to lie upon; but here there was a great scarcity of that, and the men had to sleep as they could, on the floors or in the gardens. The greatest difficulty prevailed in getting any accommodation for horses; all the stables were occupied by the horses of generals, and inferior officers would fain have had sheds, cowhouses, or any place with a cover, for the weather looked lowering, and it seemed that it would probably rain, but all the sheds were occupied by the troops, and most of the horses had to spend the night in the streets.

But there were advantages here which compensated for more than a little overcrowding. Large Austrian stores of bread, beer, and cigars had been found, and the soldiers were delighted to think that they would again have their rations of tobacco served out to them, which they had not had since they left Saxony; for to a German soldier tobacco is almost as necessary as meat, but transport had not been found for tobacco with the army, as there had been lately a difficulty in bringing up even food.

The headquarters of the armies halted on the 6th July in the same position as they took up the previous evening. The First Army at Przelautsch. The crown prince with the Second Army was at Pardubitz, whither the king himself went the same evening. Detachments were pushed along the railway towards Prague. On the morning of the 6th, an advanced guard was pushed out to feel the country south of the Elbe. It consisted of light cavalry, horse artillery, and some infantry.

The Weissenfels hussars led the way, followed by the hussars of Ziethen, and the 3rd dragoons, whose squadrons were very weak, for their ranks had been terribly thinned by the Battle of Königgrätz. As soon as the columns got out of the town the hussars spread themselves out over the fields by the side of the road, and studded the country with horsemen. Some went pushing through the corn, others galloped forward to gain every piece of rising ground, and from the summit to scan the country beyond. Every wood was carefully beaten, and every village inspected by the nimble horsemen before the main body approached, for Austrian marksmen might be lurking among the trees, or cavalry might lie in ambush behind the houses. But no signs of an enemy could be found; and, although at every moment they expected to hear the sharp crack of a rifle and the puff of blue smoke which would tell that an outlying post had been disturbed, they pursued their way unmolested, and it was evident that the Austrians had retreated far south or east.

But, though the headquarters halted at Przelautsch and Pardubitz, the 6th was a busy day there. All the sickly and weak were draughted out of the ranks, and were sentenced to be left behind—a sure sign that long and severe marches were expected, and that it was intended that the army should move free of all possible encumbrance. In vain did those who were selected to be left behind protest that they were the strongest men in the regiment, and call upon their comrades to bear witness to their marching powers. The doctors were good-naturedly obdurate, and the men selected had to bear the disappointment of not going forward with the army, being solaced with the assurance that they should rejoin as soon as possible. Those destined to be left behind were far from numerous—indeed, their number was surprisingly small, for the army had been making long marches and bivouacking out nearly every night in most changeable weather.

Although the Austrians had been obliged to leave the railway, they had taken care to make it of as little use as possible to its subsequent possessors. All the engines and carriages had been sent away, and until Prague was occupied none could be brought by the Prussians to supply their place. So the line stood idle, and the station had a desolate look, made only more remarkable by the one or two officials of the indefatigable telegraph corps, who had occupied one of the rooms, and were at their work there early that morning flashing despatches and reports to the king's staff, and receiving rapid answers which were to direct the marches of the troops.

A number of Austrian baggage waggons had after Königgrätz fallen into the hands of the conquerors, and, after being employed in helping to carry the wounded from the field on the 6th, joined in the long lines of carriages which followed the Prussian armies. They were easily distinguished in the line of march by their light yellow colour, which contrasted strongly with the dark blue with which all the Prussian military carriages are painted. Every hour showed how much more severely the Austrians had felt their defeat at Königgrätz than was at first supposed in the Prussian army. The unopposed passage of the Elbe, the mission of Marshal Gablenz, the abandonment of the country south of Przelautsch, were successive proofs of the completeness of the Prussian victory.

The morale of the army had now risen high, and the soldiers were convinced that the Austrian troops could not stand against them—a feeling which was no contemptible augury of future victories. But, though the soldiers were confident in themselves, their arms, and their leaders, their confidence never stepped beyond just bounds; they were tender and kind to the wounded and prisoners, not only by attending to their wants, but by showing them much consideration, and never exulting over the victory in their presence, which could hardly be expected from men serving in the ranks. But the Prussian system of recruiting enlists in the army as privates men of high education and refined feelings, and these easily influence their comrades, who are naturally warm-hearted, to act kindly and charitably to the unfortunate.

On the 7th July the Prussian armies advanced from the Elbe. The crown prince moved from Pardubitz along the railway towards Brandeis, with the object of pushing towards Olmütz. Prince Frederick Charles, leaning slightly in the same direction, made for the road which leads from Pardubitz by Chrudim to Brünn. On the 7th he reached Hermanmestetz. The Army of the Elbe marched on the road which leads from Przelautsch to Iglau and Znaym.

The march of the 7th was very different from that of the 5th. The panic among the country people caused by the defeat of the Austrians at the Battle of Königgrätz did not extend into the country lying south of the Elbe, and here the inhabitants had not left their houses. All was busy and full of life, peasants were working in the fields, women and children were abundant in the villages, and the soldiers, who seemed to be supplied plentifully with money by their friends at home, for their pay is small, bought eggs, butter, milk, and poultry

348

as they passed along, but in many cases they had little return for their money, for eggs are difficult to carry in crowded ranks, and butter is inclined to melt when stowed away in a knapsack, so that many found when they reached the halting place that their prudence in providing themselves with eatables was vain, and that they were disappointed of the luxuries they had meant to enjoy with their mid-day meal.

The march was little on the high road, but chiefly by country lanes, over ground covered with short, crisp grass, past water-mills sunk in the hollows by little streams, and through villages whose wide open greens covered with geese and ducks reminded one of England. From the top of every rise the country before the army could be seen stretching away in a wide rolling plain, and bounded by the dark blue line of mountains which, thirty miles distant, separates Bohemia from Moravia. The corn was rapidly ripening; but the day was cool, yet without rain, and the troops, marching easily, did not care to avail themselves of the water along the road, which was abundant, and which would have been so grateful on many former marches.

The town of Hermanmestetz is thoroughly Bohemian; few of even the better class of inhabitants could speak German. The signboards of the shops and inns were written only in Bohemian, and not in German also, as is generally the case further north. As soon as the troops marched in and were dismissed from their parades, a rush was made at the shops. The soldiers crowded in at the doors and up to the counters, calling loudly for tobacco and cigars. These were not to be had in any quantity, but coffee was plentiful at first, though the whole in the town was soon bought Then arose difficulties about money, for the soldiers did not yet thoroughly understand the Austrian coinage, and the shopkeepers tried to take the utmost advantage of their ignorance; but the men protested loudly against flagrant cases of imposition, and, amid a great deal of noise and loud talking, the bargains were concluded generally considerably to the advantage of the dealer.

Every taproom was filled by an importunate crowd eager for food, beer, and wine; knapsacks were piled on the benches, rifles stood thickly in the corners, and their owners pressed round the bar, each trying by dint of noise to secure the services of the landlord for himself. But though they were hungry and thirsty, the soldiers were always good-humoured. Differences of opinion often arose as to the comparative value of *kreutzers* and *silber groschen*; but when the dispute ran high the landlord called in the assistance of his wife, and then almost invariably the soldier had to retire worsted from the contest, exposing discontentedly to his comrades the small handful of little coins he had received in change for a dollar. As soon as it became dark all noise ceased and all bustle was stilled. The men disappeared to go to sleep. Some lay in the houses on straw, others in sheds, many in the gardens, for the house accommodation was not sufficient for them, and many seemed wisely to prefer the summer air to a crowded room. Thus the town, before so noisy, grew perfectly still, and no sound was heard except the monotonous step of a sentry or the uneasy neigh of some restive horse; but the arms piled, with the bayonets fixed, beside each house, with the knapsacks laid close to the butts packed and ready to be instantly taken up, told that the soldiers were ready, and that the least alarm would fill the streets with armed men ready to march.

The king came to Pardubitz on the morning of the 7th, held a meeting of the principal generals, and probably the future plan of the campaign was then discussed. It was still uncertain whether the two armies were making for the line of railway which runs by Brünn to Vienna, or whether they were moving towards Olmütz.

The king remained on the 8th at Pardubitz, where it was determined that the Second Army should move against Olmütz with the first *corps d'armée* and the cavalry corps leading. This advanced guard was if possible to feel the enemy, and discover what amount of his army Benedek still held in the intrenched camp and what troops he had sent to the south. A serious attack on the fortress was not, however, contemplated. Any retreat of the Second Army, which might become necessary, was to be made, not in the direction of the First Army, but on the county of Glatz, with which the Second Army now formed a line of communication.

The First and Second Armies, on the 8th, moved forwards in a south-easterly direction; the crown prince, with the Second Army, marched that morning in the direction of Mährisch Trübau, and halted for the night somewhere short of that town. The First Army, under Prince Frederick Charles, was that evening scattered round Chrast; the 8th division, under General Horne, was in the town itself, the main body along the road towards Mährisch Trübau; the 7th was a little to the south at Zumberg; the 6th at Kamenitz, a village still further to the south; and the cavalry, marching by roads more to the southwards still, covered the right flank of the army. General Herwarth von Bittenfeld, with his corps, was moving on Iglau. Eight battalions had been detached to Prague, and that town was occupied on the morning of this day, the 8th.

Marshal Gablenz passed through the outposts again the same morning, and went to Pardubitz to see the king, as a commissioner from the Austrian Government, to treat for a suspension of hostilities. He was received by General von Moltke, but his proposals could not be entertained, and his second mission was equally unsuccessful as his first He submitted that a suspension of hostilities should be concluded, which should last for at least eight weeks and for at most eight months; that during this truce the troops of both nations should retain their actual positions, and a girdle of two miles in width between the outposts be observed as neutral ground.

In return the Austrian commissioner proposed that the fortresses of Josephstadt and Königgrätz should be handed over to the Prussians, but without their garrisons and *matériel* of war. It was not in the interest of the Prussian Army after a hardly won victory, and, in its favourable circumstances, to grant such an armistice, especially as it appeared certain that Austria did not wish to definitely conclude a peace, but only to gain time to bring up her Army of the South from Italy. The passage of Marshal Gablenz through the divisions led to many reports of the speedy termination of the war, which were more or less credited

In the meantime, amid rumours of probable peace, the army still continued its steady advance, and its march was conducted with the same precautions and the same circumspection as if the campaign was only beginning, and as if an unbroken enemy was in front, ready to take advantage of the slightest error. Advanced guards were sent forward, who carefully felt the way for the marching columns, sending scouts to the top of every rise, who, standing out sharp against the sky, peered into the distance; riflemen moved in dotted lines through the fields at an even pace with the troops marching on the road, and trod through the corn as carefully as if they were sportsmen beating a covert, or, slipping into a thicket, now appeared, now disappeared in the foliage much like hounds drawing for a fox.

The troops on the road pushed along as steadily and perseveringly as on the first day they entered Saxony. The infantry, with their trousers turned up and boots often drawn on outside them, trudged along merrily, and seemed little to feel the heavy yellow cowskin knapsacks and mess tins for cooking which they carried on their backs. Their helmets had suffered in the campaign more than any other part of their equipment; many had lost the spike on the top, carried away by a bullet or the splinter of a shell at the Battle of Königgrätz. Some looked as if they had been knocked off in the hurry of action, and had been marched over heavily by the ranks behind. The belts showed a want of pipeclay, and the boots had lost all traces of blacking; but the barrels of the rifles and the blades of the bayonets were all bright and clean, and shone out cold and gray against the dark blue uniforms. The artillery horses, a little thin, and with rather prominent ribs, from hard work and scarce forage, stepped briskly out, and almost without stretching their traces the straight, steel-barrelled guns rolled along behind them, looking on the road a mere plaything to be drawn by six horses; but when the ground was heavy from falling rain, as on the morning before Königgrätz, it needed nearly all the strength of the team to get a gun over the fields uphill, and then horses were often wanting, for their bodies, larger than those of men, were more liable to be struck by shells or bullets, and many were killed or badly wounded as soon as a battery went under fire.

After the great battle, the positions that had been occupied by the field batteries on either side could be traced by the numbers of dead horses lying where the limbers and waggons had stood. Often twenty or thirty lay dead in a line near together along the front of the battery, and others limped about near them, and though always moving never tried to go away from their dead companions. They, too, were soon stretched upon the ground, for the *krankenträger*, looking for the sick, mercifully placed a carbine behind the ear of every wounded animal, and quickly put it out of pain. The mass of the cavalry scoured the country to the south of the main army, keeping watch and ward over its right flank, but here and there a few turned up in the line of march, generally a detachment of some troopers guarding waggons. These detachments were of all kinds of horsemen,—*cuirassiers* with their white flannel coats braced tightly in by the *cuirass*, and with heavy-looking high jack-boots, were followed quickly by some few men of the Ziethen hussars, with short crimson jackets, or by some of the Weimar light cavalry, with their light blue and silver uniforms looking none the worse for exposure, while every column was headed by Uhlans, the black and white flags of whose lances waved with an almost funereal aspect above their smart caps and gay red or yellow facings.

The army marched in several columns, and from every rise could be seen the different lines creeping like long blue serpents over the country. Dipping into hollows, twisting through villages, twining among trees, appearing and disappearing through woods and thickets, they stretched for many a long mile from front to rear. Always looking steadily ahead, they pushed on with the men's faces against the sun, and seemed to be bending towards the fortress of Olmütz, under the walls of which the Austrians were reported to have an intrenched camp, where there were said to be over 100,000 fighting men, with 400 pieces of artillery ensconced in fortifications. Collected here, the Austrian troops, it was said, meant to bar the road southwards from the Prussians; if these passed on disregarding them, to issue out, and, seizing the communications of the army, cut off from it all its supplies of ammunition and food from the north.

Again, on the 8th, the line of March lay through a country rich and abundant in supplies, and from which the natives had not fled away; and again the columns moved through country lanes, in some places shadowed in by fruit trees, in others leading over breezy uplands where the limestone rocks cropped up close to the surface of the ground, and left but a scanty-soil to nourish the short grass which grew thick upon it Here and there the rocks cropped out of the ground and rose up some twenty feet high, forming grotesquely-shaped natural grottoes, round which clumps of tall silver fir clustered, and at the foot of the trees, spread in great profusion, wild roses, sweetbriar, foxglove, and nightshade. All the farmhouses and cottages were built of brick, thickly coated with clean white plaster, and in the smallest hamlet there was always a church with a steeple surmounted by the large globe-like top, often gilt, which seems peculiar to Sclavonic countries.

No wooden cottages were to be seen here, for the people are richer than those north of the Elbe, and the army left behind it, when it crossed that river, the pine-wood huts, so many of which had been lately destroyed by the flames kindled by the fire of the artillery. The houses, both outside and inside, were beautifully clean; the furniture was of plain deal, without paint, scoured to a whiteness which is unknown in Northern Bohemia; the brass handles of the drawers and the steel and iron round the fireplaces shone bright from much polishing, and reflected back distorted images of the soldiers, who, in their dusty clothes and heavy boots, dirty from marching, looked much out of place in the houses in which they were billeted.

The inhabitants sighed sadly over the war, for their crops had been injured; soldiers of both armies had been billeted in their houses, for the Austrians retreated through this part of the country two days before; and some of them had sons or brothers in the Austrian service. But there was no ill-will between them and the Prussian soldiers. Indeed, the latter were always so good-natured that it would have been difficult even for churls to quarrel with them, and such the natives of the valley of the Elbe are not. They would have preferred peace to war; they suffered deeply in having their houses turned into barracks, their cornfields into bivouacs, their barns and outhouses into stables for war horses; but they did not blame the soldiers for injuries for the cause of which the latter were as innocent as the inhabitants themselves; they gave the men what they could; nor did the villagers and peasants attempt to impose upon the soldiers, though the town shopkeepers, more keenly alive to their own interests, generally managed to make a profit out of the difference of the Prussian and Austrian coinage.

The headquarters of the First Army were on the night of the 8th established in a monastery at Chrast. The priests were still there, but gave up the greater part of the house to Prince Frederick Charles and his staff. Military waggons and horses were picketed inside the usually quiet monastery close; soldier servants went whistling up and down the corridors and among the cells, saddle-bags and valises were bundled upstairs, and the monastery would soon have been very like a barrack were it not that the priests kept flitting about, good-naturedly proffering food and drink to both officers and soldiers; for, although they looked on both as the enemies of their country, and, perhaps, even of their Church, they knew that the army had marched far and fast, and they practised that charity which should be the connecting link among all Christian creeds.

From the church close by the monastery, as a centre, the little town spreads out, its white houses glistening brightly in the sun, along four streets, almost at right angles to each other. Between and behind the houses lay little gardens, in which grew most English greenhouse flowers; vines were trained in trellis-work against the walls, and beyond the fields stretched away, covered with heavy crops ripening for harvest; and between the cornfields lay long belts of gaudy-coloured poppies, which are cultivated in this country in great quantities. The church bell sounding slowly, probably for vespers, for the day was Sunday, and a few women, with shawls in Bohemian fashion thrown over their bare heads, disappearing into the church door, and just seen within crossing themselves with the holy water, would have made the whole scene one of perfect peace; but the piles of bayonets by every door, the perpetual soldiers bustling along the streets, the cantonniers who had established their itinerant stalls close outside the church door, and were squabbling with soldiers over the value of black cigars or

354

schnapps, told that this smiling little town was . the headquarters of an army which had just marched from a battlefield, and was pressing forward again to force its enemy to battle; for the policy of the Prussian Army was now to cling to the heels of the retreating Austrians and to force them to fight before they had time to reorganise their forces.

On the 9th July the whole force was again moved towards the south-east. That night the king's headquarters were at Hohenmauth; the headquarters of Prince Frederick Charles, commanding the centre, were at the village of Reichenberg, about twenty-five miles south-east of Pardubitz. The crown prince, with the headquarters of the Second Army, halted for the night at Leitomischl, one march to the east of the First Army; and the Army of the Elbe was pursuing its way, at an even pace with the two others, under General von Bittenfeld, along the road which leads to Iglau. No intelligence had yet been received of the occupation of Prague, although it was considered certain that Prussian troops must have occupied that town. Tidings of the capital of Bohemia being actually possessed were eagerly looked for, not only by those who took a strategical interest in the campaign, but by all who wished to receive private supplies from Berlin; for till the railway communication was established parcels could hardly be expected to arrive; and tobacco and cigars, which rank in Germany almost on a par with food, were very scarce, and a fresh supply was eagerly desired.

This day's was a short march, but the most unpleasant one which the army had yet had. A drizzling rain fell in the early morning, and a cold wind was blowing, which drove their wet clothes against the soldiers' bodies, and made them shiver even as they marched; but towards mid-day the rain ceased, and the sun burst through the clouds, so that the men got dry; but heavy rain again fell in the afternoon, and the bivouac at night was moist and uncomfortable. Again this day the country was found fertile, and the inhabitants still in their houses; all received kindly the soldiers who came into the cottages along the line of march to buy food or tobacco, and some even expressed a desire to become Prussians, stating as a reason that they should pay less taxes than under the Austrian rule; but whether this wish was sincere, or only elicited by the presence of the Prussian troops and from a desire of flattering their national pride, is open to question.

At this time Feldzeugmeister Benedek was working hard to reorganise the relics of the Austrian Army of the North at Olmütz, Although over sixty years old, he displayed a capacity for labour, both in the saddle and at the desk, which would have shamed many a younger man. He was at this time ordered to despatch the mass of his army by rail to Vienna, where it was to be united to the Austrian army from Italy, under the command of the Archduke Albrecht.[1]

Count Mensdorf was despatched from Vienna directly, after the defeat at Königgrätz, to the headquarters of the Army of the North, in order there to inquire into the circumstances of that disaster. The consequences of his mission were that a military commission was later assembled at Weiner Neustadt, before which Count Clam Gallas and Generals Henikstein, Krismanics, and Benedek himself were summoned to appear.

General von John was appointed chief of the staff to the Archduke Albrecht The Austrian Government wished, by bringing up its Army of the South, to oppose a force to the advance of the Prussians, but the troops from Italy did not arrive quickly enough. It was only on the 12th July that the first detachment of nine thousand men arrived at Vienna.

From the time of the Battle of Königgrätz, the Prussian armies had lost all traces of the Austrians until the 8th July, when some of the crown prince's advanced troops fell in with an outpost of the enemy before Zwittau, near the junction of the two branches of rail which lead from Olmütz and Brünn to Böhmisch Trübau. After a slight skirmish the Austrians fell back, and on the 9th the crown prince occupied Mährisch Trübau and Zwittau, two towns of Moravia. That evening the first *corps d'armée* halted at Zwittau, the Guards at Wildenschwert, the fifth corps at Landskron.

The first intelligence which the Prussians received of the retreat of the Austrian army had made it appear probable that Benedek had withdrawn the greater portion of it to Brünn, on the direct line to Vienna. Now the whole of his movements were cleared up. An Austrian field post happened to be captured in front of Mährisch Trübau, and many interesting private letters found in it, which established the demoralized condition of Benedek's army, as well as a copy of the orders of that general for the marches of his corps, and the movements of his administrative services. It was thus discovered that only the tenth Austrian corps and the heavy cavalry of the Prince of Schleswig-Holstein had been sent to Brünn, and that the rest of the Army of the North was seeking shelter under the guns of Olmütz until it should be in a fit condition to attack the Prussians.

A few days later the Austrian cavalry retaliated, and captured a

---

1. Letters from the correspondents of the *Times* with the Austrian Army.

Prussian field post, in which a despatch was found that gave them some valuable information with regard to the Prussian movements.

On the 10th July, the King of Prussia moved his headquarters to Zwittau. This day it was known to the Prussians that the Austrian Army of the South had commenced its journey to Vienna from Olmütz by railway. The transport of this army was conducted as quickly as possible, and between the 7th and the 13th Benedek despatched three corps—the 3rd, 4th, and 6th—to the capital.[2] When it was ascertained that the Austrian army was moving to the south, the march of the crown prince was directed towards Prerau, that he might there cut the railway communication between Olmütz and Vienna.

On the 10th, a long march of twenty-five miles brought the headquarters of the First Army to the little town of Neustadt, which lies about fifty miles to the northwest of Brünn. It was a wet morning; the clouds hung low, and a drizzling rain made the soft country road deep for the infantry and heavy for the artillery and baggage waggons, for this day the army did not move on one of the main *chausses*, but by one of the lesser roads which lead through the highland country dividing Bohemia from Moravia. As the road ascended, the scenery became more and more bleak and cold; the corn was in the higher parts quite short and green, and in some places not in ear; cultivation was only on patches of ground, and where the land was not tilled the grass grew short and bare. Cold, hard-looking rocks projected everywhere from the soil; the surface of the ground was thickly strewn with large stones, among which a few stunted larch-trees looked as though they had to struggle hard to obtain soil sufficient for even their roots.

Above the road on the hill-sides grow dense forests of spruce and silver fir, the tops of which were for the most part shrouded in a thick mist The dwellings along the line of march were in keeping with the aspect of the country—low, dirty, and untidy, without any gardens, and, generally standing alone on the bleak hill-side, they seemed fitting habitations for the squalid and starved-looking inhabitants who lounged in their doorways, watching with a lazy curiosity the soldiers marching on the road. The men, thin and with sharply-drawn features, seemed to have no work to do, but leant lazily against the doorposts smoking long black pipes; the women, with feet bare and garments

---

2. On no point is there so much popular misunderstanding as on the transport of troops by rail in war. The experience of the German campaign proves that 10,000 men, equipped for the field, is the most that can be safely calculated upon to be moved per day on a single railway.

scanty, shivered beside them, holding in their arms a dirty infant, or combing out their tangled hair.

The foot-soldiers trudged sullenly along; the march was long for them, and the road bad, but they kept up a good pace the whole way, and there were no stragglers. But they had had enough of wet, though, in defiance of the rain, they marched with their cloaks rolled up, mainly to keep them dry for the night bivouac, and longed for dry weather or a harder road. The horses of the artillery laboured heavily, but got the guns and ponderous waggons, weighty with ammunition and corn-sacks full of forage piled up on them, up the quickly-recurring bits of steep ascent in the road. At every sharp rise the drivers flogged and spurred, the gunners pushed behind, and, though the horses stumbled and often nearly fell, and the traces were stretched so tight that they looked as if they must break, no accident occurred, and every artillery carriage arrived safely, at its destination. The baggage-waggons did not fare so well. Less strongly horsed and not so well driven, they all dropped far behind the troops, and a few remained stranded on the side of the way with a broken axle-tree or a shivered wheel.

Near the little town of Swratka the frontier of Moravia was passed, but the road that descends from it still ran along the hill country of the frontier, and only came down into a valley near Neustadt to rise again at the beginning of the morrow's march. Within Moravia the country, though perhaps even less fertile, was more pleasing. All pretence of cultivation had been given up, for trees grew down close to the road, and where there was not wood the ground was wet and marshy, and showed no signs of ever having been drained; and the horses of the cavalry who scouted in front of the columns floundered along, sinking in it above their fetlocks.

The monotony of the march was relieved by a spirited cavalry skirmish in the little town of Saar, which is about six miles to the west of Neustadt. On the previous night the Austrian hussars of the regiment of Hesse-Cassel held Saar. The Prussian cavalry was to proceed on the 10th to Gammy, about a mile in front of Saar, and the 9th regiment of Uhlans formed its advanced guard on the march. The Austrians intended to march the same day to the rear towards Brünn, and the hussars were actually assembling for parade previous to the march when the first patrols of the Prussian Uhlans came rattling into the town. The Austrians were collecting together from all the different houses and farmyards; mounted men, filing out of barns and strawhouses, were riding slowly towards their rendezvous in the market-place; men who had not yet mounted were leading their horses, strolling carelessly alongside them, when, by some fault of their sentinels, they were surprised by the Prussians.

The Uhlans were much inferior in number at first, but their supports were coming up behind them, and this disadvantage was compensated for by the Austrians being taken unawares. The Uhlans quickly advanced, but did not charge before one Austrian squadron had time to form, and only while most of the men of the remaining divisions were quickly falling into their ranks, though some were cut off from the rendezvous by the Prussians advancing beyond the doors from which they were issuing, and were afterwards made prisoners.

In the market-place an exciting contest at once began. The celebrated cavalry of Austria were attacked by the rather depreciated horsemen of Prussia, and the lance, the "queen of weapons," as its admirers love to term it, was being engaged in real battle against the sword. The first Prussian soldiers who rode into the town were very few in number, and they could not attack before some more came up. This delay of a few minutes gave the hussars a short time to hurry together from the other parts of the town, and by the time the Uhlans received their reinforcements the Austrians were nearly formed.

As soon as their supports came up the lancers formed a line across the street, advanced a few yards at a walk, then trotted for a short distance, their horses' feet pattering on the stones, the men's swords jingling, their accoutrements rattling, and their lances borne upright, with the black and white flags streaming over their heads; but when near the opening into the broader street, which is called the Market-place, a short, sharp word of command, a quick, stern note from the trumpet, the lance-points came down and were sticking out in front of the horses' shoulders, the horses broke into a steady gallop, and the lance-flags fluttered rapidly from the motion through the air, as the horsemen, with bridle-hands low and bodies bent forward, lightly gripped the staves, and drove the points straight to the front.

But when the Prussians began to gallop, the Austrians were also in motion. With a looser formation and a greater speed they came on, their blue pelisses, trimmed with fur and embroidered with yellow, flowing freely from their left shoulders, leaving their sword-arms disencumbered. Their heads, well up, carried the single eagle's feather in every cap straight in the air; their swords were raised, bright and sharp, ready to strike, as their wiry little horses, pressed tight by the knees of the riders, came bounding along, and dashed against the Prussian

359

ranks as if they would leap over the points of the lances. The Uhlans swayed heavily under the shock of the collision; but, recovering again, pressed on, though only at a walk.

In front of them were mounted men, striking with their swords, parrying the lance-thrusts, but unable to reach the lancer; but the ground was also covered with men and horses, struggling together to rise; loose horses were galloping away; dismounted hussars in their blue uniforms and long boots were hurrying off to try to catch their chargers or to avoid the lance-points. The Uhlan line appeared unbroken, but the hussars were almost dispersed. They had dashed up against the firmer Prussian ranks, and they had recoiled, shivered, scattered, and broken as a wave is broken that dashes against a cliff. In the few moments that the ranks were locked together, it seems that the horsemen were so closely jammed against each other that lance or sword was hardly used. The hussars escaped the points in rushing in, but their speed took them so close to the lancers' breasts that they had not even room to use their swords. Then the Prussians, stouter and taller men, mounted on heavier horses, mostly bred from English sires, pressed hard on the light frames and the smaller horses of the hussars, and by mere weight and physical strength bore them back, and forced them from their seats to the ground; or sometimes, so rude was the shock, sent horse and man bounding backwards, to come down with a clatter on the pavement.

The few Austrians who remained mounted fought for a short time to stop the Prussian advance, but they could make no impression on the lancers. Wherever a hussar made a dash to close three points bristled couched against his chest or his horse's breast, for the Austrians were now in inferior numbers in the streets to the Prussians, and the narrowness of the way would not allow them to retire for their reserves to charge. So the Prussians pressed steadily forward in an invulnerable line, and the Austrians, impotent to stop them, had to fall back before them. Before they had gone far through the town, fighting this irregular combat more Prussian cavalry came up behind the Uhlans, and the Austrians began to draw off. The lancers pushed after them, but the hussars got away, and at the end of the town the pursuit ceased. One officer and twenty-two non-commissioned officers and privates taken prisoners, with nearly forty captured horses, fell into the hands of the Uhlans, as the trophies of this skirmish. Some of the prisoners were wounded; a few hussars killed, and two or three Prussians were left dead upon the ground.

One or two of the privates taken prisoners were Germans, but by far the greater number were Hungarians—smart, soldier-like looking fellows, of a wiry build; they looked the very perfection of light horsemen, but were no match in a *mêlée* for the tall, strong cavalry soldiers of Prussia, who seemed with one hand to be able to wring them from their saddles, and hurl them to the ground.

The inhabitants of Neustadt reported that there was an Austrian cavalry division of four regiments at Ostrau, a village about six miles south of Saar, and it seemed clear from the reports of the prisoners that there was a strong cavalry force in front of the advancing Prussians. On the 10th July five hundred Italians, deserters from the Austrian service, surrendered themselves to General von Bittenfeld, the commander of the Army of the Elbe, and volunteered to serve during the war in the Prussian army; but the king had no need of foreign troops, and very naturally declined the proffered services of men who had been faithless to one cause, and ordered that they should be sent to Italy, where they might perhaps have an opportunity of proving their patriotism on the Mincio.

The same day all the Saxon prisoners who had been taken during the campaign were released and sent to their homes, on condition of taking an oath not to serve against Prussia during the war. They all took the oath, and went to Saxony; but many seemed to quit their prisons with regret, for they had no money, and they feared that there would be no work to be found in their own country; but this fear ought not to have been well-grounded, for the harvest in Saxony was close at hand, and the crops there had not been trampled down by battles or bivouacs.

The weather on the 11th was better than that of the previous day. The sun shone out warm, and lighted up the dark groves of fir-wood which hung above the road, and shining on the trunks of the silver firs relieved the monotonous dark green of the foliage. The road was very hilly, and in some places bad, but it was drying quickly under the influence of the sun, and the soldiers marched cheerfully, careless of the depressing weather which had lately been the rule. The way still lay through the Moravian highlands, but the increased heat of the sun, the presence of oak and ash among the firs, the yellower crops and more abundant grass showed that the army was gradually working down towards the valley of the Schwarzawa: but the country did not become more plain, nor did the rivulcti tumble down alongside the road in less frequent miniature cataracts; on the contrary, the ground was more broken up in hills and valleys.

The former were not high, nor did they run in any chain, or in any order; sometimes they rose as huge, isolated, rounded masses, the tops of which were shrouded in fir plantations, while abutting mica rocks projecting from their sides reflected brightly the rays of the sun; sometimes they ran in tortuous ridges, breaking suddenly into a steep ravine, to allow the passage of a watercourse; or throwing up some huge masses of rock which, sparkling in the sunlight, contrasted strongly with the dark leaves of the surrounding trees, seemed to form natural castles to defend the road. In such a country a few riflemen might have delayed seriously the march of the army, but the advanced guard had patrolled the paths through all the woods, had sent scouts to the top of every hill, had looked down into every ravine, and, though the Austrian cavalry was known to be between them and Brünn, they marched on to Tischnowitz without finding an Austrian *Jäger*, or meeting with any opposition to their progress.

Fifteen miles from Neustadt, where it had halted the night before, the headquarter staff turned aside from the road, followed a rough country lane for two miles, and then plunged by a rugged, winding path into a deep ravine formed by one of the feeders of the Schwarzawa. On the side of the ravine over which the path led through a thick wood, perched high on a prominent rock, and rising above fir-trees, stood the old *Schloss* of Bernstein, where it had been considered advisable to fix headquarters for the night. The battlements and loop-holed walls of the old castle strongly lighted up by the sun, the steep ravine below sunk in shade, the helmets of the escort, the line of armed and mounted men, formed a scene which savoured more of romance than of modern war.

The Prince Frederick Charles and his staff turned down the twisting path, crossed the river by a wooden bridge close to a water-mill, and, by a more easy ascent on the other side, gained the gate, which still bore the marks of where a portcullis had been. But in the yard within every-day life was rudely recalled. The spare horses of the officers had already arrived, and indignant grooms were anathematising fiercely because they could get no stabling for their charges; the steep road forbade the approach of the forage waggons, and neither hay nor corn were to be found in the antiquated building. The appearance of the commander-in-chief for a few moments hushed the clamour, but when he rode on each aggrieved domestic made a rush at his master, and loudly poured forth the tale of his sorrows. A compromise was effected, for hay and corn had been provided at a farmhouse near at hand; and when the servants were assured that the horses should have food, they bore with resignation that they must be all night without cover.

But attention was soon called away from both the scenery and the horses by the arrival of an Uhlan officer from the advanced guard, who rode up the yard at a gallop, and, jumping off his horse before the commander-in-chief, with his hand to his forehead, delivered a hurried report

The advanced guard had found the enemy's cavalry in strong force at Tischnowitz, and the Duke of Mecklenburg had sent him to Prince Frederick Charles to report the fact and receive his orders. The orders were soon written, and Major von Capprivi, a staff-officer, who has a high reputation in this army, was entrusted to deliver them to the commander of the advanced guard.

Major Capprivi's horse was tired with a long march, and Tischnowitz lay fifteen miles off, but he had no choice but to carry the order, and in a few minutes he was ready to start. With him went three officers, who had been employed as *aides-de-camp* at headquarters, but whose regiments were in the advanced guard, and who went to join them for the action which was expected. Revolvers were inspected, and the priming carefully looked to, for Austrian patrols were expected to be on the road, and it was just possible that the little band might have to ride for their lives. But they started in high spirits, for the excitement of probable battle nerved them, and two hours of a sharp trot brought them to Tischnowitz.

Here, in a small town on the banks of the Schwarzawa, the Austrian cavalry had taken up their position. The road leading to the town goes straight along the valley, and keeping a direct course is obliged some three or four times to cross by wooden bridges the channel of the stream, which is here about fifty feet wide. When the Duke of Mecklenburg, with the advanced guard, was approaching Tischnowitz, he perceived that the enemy was in the town, and in strong force of cavalry with artillery in the plain beyond, where he occupied a position which could not be turned by cavalry on account of the rugged nature of the hills on either flank.

But the Austrians, besides the horsemen in the town and on the far side, had thrown out three squadrons in the direction of Tischnowitz, of which the centre one was in the road and between the bridges, and the right and left were thrown into the cornfields on either side. The

Prussian troopers, few in number, who formed the advance of the advanced guard, had ridden forward toward the bridges, and had almost begun to cross the first before they perceived the hostile cavalry. Then they found that both their flanks were exposed to attack, and that the squadron in the road in front of them was getting ready to charge. The Prussian advanced guard was from the 2nd regiment of dragoons of the Guard; the Austrian squadrons were lancers, and it seemed that the skirmish of the previous day between sword and lance would be repeated with the weapons in opposite hands.

But the lieutenant commanding the small Prussian advanced guard, seeing that he was too weak to force his way, and fearing to be surrounded and cut off, retreated a short distance to where a slight rise in the ground gave him a certain advantage of position, and there drawing up his little force awaited an attack, but with no intention of meeting it with the sword. While his men were yet retiring, they were unbuckling their carbines, and before they had turned to stand, their quickly-loaded arms, constructed on the same principle as the needle-gun, were ready to fire. And not too soon, for the Austrians had begun to advance quickly, and were defiling over the bridge, prepared to form line and charge, when a sudden volley from the Prussian carbines made them pull up sharp, half surprised, half frightened to find that a carbine could be of any use, except to make noise or smoke, in the hands of a mounted man.

But the Prussians did not wait to observe the discomfiture of their enemies; their officer only noticed that they were in too strong force to be allowed to get near his much smaller band, and again he retreated a little distance; and so quick were the dragoons with their loading that their carbines were almost ready to fire again before they turned to retire. The Austrians again formed to charge, and again before they had settled into their stride a rapid volley stopped their career. Again the Prussians retired, and again faced about ready to fire another volley. Again the Austrians came on, and again the fire of the dragoons stopped them short; but this was the last time, for the whole of the first squadron of the dragoons were now up, and had formed line beside the few who had hitherto prevented the advance of the lancers.

Then the dragoons advanced to charge, and the Austrians, glad to exchange the chance of close quarters for the fire of the carbines, came forward to meet them. Both sides advanced steadily: the lancers, with their spears in rest, came on in an apparently impenetrable line; but the dragoons, with their sword-points to the front and their horses well in hand, bore steadily down upon them, in the last few yards let their horses go, and dashed in through the points of the lances. Their commander. Major von Shack, went down, grievously wounded, but his men thought of his fall only to avenge it, and rushed in so close to the lancers that their spears were useless, smiting them heavily with their keen bright swords. A few moments only the *mêlée* lasted; then the lancers, turning, flew towards the town.

The dragoons pursued, but their officer kept them well in hand, and they did not lose their order. When the street was gained the lancers turned again, the swordsmen thundered down upon them, and by sheer weight and strength of blows bore them backwards along the street. The fight was long and hard. The men, too close together to use their weapons, grappled with one another; the horses, frightened and enraged, snorted, plunged, reared, and struck out But the Prussians had superior weight and strength, and pressed their antagonists back along the streets to a wider space in the centre of the town, where a high image of the Madonna, carved in stone, looked down upon the fray. Here an Austrian officer, hurled from his saddle by a tall Prussian dragoon, had his brains dashed out against the foot of the monument, and another Austrian, bent backwards over the cantle of his saddle, had his spine broken by the strength of his assailant.

The light Austrian men and horses had no chance in this close conflict, and soon they were obliged to turn, and fled down the street to where their supports were drawn up behind the town. Here there was a strong force of Austrian cavalry, and a battery of horse artillery was placed so as to sweep the road. But the cavalry drew off without waiting for an attack, and the artillery retired without firing a shot; which can only be accounted for by believing, as the country people said, that there was no ammunition with the guns. The Prussian supports came up and pushed two miles beyond the town, but the Austrians had drawn off too quickly to again allow an engagement; and the outposts were placed here for the night.

Then the Duke of Mecklenburg made his arrangements for his advance to Brünn the next morning; and when he had given a general sketch of his plans, Major von Capprivi and Captain von Bergmann, the staff officer attached to the advanced guard, retired to a back room in the small country inn of Tischnowitz, and, by the light of a single tallow candle, discussed till late into the night, and sketched upon their maps, the details of the occupation of the capital of Moravia.

The march was ordered for four o'clock in the morning, for it was expected that the Austrian cavalry would defend the approach to the town, and it was intended to surprise them before they had made their dispositions. It was after midnight that the two staff officers threw themselves on some trusses of straw to catch a few short hours of sleep before the commencement of an operation which might perhaps have been one of the most decisive of the campaign, for the plans were skilfully laid, and it seemed that if the Austrians attempted to stand in front of the town a great part of their cavalry would have been captured. All that the staff appeared to fear was that the cavalry would draw off through the town before daylight, and too early for the dispositions for their capture to be carried out—for the infantry who were required to invest the further side of Brünn had marched far in the day, and were too tired to be sent forward before daybreak.

At three o'clock on the morning of the 12th July, the soldiers of the advanced guard of the First Prussian Army were roused from their billets, and began making their preparations for the march. Horses were saddled; the cloaks in which the men had been sleeping were rolled up and buckled on the pommels, girths and bridle reins carefully inspected, and the troopers, before they mounted, drew their hands along the edges of their swords to test the sharpness of their weapons. The officers looked to the loading of their revolvers, and buckled their pistols round their waists, so that they might be easily got at in case of need; and it was expected that they would be required, for three divisions of Austrian cavalry were reported to be between the small town where the advanced guard halted the previous night and Brünn, and the Duke of Mecklenburg had only three cavalry regiments with him.

At a quarter before four, before the sun was up, the troops began marching out of Tischnowitz, and in three-quarters of an hour formed up before the little village of Hradschau, which the most advanced outposts had occupied during the former night Here the Duke of Mecklenburg called his principal officers round him, and told them that he expected to find three divisions of the enemy's cavalry, forming together a force of twelve regiments, in front of him; but that his orders were to occupy Brünn if possible, and that he intended to advance immediately. The troops were then formed in the order in which they were to move behind a ridge of rising ground, over which the Brünn road rises and falls, about a quarter of a mile beyond Hradschau. The 2nd dragoons of the Guard led; they were followed by the Ziethen Hussars and a battery of horse artillery; then came a battalion of *Jägers*, followed by the rest of the infantry and artillery, and a regiment of lancers closed the rear.

As soon as the formation was complete, the dragoons sent out their scouts, and in a few minutes the top of the ridge was studded with mounted men who showed out clear against the morning sky. Every horseman carried his carbine in his right hand, ready to fire; but the staff listened in vain for the sharp crack which would tell that the enemy was in sight; and the scouts, after peering forward for a few moments, dipped down behind the ridge, and were hidden. Then the dragoons advanced along the road. When their leading troops gained the top of the ascent they spread out right and left, and pushed across the fields that lay on either side of the way.

The hussars, in column of troops, followed along the highway, raising a cloud of dust which almost hid them, and from its midst rose the steady patter of horses' feet and the jingle of steel which mark the march of cavalry. The guns rumbled behind, with rammers and sponges ready for action, and limber-boxes, unlocked, each closely followed by its mounted gunners, prepared to spring down and twist the muzzle round towards the front. Carefully beating through the corn, and covering every piece of rising ground, the dragoons steadily advanced; but no sign of an enemy was seen, and the advanced scouts reached the village of Tschepen without finding traces of even a last night's bivouac

Here the road ran through a narrow defile, with high banks covered with plantations, and the houses of the village standing across the pass would have formed a strong position for the Austrians to hold. On approaching the village the cavalry was halted, and the riflemen were sent for to beat through the wood and push in among the houses. The halt was not long, for in a few minutes the *Jägers* came up quickly with a long swinging stride, passed by the cavalry, and burst like a pack of hounds into the village and up the sides of the slopes. Now and then a dark green uniform appeared among the trees only to disappear again; and here and there among the houses the sunlight glancing back from a rifle barrel, ever further advanced, showed that the skirmishers were working forward, but the sound of no shot came back, and it was clear that the village was deserted.

The cavalry and guns then moved on, and filed along the narrow street; but the *Jägers* were still kept in front, for the defile did not end till the village of Gurein was passed. The dragoons then spread out again, and went peeping inquisitively into every hollow, ferreting out the inhabitants of the cottages to give information, and stopping every peasant who seemed to be in too pressing a hurry to get away in the direction in which the Austrian cavalry was supposed to lie.

The country people asserted with one accord that the Austrians had retired through Brünn the night before or early that morning, and there were no troops in front of the town; that a few dragoons and lancers had bivouacked the previous evening just outside Brünn, but had passed through at daybreak, and were already far on the road to Vienna.

The road ran over successive ridges, each of which would have been an advantageous standing-point for the Austrians had they meant to oppose the Prussian advance into the town. As position after position was covered by the scouts without finding the enemy, and as the stories of the country people were always the same, the staff began to believe that the Austrian cavalry had really retired, and that their troops would seize the place without opposition. The road from Tischnowitz strikes the high road from Zwittau to Brünn about six miles before reaching the latter town, and when this point was passed it seemed almost sure that the way was clear, and that the Austrians had drawn off; and here this assurance received a further confirmation, for at this point a dragoon came in bringing with him two travellers, who had in the morning left Brünn for Zwittau, and had been stopped on their way by the foremost Prussian patrol Glad to exchange their information for permission to proceed on their journey, they willingly told that the town was deserted by troops, and that all the Austrians had retired early in the morning.

But the march was continued, notwithstanding these reports, with even greater precaution; the scouts were as alert as before, and the main body moved through the corn land by the side of the road, prepared to form line of battle. About eight o'clock the leading troops ascended a gentle slope, from the top of which the capital of Moravia could be seen lying four miles before them. Here a halt was called, and the staff-officers went forward a little way to reconnoitre.

The sun shone brightly on the spires of the churches and on the roofs of the houses, but no swords or spear-heads glittered in its light; and on the fort of the Spielberg, on the western side of the town, no guns could be seen, and no sentinels stood upon the ramparts. White flags of truce were flying from every steeple and from every tower, and, instead of the Austrian colours, a white sheet waved from the flagstaff of the fort It was evident that the town had surrendered. In a few minutes a deputation from the magistracy arrived to announce officially that the town was deserted by the Austrian troops, and praying that it might not be given up to pillage. The Duke of Mecklenburg willingly promised that the property of the inhabitants should be secure to them, for there had been no intention to allow plundering.

Then, after an hour's halt, the troops again advanced, and soon got between two lines of villas which stand outside the town on each side of the road. The scouts came cantering in, and, drawing together on the road, formed an advanced guard, behind which the Duke of Mecklenburg and his staff rode. Before the actual town was reached, a deputation—the *burgomaster* and magistrates—were seen coming to meet the troops in cabs with white flags flying from them, and each with a broad band of white round his arm. As soon as they saw the staff they sprang out of their carriages, and, with hats in hand, came forward bowing, with many prayers for the preservation of their city from pillage. They had much wealth in the city, and they feared for their property.

The Prussian commander answered them courteously, but told them that his men had marched early and had no provisions, and that, therefore, he should be much obliged to them to furnish dinner for 8,000 soldiers, and forage for 2,500 horses. The magistrates started back to the town to procure the rations.

When the deputation was dismissed the troops again advanced the line of spectators became thicker along the side of the road, crowds of inhabitants along the side of the way courted the smiles of the soldiers, white flags hung from every window, and the inmates of many houses, with a mockery of enthusiasm, had hung out green boughs and wreaths of leaves to welcome the invaders of their country.

The dragoons were sent on in advance, and went clattering through the town to occupy the bridges on the further side; *Jägers* swung swiftly forward to seize the railway station, the post-office, and the telegraph bureau; and the rest of the infantry marched in with music playing, seized the Spielbeig, and took possession of the capital of Moravia.

Prince Frederick Charles came in late in the afternoon at the head of General Manstein's division. When he reached the Platz he halted, and drew on one side to see his men march past him. The soldiers had been on the road since two o'clock in the morning, but the regiments marched as if they had not come two miles. With steady tramp and all in step, with unbroken ranks and battalions undiminished by stragglers, they marched into the town. Dusty and worn boots alone showed that they had come across Bohemia, fought a great battle, and had been marching lately over twenty-five miles a day; for they had halted outside to brush their clothes, and they came in with cloaks well folded, knapsacks as well put on, and arms as clean, as if they had been in garrison at home.

The 60th, a regiment renowned for its marching, well sustained its reputation; the men, shoulder to shoulder, close as if linked together, moved forward like a solid wall, and notwithstanding their fatigue, for they had come over thirty miles, stepped in such perfect cadence from front to rear of the regiment that only one footfall was heard upon the pavement. The 24th, tall men and well-built, came along with heads well up and rifles carried as if they could not know fatigue, and were quite unaware that they bore a heavy knapsack on their shoulders. The other regiments also marched bravely, and their chief looked that day as proud of his troops as when he stood among them victorious on the summit of the Sadowa hill; and well he might, for the Prussian army had given proof of an endurance of fatigue and of a power of marching which have rarely been equalled in the annals of war; for the marches had not been made by small detachments or over open ground, but by large masses, along deep and heavy roads, encumbered with artillery and crowded with carriages.

The headquarters of the First Army halted at Brünn on the 13th July. The troops had marched their shoes off their feet, and no repairs could be made during the late rapid marches; the horses of the cavalry wanted rest and shoeing, the saddlery required looking to, reserves of ammunition had to be brought up, and it was necessary to establish *depôts* and hospitals. The advanced guard was, however, pushing on that morning to Medritz, about six miles beyond the town, on the road to Vienna. All daylong the remaining troops of the First Army were marching in. Regiment after regiment, with band playing and drums beating, tramped steadily along the pavement, drawing behind its long line of glittering bayonets the heavy waggons which carry reserve cartridges and hospital stores, and always follow close in rear of the battalions.

The townspeople had quite recovered from the panic caused by the approach of the Prussians. All the shops were open, the manufactories were at work, the market-place was studded with country women who sat among the piled arms or on the poles of the artillery carriages, making up nosegays or selling fruit, for which there was a great demand among the soldiers. These, for many days, had tasted little but black bread and commissariat meat, carried straight to the camp cooking-fire from the newly-killed ox; for, in order to save transport, the bullocks for food were marched in rear of the regiments, and on arriving at the halting-place were killed, to be immediately cooked and eaten. But here the men had good food, for the magistracy was held responsible that they should be supplied with their rations.

Every hotel, every restaurant, every *café*, was crowded with officers, who, having laid aside their dusty marching clothes, were dressed in uniforms as bright as would be worn in Berlin; but unshaven beards, close-cropped hair, and the absence of epaulettes, showed that they were still on a campaign.

Soldiers with cleaned and pipe-clayed belt, well-brushed coats, and smart white trousers, which had been carried, by some wonderful means, unsullied in the recesses of their knapsacks, crowded the streets, filled the beershops, and drove bargains with the proprietors of the tobacco and pipe stalls.

The lower class of inhabitants mixed freely among the soldiers, and under their guidance inspected, half timidly, half curiously, the wonderful needle-gun of which they had heard so much, and numbers of which, piled four together, were standing in long lines in the market-place.

Newspapers containing Imperial decrees dated from Vienna were freely hawked about the street One of these told officially that Field Marshal the Archduke Albrecht had been appointed commander-in-chief of the whole Austrian Army, with Field Marshal von John as his chief of the staff; and another, that Austria was about to open a loan of 200,000,000 *guldens*. Cabs pushed about the town, through the crowded streets, conveying impatient staff officers, who had to find quarters for some general, or billets for some regiment which was just arriving—no easy task, for nearly the whole infantry of the First Army was in Brünn, and though the magistracy, anxious to please the Prussians, crowded the men upon the householders, accommodation was scarce.

Every house had twenty or twenty-five soldiers quartered upon it, but they did not give the inmates much trouble, for a couple of rooms with a few trusses of straw, and the use of the kitchen fire to cook their food, was all they wanted; and they did not stay much in their billets, but wandered about the town or sat in the beerhouses smoking with quiet enjoyment the long wooden pipes which, from want of tobacco, had been useless for some time past, but which had seldom been forgotten or left behind on the line of march, while some wrote long letters to their friends at home, and sent off to wives or mothers in Prussia all that they could save from their small pay.

The king arrived that afternoon, and established his headquarters in the town-hall. With him came Count Bismark and the Minister of War. Few people had collected to see him enter the town, and the populace made no demonstration of any kind; the magistrates received him with politeness, each with the white and red badge of neutrality bound broad round the left arm.

Many rumours of an armistice were flying about, for M. Benedetti, the French ambassador at Berlin, was there, and it was known that the Emperor of the French was bringing his influence to bear upon the Prussian Court in favour of peace. Count Bismark was for some time closeted with the ambassador in an upper room of the town-hall, where, undisturbed by the hum which rose from the crowded streets, they were supposed to be discussing the conditions of an armistice. The latest Austrian newspapers said that the *Kaiser* had determined that no attempt should be made to defend the capital itself, for it was thought better to let the town be occupied peaceably by an enemy than be exposed to the possibility of a bombardment But though at this time it might have been intended that the Austrian troops should abandon Vienna, preparations were being made to continue the war. The army from the Italian frontier was being brought up towards the Danube, to add 120,000 men to the troops at present round the capital

While the army halted here, reserve troops were being advanced into Bohemia to secure the communications with Saxony, and to keep order in rear of the armies, where the peasantry, having possessed themselves with weapons from the fields of battle, had begun to plunder convoys and to attack small escorts or patrols. The first reserve corps occupied Bohemia. Prague and Pardubitz were garrisoned in force, and the second reserve corps had been organised at Leipzig to act against the flank of the Bavarians. General von Falckenstein was named Prussian Commandant of Bohemia, and General Manteuffel took his place in the command of the Army of the Maine.

But many considered that all these precautions were useless, and that the army would never move south of Brünn. The visit of the French ambassador, quickly reported from billet to billet, fell as a cold chill on the enthusiasm of the troops, for they longed to go to Vienna, and conclude the campaign by an entrance into the capital. But they also wished for the end of the war, and longed for home, so they hated the idea of delay, and anticipated with disgust an armistice, by the conditions of which the army might be retained at Brünn for a considerable time. A flag of truce was sent that day to the Austrian advanced guard, which lay beyond Medritz, and the staff officer who went with it carried a letter to be given to the Austrian commander-in-chief. The contents of the letter were known only in the king's headquarters, but popular rumour did not fail to assert that the flag of truce carried with it a despatch to open negotiations which would conclude a peace.

The railway communication with Saxony was all but restored, and was actually opened on the 15th.

When Prague was occupied by the Prussian troops on the 8th, thirty locomotive engines and some thousand railway carriages were found at the railway station, and with this supply of rolling stock the railway was soon opened for military purposes between Prague and Brünn. A broken bridge between Münchengrätz and Jung-Bunzlau required several days for its repair, and still prevented communication with Berlin, but as soon as this viaduct was restored the army was able to receive supplies by the route of Türnau, Prague, and Pardubitz. The line was long, because the shorter route through Josephstadt and Königgrätz was closed by those fortresses, and the guns of Theresienstadt prevented the line to Dresden from being used; but communication by it required much less time than by the rough roads over which the convoys had hitherto to travel, and as soon as it was open supplies arrived much more quickly than while they were carried for many long miles over rough hill roads, along which the waggons jolted slowly and painfully.

The Army of the Elbe, after the Battle of Königgrätz, formed the right wing of the general advance of the Prussians from Przelautsch and Pardubitz. It followed the most direct road southwards, and on the 10th July reached Iglau, and there crossed the boundary line between Bohemia and Moravia. Here it found detachments of General Edelsheim's cavalry in its front, but they retired without making any resistance to its advance. The capture of the imperial manufactory of cigars at Iglau supplied Herwarth's soldiers with plentiful rations of tobacco, the want of which is so much missed by German troops. In the neighbourhood of Iglau Herwarth captured one hundred transport waggons. He then moved forwards in the direction of Znaym.

CHAPTER 2
Tobitschau

When the Archduke Albrecht assumed the command of all the Austrian troops in the field, he could not retain Benedek's army in Olmütz, unless he consented to sacrifice Vienna without a blow, for it was not strong enough to delay the advance of the Prussians by acting against their flank and communications. He might have determined to occupy the line of the March with the Army of the North and the troops from Italy, but he had not time to take up a strong position here before the Prussians would be upon him. The line of this river was also badly suited for a defensive position, as an army lying along it would have had a range of mountains, that of the Lower Carpathians, in its rear. An occupation of the line of the Waag, with his left wing supported on Komorn, his centre at Leopoldstadt, and his Army of the North posted along the hills on the left bank of that river, which entirely command the plain on the right bank, while his Army of the South held the Danube near Vienna, would have afforded the Archduke many advantages.

The Prussians could not have advanced against Vienna without exposing their flanks and communications to the Army of the North, nor could they have moved against this army without placing themselves in unfavourable circumstances. They would have been obliged to cross the March and the Lower Carpathians, to fight a battle where they would have had a river and a line of hills in front of them, a chain of mountains and a river in their rear. It appears, however, that the archduke feared that the Prussians, by seizing the passes of the Carpathians, might have neutralized the action of his Army of the North, and have pushed on against the capital, for he determined take up the line of the Danube from Krems to Pressburg, with his centre resting on the fortifications of Florisdorf, in front of Vienna.

Yet a battle lost here would have yielded up all Hungary to his enemy, and have placed Austria entirely at the mercy of Prussia. Benedek was ordered to send his army from Olmütz to Vienna, and by the 14th July he had despatched his third, fourth, and sixth corps by railway to the capital On the 15th, while more of his troops were actually upon the line, the railway communications between Olmütz and Vienna was cut near Lundenburg, by the cavalry of the advanced guard of Prince Charles, which had been pushed forward from Brünn.[1] Benedek could send no more troops by rail; he resolved, with the first, second, and eighth corps, which still remained at Olmütz, to march by road to the Danube. One brigade of the eighth corps, followed by a large proportion of artillery, moved by way of Tobitschau and Kremser, on the right bank of the March. The main body, accompanied by Benedek in person, moved on the left bank of the March, by way of Prerau; while a garrison of twenty-five thousand men was left in Olmütz. This movement of the Austrian general brought on the

ACTION OF TOBITSCHAU

The army of the crown prince, after leaving Pardubitz, was directed, as has been already seen, in the direction of Olmütz. On the 14th July, the advanced guard of the first *corps d'armée* reached Prossnitz, about twelve miles to the southward of Olmütz. This advanced guard consisted of General Buddenbrock's brigade, which had been reinforced by some additional artillery, and was accompanied by the first regiment of hussars. Near Prossnitz some detachments of hostile cavalry made their appearance, advancing from Wrahartz. These were Saxon dragoons, which, after a slight skirmish, the Prussian hussars drove back to Kralitz and Biskupitz, on the River Blatta. On the 12th the crown prince determined to leave only one corps to mask Olmütz and the Austrian entrenched camp. With his other corps he resolved to lean towards his right, and keep open his communications with Prince Frederick Charles.

On this day the Guards were at Könitz, the fifth corps at Plumenau. Orders were issued that on the 15th the cavalry reserve by way of Plin, and the first corps from Prossnitz, should make an attack on Prerau, and there cut the railway between Olmütz and Lundenburg. Thus on the 15th, while the main body of the crown prince's army was moving southwards by Urtschitz and Ottaslawitz, General Malotki's brigade of the first corps, consisting of six battalions and a 4-pounder battery, was at daybreak to march to the east of Plumenau, to seize

---

1. See chapter 3.

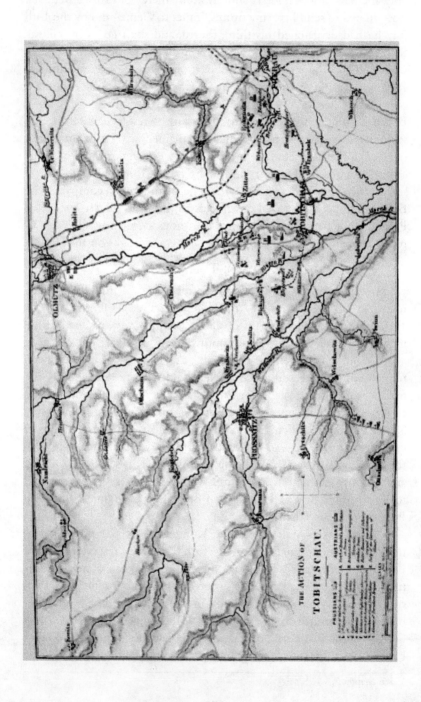

THE ACTION OF
TOBITSCHAU.

Tobitschau and Traubeck, thus to secure the passages over the Blatta, the March, and the Beczwa, and to hold them until General Hartman's division of reserve cavalry could reach Prerau, destroy the railway and return. From Plumenau, by way of Prossnitz, to Hrubschitz is ten miles. Malotki reached the heights of Hrubschitz soon after six o'clock in the morning. From this position he could see a part of the road from Olmütz to Tobitschau, and on it a heavy Austrian column moving towards the latter place. This was Rothkirch's brigade, in rear of which Benedek, either ignorant of the proximity of the Prussians, or anxious to have a strong force of artillery to cover his left flank, had caused a considerable portion of his artillery train to march.[2] At this time the Prussians were ignorant of what Austrian force still remained at Olmütz, although it was calculated, as was afterwards proved correctly, that forty thousand men could have been moved to Vienna before the railway was broken.

The Austrian troops in front of Malotki, under Rothkirch's command, consisted of the 25th Hungarian regiment, the 7th Hungarian regiment, and one *Jäger* battalion: in all, seven battalions, which were accompanied by a squadron of Uhlans and three field batteries.

Malotki deployed his brigade on the east of Hrubschitz towards Wiklitzer Hof and Klopotowitz, with the 44th regiment in the first line, the 4th in the second, and posted his artillery on the left flank of his infantry, just south of Klopotowitz.

The Austrian general brought up twenty-four guns to the hills between the Blatta and the March, and smote with them upon the Prussian flank.

These guns were engaged, but at much disadvantage, by the Prussian battery which was attached to Malotki's brigade. After a short time, however. General Hartman's division of Prussian cavalry arrived on the ground, and reinforced Malotki's guns with two batteries of horse artillery, which took up a position more to the north, and gradually advancing to the Blatta, in about an hour's time succeeded in somewhat silencing the Austrian pieces.

Already, before the artillery on either side had opened fire, the 44th regiment, which formed the first line of Malotki's infantry, began to

2. The accounts of the object with which Rothkirch's brigade moved along this road are varied. Some say that he was intended to occupy a position on the rivers which unite near Tobitschau, in order to cover the march of the main body. Others that Benedek moved him along this route ignorant that the crown prince was so close at hand, and committed the artillery train on it because of its being the better road.

advance. The fusilier battalion of this regiment moved against Wiklitzer Hof, the second battalion on its left towards Klopotowitz, and the third battalion between the two others. Without coming into collision with the enemy, these battalions gained the western bank of the Blatta. The river was so deep and broad in consequence of the late heavy rain that it could only be crossed at Wiklitzer Hof, where there were two bridges. Had the enemy occupied these passages, the advance of the brigade would have been exceedingly difficult, perhaps prevented altogether. The fusilier battalion of the 44th, which first passed the stream, came on the further side upon two Austrian companies, which had been thrown out to cover Rothkirch's right flank.

These, on account of some undulations in the ground, had as yet seen nothing of the Prussian advance. They now threw themselves into a small plantation which lay on the south of Tobitschau, and a musketry fight commenced between them and the fusiliers, during which the first and second battalions of the 44th deployed to the left of the fusiliers. Each battalion threw two companies forward in skirmishing order, and retained its two others as reserves in close column of companies. The 4th regiment, which formed Malotki's second line, crossed the stream after the 44th, with its fusilier battalion leading. Two companies of this battalion were directed to occupy Tobitschau, seize the passage over the March, and to bear upon the Austrian left flank. The rest of the regiment followed the first line.

The main body of the brigade then made an attack against the plantation, but was received with such a heavy fire of artillery and musketry that it reeled under the iron storm. It paused a few moments to steady itself, then, covered by skirmishers, sprang forwards upon the trees. The Austrians, against overpowering numbers, stood their ground with wonderful determination, and it was not till bayonets had been crossed, that they quitted the cover. The Prussians halted to rally at the further edge of the wood, while the Austrians drew slowly back along the road towards Olmütz, but lined the ditches in the fields by the wayside with sharpshooters.

All the Austrian battalions had meanwhile formed, and Rothkirch advanced them for a counter-attack, by which he hoped to recover the wood, and drive the Prussians again over the Blatta. The Prussians awaited their approach till they came within one hundred yards of the trees. Then the needle-gun opened with its deadly rapidity, and with rapid and perpetual volleys broke down the heads of the assailant columns. The Austrian battalions were crushed beneath the greeting and in partial confusion drew back. The Prussians rallied, and followed them as they retired to some open ground near the village of Wierowan, beside the road to Olmütz.

During the whole of this combat, the Austrian artillery had played upon the Prussian left flank. General Malotki directed two hundred of the 4th regiment to attack the guns in skirmishing order. The biting fire of the sharpshooters, coupled with the salvoes of the Prussian batteries on the west of the Blatta, forced the enemy's pieces to withdraw to a more convenient distance, and Malotki could make his preparations for a further advance.

In the meantime, Hartman's cavalry had not been idle. At the same time as Malotki advanced, on his left flank a Prussian detachment under Lieutenant-Colonel Kehler, who commanded the 1st Royal hussars, was pushed forward from Prossnitz, by way of Wrahowitz, towards the village of Dub on the March. This detachment consisted of the 1st Royal hussars, a 4-pounder battery, and one battalion of the 5th Prussian regiment of the Line. East of Wrahowitz, it fell in with the Austrian flanking parties. As these were apparently in much superior force, it retired behind the Wallowa, and from the right bank of this stream its artillery opened a fire which at least detained some of the Austrian artillery accompanying Rothkirch's brigade in this direction.

On the morning of the 15th July, after Malotki's brigade had marched on Wiklitzer Hof, Hartman's cavalry division of three brigades took post near and behind it, about Klopotowitz and Biskupitz. Hartman's three brigades were, the light brigade of *Landwehr* cavalry, consisting of the 2nd regiment of *Landwehr* Hussars and the 1st regiment of *Landwehr* Uhlans, a light brigade of the Line, consisting of the 2nd Royal hussars and the 10th Uhlans, and a heavy, or *cuirassier* brigade, consisting of the 1st and 5th regiments of Cuirassiers.

As Malotki pressed upon the Austrian brigade, and it began to retire from the direction of Tobitschau towards Wierowan, Hartman, in order to harass its retreat, formed the design of passing his *cuirassier* brigade, which formed his extreme left, over the Blatta, and with it acting against the Austrian right flank. Some officers sent to reconnoitre found that the bridge over the river near Biskupitz was neither held nor had been destroyed by the enemy.

When the 5th Cuirassiers had crossed the bridge and had gained the further bank, it perceived the Austrian artillery train on the road between Olmütz and Tobitschau, which, on account of the action going on near the latter place, had been halted north of Rakodau, and appeared to be without any escort

Colonel Bredow, who commanded the 5th Cuirassiers, sought permission from General Hartman to attack the artillery train. This permission was accorded to him, not, however, till the Austrian artillery had noticed the Prussian cavalry. The gunners unlimbered, and opened upon the horsemen with shell, but at a long range, for they saw not the 5th Cuirassiers, who were on their own side the stream, but the 1st, who were still near Biskupitz.

Bredow, under cover of some undulating ground, formed his regiment in *échelon* of squadrons, for the attack of the guns. The first squadron he kept towards his right to cover the flank of his attack from any Austrian cavalry which might lie in that direction, the second and fourth squadrons he directed full against the front of the battery, and supported the second with the third as a reserve.

The squadrons moved forward in perfect lines, slowly and steadily at first, seeming to glide over the field, gradually increasing their pace, regardless of the tremendous fire directed upon them, which emptied some saddles. When within a few hundred paces of the battery they broke into a steady gallop, which increased in rapidity at every stride that brought the horses nearer to the Austrian line. All the time of their advance the gunners poured round after round into them, striving with desperate energy to sweep them away before they could gain the mouths of the cannons. Rapid flashes of flame breaking from the mouths of the guns accompanied the discharge of the shells, which were being blurted forth with a nervous haste through the thick clouds of smoke that hung heavily before the muzzles.

The flank squadrons, bending a little away from their comrades, made for either end of the line of guns, in expectation of finding there some supporting cavalry. The two centre ones went straight as an arrow against the guns themselves, and hurled themselves through the intervals between them upon the gunners. Then the firing ceased in a moment, and the smoke began to drift slowly away, but all noise was not hushed; shrieks from men cut down by the broad blades of the *cuirassiers*, cries for quarter, the rapid tramp of snorting and excited horses, the rattle of steel, shouts, cheers, and imprecations from the excited combatants, rose up to heaven in a wild medley, along with the prayers which were being offered up by another armed host not many miles distant at Brünn, where on this Sunday the army of Prince Frederick Charles was engaged in a solemn thanksgiving for their hitherto victorious career.

Eighteen guns, seven waggons, and one hundred and sixty-eight horses, with one hundred and seventy prisoners, fell into the hands of the Prussian force—a noble prize to be won by a single regiment. It lost only twelve men and eight horses, for the swelling ground and rapid motion of the gliding squadrons baulked the aim of the gunners, who mostly pointed their pieces too high, and sent their shells over the heads of the charging horsemen. Of the eighteen captured guns seventeen were conveyed to Prossnitz. One was too much disabled to be moved.

While the Prussian *cuirassiers* were engaged in drawing the captured guns to a safe place, a squadron of hostile cavalry deployed from Nenakowitz. Colonel Bredow placed himself at the head of his first squadron, and charged to cover the retreat of his regiment's spoils. This squadron dashed with a heavy surge upon the hostile ranks. The lighter Austrian horsemen, borne down and scattered by their ponderous shock, broke in wild confusion, could not rally, and were driven far beyond Nenakowitz.

The Austrian infantry still held Wierowan, and was thus in rear and flank of the cuirassiers, who, under the fire of musketry, could not hold their position on the plateau in front of the Blatta, and were obliged for a time to retire towards Klopotowitz.

The village of Wierowan was, however, soon carried by the Prussian infantry, as well as that of Rakodau, which lay behind it. Both places were occupied, and one of the Prussian batteries crossing the Blatta opened upon the retreating Austrians, who drew off towards Dub. About mid-day the combat terminated at this point. But while this action had been going on northwards of Tobitschau, the Prussians had reaped other successes in the direction of Traubeck. The two fusilier companies of the 4th regiment, which soon after the commencement of the action had been directed upon Tobitschau, at that place fell in with three Austrian companies. These they drove out of the town, after a short though sharp engagement, and captured from them several prisoners.

Another battalion and the two remaining companies of their own battalion were then sent by Malotki to support the Prussian advance in this direction. They advanced towards Traubeck, and occupied that place without any serious opposition, although some stray detachments of the Austrians were in its immediate vicinity. Under the cover of the garrison of Traubeck, a detachment of Hartman's cavalry advanced against Prerau. This detachment consisted of three squadrons of the second Royal hussars, the regiment of *Landwehr* hussars, a squadron of Polish Uhlans, and a battery of horse artillery, and was accompanied by a company of fusiliers, who were quickly mounted on some waggons near at hand. Before Hartman could develop his attack towards Prerau, an Austrian column was seen advancing from Olmütz towards Dub. It consisted of six battalions, a battery, and some squadrons. These had been despatched by the commandant of the fortress to support Rothkirch's brigade in the neighbourhood of Tobitschau.

At the same time as these Austrian reinforcements approached the scene of action, Prussian supports were also coming up. General von Bonin, who commanded the first Prussian *corps d'armée*, and had ordered Malotki's advance, at the commencement of the engagement, not knowing in what strength the Austrians were, had sent his *aides-de-camp* to order the remaining brigades of his corps to move on Tobitschau. The commanders of these brigades, hearing the cannonade, had of their own accord moved in the direction of the sound, and the advanced guard, formed of Barnekow's brigade, which mustered six battalions and a battery, had already reached Biskupitz when the Austrian reinforcements from Olmütz came into sight Biskupitz lies about a mile to the west of Wierowan.

The rifled battery of Barnekow's brigade immediately came into action, and fired against the right flank of the Austrian advance. At the same time a battery for which Bonin had sent came up, and, joining the battery Malotki had previously with him, took up a position on the west of the main road. The Austrian guns advanced to Dub, and there near the church came into action to cover the deployment of their infantry. But the quick handling of the Prussian guns and the advance of Barnekow were too formidable for the sallying troops, and they, without engaging with Malotki, retired again to the fortress.

About five o'clock in the afternoon General Hartman, with his detachment of cavalry, approached Prerau. He found a good ford through the Beczwa near Wichowitz, and passed the stream by means of it, leaving his company of fusiliers to secure the passage. With his horsemen he passed on towards Dluhonitz and Roketnitz. As soon as he had crossed the railway he discovered an Austrian battalion on the west of Dluhonitz, and other detachments of hostile infantry could be made out partially concealed in the ripe corn. General Hartman deployed his cavalry. In the first line he placed the *Landwehr* hussars and the squadron of Uhlans with the battery on their left flank, covered by the fourth squadron of Royal Hussars. The second and third squadrons of the latter regiment formed his second line. As soon as the battery had shaken the detachments of Austrian infantry, Hartman attacked them. In vain the Austrians attempted to form company squares; the horsemen were too quick for them, got among them before their formation was complete, and made a large number of prisoners, but however without very severe loss to themselves.

During this attack a large number of Austrian baggage waggons were hurrying along the road from Roketnitz towards Prerau. Hartman sent his three leading squadrons, under Colonel Glasenapp, against the road to cut off the baggage trains, and sent away his prisoners with an escort to Tobitschau. The drivers of the baggage waggons, perceiving the threatened attack, began to overturn the carts in the ditches alongside the way. In the meantime some Austrian artillery had come into action on the hills north of Roketnitz, which told with effect on the Prussian troops. At the same time five squadrons of an Austrian *cuirass* regiment appeared on the left flank of the Prussians, while five squadrons of Austrian hussars also dashed into the field to protect Feldzeugmeister von Benedek, who with his staff had been mixed up with the escort of the baggage train, and had been personally engaged in the *mêlée* with the Prussian cavalry.

Colonel Glasenapp tried to retire, but the Austrian Haller hussars came down upon him, and he was forced to turn to face them. The attack on both sides could only, on account of the standing corn, be made at a trot. The hand-to-hand combat which ensued endured for some ten minutes. Man pressed against man—horse against horse; swords and revolvers were freely used, Glasenapp himself went down, and many of his troopers beside him were borne to earth. At last the relics of his squadrons shook themselves free from the rough embrace of their assailants, and managed to gain a retreat As far as possible in the time they could spare they broke the railway and the telegraph; and then, recrossing the Beczwa, took up a position on its western bank.

The Austrian cavalry did not pursue. Benedek, threatened on his right flank by the approach of the crown prince's army, pushed by forced marches towards Vienna, and Rothkirch's brigade, which had been engaged at Tobitschau, retreated by Kobe, and followed him along the Prerau road. When the Austrian general reached Hradschin he heard that the railway at Lundenburg had been cut by Prince Frederick Charles. He then crossed the Carpathians, and by a flank march down the valley of the Waag, gained Pressburg by way of Tyrnau. Here, on the 21st July, he placed the leading divisions of his army in direct communication with that of the Archduke Albrecht, which was round Vienna.

On the 17th the army of the crown prince occupied Prerau, which by that time was entirely deserted by the Austrians. This was the result of the action of Tobitschau, which cost the Austrians about Ave hundred killed and wounded, five hundred prisoners, and seventeen guns; the Prussians about three hundred killed, wounded, and missing.

The army of the crown prince, after the action of Tobitschau, left the fifth *corps d'armée* to watch Olmütz, and moved in two columns upon Brünn, which place it reached on the 19th July.

CHAPTER 3

Further Advance of the Prussian Armies From Brünn to the Danube

While the crown prince had moved in the direction of Prerau, Prince Frederick Charles had occupied Brünn on the 12th July. Here the First Army halted on the 15th.

All the 14th the possibilities and probabilities of an armistice and of a subsequent peace were discussed warmly by the officers and soldiers of the Prussian Army at Brünn. In every restaurant and in every taproom, over bottles of champagne or flagons of beer, amid the light blue smoke of cigars and the dark clouds of strong tobacco, there was only this one subject of conversation. All kinds of theories were broached; knots of officers discussed it quietly in the hotels and in their quarters, crowds of soldiers in the streets stopped every orderly to question him as to his knowledge of passing events, or collected round some comrade supposed to have good information, to hear him dilate upon the intentions of the Emperor of the French, or the private views of the *Kaiser*. But those who really knew what was to happen preserved a profound silence, and nothing was authentically known beyond the precincts of the headquarter-house, and there only to a very few.

In the meantime the advanced guard was ordered to march forward the next morning as far as Moschau, twenty miles from Brünn, on the road to Vienna, and the greater part of the troops who were at Brünn that night were at the same time to move in that direction. But the king remained in the Moravian capital, and the headquarters of Prince Frederick Charles also halted there another day. The town was still thronged by a multitude of Prussian soldiers, who wandered about idly, looking into the shop windows, or trying to read the notices placarded on the walls in the Moravian dialect Prussian sentries were mounted on the main guard, and looked out of place by the side of the sentry boxes and door posts painted with the black and gold colours of Austria.

In front of the *rathhaus*, where the king was lodged, a Prussian guard and numerous sentries had taken the place of the civil watch, who usually stand at the gate of the meeting-house of the town council. In front, in the Platz, artillery carriages were closely parked, and were surrounded by the piled arms of a regiment which, billeted in the houses round, had here its place for assembly. Thick crowds of the inhabitants, with soldiers sprinkled among them, stood to listen to the music of a regimental band which, standing between the gate of the *rathhaus* and the guns, was playing Prussian airs. Country women with bright coloured handkerchiefs over their heads, and dressed in highly tinted muslins, wandered about the crowd, selling from their baskets gingerbread and sweetmeats to the people and the soldiers equally. The theatre was crowded with uniforms, knots of officers were smoking at every hotel door, and the whole town was alive with a lazy activity, except where the closed railway station looked down upon the bare line and its deserted warehouses.

There were sentinels now upon the Spielberg, and Prussian colours floated from its flagstaff. Numbers of soldiers were leaning against the parapets talking with earnestness, for they were deep in discussion of the probabilities of peace, and questioned everyone who came into the fort as to the latest news, half afraid to hear that an armistice was already concluded, and that they would never see the capital of Austria. Nor were the privates alone ill pleased with the prospect of so speedy a peace; the officers wished for the glory of marching into Vienna, and of ending the campaign by the occupation of the enemy's capital; high and low seemed to think that this would only be the just reward of their hard work; and while the younger ones only looked forward to the excitement of entering a large town, and hoped for a little more fighting and higher promotion, those who had planned and carried out the strategy of the campaign regarded the visit of M. Benedetti to headquarters much in the same light as that in which a skilful chess-player about to check-mate his adversary's king would view the intrusion of an officious stranger, who suddenly stopped the game by sweeping the men off the board and putting them into his pocket.

The order for the march of the troops on the following morning gave rise to hopes that a further advance was actually decided upon.

By the evening of the 14th it was known that the negotiations for an armistice had failed. The Prussians sent to the Austrians the conditions on which they would agree to a cessation of hostilities, and at the same time stated that no alteration in the terms would be permitted. One of these conditions was that the Prussian Army should occupy the line of the Thaya, and consequently have possession of the railway station at Lundenburg. The Austrians sent back a proposal that an armistice should be granted for three days, and during this time that the Prussian Army should remain in its actual position. As the acceptance of this proposal would have allowed time for the Austrian Army at Olmütz to be withdrawn to the neighbourhood of Vienna, and to be placed across the line of march of the Prussians towards the capital, it seemed clear that the intention of the Austrians was not to conclude peace, but only to gain time for the concentration of their troops. Negotiations were in consequence broken off, and the march southward was ordered to be continued.

All was again activity and excitement in the Prussian Army; the whole of the troops who were at Brünn on the 14th, with the exception of one division, marched out on the morning of the 15th, and pushed forwards towards Thaya. The men, refreshed by their halt, equipped anew with supplies of the articles which had been worn out or lost during the late marches and actions, went forth in high spirits, for they thought that now they were certain to reach Vienna. They had no doubt of the result of a battle, if one should have to be fought on the way to the Austrian capital, and their fears that peace might be concluded had been allayed by the news of the failure of the negotiations; for it was known early on the 15th, that the armistice had not been agreed to, and the intelligence spread quickly from company to company, and from regiment to regiment.

General von Moltke retired to his quarters, and was closeted with his maps, making new plans for the further progress of the campaign, and for the occupation of Vienna. This skilful strategist, who had been the chief director of the movements by which the three Prussian armies, starting from different points, were collected at the necessary hour on the field of Königgrätz, never, except at that battle, appeared in the front of the armies. Some distance in the rear, sitting calmly at his desk, he traced on the map the course of his troops, and, by means of the field telegraph, flashed his orders to the different generals in more immediate command, with such skill and foresight that not a movement failed, and every combination was made at exactly the right moment.

A quick, light-blue eye, a high forehead, and a well-set figure, mark him an intellectual and energetic man, but though quick in action he is so prudent in discourse and so guarded in his speech, that from this quality and his wide knowledge of European languages he is known in the Prussian Army as the man who is silent in seven tongues. Careful and laborious, he worked out with his own hand, and himself calculated, almost every detail of the operations in which he took Europe by surprise from the lightning rapidity of his strokes and the tremendous consequences of his dispositions, before which the Austrian army withered away almost before it was gathered together, and which have won for him from his countrymen the title of the first strategist in Europe.

But though General von Moltke in so short a time deservedly obtained such a high reputation in Prussia, the soldiers and officers of the two armies thought almost as highly of the Princes who have carried out so ably the plans which were formed by the chief of the Royal Staff. Prince Frederick Charles, with all the dash and fire of a cavalry officer, can equally well lead his squadrons to pursue the broken enemy, and direct with patience his infantry and artillery in an attack against a firm and steady line; but his qualities as a general do not shine out more in the exciting duties of the battlefield than they do in the more tedious and laborious work which is necessary for the comfort of his soldiers in quarters or on the line of march. He has a singular power of making his troops care little for fatigue and hardship; on the line of march he is always with them, and often, from his knowledge of how to deal with his men, can, by a few happy words, dose up the straggling ranks of a weary battalion, and send the men forward cheering loudly. In the bivouac, often in person, he inspected the rations and heard the applications of the men for favours or indulgences, and few applied in vain to their commander-in-chief He had both the confidence and love of his troops, who regarded him as a skilful leader and a powerful friend.

The crown prince, by a series of victories in three successive days, established his title to be considered a general In the Second Army he was looked upon with the same affection and confidence as Prince Frederick Charles is in the First. By the men of Silesia he was particularly beloved; for he, as a colonel, commanded a regiment at Breslau, and became well known then to the whole province. Careless of trouble, ever anxious for the welfare of his troops, he visited, personally, billets and hospitals, and took the most kindly interest in every individual soldier. But in the hour of need he did not spare his troops, for his affection for them sprang from a sense of duty and from no mere desire of popularity. The march from Miletin to Königgrätz, and the attack on the Austrian right in that battle which crushed Marshal Benedek's army and shook the Austrian dynasty, say more for his energy in action than could be written in any words.

With such leaders and so well led, with a better arm than their enemies, with every mechanical contrivance which modern science could suggest adapted to aid the operations of the army, it is little wonder that the stout-hearted and long-enduring Prussian soldiers proved victorious on every occasion on which they went into action.

The headquarters of the First Army were ordered to move forward on the 16th, to Pawlowitz, a small village twenty-five miles from Brünn. The advanced guard, on the 15th, moved upon Moschau; the whole of the army, except one division, which stayed another day here to guard the king's headquarters, marched to the vicinity of Medritz, and the campaign already recommenced with energy.

M. Benedetti, unsuccessful in his attempt to procure an armistice through the mediation of France, left the Prussian headquarters on the afternoon of the 15th. He was accompanied by Count Colleredo, an Austrian officer, who had come in with a flag of truce, and a Prussian staff-officer went with him to take him through the outposts, for he went to Vienna,

The Prussians had now quite got their blood up; in the army it was regarded as an established fact that the conditions proposed by Austria for an armistice were intended only to gain time to move the army of Feldzeugmeister Benedek from Olmütz to the south, and their national feelings were wounded by the idea that the Austrians should imagine that they could be so easily duped. On the afternoon of the 15th, the patrols of the cavalry of the Prussian advanced guard pushed forward as far as the railway station of Göding, which lies on the line that leads from Olmütz to Lundenburg. When the leading horsemen came in sight of the railway they could distinguish two trains, one close behind the other, with engines puffing and snorting violently, as if drawing a heavy load, steaming slowly in the direction of Lundenburg.

There could be little doubt that in these trains were portions of the Austrian Army from Olmütz, which were on the way to Vienna.

To prevent any more troops from being taken south by this line, it was immediately resolved to break up the line. Some troopers dismounted, a few pickaxes, spades, and axes were found in the neighbouring cottages, and the men on foot quickly set to work, while the others held their horses. There was no Austrian cavalry to guard the line, no infantry picket in the station-house, and the demolition of the line by which alone General Benedek could hope to reunite his army to protect the capital of the empire began without any opposition.

Blows fell heavily on the rails and on the sleepers, the rails were wrenched out of their places, thrown upon one side, and in a few minutes the line was useless for railway traffic The work was hardly completed when another train came in sight, but before it came up to where the rails were taken away the engine-driver saw the Prussian cavalry, reversed his engine, and the train drew up short, and after a moment's pause began to back slowly in the direction from which it came.

The great problem now for the Prussian staff was to discover how much of their northern army the Austrians had been able to move to Vienna, and how many troops were still in the camp before Olmütz. From the experience of this war many facts have been ascertained relative to the railway transport of troops which were now useful in assisting this calculation. When the Prussians were concentrating their army for the invasion of Saxony they found that it required 100 trains to move a *corps d'armée* of 30,000 combatants with all its train and baggage, and that it was rarely possible to despatch more than twelve trains a day—so that it required nearly ten days for the movement of a corps. The Austrians, during the concentration of their army, despatched fifteen trains a day; but at that time they are supposed to have moved with baggage and train complete.

On such a pressing occasion as the present, they probably might let the troops move with almost no baggage and little train, and might have managed to despatch twenty trains per day, for they had most of the rolling stock which used to run upon the line between Vienna and Türnau by Josephstadt, and on this calculation 40,000 men could be moved in about six days. This calculation was subsequently found to be correct.

Another fact concerning railway transport dictated by common sense has been fully confirmed by the experience of the German war. Railways in an enemy's country have been proved to be of no use for the transport of the troops of the invader during his advance; the army acting on the defensive always breaks them up, and they cannot be repaired quickly enough to allow of troops being moved by them. But for the carriage of provisions and stores they are invaluable.[1] The more quickly an advancing army can lay down the rails the more quickly can it move forward, and the more free are its motions, for the line of railway is the great artery which leading from the heart supplies the extremities of the army with means of life and action. In laying down the broken lines the band of workmen who accompany the Prussian army were singularly rapid and successful, but quick as they were they were not yet quick enough, for the army transport was conducted by road for some days, even after Prague was occupied, and no enemy on the line stopped the passage of convoys. A broken bridge, even though the breach was but only a few yards wide, caused a dead stoppage in the locomotion, and the time required to shift stores from a train on one side of the impediment to that on the other was very great.

An engineer who would find means of constructing rapidly field bridges which would bear the weight of a railway train, would cause an advance in the art of war. The road transport of the Prussian army was very well organised, but long distances, rapid marches, hilly roads, and accidents, were too much in some cases for even its powers. With each army corps there were five provision columns, in every column there were thirty-two waggons, each drawn by five horses, some spare horses being also supplied to the column to replace animals which may fall lame or get galled by the saddle or collar. These five columns were under the control of the *intendantur*, and were never used for any other purpose than the supply of food for the soldiers; the forage for the horses was carried in waggons hired in the country where the war was being carried on, which were also placed under the control of the commissariat.

Stores of clothing and arms were carried as much as possible by railway, and were brought to the army from the nearest practicable railway station by trains of waggons, which were also under the control of the *intendant*-general; but each battalion carried with it, besides a medicine cart, a waggon for spare ammunition, and an officers' baggage waggon, a waggon which held materials for the repair of clothes and shoes, and which were thus always present with the troops, so that the old proverb that "*a stitch in time saves nine*" might be, as far as possible, acted upon.

For the transport of ammunition the commanding officer of artil-

1. This has been amply verified by the late campaign in France.

lery was entirely responsible; and it was conducted by means of trains of waggons, which were under his sole control There were nine ammunition trains with each *corps d'armée*. Each train consisted of thirty-three waggons, and was individually organised so as to carry ammunition for infantry, cavalry, 4-pounder, 6-pounder, and 12-pounder guns.

A long, hot march, over a road covered deep with dust, which rose in thick stifling clouds from under the horses' feet, and deposited gritty particles in every pore of the skin, brought the headquarters of Prince Frederick Charles to Pawlowitz, which is about six miles south-west of the town of Auspitz, and about twelve north-east of the railway junction at Lundenburg. This day the army entered a country where the low, rounded hills were covered with vineyards, and from which, as a consequence, trees had almost disappeared. Down by the courses of the streams there were a few pollard willows dotted along the narrow belts of sward which fringed the banks, and some clumps of fir-trees could be made out, stuck like black patches against the blue sides of the Pollauer-Gebirge, which stands up high above the surrounding country; but everywhere else nothing could be seen except, on the lower ground nearer the water-courses, long stretches of unbroken corn-land, backed on either side by the undulating mounds rather than hills on which the vines twined round their poles, planted in straight lines with a monotonous regularity.

The aspect of the little town showed its proximity to the Hungarian frontier. The men, dressed in white trousers gathered tight in below the knees, and contained by a long black boot, with their black jackets trimmed with a bright edging and braided almost like a hussar's *pelisse*, and with their low broad-brimmed black hat, round which a red riband was bound with the ends hanging down, looked rather like stage peasants, and had little resemblance to the heavy bloused vine-dressers that are seen on the banks of the Rhine. The women, with their short bright-coloured skirts, white bodices, and handkerchiefs for the head, kept up the theatrical appearance of the population. The houses were low and small, and not nearly so large as the stable which, without exception, was an adjunct to every cottage.

On the night of the 16th the First Army had its advanced guard at Lundenburg, and the Duke of Mecklenburg, who commanded it, threw some detachments across the Thaya by means of a pontoon bridge, for the Austrians had destroyed all the bridges which led across the river. General Manstein also threw a pontoon bridge near Wisternitz, and led the sixth division across at that point, and two other divisions crossed the stream a little higher up. The cavalry was at Feldsburg; and the eighth division was at Göding, on the line to Olmütz. The rest of the army was round Pawlowitz.

On the 15th July, the same day that Prince Frederick Charles pushed forward his troops from Brünn and with his advanced guard cut the railway from Olmütz to Vienna, near Lundenburg, and that the crown prince's cavalry after the action of Tobitschau cut the same railway near Prerau, Herwarth, with the Army of the Elbe, occupied Znaym, and secured there the passage of the Thaya, the boundary between Moravia and the Crown lands of Austria.

On the 16th, Herwarth was to have pushed his left wing down the Thaya, to assist in cutting the railway. As its advanced guard approached the road from Nikolsburg to Vienna, it received intelligence that Prince Frederick Charles had already secured the railway, and that Manstein's division of his army was moving along that road. Herwarth, on the receipt of this intelligence, drew his left back to the Znaym road, and pursued his way along it towards the Danube. At Jetzelsdorf the advanced guard of Herwarth's centre, which had been pushed along this road, fell in with the Austrian cavalry of Wallis's brigade. A slight skirmish took place between Wallis's horsemen and the first Prussian light cavalry division, after which Wallis drew his troops off, and the Prussians occupied Hollabrun, thirty miles south of Vienna. Etzel's division was at the same time directed in a south-westerly direction on Krems, where the Austrians, on its approach, blew up the bridge over the Danube.

On the 20th July, Herwarth's outposts were pushed forward to Stockerau, within fifteen miles of Vienna. From the hills near Weikersdorf, the advanced guard first saw the Imperial city, which could be distinguished easily from afar off by the tall spire of the Cathedral of St. Stephen, and the tower of the Castle of Schönbrunn, glittering in the sloping rays of the evening sun. In the foreground, on the Marchfeld, lay the famous villages of Wagram, Aspern, and Eszling, in the midst of rich corn-land and fields of bright poppies, which from the distance looked like pieces of dazzling mosaic let into a golden pavement, fringed by the silver band of the Danube studded with emerald islets. Near the stream were the swelling undulations of the Bisamberg, and beyond the river were seen the purple highlands of Austria, with the heavy masses of the Wiener Wald, while the dark blue Carpathians bounded the prospect towards Hungary. Such a view was a fitting reward for Königgrätz. No Prussian army, not even that of the Great Frederick, had ever gazed upon the same.

Late on the night of the 16th, it was ascertained that the Austrians had sent forty trains from Olmütz to the neighbourhood of Vienna before the railroad between those towns was broken up by the Prussian cavalry on the 15th. The last six trains were known to have been filled with Saxon troops. It was tolerably certain that all the trains contained infantry only, and that the proper complement of cavalry and artillery to accompany these foot soldiers had in all probability marched by road. This being the case, every train was estimated to have carried 1,000 men, so that the Austrian army round Vienna had been reinforced by 34,000 Austrian and 6,000 Saxon infantry, and very likely also by some cavalry and artillery.

Under these circumstances the headquarters of the First Army were on the morning of the 17th moved forward to the important railway junction of Lundenburg; the cavalry was retained for the morning at Feldsberg; the Army of the Elbe and some portions of the First Army were on the right flank, and the advanced guard was pushed forward a short distance on the road to Vienna. But at the same time the eighth division, which had been detached to the left bank of the March, marched by way of Göding, and occupied Holitsch. From that point this detachment was held able either to combine with the rest of the army in a movement upon Vienna, or to be pushed forward further into Hungary as an advanced portion of the First Army; for the previous night information was received by Prince Frederick Charles which showed that the Austrians had been moving troops from the country round Vienna towards Pesth, and it was possible that the regiments taken from Olmütz might have been also sent into Hungary by Preszburg, in order there to concentrate an army for future operations. If the Austrians had concentrated in Hungary, it is probable that Prince Frederick Charles would have been sent across the Carpathians to act against them there.

The 17th was a fearfully hot, burning summer day, not a bit of shade was to be found on the road by which the army marched, except where sometimes the way ran close by the side of the Thaya, and a few pollard willows which fringed the edges afforded a moment's relief from the scorching rays of the sun, but not from the dust which rose in a thick, heavy cloud from the soft deep powder on the road every time a man stepped on it, or a horse, restive from the attacks of innumerable flies, stamped savagely upon the ground. The bright, thick groves of poplars, intermingled with oak, springing from beautifully soft and velvety turf which fringed the further bank of the river, tantalized the troops by their proximity.

At Lundenburg the midday sun was pouring down on the wide, unpaved, dusty streets, and glaring while houses. Von Tümpling's division lay here that day, and the soldiers wandered about slowly, seeking for anything to drink, or for shade from the rays of the sun. Every house was a billet, and the atmosphere of the close, small rooms was stifling, while the sun poured hotly in through the small windows, and made the insides of the houses almost as hot and more disagreeable than the open. Several of the houses had no roofs, the thatch bore signs of having been recently torn off, and was thrown away to some distance; the bare timbers stood out against the cloudless sky, and some rough, rugged openings made in the walls, which looked as if an unskilful mason had been trying to break down the walls, were in reality loop-holes; for in the evening of the 15th the Austrians held Lundenburg, and meant to fight to keep it.

Here that day were collected Mondel's infantry brigade, consisting of the 12th battalion of *Jägers*, the 10th regiment of Foot (Mazuchelli's), and the 24th regiment of Foot (Duke of Parma's), with some artillery and some of the cavalry of General Edelsheim's division. They had orders to hold the town to the last extremity, and they began to make some of the houses into temporary fortresses. The inhabitants, afraid of coming involuntarily under fire, mostly fled, and left their town, expecting never to return and see its houses standing; but before the preparations for defence were concluded the Prussian cavalry had broken up the line at Göding, and the railway junction of Lundenburg had lost its military value;.

Before, however, the Austrians evacuated the town, Lieutenant von Radowitz, who had been sent by Prince Frederick Charles to take M. Benedetti, the French ambassador, as far as the Austrian outposts, arrived with the minister at Lundenburg. The Austrians would not allow the Prussian officer to return at once to his headquarters, for fear that he might carry back with him intelligence that the place was being given up, but thought it necessary that he should follow the ambassador to Weibendorf; so he was put into the railway and taken to that station. As soon as he arrived there he got leave to return, but, only able to come by road and in a country waggon, he did not reach Pawlowitz, the headquarters of Prince Frederick Charles, till the evening of the 16th. So far the Austrians were successful, for they managed to detain the staff-officer; but long before his arrival at Pawlowitz, Prince Frederick Charles knew of the evacuation of Lundenburg; and the staff-officer, by being taken south among the Austrian troops, saw a great deal which could never have been known at the Prussian head-quarters, had he not been forced to make his involuntary railway journey in the direction of Vienna,

General von Manstein had occupied Nikolsburg with his division, after crossing the muddy Thaya by a pontoon bridge, which he had to throw across the stream to replace one that had been destroyed by the retreating Austrians. It was anticipated that the boggy banks and unsound sides of the river would cause a good deal of difficulty in throwing the bridge; but if there were difficulties Manstein overcame them, and said nothing about them. But this is no proof that his passage, although unopposed by the enemy, was an easy one, as he was renowned in the army for a quiet determination combined with a high daring, and gave many proofs of both as well in the war with Denmark as in the Bohemian campaign.

A short halt in the hot, bare town of Lundenburg, and then the march was continued to Feldsberg, through the beautifully wooded park of the Prince of Lichtenstein. The cavalry corps moved forward in the evening, and there were no troops in Feldsberg, on the evening of the 17th, except the headquarter staff, for whom the Prince's large castle afforded plenty of accommodation, and a few battalions who were billeted in the town for the night The little town nestles round the foot of the castle in a dip in the ground, beyond it to the south rises a gentle rounded elevation, and beyond that lay nothing but flat plains as far as the Danube.

Nothing, on the evening of the 17th, was known of the direction of the morrow's march; at nine o'clock at night, no orders had yet come from the king, and it was all uncertain whether the First Army was to move on Florisdorf or Hungary. There was a general impression that there would be fighting in a few days. The troops looked forward to the possibility of meeting the enemy with the most perfect confidence of success, and they had every reason to do so on account of both their generals and their arms. It cannot, however, be denied that the army had a most difficult, and perhaps even dangerous, operation before it if it meant to go to Vienna, had the Austrians held fast by Florisdorf and the Bisamberg.

The passage of a river is always a dangerous undertaking, and as the Austrian army from Italy was in Vienna, and garrisoned the intrenchments in front of the Danube, while a strong force of troops brought from Hungary, whither Benedek was also hurrying, was at Preszburg, the Prussian generals had a piece of work before them difficult of execution.

On the morning of the 18th the sun shone bright and warm on the *schloss* and town of Feldsberg. The day seemed likely to be as hot as the previous, and consequently the march was ordered for the evening. But about two o'clock a sudden change occurred in the weather. The sky became in a few moments covered with clouds, and an extraordinary darkness set in. Up to windward a thick, dense black cloud could be seen bearing down steadily towards the castle; but not on the sky alone, for like a great volume of heavy smoke it seemed rising from the earth, and filled the air for miles. Nearer and nearer it came. When it got within a quarter of a mile a sudden tempest of wind, which seemed bearing this cloud behind it, burst upon the place.

The trees swayed about, rocked by the strong continuous gust, branches were torn off, sheaves of corn were torn up, and taken through the air, the Indian corn and standing crops in the fields were swept down almost level with the ground, and the heavy cloud of dust, which looked in the distance like smoke, was driven about by the wind and whirled up and down in a most fantastic manner. For a few minutes only this tornado lasted, and then was followed by a tremendous downpour of rain, which fell for about half an hour; but so dry and parched was the ground that though the water came down in torrents it was sucked in in a moment, and when the rain ceased not a puddle stood upon the surface of the thirsty earth.

But the rain laid the dust, and the march was more agreeable than it had been for some days past. The way lay down the valley of the March, which divides the Crown lands of Austria from Hungary. Flat wide-stretching plains lay on the right, in parts covered with standing barley or Indian corn; in parts black and bleak where the soil had already been turned up and prepared to take the seed for the second crop; and here and there, where the corn had been cut, the sheaves, which had been carried hither and thither by the afternoon's tempest, were strewn about in confusion.

On the left the sluggish March twisted about in many channels through numerous marshy islets, on which short willows grew densely springing up from sedgy ground, which is covered with beds of tall bulrushes or tangled water plants. Further on the left the blue ridge of the Carpathians stood out against the sombre sky, lighted up here and there by some rays from the watery sun, which, sinking rapidly, had before going down lighted up in the west one small portion of the cloudy sky.

The road lay close along the railway, upon which the officials of the field telegraph division, the principal instrument of the success of the campaign, were riding, carefully inspecting the wires. Every post was looked at, every joint inspected with a careful scrutiny; but as long as the diligent inspectors could be seen, no break was found which called for the assistance of their workmen, who followed alongside with their waggons filled with tools and materials to repair a flaw, and that night telegraphic communication was open between Prince Frederick Charles at Hohenau and the King at Nikolsburg. And it was required, for the approach to the Danube required new combinations, and again the whole forces of the field were about to be removed in unison by orders flashed from the headquarters of the king.

When the staff reached Radensburg, a little village about two miles from Hohenau, a Vienna *droschky* was seen drawn up on one side of the road, with two gentlemen in plain clothes and wide-awake hats standing beside it, chatting quietly with a group of Prussian officers who had their billets in a roadside public-house. A little flag beside the coachmen showed that the travellers who had come by the carriage were engaged in some neutral duty, and a footman dressed in livery, with a broad lace band round his cap, who stood with the handle of the carriage door in his hand, showed by his dress that he was the servant of some high official.

A nearer approach showed that the travellers were M. Benedetti, the French ambassador at Berlin, and his secretary, who had gone to Vienna after the unsuccessful attempts to procure an armistice at Brünn, and were now on their way back to the king's headquarters, which had been established on the 17th at Nikolsburg, in the old castle of Prince Dietrichstein. The King of Prussia during his stay here slept in the same room which Napoleon had occupied in 1805 after the battle of Austerlitz, and before his entry into Vienna on the 9th December.

Prince Frederick Charles dismounted from his horse, and in the middle of the road held a long conversation with the Ambassador. Perhaps they were discussing on that rainy evening, in the middle of the country road, questions which might affect the destinies of Europe—perhaps they were only having a friendly chat Numbers of suppositions were broached by the officers of the staff, but no one except the two who engaged in that conversation know what passed, for all others drew out of earshot as soon as the ambassador approached the prince.

The officers of the staff were not so delighted to see the bearer of news which might possibly lead to an armistice as they would have been to receive him if he had come in a private capacity, for they feared that negotiations might stop the campaign before it found its just conclusion in the occupation of Vienna, and with the feelings of true soldiers they had little sympathy with the diplomacy which might arrest the progress of their armies.

The marches of the 18th were short, for the armies were drawing together, perhaps for the attack of the Austrian intrenched position at Florisdorf, perhaps to force the passage of the Danube at some other point, and the army had to move slowly in order to give General Herwarth time to close towards it from the right, and to let the Army of Silesia come up into line. On the 19th Prince Frederick Charles's headquarters were established at Duernkruth; his advanced guard, with part of the seventh division, that afternoon reached and occupied the railway junction at Gänserndorf, where the lines of Preszburg and Vienna unite. Another portion of the seventh division occupied the passage of the March at Marchegg. The cavalry corps under the command of Prince Albrecht was round the little town of Anger, about five miles north of Gänserndorf. The light infantry division was across the March, and on the road which leads from Holitsch down the left bank of that river billeted in and about St. Johann and Malarzka, while the rest of the army was clustered round the headquarters of its commander-in-chief.

The crown prince in person this day reached Brünn, but his army was pushing rapidly forward, and the Guards had already arrived at Lundenburg; he had left a force to mask Olmütz, but the garrison of that place was not watched by this detachment alone, for Knobelsdorf's troops from Silesia were being pushed on to aid in preventing the occupants of the great fortress of Moravia from making any demonstration against the Prussian line of communications.

It was quite evident from the movements of the Prussian troops that some great operation was meditated, and it was but natural to suppose that the present combinations were being made with the design of striking a heavy blow against the capital of the Austrian empire.

The Prussian cavalry was being collected together into one mass, and when united formed an enormous number of sabres, of which it was expected that some use would be made within the next few days; for from Gänserndorf to the Danube stretches the wide flat plain of the Marchfeld, on which the Austrian cavalry might have a fair field for action, and where it might strive to regain the world-wide reputation which was so rudely shaken by the charges of the Prussian squadrons in the earlier parts of the war.

The Austrians had, in retreating, destroyed the bridges across the March, in order to prevent communication between the Prussian columns which might advance on either bank of the stream. That of Anger had been burnt, and a few charred piles peeping above the water were all that showed where the bridge stood; but the Prussian engineers had already replaced it by another bridge, made out of such materials as came readily to hand, and had thrown another, supported upon trestles, at Duernkruth, so that by these means infantry and artillery could cross from one side of the river to the other, and many fords had been found of which the cavalry could make use.

On the morning of the 19th, Count Hasler, an officer of the staff, rode forward beyond the outposts on the northern bank of the Danube to destroy the telegraph which communicates between Vienna and Preszburg. At Gänserndorf he found two *cuirassiers*, who formed his working party, and picked up a hatchet near a roadside house, which formed the whole of the tools required. When the point at which the wires were to be broken was reached, the chief difficulty of the undertaking was found, for the lines ran along the tops of a succession of bare slippery poles, up which it was very difficult to climb. Several attempts were made to ascend up the pole, but just as the piece of bent iron which supported the porcelain knob round which the lowest wire was turned for a support was reached, arms and legs gave way and the man came sliding down the dry polished wood.

At last one of the *cuirassiers*, making use of his comrade's shoulders as a starting point, began on better terms than before, and got his hand upon the bent iron; then to haul himself up to the top was comparatively easy; and as he had got the hatchet between his teeth he began to deliver some smart, quick blows upon the uppermost wire. A few strokes severed it, and the two portions of the broken line, parting from each other, came surging down to the ground. The same process was repeated with the others, and in a few minutes, all the wires being broken, the man threw his hatchet to the ground, saying, "There, they won't be able now to telegraph from Vienna to Preszburg," and came sliding down the post. There was no need to break up the railway, for the Austrians had already blown up the bridge over the March; and if they had not, the Prussian advanced guard had arrived at Gänserndorf, and their outposts were pushed in advance of the railway junction.

Rumours of peace were flying about the camp all the 19th; some people asserted that a three days' armistice had been agreed upon, and that this was the reason that the marches were so short, but that M. Benedetti had terms to propose from the *Kaiser*. Nothing certain with regard to a cessation of hostilities was yet decided upon, and the shortness of the marches can be accounted for by the necessity of allowing time for the Army of the Elbe to make its lateral movement, and for that of the crown prince to come up close to the First Army.

In the army, at this time, no one except those in high command had any idea of whither the next advance would lead: some supposed that the whole Prussian force was to be dashed against the parapets and heavily-armed embrasures of Florisdorf; others that a sudden raid was to be made by a large force into Hungary to beat up the quarters of the *Kaiser* at Pesth, whither the Imperial family had retired from Vienna. But all feared the results of M. Benedetti's mission, and were much afraid that diplomacy would stand in the way of an entry into the capital of Austria, and would deprive the army of what they considered would be only a just and fitting termination to their rapid but glorious campaign.

A welcome capture had been made by the commissariat of the First Army by the occupation of Göding, the place near which the cavalry of the advanced guard broke up the railway between Olmütz and Lundenburg on the 15th. Immense magazines of Austrian stores had been found there, and among other valuable commodities about 50,000*l*. worth of cigars, intended for issue to the Austrian troops, which were confiscated for the use of the Prussians, and, in consequence, the soldiers received liberal supplies. They were most grateful, for in the German armies tobacco is considered almost necessary to existence, and in importance as a ration ranks only second to bread or meat

Headquarters were established on the 19th at Duernkruth, in a small white *schloss*, which afforded the most limited accommodation even for the small number of officers who comprised the headquarter staff. Few, very few, indeed, had beds; colonels and subalterns lay side by side on mattresses or trusses of straw upon the floor; a few specially favoured had sofas. Among these was Count Stölberg, the President of the Prussian House of Lords, who was with the army as a Knight of St. John of Jerusalem. But all were very cheerful and happy, and would have been perfectly well pleased with everything, except that the younger officers expressed loud wishes that M. Benedetti was anywhere except in the king's headquarters, for they feared that his presence meant peace, and they wanted more fighting, more promotion, and more glory, and were extremely anxious to march into Vienna. And, although their elders did not express their opinions, it was tolerably evident that in their eyes also the prospect of an immediate peace was looked upon as anything but a blessing.

On the further side of the March, which lay about half a mile from the headquarter *schloss*, wide pasture lands, dotted with clumps of willow-trees, stretched over a flat plain, which was raised but a few feet above the level of the water in the river towards the Carpathian Mountains, that rise about fifteen miles to the east. This plain was covered with droves of horses, pigs, and large white cattle, with broad outstretched horns about as large as those of buffaloes. These droves were tended by boys, clad some in proper Hungarian costume, but more frequently in a white flannel cloak, which, hanging from their shoulders down to their ankles, formed their only covering. But, wild though the country might be, the Prussian generals viewed it with favour, for it was generally clear and open, and would be a fair field for their needle-guns and rifle artillery. Over this plain, on the left bank of the March, the eighth Prussian division scoured the whole country between the stream and the mountains.

But it did not seem probable that these weapons would be required till the Prussians advanced on Vienna. No Austrians were reported in front of the outposts, and it appeared that the Archduke Albrecht intended to wait in his works at Florisdorf until the Prussians either attacked him there, or attempted the passage of the Danube at some other point In the meantime, while the needle-gun was not in active use, its merits formed an endless topic of conversation in the army. Of course, its success had made it a great favourite, and the Prussians, both men and officers, considered the victories which were won at Gitschin and Podoll by its means to have established its claim to be regarded as the best weapon in existence.

It has certainly been most satisfactorily proved that the *zündnadel-gewehr* is better than the Austrian muzzle-loader, but we had a pretty good idea before this war took place that any breech-loader would be a better arm for infantry than any muzzle-loader; and though the great slaughter of the Austrians in the actions of this campaign brought the fact more forcibly before our notice, nothing has been elicited in the late war to prove that the needle-gun is better or even equal to many breech-loading rifles that have been invented more lately. The success of the needle-gun has established the superiority of the breech-loading over the muzzle-loading principle; but there are many breech-loaders better adapted for all the purposes of warfare than the needle-gun, and any nation which may arm its troops with a servile imitation of the Prussian arm may probably find that the next European war will show the trouble to have been in vain, and the expenses of the armament thrown away.[2]

Many attempts were made on the afternoon of the 19th to see the Stephanenthurm of Vienna, but the tower could not be seen; for, although the country is in general flat, many swelling undulations of ground lay between Duernkruth and the capital, which impeded the view. Even from the railway embankment at Gänserndorf it could not be made out, for a rising ground covered with corn lay directly between the village and the city, and a man standing on the embankment was not raised high enough to see over the swell Nor could a glimpse be caught of the position of Florisdorf, or even of the Bisamberg, which was also reported to be intrenched, and defended by heavy artillery. The Prussian advance had been so rapid that it was almost impossible to realise that the army was within thirty miles of the Austrian capital, and the troops of the First Army would have been glad of some visible proof which would assure them of its proximity; but as yet they could have none, and many thought that perhaps the first palpable proof of their near approach to Vienna might be the reports of the Austrian guns, which were to dispute the passage of the Danube,

On the evening of the 21st July the Cabinet of Vienna expressed itself willing to enter upon a suspension of hostilities for five days, on the basis of the Prussian proposals, and on the evening of the 22nd an armistice for that time was agreed upon at Nikolsburg. It came into effect at noon on the 22nd, and was to expire at mid-day on the following Friday, the 27th. But an action was fought on the morning of the 22nd, by the seventh and eighth divisions, who moved at daybreak that day on Preszburg, by the left bank of the March. The eighth division had moved down the left bank of that river from Göding by way of St. Johann and Malaczka in Hungary, and on the 21st had neared

---

2. In 1870-71 the *chassepot* was universally acknowledged to be a better weapon than the needle-gun.

Stampfen.

On the 21st the seventh division crossed the March, at Marchegg, under General Franzecky, who was placed in command of all the troops on the left bank of the stream. Prince Frederick Charles knew that on the 22nd General Benedek would throw his leading divisions over the Danube at Preszburg. If then he could seize that place, the remainder of the *feldzeugmeister's* troops would have to make a *détour* by Komorn before arriving at Vienna. The commander-in-chief of the First Army, not being aware that any decision had been arrived at relative to the suspension of hostilities, on hearing on the night of the 21st that the Austrians were in position to bar the way near the village of Bystenitz, was forced to order General Franzecky to attack them, and so a combat was commenced.

On the evening of the 21st the seventh and eighth divisions, under the orders of General Franzecky, were bivouacked on the road which leads down the left side of the March from Göding to Preszburg, and occupied a position on that road between the villages of Stampfen and Bystenitz, with their advanced guard pushed forward a little in front of the latter village. The quartermaster-general of the First Army, General Stülpnagel, attended by Count Hasler, of the general staff, had that afternoon been making a reconnaissance of the Austrian positions on the north of the Danube, and arrived in the evening at the bivou-acs of Franzecky's divisions. It was soon found that the Austrians held the village of Blumenau, which lies on the same road, about five miles nearer Preszburg, in strong force; and as it was extremely desirable to secure the town of Preszburg as quickly as possible, Count Hasler was despatched to Ebenthal to request Prince Frederick Charles's permission for an attack to be made on Blumenau.

The staff-officer reached headquarters towards midnight At this time Prince Frederick Charles was ignorant that an armistice would be agreed to, and he sent back the desired permission. A little after midnight Count Hasler left the headquarters of the First Army at Ebenthal, and started on his return journey, carrying this important order, on which so much might depend. Thirty miles of bad road lay between Ebenthal and Bystenitz; the night was very dark, there was no moon, and clouds shut out even the dim light which the stars might have afforded; but the staff-officer pushed his horse resolutely over the March by the repaired bridge at Anger, along twisting country lanes, past wide ditches and morasses, reached Bystenitz safely at the first streaks of dawn, and communicated the Prince's message to General

Franzecky. Franzecky at once made his dispositions for attack. At the same time Prince Frederick Charles sent orders to General Hann to support Franzecky with his division of cavalry.

The road from Bystenitz to Blumenau, which is a distance of about five English miles, runs close below the extreme westerly spurs of the Lower Carpathians, which rise high on the left of a traveller journeying from the former to the latter place. The ground on the right until the road strikes the railway from Gänserndorf to Preszburg is flat and level. The mountains on the left are broken by steep and rough ravines, down which run little rivulets, making their way with perpetual cascades towards the March or the Danube; between the courses of these rivulets the spurs of the mountains swell out in bluff undulations into the plain through which runs the river March. The ground on the mountain sides is everywhere rough and broken, large stones are scattered over it, and in many places jagged lumps of rock start out of the soil and form natural fortresses to oppose the passage of troops up the hills.

A dense forest of oak and pine trees, which, from being untended, have grown close together, and intertwined their branches so as to form a network of dark-green foliage, through which a man can hardly penetrate, grows upon the sides of the ravines and the less steep spurs of the mountains, and runs up the sides of the hills all the way from Bystenitz to Preszburg. The roads through the wood are few and at long distances apart; none are practicable for any troops except foot soldiers, and only for these when moving with a very narrow front. At Blumenau the road leads to the left, and runs straight to Preszburg through a defile in the hills, being crossed near to this village by the railway which leads from Gänserndorf to Preszburg, and which, after crossing the road, runs along the left-hand side of the latter through the same defile.

On the side of the road and railway opposite to Blumenau, and about three-quarters of a mile to the right, lies the little village of Kaltenbrun, situated on rough, broken hills called the Theben-Berger, which are thickly clothed with fir woods, and fill up the whole triangle enclosed between the railway, the March, and the Danube. About three miles from Blumenau, nearer Preszburg, the road and railway, side by side, pass over a little rivulet which supplies the stream to turn the wheels of two watermills—one situated upon each side of the way; above these mills on the left-hand side rises a portion of hill rather higher than the surrounding spurs and less thickly covered with forest, called the Gämsen-Berg; a footpath which leaves the high road at Bystenitz leads up the mountain side to the left of the road, and after a steep and rugged ascent descends equally roughly, and again joins the main road behind the watermills coming down beside the Gämsen-Berg.

The Austrian position was shrouded by the woods and by the broken ground, but a reconnaissance, made with considerable difficulty, showed that they were in great force. Their centre held the villages of Blumenau and Kaltenbrun and the ground between, the left was in the fir woods on the Theben-Berger stretching toward the March. Their right extended from the village of Blumenau about half a mile up the lower spurs of the Carpathians. The position was strong and formidable, the ground was extremely favourable to the defenders, and gave no open field for the play of the needle-gun; but Franzecky not only determined to carry the position, but also had the bold design of cutting off from Preszburg and capturing the greater part of the defending force and all their artillery, and in all human probability he would have done so had not the good fortune of Austria brought the combat to a premature close.

General Bose was directed to take two regiments, the 21st and 71st, each of three battalions, making a total force of under 5,000 men— for these regiments had had their ranks thinned by the war—by the mountain path leading from Bystenitz, and gain the rear of the enemy near the Gämsen-Berg, so as to cut off their retreat to Preszburg, while Franzecky himself determined, with the remainder of his troops, to attack the position in front. About half-past four in the morning Bose's men began their march, and, disappearing into the wood to the left, began their ascent of the difficult mountain path. Their way was long and rugged, so that time had to be allowed them to gain the Gämsen-Berg, and it was not till after six that Franzecky gave the signal for the advance of the troops on the main road.

Then the advance guard began to move briskly forward, and the rest of the little army followed in battle array. Skirmishers pushed forward through the fields on the left, pushing up close to the wood on the mountain side; their supports moved in small clumps here and there behind them; a larger body marched along the road, and behind them, spread out right and left, came the heavy columns of the infantry and the broad-fronted batteries of guns. On the right of the road a squadron of the 10th Hussars glided with the cheery noise of clinking sabres and ringing steel over the meadows and flat stubble field, pushing forwards to feel their way—scouts, who, carbine in hand, spread, a thin curtain of horsemen, before the main body. Scarcely had the troops begun to move when the morning sun burst brightly from the clouds over the Carpathians, and fell upon the bright swords of the cavalry, the glittering bayonets and rifles of the infantry, and even managed to draw a twinkling reflection from the darkly-browned steel of the artillery guns. The Prussian soldiers greeted it with joy, for their frames were chilled with their night's bivouac, and they marched in the full confidence that before it set it would have lighted them to another victory.

Slowly and steadily the columns moved; the men were very silent, for they all felt that stem subdued excitement which always appears to pervade every breast when a battle is close at hand; and the sound of the measured tread of the battalions, and the heavy nimble of the guns, rose into the air almost unbroken. The advanced guard, consisting of the 72nd regiment, approached to within three thousand paces of the point where the railway, marked by its long line of spectral telegraph posts, could be seen closing into the road from the right, and where the dark green fir-woods behind it showed that there was the Austrian position; but no signs of the enemy could be seen, except two squadrons of lancers, one considerably in rear of the other, which stood on the level ground to the right of the road in front of the railway, motionless as statues, with the pennons of their lances faintly fluttering in the breeze.

Then suddenly the well-known cloud of white smoke, which shows where a gun has been fired, rose from the raised ground between Blumenau and Kaltenbrun, and a whizzing whistling shell rushed through the air, over the heads of the hussars on the right of the road. The Prussian guns came quickly into action, and opened on the spot where the cloud of smoke had risen, and where, in a few moments, repeated flashes of fire and many more clouds of heavy hanging smoke announced that a strong Austrian battery had its post. While the artillery fight was going on, the dark green hussars on the right began to move quickly forward, and rushed in full career against the foremost squadron of Austrian lancers. These did not stand motionless now. Slowly at first, and then more quickly, they began to advance against the hussars; and when the two squadrons came within a few hundred yards of each other, both urged their horses to their utmost speed, and with a mighty clatter dashed together.

The rough embrace lasted but for a moment; then the lancers scattered and fled, for the hussars were stronger and better mounted, and their mere weight smashed the lancers' ranks. These pursued a short distance, capturing several prisoners; but they could not follow far, for the other squadron of lancers looked threatening, and the hussars had no reserves near at hand The cavalry combat, though so short, was severe; many men were down on both sides, and Major von Hymen, commanding the hussars, had the whole side of his face laid open, but refused to quit the field, and commanded his squadron throughout the day.

In the meantime the cannonade increased in the centre, more Prussian guns were brought into action, and more Austrian pieces were firing between Blumenau and Kaltenbrun; and at eight o'clock, when the action had lasted about an hour, forty Austrian and thirty-six Prussian guns were pounding against each other. Casualties began to increase; one Prussian battery in particular was rapidly being unhorsed, for the Austrians were making good practice, and their shells were generally bursting at the proper moment

Half an hour later an officer arrived from Prince Frederick Charles to announce that an armistice was agreed upon, and that it was to commence at mid-day; but Franzecky could not stop the fight, for Bose was with his brigade committed in the mountains, and if the grand front attack ceased he would probably before noon be captured. But no infantry was sent forward, and the combat was confined to artillery fire alone for more than two hours.

Then Franzecky, fearing for Bose, determined to attack the Austrian position with energy, and made his dispositions for a general advance. General Gordon, with four battalions, was ordered to move by a mountain path, which, leaving the road near where the artillery was at present, runs lower down the hills than the way taken by Bose, and comes out on the road again near Blumenau; when he felt the Austrian right, he was to attack it with vigour and occupy the village of Blumenau. At the same time, two battalions were sent against the fir-woods near Kaltenbrun to attack the Austrian left, and, if possible, to seize that village, while the main body and the artillery were to move straight against the front

The guns were limbered up; the two battalions began moving over the plain towards the wood of Kaltenbrun; Gordon was already on the hillside, and the main body advanced for about one thousand paces, when the guns, again unlimbered, came into action, and renewed their fire on the Austrian batteries. About eleven o'clock the two battalions came within easy distance of the wood near Kaltenbrun, and were received by a biting fire from the Austrian sharpshooters among the trees, while to the rear of the guns between Blumenau and Kaltenbrun they could see heavy masses of infantry ready to resist the front attack. The Prussian battalions immediately opened out and began to fire against the infantry in the wood; but the trees hid their antagonists, and they did not seem to cause much diminution of the fire from the forest.

In the meantime a message came from Bose to say that he had debouched on the Gämsen-Berg, and had there met the celebrated Austrian Schwarz and Gelh brigade. A severe fight took place here; the Austrians poured volley after volley into the head of Bose's column as it attempted to come out of the trees, and so tangled was the jungle that the Prussian marksmen could hardly force through it in order to spread out on either side and open fire against the Austrians. But after a time they succeeded in penetrating through the thick trunks and interwoven branches, and the Prussians debouched and deployed on the Gämsen-Berg. Still the fight went on, but the Austrians were driven back step by step, and at last Bose seized the water-mills and planted his brigade across the road and railway to Preszburg, sending a messenger to General Franzecky to say that the enemy's retreat was cut off, and that now the front attack might be pressed hard. It was the receipt of this message that caused Franzecky to order the general advance, but before the combat could be finished the laurels that he would have gained by the capture of the enemy, which would have certainly been the result of his skilful dispositions, were snatched from his grasp.

Time was getting on; and before the front attack was developed, the sun, standing high up in the heavens and directly south, showed that mid-day had arrived. In a few minutes an Austrian officer came out from the Blumenau position with a flag of trace, and advanced towards the Prussian lines. He was met by a Prussian officer, to whom he reported that an armistice had been agreed upon, to date from mid-day, and that it was already past the hour. In a few minutes the signal to cease firing was sounded along the Prussian ranks, and the combat was broken off. The sudden silence was curious and abrupt; there were none of the dropping shots or single occasional reports in which a cannonade generally dies away; in a moment the roar of the artillery and the patter of small arms ceased, and a curious hum of conversation rose from the astonished soldiers.

At first the Austrians would not believe that their retreat was cut off, and that they had been in such imminent danger of being captured, for no report had been sent up from the rear, and they still thought that they commanded the road to Preszburg. But they were soon convinced that they were really surrounded, when, on sending back, it was found that Prussian troops were drawn up across the only line of retreat for their artillery.

The Austrians lost in the combat between five hundred and six hundred men, of whom one hundred were taken prisoners, and over three hundred were wounded. The Prussian loss was reported only one hundred killed and wounded.

To speculate on what would have been is generally unprofitable, especially so in war; but as the Austrians fully acknowledge that they were only saved by a lucky fortune from a terrible disaster, it may not be too much for impartial observers to believe that the action was virtually gained by the Prussians, and that if it had continued all the Austrian artillery must have been taken, and probably the greater part of their infantry captured; for there is no road except the one occupied by Bose by which the guns could have been withdrawn from Blumenau; and though there is a rough country lane by which men on foot could from Kaltenbrun reach the banks of the Danube, it is extremely doubtful if the Prussians would not have been in Preszburg before the Austrian infantry could have gained that line by this roundabout route, and then their capture was certain.

The number of men engaged on each side was about equal. The Prussians had two divisions, which together consisted of twenty-five battalions, in the field, with forty-eight guns, but twelve of these were always in reserve. The Austrians had the 1st, 2nd, and 4th brigades of their second *corps d'armée* and Mendel's brigade of the tenth corps engaged, and had forty guns.

Had this action been allowed to proceed, and had it been a victory for the Prussians, it would have been won, not by the needle-gun so much as by the brilliant dispositions made by General Franzecky for turning his enemy's right flank. This was confessed by an Austrian officer, who, talking to a Prussian officer after the armistice was declared, said, "Your needle-gun may be a terrible weapon, and we know by experience how well it shoots; but it has not been so bad for us as your generals, who have a most diabolical power of manoeuvring."

Directly the action was over, General Stülpnagel and Count Hasler rode into Preszburg to settle with the commandant of that place the line of demarcation which should be observed by the troops during the armistice. The Prussian troops were all in front of the line that was agreed upon, and ought, according to the strict letter of the law, to have withdrawn at once, but it was late in the day when the line was fixed. The Austrian officer consented that for the night the Prussians should remain where they were, and retire to their new ground in. the morning.

Then occurred a curious scene. The men of Bose's Prussian brigade, who had been planted across the Preszburg road, and a few hours before had been standing ready, rifle in hand, to fire upon the retreating Austrian battalions, were surrounded by groups of those very Austrian soldiers whom they had been waiting to destroy. The men of the two nations mingled together, exchanged tobacco, drank out of each other's flasks, talked and laughed over the war in groups equally composed of blue and white uniforms, cooked their rations at the same fires, and that night Austrian and Prussian battalions lay down bivouacked close together, without fear and in perfect security.

On the morrow all along the line of the front of the Prussian Army the divisions took up the positions they were to occupy during the temporary peace.

Early on the morning of the 22nd, commissioners from the Austrian and Prussian Armies had a meeting at a small village between Gänserndorf and the Danube, in order to decide upon a line which should, during the armistice, form the boundary between the troops of the two nations. The Prussian commissioners were General von Podbielsky, of the king's headquarter staff, and Major von Capprivi, of the staff of Prince Frederick Charles; their colleagues from the Austrian camp were General von John and some of his assistants in the Austrian headquarter staff. After some hours of consultation the line of demarcation was decided upon. It started on the Prussian right at Krems, on the Danube; followed the north bank of the river down as far as Stockerau; from that town ran up the curve of the Gollsbach rivulet to the neighbourhood of Fellabrun; then, by taking a line to the village of Weinsteig, it struck the Rossbach rivulet close to that village, followed this stream as far as Leopoldsdorf, then ran along the road between that village and Lasse, and was then drawn along an imaginary straight line to the railway bridge over the March, near Marchegg.

On the left side of the March a straight line from the railway bridge carried it to the village of Bistritz, whence it followed the eastern edge of the Fahren Wald till it struck the main road from Skalitz to Tyrnau.

It was further agreed that commanders of detachments and of troops left to mask fortresses should decide with the commanders of the troops opposite to them upon the lines of demarcation to be observed in the vicinity of their own commands.

The Prussian cavalry corps, under the command of Prince Albrecht, was pushed forward to the line of the Roszbach, and had its headquarters in the neighbourhood of Deutsch Wagram, whence the fortifications of Florisdorf could be seen, but their details could not be made out.

While the action of Blumenau was actually being fought. General Degenfeld and Count Karolyi, the former Austrian ambassador at Berlin, crossed the space between the outposts on the other side of the March, and went to the king's headquarters, empowered by the Austrian Government to conclude a treaty of peace.

At the time of the suspension of hostilities, the Prussian armies on the Marchfeld and between Vienna and Brünn consisted of the three corps of Prince Frederick Charles, the cavalry corps of Prince Albrecht, three divisions under General Herwarth, and three and a half corps under the crown prince. These formed a force of about two hundred and sixty-five thousand combatants. Behind these lay the first reserve corps under General Mülbe at Brünn, half a corps from the crown prince's army in front of Olmütz, and near the same fortress Knobelsdorf's corps, forming together an additional force of about fifty-five thousand men. The corps of Knobelsdorf had occupied the Austrian town of Troppau on the 9th July, and had then been pushed forward to observe Olmütz and garrison the line of railway to Brünn. Count Stölberg was left in Silesia with about ten thousand men to watch the Austrian detachments in Gallicia, The division of *Landwehr* of the Guard was in Prague. Detachments of *Landwehr* held Saxony, and garrisoned the capital and fortresses of Prussia.

On the western theatre of war, Manteuffel had sixty thousand men in the field. The Grand Duke of Mecklenburg had about twenty-five thousand. Five thousand men held Frankfort and Hanau, and *Landwehr* garrisoned Nassau, Hesse-Cassel, and Hanover. In all, Prussia had at the lowest computation five hundred and twenty thousand fighting men in the field—a stupendous force to be supplied by a country which with its allies did not possess a population of twenty million inhabitants. Besides these, there were *depôt* and garrison troops retained in the provinces, which numbered at least one hundred thousand additional soldiers.

CHAPTER 4

The Truce

During the armistice of five days, the Prussian troops remained in the Marchfeld.

On the morning of the 23rd, the troops who had been the previous day engaged in the combat of Blumenau marched back to their positions on their own side of the line of demarcation which was to be observed by the Prussians during the armistice. Between this line and that up to which the Austrian outposts were pushed forward extended a narrow belt of neutral ground, on which the soldiers of either side were forbidden to tread, and where the labourers were cutting the corn and carrying in the harvest as peaceably and diligently as if there was no enemy in their country, and no Prussian *vedettes* were posted along the course of the Roszbach. The troops, not ungrateful for a little idleness after their hard work, lay billeted in the villages between Ebenthal and the line of demarcation, knapsacks were unpacked, and their motley contents laid out on the banks by the roadside to be dried and aired in the sun.

The artillery ammunition went under a careful inspection; groups of soldier-tailors sitting together under the trees patched up holes made in uniforms either by the wear and tear of the campaign, or by the too near approach of a bullet or the splinter of a shell. Everywhere through the cantonments there was a listless, idle air of careless comfort and rest, such as can only be thoroughly appreciated by those who have been marching and fighting for weeks past under a burning sun or heavy soaking rain; except where the sentinel paced up and down before some cottage improvised into a guardhouse, where the regimental colours were deposited, or where the *vedette* sat mounted, with pistol in hand, peering as carefully towards Florisdorf and the Danube as if there were no truce agreed upon, and as if he expected

413

every moment to have to give the signal of the approach of the enemy's columns.

No one who bore any look of being a spy was allowed to pass either out of the lines or into them, and so suspicious were the sentries that the country people going out to or returning from work had to give satisfactory accounts of themselves before they were allowed to pass. The Austrians were equally careful on their side, so that no communication could take place with Vienna; and the Stephanenthurm, which looked down on the city where so many would like to go if only for an hour, only tantalized those who could see it from the line of outposts, and drew forth many exclamations of impatience from those who fretted and fumed at being tied down to the flat plain of the Marchfeld, in the very sight of the capital, where many little luxuries which were greatly missed and wanted in the army could so easily have been purchased.

In the meantime the military authorities were not idle in their preparations for the continuance of the campaign, in case the diplomatists, who were working in mysterious silence at Nikolsburg, should fail to come to terms upon the conditions of peace. The railway was crowded with trains all the way from Görlitz to Lundenburg, which were bringing up reserves, heavy guns, stores, pontoons, and all the other materials which would be required for the passage of the Danube. The armistice had not done the Prussians much harm, even if the war should have broken out afresh, except by stopping the action of Blumenau, for they would probably have had to pause in the middle of active operations to await the arrival of their siege guns and their bridge material, even if there had been no suspension of hostilities; and the five days which gave rest to the battalions in the front of the army also afforded time to get forward the immense train of boats, pontoons, and planks which the engineers would have required if they had been called upon to throw bridges across the broad, rapid stream which flows between the Marchfeld and Vienna, although the Danube is not so difficult to cross as most rivers with an equal amount of water, for it is broken up into many channels, enclosing numerous islands which much aid the construction of a bridge.

Now in the different billets many stories were related of individual prowess and personal bravery during the campaign. There was not a battalion or a squadron which had not its special hero, about whom some particular anecdote was recorded; no two opinions were stated concerning the organisation and equipment of the different branches

414

of the army from those who have had the most practical proofs of the working of them, by being dependent upon them in the real work of war. There were no grumblers; and though the staff officers, who observed carefully every incident of the campaign, with a view to profit by its experience for further improvement and for further progress, had noted many things which were changed or adopted as soon as peace gave time and opportunity, the regimental officers were well content with everything, and were ready to stand or fall by their conviction that the Prussian army was the most smoothly-worked piece of machinery in the whole world.

It was curious to find from those who had taken part in the cavalry fighting that the epaulette, which has of late been discarded in many armies as a useless incumbrance, had again risen into high favour. None of the Prussian cavalry wore their epaulettes on service except the Uhlans, but some officers of these regiments spoke most highly of the good service the little plates of shoulder armour had done in warding off sword cuts. The *cuirass*, too, proved more useful in close encounter than most people would have given it credit for, and was in more than one case the instrument of saving a man's life, and yet the Prussian *cuirasses* are thin, ill made, and ill fitted in comparison with those of the British Household Cavalry. Still, there was a strong party against this defensive armour, for many in the army held that its use does not repay the extra weight it puts upon the horse, but this party was for the present silenced by the great success which the 5th regiment of Cuirassiers, attached to the crown prince's army, had lately been in the combat near Tobitschau, where it took seventeen guns.

The needle-gun was of course an immense favourite, and the Prussian officers justly held that an army provided with a muzzle-loading arm can never hope to stand up to their troops in the shock of open battle; but their conclusion that the needle-gun is the best possible breech-loader was founded on nothing more than the fact that it is superior to a muzzle-loading rifle, and they advanced no good grounds for supposing that no breech-loader has been invented since the introduction of the needle-gun into the Prussian service, which can be superior to the arm that did such fearful execution in the Austrian ranks at Podoll, and in the actions before Gitschin.

The Prussians entered upon the campaign with their horse artillery armed with smooth-bore 12-pounder guns. They had long before the armistice bitterly repented this error, and will take care to remedy it before they are embroiled in another war. The whole of their field artillery is to be armed with steel breech-loading rifled guns constructed on Krupp's system—good ordnance doubtless, but the Prussian guns did not appear in action to make such good practice as the Armstrong guns did in China, when the English gunners were still unaccustomed to them, and as yet looked upon all breech-loading ordnance with considerable suspicion.[1]

The Prussians on the 24th commenced massing troops towards the left of their position, with the view of being able to make an immediate dash on Preszburg on the afternoon of the 27th, if peace should not be concluded during the time that the armistice lasted; but most in camp looked upon this concentration as a needless precaution, for it was considered that peace was perfectly certain. But neither the staff nor the outposts were prevented by this feeling of certainty from using all precautions from being taken unawares; the railway still teemed with trains loaded heavily with troops and stores.

No news could be obtained of how the negotiations were going on at Nikolsburg, for the diplomatists preserved the correct diplomatic silence, and took care that the *profanum vulgus* should gain no clue either to the progress or probable result of the discussions held at their mysterious meetings.

Rumours, of course, were rife, and all of them prophesied peace; some went so far as to assert that the treaty would actually be signed on Thursday, the 26th; but how flax such reports were to be trusted could not be established, as popular opinion was now swayed about in the most extraordinary way. The sudden glance of a minister, or the wearied look of a plenipotentiary, was interpreted according to the inclination of the observer, and had some deep meaning attached to it, possibly very remote from what it might really signify.

Nothing was doing at headquarters, so a party of officers of the staff was made to visit the outposts, partly for the sake of something to do, partly in hopes of being able to catch some glimpses of the fortifications round Florisdorf, which are rapidly becoming famous. A ride of fifteen miles over the flat, wide-spreading Marchfeld, carpeted with meadows, clover-fields, and broad belts of stubble, from which most of the corn had been removed, past dark woods of fir and lighter copses of dark oak, took them to Wagram. More than once someone exclaimed, "What a beautiful battlefield for cavalry!" as they rode for

---

1. In 1870-71, a portion of the Prussian field artillery was armed with bronze breech-loading guns, and probably in future all the guns for the field artillery will be made of bronze.

miles over ground unbroken by fences or brooks, and in which the only obstacles to the free gallop of horses were a few small ditches, and here and there a tiny bank.

The village of Wagram, celebrated by the battle won here by the first Napoleon, contains a chapel where are collected many of the arms that were found on the field after that great fight. A strange feeling of awe comes upon one when brought face to face with these truest monuments of the great conflict waged here by the mighty dead; and the loud talk and laughter of careless soldiers fresh from a field of battle, and reckless of how soon they might march to another, were hushed, not more by the sanctity of the place than by an almost involuntary reverence for the visible memorials of the great battle and of the warriors who fell in it.

But disappointment has also its place in the mind; for how clumsy, how old-fashioned, according to our ideas, look those old flint muskets and heavy swords with which but a few years back the fate of Europe was decided! Could the question fail? Shall we to our successors in the next generation appear to have known so little of what science has in such a short time developed, and to have been so ignorant of mechanical appliances, which, when once unfolded, appear so simple and so palpable? And another thought came into every mind, which struck home to the heart; for it told that in a few short years those who had fought at Königgrätz and survived the long summer day's slaughter on the Sadowa hill would individually be equally lost to memory as those who fell at Wagram—their names mostly unknown, their private deeds unrecorded by any historian.

About two hundred yards south of the village of Wagram lies the watercourse of the Roszbach rivulet. This world-known brook is about ten feet wide and fifteen feet deep. With sharp sides cut almost straight down, and the earth thrown up on either bank to form dykes which prevent its winter floods from inundating the surrounding country, it looks more like a huge artificial drain than like a natural rivulet. Along its banks grow rows of pollard willows, closely planted together, which formed a grateful shade from the burning July sun. The road which leads to Florisdorf crosses the brook by a slight wooden bridge which could be destroyed in a few minutes by the pioneers of a single battalion.

On the Wagram side of the bridge were two *vedettes* from Hohenlohe's fine regiment of Uhlans, crouching for shade under the willow-trees, but steadily gazing out towards Florisdorf, though not an

Austrian *vedette* could be seen, for they were all hidden by trees.

But, though no enemy was in sight, a view was there which well repaid the long ride, and which even the soldiers, accustomed as they had been to marching through fine scenery, were admiring to each other. On the right lay the rounded hill of the Bisamberg, studded with vineyards, cornfields, and woods, among which vain search with glasses was made to discover any signs of the hostile batteries. Beyond the Bisamberg could be seen the narrow gorge from which the Danube issues, and further still the rough rugged recess of the hills above Klosterneuberg, rising steeply up from the water's edge, with their summits capped with heavy masses of dark green foliage, and their sides sprinkled over with fir-trees.

A little to the left, and at the foot of the hills, the city of Vienna lay sparkling in the sun; the tops of the steeples and the roofs of the houses glittered in the bright flood of light, but not too powerfully, for the air between Wagram and the town seemed converted by the heat into a heavy transparent ether, which spread a halo round the city. In the foreground, a little to the left, a high church spire, surrounded by tall poplar-trees, showed the situation of the village of Florisdorf; but no intrenchments could be seen, no working parties could be discovered; they were all hidden by a long gentle wave of the ground, which would not have been noticed except because it excluded from the view. Far away on the left front spread the Marchfeld, beyond which could be seen the dim blue line of hills which gird the valley south of the Danube, while directly to the left the dark Carpathians towered up to the sky, and the gap between the Theben-Berger and the main ridge showed where the road ran to Preszburg, and pointed, out the situation of the village of Blumenau, the scene of the combat of the 22nd.

After a long and fruitless search among the poplar-trees for any signs of intrenchments, during which heaps of earth were pointed out as redoubts, which may have been or may not, the officers turned to ride down the Roszbach. The brook was almost entirely dry; here and there for a few yards a thin sheet of water a few inches deep covered the soft muddy bottom, and gave a refuge to flocks of mud-bedaubed ducks, but in general the mud which forms the sole of the water-course lay exposed to the sun, and was dried and broken into cracks and fissures, which ran into each other, forming a tracery not unlike hieroglyphic writing. All along the brook were constant *vedettes*, all hidden in the willows on the bank, which the conditions of the armistice had declared to be for the present Prussian ground The sound of horses' feet coming along drew the sentries out of their ambush far enough to let them be seen, but as soon they saw the uniforms of the Prussian staff-officers they resumed their steady stare to the front, retiring into the shade, and let the officers pass them as if they were not aware of our existence; for outlying sentinels pay no compliments in the presence of the enemy.

The Prussian armies were by the 25th drawn close together, and, concentrated in one huge mass, lay like a crouching lion, ready to spring upon the Danube, should the negotiations for peace fail, and the orders for an advance be flashed by telegraph from Nikolsburg to the different commanders. The First Army, under Prince Frederick Charles, was close up to the Roszbach and the line of demarcation, with a strong corps on the left bank of the March to guard its flank or form its advanced guard as might be required, in case the signal should be given to move forward. General Herwarth, with the Army of the Elbe, was on the right, perhaps with the object of crossing the river at a lower point of its course. The crown prince was in rear of the first, ready to move in any direction which occasion might require.

On the 27th, at mid-day, the armistice would expire, and, in case that it should not be prolonged, or preliminaries of peace were not agreed upon by that hour, the Prussian troops were on the 26th held in readiness to march at the shortest notice. If an advance had been made, there can be no doubt, from the positions of the different divisions, that the great attack against the line of the Danube would have been made towards Preszburg; probably, at the same time, a demonstration might have been made towards the Prussian right, and a false attack directed on Florisdorf, in order to retain the garrison in their fortifications. The action of the 22nd, which at the moment of certain victory for the Prussians was interrupted by the armistice, had shown the Austrians where the chief attack could be made, and the Prussians thought that by the 27th the position of Blumenau would in all likelihood have been artificially strengthened, and the road by which Bose advanced and gained the rear of the villages would certainly be watched on a future occasion.

Yet, though there could be no hope of succeeding so suddenly as on the 22nd in gaining the command of the defile which leads to Preszburg, and though there was no chance, as would probably have been the case if the previous Sunday's action had continued, of driving the enemy so quickly through the town as to prevent him from destroying the bridge, the advantages to be gained from attempting to pass the Danube at Preszburg were so great, that an attempt would probably have been made to force the defile and to secure that town. The fortifications of Florisdorf, a part of which could be seen from the church-tower of Wagram, shut out the access to such a broad piece of the river bank that very different measures had to be taken for securing the passage than would have been most expedient, if no intrenchments had covered the approach across the flat plain from Wagram and Aspern. The portion of the works which could be seen through the clear air from the church spire embraced four redoubts on the Bisamberg hill, and three on the flat ground between the Bisamberg and Florisdorf; there was also another work on the hill to guard the left flank of the position, which lying more towards the river could not be seen from Wagram.

The Prussian cavalry had gained much from the rest afforded by the armistice; fatigued by long marches through the Moravian highlands, and stinted for forage, it had a sufficiently long period of repose when the army halted at Brünn to restore it to the splendid condition in which it entered upon the campaign; but the long rest in the Marchfeld had done it an immensity of good, though even here forage had not been plentiful. Notwithstanding small rations, the horses had profited by their rest, for time had been given to replace their worn-out shoes, and to afford relief to chafed backs caused by the late long marches. The troopers were in high spirits, for they had overcome the famed Austrian cavalry in several encounters, and now claimed a higher reputation than that which for several years past had been accorded to their antagonists.

The failures of the Austrian cavalry in their encounters with the stronger and better-mounted horsemen of Prussia had not so much astonished the thinking officers of this army as had the singularly little use which General Benedek had made of his light horse. Although operations had been conducted in its own country, where every information concerning the Prussian movements could have been readily obtained from the inhabitants, the Austrian cavalry had made no raids against the flank or rear of the advancing army, had cut off no ammunition or provision trains, had broken up no railway communication behind the marching columns, had destroyed no telegraph lines between the front and the base of supplies, had made no sudden or night attacks against the outposts so as to make the weary infantry stand to their arms and lose their night's rest, and, instead of hovering round the front and flanks to irritate and annoy the pickets, had been rarely seen or fallen in with except when it had been marched down upon and beaten up by the Prussian advanced guards.

Yet the Prussian cavalry had in many cases lost severely in the campaign, especially the 3rd regiment of Dragoons. This regiment suffered fearfully from its rough hustle with the Austrian *cuirassiers* at Königgrätz, and now mustered but half the men and horses with which it entered upon the campaign. More than half the officers and quite half the men who followed across the Bohemian frontier the standard which has been cherished in their regiment since the year 1704 are now lying under the earth of Lipa, or were in the hospitals of Türnau and Görlitz, for this was the regiment which dashed against the heavy mass of *cuirass* horsemen who sacrificed themselves to cover the retreat of the Austrian battalions, and it supported its character for dashing courage at a tremendous cost. Very many of both the officers and men who were not now in the ranks were victims to terrible sword cuts, which, coming down upon the shoulder, cut clean through the shoulder-blade, and often deep down into the body—awful memorials of the strength of arm of the Austrian horsemen.

Much did the officers of this regiment complain of the absence of epaulettes, which they estimated would, by defending the shoulder, have saved half the men they had left behind them—a complaint which was to some extent borne out by the fact that the ultimate overthrow of the *cuirass* regiments of Austria was due to the arrival of some of Hohenlohe's Uhlans, who took them in flank. Then, though the heavy horsemen turned upon Hohenlohe's men, their swords were shivered upon the brass plates which lay upon the shoulders of the Uhlans, for these, unlike the rank and file of the rest of the Prussian cavalry carried epaulettes, and though the blows were aimed at the head, the smaller object was nearly always missed, and the sharp edge descended only to be dinted or broken upon the protected shoulder, while the Uhlans, with their lances held short in hand, searched out with their spear-heads unguarded portions of their antagonists' bodies, or, dealing heavy blows with the butt ends of their staves, pressed through the thick ranks of the heavy horsemen, marking their track with great heaps of dead, dying, or wounded.

On the evening of the 26th, there was still no definite news from Nikolsburg, but every rumour which arrived from headquarters pointed more and more to peace; still the army was held in readiness to move, and the *officiers d'ordonnance*, or "gallopers" as they would be termed in the vernacular of Aldershot, were ordered to be prepared to start with orders to the different divisions at three in the morning.

The preliminaries of peace had been agreed upon at Nikolsburg on the evening of the 26th, and the war was certainly at an end as far as Austria and the North German States were concerned. Late on the night of the 26th, a courier arrived from the king's headquarters at Nikolsburg, bringing a letter from General von Moltke to Prince Frederick Charles, which gave no details and no information as to the conditions of the peace, but said simply that a glorious peace had been arranged. The news spread in a moment, and suddenly all was changed. In the evening information was being obtained about the strength of the Austrian position at Florisdorf, the preparations to guard the defile which leads to Preszburg, the nature of the bridges over the Danube, or the chance of Edelsheim's cavalrry coming forward to break a lance in the Marchfeld.

On the morning of the 27th, these things were held of no account; no one would have cared to hear accurately where every battalion and every gun was posted in the Austrian lines; the number of Edelsheim's sabres and of the Archduke Albrecht's corps were alike disregarded; no one would have cared to hear how many of the regiments from Italy were actually in Vienna, and the intrenchments of Florisdorf were considered a matter of history. These who the previous night seemed to have no thought but of battle, promotion, and an entry into Vienna, could speak on the 27th of nothing but home, and hardly thought of anything except their speedy return to Prussia. Now and then a faint discussion arose on the subject of the conditions of peace, but so little was known in the army, and so many reports were flying about, that these soon subsided, and gave place to conversations about home and home friends.

Though peace had been actually decided upon, no one connected with the army was able to go across the two miles of neutral ground which separate the Prussian from the Austrian outposts, so that there was almost no communication with Vienna.

The great desire of marching into the Austrian capital had melted away under the genial influence of certain peace, and there had sprung up instead a feeling of satisfaction that it was not necessary to humiliate Austria so far; for of a sudden all the affection for their old comrades of the Danish war, which had lain latent in the hearts of the Prussian soldiers during the campaign, had again burst forth into life, and there were prevalent in this army almost a kindly pity for the mis-

422

fortunes of those who but on the yesterday were regarded as deadly enemies. The soft, stout hearts of the Prussians were easily turned from anger to sympathy, as was so often shown by their tender treatment of the Austrian wounded.

During the armistice there was a feeling of suspicion that the Austrian diplomatists would be shifty, and break off the negotiations as soon as their troops were concentrated. This feeling, combined with a desire of mere glory, made the armistice very unpopular; but now that it had been proved that the Austrians were really honest, and that peace was really to be concluded, the memory of all the old grudges was obliterated, and had been replaced by a rapidly increasing feeling of friendship. If an Austrian officer had now come into the Prussian lines he would have been received by the officers with the same open-hearted hospitality which they show to their own comrades; the day before he would have been treated with the most polite courtesy.

The troops were in excellent condition, both as to health and spirits, and quite prepared to march back to the frontier at the same rate as they advanced.

On the evening of the 26th the preliminaries of peace[2] were signed at Nikolsburg between Prussia and Austria; the terms which were agreed to were—that Austria should go out of the Germanic Confederation, should pay a contribution towards Prussia's expenses in the late war, and should offer no opposition to the steps which Prussia might take with regard to Northern Germany: these steps were, to annex Hanover, Hesse-Cassel, Nassau, and the portion of Hesse-Darmstadt which lies on the north bank of the Maine; to secure the reversion of Brunswick on the death of the present duke, who has no children, to force Saxony to enter into the new North German Confederation headed by Prussia, and to hold the entire military and diplomatic leadership in that Confederation. The war contribution to be paid by Austria was fixed at 40,000,000 *thalers*, of which 15,000,000 were to be paid up, 15,000,000 were credited to Austria for the Schleswig-Holstein expenses, 5,000,000 for the support of the Prussian armies in Bohemia and Moravia, and 5,000,000 were to be paid at a future date to be afterwards settled. The Prussian armies were on the 2nd of August to retire to the north of the Thaya, but were to occupy Bohemia and Moravia till the signature of the final treaty of peace, and to hold Austrian Silesia until the war contribution was paid.

To allow time for the preparation and determination of the de-

2. See later in this chapter.

finitive treaty of peace, an armistice for five weeks was concluded, to commence on the 2nd August, to which day the five days' suspension of hostilities was extended. The convention for the armistice determined as follows:—

That the line of demarcation during the armistice should run from Eyer by Pilsen, Neuhaus, Zlabings to the Thaya: then follow the course of that stream to its junction with the March, along the March to Napajedl, and in a straight line from Napajedl to Oderberg, on the Prussian frontier.

Round each of the Austrian fortresses lying within the territories occupied by the Prussians a space was to be left, in order that the fortress might draw provisions therefrom. Round Olmütz this space was to be ten miles, round Josephstadt, Theresienstadt, and Königgrätz five miles.

The Prussians were to have the free use of all land and water communications within the ground occupied by their armies, and to have the right of transport by the railway from Prerau to Böhmisch-Trübau, which runs past the fortress of Olmütz.

The Austrian troops were not to advance from their actual positions until the Prussian troops were entirely beyond the Thaya.

The sick, who were left by the Prussians with doctors and attendants in their actual positions, were to be supplied by the Austrian Government, and no impediment was to be made to their removal to their homes as soon as possible by the Prussian Government

The Prussian troops were to be rationed from the territories occupied. No money contributions were to be raised.

Negotiations were to be opened at Prague for the definitive conclusion of peace.

By some unfortunate misunderstanding, the garrison of Theresienstadt on the 28th July, although peace was agreed upon on the 26th, sallied from their fortress, destroyed the railway bridge near Kralup, north of Prague, broke the telegraph wires near the same spot, and captured two Prussian officers, two officials, and fifty soldiers. When the commandant of Theresienstadt directed this sally, he was unaware that the preliminaries of peace had been agreed to; but his inopportune vigour caused a great deal of inconvenience to the Prussian army, for the destruction of the bridge broke the line of communication with Türnau, which was a large *depôt* of stores. During the armistice, too, some Austrian hussars, unconscious of the existence of a truce, made an attack on a park of reserve artillery at Znaym, and did some damage, for, on account of the conclusion of the armistice, the guards bad not taken precautions against a surprise.

On the evening of the 27th, preliminaries of peace were also agreed upon with Bavaria. The Bavarian ambassador, Herr von der Pfordten, had been for some days at Nikolsburg unable to obtain an audience of Count Bismark, and only in the afternoon of the 27th secured a few moments' conversation with the Prussian prime minister. The terms of peace were quickly stated: the cession of all Bavarian territory north of the Maine to Prussia, and the payment of a war contribution. The Bavarian demurred, pleaded he had no instructions to give up territory, and wished to enter into diplomatic negotiations in a more orthodox manner, for to the ambassador, trained in the rules of his art it seemed almost sacrilege to turn over provinces in a meeting of only some moments' duration, and to scratch out frontier lines with one or two dashing strokes of a hurried pen; but the plenipotentiaries of Prussia, Count Bismark and General von Moltke, would listen to no propositions and hear no objections, they required an immediate assent; the representative of the Court of Munich did not feel justified in agreeing to such conditions, the meeting abruptly terminated, and orders were telegraphed to General Manteuffel to press the war in Bavaria.

News came in from that country of Prussian successes; the Armies of the Elbe, of Prince Frederick Charles, and of the crown prince were ready to hurry off detachments to the theatre of war south of the Maine, the cause of the decaying Bund was evidently hopeless, every day of indecision must heighten the war contribution; so in the evening the Bavarian ambassador was fain to declare his agreement to the terms dictated. Orders were then telegraphed to General Manteuffel to arrest the progress of his army, and preliminaries for a peace were signed.

On the 27th, after the preliminary treaty with Austria had been signed, the king, much to the satisfaction of the officers at Nikolsburg, who in this case certainly represented the public opinion of the whole army, conferred on General von Moltke the Order of the Black Eagle, the highest of the decorations of Prussia, not more as a sign of approval of the skill with which the general had carried through the negotiations, than of the strategy he had displayed in the conduct of the campaign.

The army was delighted with the terms of the peace; all the hardship, all the danger of the campaign were quite forgotten—all desire of war and regret that peace had been made so soon had utterly vanished, giving way to feelings of congratulation and happiness, because few men really thought that the dreams of a United Germany and of a common Fatherland for the whole Teutonic race were now visionary speculations, but were results which must follow sooner or later from this campaign. Count Bismark was immensely popular in the army; he was regarded as the author and origin of this success, so rapid, so complete, that no Prussian dared to hope for half such a triumph when the troops dashed into Saxony nearly seven weeks before.

A review was ordered in the Marchfeld for the 31st, but only of the main body of the First Army and of the cavalry corps. The Second Army and the Army of the Elbe were already preparing to march back over the Thaya, and as soon as the roads were clear the army of Prince Frederick Charles was to follow. The greater part of the crown prince's army was to hold Austrian Silesia and Moravia, while the First Army and the Army of the Elbe occupied Bohemia. There was one dark shadow cast over the troops, although it was almost disregarded amid the universal joy caused by the glorious terms of peace which had been obtained. The cholera had broken out in the camp, several men and officers were already down with it, and great fears were entertained that the hot weather might cause it to increase.

The cases at first were not very numerous, but they were not confined to one particular regiment, or one particular locality, which makes it appear as though the disease were lurking all through the lines, ready to burst forth everywhere if a day hotter than usual or a slight failure of good water should occur. The medical men, however, spoke confidently of their power to keep the pestilence under, and it was hoped that when the troops turned their faces homewards they might shake it off by change of quarters, and suffer no more when well away from the flat land which borders on the Danube. But it pursued them as they moved, and during the whole of the remaining time which the Prussian Army remained on Austrian territory it suffered much from disease.

By the 29th the Prussian Army began to withdraw from the duchy of Austria; the crown prince's army was already moving back towards Austrian Silesia, passing through Moravia. The second *corps d'armée* of the First Army had commenced its movement towards Prague, and the rest of the First Army was also to begin its retrograde march on the 1st August, after it had been reviewed by the king in the Marchfeld on the 31st July. General Mülbe, who had come with his reserve corps

426

from Prague to Brünn before the preliminaries of peace were agreed upon, was retracing his steps. It could not be expected that the return march would be nearly so rapid as that of the advance. There was no enemy now in the front to be turned or hurriedly pushed back, so the troops moved by easy stages until they reached the positions they had to occupy till the treaty of peace was finally signed

The troops were not at all sorry to be called upon to march again; they had had more than enough rest after the quick marches of the advance, and began now to find time hang rather heavy on their hands. Even smoking gets tiresome when it has been indulged in for almost a week continuously without the interruption of parades or inspections. Helmet tops had been polished and repolished, needle-guns had had their complicated mechanism taken to pieces, cleaned, and put together again, swords and bayonets had been burnished over and over again, accoutrements and appointments had been inspected closely and more closely, almost in the hope of finding some rent or hole which might have to be repaired, all for the sake of something to do. But all the occupation which their accoutrements could afford to the men had been exhausted, and now they were reduced to strolling about listlessly, or hanging over the fences which surround the gardens of the cottages where they were billeted, sucking gravely at their long wooden pipes.

Now and then a soldier might be seen starting off to cut Indian corn for the cow of the villager on whom he was billeted, but he was seldom allowed to enjoy alone his temporary occupation; a group of comrades, eager for employment, joined him, and in consequence the basket, the filling of which might have given one man work for a couple of hours, was crammed full in a few minutes by the thick group of voluntary labourers. The village children alone were perfectly satisfied with the existing state of affairs; they, unlike their elders, had no misgivings about heavy taxes which they would be required to pay for the expenses of the Austrian Army or the war contribution to Prussia; unlike the soldiers, they were not far away from friends and homes, to whom, now that the legitimate work of the campaign was over, these were eager to return; careless of tomorrow, they were only delighted to have so many playfellows, for the great strong men, who had been but the other day pursuing the flying Austrian battalions from König-grätz, were now content to let the children beat them, pull their hair, or sometimes run about with their newly cleaned swords trailing in the dust, and were well pleased afterwards to instruct the urchins in the arts of converting a lump of deal into a boat, or a stick of sycamore wood into a whistle.

A little after nine o'clock on the morning of the 31st July, 1866, the 5th, 6th, 7th, and 8th infantry divisions and the cavalry corps of the First Prussian Army were drawn up on the Marchfeld, within fifteen miles of Vienna, to be reviewed by the King of Prussia. The troops were formed in four lines, facing towards the south, where, through the haze which always on a warm day overhangs a large city, could be indistinctly seen the tall Stephanenthurm that marked the situation of the Austrian capital; their left rested close to the village of Gänserndorf, whence the lines stretched for a distance of a mile and a half over a slightly undulated plain, from which the crops had already been removed, in the direction of Auersthal, but did not extend so far as that village. The two front lines were formed of heavy battalions of infantry, each clumped together in close columns of companies, standing out a dark blue square against the yellow stubble; a hundred yards behind the battalion stood a long line of the cavalry corps under the command of Prince Albrecht, forming, with the cavalry regiments attached to the infantry, a force of close upon 10,000 sabres and lances.

On the right stood the heavy brigade of General Pfuel, consisting of the two *cuirassier* regiments of the emperor of Russia and of the Duke of Coburg, tall strong men, mounted on massive horses, with their yellow helmets and armour glittering in the hot sunshine like burnished gold; next on the left stood Rheinhaben's brigade formed from cavalry of the Guard, one regiment of dragoons in light blue uniforms with red facings, and shining black japanned helmets; and two of Uhlans, the black and white flags of whose lances formed a strong contrast to the bright red facings and lancer caps over which they waved. Next to the Guard brigade was drawn up the brigade of Duke William of Mecklenburg, which had formed the advanced guard of the First Army since it crossed the Elbe at Przelautsch, and which did such tremendous havoc among the Austrian *cuirassiers* at the end of the Battle of Königgrätz.

The regiments in this brigade are the red hussars of Ziethen, the celebrated yellow Uhlans commanded by Prince Hohenlohe, and the 2nd dragoons of the Guard, one of whose squadrons rode down the Austrian lancers at Tischnowitz. In the next brigade stood the thinned squadrons of the 3rd dragoons, who lost more than half their numbers at the great battle, side by side with the light blue and silver clad Thuringian hussars, who also suffered much in the same charge as the

428

3rd Dragoons. The left of the cavalry brigade was formed by Goltz's heavy brigade, the Queen's Own Cuirassiers, and the 9th Uhlans, the regiment in whose hands the lance asserted its supremacy over the sword in the cavalry combat at Saar. In the fourth line, some two hundred yards in the rear of the cavalry, were drawn up the ambulance waggons, ammunition waggons, field telegraph division, a long line of light blue carriages with companies of side bearers, and engineers here and there between them, while on the left lay the batteries of the reserve artillery. Between the batteries of infantry and the long line of horsemen stood the field batteries attached to the infantry divisions, each division in a closed column of four batteries, with a cavalry regiment beside it

About half-past nine Prince Frederick Charles galloped on to the ground and took the command of the whole force. The troops were not quite formed up when he arrived, and in a short time they had all taken up their positions. Officers were sent to look out for the approach of the king, and the cavalry dismounted and stood beside their horses, the infantry piled their arms and rested beside them to await his arrival. In about half an hour an officer who had been acting as scout towards the right was seen coming at full gallop towards the prince, but the purport of his message was understood—he had no need to deliver it. Before he had reached the commander-in-chief the sharp words of command calling the battalions and squadrons to "attention" were passing quickly along the line, and in two or three minutes the troopers were in their saddles, the companies were reformed, the gunners sprang to their posts beside their guns, and the whole army stood silent and motionless; the bayonets bristled stiff among the serried ranks of the infantry, the lance-staves and swords formed a perfect unbending line along the whole cavalry division, the troopers sat as still as statues, for the horses had been perfectly quieted by the campaign, and the only moving things among the widespread hosts were the standards of the infantry, and the pennons of the Uhlans.

A little knot of horsemen appeared over the brow of a gentle undulation, and came quickly towards the centre of the line; a tall man with grey hair and moustache, in the uniform of a general officer, rode in front When he came nearly opposite the centre of the army, the sword-point of Prince Frederick Charles was lowered quickly towards the ground. At this signal every officer's sword went down, with a rapid clatter every musket came to the "present," the lance-staves and glittering sword-blades of the cavalry stood straight up at the "carry," while every band struck up the Prussian national hymn to salute the king. He bowed down to his horse's neck to return not only the salute, but the loud cheer which went up from the ordered crowd, and which drowned the music almost as soon as it began to sound. For a few minutes this lasted, and then it died away, giving place to the last few notes of the bands. All was again silent.

The king moved to the right of the foremost line, and rode along it, stopping here and there to speak to soldiers who had specially distinguished themselves, or to shake hands with the commanding officers. Every battalion cheered him as he walked along its front, pausing to address to each a few words of praise for some particular action during the campaign. Along the second line, the cavalry, and the carriages in the rear he also rode, before he took up his position for the army to march past hint

The first troops that went by were those of the fifth division, commanded by General Tümpling, who fought and won, from a superior Austrian force strongly posted, the action of Brada, near Gitschin. The whole of the Prussian infantry had well proved during the war its power of marching long distances on bad roads and in unfavourable weather, and that day the battalions who were reviewed on the Marchfeld amply demonstrated that this power can co-exist with the most beautiful exactness of parade movements. With a long swinging stride the men passed by, keeping perfect line, and stepping together in such exact time that they could not have done better if, instead of campaigning and bivouacking, they had spent the last two months at marching drill. In the centre of each battalion was carried the standard, often riddled with bullet-holes, sometimes so torn away that only a few patches of tattered silk were left hanging on the bare pole.

In the fifth division were the 8th, 12th, 18th, and 48th regiments, all below their proper strength, for the losses at Gitschin had not yet been replaced, as the reinforcements which were coming up were stopped as soon as peace was agreed upon. After the infantry came the 3rd regiment of Uhlans, which was attached to this division. The perfect marching of the foot soldiers seemed to be contagious, for the squadrons moved in such even lines that as they passed the horseman on the flank utterly hid all the rest from view. Then came the batteries, two abreast, dark and business-like, with the guns uncovered, and the rammers ready, as if pressing forward into action.

The sixth division, under General Manstein, followed the fifth, in the same order; it consisted of the 24th, 64th, 60th, and 35th regiments, all marching with the same steady step, and in equally perfect lines as those who had gone before them. Well they looked and well they went; stout, broad-shouldered men, well grown in years, with thick beards and moustaches, who swung along quickly, without a thought about the heavy yellow knapsack which hung upon their backs. After them followed a dark-green battalion of *Jägers*, linked shoulder to shoulder in four wall-like lines, marching as if they were always in this close formation, though really they have been used in nothing but skirmishing order during the war. The cavalry of this division, the well-known black dragoons of Brandenburg, with their light-blue tunics and dark velvet collars, from which they get their name, formed a bright contrast in colour to the dark-green riflemen, but moved with unwavering squadrons, which showed perfectly trained horses and skilled horsemen.

Franzecky's division came next, the heroes of Benatek and of the attack against the Austrian right on the Bistriz, where they left so many of their comrades. Behind this general marched the 26th, 66th, 67th, and 97th regiments, the last showing by its diminished front the severity of the fire to which it was so long exposed in the hardly-contested wood above Benatek, and the sharp fighting of a later date near Blumenau. With this division passed the dark-green and gold Magdeburg hussars, one squadron of which made the successful charge against the Austrian Uhlans in front of Kaltenbrun.

The last infantry regiment which marched past was the 8th, formerly commanded by General Horne, but, since that general had gone to take the command of the whole of the infantry of the first reserve corps, under General Schoeler. It was a brigade of this division which fought by night the first infantry combat of the campaign in the narrow street of Podoll, where it suffered severely. This division also stormed the village of Sadowa on the morning of the 3rd of July, and spent the greater part of the day in the wood above, exposed to both artillery and musketry fire. The companies looked weak, for their ranks had been thinned by much fighting; but the men who had come through it went past their king with a proud bearing, more like fresh troops going upon service than like men who had just finished a campaign.

All looked splendid, all called forth admiration, and a loud murmur of delight went up from the groups of officers behind the king as the tall *Jägers* of Magdeburg passed in unbending line before them. These men, recruited from the Hartz mountains, and bred up to a forest life, are the very *beau idéal* of light infantry soldiers; tall, muscular, and wiry, quick of sight, and rare marksmen. They are so cool under fire and so certain of their aim, that it is asserted that, like the English archer of old, the Magdeburg *Jäger* carries a foeman's life in every bullet in his *cartouche.*

When the infantry had passed away, the cavalry in a long column of squadrons filed before the king, and in the column was seen every class of cavalry soldier which exists in the Prussian service: heavy, broad-shouldered *cuirassiers*, clothed in white uniforms, with high black boots, mounted on tall, strong horses, which tramped along under the weight of their armour-clad riders, raising clouds of dust, which half obscured the dazzling reflection of the sun from the helmets and *cuirasses*; tall and lithe Uhlans, carrying with an easy balance their long lances, of which the bannered points rose in an even line above their heads; light dragoons—for in this service all the dragoons are light cavalry, armed with sword and carbine; and lighter still, bright-coloured, rakish-looking hussars, active little men, on strong, short-legged horses, decked out with gaudy trappings, which gave them an almost Oriental appearance. In rear of the cavalry the reserve artillery rolled slowly past, followed by the hospital trains, now empty, and with the stretchers, which used to be carried by the *krankenträgers*, now folded up and strapped upon the carriages; but ugly red stains upon the curtains of the ambulance waggons showed that all had been lately used. Last of all came the very useful field telegraph detachment, nine carriages, carrying means for laying down instantly and for using thirty miles of wire. When all had passed, the king called the commanding officers round him, and said:—

Gentlemen,—I cannot speak to all the soldiers under your command—they are too many; but to you, for all, I must express my thanks for the conduct and behaviour of this army during the campaign, which your exertions have brought to such a glorious conclusion. I shall not enter into the details of the gallant conduct of your troops at the battle of Königgrätz, where for hours you stood under the whole artillery fire of the Austrian Army, and resisted successfully all the attempts of the enemy to crush you, and thus break the centre of the line of our battle. I cannot speak as I should wish of Sichrow, Münchengrätz, Podoll, and Gitschin. I can but embrace my nephew, your commander, as the representative of you all. I can but tell you that I thank you, and that your King and your Fatherland feel that you have nobly done your duty. I am sure there is nothing I could say which could be more pleasing to Prussian soldiers.

Loud cheers greeted the conclusion of this speech, when the king turned his horse, and rode away.

On the morning of the 31st, Prince Charles, the father of Prince Frederick Charles and Prince Adalbert, received the Order of Merit from the king, the same Order as the crown prince received on the battlefield of Königgrätz. General von Voigt-Rhetz was appointed Governor of Hanover, and many other officers and soldiers received military honours. Prince Frederick Charles received nothing, for there was nothing left to give him; he had already won every decoration which it was in the power of the monarch to bestow; but he was well contented, for the troops under his command had won a reputation, not only for courage, discipline, and endurance, but also for tenderness to their wounded enemies and for a kindly consideration for the peaceful inhabitants of the conquered countries, which must endure as long as history lives. The king's speech closed the last scene of the war of 1866.

The king started for Berlin immediately, and the troops of the First Army, who were reviewed on the 31st, began their northward march the following morning. During the occupation of the Austrian provinces the headquarters of Prince Frederick Charles were ordered to be established at Prague, and his army to lie between that city and the Thaya, with the Army of the Elbe on its west and the Second Army on its north and east. On the morning of the first of August, the last of the Prussian troops broke up from their positions on the Marchfeld, and began to retrace their steps towards the north. There was no need now to advance prepared to form up for battle, no scouts were required to steal along in front of the columns, skirmishers were not required to beat through the woods and search the villages alongside of the line of march, the staff-officers did not need to ride forward to gaze anxiously through their field-glasses for indications of an enemy, so the troops were allowed to march easily and carelessly along, and as far as possible the marches were arranged so that the infantry might move by separate roads from the cavalry and artillery, and press forward at their own pace, unincommoded by horsemen or waggons.

Though only two-thirds of the First Army remained to be reviewed by the king on the 31st, and the rest were already several marches before them, it was wonderful to see what an extent of country was occupied by the same troops when moving which two days before were clumped together on the small strip of ground near Gänserndorf Along every road and every lane poured long columns: here battalions of infantry, formed of soldiers swinging along carelessly in loose formation and with open ranks, generally singing in loud chorus the Prussian equivalent to "Home, sweet home," "*Mein schönes Heimath's Land;*" there, long glittering lines of *cuirassiers* twisted and twined between willow-trees and vineyards, standing out with their burnished armour bright and dear against the green foliage of the copses or thickly-planted vines; further off the march of a regiment of Uhlans could be detected by the tall spears and fluttering pennons which rose above a swelling piece of ground or a plantation of dwarfed oak; while a heavy, rumbling noise, toned down by distance, through which rose faintly the voices of the singing soldiers, told that the batteries were moving along the main road to Nikolsburg.

Every village was teeming with soldiers, who were quartered in every house, but, though the inhabitants were often inconvenienced by having to find the requisite accommodation for the men, they were very friendly, though they did not scruple openly to say they were extremely glad it was the last time they would be obliged to be the involuntary hosts of the multitudes of foreigners who, however agreeable and friendly, still took up a great deal of room. The villages of this part of the country had a harder time than those of Bohemia and Moravia, inasmuch as for many days the whole of the Prussian armies had been concentrated between Nikolsburg and the Roszbach, but by some wonderful means every village now had plenty of food and wine to sell to hungry and thirsty officers and soldiers—a marvellous fact, for they had been long shut out from Vienna, whence the inhabitants said they drew all their usual supplies; but as this was a good wine country, and poultry and eggs do not generally come out of capital cities, it is just possible that these statements might have been advanced as an excuse for the high prices by means of which they were doing their best to wring from the pockets of the passing Prussians a set-off against the heavy taxes they expected to be levied by the Austrian Government to pay the expenses of the war.

Still, the villagers and the soldiers were on excellent terms; and as the troops were parading on the 1st, to march away, there was a good deal of handshaking and loud protestations of mutual esteem and goodwill. The inhabitants made no complaints against the troops, and had no grounds to make any. The soldiers spoke well of their entertainers, though there was a theory in the ranks that the wonderful abundance of wine was only a direct consequence of the admirable supply of water which the valley of the March boasts, and some of the men could detail graphically the different gradations of colour, from purple to very light red, which their daily beverage underwent during the period of the Prussian occupation of the district

On the afternoon of the 1st, the headquarters of the First Army were all ready to march in the direction of Iglau, *en route* for Prague, where they were to be established until the conclusion of peace, or until such an apparently improbable event should occur as the expiration of the armistice without the conclusion of a treaty. When all was ready, horses saddled, saddle-bags packed, and every preparation had been made to evacuate Ebenthal, a telegram arrived ordering Prince Frederick Charles to march to Lundenburg, and thence to proceed by rail with some of his troops to the capital of Bohemia. The field post-office and some of the baggage had already moved off and were well on their way to a village named Peirawerth, which would have been the first halting-place had the original route been adhered to. It was useless to recall them, so orders were sent to them to move to Zisterdorf, where the staff joined them on the morning of the 2nd, after a short march over the undulating country which lies between the March and the great highway from Nikolsburg to Vienna.

The land was now bare of its corn crops, for the harvest was already nearly over, and stretched away in a rolling plain of bare stubble land, broken here and there by bright green patches of vineyard, which contrasted refreshingly with the monotonous yellow, or by clumps of pollard willows or stunted oaks, which cluster round the little watercourses in the hollows. A miserable little town at the best of times, off the main road, hot, white and dusty, Zisterdorf that day looked worse than usual; it had been for some time occupied by troops, who had left untidy *souvenirs* of the encampments of horses in the market-place and streets in the shape of remnants of down-trodden straw and fodder.

Every house had been more or less tenanted by soldiers, and the traces of their visit were still extant in the crushed bundles of straw which formed their sleeping-places, and now lay in most of the rooms disregarded by the dirty inhabitants, and afforded a copious supply of waifs and strays to be carried by the feet of everyone who went out of the house along the passages and into the unpaved street, where the marks of the numerous waggons which had passed through the town were preserved in deep rough ruts sunk far into the mud, which had since been hardened by the heat of the sun. But men who were turning homewards from the end of a successful campaign faced cheerfully even the dirty rooms and straw-covered floors of this worst class of German village; so the staff-officers did not grumble, but made up their minds to it, and looked forward to Prague as a happy haven, where clean beds would at last be found.[3]

A march of twenty-five miles brought the headquarters of the First Army on the 3rd August to the village of Eisgrub, where they were established in the *château* of Prince Lichtenstein, said to be the most beautiful country-seat in the territories of the *Kaiser*. The *château* inside consisted of long series of wide halls, high corridors, and magnificent rooms, decorated and adorned with oak carving of rare workmanship, and precious suits of ancient armour, where stood furniture of exquisite finish and taste, and the walls of which were hung with glorious old pictures recording the noble deeds done by the house of Lichtenstein. Outside stretched away into the far distance long *vistas* of pleasure-grounds, the green turf of which was thickly studded with clumps of full-grown cedars, tulip-trees, and coppice-beech, grouped among other more common but not less beautiful trees, with so high a skill that all trace of art was concealed, and Nature was courted so skilfully as to be outrivaled.

The River Thaya, which flows through the grounds, was by hidden means constrained to form wide lakes or narrow winding creeks

3. It may not be uninteresting for anyone who happens to have that rare piece of property, a good map of this part of the country, to see how the different divisions of this army were billeted, as it serves as an example of the manner in which divisions have been quartered during the advance, and shows what extent of country each body of troops occupies in its nightly quarters when moving. The fifth infantry division occupied Laab, Hoflein, Ruhhof, Rothenseehof, Neudorf, Neusiedl, Hanitthal, Reiselbrechtsdorf, Wülzershofen. The sixth division was in Gross Teijar, Erdberg, Klein, Grillowitz, Waltrowitz, Klein Olkowitz, Zulb, Klietemanns, Raissenbrück, Josewitz, Isefeld, Malberg, Zwingendorf, Derhhof, Carlhof; the seventh division, in Guttenfeld, Bartelsbrünn, Schafferhof, Stuttenhof, Prerau, Wildendürnbach, Poltenhof, Ruffersdorf, Kirchstätden, Zabern, Falkenstein, Pugsbrünn, Stutzenhofen, Gutenbrünn, Offenthal, Schwenwarth; the eighth division, in Nikolsburg, Voitelsbrünn, Drasenhofen, Tunstkirchen, Steinabrun, Garrenthal, Haithof, Feldsberg, Eisgrub, Keudek, Pilgram, Evrett, Mitlowitz. The reserve artillery was parked in Grussbach, Neuhof, Sihoenau, Grafendorf, Auschanhof, Tröllersdorf, Neusiedl, Pardorf, Illemnitz, Bergen, Dannowitz, Weistenitz, Guldenfurth. It may be seen from this what an extent of country even a small portion of this army required, for the above list does not include the quarters of the cavalry corps, but of only four infantry divisions, with their reserve artillery.

of dark blue water, which in some places washed with a tiny wave raised by the gentle summer breeze against sloping banks of emerald turf, sometimes lay calm and still under the shelter of the woods, reflecting the light green weeping willows which overshadowed it, and floated their lowest leaves upon the surface. Where the trees did not occupy the ground, bright beds of carefully-tended flowers, jets of water springing from quaintly constructed fountains, orange-trees loaded with bright yellow fruit, flowering shrubs covered with full blossoms, and bushes of nearly full-blown roses of every shade and hue, threw just the proper amount of life into the picture to prevent it from being melancholy, and make it sublime.

Never had it been more admired than on this day. Men who had come over down-trodden cornfields, destroyed villages, woods cut away for palisades or abattis, and trees torn down and shivered by tempests of shells, required no knowledge of landscape gardening, no wisdom in architecture, to make them heartfelt admirers of the peaceful prospect here; they saw its beauty, and felt it. Prince Lichtenstein himself could not have been more satisfied than his unknown guests that his property lay where no skirmish had to be fought, no defence made in his *château*, and no attack directed against it

The headquarters of the crown prince had been here for twelve days before the place was occupied by Prince Frederick Charles, but no traces had been left of the former tenants, either in the house itself or the adjoining grounds. Troops had been in and around Eisgrub for more than a fortnight, yet no trees had been broken, no grass cut up by horses' feet, no flower-beds trampled down; all the servants and inhabitants, with two exceptions, were well pleased with the Prussians, and were perfectly satisfied that the soldiers they had been told were little better than barbarians were very easy-going quiet sort of people after all. The two exceptions were the chief butler and the head game-keeper. The former had a great grievance—the whole of the wine in the cellar of Feldsberg, a neighbouring property which also belongs to the Lichtenstein family, had been "required" by the Prussian commissariat It was in vain to urge that some of it had been thirty years in bottle, that it would not bear carriage, or even that the key of the cellar had been lost.

The commissariat officers would take no denial; if keys were not forthcoming, doors could be broken open; as for the not standing carriage, the troops would take their chance of that, and probably the great age of the wine would compensate for any deterioration it might undergo by shaking. Finding all excuses unavailing, the unwilling functionary had to yield up his keys, and in silent agony to see what he had watched with an almost fatherly care for many years, and had been intended for the consumption of far more delicate connoisseurs, carried out of the cellars by working parties of soldiers, stowed away in rough provision waggons, and carted off to be served out as rations to Prussian troops. What comfort was it to him that he was assured the wine would be paid for when the war was over? No money could buy such vintages again, and even if it could, the present generation could barely hope to drink it.

The second complainant, the gamekeeper, was more indignant than sorrowful; it appeared that a number of soldiers belonging to some regiment of the Second Army quartered near Eisgrub organised a *battue* on their own account, and with their needle-guns succeeded in killing a large number of the deer which were in the park. "But," as he said triumphantly, "we forwarded a complaint to the crown prince himself. This step, by the tone in which it was announced, seems to be supposed to have resulted in some terrible punishment being inflicted on the nefarious sportsmen who expended Prussian Government ammunition on unoffending stags, instead of against the enemies of their country; but what was actually the fate of these violators of the game laws, or whether, as the gamekeeper evidently thinks, the commander-in-chief of the Second Army carried out some such penalty against the delinquents as those which were enacted by the laws of William the Conqueror against similar offenders, has not been recorded. It is certain that a body of military police remained as watchers of the deer park during the rest of the time that the Army of Silesia was here, and that after the appeal to its commander no *zündnadel-gewehr* prevented the deer from roaming about in undisturbed safety.

On the 2nd August the king's headquarters moved to Prague; the next day he went to Berlin, whither he was accompanied by the crown prince, to be present at the opening of the Prussian Chambers. The troops of the First Army were about Eisgrub that night, the next day most of them crossed the Thaya. The headquarters of Prince Frederick Charles left Lundenburg on the morning of the 4th, and by that evening every Prussian soldier was out of the Crown lands of Austria. There was great reason to rejoice that the army was now free to move its position, and was not tied down by the necessities of war to the Duchy of Austria, for cholera had within the last few days broken out among the inhabitants with great violence.

In Lundenburg the people were said to be dying at the rate of ten an hour; this appeared to be the exaggerated report of the frightened inhabitants, but there is no doubt that the pestilence was very prevalent, and was causing much mortality among the country people. The Prussian troops had suffered, but not to a very great extent, and more cases had been cured than had proved fatal. It was hoped that change of quarters, rest, and plenty of food would soon free the troops of the disease; but it was feared that it would rage among the natives, who had little to eat, and could hope for little from the vintage, for the late frost in this spring nipped the early vines, and almost ruined the crop of grapes.

On the morning of the 5th August, at four o'clock, the headquarters of the First Prussian Army broke up from Eisgrub, by a short march reached Lundenburg station, and thence by railway to Prague, where Prince Frederick Charles remained until peace was definitely signed, and no possibility remained of his army being required again for the present. Although only one battalion of *Jägers* formed the escort of the train which brought the prince and his staff, yet the number of carriages required to convey the whole of the heads of departments who moved with headquarters, their servants and horses was very great; and on account of the numerous curves in the line, the long train was only able to jolt so slowly along that, although it left Lundenburg at half-past six in the morning, it did not arrive at Prague till midnight.

Slow and tedious as the journey was, and much as at the time the impatient officers grumbled, they had good cause to be grateful for the tardiness with which it was driven, for the next morning intelligence was received which told that a train, following a few hours after, in trying to go faster, met with a terrible accident. On account of the great amount of military traffic on the line, which had lately formed the artery of communication and supplies for the three united Prussian armies, railway carriages had been brought from Saxony and even Prussia to supply the necessary transport. These carriages for the most part ran on three pairs of wheels, instead of on two, as do those which in time of peace run along this line, and which for the most part the Austrians drew back with them when they retreated. The Saxon carriages, built for straighter lines and gentler curves, were very liable on such a line as that which from Brünn twists and winds up the valley to Prerau to run off the rails.

It was thus that the accident occurred. One of the six-wheeled carriages flew off the rails, turned over, and formed a barricade, against which and each other the twelve succeeding ones were shivered. Five men were killed, and eight were seriously hurt; many horses suffered, and seven belonging to the king were killed. This unfortunate accident affords a moral, inasmuch that it shows that not only must the permanent way be entire and safe, but the rolling stock used must be suited to the particular line, if railways are required to afford in time of war not only powerful but also rapid means of transport.

The railway journey was from the front to far in the rear of the great Prussian armies. At Lundenburg, and for some distance north, all the roads which could be seen from the line were swarming with infantry, cavalry, and artillery, winding slowly along in a northerly direction; further on were reserve store trains, ammunition columns, heavy artillery, and all the numerous waggons which must follow in the rear of a great host of fighting men; at Brünn was a garrison of Mülbe's reserve corps, the soldiers of which crowded the station to catch a glimpse of the commander-in-chief of the First Army; here too, were the officers of the staff of the crown prince, who were waiting here till they received definite orders as to their further journey from their commander, who had been hurried to Berlin to take part in the opening of the Chambers. Further north, beside roads and near villages, could be seen dark blue heavy waggons, packed in regular order, which formed the rearmost line of the reserve artillery and ammunition trains, and further north still the stations and towns were garrisoned by regiments of *Landwehr*.

Nothing could be more striking to Englishmen, who had long been accustomed to hear the Prussian army described as a sort of hurried levy of untrained militiamen, than the appearance of these troops. Fine and strong as were the men who fought in the foremost ranks during the campaign, Prussia had in reserve behind them troops formed of soldiers equally tall, equally strong, older and better grown, in these *Landwehr* levies. Most of the privates are men of good situation in life, for, after completing their terms of service in the line, they go into business or professions, and generally have secured comfortable incomes; but at the call of their country they quit their affairs, and return to serve in the ranks, and bring with them to their soldier's duty an education and intelligence which can be found in the armies of no other country in Europe; nor, as can be seen from the garrison of this place, have they in private life forgotten one item of their former military training.

They are grand troops, the very *beau idéal* of a soldiery; and they are well led, for their officers, nearly all of noble birth, are men who have formerly served in the army, and who in time of peace live upon their estates in the same districts as the soldiers they command in war are drawn from; so that these *Landwehr* levies unite with their superior education and intelligence a chivalrous affection for their chief, such as characterised the privates of the bands who fought so gallantly for the House of Stuart.

The *Landwehr* soon began to move back into Prussia, and were disbanded to return to their homes; their places were taken by the troops of the armies, which had been engaged in the field, and which occupied the greater part of Bohemia and Moravia until the conclusion of the definite treaty of peace.

The city of Prague was not visibly affected by the presence of a Prussian garrison. The shops were all open; trade went on even more briskly than usual, for the *Landwehr* officers were generally rich, and spent their money freely; but it must have taken the citizens some time to recover from the officers and soldiers of the garrison the money they had to contribute for the expenses of, the occupation of their town by the Prussians.

Prince Albrecht, the commander of the cavalry corps, reached Prague on the 10th of August, but he did not bring his troops with him, for they had been scattered through the country to facilitate the supply of the large amount of provisions and forage which so many horsemen daily required. The infantry of the armies of Prince Frederick Charles, the Crown Prince, and the Army of the Elbe, were also scattered through Bohemia and Moravia in small divisions, which took up the positions they held until the plenipotentiaries who were assembling at Prague had affixed their signatures to the definitive treaty of peace.

Some of the infantry corps of the Guard were stationed at Prague for a few days, but only as a temporary measure.

On the 10th August a brigade of cavalry of the Guard corps marched through the town on their way to the north, for the whole of this corps was to be scattered among the villages between Prague and Theresienstadt This brigade consisted of the *garde du corps*, the *cuirassiers* of the Guard, and a battery of the horse artillery of the Guard; it was the heavy brigade of the Guard cavalry, and corresponds in the Prussian service to our Household cavalry. The *garde du corps* were dressed in the same way as our *cuirassiers*; their men, though not so tall as the soldiers of the Life-guards, looked as if they rode heavier upon their horses, for they carried, even upon active service, the long black boot, and were encumbered with an enormous kit.

Their uniform was white, their *cuirasses* and helmets of a burnished golden colour; the men looked strong, solid, and healthy; the horses were thin, but in wonderful condition, considering that they had within seven weeks marched from Prussian Silesia to the banks of the Danube and back to Prague. The Guard *cuirassiers*, who followed, were dressed in the same manner as the *garde du corps*, except that they had blue facings instead of scarlet, and wore the ordinary cavalry overall The long squadrons of bright bay horses looked exceedingly well, and even the most prejudiced advocate of light cavalry, and nothing but light cavalry, if he had that day seen Prince Albrecht's heavy horsemen returning from their campaign, must have owned that the days in which heavy cavalry are of use in war are not yet numbered. The experience of this campaign has taught that needle-guns and rifled artillery have no more driven cavalry, and even very heavy cavalry, from the field of battle than they have from the theatre of war; but it has been found that, in the shock of closing squadrons, small men and light horses must go down before the powerful onset of stouter assailants.

The Prussians found that, in future, cavalry must be formed and equipped so as to allow strong troopers to be brought into the field; but strong troopers ride heavily, and heavy loads tell fearfully on horses on the line of march; so, to secure power in the charge with rapidity of movement, the dead weight which cavalry horses now carry must be reduced almost to nothing, and the horse must be required to bear little more than the rider, his arms, his cloak, and a light saddle. Valises will have to be carried in waggons in rear of the regiments, or left at some convenient place whence they can be forwarded to the front by railway or water transport when the army halts.

In this war the Prussian cavalry gained a glorious and unexpected reputation from its conduct in the field; but its horses suffered much from marching, especially in crossing the highland country which lies on the frontiers of Bohemia and Moravia. The cavalry felt the effects of the rapid movements more than the infantry; yet the Prussian foot-soldier marched under almost every disadvantage which dress could inflict. His helmet was horrible, both as to comfort and appearance, his clothes were uncomfortable, the trousers without gaiters hung clammily against the calf on a rainy day, or collected inside them a layer of mud which rubbed uneasily against the ankle. The inconvenience of the dress was shown whenever a battalion started to march; the first thing the soldier did was to divest himself of his helmet, and sling it from his waist-belt, where it dangled uncomfortably against his legs; he unbuttoned his coat, and after a few days' experience scarcely ever omitted to stuff the lower parts of his trousers into his boots, which thus afforded a gaiter with the advantage of requiring neither buttons nor straps, as do those in use in most armies.

Prussian officers themselves acknowledged that the dress of their army could not be compared to that of the Austrians either for efficiency or appearance. It only shows what splendid stuff the Prussian troops are made of when they performed such prodigies of marching as marked their victorious course under these disadvantages, and also weighed down by their heavy knapsacks, which, although of a better construction than those of most armies, were hardly required, and though present were seldom looked into in the actual campaign.

Railways and improved roads have made great alterations in the necessities of a warrior, both by shortening the duration of campaigns and facilitating transport. Europe will never again see any decently-organised army waiting many weeks for the arrival of a siege train, for the carriage of which all available transport is required, so that from want of means of sending stores forward the troops in the front are shivering in tattered clothes and suffering painfully from unbooted feet. Soldiers need no longer be weighed down by heavy loads upon their backs, held back from their real use—marching and fighting—to be converted into beasts of burden. A spare shirt, a change of shoes, and a pot of grease, is about all that a foot-soldier need carry with him, besides his arms, ammunition, and some food.

On the morning of the 17th, the greater part of the first division of the infantry of the Guard marched into the town, and marched past before Prince Frederick Charles. Some of the division had arrived a few days before, but only that day made their formal entrance with their comrades, who early that morning reached the suburbs. In an open space about a mile and a half without the ramparts the whole of the troops who were to march in were assembled about eight o'clock, and a little after began moving towards the Ross Thor. There they filed through the gate, halted at the top of the market-place for a few moments to form their columns, passed before the prince, and disappeared into the narrow winding streets beyond, some to take up billets for a few days in the town, others to pass through and move to their positions in the villages further north.

The scarlet and gold squadrons of the Guard hussars led the way, the most smartly-equipped regiment in the Prussian service, whose officers wear the Hessian boot, the true leg-dress of the cavalry soldier. Behind them came the first infantry regiment of the Guard, with their white facings and silver ornaments; this is the celebrated regiment of Potsdam grenadiers, to fill the ranks of which with enormous men Frederick William I. culled giants out of every country in Europe, and made every Prussian Embassy, from London to Vienna, a recruiting-office. The men are not quite so tall now as those handed down to Frederick the Great; but still they worthily support the title of grenadiers, for no private in the battalions was less than six feet high, and the stature of the greater part exceeded that figure.

The companies were weak, for many of the tall soldiers who marched with their eagles from Prussia sleep at Chlum beside the chief who led them forth, General Hiller; many were in hospital with wounds, and not a few had been left behind on account of sickness; for the cholera had been among those who passed through the action of Trautenau and came scatheless out of the battle of Königgratz. Then came the fusiliers of the Guard, not quite so big as those who had gone before, but on the average taller men than the English Footguards. Behind these marched the dark green sections of the *Jägers* of the Guard, whose recruits are picked from all the foresters and gamekeepers of Prussia—marksmen of unerring aim, skirmishers of high intelligence, who know full well how to avail themselves of every stump and hillock, and how, lurking behind shelter, themselves in safety, with every bullet to bring down an enemy.

A gap of some hundred yards separated the *Jägers* from the second brigade, first in which came the 2nd regiment, men and officers marching in forage caps. There was not a helmet to be seen in their ranks, for on going into action at Trautenau this regiment to a man threw away then: heavy helmets, and thus rid themselves for the campaign of a cumbrous head-dress in a manner which did not draw forth such unqualified approval from the military authorities as did their conduct on the line of march or under fire. Behind the foot soldiers came the artillery of the division, followed by the provision columns and ambulance waggons, whose fine-drawn horses told of many a heavy pull over the rugged roads of Bohemia and Moravia.

The parade marching of the infantry of the Prussian Guard has been renowned ever since its recruits were so harshly drilled by the stem soldier who first formed it. Since that time great alterations have been made both in the tactics and treatment of the men; the Prussian grenadiers no longer move in the field in the stiff unbending formation which regarded soldiers only as machines.

But while the Prussians have lately adopted a system of manoeuvres for field service which unites immense elasticity with great rapidity of movement, they have not failed to observe that the foundation of all tactical pliability lies in previous solidity and precision; that troops who cannot move well on parade rarely can be of much use in service, and that before infantry soldiers can dash about as skirmishers they must be able to move accurately in more solid formation. This was well shown by the Guards who marched into Prague on the 17th August. As the battalions passed the prince not a line wavered, not an opening was seen between the shoulders of the men; solid and compact, the companies swept rapidly along in lines as even as if they had been ruled, while every foot fell in measured cadence to describe a step of equal length.

The 18th was the birthday of the emperor of Austria. Notwithstanding the presence of the Prussian garrison, it was celebrated with all due honours by the civil guard of the town. Early in the morning the town guards paraded, and marched through the street with sprigs of oak leaf in their hats, music playing, and swords drawn, while numbers of Prussian soldiers off duty crowded the foot pavements to gaze at them, and Prussian guards turned out to present arms to the Austrian standard of the ancient city of Prague, which was carried in their midst. After the civil guard had marched through the principal streets, the fire engines followed, decked with flags and preceded by a band.

The Prussian authorities made no objection to the celebration of the day; in fact, they encouraged it, for they made a point of allowing everything to go on in the Austrian towns they occupied as if no foreign troops were present, and no Prussian sentries stood upon the ramparts or occupied the guard houses. In consequence there was good feeling between the soldiers and the townspeople, between whom there arose many personal friendships, though the latter did not scruple, even openly, to say that, though they found the Prussians much more pleasant than they could have expected any enemies to be, they would not be sorry when their visit was over, and Prague was again garrisoned by the white uniforms of the *Kaiser*.

On the 19th, some more of the Guard corps marched into the town, while those that arrived two days before marched out to die north to occupy positions nearer Theresienstadt, and to make room for the new arrivals. The troops that came in were the yellow Uh-lans of the Guard and the Elizabeth regiment. The infantry arrived very dusty, for they had a long march in the morning; but they went through the streets up to the Pulver Thurm, near which Prince Frederick Charles was waiting to receive them, with the same even front and steady tramp as the grenadiers who came in two days before, and swept past the commander-in-chief of the First Army in the unwavering lines which always characterize a Prussian parade. The men of this regiment, destined for lighter duties, were not so tall or stout as those of the first brigade, but they were still large men, with great depth and breadth of chest, and, though dusty, looked anything but tired from the hot march.

The cavalry, like all lancers, looked smart, and, except that the horses were thinner than when they left Berlin, and that some of the squadron did not show then: proper strength, exhibited small signs of having just come off a campaign. The people of Prague were so much accustomed now to the perpetual arrival of troops that few generally collected to see a regiment march in, but on this day, as the troops arrived just as mass was over and the congregations were pouring out of the churches, a considerable crowd stopped to gaze upon the Prussian guardsmen, who marched along between the thronged pavements, overtopping like giants the staring Bohemians. Some Austrian officers who were prisoners on parole, several having their arms in slings, on account of wounds received at Münchengrätz or Sadowa, could not conceal their admiration of the Prussian troops. For a time they gazed silently; but as company after company swept along, their countenances brightened up, and as the last battalion came they could no longer refrain from expressing in words their surprise and wonder that soldiers could be so perfectly trained within a period of three years' service.

Fine as the men were who marched into Prague, many held that they did not come up to the *Landwehr* levies. The latter are older men and better filled out, and their ranks contain those whose education has been supplemented by application to trades or professions; and *Landwehr* men are not men who have been hastily recruited and rawly trained, they have all served for three years in the regular ranks, they are all true soldiers, and soldiers of such a sort as every general and every statesman would wish to see available for the service of his country.

The definitive treaty of peace was signed between Austria and

Prussia at the Blue Star Hotel at Prague, on the 23rd August Austria was represented by Baron Brenner, Prussia by Baron Werther, as Count Bismarck had gone to Berlin at the same time as the king, to be present at the opening of the Chambers on the 5th August.

The treaty of peace definitively signed, was as follows:—

In the name of the Holy and Indivisible Trinity.

His Majesty the King of Prussia and His Majesty the Emperor of Austria, animated by a desire of restoring the blessings of peace to their dominions, have resolved to convert the Preliminaries signed at Nikolsburg on the 26th of July, 1866, into a definitive Treaty of Peace.

To this end Their Majesties have appointed their plenipotentiaries as follows:—

His Majesty the King of Prussia:—

His *Kammerherr*, Effective Privy Councillor and Plenipotentiary, Charles Baron von Werther, Grand Cross of the Royal Prussian Order of the Red Eagle with Oak-leaves, and of the Imperial Austrian Order of Leopold; and,

His Majesty the Emperor of Austria:—

His Effective Privy Councillor and *Kammerherr*, Ambassador Extraordinary and Plenipotentiary, Adolph Marie Baron von Brenner Tilsach, of the Imperial Austrian Order of Leopold, and Knight of the Royal Prussian Order of the Red Eagle, First Class, &c.

Who have met in Conference at Prague, and having exchanged their powers, drawn up in good and proper form, have agreed to the following Articles:

Article 1—For the future there shall be lasting peace and friendship between His Majesty the King of Prussia and His Majesty the Emperor of Austria, as well as between their heirs and descendants, their Stales and subjects.

Article 2.—That the 6th Article of the Preliminaries of Peace signed at Nikolsburg on the 26th of July of this year may be carried out; and inasmuch as His Majesty the Emperor of the French, by his authorised emissary to His Majesty the King of Prussia, officially declared at Nikolsburg on the 29th of the same month of July, *qu'en ce qui concerns le Gouvernement de l'Empereur la Vénise est acquise à l'Italie pour lui être remise à la paix*, His Majesty the Emperor of Austria on his part conforms to this declaration, and gives his consent to the union of the Lombardo-Venetian Kingdom with the Kingdom of Italy, without imposing any other condition than the liquidation of those debts which have been acknowledged charges on the territories now resigned, in conformity with the Treaty of Zurich.

Article 3.—The prisoners of war shall be at once released on both sides.

Article 4.—His Majesty the Emperor of Austria recognises the dissolution of the late German Bund, and gives his consent to a new formation of Germany, in which the Imperial State of Austria shall take no part. Moreover, His Majesty promises to recognise the closer Federal relations which His Majesty the King of Prussia is about to establish north of the line of the Maine, and also agrees that the German States to the south of this line shall form an union, the national connection of which with the Northern Confederacy is reserved for a more defined agreement between both parties, and which is to maintain an international independent existence.

Article 5.—His Majesty the Emperor of Austria transfers to His Majesty the King of Prussia all the rights he acquired under the Peace of Vienna on the 30th of October, 1864, to the Duchies of Holstein and Schleswig, with the understanding that the people of the northern district of Schleswig, if, by free vote they express a wish to be united to Denmark, shall be ceded to Denmark accordingly.

Article 6.—At the desire of His Majesty the Emperor of Austria, His Majesty the King of Prussia declares himself willing, on the approaching changes in Germany, to allow the territory of the Kingdom of Saxony to remain within its present limits, reserving to himself the right of settling in a separate Treaty of Peace with the King of Saxony the share to be contributed by Saxony towards the expenses of the war, and the position henceforth to be held by the Kingdom of Saxony within the North German Confederation. On the other hand. His Majesty the Emperor of Austria promises to recognise the changes about to be made in North Germany by His Majesty the King of Prussia, territorial changes included.

Article 7.—In order to settle the property of the late *Bund* a commission shall meet at Frankfort-on-the-Maine within, at most, six creeks after the ratification of the present Treaty, at which all formal claims and demands upon the German Bund are to be made, and to be liquidated within six months. Prussia and Austria will be represented in this commission, and all the States belonging to the late *Bund* are allowed the same privilege.

Article 8.—Austria is at liberty to take from the forts of the late *Bund* all that belongs to the Empire, and from the moveable property of the *Bund* the proportionate share of Austria, or otherwise to dispose thereof. This provision extends to all the moveable property of the *Bund*.

Article 9.—The civil officers, servants and pensioners of the Bund will receive the pensions already accorded in due proportion, but the Royal Prussian Government undertakes to manage the pensions and allowances hitherto paid from the Treasury of the *Bund* to the officers of the late Schleswig-Holstein army and their families.

Article 10.—The allowance of the pensions granted by the Imperial Austrian Government in Holstein is agreed upon. The sum of 449,500 dollars Danish in 4 *per cent* Danish bonds now lodged in the hands of the Imperial Austrian Government, and belonging to the Holstein Treasury, will be repaid immediately after the ratification of this Treaty. No adherent of the Duchies of Holstein and Schleswig, and no subject of Their Majesties the King of Prussia and the Emperor of Austria, is to be prosecuted, troubled, or in any way molested in his person or his property on account of his political position during recent events and the recent war.

Article 11.—In order to defray a portion of the expenses incurred by Prussia on account of the war, His Majesty the Emperor of Austria promises to pay to His Majesty the King of Prussia the sum of 40,000,000 Prussian dollars. From this sum, however, the amount of the costs of war which, by virtue of the 12th Article of the before-mentioned Treaty of Vienna of the 30th of October, 1864, His Majesty the Emperor claims from the Duchies of Schleswig and Holstein, and which are valued at 15,000,000 Prussian dollars, together with 5,000,000 Prussian dollars as an equivalent for the free maintenance of the Prussian army in the Austrian States which it occupied till the conclusion of the peace, is to be deducted, so that only 20,000,000 Prussian dollars remain to be paid. Of this sum half is to be paid on the exchange of the ratifications of this Treaty, the other half three weeks afterwards.

Article 12.—The evacuation of the Austrian territories now occupied by the Royal Prussian troops will be completed within three weeks after the exchange of the ratifications of the Treaty. From the day of such exchange the Prussian General Governments will confine their operations to purely military matters. The details with respect to the manner in which this evacuation is to be effected are settled in a separate protocol, which forms an appendix to this Treaty.

Article 13.—All treaties and agreements made by the high contracting parties before the war are hereby revived in full force, so far as they are not invalidated by the dissolution of the German Bund. More especially the General Convention between the States of the German Confederation on the 10th of February, 1831, together with more recent resolutions thereto appertaining, will remain in full force as between Prussia and Austria. The Imperial Austrian Government declares, however, that the Coinage Treaty of the 24th of February, 1857, is deprived of its chief value for Austria by the dissolution of the German *Bund*, and the Royal Prussian Government declares itself ready to join with Austria and the other interested parties in the negotiations that may arise on the abolition of this Treaty. The high contracting parties likewise agree that as soon as possible they will enter into negotiations for a revision of the Commercial Treaty of the 11th of April, 1865, with a view to a further alleviation of burdens on both sides. In the meanwhile, the said Treaty is restored to its full force, with this provision, that both the high contracting parties reserve to themselves the right to cancel it after six months' notice.

Article 14.—The ratifications of the present Treaty shall be exchanged at Prague within a week, or, if possible, within a shorter period.

In witness whereof, &c.

Werther.

Brenner.

Prague, August 23rd, 1866.

The ratifications of this treaty were exchanged on the 29th August at Prague.

On the 28th, Prince Frederick Charles broke up his headquarters at Prague, and the whole of the Prussian troops who had been lying in Bohemia and Moravia during the progress of the negotiations for peace between Prussia and Austria commenced their march back towards the Prussian frontier. The men were not sorry to leave Bohemia, for the cholera had been among them during their stay in that country, and many had fallen victims to it

On the evening of the 26th, General von Lengsfeld, the commander of the artillery of the First Army, was carried off after two days' illness—the third Prussian general who had died from cholera since the commencement of the armistice.

As a consequence of the exchange of the ratifications of peace, the Prussian troops began to vacate Austrian territory, and by the 18th of August there was not a spiked helmet or a needle-gun in Bohemia or Moravia. The Guards, the third, fifth, and sixth *corps d'armée* marched by road; the other corps were moved by railway. The first corps moved by Oderberg, the second by Görlitz, the fourth from Brünn by Prague, the eighth by Nürnberg and Aschaffenburg, the fourteenth division by Gera and Cassel to Hanover, the second reserve corps by Hof. The Army of the Maine held its position until peace was concluded with Hesse-Darmstadt.

A Prussian garrison had already occupied Mayence, the keys of the fortress having been handed over by the Bavarians, who were in garrison there, as soon as peace was concluded between Prussia and Bavaria.[1] What right Bavaria had to deliver up the fortress, which her troops avowedly only held as representatives of the forces of the Bund, no one can tell; but as no German Power was in a position to remonstrate, and as France, who was more concerned than any other European Power in the fate of Mayence, appeared to consent, though not quite tacitly, to the arrangement, the Prussian colours waved without molestation over the fortifications which guard the mouth of the valley of the Maine.[2]

On the 27th the unwounded prisoners who had been captured during the campaign were exchanged at Oderberg. The Prussians liberated 523 Austrian officers and 35,036 non-commissioned officers

1. See chapter 4.
2. On the 6th August, France demanded Mayence from Prussia, but afterwards withdrew the demand.

and men; but this was not the total muster-roll of the Austrian prisoners who fell into the hands of the enemy, for 13,000 wounded who could not yet be removed still remained in Prussian hospitals. Austria gave back about 450 Prussian unwounded non-commissioned officers and men, and about 120 wounded were unable to be moved. There were also seven Prussian officers liberated. On the same day about 5,000 prisoners, who had been taken from the Bavarian and Hesse-Cassel troops, were released.

Count Bismark, who was formerly a major of *cuirassiers* was promoted to the rank of lieutenant-colonel; but this promotion was not his reward for the part he has taken in late events; it occurred only in the natural order of things. The headquarters of Prince Frederick Charles moved by rail to the Prussian capital.

Berlin was very empty: the usual garrison and the crowds of officers who generally fill the streets were all away with the army. Over many doors were painted up the red crosses which marked that within subscriptions were received for the military hospitals and wounded. At the doors of the public offices, and at those of several shops and hotels, little padlock-boxes painted with the black and white stripes of the Prussian colours, and labelled "*Für die Verwundete*," invited the alms of those who loitered or who passed by. Here and there a convalescent soldier was seen, with his hand bandaged up or his arm in a sling.

Preparations were, however, being made for the triumphal entry of the army, when the lamentations of the maimed and the wailings of widows and orphan children were to be drowned in the clash of military bands, and the applause of the crowd. Would not the money that this festival cost have been better expended on the families of those who died, and on the men who had been rendered unable to work for their livelihood, in fighting the battles which had given so much glory and so many broad miles to Prussia? Military pensions were very low. Widows with helpless children and disabled men who could labour no longer for bread could hardly regard one day's acclamations from an excited populace as a compensation for a life-long misery.

In the first sitting of the Special Committee of the Prussian House of Deputies on the loan demanded, which was held on the 29th August) the total cost of the war was stated by government to amount to 88,000,000 *thalers*. The single items were as follows:—

1. Mobilization of eleven *corps d'armée* at 42,000 men each, 25,500,000 *thalers*.

452

2. Current expenditure of the war till the end of August, 33,800,000 *thalers*.

3. Demobilization of the troops, 1,700,000 *thalers*.

4. Resupplying the *depôts* of arms and clothing after the war, 27,000,000 *thalers*. To the total of 88,000,000 resulting from the above must be added 20,000,000 to defray the cost of keeping the army on a war footing till January 1, 1867. The liabilities incurred mostly remained to be liquidated, having hitherto been met only by 20,000,000 of cash taken from the reserve fund, 4,343,000 *thalers* obtained by the sale of railway stock, and some 12,000 *thalers* of surplus moneys from the finance administration of 1865. Large quantities of victuals and other stores were furnished by Prussian and foreign subjects, but the former, though legally obliged to contribute *gratis* horses, corn, &c. while the war lasted, had to be paid within a year of its close. The amount of this and other debts contracted by the Government for railway transport, &c was not specially mentioned in the reports published.

About one-half of the costs were covered by the sums exacted from the defeated States, estimated at a total of 45,143,000 *thalers*. Surely the Prussian successes have been cheaply acquired, if about 43,000,000 *thalers*, with 20,000,000 more to insure the maintenance of peace during the next three months, were all that had to be actually invested. To pay off debts and replenish the Exchequer, a loan of 60,000,000 *thalers* was demanded by the government.

The ministers also asked to be empowered to sell some 30,000,000 *thalers'* worth of railway shares belonging to lines hitherto in part the property of government, but lately disposed of for the above-mentioned sum. Of the money thus realized 27,500,000 *thalers* were to be added to the reserve fund to raise it to the normal height of 40,000,000 *thalers*, while the remainder was to be employed on two iron-plated vessels, which were being constructed and already partly paid for.

Another interesting item of future expenditure occasioned by the war was formed by the contemplated purchase of one more iron-plated vessel for 2,800,000 *thalers*, and the strengthening of fortresses at a cost of 3,500,000 *thalers*. To meet these sums the Finance Minister had 4,000,000 *thalers*, the contribution levied on Frankfort, in hand, and hoped to realize 2,557,000 *thalers* more from the sale of horses on the demobilization of the army.

On the 20th and 21st September, the Prussian *fêtes*, to celebrate the return of the army, took place at Berlin. All the evening of the 19th and till late in the dark hours of the morning of the 20th workmen were busy by torchlight finishing the preparations for the festival, and at sunrise on the 20th the whole of Berlin was decked in holiday garb. From every spire, steeple, and dome, from the heavy tower of the Cathedral and rounded cupola of the Royal *Schloss*, from every housetop and balcony, waived or fluttered a thick, rustling crowd of banners, streamers, and *gonfalons*. In most of the side streets lines stretched from house to house across the way supported flags, which swayed backward and forwards above the heads of the restless, ever-moving crowd which thronged the avenues leading to the Linden, while in the Linden itself every house was decorated with festoons of evergreen and laurel, and showed prominently from some balcony or window the black and white colours of Prussia, often coupled with the crimson and white of the town of Berlin, which, fluttering in the light breeze and the bright sunlight, gave an appearance of intense lightness and life to the heavy masses of building which fringe the street.

In the centre, where between the two paved carriage-roads the avenue of the lindens runs from the Brandenburg Gate to the open space in front of the Royal Palace, the captured guns were ranged in double line below the trees, with their muzzles pointed inwards towards each other, but with a wide space of some fifteen yards' interval between them, through which the troops that were to make their triumphal entry were to pass. Round the bright yellow barrels of the brass ordnance were wreathed garlands of green leaves, which were in many cases prolonged so as to cover the spokes of the wheels or the yellow-painted trails.

In line with the guns and the intervals between them were erected trophies, some representing golden cannon grouped together in artistic confusion, others swords, bayonets, helmets, and muskets, but all bearing groups of the special flags of the different provinces of the kingdom, surmounted by a black and white banner, which carried in its centre the double eagle of Prussia. From lamppost to lamppost, themselves hidden in masses of foliage, from trophy to trophy, stretched garlands of evergreens, so that from the top of the avenue near the Brandenburg Gate to the equestrian statue of Frederick the Great, opposite the palace, one long wreath of laurel fringed the way by which the home-returning warriors were to advance to the open space in front of Blücher's statue, where they were to march past the king. The Brandenburg Gate itself was converted into a temporary arch of triumph. On its summit stood a line of flagstaffs, from which waved long standards that floated heavily even in the brisk breeze above the head of the bronze figure of Victory which adorned the summit, while on either face heavy draperies of bright-coloured bunting hid beneath their well-arranged folds the stonework and the preparations for the evening's illuminations.

Before daylight people began to assemble in the street, and to take up places from which the march of the troops could be advantageously seen, and by nine o'clock a double line of spectators fringed the Linden Avenue, while the pavement of the street, which, being a little higher, gave an advantageous position, was thickly crowded. Most of the windows were well filled, but the number of lookers-on was not so great as might have been expected, and neither the streets nor the houses were so thickly occupied as were those in London on the entrance of the Princess of Wales before her marriage. Still, the number of people that collected to see the entrance was very large, and large tribunes which had been erected in the Pariser Platz, just within the Brandenburg Gate, were thickly crowded with ladies.

A little before eleven, the hour arranged for the troops to enter the town, the king left the palace, and, followed by his staff, rode up the avenue towards the Brandenburg Gate, outside of which he was to meet the troops. He was enthusiastically greeted, and a loud swell of shouts of welcome traced his path till he disappeared through the gate. The queen and the crown princess, with the royal children, followed in a carriage, and met with a similar reception from the people, and in other carriages, which were equally cheered, the Queen Dowager, the Princess Frederick Charles, and the Princess of the Netherlands, who all drove out to the place where the soldiers assembled before their entrance into the town.

Outside the gate the king was received by the troops with due honours and some ringing cheers, which had hardly died away before he had passed along the line, quickly followed by the carriages which contained the ladies of the court, and then took up his post in front of the troops. The line of march was rapidly formed, and the head of the column began moving towards the Brandenburg Gate, while the royal carriages turned and drove quickly back again down to the Linden

Avenue, where their occupants were again loudly greeted, so that the ladies might from the windows of the crown prince's palace witness the parade in front of Blücher's statue.

A few minutes after the carriages had passed down, the head of the triumphal column began to wind in at the gate, led by Field Marshal Count Wrangel, behind whom came a large mass of staff-officers and the military attaches to the various embassies. After a short interval rode General von Roon, the Minister of War, and General von Moltke, the chief of the staff of the king. The greeting accorded to these two, the organiser and the director of the movements of the army, was loud and long, as also that to the two generals who immediately followed them, Von Voigt-Rhetz and Blumenthal, who had been the chiefs of the staff of the First and Second Armies during the campaign. Behind these generals came their adjutants, assistants, and *aides-de-camp*, and the whole of the staff-officers of the two armies.

There was then a pause, and an interval of some hundreds of yards in the column, for the king had halted inside the gate to receive an address from the magistracy of the town, and it was some minutes before he himself appeared. But when he came, and close behind him the crown prince and Prince Frederick Charles were seen riding side by side, the enthusiasm of the people rose high. Hats were taken off and waived in the air, handkerchiefs fluttered from every window, and the cheering went up from the crowded street, and was echoed by the houses with that mighty roar which rises from a great multitude when its heart is touched. Behind the commanders-in-chief of the First and Second Armies rode Prince Charles, the commander of the whole artillery, Prince Albrecht, the leader of the cavalry crops of the First Army, Prince Alexander, and Prince Adalbert.

The troops followed, preceded by a small detachment carrying the standards taken in the war, which were borne this day through Berlin by the men who had taken them in battle. Close behind came the Potsdam regiment of Guards, with the Prince of Würtemberg at its head, but the usual fine marching of this splendid regiment was spoilt by the narrowness of way along which it moved, and by the anxiety of the soldiers to exchange greetings with their friends in the crowd, a lack of discipline which today was excused. Nor did the big men of this regiment present the same imposing appearance as usual, for most spectators saw them from windows raised above the street, the result of which was to give even these large men a dwarfed appearance, and it was only by comparing them with the lines of people through whom they passed that one could actually realize their true stature. Behind these followed the 3rd infantry regiment of the Guard.

These two regiments formed the first brigade of the Guard, and were commanded by General Alvensleben. The second brigade consisted of the fusiliers of the Guard and of the 2nd Infantry regiment The latter marched into Berlin without helmets, for the cumbersome head-dresses of which they undertook to relieve themselves at the action of Trautenau had not yet been replaced; but the people cheered them enthusiastically, for they were the heroes of Rosberitz, and the regiment which left so many of its soldiers round the spot where General Hiller fell.

The next brigade was composed of the *Jägers* of the Guard—riflemen recruited from all the foresters and gamekeepers of Prussia, renowned marksmen, who had done much hard duty during the campaign, and reaped their reward in the loud applause of the people of Berlin—and of a battalion of the Guard of the Grand Duke of Mecklenburg. The entrance of this battalion was a compliment on the part of the Prussian Government to Mecklenburg in return for the loyal manner in which that State stood by Prussia before and during the war, and the people ratified the compliment by the loud greeting they gave to these troops as they passed down the Linden by bursts of cheering, which were renewed again and again.

After the infantry dame the scarlet and gold regiment of hussars of the Guard, followed by small detachments which represented the 12th light blue and silver Weissenfels Hussars, who suffered so severely at Königgrätz, the 3rd Dragoons, who were nearly cut to pieces by their rough *mêlée* with the Austrian *cuirass* brigade at the same battle, and the Magdeburg hussars, who cleared the way for the Prussian infantry at Blumenau; after these the artillery, in a long column, which marched with two guns abreast, decorated with flowers and garlands.

As the troops came out of the Linden Avenue and entered the wide, open space in front of the Palace, they formed upon a broader front, and marched past the king, who took his place in front of the statue of Blücher, with his staff around him, when by an accidental but curious coincidence General Moltke as placed below the statue of Gneisenau, the chief of the staff in the War of Independence. Here the whole of the force passed before the sovereign, and then filed across the bridge over the Spree, and their glittering bayonets and shining helmet spikes disappeared into the streets beyond, still cheered by the crowds in the street and houses until the last were lost sight of. By one o'clock the whole of the troops had passed, and the people quickly separated to go to their homes, for every citizen of Berlin entertained a detachment of the men who made their entry—the rich larger, the poorer smaller numbers, but all some.

A fall of rain during the night of the 20th laid the dust, which the previous day blew unpleasantly about the streets. A cloudy morning allowed the people who took up their places early to see the entry of the second portion of the troops who marched publicly into the town to pass the hours of waiting without being incommoded by the glare which the day before was dazzling to the eyes, and after a time became almost painful. Those who had wished to obtain good places from which to see the troops pass did not this morning take up their positions so very early as they did the day before, since it was found that the crowd was not so great as might have been expected, and many discovered that they had taken a needless precaution by being in the Linden before daybreak. The consequence was that the people were more animated, since they were not already weary before the proceedings commenced. The enthusiasm was greater, the cheering was louder, and there was generally an appearance of more vivacity, enjoyment, and relish on the part of both the populace and the soldiery.

The arrangements and general decorations were much the same as on the previous day. The ground between the Brandenburg Gate and the *schloss*, or old palace of Berlin, which is now not inhabited by the Sovereign, but used for official and state occasions, was divided into four portions. The first was the Pariser Platz, which lies just inside the Brandenburg Gate, and was used as the place of the formal greeting of the king by the magistracy and a detachment of fifty-five young ladies, who presented an address in poetry. The second portion was the Linden Avenue, in the centre of the Linden Street, down which the troops marched, and which in the Berlin triumph played the same part as the Via Sacra in those of Ancient Rome. The third portion was the open space which extends from the statue of Frederick the Great to the bridge over the Spree, in which the troops marched past the king; and the fourth was the open place and garden in front of the *schloss*, which was used for the celebration of the *Te Deum,* which this afternoon was sung after the last of the troops had marched past.

On each side of the Pariser Platz tribunes were raised for spectators, which were entirely draped with the red and white colours of the town of Berlin. Behind these, numerous masts were raised, which bore gonfalons of the black and white Prussian colours, with silver-coloured shields deviced with the eagle of Prussia or the bear of Berlin. On either side of the entrance to the Linden Avenue from the Pariser Platz tall trophies were erected, which bore groups of alternate Prussian and Berlin flags, raised above pedestals formed of gilt cannon. Along either side of the Linden Avenue were raised on pedestals, hidden in masses of garlands of laurels and oak leaves, gilt bronze figures of Victory, each of which bore upon a shield with azure ground the name and date of one of the actions of the war, inscribed in golden letters; round these shields were bronze borders, on the top of which was placed the Prussian eagle, while above the head of the figure drooped the national flag, supported on either side by the more cheerful colours of the metropolis. The height from the ground to the top of the flagstaff over each figure was thirty-two feet.

The names of the battles inscribed on these shields were:—June 26, Liebenau, Türnau, Podoll; June 27, Nachod; June 27, Langensalza; June 27, Oswiecin; June 27, Hünerwasser; June 28, Münchengrätz; June 28, Soor; June 28, Trautenau; June 28, Skalitz; June 29, Gitschin; June 29, Königinhof; June 29, Jaromier, Schweinschädel; July 3, Königgrätz; July 4, Dermbach; July 5, Hünfeld; July 5, Zell; July 10, Waldaschach, Hausen; July 10, Hammelburg, Friedericshall; July 10, Kissingen; July 13, Laufach; July 14, Aschaffenburg; July 15, Tobitschau; July 22, Blumenau; July 23, Hof; July 24, Tauber-Bischofsheim; July 24, Werbach, Hochhausen; July 25, Neubrunn, Helmstadt; July 25, Gerchshein; July 26, Roszbrünn; July 28, Würzburg; July 28, Baireuth.

In the alternate spaces between these figures stood on each side of the avenue square pedestals ten feet high, each crowned with a gilt eagle with wings outspread. On the sides of these pedestals were inscribed, as a memorial of the manner in which Berlin heard of the successes of the army, the telegrams received from the seat of war which told of each victory. In the space of each of these pedestals and the trophies on either side bearing the names of the battles were placed two candelabra, each ten feet high, formed of a bronze stalk, standing on a triangular pedestal swathed with laurel wreaths, and terminating at the summit in a gilt basin, which was used in the illumination for burning coloured lights.

All these trophies, pedestals, and candelabra were connected together by festoons of green foliage, which drooped down so as almost to kiss the bright barrels of the captured guns, which were placed between the works of art, and were themselves wreathed with garlands. Two hundred and eight guns, one hundred and four on each side, stood in the Linden Avenue, with their muzzles still begrimed with powder, in a line with the pedestals and figures, and their trails just inside the lines of linden trees which give the name to the street. More cannon might have been exhibited as spoils of the war, for many more were taken; but it was resolved that only those which were captured in open battle should be here, and those which were seized in arsenals or fortified places that fell into the hands of the victors were not brought out for this festival.

Only at the places where cross streets cut the Linden Avenue were these festoons interrupted. At the four corners of each crossing four tall obelisks were raised on triangular bases, which were wound round with spirals of foliage and decorated with the flags of the provinces and allies of Prussia, while from the top of each the national standard floated fifty feet above the ground. On each corner of the triangular pedestal was placed a golden eagle, and diagonally from obelisk to obelisk festoons were stretched, from which hung shields carrying the arms of Prussia and Berlin on either side.

From the end of the Linden Avenue to the bridge over the river the open space was left clear for the marching past of the troops, but tall masts were raised on either side, from the summits of which long streamers fluttered, and festoons were led from one to the other. On either parapet of the bridge four marble statues of Victory were placed, behind which hung flags and drapery, supported by masts raised from rafts anchored in the river.

The large square in front of the *schloss* beyond the bridge was surrounded with black and white painted poles, each of which carried the Hohenzollern shield, surmounted by a banner. In the centre was placed the altar for the public *Te Deum*. A square pedestal, four feet high and forty-eight feet long, supported at each corner a figure of the Angel of Peace, with a palm branch in her hand, and in the centre of each side a statue of Victory distributing laurel crowns, while between the figures flights of low and easy steps, covered with rich carpeting, were placed for the officiating priests. Further steps led from the pedestals to the altar-place, which was raised seven feet higher, and, surrounded by golden candelabra, supported the altar, draped in velvet, above which stood the golden cross, heavy with mouldings of exquisite workmanship.

Behind the altar, between it and the heavy pile of the dome-topped *schloss*, rose a towering statue of Borussia, the classical cognomen of Prussia. With eagle-crowned helmet on her head, the sceptre with the

460

iron cross grasped in her left hand, and her right stretching forth the crown of victory, the figure was placed there as a token to signify that their country considered that her warriors had done well. On either side stood tall trophies of drooped flags and intermingled arms, the pedestals of which bore the names of the most glorious deeds of Prussian arms in the last two centuries.

Emblazoned in letters of gold beside Königgrätz, Kissingen, and Skalitz, were Fehrbellin, 1675; Stralsund, 1678; Hohenfriedberg, 1745; Prague, 1757; Rossbach, 1757; Leuthen, 1757; Zorndorf, 1758; Leipzig, 1813; Paris, 1814; Belle-Alliance, 1815. On either side these trophies were ranged figures of the Electors of Brandenburg and Kings of Prussia; under each was written his motto, war-cry, or favourite expression, with the date of his accession and death. Some of the most striking of these were those of Albrecht Achilles, 1470—1486, "*Nowhere is it more glorious to die than on the field of battle;*" of Friederich Wilhelm, 1640—1688, "*Mit Gott;*" and Friederich Wilhelm III., 1797—1840, "*My time in trouble, my hope in God.*"

A few minutes before eleven, the king, at the head of his staff, and closely followed by the crown prince and Prince Frederick Charles, passed quickly up the Linden towards the Brandenburg Gate. A long, rolling cheer marked his approach, which swelled into a louder and louder shout as he came nearer; from every window handkerchiefs were waved and Prussian colours fluttered, while in the street below every head was uncovered, and the exultant people, with all the strength of their hundred thousand voices, roared out their greeting to their sovereign. The king stopped for a few minutes in the Pariser Platz, and spoke to the wounded, who, still not recovered sufficiently to march in the ranks, were seated in front of the tribunes on either side, then went through the Brandenburg Gate, to place himself at the head of the troops and lead them into the town.

The carriages of the ladies of the Royal family followed soon after, and met with an equally enthusiastic reception as the king himself, both as they went up toward the Brandenburg Gate and on their return after a short inspection of the troops outside the town. Soon the Count Wrangel, who again led the column, came down the avenue, and was greeted very warmly. After him the king's staff followed in the same order as before, last of whom rode side by side the *triumvirate* to whom so much of Prussians success was due—Bismarck, Roon, and Moltke, today all three generals, for the prime minister was promoted to that rank the previous day.

461

A considerable space separated the staff from the king himself, for he had to hear again today the address of the magistracy which he had already received on the former day, and to listen to the poetical welcome delivered by the chief of the detachment of fifty-one young ladies. When he came he was welcomed as loudly, or even more so, than before, more loudly than the day before, for the people were less fatigued by waiting, and were not annoyed by the dust which blew about among them yesterday. From the time the king came down the avenue with the crown prince and Prince Frederick Charles close behind him one incessant shout was maintained until the whole of the troops had passed, which sometimes rose very loud, sometimes slightly fell, but never died away entirely.

The troops which marched in this day were the brigades of the Guards which did not come in before, and some detachments as representatives of line regiments. All were greeted loudly, especially the 2nd Dragoons of the Guard, who defeated the Austrian cavalry at Tischnowitz. To those, however, who had seen the same troops in the field, or directly after the campaign, their appearance was disappointing. The soldiers marched carelessly, and did not preserve either the even formation or the measured swinging stride which distinguishes the Prussian infantry on its usual parades. The day seemed to be regarded only as a holiday and festival, and much more attention was paid to friends in the houses, or alongside the avenue, than to the maintenance of that perfect order in the ranks which is generally so rigidly observed.

After the troops had marched by the king, a portion of them were formed up in the square in front of the *schloss* around the altar. The king, the prince, the staff, and the generals came to the same place, and in the name of the army and nation yielded up their hearts in thanksgiving to Heaven, while hundreds of priests burst forth into the noblest of all songs of praise to the Lord of Hosts and the God of Victories.

On the evening of the 21st, the king assembled twelve hundred of the generals and principal officers who had served in the campaign at dinner in the *schloss*. In the later part of the evening the town was illuminated. Directly after dark the whole city was lighted up. The *schloss* was surrounded by rows of lamps, which stood out bright against the heavy and indistinct background of the massive building, while circlets of coloured lights, high up in the dome, seemed as if suspended in the air without support Opposite the *schloss* bright blue lights burnt, and, raised high upon lofty poles, glistened like stars of dazzling brightness above the museum. These cast a fitful and almost mysterious glow upon the restless crowds, who, notwithstanding the rain, which began to fall early in the afternoon, thronged every street, and clustered in thick swarms around the fountain in front of the museum, where gas jets, introduced among the pipes, from which the water played, glistened through the sparkling cascade.

Every house was illuminated. On public buildings and in many private residences were fiery copies of the national arms, or names of victories inscribed in flame. Down the Linden Avenue and round the statue of Frederick the Great large basins raised on bronze stalks contained blazing *flambeaux*, which blew about wildly in the breeze. In many places words of welcome to the returning soldiers or mottoes recording victory were traced in lamps, which burnt with coloured flames, but nowhere was to be seen a single signal of congratulation for the return of peace. Every fiery inscription, every device of flame, told the fierce joy of the people for victory and conquest, and to the minds of many men foreboded that thirst for further war and for military glory was taking a strong seat in the heart of Prussia.

Where the exterior of the houses was not decked with lamps, or where burning gas did not trace the outlines of the national eagle or the names of victories, inside of the windows were fringes of candles. Everywhere there was light. No window was dark, no house not illuminated, except where the Austrian or some of the neutral embassies broke, by a gap of darkness, the brilliant aspect of a lighted street There were few carriages. The people moved through the city a restless, feverish crowd, from which rose a loud continuous hum of approbation and of triumph, that here and there swelled into a cheer before the residence of a minister or the palace of the king.

A long list of promotions and military advancements was published that day, and it was also notified that a cross of bronze cast from the metal of the captured cannon was to be given to every officer and soldier who had passed through the campaign.

An amnesty, dated the 20th June, was published the same morning, which remitted any punishments not yet completed, or any fines which had been decreed by courts of justice against persons convicted of offences under the 87th to 93rd paragraphs of the statute-book inclusive, and under the 97th to 103rd, or under the law for the control of the press.

In the evening special performances were given in all the theatres in honour of the triumphant termination of the war. Prologues were delivered which detailed the glorious deeds of the army, and the plays, which were written for the occasion, dwelt upon the actions and personal adventures of the late campaign, and recalled the memories of the concluding wars of the first French Empire.

CHAPTER 5

Peace With the South-German States

On the 2nd August, armistices between Prussia and Bavaria, Baden, Würtemberg, and Hesse-Darmstadt, were established, which were to endure until the 22nd August The terms of these armistices were similar to those made with Austria; by them stipulations were also made for the delivery of the fortress of Mainz to the Prussians, and for the unimpeded departure of the South-German contingents from the other Federal fortresses.

By the 22nd August, peace was definitely concluded between Prussia and the governments of all those countries except that of Darmstadt.

The treaty of peace with Bavaria was signed at Berlin on the 22nd of August, by Count Bismarck and Herr von Savigny for Prussia, by Herr von der Pfordten and Count Bray Steinburg for Bavaria. By it Bavaria agreed to pay Prussia thirty million *gulden* as a war contribution in three instalments, the last instalment to be paid within six months of the exchange of the ratifications; to abolish the shipping dues on the Rhine and Maine; and to give up the telegraph stations on the north of the Maine to Prussia. The ratifications were exchanged within twelve days. Peace with Würtemburg was concluded at Berlin on the 13th August The text of this treaty was as follows:—

Their Majesties the King of Würtemberg and the King of Prussia, actuated by the desire of securing to their subjects the blessings of peace, have determined to come to an agreement as to the clauses of a Treaty of Peace to be concluded between them. For this purpose their Majesties have appointed as plenipotentiaries—The King of Würtemberg, his Minister for Foreign Affairs, Baron Karl von Varnbuler, Grand Cross, &c; and his

War Minister, Lieutenant-General Oscar von Hardegg, Grand Cross, &c.; and the King of Prussia, his President of the Council and Minister for Foreign Affairs, Count Otto von Bismarck-Schönhausen, Knight of the Black Eagle, &c., and his Privy Councillor, Chamberlain and Ambassador Karl Friedrich von Savigny, Grand Cross, &c. These plenipotentiaries having exchanged powers and found them sufficient, have agreed upon the following clauses:—

1. Peace and friendship shall henceforth subsist for ever between His Majesty the King of Würtemberg and His Majesty the King of Prussia, their heirs and successors, their States and subjects.

2. His Majesty the King of Würtemberg engages to pay His Majesty the King of Prussia the sum of 8,000,000 *fl.* within two months, towards covering part of the costs incurred by Prussia in the war. By payment of this sum the King of Würtemberg fulfils the compensation obligations undertaken by him in paragraphs 9 and 10 of the armistice convention, signed August 1, 1866, at Eisingen and Würtzburg.

3. As pledge for the payment of this sum the King of Würtemberg will deposit 3½ and 4 *per cent.* Würtemberg State bonds to the amount of the sum to be guaranteed. The bonds to be deposited will be calculated at the quotations of the day, and the guarantee sum will be increased by 10 *per cent,* accordingly.

4. His Majesty the King of Würtemberg retains the right of paying the above-mentioned compensation in part, or wholly at an earlier date, at a discount of 5 *per cent, per annum.*

5. Immediately after the guarantee being given, ,in accordance with Article 3, or after payment of the war contribution has been made, the King of Prussia will withdraw his troops from Würtemberg territory. The provisionment of the troops daring their withdrawal shall be according to the hitherto existing Federal dietary scale.

6. The apportionment of Federal property belonging to the former Germanic Confederation is reserved for a special agreement.

7. The high contracting parties will enter into negotiations for the settlement of the Zollverein relations immediately after the

conclusion of peace. In the meantime the Zollverein Union Treaty of May 16, 1855, and the conventions connected therewith, which have been rendered inoperative by the outbreak of the war, shall again come into operation from the day the ratifications of this present treaty are exchanged, with the understanding that it remains reserved to either of the high contracting parties to allow them to lapse after a notification of six months.

8, Immediately after the restoration of peace in Germany the high contracting parties will cause the assembly of commissioners to agree upon bases calculated to further passenger and goods' traffic upon the railways as greatly as possible, especially to regulate the relations of competition in a suitable manner and to oppose the efforts of individual companies disadvantageous to the public interests of traffic While the high contracting parties are agreed that the establishment of every new railway line conducive to the public advantage is to be permitted and supported as fully as possible, they will also have the principles demanded in this respect by the general interests laid down by the aforesaid commissioners.

9. His Majesty the King of Würtemberg recognises the arrangements made by the preliminary treaty concluded between Prussia and Austria at Nikolsburg on the 20th of July, 1866, and acceded thereto upon his part also, so far as they affect the future of Germany.

10. The ratification of this present treaty shall take place at latest by the 21st of August of this year. In token whereof the abovenamed plenipotentiaries have executed the same this day in duplicate, and appended their signatures and seals.

Done at Berlin this 13th of August, 1866.

Varnbuler,   Hardegg.
Von Bismarck,   Savigny.

Peace with Baden was concluded at Berlin on the 17th August .The first, fifth, sixth, seventh, and eighth articles were the same as those of the treaty with Würtemberg; the tenth and eleventh the same as the ninth and tenth of that with Würtemberg, By the second, third, and fourth articles, Baden agreed to pay Prussia six million *gulden* within two months, as a war contribution. By the ninth article, Baden agreed to abolish the shipping dues on the Rhine.

Peace with Hesse-Darmstadt was only concluded on the 3rd September, to which day the armistice was extended. The text of this treaty was, exclusive of the prologue, as follows:—

1. Peace and friendship shall exist between the Grand Duke of Hesse, and on the Rhine, &c, and His Majesty the King of Prussia, their heirs and successors, for eternal time.

2. The Grand Duke of Hesse engages to pay to the King of Prussia within two months the sum of 3,000,000 florins, to cover a part of the expenses caused to Prussia by the war. By the payment of this sum the grand duke is released from his obligation to pay the war contribution which he undertook by the Treaty of Armistice on the 1st of August, 1S66.

3. The grand duke provides guarantees for the payment of this money by depositing bonds of the Grand Ducal Loan, when the 4 *per cent.* bonds will be accepted at 80 and the 3 *per cent,* at 70.

4. The grand duke has the right to pay the above contribution either in whole or in part at an earlier date, and if he does so will be allowed a discount at the rate of 5 *per cent,* per annum.

5. Immediately after the deposit of the guarantees mentioned in Article 3, the King of Prussia will withdraw his troops from the Grand Ducal territory. The supplying of the troops in their return march will be conducted in accordance with the supply regulations of the late *Bund.*

6. The regulations for the disposal of common property which belonged to the late *Bund* are reserved for special agreement.

7. The high contracting powers will enter into negotiations directly after the conclusion of peace for the reform of the Zollverein Treaty. In the meantime the Zollverein Treaty of the 16th of May, 1865, and the agreements connected with it, will come again into force on the day of the exchange of the ratifications of the present tre.ity. Each party reserves the right to annul the same after six months' notice.

8. All other treaties and stipulations concluded between the high contracting powers previous to the war come again into force.

9. The high contracting powers will, immediately after the establishment of peace in Germany, cause commissioners to

meet, in order to establish rules to facilitate as much as possible the railway transport of passengers and goods between the two States, and to oppose the pernicious effects of individual administration in favour of common interests; and as the high contracting powers are agreed that the establishment of a new railway communication based on their common interests should be allowed, and, as far as possible, furthered, they will cause the plans thereof to be settled by the above-mentioned commissioners.

10. The Grand Ducal Government declares itself agreed to the conventions which Prussia has made with the princely House of Taxis for the abolition of the Thurn and Taxis postal monopoly. In consequence the whole postal administration of the Grand Duchy of Hesse is to be given over to Prussia.

11. The Grand Ducal Government binds itself to allow no other than a Prussian telegraph station in Mayence. In like manner the Grand Ducal Government cedes to Prussia unlimited power to construct and to use telegraph lines and telegraph stations in the other districts of the Grand Duchy.

12. The Grand Ducal Government will completely discontinue to levy navigation tolls on the Rhine, and also navigation dues (Tariff B in the Convention of the 31st of March, 1831), as also dues for lading (Supplementary Articles to the Convention of the 31st of March, 1831), from the day on which the same measure shall be adopted by the other German States on the banks of the Rhine. The high contracting parties undertake to do the same with regard to the still existing navigation tolls on the Maine.

13. The Grand Duke of Hesse recognises the Definitions of the Preliminary Treaty concluded between Prussia and Austria at Nikolsburg, on the 26th July, 1866, and also on his part enters into the same as far as the future of Germany is concerned.

14, His Royal Highness the Grand Duke of Hesse cedes to the King of Prussia with all rights of sovereignty and dominion—

(1) the country of Hesse-Homburg, inclusive of the district of Meisenheim, but exclusive of the two demesnes Hötensleben and Oebisfelde belonging to Homburg, which lie in the Prussian province of Saxony.

(2) The following portions of territory which belong to

the province of Oberhessen:—(1.) the district of Bie-donkofp; (2.) the district of Vöhl, including the enclaves Eimelrod Höringhausen; (3.) the north-western part of the district of Giessen, which includes Frankenbach, Krumbach, Königsburg, Fellingshausen, Biber, Haina, Rodheim, Waldgirmes, Nauheim, and Hermannstein, with the ground within their landmarks; (4.) the district of Rödelheim; (5.) the part of the district of Nieder-Urfel which is under the Grand Ducal Sovereignty.

15. The Grand Duke of Hesse enters into the North German Confederation on the basis of the reform project of the 10th June, 1866, with all his territory lying north of the Maine, while he binds himself to cause the elections to Parliament to be in proportion to the numbers of the population. The Grand Ducal contingent from the territory separated in consequence of this and belonging to the Northern Confederation passes under the supreme command of the King of Prussia.

The King of Prussia cedes to the Grand Duke of Hesse, in lieu of the territorial cessions in the province of Oberhessen the following districts, with all rights of sovereignty and domin-ion—

(1.) The formerly Hesse-Cassel district Katzenberg, with the places Ohmes, Wolkenrode, Ruhlkirchen, Leibelsdorf.

(2) The formerly Hesse-Cassel district Nauheim, with all rights of property, the bath establishments and salt works in Nauheim, as well as the places Dorheim, Nauheim, Schwalheim, and Rödchen.

(3.) The district of Reichelsheim which lies to the east of the above, and formerly belonged to Nassau, with the places Reichelsheim and Dornassenheim.

(4) The enclave of Trais on the Lunda, which formerly belonged to Hesse-Cassel.

(5.) The woodland demesne formerly belonging to Hesse-Cassel which lies between the Grand Ducal dis-tricts of Altenstadt and Bönstadt.

(6.) The districts of Dortelweil and Nieder-Erlenbach, which formerly belonged to Frankfort.

(7.) The district of Massenheim, which formerly be-longed to Hesse Cassel.

(8.) The district of Haarheim, which formerly belonged to Nassau.

(9.) The portion of the district of Mittel-Gründau, of about 1,700 acres, which formerly belonged to Hesse-Cassel.

These districts enter into the province of Oberhessen. In the next place, the district of Rumpenheim, which formerly belonged to Hesse-Cassel, lying on the left bank of the Maine, is ceded to the grand duke, with all rights. The descriptions of the boundary lines lie over.

16. Agreements between the contracting powers with reference to the archives, officials, military stores, &&, of the ceded districts will be concluded by special commissioners.

17. The books, manuscripts, and other articles which were in the library of the Cathedral of Cologne previously to the year 1794, and are now in the Grand Ducal museum and library, are to be handed over to the King of Prussia that they may be restored to Cologne, to which the different volumes and articles belong. There shall be one commissioner of either side, who in case of dispute are to choose each an impartial referee, to whom the case shall be referred.

18. The Grand Ducal Government agrees to prolong the present contract between a number of bathing-house proprietors in the town of Kreuznach and the Grand Ducal salt work of Karl Theodor Hulle, for the supply of lixivium and salt water at the present rate, until the Prussian Government shall find itself able to acquire this salt work.

The Grand Ducal Government will also lay down pipes for the supply of this to Kreuznach.

19. The ratification of the present Treaty shall take place at the latest on the 15th of September.

| (Signed) | Dalwigk | Bismarck. |
| | Hofman | Savigny." |

A supplementary convention with reference to Articles 14 and 15 was to the following purpose:—

1. Prussia enters into all rights hitherto possessed by the Hessian Government in the ceded districts, and pays pensions in the

hitherto existing way. Officials and servants are guaranteed to be allowed to remain in their present situations if they will enter the Prussian service; if they, however, return to the Hessian within three months after the close of this treaty, they are to be paid up to the time of their return by the Hessian Government. The same rule applies to the districts ceded to Hesse, which formerly belonged to Nassau and Cassel. Soldiers who are of the rank of officers in the ceded districts shall be sent to their homes; and their time of service in the Hessian Army will be reckoned as if in the Prussian service. Officers and military officials ranking as officers are to be allowed to choose into which service they will enter.

2. The commissioners chosen by Article 16 of the Treaty will settle all matters of detail which are connected with the present negotiations.

3. All the inhabitants of the ceded districts are to be allowed full freedom to settle in whichever country they choose for a year after the exchange of the ratifications.

4. In the cession of the country of Hesse-Homburg, the pictures, library, and such things in the Ducal Castle are not included, as likewise the orangery. These all remain the private property of the Grand Ducal House.

5. At the same time as the Prussian troops withdraw, the civil officers in the lands at present occupied will cease to act, and the Grand Ducal officials will return to their duty.

6. It is understood that the same regulations for the post and telegraph services as are to come into force in the province of Oberhessen, from its feeing included in the *Bund*, are by this Treaty to be extended to the provinces of Stachenburg and Rheinhessen, which are south of the Maine.

7. All prisoners of war are to be exchanged in eight days after the ratification of this Treaty.

8. In reference to the right of garrisoning Mayence, which is to remain to Prussia, the same arrangements are to hold good between the Prussian garrison and the territorial government as did between the former garrison of *Bund* troops and the territorial government.

9. All telegraphic offices in Mayence must be entirely in the

hands of the Prussian Government The railway telegraphs will not be disturbed unless in cases of absolute necessity for the security of the fortress.

10. The Grand Ducal Government is ready to surrender the direction of the administration of the Main-Weser Railway from the Hesse-Cassel frontier to Giessen into the hands of the Prussian Government, provided that the latter will give to the former a yearly account of its receipts.

11. If the Prussian Government wishes to send troops returning from Bohemia or Bavaria by the Schwandorf to Würzburg line, the Grand Ducal Government will transport them, and will be paid for the same by the Prussian Government.

12. No subject of the grand duke or of the King of Prussia is to be annoyed or disturbed in person or property on account of his conduct during the time of the war.

13. In reference to Article 18 of the Treaty, it is understood that this article only holds good till the year 1892, if the said salt-work is not acquired by Prussia before that year.

14. The ratifications of this convention are to be exchanged at the same time and place as those of the above Treaty.

CHAPTER 6

Formation of the North-German Confederation

After the war the Prussian Government determined to annex the territories of Hanover, Hesse-Cassel, Nassau, and the free town of Frankfort On the 17th August, Count Bismarck introduced a bill into the Prussian House of Deputies for this annexation, which was carried by two hundred and seventy-three votes, in a house of three hundred members; and these territories became provinces of the Prussian monarchy. By the treaties with Austria, made before and after the war, Schleswig, Holstein, and Lauenberg were also united to Prussia. The area of Prussia, which before the war was 127,350 square miles was increased to 160,000. Her population was raised from 19,000,000 to 23,000,000 inhabitants.

In August the governments of Prussia, Mecklenburg-Schwerin, Mecklenburg-Strelitz, Saxe-Weimar, Oldenburg, Brunswick, Sachsen-Altenburg, Sachsen-Coburg-Gotha, Anhalt, Schwarzburg-Sonder-shausen, Schwarzburg-Rodolstadt, Waldeck, Reusz (of the younger line), Schaumburg-Lippé, Lippé, Lübeck, Bremen, and Hamburg, concluded an offensive and defensive treaty for the maintenance of the independence and integrity as well as of the internal and external security of their States, and undertook a common defence of their territory, which they guaranteed by this treaty.

2. The aims of the Confederation shall be definitely laid down by a Confederate Constitution on the basis of the Prussian outlines of the 10th of June, 1866, with the co-operation of a common Parliament which is to be called together.

3. All existing treaties and agreements between the Confeder-

ates are to remain in full force, as far as they are not expressly modified by the present Federation.

4. The troops of the Confederates are to be under the supreme command of the King of Prussia. The duties during war will be arranged by special settlements.

5. The Confederate Governments will appoint votes to be taken on the basis of the elective law of the Empire of April 12, 1849, for deputies to the Parliament, and will call the latter together in common with Prussia. They shall also send Plenipotentiaries to Berlin, in order to settle the Bill of Confederation in accordance with the outlines of the 10th of June, 1866, which is to be laid before the Parliament for its consideration and approval.

6. The duration of this agreement is until the formation of the new Confederation, and is settled for one year if the new Confederation is not concluded before the expiration of a year.

7. The above Treaty of agreement shall be ratified and the ratifications exchanged as soon as possible, at the latest within three weeks of the date of its conclusion, at Berlin.

The only States north of the Maine which, on the conclusion of this treaty, were not united to Prussia in the North-German confederacy, were Reusz (of the older line), Saxe-Meiningen, and the Kingdom of Saxony. The Regent, Princess Caroline of Reusz, soon, however, concluded the same treaty with Prussia.

On the 20th September, Duke Bernhard of Saxe-Meiningen, who did not approve of the new order of things, abdicated, and the new duke, George, declared himself ready to enter the confederation.

After a long delay, peace was finally concluded between Prussia and Saxony, on the 21st of October. By this treaty, Saxony entered the North-German Confederation. The Saxon troops were to form an integral portion of the North-German army, under the supreme command of the King of Prussia. Saxony was to pay a war contribution of ten millions of *thalers*,[1] in three instalments; the last instalment was to be paid on the 30th April, 1867; one million, however, was to be remitted, in consideration of Saxony giving up to Prussia so much of the railway between Görlitz and Dresden as ran on Prussian ground. A direct railway was to be constructed from Leipsic to Zeitz. All the Saxon telegraphs were to be given up to Prussia. The salt monopoly in

---

1. £1,500,000.

Saxony was to be abolished. The fortress of Königstein was to be given over to Prussia; Dresden was to be held by a garrison half Prussian half Saxon, the latter not to muster more than three thousand men. The commandant was to be appointed by the King of Prussia, the second in command by the King of Saxony.

The conclusion of the treaty of peace with Saxony was virtually the last act in the formation of the North-German Confederacy. The Parliament had afterwards to agree formally to the settlement of the Confederation, as it did in the early months of 1867, but practically, Northern Germany was united into one confederate power under the sceptre of the House of Hohenzollern by the end of October, 1866.

BOOK 10

CHAPTER 1

The War in Italy

When Prussia declared that she regarded the Austrian proceedings at Frankfort as a declaration of war, King Victor Emmanuel, in consequence of his alliance with the government of Berlin, declared war against Austria. On the 20th of June, General La Marmora, the chief of the Staff of the Italian army, sent an intimation to the commandant of Mantua that hostilities would commence on the 23rd. The Archduke Albrecht accepted the intimation, and made ready for action.

The theatre of war [1] in which the troops of Italy and those of the Austrian Army of the South were about to engage has formed one of the ordinary battlefields of Europe. Its communications with Vienna lay along two lines. The railway which from the capital by way of Trieste runs through Goerz, Udine, Treviso, and Padua to Verona, connects Vienna with the quadrilateral: and the line by Salzburg, Innsbrüch, Botzen, and Roveredo, although not completed between Innsbrüch and Botzen, afforded a subsidiary line for the supply of troops camped under the protection of the fortresses.

The quadrilateral itself consisted of the strongly intrenched camp of Verona, on the Adige, the smaller and less important fortress of Legnano, on the same river, the lately strengthened fortifications of Peschiera at the issue of the Mincio from the Lago di Garda, and the fortress of Mantua, which lies further down the Mincio, with its citadel and Fort St George on the left bank, and its minor works on the right banks of the stream. The fortified Borgo Forte supports the line of the Mincio in front of the confluence of that river with the

---

1. This theatre of war has been so frequently and so lately the scene of memorable campaigns, and so many good maps of it exist, that it is thought unnecessary to supply one.

Po, while Venice, with many adjacent forts, protected the rear of the quadrilateral towards the sea.

The Italians, in acting against the quadrilateral with their army concentrated, could either advance across the Mincio and rush headlong against its parapets and embrasures, or, by advancing from the Lower Po, push towards Padua to cut the main line of communication with Vienna. General La Marmora had a very difficult problem to solve, and was not fortunate in the conditions he introduced into its solution. His information as to the Austrian designs was manifestly exceedingly faulty, while that of the Archduke Albrecht was excellent The Italian general was bound to assume the offensive, for political reasons. Neglecting a plan for his campaign which had been forwarded from Berlin,[2] he adopted one which, as is believed, had been determined upon in case of the prosecution of the war of 1859, by a mixed council of French and Italian officers.

The main attack was to be made against the Mincio and the Adige by the principal army, under the personal command of King Victor Emmanuel. Each corps of this army was reinforced by one division, so as to consist of four divisions. These corps were the first corps of General Durando, consisting of the divisions of Cerale, Pianelli, Sirtori, and Brignone; the second corps, under Cucchiari, consisting of the divisions of Angioletti, Longoni, Cosenz, and Nunziante; the third corps, under Della Rocca, consisting of the divisions of Cugia, Govone, Bixio, and the Crown Prince Humbert. If, as has been before observed, each division may be reckoned at twelve thousand men, with eighteen guns, the whole army, including the division of reserve cavalry, mustered about one hundred and forty-six thousand men, with two hundred and twenty-eight guns.

The Italian staff from its information concluded that the Archduke Albrecht would await an attack behind the Adige, and determined to cross the Mincio, and occupy within the quadrilateral the ground not held by the Austrians. After taking up this position, and so separating the fortresses from one another, the main army was to give a hand across the Adige to General Cialdini, who with his corps was to cross

---

2. The plan of campaign forwarded from Berlin is supposed to have been the product of General von Moltke, and to have been as follows:—A corps of Italians of about one hundred thousand men was to cross the Lower Po to the east of the Mincio, and take up a strong position between Mantua and Legnano, and by their presence hold the Austrian Army within the quadrilateral, while the remainder of the Italian army, by aid of the fleet, disembarked in the neighbourhood of Trieste, and pushed directly upon Vienna.

the Lower Po from the direction of Ferrara. General Garibaldi, with his volunteers, was to support the movement on the left by attacks on the passes which lead from Northern Lombardy into the Tyrol. On the day immediately succeeding the declaration of war, the main body of the king's army was moved towards the Mincio. On the 22nd June, the day before hostilities were to commence, the headquarters of the first corps were at Cavriana, those of the third at Gazzoldo, those of the second at Castelluccio. On the night between the 22nd and 23rd, the king in person moved to Goito.

The passage of the Mincio was intended to take place at seven o'clock on the morning of the 23rd, by the division of reserve cavalry, the whole of the third corps, and Cerale's, Sirtori's, and Brignone's divisions of the first corps,—altogether about eighty-seven thousand combatants, with one hundred and thirty-eight guns. To cover this advance, Pianelli's division of the first corps was to remain on the right bank of the Mincio, and watch the garrison at Peschiera. Cosenz's division of the second corps and one brigade of Nunziante's division were detached towards Mantua; the other brigade of Nunziante's division was posted on the right bank of the Po, to keep open the communications with Cialdini, and to observe Borgoforte.

Angioletti's and Longoni's divisions of the second corps were to remain near Castelluccio, and if they received no further orders, to cross the Mincio on the 24th and support the other two corps, which on that day were to be in position between the Mincio and the Adige.

On the morning of the 23rd the passage of the Mincio by the Italians commenced. Cerale's division crossed at Monzambano, Sirtori's at Borghetto and Valeggio, and Brignone's at Molino di Volta, between Volta and Pozzolo. The reserve division of cavalry passed at Goito, and was followed by the four divisions of the third corps. The two divisions of Bixio and of Prince Humbert were pushed to Belvedere and Roverbella, the divisions of Govone and Cugia encamped near Pozzolo and Massimbona. The three divisions of the first corps bivouacked near the points where they had crossed the stream on the left bank of the Mincio.

The reserve cavalry pushed patrols to Villafranca, which fell in with a few weak detachments of Austrian cavalry, but no other signs of the enemy were perceived.

A coronet of heights lies on the south side of the Lago di Garda, upon the left bank of the Mincio, which, on the south, between Valeggio and Somma Campagna, sinks into the plain of Villafranca, on the east, between Somma Campagna and Santa Giustina, drops towards Verona and the valley of the Adige. Since the very slight nature of the enemy's detachments discovered by the cavalry confirmed the Italian headquarter staff in the idea that the Archduke Albrecht did not intend to hold the ground between the Mincio and the Adige, but to await an attack behind the latter stream, it was resolved to occupy these hills, and, on the 24th, to take up a position on the heights between Valeggio, Castelnovo, and Somma Campagna.

The orders issued for the Italian advance of the 24th June were, that the first corps should leave the division of Pianelli on the right bank of the Mincio, and should move the headquarters of its main body to Castelnovo. There Cerale's division was to assume a position facing towards Peschiera, while those of Sirtori and Brignone at Santa Giustina and Sona should form front towards Pastrengo and Verona, The line taken up by the first corps was to be prolonged through Somma Campagna and Villafranca by the third corps, and to Quaderni and Mozzecane by the division of the reserve cavalry. The divisions of Angioletti and Longoni were to cross the Mincio at Goito, and take post at Marmirolo and Roverbella, as reserves. Orders were also issued that a field bridge was to be thrown at Torre di Goito, above Goito, and that the field-bridge at Molino di Volta, as well as the permanent bridges at Monzambano, Borghetto, and Goito, should be covered by bridge-heads.

Confident of his information, and without scouring the country with his cavalry, General La Marmora ordered the advance of the 24th to be made only according to the ordinary habit of route marching. The troops did not breakfast before starting, proper rations were not served out to them, and the provision trains followed the columns. No preparation appears to have been made for combat. Scouts do not seem to have been sent out to observe the roads from the fortresses, and the soldiers of the infantry were loaded with their knapsacks under the broiling sun of Italian midsummer. This negligence and temerity met with its just reward.

The Archduke Albrecht had as field troops under his command, the fifth Austrian *corps d'armée,* led by Prince Liechtenstein, the seventh corps, under Field Marshal Maroicic di Madonna del Monte, the ninth corps, under General Hartung, and a division of reserve infantry formed out of fourth and border battalions under General Rodich. After a short time Rodich replaced Prince Liechtenstein in the command of the fifth corps, and General Rupprecht received the command of the reserve division.

As soon as the Prussians entered Holstein, the Austrian commander in Italy concentrated his troops between Pastrengo and San Bonifacio,[3] so that they could be united with facility on either bank of the Adige, in case of necessity for action. After deductions for necessary detachments, the Archduke had three brigades of each corps, and a strong brigade of the reserve division ready for battle. His force was thus ten brigades, mustering about sixty thousand combatants, which the cavalry raised to sixty-two thousand five hundred. To these, two hundred and seventy guns were attached.

At the time that Italy declared war, the reserve division was posted at Pastrengo as the right Austrian wing, the seventh corps at San Bonifacio as the left wing, the fifth and ninth corps were concentrated at Verona. A few brigades were pushed forwards towards the line of the Lower Po, to watch Cialdini. A light cavalry brigade, pushed forward towards the Mincio to watch the army of King Victor Emmanuel, received orders, in case the latter crossed that river, to fall back, without committing itself to any serious action, by way of Villafranca.

This brigade of cavalry withdrew on the 22nd, as soon as the Italians seriously showed that they intended to cross the Mincio, to Villafranca. On the 23rd, when the Italians crossed it, they withdrew further, with no more resistance than the exchange of a few cannon shots near Dossobuono, and that evening took post under the forts of Verona.

On the afternoon of the 23rd, a staff-officer, who had been sent to Somma Campagna, reported to the Archduke Albrecht that the heights near that place were not yet occupied by the Italians, but that heavy clouds of dust could be seen to the south moving towards the Adige.

Archduke Albrecht, who had before thought that the Italians after crossing the Mincio, would move directly upon Isola della Scala to join Cialdini on the Lower Po, was confirmed in his idea by this report from Somma Campagna. He concluded that King Victor Emmanuel was moving, by way of Isola, to Albaredo on the Adige, there to throw a bridge and cross that river. From Goito to Albaredo the distance is over thirty miles. The archduke calculated that the Italians could not reach Albaredo before the evening of the 24th, and that, as they must then throw a bridge, they could only with difficulty com-

---

3. A station on the railway between Verona and Vicenza, and about midway between those towns.

mence the passage of the Adige on the morning of the 25th. The arch-duke calculated that on the 23rd he could occupy the heights by Sona and Somma Campagna, and could, on the morning of the 24th, attack with strong force the Italian flank near Villafranca, while his reserves could at the same time be at Castel d'Azzano.

Acting with this idea, on the afternoon of the 23rd, the Arch-duke removed one brigade of his reserve division to Sandra, whence it pushed detachments towards Castelnovo. The fifth corps, under General Rodich, was at the same time to move to Sona, and send its advanced guard to Zerbare in the direction of Custozza and Valeggio. The ninth corps, which had to make a march of fifteen miles from San Bonifacio, could only reach Verona on the evening of the 23rd, and was therefore ordered to be held as the reserve. The cavalry attached to the different *corps d'armée* was formed into an independent cavalry brigade, so that the archduke now had two brigades of that arm.

On the night between the 23rd and 24th, the Austrian headquarters were moved to San Massimo, and orders were issued that on the 24th, at early morning, the line between Sandra, Santa Giustina, Sona, and Somma Campagna should be occupied, and that then a wheel to the left should be made on Somma Campagna, as a pivot, which would bring the troops on a line from Castelnovo by San Giorgio and Zerbare to Somma Campagna. This movement was to be covered by the two cavalry brigades, which were to advance by Ganfardine and Dossobuono towards Custozza and Villafranca.

The dispositions on both sides thus rendered a collision between the two armies imminent, and brought on the

Battle of Custozza

In the night between the 23rd and 24th, a heavy fall of rain took place, which laid the dust, and made the air cool on the following day.

At three o'clock in the morning of the 24th, the sixth Austrian corps moved on Somma Campagna, the fifth corps, leaving a detachment in Sona, moved on San Giorgio; the reserve division from Sandra, on Castelnovo. The advanced guards of all three corps were pushed further forward, and the cavalry brigades spread themselves in the plain, on the left of the ninth corps. These advanced guards fell in with those of the divisions of King Victor Emmanuel, which were moving in the opposite direction, first with those of the reserve cavalry division and that of Prince Humbert, which were moving from

Villafranca on Dossobuono and Ganfardine, then on that of Bixio, which followed on the left of Prince Humbert, as well as on that of Cugia's division, which was moving on Staffalo, and which was supported by the divisions of Govone and Brignone.

The above-named Italian divisions were engaged on the eastern bank of the Tione. On the western bank of that stream the advanced guard of Cerale's division fell in with the Austrian reserve division near Alzarea, and under the pressure of superior force was compelled to retire to Oliosi, where Cerale made a determined stand. The Archduke Albrecht reinforced his reserve division by Piret's brigade of the fifth corps, from the eastern side of the Tione, while Möring and Bauer's brigade of the same corps advanced against San Rocco di Palazzuolo. The communication between his fifth and ninth corps was secured by the advanced guard of the seventh corps, which was marching from Sona by Zerbare. After a hot fight, in which great bravery was displayed by both sides, Oliosi caught fire, and Cerale was forced to retreat about one o'clock, to Monte Vento. Cerale himself was wounded, and General Villarey, the commander of one of his brigades, was killed.

At Monte Vento, Sirtori's division, which had advanced from Valeggio to Santa Lucia, on the Tione, covered the right wing of Cerale's troops, yet without effect, for the Austrians stormed Monte Vento and drove out Cerale, who was forced to retreat on Valeggio. He was not, however, pursued. General Pianelli, who had been left on the right bank of the Mincio, near Monzambano, hearing that Cerale was hard pressed at Oliosi, on his own responsibility led one brigade of his division across the river, and threatened the right flank of the Austrian advance against Monte Vento.

As soon as Monte Vento was evacuated by the Italians, Bauer's and Möring's brigades advanced against Sirtori, at Santa Lucia. The Italian general quitted his position here because he was not supported on his left, and retreated about three o'clock to Valeggio. The Austrian reserve division had in the meantime advanced against Salionze and Monzambano. By this hour the left wing of the Italian Army had been completely driven from the field, but the battle still was maintained on the eastern bank of the Tione. In this part of the field the Austrian ninth corps had received orders to halt near Somma Campagna, when Cugia, about eight o'clock, advanced by way of Madonna della Croce. General Hartung occupied Berettara and Casa del Sole in force. He soon received orders to advance on Custozza, when he fell in with

Cugia's division, which was supported on the right by that of Prince Humbert The latter was exposed to frequent attacks of the Austrian cavalry, and was often obliged to throw its battalions into square, in one of which the Prince himself found shelter from the enemy's horsemen.

On Cugia's left Brignone was engaged. The latter division was led into action by General La Marmora himself. At Monte Godio it was attacked by the Austrian brigade of Sardier, supported by two other brigades of the seventh Austrian corps. Shortly after mid-day, and after two commanders of his brigades, Gozzani and Prince Amadeus, had been wounded, Brignone was forced to retreat to Custozza. Govone's division was pushed forward in his place.

After Cerale had been driven from Monte Vento, and Sirtori had retired from Santa Lucia, the seventh Austrian corps, supported by the left brigade of the fifth corps, which had now nothing before it, pressed hard on Govone at Bagolino, and took this place from him. Cugia, now outflanked on his left, was forced to quit Madonna della Croce, and at five o'clock the retreat of the Italian army was general. Slowly the third corps retired beyond Custozza, with its left wing on Prabiano, its right on Villafranca. It was not till seven o'clock in the evening that the Austrians occupied the heights of Custozza. Bixio's division and the reserve cavalry covered the retreat across the plain, where some detachments of the second corps also came into action.

The two divisions of Angioletti and Longoni, of the second corps, were to have marched from Castelluccio early on the 24th, and crossing the Mincio at Goito, have moved on Villafranca, where they could easily have arrived by ten o'clock in the morning. They did not, however, march at daybreak, and when General La Marmora, who during the action, for some unexplained reason, instead of sending a staff-officer rode to Goito to send these troops forward, he found there, between three and four o'clock, only a weak advanced guard of those divisions. This was sent forward towards Villafranca, and took a slight part in covering the retreat, but the main body of the second corps had not moved from Castelluccio.

The Italian retreat was made, without any orders from the commander-in-chief, by order of the commanders of divisions. Pianelli's division, after repelling a sally against it by the garrison of Peschiera, retired on Monzambano, Cerale's and Sirtori's on Valeggio, Brignone's on Molino di Volta. Of the third corps Govone and Cugia retired to Valeggio, Prince Humbert and Bixio to Goito. The first corps re-crossed the river on the afternoon and evening of the 24th; the third corps and the cavalry in the night The third corps rallied at Volta, the cavalry between Goito and Cerlango. The bridge of Valeggio was destroyed.

The army of King Victor Emmanuel was withdrawn behind the Oglio. Cialdini, who, on the news of the Battle of Custozza, did not cross the Lower Po, moved towards his left, and posted his troops near Mirandola and Modena, so as to be in close communication with the army of the king.

The Austrians lost nine hundred and sixty killed, three thousand six hundred and ninety wounded, and nearly one thousand prisoners, who were for the most part captured by Pianelli. The Italians lost seven hundred and twenty killed, three thousand one hundred and twelve wounded, and four thousand three hundred and fifteen missing.

A pause in the operations was necessary to allow the Italian army time to recover from the disaster of Custozza. On the 30th, detachments of the Austrian cavalry crossed the Mincio, and pushed as far as the Chiese, but the Archduke Albrecht bad no intention or design of invading Lombardy.

The volunteers under General Garibaldi amounted to about six thousand men. They were divided upon three lines. The main body was collected by the 20th June, in front of Rocca d'Ans, a small detachment was placed near Edolo, on the road which leads through the pass of the Monte Tonale into the Tyrol, another detachment near Bormio on the road which leads over the Stelvio.

On the 22nd June, Garibaldi's main body crossed the frontier near Storo, but found the population of the Tyrol entirely opposed to them, and staunchly loyal to the House of Hapsburg. On the 25th, a sharp combat took place at the frontier bridge of Cassarobach, in which the Italians were worsted. They retired towards Bogolino. Near this town they were attacked by an Austrian detachment on the 3rd July, and again suffered a reverse. In this engagement General Garibaldi was wounded.

The Austrians crossed the frontier by the Tonal and Stelvio roads with small detachments, and several skirmishes took place in these directions between the 23rd June and 3rd July.

As soon as after the battle of Königgrätz Venetia was offered by the Government of Vienna to the Emperor of the French, the fifth and ninth Austrian corps were withdrawn from Italy, and forwarded to the Danube. There then remained in Venetia, besides the garrisons of the fortress, only one Austrian corps, and in the Tyrol a weak detachment under General Kuhn.

The Italian army rested for a space after the battle of Custozza, but an advance was rendered necessary by the alliance with Prussia. The disaster of Custozza had caused both the country and the army to lose confidence in La Marmora. The command-in-chief was given to General Cialdini, who was ordered to cross the Lower Po, and push troops against the Tyrol and into Eastern Venetia.

On the evening of the 7th July, Cialdini, leaving a division to watch Borgoforte, and another near Ferrara, concentrated seven divisions near Carbonara and Felonica, and that evening threw some detachments of light troops across the Po at Massa. On the night of the 8th, three bridges of boats were thrown across the stream at Carbanarola, Sermide, and Felonica, and on the 9th the army crossed at these points, covered from any attack by the marshes which in this direction lie between the Po and the Adige. After having passed the Po under cover of this natural obstacle, Cialdini made a flank march to his right, gained the high road which leads from Ferrara by Rovigo to Padua, and opened his communication with Ferrara by military bridges thrown across the river to replace the road and railway bridges which, on the night of the 9th, the Austrians blew up, as well as the works of Rovigo. On the 10th Cialdini's headquarters arrived at Rovigo, and on the 14th, after securing the passage of the Adige at Monselice, his advanced guard occupied Padua.

The division which Cialdini left under Nunziante, in front of Borgoforte, besieged that place. The batteries were armed by the 16th and opened on the 17th. On the night of the 18th, the place was evacuated by the Austrian garrison, which retired to Mantua, and was occupied by the Italians, who captured there seventy guns, and magazines of all kinds.

As the progress of events in the north pointed to the conclusion of an armistice, the terms of which would compel, in all probability, the troops on both sides to remain in their actual positions, the Italians determined to gain as much ground as possible before diplomacy might cause their army to halt.

Cialdini, on the 19th, had with him about seventy thousand men, and an expeditionary force to reinforce him was being prepared, which would bring into the field about seventy thousand additional combatants. The Austrian troops in Italy which could take the field mustered little over thirty thousand men. That day, the Italian general

486

commenced his advance from Padua. To Vicenza, which on the 15th had been entered by a weak advanced detachment, one division was sent; the remainder of the army moved to the left bank of the Brenta. The right wing marched to Mestre, to cut Venice off on the land side, while the fleet, as was intended, should attack it from the sea. The centre was directed along the railway which leads by Treviso and Udine to the Isonzo; the left wing was to act against the Tyrol. The reserve, which was being brought rapidly forward, was to hold the line of the Adige. Medici's division was to move on Primolano and through the Sugana valley upon Trent, while Garibaldi, with his volunteers, was to act from the west against the same place.

As Cialdini advanced, the Austrian field troops under General Maroicic withdrew from the quadrilateral, and retired gradually behind the Piave, the Livenza, the Tagliamento, and finally, behind the Isonzo. On the 22nd, they evacuated Udine, which, on the 24th, was occupied by the Italians, with two corps. No resistance was made by the Austrians until the Italian advanced guard, on the 25th, passed beyond Palmanovo, when a sharp skirmish took place with the Austrian rearguard. As a truce had, however, been concluded on the 25th, it led to no results. In the meantime, Cialdini had pushed detachments by Schio towards Roveredo and by Belluno, as far as Avronzo, on his left, while on his right his troops were close up to Venice and Chioggia. A truce was agreed upon on the 22nd, which was extended from week to week, until on the 12th August an armistice was concluded. The line of the Indrio was fixed as the line of demarcation between the troops on either side.

As soon as the armistice between Prussia and Austria had been agreed to upon the 22nd July, the Austrian troops which had been transferred from Venetia to the Danube were sent back to the Isonzo, but on account of the subsequent peace were not called upon to act.

In the meantime operations had been carried on against the Southern Tyrol. On the 20th July, Medici received orders at Vigo d'Arzere to push through the Val Sugana upon Trent. He reached Bassano on the 21st, with about twelve thousand men and eighteen guns: the same evening he pushed his advanced guard to Carpano. Hence he detached a regiment to his right and one to his left to turn the works which the Austrians had thrown up at Primolano, to cover the junction of the roads to Feltre and Trent.

On the 22nd, with his main body he marched against these works, which the Austrians evacuated as soon as they heard of their being threatened to be turned. On the 23rd, Medici found the bridge over the Strigno barricaded, but not defended, and, after a slight opposition, that evening entered Borgo. On the 24th he pushed his advanced guards to Pergine and Vigolo. That day General Kuhn telegraphed to Verona for reinforcements, and on the 25th received from that place about eight thousand men. With them and the four thousand he had near Trent, he determined to fall upon Medici, and push him back.

On the 25th a slight combat took place between some of Kuhn's outposts and the Italian advanced guard near Sorda; but nothing further occurred on account of the receipt of the intelligence of the conclusion of the armistice. Garibaldi had made some movements from the west against the Tyrol, but without great success. On the 14th, after crossing the frontier, he fixed his headquarters at Storo. On the 19th he captured the small fort of Ampola. The Austrians made several attacks against the Italian volunteers, who tried to secure the roads leading through the mountains. This irregular warfare led to no great successes on either side. Though Garibaldi attempted to gain as much ground as possible, he did not occupy much at the . time of the conclusion of the armistice. By that date he held the valley of the Chiese for a length of only ten miles from the Italian frontier, and in the Val di Conzei, one of his regiments was advanced two miles to the north of Riva. On the pass over Monte Tonale the Italians were repulsed by an Austrian detachment, and never effected a lodgement beyond the frontier.

CHAPTER 2

Naval Operations

Of the Italian fleet great things were expected. The long coast-line of Italy, and the mercantile habits of the natives of many of her seaboard towns, had for a long succession of years been calculated to foster seamen, and to lay the foundation for an efficient navy. The result of the war caused bitter disappointment to the Italian people.

The Italian fleet was assembled at Tarento in the middle of May, and the command of it given to Admiral Persano. He divided it into three squadrons. The first squadron, under the immediate command of Persano himself, consisted of the ironclad vessels *Re d'Italia, Re di Portagallo, San Martino, Ancona, Maria Pia, Castelfidardo*, and *Affondatore*; a flotilla of five gunboats was attached to this active squadron. The second, or auxiliary squadron, was formed of unplated vessels. In it were the frigates *Maria Adelaide, Duca di Genova, Vittorio Emanuele, Gaeta, Principe Umberto, Carlo Alberto, Garibaldi*, and the *corvettes Clotilda, Etna, San Giovanni*, and *Guiscardo*. The third squadron consisted of three battering vessels and two gunboats; and the transport squadron included fifteen vessels, which could convey in all about twenty thousand men across the Adriatic.

On the declaration of war the fleets sailed from Tarento to Ancona, and cast anchor there on the 25th of June.

Here Persano heard of the disaster of Custozza, and resolved to wait until the new plan for the operations of the land army had been decided upon, leaving one vessel, the *Esploratore*, to cruise outside of the harbour.

On the 27th the Austrian fleet, under the command of Admiral Tegethoff, appeared in front of Ancona. Some shots were exchanged between the *Exploratore* and the leading Austrian vessel, the *Elisabeth*, but no further engagement took place, for, before Persano could weigh anchor and come out to fight, the Austrian fleet retired.

For a length of time Persano remained inactive in Ancona. When Cialdini advanced into Venetia, he was, however, ordered to act, and he determined to attack Lissa.

The island of Lissa lies in the Adriatic, some thirty miles south of Spalato. Between it and the main land lie the islands of Lesina, Brazza, and Solta. Between Lissa and Lesina there is a strait of a breadth of about fifteen miles. In Lissa there are two ports, those of San Giorgio and of Comisa.

On the 16th July Persano weighed from Ancona, The fleet which accompanied him consisted of twenty-eight vessels, of which eleven were iron-plated, four were screw-frigates, two paddle-wheel corvettes, one a screw corvette, four despatch-boats, four gunboats, one hospital ship, and one store ship. The frigate *Garibaldi* remained at Ancona on account of necessary repairs. Messages were sent to all vessels at Tarento or Brindisi to sail towards Lissa, especially to the ram, the *Affondatore*.

On the evening of the 17th, Persano issued orders that Admiral Vacca, with three ironclad vessels and a corvette, should bombard Comisa; that the main force, consisting of eight ironclads, a *corvette*, and despatch-boat, should assail San Giorgio; and that Admiral Albini, with four wooden frigates and a despatch-boat, should effect a landing at the port of Manego on the south side of the island, in rear of the works of San Giorgio. Two vessels were to cruise on the north and east of Lissa during these operations, in order to give timely warning of the approach of the Austrian fleet.

On the morning of the 18th, Vacca began to bombard the works of Comisa, He soon found, however, that his guns could not attain sufficient elevation to do much damage. He gave up the attack, and sailed for Port Manego. Albini at Manego, for similar reasons as Vacca, could not effect a landing, and Vacca sailed to join Persano. The latter had begun to bombard San Giorgio at eleven in the rooming; by three o'clock, when Vacca arrived, he had blown up two magazines, and silenced several of the Austrian batteries. He could not, however, succeed in sending his ships into the harbour, and the prosecution of the attack was postponed till the next day.

On the evening of the 18th the whole of Persano's fleet was assembled in front of San Giorgio, and in the night it was joined by the ram *Affondatore* and three wooden vessels. That evening Persano heard that the Austrian fleet was leaving Fasana to attack him. He calculated, however, that it could not approach Lissa before nightfall on the 19th, and determined to make a second attack upon the island on that day, and issued in consequence the following orders:—

Albini, with the squadron of wooden ships and the gun-boats, was to attempt a landing at Port Carobert, south of San Giorgio. The iron-clads, *Terribile* and *Varese*, were to bombard Comisa, in order to prevent the garrison there from reinforcing that of San Giorgio. The float-ing battery, the *Formidabile*, was to enter the harbour of San Giorgio, and silence the batteries inside. Vacca, with the *Principe de Carignano, Castelfidardo*, and *Ancona*, was to support the *Formidabile*; the *Re di Por-tagallo* and the *Palestro* were to bombard the outside batteries; while Persano himself, with the *Re d'Italia*, the *San Martino*, and the *Maria Pia,* were to prevent opposition being offered to Albini's landing.

The attack was postponed from hour to hour in case Tegethoff might arrive; but when, in the afternoon, the cruisers signalled that no smoke was to be made out on the horizon, the attack began.

The *Formidabile* entered the harbour, and, taking post four hundred yards distant from the Austrian batteries at the extreme end, opened fire. A battery on the northern side told severely upon her, and Per-sano ordered the *Affondatore* to open upon this battery through the mouth of the harbour. This was done, but without much effect.

Vacca formed his three ironclads in single line, steamed into the harbour, and opened on the batteries inside; but he could not effi-ciently support the *Formidabile*, both because she herself covered the Austrian batteries, and on account of the difficulty of manoeuvring in the narrow space within the harbour, which is only about one hun-dred fathoms wide.

He was soon forced to quit the harbour, and was followed by the *Formidabile*, which had lost sixty men, and suffered considerably. The latter was sent the same evening to Ancona for repairs.

The landing was equally unsuccessful. The wind blew fresh from the south-east, and the boats could with difficulty approach the beach on account of the surf.

On the night of the 19th, the ironclads were assembled in order of battle outside of the harbour of San Giorgio. Early the next morning the *Piemonte* joined Persano, who had now in all, thirty-four vessels under his command. On the 20th at daybreak the weather was stormy; yet Persano ordered another attempt to land. The ironclads, *Terribile* and *Varese*, bombarded Comisa. Albini and Sandri, with the wooden vessels and the gunboats, supported the landing at Port Carobert. *The*

Re di Portagallo and the *Castelfidardo* were engaged in some repairs to their machinery; the ironclads remained under steam in front of San Giorgio, awaiting orders.

The surf ran so high that the landing could not be effected, and it was about to be abandoned, when one of the cruisers bore hastily down through the rainy mist, and signalled that the enemy was approaching from the north. Tegethoff with the Austrian fleet was at hand, to raise the attack upon the island.

BATTLE OF LISSA

On the 17th July, Admiral Tegethoff at Fasana heard by telegram of the Italian fleet being near Lissa. He concluded that its appearance there was but a demonstration to draw him away from the coast of Istria. On the 19th, however, fresh telegrams assured him that the attack on the island was serious. He determined to proceed there. His fleet was in three divisions. The first division, consisting of the ironclads *Archduke Ferdinand Max, Hapsburg, Kaiser Max, Don Juan d'Austria, Prince Eugene, Salamander*, and *Drache*, was under the immediate command of Tegethoff. The second division, consisting of the large wooden vessels *Kaiser Novara, Prince Schwarzenberg, Count Radetzky, Adria, Danube*, and *Archduke Frederick*, was led by Commodore Petz. The third division consisted of the smaller wooden vessels, *Hum, Dalmat, Reka, Seahound, Streiter, Velebich*, and *Wall*. Each division of the fleet consisted thus of seven vessels. To it four despatch boats were attached, the *Kaiserin Elisabeth, Andreas Hofer, Stadini*, and *Greif*. Tegethoff had with him thus twenty-five vessels, mounting about five hundred guns.

The Austrian admiral left the roads of Fasana about mid-day on the 19th of June. On the morning of the 20th his despatch boats reported a vessel of the enemy in sight The wind was blowing strong from the north-west At first Tegethoff steered a course from the north-west to south-east, parallel to the Istrian coast, but off Zirona and Solta he altered his course to one directly from north to south.

Persano, as soon as he heard of the Austrian approach, ordered his vessels to form line of battle. The Terribile and Varese were in front of Comisa, so that he had only ten ironclads. The Italian wooden vessels never came into action at all, except by firing some long-range shots.

About nine o'clock the Italian ironclads, formed in single line, were steering almost from west-south-west to east-north-east in three divisions. The first division consisted of the *Maria Pia*, the *Varese*, which arrived about this time, and the *Re di Portagallo*; it was under

492

the command of Ribotty. The second group consisted of the *San Martino, Palestro, Affondatore*, and Persano's flag-ship, the *Re d'Italia*. The third group, under the command of Vacca, consisted of the *Ancona*, the *Castelfidardo*, and *Principe di Carignano*. The *Maria Pia* was at the head of the column; the *Carignano* was the sternmost vessel. When the Austrian fleet came nearer, Persano signalled each ship to go about, so that the *Carignano* led, and the column took a course from west to east.

Persano, at the same time, moved in person from the *Re d'Italia* to the *Affondatore*, which he ordered to take up a position on the flank of the column furthest from the Austrian attack. When Admiral Tegethoff could clearly make out the Italian fleet, it was steering from west to east. He bore down upon it in the following order:—His twenty-one vessels were arranged in three divisions of seven ships each. The first division consisted of ironclads; the two other divisions of wooden vessels. The line of ironclads led, with the admiral's flag-ship slightly in advance, from which the other vessels, falling a little astern, formed a wedge-like order. The seven heaviest wooden vessels followed the ironclads, and were themselves followed by the lighter vessels in a similar formation.

Tegethoff bore down upon the gap between Vacca's three vessels and the central Italian group, and drove his own flag-ship, the *Ferdinand Max*, straight upon the *Re d'Italia*, which he rammed several times, and sank. Only a small portion of the crew were saved. The *Palestro* attempted to aid the *Re d'Italia*, but Tegethoff turning upon her, ruined her steering apparatus. At the same time she was attacked by other ironclads, and quickly caught fire. She fell away before the wind; the fire could not be got under, and with all her ship's company, except sixteen men, she blew up. Thus of the Italian central division two vessels were lost, while the *Affondatore* remained inactive, apart from the battle. The third vessel of this division, attacked by the seven Austrian ironclads, as well as by three wooden vessels, was severely handled, and forced to retreat.

The Italian division under Vacca had, with a north-easterly course, sailed along the flank of the Austrian ironclads as they advanced, and exchanged some broadsides with them. When his leading ship, the *Carignano*, was clear of Tegethoff's ironclads, Vacca ordered a change of direction, and brought his three vessels in line between the second and third Austrian divisions. His fire told severely on both, especially on the *Kaiser*, the flagship of the Austrian second division.

The Italian division under Ribotty, when it saw the central division engaged, altering its course, moved against the Austrian wooden ships, and thus brought them between two fires. Ribotty fiercely attacked the *Kaiser*, commanded by Commodore Petz. Petz, using his wooden vessel as a ram, ran with full steam against the *Re di Portagallo*, and lay then alongside of her. At the same time he was attacked by the *Maria Pia*, and his vessel suffered fearfully.

Tegethoff, by this time, had disposed of the Italian central division, and he brought his ironclads back to aid his wooden vessels. Under their protection the *Kaiser* got away, and was taken to Lissa. A close and fierce battle began now between the whole of the Austrian vessels and the six Italian ironclads, during which the Italian wooden squadron and the *Affondatore* looked on from the distance. The smoke was so thick that either side could with difficulty tell their own vessels; and soon the necessity of hauling off was felt.

Tegethoff signalled to his fleet to form in three columns, with a north-easterly course; the ironclads formed the northern-most line, nearest to the Italians. By this manoeuvre the Austrian fleet was brought in front of the strait between Lissa and Lesina. Vacca, under the impression that Persano had gone down in the *Re d'Italia*, ordered the Italian ironclads to assemble, and with them in a single line steered slowly towards the west, waiting for the Palestro. She soon blew up. It was now about two o'clock, and the action had lasted about four hours. At this time Persano, with the *Affondatore*, joined Vacca's squadron, placed her at the head of the line, and ordered the other vessels to follow her movements. These movements appear to have consisted in no more than a steady pursuit of a westerly course to the harbour of Ancona. By the Battle of Lissa the Italians lost two ironclads, the *Re d'Italia* and the Palestro. The *Affondatore* sunk at Ancona, after reaching harbour. For three days the Italian people were led to believe that a victory had been won at Lissa. The mortification of the defeat which then became known was thereby increased Persano was summoned before the Senate, and was deprived of all command in the Italian navy.

One remark appears patent, even to those who are quite unskilled in naval matters, that in this sea-fight Tegethoff led his fleet, Persano only directed his. Another, that the Italian admiral, with superior forces at his command, allowed an inferior force of his own vessels to be attacked and defeated at the decisive moment by a smaller force of his adversary.

On the 21st, the Austrian admiral returned, without a missing vessel, to the roads of Fasana.

CHAPTER 3

Peace Between Italy and Austria

The armistice concluded between Austria and Italy was to last from mid-day on the 13th August to the 9th September.

In the meantime, negotiations for peace were opened at Vienna; and on the 3rd October a definite treaty was signed. By it Austria recognised the kingdom of Italy, and the cession to it of Venetia by the Emperor of the French. The ratifications were exchanged as soon as possible. The Austrian commissioner-general, Möring, formally gave over Venetia to the French commissioner, General Leboeuf, when a plebiscite took place. The annexation to the kingdom of Victor Emmanuel was almost unanimously voted by the people of Venetia, and Italy became one great country, united under the sceptre of the House of Piedmont, and free of any foreign dominion, from the Alps to the Adriatic.

Appendix 1

Peace concluded at Vienna on the 30th October, 1864, between Austria (Emperor Francis Joseph I.) and Prussia (King William I.) on the one side, and Denmark (King Christian IX.) on the other.

Introduction.—In the name of the Most Holy and Inseparable Trinity, His Majesty the King of Prussia, His Majesty the Emperor of Austria, and His Majesty the King of Denmark, are decided to convert the Preliminaries signed on the 1st August into a definitive Treaty of Peace.

To this end are named as Plenipotentiaries, Baron Charles von Werther, authorised Minister at the Austrian Court, &c., and Mr. Louis von Balen, present Privy Councillor, by His Majesty the King of Prussia; Bernhardt Count von Rechberg, Knight of the Golden Fleece (until 27th October, Austrian Minister for Foreign Affairs), and Baron Adolph von Brenner Felsech, Ambassador Extraordinary to the Danish Court, by His Majesty the Emperor of Austria; Mr. Quaade, Minister without Portfolio, &c., and Mr. Theodor von Kaufmann, Colonel in the General Staff, &c., by His Majesty the King of Denmark. These met together at the Vienna Conference, and having exchanged their powers of action, and proved them in due order, are agreed on the following articles:—

Article 1.—May peace and friendship exist from this time forth between their Majesties the King of Prussia, the Emperor of Austria, and the King of Denmark, and between their heirs and successors, their states and subjects.

Article 2.—All stipulations and agreements which existed between the contracting Powers before the war shall again come into force, in so far as they have not become annulled or modified by the sense of the present treaty.

Article 3.—His Majesty the King of Denmark gives up all rights in the Duchies of Schleswig-Holstein and Lauenburg, in favour of their Majesties the King of Prussia and the Emperor of Austria, and binds himself to acknowledge any arrangements relative to these duchies which their aforenamed Majesties may make.

Article 4.—The abdication of the duchy of Schleswig includes all those islands belonging to it, as well as the territory situate on the continent To facilitate the determination of boundary, and to avoid the inconveniences which arise from the position of the Jutland territories, which are circumscribed with those of Schleswig, His Majesty the King of Denmark gives up to their Majesties the King of Prussia and the Emperor of Austria those Jutland possessions lying south of the southern boundary of the Ribe district, as well as the Jutland territory of Mogel-Tondern, the Island of Amrum, the Jutland share of the Tohr, Sylb, and Roms Isles. In exchange, their Majesties the King of Prussia and the Emperor of Austria concede an equivalent portion of Schleswig, which includes territories serving to secure the connexion of the above-mentioned district of Ribe, with the remainder of Jutland, and mark the boundary between Jutland and Schleswig, on the Koldnig side, which portion shall be separated from the duchy of Schleswig, and incorporated with the kingdom of Denmark.

Article 5.—The new boundary between the kingdom of Denmark and the duchy of Schleswig will proceed from the centre of the mouth of the Bay of Heilsminde, on the little belt, and after passing this bay, will follow the present southern limits of the Heyl, Weystrup, and Taps parishes, as far as the course of the river, which is on the south of Geylbjerg and Brönore. It will then follow the course of this river from its mouth in the Fövs Aa, the extent of the southern limits of the parishes of Peddis and Vandrup, and the west boundary of the latter, as far as Konge Aa, to the norm of Holte. From this point the valley of Konge Aa will represent the limits as far as the eastern boundary of the parish of Hjort-Lund.

From this point the boundary line will follow this east limit and its prolongation, as far as the jutting angle to the north of the valley of Abbekjar, and lastly the eastern boundary of the village, on to Gyels Aa. From there the east boundary of Seem parish, and the south borders of the Seem, Ribe, and Wester-Wedstedt parishes, will represent the new limits, which will run in the North Sea, at equal distance between the islands of Mäno and Römo. In consequence of this new

determination of boundary, the common title to rights and possessions, as well those which relate to the secular as the ecclesiastical, and
which till now have existed on the islands and in the various parishes
of die district, will be declared null. Therefore the new sovereign powers will have full right in every relation to the territories separated by
the new boundaries.

Article 6.—An international commission, composed of the representatives of these high contracting powers, will, immediately after
the exchange of the ratifications of the present treaty, be authorised to
undertake the drawing of the new boundaries, according to the stipulations of the above article. This commission will also have to divide
the restoration expenses for the new high road from Ribe to Tondern,
even to the extension of the mutual territories through which it runs.
Lastly, the same commission will lead the presidentship in the division
of the institutions and capitals which till this time belonged in common to the districts or parishes now severed by the new boundaries.

Article 7.—The arrangements of the 20th, 21st, and 22nd Articles
of the Treaty of the 3rd May, 1815, between Austria and Russia, which
represents an essential part of the arrangements relating to mixed possessors, to the rights which these may exert, and neighbourly relations,
with regard to the possessions separated by the boundary line, will find
their application to the possessors, as well as to the possessions, which
are to be found in Schleswig as in Jutland, in the cases given in the
above-mentioned arrangements.

Article 8.—To arrive at a just division of the Danish monarch's
public debt, according to the proportion of the population in the
kingdom and duchies concerned, and at the same time to ameliorate
the insuperable difficulties which a detailed liquidation of the mutual
claims and pretensions would call forth, the high contracting powers
have fixed the debt of the Danish monarchy with which the duchies will be burdened at the round sum of 20,000,000 *thalers* (Danish
currency).

Article 9.—The share of the public debt to the Danish monarchy,
which according to the above article is to fell on the duchies, shall,
under the guarantee of their Majesties the King of Prussia and the
Emperor of Austria, reckon as to the debt of the above-mentioned
duchies to the kingdom of Denmark, after the expiration of a year, or
earlier if it be possible, from the time of the definitive organisation of
the duchies. For the payment of this debt the duchies can avail them-

selves, wholly or in part, of one or other of the following means:—

1. Payment in silver currency, 75 *thalers* (Prussian) equal to 100 *thalers* (Danish);

2. Parent to the Danish Treasury, by indissoluble bonds at 4 *per cent*, on the internal debt of the Danish monarchy;

3. Payment to the Danish Treasury, in new Treasury bonds, given out by the duchies, and the value of which shall be determined in Prussian *thalers* (30 to the pound), or in Hamburg marks. These will be liquidated by a half-yearly annuity of 5 *per cent* upon the original amount of the debt, of which 2 *per cent*, represents the interest ad judged to the debt for each term, while the rest will serve to pay it off. The above-mentioned payment of the half-yearly annuity will be made through the public coffers of the duchies, or through the bankers of Berlin and Hamburg. The bonds named under 2 and 3 will be accepted by the Danish Treasury at their nominal value.

Article 10.—Up to the time when the duchies definitively receive the sum, which according to the 8th Article of the present Treaty is that which the Danish monarchy has to pay as its share of the mutual debt, they will pay 2 *per cent*, on the settled sum, that is 580,000 *thalers*, Danish currency. This payment will be so effected that the interest and the account settlement of the Danish debt, which to the present has been assigned to the public offices of the duchies, shall, as before, be paid by them.

These payments will be made every half year, and in case they do not reach the above-mentioned sums, the duchies will pay off the remainder in cash to the Danish Finance Administration; if the reverse, the overplus is to be likewise repaid to them in cash. The liquidation will take place between Denmark and the highest managing authorities of the duchies, commissioned for the purpose, according to the stipulated manner of the present list, or even quarterly, if it be considered necessary on both sides. The first settlement shall be for the especial purpose of arranging the interest and account payment of the Danish monarchy, which were made after the 2nd December, 1863.

Article 11.—The sums which represent the so-called Holstein-Plousche equivalent, the remainder of the compensation for the former possessions of the Duke of Augustenburg, including the debt of precedence with which it is burdened, and the government bonds of Schleswig and Holstein, shall fall exclusively to the duchies.

Article 12.—The governments of Prussia and Austria will repay themselves the expenses of the war through the duchies.

Article 13.—His Majesty the King of Denmark binds himself, immediately after the ratification of the present treaty, to give up, with their freights, all the merchant ships of Prussia, Austria, and Germany, which have been taken during the war, also the cargoes belonging to Prussian, Austrian, or German subjects, which have been taken from neutral vessels; lastly, all vessels which Denmark had taken with a warlike design from the abdicated duchies. These objects shall be given back in the same condition in which they really are up to the time of restoration. In case the objects to be returned no longer exist, the worth shall be given in restitution; and should the value have considerably diminished since their seizure, the owner shall receive a proportionate remuneration.

It is also acknowledged as binding to make amends to the owners and crews of the ships, and to the owners of the cargoes, for all outlay and direct loss which are proved to have fallen on them through the seizure of the vessels; also for the port duties, quarantine duties, law expenses, costs of maintenance, and expenses of sending back the ships and crews. Concerning the vessels which cannot be restored, the value of these at the time of seizure will be accepted as remuneration. Concerning the average freights, or those objects which exist no more, the indemnification will be fixed according to the value which they would have borne at the place of their destination, at the time when the vessel would have reached it, according to probable calculation.

Their Majesties the King of Prussia and the Emperor of Austria will also give up the merchant ships which have been taken by their troops and men-of-war, with their freights, as far as these are the properties of private individuals. If the restoration cannot be made *in naturâ*, the indemnification will be settled according to the abovementioned principles. At the same time their Majesties bind themselves to bring to a settlement the sum total of the war contributions which were received in advance by their troops in Jutland. This sum will be deducted from the indemnification which was to be paid by Denmark, according to the principles of the present act. Their Majesties the King of Prussia and the Emperor of Austria, and the King of Denmark, will name a special commission to fix the sum total of the indemnifications. This commission will assemble at Copenhagen, at latest six weeks after the ratification of the present Treaty, and will endeavour to complete their task in three months. If at the end of this term they have arrived at no understanding about the claims brought before them, those which are not yet arranged shall be submitted to a court of separation (*Schneide*), To this end their Majesties the King of Prussia, the Emperor of Austria, and the King of Denmark, will agree on the choice of a judge (of separation?). The indemnifications will be paid, at latest, one month after their definitive appointment

Article 14.—The Danish Government remains burdened with all sums which are paid through the subjects of the duchies, communities, public institutions, and corporations, to the Danish pay offices, as cautions, deposits, and consignments. Moreover shall be restored to the duchies—

1. The deposit fixed for the payment of the Holstein Bank certificates;

2. The funds appointed for the prison building;

3. The fire insurance funds;

4. The Savings' Bank;

5. The capital proceeding from legacies belonging to the parishes or public institutions of the duchies;

6. Bank reserves from the special receipts of the duchies, which were *bonâ fide* in the public coffers, at the commencement of the Germanic execution and occupation of these lands. An international commission shall be authorized to liquidate the amount of the above-mentioned sums, deducting the expenses which the special administration required. The collection of antiquities at Flensburg, relating to the history of Schleswig, and which during the late occurrences have been for the most part dispersed, shall, by the assistance of the Danish Government, be again gathered together. Likewise shall those Danish subjects, communities, public institutions, and corporations which have paid sums of money into the public coffers of the duchies, as cautions, deposits, or consignments, be most promptly satisfied by the new government.

Article 15.—The pensions which depend on the special budgets, be it of the kingdom of Denmark or of the duchies, shall in future be paid by the country concerned, and the holders of them shall be free to choose their domicile, either in the kingdom or in the duchies. All other pensions, civil as well as military (including the pensions of the functionaries of the civil list of His late Majesty King Frederick VII., of His late Royal Highness Prince Ferdinand, of Her late Royal Highness the Margravine Charlotte of Hesse, *née* Princess of Denmark), and the pensions which till now have been paid through the Privy Purse, will be divided between the kingdom and duchies, according; to the proportion of their population. To this end, a list of all these pensions will soon after be drawn up, the value of the life rents converted into capital, and all the pensioners invited to declare whether in future they desire to receive their pensions in the kingdom or the duchies.

Should it happen that, in consequence of this declaration, the proportion between the two parts, that is, between that which falls to the duchies and that which remains as a charge on the kingdom, should not be according to the proportionate population, the difference shall be equalized by the parties concerned. The pensions which are assigned to the General Widows' Pay-office, and the Pension-fund of the subordinate military, will for the future, as formerly, be paid as far as the funds reach.

As regards the additional sums which the State will have to advance to these funds, the duchies will be charged with a share, according to the proportion of their population. The share of the Income and Life Insurance Institution, founded at Copenhagen in 1848, which the individual rights belonging to the duchies have attained, they shall expressly retain. An international commission, composed of representatives of both sides, shall assemble at Copenhagen, immediately after the exchange of the ratifications of the present Treaty, and regulate singly the stipulations of this article.

Article 16.—The Royal Government of Denmark undertakes the payment of the following royal annuities: Her Majesty the Dowager Queen Caroline Amelia; Her Royal Highness the Hereditary Princess Caroline; Her Royal Highness the Duchess Wilhelmina von Glücksburg; Her Serene Highness the Princess Caroline Charlotte Marianne of Mecklenburg-Strelitz; Her Serene Highness the Dowager Duchess Louise Caroline von Glücksburg; His Highness the Prince of Hesse; and their Serene Highnesses the Princesses Charlotte Victoria, and Amelia of Schleswig-Holstein-Sonderburg-Augustenburg. The share of these payments which according to the proportion of the population falls to the duchies will be repaid to the Danish Government by the administration of the duchies. The selected commissioners mentioned in the preceding article will also be charged to fix the arrangements for the performance of the present article.

Article 17.—The new government of the duchies undertakes the rights and obligations of all contracts and objects of public interest (especially those which concern the abdicated country) which have been concluded, conformable to the law of the administration of His Majesty the King of Denmark. It is, of course, understood that all obligations resulting from contracts which the Danish Government had concluded, in reference to the war and the Germanic execution, are not included in the preceding determinations. The new government of the duchies will respect every right or title of individuals or civilians, legally acquired in the duchies. In case of dispute, the Law Courts will find their matters under this category.

Article 18.—The native subjects of the relinquished countries serving in the Danish army or navy have the right to be immediately exempted from military service, and to return to their homes. It is understood that those among them who remain in the service of His Majesty the King of Denmark need not therefore be in fear, either in reference to their persons or their estates. The same rights and guarantees will be mutually assured to the civil functionaries born in Denmark or the duchies, and who hare the intention either to give up or retain the offices they hold, either in Denmark or the duchies.

Article 19.—The subjects domiciled in the countries relinquished under the present Treaty have, during an interval of six years (reckoned from the day of the exchange of the ratifications), by means of a preliminary declaration before the authorized jurisdiction, full and entire freedom to carry out their moveable possessions free from all tax, and to retire with their families into the states of His Danish Majesty, in which case they will retain the quality of Danish subjects. At the same time they are permitted to keep their estates in the abdicated countries. The same freedom is also mutually allowed to Danish subjects and individuals born in the duchies, who are established in the states of His Majesty the King of Denmark.

The subjects who make use of these arrangements need suffer no inquietude, either for their persons or with reference to the properties situate in both states, on account of their choice of either one side or the other. The above-mentioned respite of six years is also available to those belonging either to the kingdom of Denmark or to the ceded country, who are staying out of the territories of the King of Denmark, or of the duchies at the time of the exchange of the ratifications of the present Treaty. The nearest Danish Embassy, or any high provincial jurisdiction of the kingdom or the duchies, will receive their declaration. The naturalization in the kingdom of Denmark, as in the duchies, belongs to any individual who has possessed it up to the time of the ratification of this Treaty.

Article 20.—The titles of possession, the acts of administration and civil justice, which relate to the ceded countries, and which are in the archives of the kingdom of Denmark, shall be surrendered to the commissioners of the new government of the duchies as soon as possible. All those divisions of the archives at Copenhagen, which belonged to the ceded country, and which were taken from their archives, shall be given up. The Danish Government and the new government of the duchies mutually bind themselves to divide all documents and manuscripts which bear reference to the common concerns of Denmark and the duchies, on the demand of the high administrative jurisdiction.

The trade and navigation of Denmark and the ceded duchies shall enjoy the rights and privileges of the most favoured nations, and indeed, until a special. Treaty settles the conditions, the exemptions and facilities relating to the transit duty, which, according to Article 2 of the Treaty of the 14th May, 1857, is allowed to the goods which are conveyed on the highways and canals which unite, or will unite, the North Sea and the East Sea, will find their application to all goods which the kingdom or the duchies convey, whatever mode of communication it be.

Article 21.—The evacuation of Jutland by the allied troops will be accomplished in as short a time as possible, at latest in the course of three weeks after the exchange of the ratifications of the present Treaty. The extra arrangements concerning the evacuation are fixed in a protocol appended to the present Treaty.

Article 22.—And to contribute all in their power to the tranquillity of every mind, the high contracting powers declare and promise that no person who is compromised on the occasion of the late events, because of His position and political opinions, shall be at all persecuted, molested, or alarmed, either in his person or with reference to his possessions, whatever be his rank or situation.

Article 23.—The present Treaty will be ratified, and the ratifications will be exchanged in Vienna, within three weeks, or sooner. In witness whereof the plenipotentiaries have signed and sealed it with their arms.

Passed at Vienna the 30th October, in the Year of Grace 1864.

> Werther,
> Balen.
> Rechberg.
> Brenner,
> Quaade.
> Kaufmann.

(Here follows, as Appendix, a protocol, which decides the manner in which the evacuation of Jutland shall take place within three weeks. Then also a second protocol of the same 30th October, which says: "Immediately after the exchange of the ratifications of the above-mentioned Treaties, His Majesty the King of Denmark will issue proclamations to the inhabitants of the ceded countries, to notify the change which has taken place in their situation and to release them from their oath of fidelity.")

Appendix 2

1865. *February 21.*—Prussian Despatch to the Austrian Ministry, pronouncing the conditions the fulfilment of which is demanded by the Prussian Cabinet in the duchies of Schleswig Holstein, for the safe position of the German interests. There are six Articles.

1st.—Lasting and indissoluble defensive and offensive alliance of the duchies with Prussia. To make this feasible, Prussia binds herself to give protection and defence to the duchies against all attacks, in return the future duke will place the whole defensive power of the duchies at the disposition of the King of Prussia, to apply it in the army and navy to the protection and interest of both countries. The whole military disposition of the duchies shall be placed on Prussian footing. It shall be yielded to the Prussian Government, to appoint the quarters of the duchy troops, either in Prussia, or the duchies; the troops shall take the oath of allegiance to the king. The same principles apply to the navy.

2nd.—The Federal obligation of the sovereign of the duchies remains unaltered. He will organise his Federal contingent from the Holstein-Prussian troops not belonging to the Prussian Federal contingent.

3rd.—Rendsburg shall be a Federal Fortress, and remain occupied by the Prussians as hitherto.

4th.—On behalf of the protection of the duchies, the following territories, with full sovereignty, shall be resigned: (a) The town of Sonderburg, Math corresponding dominions, on both sides of the Alsen Sound, (b) The fortress of Friedricksort, with corresponding dominions, for the protection of Kiel. (c) The ground necessary for the establishment of fortifications at the mouths of the canal joining the East and North Seas. Prussia demands that the levelling of the canal, the guidance of the structure, and the supreme direction, shall be given up to her.

5th.—The duchies, with their entire dominions, shall assent to the Pussian tariff system (Prussian tariff union).

6th.—The postal and telegraph affairs of the duchies shall be united with those of Prussia. The surrender of the duchies to the future sovereign will follow on the fixing and perform-ance of the above conditions. Be they not executed, Prussia will again enter on the rights appertaining to her from the Peace of Vienna, and will reserve to herself the monetary winding up (*Geltendmachung*) of her other appertaining pretensions with regard to the duchies.

The Austrian Cabinet answered this despatch on the 5th March. It declared that each one of the Prussian demands contradicted either the Federal law, or the independence of the new Federal state. The Austrian minister, Count Mensdorff, had however, directly from the beginning set up the principle in regard to constituting the duchies, that the new Federal state should be independent, and that the regu-lation of its future relations to Prussia should take place within the limits of the Federal legislation. As soon as these two demands shall be fulfilled, Austria will willingly agree to those arrangements, which Prussia may judge necessary for the preservation of her interests in the formation of the new state.

Appendix 3

ORDER OF BATTLE OF THE PRUSSIAN ARMY.

Commander-in-Chief   His Majesty the King.
Chief of the Staff   General von Moltke.
Inspector-General of Artillery   Lieutenant-General von Hindersin.
Inspector-General of Engineers   ,,   von Wasserchleben .

FIRST ARMY.

Commander-in-Chief   H. R. H. Prince Frederick Charles,
    General of Cavalry.
Chief of the Staff   Lieutenant-General von Voigts-Rhetz.
Quartermaster-General   Major-General von Stülpnagel.
Commandant of Artillery   ,,   von Lengsfeld.
    ,,   Pioneers   ,,   von Keiser.

Second Corps D'armée.

General Commanding   Lieutenant-General von Schmidt.
Chief of the Staff   Major-General von Kamecke.
Commandant of Artillery   ,,   Hurrelbrink.
    ,,   Pioneers   Lieutenant-Colonel Leuthaus.
Commandant of 3rd Division   Lieutenant-General von Werder.
    ,,   5th Brigade   Major- General von Januschovsky
    (2nd and 42nd Regiments)
    ,,   6th Brigade   Major-General von Winterfeld (14th
    and 54th Regiments).
    Blücher's Hussars, No. 5.
Commandant of 4th Division   Lieutenant-General von Herwarth.
    ,,   7th Brigade   Major-General von Schlaberndorf (9th
    and 49th Regiments)
    ,,   8th Brigade   Major-General von Hanneken (21st
    and 61st Regiments).
    Pomeranian Uhlans,
    No. 4. 2nd Jäger Battalion.

Third Corps d'Armée.

General Commanding   *None.*
Commandant of 5th Division   Lieutenant-General von Tümpling.
    ,,   9th Brigade   Major-General von Schimmelman (8th and 48th Regiments)
    ,,   10th Brigade   Major-General von Kaminsky (12th and 18th Regiments).

1st Brandenburg Uhlans, No. 3.

Commandant of 6th Division   Lieutenant-General von Manstein.
    ,,   11th Brigade   Major-General von Gusdorf (35th and 60th Regiments)
    ,,   12th Brigade   Major-General von Kotze (24th and 64th Regiments).

Brandenburg Dragoons, No. 2.

3rd Jäger Battalion.

Fourth Corps d'Armée

General Commanding   *None,*
Commandant of 7th Division   Lieutenant-General von Franzecky.
    ,,   13th Brigade .   Major-General von Schwarzhoff (26th and 66th Regiments).
    ,,   14th Brigade   Major-General von Gordon (27th and 67th Regiments).

Magdeburg Hussars, No 10.

Commandant of 8th Division   Lieutenant-General von Horne.
    ,,   15th Brigade .   Major-General von Bose (31st and 71st Regiments).
    ,,   16th Brigade   Colonel von Schmidt (72nd and 4th Jäger Battalions).

Thuringian Uhlans' No. 6.

Cavalry Corps of the First Army.

H.R.H. Prince Albrecht, General of Cavalry.

Commandant of 1st Cavalry Division.—Major-General von Alvensleben,

Commandant of 1st Heavy Brigade.—Major-General H.R.H Prince Albrecht.

Garde de Corps.

Cuirassiers of the Guard.

Commandant of 2nd Heavy Brigade.—Major-General von Pfuel.

Brandenburg Cuirassiers, No. 6.

Magdeburg Cuirassiers, No. 7.

Commandant of Light Brigade.—Major-General von Rhembaben.

1st Dragoons of the Guard.

1st Uhlans   ,,

2nd „ „

Commandant of 2nd Cavalry Division Major-General Hann von Weyhern.

Commandant of 2nd Light Brigade „ Duke William of Mecklenberg.

2nd Dragoons of the Guard.
Brandenbur Hussars, No. 3.
2nd Brandenburg Uhlans, No. 11.

Commandant of 3rd Light Brigade.—Major-General von Groeben.
Neumark Dragoons, No. 3.
Thuringian Hussars, No. 12.

Commandant of 3rd Heavy Brigade.—Major-General von Der Goltz.
Queen's Own Cuirassiers, No. 2.
Second Pomeranian Uhlans, No. 9.

SECOND ARMY.

Commander-in-Chief   H.R.H. the Crown Prince.
Chief of the Staff   Major-General von Blumenthal
Quartermaster-General   „   von Stosch.
Commandant of Artillery   „   von Jacobi.
„   Engineers   „   von Schweinitz.

First Corps d'Armée

General von Bonin.
Chief of Staff   Lieutenant-Colonel von Borries.
Commandant of Artillery   Colonel Knotke.
„   Engineers   Lieutenant Colonel Weber.
Commandant of 1st Division   Lieutenant-General von Groszman.
„   1st Brigade   Major-General von Pape (1st and 41st Regiments)
„   2nd Brigade   Major-General von Barnekow (3rd and 43rd Regiments).
Lithuanian Dragoons, No.1.
Commandant of 2nd Division   Lieutenant-General von Clausewitz.
„   3rd Brigade   Major-General von Malotki (4th and 44th Regiments).
„   4th Brigade   Major-General von Buddenbrock (5th and 45th Regiments).
1st Royal Hussars, No. 1.
1st Jäger Battalion.
Commandant of Reserve Brigade of Cavalry of First Corps.—Colonel von Bredow.
East Prussian Cuirassiers, No. 3.
East Prussian Uhlans, No. 8,

510

Lithuanian Uhlans, No. 12.

Fifth Corps d'Armée

General Commanding   General von Steinmetz.

Chief of the Staff   Colonel von Wittich,

Commandant of Artillery   ,,   von Karwel.

,,   Engineers   ,,   von Kleist

Commandant of 9th Division   Major-General von Löwenfeld

,,   17th Brigade   Major-General von Ollech (37th and 58th Regiments).

,,   18th Brigade   Major-General von Horn (7th Regt.).

1st Silesian Dragoons, No. 4.

Commandant of 10th Division   Major-General von Kirchbach.

,,   19th Brigade   ,,   von Tiedeman (6th and 46th Regiments).

,,   20th Brigade   Colonel von Wittig (47th and 52nd Regiments).

2nd Royal Hussars, No. 2.

5th Jäger Battalion.

Sixth Corps d'Armée

General Commanding   General von Mutius

Chief of the Staff.   Colonel von Sperling

Commandant of Artillery.   Major-General von Herkt

,,   Engineers   Colonel Schulz.

Commandant of 11th Division   Lieutenant-General von Zastrow.

,,   21st   Brigade Major-General von Hahnenfeld (10th and 50th Regiments).

,,   22nd Brigade   Colonel von Hoffman (38th and 51st Regiments).

2nd Silesian Dragoons, No. 8.

Commandant of 12th Division.   Lieutenant-General von Prodzinsky.

,,   24th Brigade   Colonel von Krauach (22nd and 23rd Regiments).

2nd Silesian Hussars, No. 6.

6th Jäger Battalion.

N.B.—Two infantry regiments of the 12th Division were detached, the 63rd to garrison Neisse, the 62nd to the command of General von Knobelsdorf, who protected Silesia at Ratibor, and to whom the Silesian Uhlans were attached.

Guard Corps.

General Commanding	Prince August of Würtemberg
Chief of the Staff	Colonel von Dannenberg.
Commandant of Artillery	Major-General von Colomier.
,,　　Engineers	Colonel Bichler,
Commandant of 1st Division of the Guard	Lieut.-General Hiller von Gättringen.
Commandant of 1st Brigade	Colonel von Obernitz (1st and 3rd Guards).
Commandant of 2nd Brigade	Major-General von Alvensleben (2nd Guards and Guard Fusiliers).

Hussars of the Guard.
Jägers of the Guard.

2nd Division of the Guard.

Commandant of 3rd Brigade	Major-General von Budritzki (Grenadiers of Kaiser Alexander, and 3rd Grenadiers of the Guard.
,,　　4th Brigade	Major-General von Loën (Grenadiers of Kaiser Franz, and 4th Grenadiers of the Guard).

3rd Uhlans of the Guard.
Sharpshooter Battalion of the Guard.

N.B.—The 4th Regiment of the Guard was retained at Berlin, and sent later to the Second Reserve Corps.

Reserve Cavalry of the Second Army.

Divisional Commander	Major-General von Hartmann.
Commandant of 9th C. Brigade	Major-General von Witzleben (West Prussian Cuirassiers, No. 5, Polish. Uhlans, No. 10).
,,　　10th C. Brigade	Major-General von Schoen (West Prussian Uhlans, No. 1).
,,　　11th C. Brigade	Major-General von Verstell (Silesian Cuirassiers, No. 1, Silesian Hussars, No. 4).
,,　　12th C. Brigade	Major-General von Kalkreuth.

2nd Landwehr Hussars.
1st Landwehr Uhlans.

ARMY OF THE ELBE.

Commander-in-Chief	General von Herwarth.
Chief of the Staff	Colonel von Schlotheim.
Commandant of Artillery	,,　　von Rozynski.

,,   Engineers   Lieutenant-Colonel von Forell.

Commandant of 14th Division   Lieutenant-General von Münster.

,,   27th Brigade Major-General von Schwarzkoppen
(16 and 56th Regiments.)

,,   28th   ,,   Major-General von Hiller (17th and
57th Regiments).

Westphalian Dragoons, No. 7.

Commandant of 15th Division   Lieutenant-General von Canstein.

,,   29th Brigade Colonel von Stückradt (40th and 65th
Regiments).

,,   30th Brigade Colonel von Clasenapp (28th and 68th
Regiments).

Royal Hussars, No. 7.

Commandant of 16th Division   Lieutenant-General von Etzel.

,,   31st Brigade Major-General von Schöler (29th and
69th Regiments).

,,   32nd   ,, (31st and 8th Jäger Battalion).

2nd Westphalian Hussars, No. 11.

Reserve Cavalry.

Rhenish Cuirassiers, No. 8.

Rhenish Uhlans, No. 7.

Westphalian Uhlans, No. 5.

First Reserve Corps.

Lieutenant-General von Mülbe.

Landwehr Division of the Guard.—General von Bentheim.

1st Brigade of Guard Landwehr (1st and 2nd Guard Landwehr
Regiments).

2nd Brigade of Guard Landwehr (1st and 2nd Guard Grenadier
Landwehr Regiments).

1st Landwehr Division.—General Rosenberg.

1st Landwehr Brigade (9th and 21st Landwehr Regiments).

2nd   ,,   ,, (13th and 15th   ,,   ,,).

2nd Landwehr Division.

1st Landwehr Brigade (2nd and 12th Landwehr Regiments).

2nd   ,,   ,, (24th and 31st   ,,   ,,).

Landwehr Cavalry Division.—Major-General Dohna.

6th Landwehr Cavalry Regiment.

1 Battery.

ARMY OF THE MAINE.

Commander-in-Chief   General Vogel von Falckenstein.

Chief of the Staff   Colonel von Kraatz-Koschlau.

A. 13th Division.—Lieutenant-General von Goeben.

Commandant of 25th Brigade   Major-General von Kummer
(13th and 53rd Regiments).

,,   26th   ,,   Major-General von Wrangel (15th and
55th Regiments).

Westphalian Cuirassiers, No. 4.

1st Westphalian Hussars, No. 8.

B. Combined Division.—Major-General von Beyer.

19th, 20th, 30th, 32nd, 34th, 39th, and 70th Regiments.

N.B.—The 30th and 70th were detached to garrison Hesse-Cassel.

2nd Rhenish Hussars, No. 9.

C. Combined Division (formerly in Holstein).

Lieutenant-General von Manteuffel.

Commandant of 1st Com. Brigade Major-General von Freyhold (25th
and 36th Regiments).

,,   2nd ,,   ,,   (11th and 59th Regiments).

Commandant of Cavalry Brigade Major-General von Flies (Rhenish
Dragoons, No. 9, Magdeburg
Dragoons, No. 6).

Two Battalions of Coburg-Gotha.

One Battalion of Lippe.

Five Fourth Battalions.

9th Jäger Battalion.

Three newly-raised Regiments of Landwehr Cavalry.

Oldenburg, Hanseatic Brigade (nine Battalions, three Squadrons, two
Batteries).

Second Reserve Corps.

Commander-in-Chief.—His Royal Highness the Duke of
Mecklenburg-Schwerin.

a. Mecklenberg Division (five battalions, four Squadrons, two Batteries).

b. Combined Prussian Division (sixteen Battalions).

c. Two Anhalt Battalions.

Two Reserve Regiments of Landwehr Cavalry.

Eight Batteries.

ORDER OF BATTLE OF THE IMPERIAL AUSTRIAN ARMY OF THE NORTH.

General-in-Chief   Feldzeugmeister Ritter von Benedek.

Chief of the Staff   Lieutenant Field-Marshal von Henikstein.

Director of Artillery   Lieutenant Field-Marshal Archduke William

. ,,   Engineers Colonel von Pidoll.

First Corps d'Armée.

General Commanding General of Cavalry, Count Clam Gallas.

Assistant   General Count Gondrecourt.

Chief of the Staff   Colonel von Litzelhofen.

Commandant of Brigade.—Major-General Poschacher.

18th Field Jäger Battalion.

30th Infantry Regiment (Martini).

34th Infantry (King William of Prussia).

Commandant of Brigade.—Colonel Count Leiningen.

32nd Field Jäger Battalion.

33rd Infantry Regiment (Giulay).

38th Infantry Regiment (Haugwitz).

Commandant of Brigade.—Major-General Piret.

29th Field Jäger Battalion.

18th Infantry Regiment (Constantin).

45th   ,,   ,, (Sigismund).

Commandant of Brigade.—Major-General Ringelsheim.

26th Jäger Battalion.

42nd Infantry Regiment (Hanover).

73rd Infantry Regiment (Mensdorf).

To each Brigade one squadron of the Nikolaus Regiment of Hussars (No. 2), and one 4-pounder Field Battery, were attached.

N.B.—To the Corps were besides attached one Sanitary Company, two Field Ambulances, five Companies of Pioneers, four Companies of Engineers, two 4-pounder and two 8-pounder Field Batteries, one 4-pounder and one 8-pounder Horse Artillery Battery, and a Rocket Battery.

Second Corps d'Armée.

General Commanding   Lieutenant Field-Marshal Count Thun-Hohenstadt.

Assistant   Major-General von Philippovich

Chief of the Staff   Colonel von Döpfner.

Commandant of Brigade.—Colonel Thorn.

2nd Field Jäger Battalion.

40th Infantry Regiment (Roszbach).

69th   ,,   ,, (Jellachich).

Commandant of Brigade.—Major-General Henriquez.

9th Field Jäger Battalion.

14th Infantry Regiment (Hesse).

27th   ,,   ,, (Belgium).

Commandant of Brigade.—Major-General von Saffrau.

515

11th Field Jäger Battalion.
64th Infantry Regiment (Saxe-Weimar).
80th   ,,   ,,   (Holstein).
Commandant of Brigade.—Prince Würtemberg.
20th Field Jäger Battalion.
47th Infantry Regiment (Hartung).
57th   ,,   ,,   (Mecklenburg).

To each brigade one squadron of the Imperial Uhlans (No. 6), and one 4-pounder Field Battery, were attached.

To the Corps were attached the same as to the First Corps.

Third Corps d'Armée.

General Commanding Lieutenant Field-Marshal Archduke Ernst.
Assistant   Major-General von Baumgarten.
Chief of the Staff   Colonel Baron Catty.
Commandant of Brigade.—Major General Kalik.
22nd Field Jäger Battalion.
35th Infantry Regiment (Khevenhüller).
72nd   ,,   ,,   (Ramming).

N.B.—This brigade, which had garrisoned Holstein on the outbreak of hostilities, was attached to the First *Corps d'Armée.*

Commandant of Brigade.—Major-General Appiano.
4th Field Jäger Battalion.
46th Infantry Regiment (Meiningen).
62nd   ,,   ,,   (Archduke Henry).
Commandant of Brigade.—Colonel Benedek.
1st Field Jäger Battalion.
52nd Infantry Regiment (Archduke Franz Karl).
78th Infantry Regiment (Sokcsevics).
Commandant of Brigade.—Colonel Kirchsberg.
3rd Field Jäger Battalion.
44th Infantry Regiment (Archduke Albrecht).
49th Infantry Regiment (Hesz).
Commandant of Brigade.—Colonel Prohaszka.
13th Border Infantry Regiment.
Four Battalions of the 55th Regiment.
      ,,   ,,   56th

To each brigade were attached one squadron of the Lichtenstein Uhlans (No. 9) and one 4-pounder Field Battery. To the Corps were attached the same as to the First Corps.

Fourth Corps d'Armeé.

General Commanding Lieutenant Field-Marshal Count Festetics.
Assistant   Major-General von Mollinary.
Chief of the Staff   Colonel von Görz.

Commandant of Brigade.—Colonel Kopal.
27th Field Jäger Battalion.
12th Infantry Regiment (Archduke William).
26th Infantry Regiment (Michael).

Commandant of Brigade.—Colonel Fleischhacker.
13th Field Jäger Battalion.
6th Infantry Regiment (Coronini).
61st   ,,   ,,   (Prince of Russia).

Commandant of Brigade.—Colonel Poekh.
8th Field Jäger Battalion.
37th Infantry Regiment (Archduke Joseph.
51st Infantry Regiment (Archduke Charles Ferdinand).

Commandant of Brigade.—Major-General Archduke Joseph.
30th Field Jäger Battalion.
67th Infantry Regiment (Schmerling).
68th   ,,   ,,   (Steininger).

To each Brigade one squadron of the 7th Hussars and one 4-pounder Field Battery were attached.

To the Corps the same were attached as to the First Corps.

Sixth Corps d'Armée.

General Commanding   Lieutenant Field-Marshal Baron
                                    Ramming.
Assistant   Major-General von Kochmeister.
Chief of the Staff   Colonel Frölich.

Commandant of Brigade.—Colonel von Waldstatten.
6th Field Jäger Battalion.
9th Infantry Regiment (Hartmann)
79th   ,,   ,,   (Frank)

Commandant of Brigade.—Colonel Hertwegh.
25th Field Jäger Battalion.
41st Infantry Regiment (Kellner).
56th   ,,   ,,   (Gorizutti).

Commandant of Brigade.—Major-General Rosenweig.
17th Field Jäger Battalion.

4th Infantry Regiment (Deutschmeister).
55th   ,,   ,,   (Bianchi).
Commandant of Brigade.—Colonel Jonak.
14th Field Jäger Battalion.
20th Infantry Regiment (Prussia).
60th   ,,   ,,   (Wasa).

To each Brigade one squadron of the 10th Uhlans and one 4-pounder Field Battery were attached.

Besides were attached to the Corps one Sanitary Company, two Field Ambulances, one battalion of Engineers, one battalion of Pioneers, two 4-pounder and two 8-pounder Field Batteries, two 8-pounder batteries of Horse Artillery, and a Rocket Battery.

Eighth Corps d'Armée.

General Commanding   Archduke Leopold.
Assistant   Major-General Weber.
Chief of the Staff   Lieutenant-Colonel von Majnone.
Commandant of Brigade.—Colonel Fragner.
5th Field Jäger Battalion.
15th Infantry Regiment (Nassau).
77th   ,,   ,,   (Archduke of Tuscany).
Commandant of Brigade.—Major-General von Docteur.
31st Field Jäger Battalion.
8th Infantry Regiment (Archduke Louis).
74th   ,,   ,,   (Nobili).
Commandant of Brigade.—General Count Rothkirk.
25th Infantry Regiment (Mamula).
71st   ,,   ,,   (Leopold of Tuscany).
Commandant of Brigade.—Major-General Brandenstein.
24th Field Jäger Battalion.
21st Infantry Regiment (Reischach).
23rd   ,,   ,,   (Este).

To each Brigade one squadron of the Archduke Charles's Uhlans (No. 3) and one 4-pounder Battery were attached.

Besides were attached to the Corps the same as to the First Corps.

Tenth Corps d'Armée..

General Commanding   Lieutenant Field Marshal von Gablenz.
Assistant   Baron Roller.

Chief of the Staff   Colonel Bourgignone.

Commandant of Brigade.—Colonel Mondel.

12th Field Jäger Battalion,

10th Infantry Regiment (Mazuchelli).

24th   ,,   ,,   (Parma).

Commandant of Brigade.—Colonel Grivicics.

16th Field Jäger Battalion.

2nd Infantry Regiment (Alexander).

23rd   ,,   ,,   (Airoldi).

Commandant of Brigade.—Major-General von Knebel.

28th Field Jäger Battalion.

1st Infantry Regiment (Emperor Francis Joseph).

3rd   ,,   ,,   (Archduke Charles).

Commandant of Brigade.—Major-General Wimpffen.

13th Infantry Regiment (Bamberg).

58th   ,,   ,,   (Archduke Stephen).

To each Brigade were attached one squadron of the 1st Uhlans and one 4-pounder Field Battery.

The same were attached to the Corps as to the First Corps, except that this Corps had only one 4-pounder Field Battery.

First Light Cavalry Division.—Major-General Baron Edelsheim.

Chief of Staff.—Major Wäldestatten.

Commandant of Brigade.—Colonel Appel.

2nd Dragoons (Windischgrätz).

9th Hussars (Liechtenstein).

Commandant of Brigade.—Colonel Wallis.

1st Dragoons (Savoy).

10th Hussars (King of Prussia).

Commandant of Brigade.—Colonel Fratricievics.

5th Hussars (Radetzky).

8th   ,,   (Hesse-Cassel).

Second Light Cavalry Division.—Major-General Prince Thurn
and Taxis.

Chief of the Staff.—Colonel Rodakovszky.

Commandant of Brigade.—Colonel Bellegarde.

4th Hussars (Eseh).

12th   ,,   (Haller).

Commandant of Brigade.—Colonel Westphalen.

6th Hussars (Würtemberg).
11th   ,,   (Palffy).

First Reserve Division of Cavalry.—Lieutenant Field-Marshal Prince
Schleswig-Holstein.
Commandant of Brigade.—Major General Prince Solms.
4th Cuirass Regiment (Ferdinand).
6th   ,,   ,,   (Hesse).
8th Uhlans (Emperor Max.).
Commandant of Brigade.—Major-General Schindlöcker.
9th Cuirass Regiment (Stadion).
11th Cuirass Regiment (Emperor Francis Joseph).
4th Uhlans   (,,   ,,   ).

Second Reserve Division of Cavalry.—Major General von Zajtsek.
Commandant of Brigade.—Major-General Borberg.
3rd Cuirass Regiment (Saxony).
7th   ,,   ,,   (Brunswick).
2nd Uhlans (Schwarzenberg).
Commandant of Brigade.—General Count Soltyk.
1st Cuirass Regiment (Emperor Francis Joseph).
5th Cuirass Regiment (Nicolas).
5th Uhlans (Walmoden).
Third Reserve Division of Cavalry.—Major-General Count
Coudenhove.
Commandant of Brigade.—Prince Windischgrätz.
2nd Cuirass Regiment (Wrangel).
8th   ,,   ,,   (Prince of Prussia).
7th Uhlans (Archduke Charles Louis).
Commandant of Brigade.—Major-General Mengen.
10th Cuirass Regiment (Bavaria).
12th   ,,   ,,   (Horvath).
11th Uhlans (Alexander).

To each Cavalry Brigade was attached one battery of Horse Artillery.

IMPERIAL AUSTRIAN ARMY OF THE SOUTH.
General-in-Chief   Field-Marshal Archduke Albrecht.
Chief of the Staff   Major-General von John.

Fifth Corps d'Armée.
Major-General Rodich.

Commandant of Brigade.—Major-General Daun.

19th Field Jäger Battalion.

38th Infantry Regiment (Benedek).

70th   ,,   ,,   (Also-Szopor).

Commandant of Brigade.—Major-General Möring.

21st Field Jäger Battalion.

53rd Infantry Regiment (Archduke Leopold Louis).

54th   ,,   ,,   (Grueber).

Commandant of Brigade.—Major-General Piret.

5th Imperial Jäger Battalion.

50th Infantry Regiment (Baden).

75th   ,,   ,,   (Crenneville).

Seventh Corps d'Armée.

Lieutenant Field-Marshal Marivici di Madonna del Monte.

Commandant of Brigade.—Major-General Emmerich von Thurn and Taxis.

7th Field Jäger Battalion.

29th Infantry Regiment (Thun).

43rd   ,,   ,,   (Alemann).

Commandant of Brigade.—Major-General Scudier.

10th Field Jäger Battalion.

19th Infantry Regiment (Crown Prince Rudolf).

48th   ,,   ,,   (Archduke Ernest Charles).

Commandant of Brigade.—Major-General Hammerstein.

4th Imperial Jäger Battalion.

66th Infantry Regiment (Grand Duke of Tuscany).

76th   ,,   ,,   (Paumgarten).

Commandant of Brigade.—

6th Imperial Jäger Battalion.

11th Infantry Regiment (Crown Prince of Saxony).

59th   ,,   ,,   (Archduke Rainer).

Ninth Corps d'Armée.

Commandant of Brigade.—Major-General Weckbecher.

23rd Field Jäger Battalion.

63rd Infantry Regiment (Netherlands).

65th   ,,   ,,   (Archduke Louis Victor).

Commandant of Brigade.—Major-General Appiano.

15th Field Jäger Battalion.

5th Infantry Regiment (Wetzlar).

7th   ,,   ,,   (Maroicic).

Commandant of Brigade.—Major-General Gaal.

3rd Imperial Jäger Battalion.

31st Infantry Regiment (Mecklenburg-Strelitz).

39th   ,,   ,,   (Don Miguel).

Besides these, to the Army of the South were attached the 1st and 2nd Imperial Jäger Battalions, and the 17th Hohenlohe), 22nd (Wimpffen), 36th (Degenfeld) Infantry Regiments.

The Cavalry consisted of the 12th and 13th Uhlans, and the 1st, 3rd, 11th, and 14th Hussars, the Artillery of the 5th and 7th Regiments.

N.B.—The Border Regiments garrisoned the fortresses and the Littorale.

Appendix 4

"Their Majesties the Emperor of Austria and the King of Prussia, after declaring that they are animated by a desire to restore to their peoples the blessings of peace, appoint as their plenipotentiaries—

"His Apostolic Majesty—Count Karolyi and Baron de Brenner; and the King of Prussia—Count Bismarck, who have agreed upon the following points:—

"The integrity of the Austrian monarchy, with the exception of Venetia, shall be maintained.

"The King of Prussia shall withdraw his troops from the Austrian territory as soon as a peace shall have been signed.

"The Emperor of Austria recognises the dissolution of the Germanic Confederation as it heretofore existed, and accepts the new organization of Germany without the participation of Austria; he undertakes to recognise the closer Federal relations (*die engern Bundesbande*) which the King of Prussia shall establish to the north of the line of the Maine; he also accepts the formation by the States of the South of a separate Confederation, and that the national connexion with the North shall be reserved for future arrangement between the two Confederations.

"His Apostolic Majesty transfers to the King of Prussia all the rights which he had acquired by the Treaty of Vienna of the 30th of October over the Duchies of Schleswig and Holstein, with the reservation that the population of Northern Schleswig, if they should express such a desire by a free vote, should be reunited to Denmark.

"The war indemnity is fixed at forty million *thalers*. From this sum fifteen millions shall be deducted as the equivalent of the amount which the Emperor of Austria, by virtue of the Treaty of 1864, would still be entitled to claim from the Elbe Duchies, and five millions as the equivalent of the provisioning of the Prussian troops which still continue to occupy the Austrian provinces until the conclusion of peace. There will, therefore, remain a sum of twenty million *thalers* to be paid in specie.

"The King of Prussia, at the request of Austria, consents to allow the kingdom of Saxony to retain its present territorial limits, but he reserves to himself the power of settling, by a special treaty to be concluded with the King of Saxony, the question of the war indemnities as well as the future position which Saxony shall hold in the Northern Confederation.

"The Emperor of Austria will recognise the new territorial arrangements effected by the King of Prussia in the north of Germany, and also any territorial changes which he may complete.

"The King of Prussia engages to obtain the adhesion of his ally of Italy to the preliminaries of peace and to the armistice as soon as the Emperor of the French shall have declared that the kingdom of Venetia is at the disposition of the King of Italy.

"The Emperor of Austria and the King of Prussia, after the exchange of ratifications of the present preliminaries has been completed, shall appoint plenipotentiaries, who shall meet at a place to be hereafter selected, in order to conclude a peace upon the bases of the present preliminary convention, and to negotiate upon questions of detail.

"For these purposes, after having agreed upon the present preliminaries, the high contracting parties shall conclude this armistice between the Austrian and Saxon military forces on the one part, and the Prussian military forces on the other part.

"The conditions of this armistice shall be settled immediately.

"The armistice shall commence from August 2nd, and the present suspension of arms shall be prolonged until that date.

"There shall also be concluded at the present state of the negotiations an armistice with Bavaria, and General Baron de Manteuffel shall be required to conclude armistices, to commence also from the date of August 2nd, upon the bases of the military *status quo*, with Baden, Würtemberg, and Hesse-Darmstadt, as soon as these states shall require."

Appendix 5

Much was said and written at the time of the armistice on the state of the Prussian hospitals. While the headquarters of the fine army lay at Prague, the utter stagnation of affairs and a favourable opportunity induced the author to pay a visit to the line by which the crown prince advanced with the Second Army from Silesia to the Battle of Königgrätz. The train glided without stopping past the station of Königgrätz, which is a short distance from the advanced works of the fortress, and where a guard of the Austrian garrison were standing beside their piled arms, past Josephstadt, close under the guns of the bastions, and between the main body of the place and an outwork on which an Austrian sentry was pacing along the rampart, and Austrian soldiers were lying listlessly beside the big guns looming out of the embrasures.

The line of railway was itself, by the conditions of the armistice, available for Prussian transport, but no Prussian was allowed to get out of the train either at Josephstadt or Königgrätz, nor did the trains stop at either place unless someone unconnected with the Prussian army wished to be put down or to get in, in which case a momentary halt was made at the station. On arriving at Königinhof, we found a large number of hospital tents filled with men who had been wounded at Nachod, Skalitz, or the great battle. Prussian and Austrian soldiers lay side by side, all under the care of Prussian surgeons, but tended and nursed by a large number of Prussian ladies, and by many sisters of charity. Many of the Austrian soldiers were Poles, many Italians who spoke no German, but relied upon the Prussian ladies to act as interpreters between them and the surgeons.

Many of the men were on the road to rapid recovery, and were able to talk cheerfully and smoke, while with a piece of green bough they brushed away the flies which in this warm climate clustered thickly in the hospital tent, and tried to fix themselves upon the healing wounds. In one tent lay two or three who were considered hopeless cases; one poor fellow, an Austrian artilleryman, who had lost both legs, lay upon his mattress, moving his head feebly with a restless motion. "He must die," whispered the surgeon; "he cannot get over it." But going forward he stooped over the much-suffering man, patted his forehead, and spoke some words of consolation to him.

As the doctor turned to leave the bedside, the man, who seemed to derive some hope from his presence, began to moan feebly, but a lady who was sitting near him came over to him, smoothed his pillow, and by a few kind words quieted him, and induced him to try to go to sleep. The sufferer, with a child's obedience, closed his eyes, while his nurse sat down by his bed-head, ready to frighten away any fly that might threaten to disturb the fitful slumbers of the patient.

In another tent were a number of convalescents, with bright eyes, very different from those which, dull and hazy, betokened more dangerous cases. Here Baroness Seydlitz was serving out plentiful portions of cigars and tobacco, which were eagerly accepted by the men who were still unable to leave their beds, and whose thinned white hands told how much pain and illness can be caused even by the tiny bullets of the needle-gun. This noble lady had two sons in the Prussian army, both of whom had served during the campaign. At the beginning of the war she was made superintendent of one of the many companies of Prussian ladies who formed themselves into charitable bands for nursing the wounded, and was now with her division of benefactresses stationed in the hospital tents of Königinhof. Fortunately, her sons had passed unscathed through the actions; but if every wounded soldier who came under her care had been her own child she could not have shown more solicitude for them than she did. The Prussian wounded had made us acquainted with their love and estimation for her before we found her in the hospital tent, and every Sclave, Pole, or Italian-Austrian, when asked who had given him any little luxury which we saw by his bed-head, knew enough German to answer, "*Du gute Fran von Seydlitz*."

General von Löwenfeld, who was passing through Königinhof on his way to review the battlefield of Nachod, where he with six battalions repulsed the fierce attacks of the Austrians until his supports arrived, was visiting the hospitals, and with a wonderful power, not only of language but dialect, was talking kindly to every patient Many of the Austrians who were lying in the shaded tents of Königinhof had fallen under his own guns or the deadly fire of his own infantry at Nachod or Skalitz, but they bore no ill-will to the Prussian general The Prussian *krankenträgers*, Prussian surgeons, and Prussian ladies had removed any animosity which they might at first not unnaturally have felt to not only an enemy but a conqueror.

All were asked how long they had lain on the field of battle; some four hours, some ten, some said thirty-six; one now merry Austrian boy, about eighteen years old, told us that he had been wounded in the Maslowed Wood during the Battle of Königgrätz, and had lain there lost and hidden in the trees, and suffering fearfully from thirst and hunger, until found at the end of three days by some Prussian soldiers. An amputated foot showed that he had been badly wounded, but it is probable that suffering exaggerated to his mind the length of time he lay upon the ground, for the woods were searched by the Prussian *krankenträgers* the day after the battle, though it is quite possible that in such thick foliage a wounded man may have lain long undetected, and perhaps been missed altogether.

No one who did not see the country in which the battles of the war were fought would realize the enormous exertions made by the Prussian *krankenträgers* to bring in wounded men. It must be remembered that every piece of rising ground was covered with thick wood or high standing corn; that down by the watercourses the long grass and the bulrushes rose tall in all their summer luxuriance. The wounded invariably, if possible, crawled under cover after Königgrätz, and sought by the brooks for water to quench their thirst, or in the trees and crops for shelter; the *krankenträgers* had to beat carefully over every yard of ground which lies between Horonowitz and Nechanitz, between the Bistritz and the Elbe—a space of nearly forty-five square miles, over which they had to search for and carry to the ambulances many thousands of wounded men, Austrians and Prussians alike; and there are but 1,900 of these men with the whole Prussian armies.

The usual answer to the question, "Who first relieved you after the battle?" was that a Prussian soldier had given the speaker something to drink out of his water-bottle directly after the action had ceased, and that, after some time, two Prussian soldiers with a stretcher had lifted him up and carried him to the divisional hospital. A drive down the valley of the Elbe towards the mountains brought us to the Castle of Nachod, which lies at the entrance of the Nachod Pass, and about half a mile nearer to the main ridge than the hill upon which the action was fought. From every large country house waved the white flag with its red cross, which showed that the building was being used as a hospital, and that under its roof wounded men were being coaxed slowly to recover.

The castle of Nachod, itself standing on a high spur of the mountain chain, and overlooking most beautiful scenery, was occupied by 800 wounded, under the voluntary superintendence of the Prince of Salm-Horstmar, who had left his beautiful property of Rheingraf to work for charity in the hospitals of wounded soldiers. Long lines of beds stretched on both sides of the oak banqueting halls and the tapestried chambers of the castle—beds occupied by suffering but patient men; Prussian ladies in black dresses were gliding about, noiselessly carrying medicines or medical comforts to their grateful patients; Sisters of Mercy were sitting by the bedsides reading to the listening occupant, or propping up a feverish head on a snowy white pillow; while in the corridors outside noble ladies, both in the dresses of the Prussian lady volunteers and in those of Sisters of Mercy, were preparing food for the sick, or tearing up linen and soiling cotton wool to assist the surgeons. Most of the patients were doing wonderfully well. The fine mountain air and the tender care of the nurses had a cheering effect upon them, which led them on to recovery.

Many officers were in separate rooms, most of them Austrians, brave men who, undaunted even by pain, expressed their opinion that their defeat was due to the needle-gun alone, and showed no want of desire to fight the war over again with equal arms. All, fortunately, so nearly well that a few weeks more restored them to their regiments.

There were still tenants of the castle hospital at Nachod and of the tents of Königinhof long after peace had been signed, and after the Prussian armies had marched out of Bohemia; but it was quite wonderful how many of the men who were wounded at Nachod and Skalitz had already been dismissed from hospital.

After the action of Nachod, 3,000 wounded were brought into the castle and town of Nachod alone, besides many who were withdrawn by the retreating Austrians to Skalitz and Königinhof, and afterwards fell into the hands of the Prussians. Of the 3,000 brought to Nachod, 800 still remained; but the rest had been sent away as convalescent, for but few had died, defeating the cares of their nurses. The soldiers still in hospital could not find words to express their gratitude to the ladies, both Catholic and Protestant, who had been their constant attendants night and day, since they were lifted from the stretchers of the *krankenträgers* into their beds in the hospitals. Many of the recoveries must also be attributed to their care, for they, as all women by a bed of sickness, had a power to soothe suffering men which no surgeons or professional hospital attendants ever seemed to attain to.

CPSIA information can be obtained
at www.ICGtesting.com
Printed in the USA
BVHW080810231221
624644BV00001B/6